THE RISE OF
AMERICAN ECONOMIC LIFE

THE RISE
OF AMERICAN
ECONOMIC LIFE

FOURTH EDITION

Arthur Cecil Bining
Thomas C. Cochran
University of Pennsylvania

CHARLES SCRIBNER'S SONS　　NEW YORK

Contents

10

11

12

13

14

15

Preface

Arthur C. Bining was a true historian with a gift for writing simple and colorful narrative. He had a deep interest in artifacts, technology, and how processes actually worked. In revising this text to bring it more in tune with present-day hypotheses regarding economic growth, I have tried to preserve as much as possible of the original narrative. The major deletions, necessary to make room for more explanatory discussion, have been in the large amount of political and diplomatic background included in the original edition. I have tried, however, to add to rather than subtract from the historical facts bearing directly on economic life. In other words, while there is recognition of the new concepts and theories developed by economists in recent years, the book is primarily an historical description of trends and events rather than a speculative analysis of factors of growth. The book provides a framework of factual knowledge which leaves the teacher free to add further interpretation.

Revision in the direction of emphasizing current interests has led to relatively little change in the chapters on the Colonial period, more in those on the nineteenth century, and a fairly complete rewriting of the section since 1914. In revising the recent chapters, however, I have tried to preserve the good, chronological accounts of government action. The book is a better reference than most for economic legislation to 1960.

Technical economic language has generally been avoided, but when used, because new phrases such as "social overhead capital" seem aptly descriptive, terms are first defined and then employed in contexts in which the student could guess their meaning.

THOMAS C. COCHRAN

July 4, 1963

Maps, Diagrams, and Tables

TABLES

Illustrations

THE RISE OF
AMERICAN ECONOMIC LIFE

CHAPTER I

The Economic Awakening of Medieval Europe

The roots of American economic life extend deeply into that period in the history of the world usually known as the Middle Ages. It is true that these fibrous roots may be traced much deeper—into the soil of ancient empires whose cultures rose to great heights only to decline and fade into the twilight of obscurity. But it was in the latter part of the medieval era when Europe was awakening to increased activities, and the cross currents of European civilization were becoming more complex, that ideas and patterns took shape which were to provide the background for a new order of society on the virgin continent of America. Not only were the political and social concepts of a changing Europe transplanted, but the earliest economic activities were also patterned after those of the Old World. This culture was to be modified and changed in many ways by a new environment, the rigors of pioneering, the mingling of various racial groups, and the alchemy of rapid growth and expansion. In the course of time, a new society—distinctly American—took form.

Since the story of America begins in Europe, it is necessary to take a glance at medieval society, whose customs and concepts had an influence on many phases of early American life. With the collapse of the great structure of Roman material civilization and the destruc-

1

tion of universal law and order, an inferior form of society arose in Europe. Attacks from without and disintegration from within had put an end to the great Roman Empire. In the West, culture in all its aspects crumbled, although for centuries Byzantium in the East retained an important civilization and many of Rome's traditions. But gone was the vast military machine whose well-disciplined troops had successfully sought world conquest; gone was protection and security to person and property afforded by a strong government; gone was the bond of unity such as the Western world had never known before; and gone was Roman peace, which, although brief, had given mankind a fleeting vision of a brighter and happier world. The old commercial prosperity disappeared as commerce and industry declined. The Western seas were once more infested with pirates. The great roads fell into decay and were plagued with robbers and brigands. Urban life disintegrated, and, apart from the cities of the Eastern Empire, only Rome and a few other centers continued to exist as cities, though with greatly diminished populations. Out of the turbulence of long years of disorder, a different type of society and a new form of government emerged in Western Europe.

Medieval society must be considered in terms of suzerains and vassals, of barons and lesser nobles of different ranks, of tenants, freemen, and a great body of peasants or serfs. Then too, the procession of clergy—archbishops, bishops, abbots, and priests—as well as those pious individuals in the various monastic orders who took the fundamental vows of poverty, chastity, and obedience must be included among the actors in the medieval pageant. Europe was shattered into thousands of estates and manors, ruled over by nobles who consumed most of their energies in continual petty warfare. Clustered in villages, protected by the castle or stronghold of the overlord, were the hovels of the miserable serfs, who spent their days in providing for the needs of their superiors, taking comfort in the thought and hope of a better life beyond the grave. The Church, as it grew in power, became a unifying influence, and its abbeys and monasteries preserved the smouldering embers of learning, scholarship, and scientific endeavor that remained of the heritage of the past.

Feudalism grew up because there was no settled government to protect life and property and to regulate the dealings of men. In its principles and usages, it was a system of polity based on the relations of men to one another rather than on the obedience of men to government and law. It centered in the relationship of the lord to the vassal in connection with the holding of land in fee. It developed many practices and customs, the most important of which were fealty, homage, personal services, wardship, reliefs, aids, escheat, forfeiture, and finally chivalry. Feudalism, based almost exclusively on agriculture, gradually weakened with the passing of the medieval period. Among the circumstances that brought about its decline were the revival of towns and cities, the gradual expansion of economic life, the rise of a middle class, the Crusades, the change in the purpose and nature of warfare, the beginning of modern states, the emergence of monarchy and autocracy, and the colonization of distant lands. Although feudalism finally died, many of its concepts and customs remained well into the modern period, and like vestigial remains in the human body, a few, such as hereditary titles and great landed estates, still survive and persist as reminders of a bygone age.

THE REVIVAL OF TOWN LIFE

By the eleventh century, as feudalism was reaching its height, certain forces became manifest that in the course of time were to change the entire complexion of European society. The feudal world seemed to be starting a process of organization. Anarchy gradually grew less violent in degree and extent; many nobles attempted to exploit their holdings economically rather than continue to risk the perils involved in seizing the lands and possessions of others; agricultural surpluses from the curiously arranged strips and fields of the manors sought outlets; increasingly men exchanged commodities; new markets were opened; and commercial relations developed between the manors and the reviving towns, and among the towns themselves. Thus, a revival of labor and production in many new forms began to stir Europe, resulting once again in the rise of town and city life. This marked the beginning of a new commercial era and the threshold of another epoch in the history of mankind.

The first cities and towns to show renewed activity were on the shores of the Mediterranean, in Italy and Provence. Commerce, trade, and urban life had never entirely disappeared at any time during the Middle Ages. The expanding Church required stone, marble, mosaics, and stained-glass windows for its towering cathedrals; its activities kept town life alive. For its decorations and reliquaries, the Church also sought gold, silver, precious stones, and tapestries, much of which came from the Byzantine Empire and even from the far-off Orient. Many a great feudal noble, also, was able to secure coveted articles through the instrumentality of the decadent cities, and during the period of greatest disorganization, there remained a semblance of commerce which from time to time ebbed and flowed like the tides, never reaching great heights because of the hazards and perils of the times.

The older towns, such as Naples, Ravenna, Florence, Milan, Amalfi, Pisa, Genoa, and the one destined to become the greatest of all—Venice, began to grow and prosper. Several became great city-states. New towns that owed their origin to medieval conditions arose. Many grew up under the shadowy protection of a monastery or castle. Others began as villages at the junction of roads, the headwaters of rivers, or where main routes of travel converged. Locations suited to trade became market centers. Towns like Bruges, Cologne, Ghent, and Nuremberg began to thrive as unstable conditions slowly gave way to more peaceful times.

The towns that arose in later medieval times, and the older ones that took on new life as feudalism weakened, varied somewhat in appearance and organization, but all had certain similarities. They had walls of earth or stone. Each had its watchtowers to guard it by day and by night. Bells sounded alarms of danger from enemies without and fires within. Streets were narrow, crooked, unpaved, and in most cases were stenching with filth and refuse distributed by the inhabitants and by domestic animals that roamed through them. Buildings varied from great structures to hovels. In the town hall, the charter, wrested by one of various methods from the king or a great baron, set forth the privileges of the town and the degree to which it was free. In the larger towns or cities, magnificent cathedrals with spires and steeples pointing skyward denoted the religious aspirations of the people as well as the skill of architects, sculptors, masons, and other workers.

Within the towns the guilds developed and held control in their respective spheres. They were associations of men with kindred pursuits or common interests formed for mutual aid and protection, and included religious, commercial, and industrial groups. The chief aim of the merchant guilds was to secure a monopoly of the trade of the town and its neighborhood and to protect its members from the competition of strangers. The primary purpose of the craft guilds was to secure complete control of the production of the articles of a particular craft. They regulated the way goods were produced, the hours and wages of the craftsmen, the price of the commodities, and enforced rules in regard to learning the trade. The guilds included three groups: apprentices, journeymen, and masters. The members of the various craft guilds usually lived together in one section of the town. Many surnames, such as Smith, Weaver, Cooper, Taylor, and Currier, denoting the original occupation of the workers, have come down from the crafts of the Middle Ages. The early guilds often formed a bulwark against the oppression of the nobility and thus played an important part in securing municipal and civil liberty.

In spite of its walls, the medieval town was not cut off from the surrounding countryside. Peasants, continuing to cultivate their fields and pastures, moved close to it for protection and for social life. Towns that grew out of villages retained around them their old common fields, strips, and pastures. Villagers and others visited the markets and fairs, trading under the conditions and regulations laid down by the guilds. In spite of the guilds, certain questionable practices arose. Among commercial terms relating to them were forestalling (preventing normal trading by buying or diverting goods before they got to the markets or fairs), engrossing (monopolizing, controlling or cornering the market), and regrating (buying to sell again at a profit). At the pie powder courts (from *pied poudré* or "dusty foot" courts) the law merchant—legal rules applied to cases arising in trade transactions—was quickly administered in cases of dispute. The commercial, industrial, and social aspects of town life, as they unfolded, were important factors in the economic awakening of Europe.

The new activities in manufacture and exchange produced a class of successful townsmen, usually called the bourgeois or middle class. Some came from the lower orders of nobility; others were freemen; and some were emancipated or escaped serfs who became free, according to custom and law, if they could maintain their freedom for a year and a day. Those townsmen who were able to attain wealth and power above that of their fellows became the governing class. They were the masters of the guilds, the prosperous merchants, and the officials. Having made use of the lower classes to destroy the control of the feudal lords, they denied them a share in government. Thus, a medieval town was in no way democratic, for government was vested in the hands of a few. New class distinctions arose between the bourgeois (the prosperous groups) and the proletariat (the lowest groups), which have been bequeathed to modern times. Class hatreds developed and serious revolts occurred from time to time. Having fought their way from serfdom, the masses fell prey to the domination of the rising and prosperous middle class. It was this influential group that laid the foundations for the commercial and industrial expansion which in time was to affect all parts of the globe.

THE ECONOMIC IMPORTANCE
OF THE CRUSADES

Throughout the Middle Ages much value was attached to pilgrimages to the shrines of saints. The long journey from western Europe to the Holy Land was the greatest religious service or duty one could undertake. It was attempted by nobles and others because of deep religious feeling or in the hope of securing pardon for sins—often for both reasons. The Mohammedans, who controlled much of the Near East, did not object to the Christian pilgrims, for they exploited them in this profitable tourist trade. But by the eleventh century, the Arab empire was falling into decay and a number of separate kingdoms were forming within it. On these the warlike Turks descended, wresting control and power from the Arabs. The Crusades began as a religious war to recover the Holy Places from the fierce Seljuk Turks, who, by becoming converts to Islam, made easier their conquest of Asia Minor. With the sign of the cross sewed on their jackets and the words, " 'Tis the will of God," on their lips, the crusaders turned eastward for almost two centuries (1096–1270). In addition to the religious motive, many set out in the hope of securing new principalities for themselves in the expectation of obtaining riches or from a thirst for adventure. The story of the movement is a strange blend of religious fanaticism, greed, and recklessness.

While the Crusades cost Europe a million lives and in general failed in their objectives, except for the control of Jerusalem for about a hundred years, they constituted another blow to the feudal system. Rich barons were compelled to sell their possessions in order to raise money to equip troops and to transport them to the Syrian coast. The personal power of many princes who stayed home was increased as a result, especially through the reversion and seizure of feudal holdings which became vacant. The failure of many to return meant freedom for the serfs who were able to flee to the towns, and also resulted in the extension of the power and influence of the ruling classes in the towns. The Crusades did much to bring in the new commercial era, as well as to increase the power and authority of the Church and the Papacy.

The crusaders traveled by land and sea. Their activities benefited the rising Italian commercial cities. Venice, Genoa, Pisa, Barcelona, Marseilles, and others made increasing contacts with Constantinople (Byzantium), which as an independent state had stood guard throughout the Middle Ages against the inroads of the barbarians and had preserved from destruction much of the best in civilization. The rivalry between the Italian cities, especially Venice and Genoa, for trade with Constantinople and the southeastern Mediterranean was woven into the warp and woof of the Crusades.

The economic awakening of Europe had begun more than a century before the Crusades. That movement, however, stimulated commerce by creating new markets in the East for European products—mostly raw materials, especially metals and minerals—and by extending into the West the use of oriental products, such as sugar, spices, tapestries, dyestuffs, fragrant woods, perfumes, cotton, silk, calicoes, muslins, satins, velvets, and other products. The crusaders were amazed at the high culture of the Saracens with whom they came in contact. Those fortunate enough to get back home carried with them desires for the luxuries of the East and a determination to get them. At this time in western Europe, Italy was foremost in the production of luxury goods, but Italian arts and crafts were inferior in many ways to those of the Levant and the more distant Orient. As a result of the Crusades, the increased trade and commerce brought many foreign countries into more intimate relations with each other. In consequence, much progress was made in transportation, especially in navigation and shipbuilding. The Italian cities acquired wealth and attained vast commercial importance. Many men became curious about distant parts of the East. Travelers, like the great Venetian, Marco Polo, visited China and other eastern countries. In addition to important economic results, the Crusades also influenced the culture of Europe profoundly, although Arabian culture entered Europe in other ways as well, notably through Spain and Sicily.

THE EXPANSION OF COMMERCE

Trade routes became more complex as commerce expanded. The Levant once more was the crossroads of civilization. That eastern end of the Mediterranean marked the routes of conquest and martyrdom of generations of warriors and traders. From this region early Phoenician merchants had extended their commercial imperialism; vast Roman legions trod these shores as they turned eastward for conquest; here the crusaders sought the protection of God for their deeds of piety and cruelty; and in this active but troubled area Venetians, Genoese, and other Italian traders built trading posts, carried on diplomatic intrigues, and made deals with the Arabs.

From the Far East to the Levant, goods were brought by the Arabs over three main routes. Merchandise was carried by sea from eastern

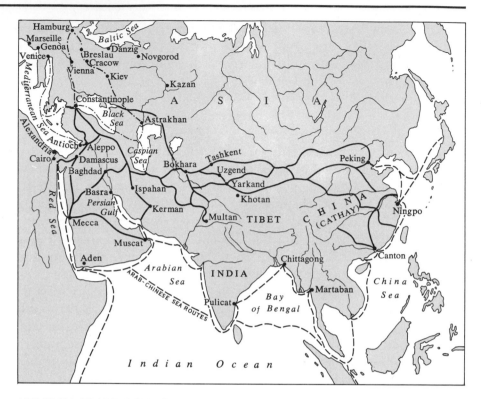

MEDIEVAL TRADE ROUTES, LAND AND SEA

Asia to Ormuz, to the north end of the Persian Gulf, thence up the
ancient Tigris valley to fabulous Baghdad. From this city, the center
of Mohammedan wealth and learning, several caravan routes branched
out, north to Tabriz, westward to Antioch, Damascus, or Jaffa. A
northern land route, across mountain, valley, plain, and desert led
from inland China and India to Bokhara and from there several routes
met from the West, one branching out into the Caspian, up the Volga
to central Russia and the Baltic, while another continued west to Trebi-
zond on the Black Sea. The third or southern route was an all-water
way from India across the Indian Ocean and the Arabian Sea to the
Red Sea, where goods were landed at Berenice on the African coast
and transported by caravan to the Nile, thence down that river to
the great metropolis of Alexandria or to other seaports on the Mediterranean.

From the cities of the Levant, the Italian traders had a monopoly
over the distribution of Eastern goods into Europe, for they controlled
the Mediterranean. This great sea remained the center of European

commerce until the latter part of the fifteenth century, when triumphant Venice, after reaching the height of vigor and prosperity with her oligarchy, fleets, colonies, and commercial control, gradually declined. The age of discovery marked the doom of Italian commercial monopoly as the supremacy and power of the Italian cities were seized by the rising national states on the western coast of Europe.

During the period when the Italian merchants dominated the expanding commercial scene, it was natural that inter-regional trade should greatly increase as town life expanded and the demand for exotic luxuries grew. European trade routes, many of them ages old, saw increasing activity. Over the passes of the Alps, along the Rhone River, and through the Strait of Gibraltar to northern countries, prosperous trading was carried on by many different peoples. Associations of individuals, groups, and towns gave impetus to commercial activities. Such, for example, were the Merchants of the Staple comprising an association of Englishmen for the export of English wool and other raw materials; and the Merchant Adventurers constituting a company of English merchants dealing in cloth and other commodities, especially with Germany and the Low Countries. The outstanding association of towns was the famous Hanseatic League of North Germany whose commercial activities were carried on with England, the Netherlands, Norway, Denmark, Sweden, and Russia. This league served in a sense as a government and waged wars, made treaties with foreign states, taxed its members, and took a leading part in the affairs of northern Europe until about 1500. Many individual merchants or mercantile houses also became wealthy and powerful. The Bardi and Medici of Florence who rose to heights of magnificence through mercantile and banking pursuits; Jacques Coeur, the merchant-prince of Bourges, whose dazzling career brought him into the royal favor of Charles VII, but whose wealth led to his ruin at the hands of that fickle and covetous monarch; and the generations of the Fuggers of Augsburg, who had commercial and financial connections all over Europe, are examples of great individual merchants of the period. Although the Italian cities held a monopoly of trade on the Mediterranean, inter-regional trade was carried on by the peoples of all the important countries of Europe.

THE ORIGINS OF MODERN CAPITALISM

An early writer classified medieval society into three groups—the prayers, the fighters, and the workers. The latter were chiefly the miserable serfs whose toil largely supported the rest of society. By the thirteenth century, the new middle class had arisen in the towns and was increasing rapidly. Before the fifteenth century, wealthy middle-class families, such as the Medici in Italy and the Fuggers in Germany, were becoming important and influential. They possessed an abundance of floating wealth and became the financiers of commercial undertakings, of banking projects, of industrial enterprises, of rulers, and of nations. In the accumulations of money, the development of new methods to obtain profits, and the growth of the profit-making spirit may be found the origins of modern capitalism.

The medieval way of life was essentially religious, and religion colored economic ideas as well as political and social thought. In the strictest view, profits of any sort were sinful. According to the Church, one risked his soul in such gainful transactions, for it might lead to avarice or greed. The Church strove to enforce its prohibition of usury by the denial of communion, the refusal of Christian burial, and in other ways. Its courts, as well as those of the rising towns and states, also tried to punish such offenders by imposing heavy fines. But as early as the thirteenth century, the Church's stand on usury and profit-seeking was beginning to weaken. Dante, Italy's most famous poet, gave the moneylenders of Cahors a particular place in hell, but a Pope called them "peculiar sons of the Church." In the centuries that followed, preachers, teachers, and writers began to justify usury and profits. At the same time, the guilds, which made regulations for the benefit of all their members, gradually began to lose some of their power. These factors slowly but surely brought about the acceptance of the capitalist spirit.

The accumulation of early capital goes back to the eleventh century. At that time agriculture was still the chief form of economic life. It required the use of little or no money and was carried on not for profit but for the subsistence of the inhabitants of each manor or estate. But with the rise of town life once again, money slowly came into circulation and tended to accumulate in the hands of aggressive or fortunate individuals. In some cases, profits were obtained from the existence of agricultural surpluses, which were sold at markets and fairs. Important, also, was the growing use of money for ever-increasing taxes and dues, collected by nobles, kings, and the Church. Profits in rising commerce and the output of new gold and silver mines in Europe also enabled merchants to amass wealth. The economic awakening of Europe brought increases in rents of lands and houses, with resulting stores of capital. Moneylending and financial undertakings were means of building fortunes. Wealth also accumulated as export industries developed, such as the Florentine and Flemish woolen manufactures, the silk industries of Italian cities, and the metalware production of Belgium and the Rhineland. From various sources, therefore, medieval accumulations of money of simple origin provided the basis for capital. Fully developed capitalism, however, did not appear until after the industrial revolution of the eighteenth century. By that time broad markets, a highly developed money and credit economy, and the expansion of the wage system, as well as strict private ownership of the means of production and exchange, became the outstanding aspects of modern capitalism.

Even in the late medieval period, however, infant capitalism accelerated the growth of national states, especially as the rising nations came to realize the importance of economic matters. They began to develop more intense trade rivalries and, finally, a scramble for colonies. Capital was necessary if a country was to expand economically. The origins of mercantilism, which dominated Europe for several centuries, can be found in this period. Mercantilism may be defined as a system of economic nationalism by which a state put into practice methods and means of economic control to secure unity, power, and wealth. The striking political developments in the rise of national states were paralleled by economic ideas and practices. It should be emphasized that mercantilism, as it developed, varied in its operations and details in each country.

OCEAN TRADE ROUTES

From the beginnings of the Crusades, European trade and exploration had taken an eastern direction—toward the lands of the rising sun. As commerce was reaching a new height in the thirteenth century, a terrible horde of invaders from central Asia—the Mongols under Genghis Khan—swept down and broke the power of the Seljuk Turks. When the tide of Mongol invasion rolled back, Asia Minor was divided into a number of small districts, each ruled by a petty chief. One of these was Othman, the leader of a band of Turks from Central Asia. His followers became known as Ottomans. The warlike Ottoman Turks conquered other groups and extended their conquests. For a century and a half, they possessed Asia Minor, the coasts of the Black Sea, the Aegean Islands, and in 1453 Constantinople itself fell to them. Caring little for trade, the raiders lived largely by plunder. The Italian cities, especially Venice, suffered greatly by these conquests and sought new routes of commerce southeastward from Asia Minor. But here, too, the marauders spread until by 1517 they had occupied Syria and

Egypt, checking the flow of goods east and west through their raids and depredations and imposing heavy duties, but not entirely closing the trade routes.

While there were many reasons for the decline of the Italian cities, the disruption of trade by the Turks was an important one. At the time that Turks and Mongols controlled eastern Europe, many Europeans began to turn their attention in other directions. As a result of trying to get to Asia in a roundabout manner, either by way of a southern and eastern route or directly westward, they accidentally found themselves on the portals of a new world, which became known as America. As the Italian cities declined, Portugal and Spain took the lead in the new age of discovery. Venice held her own in the Mediterranean for a time, but that great power also went down in defeat. The exhaustion of Italian oak forests and revolutionary changes in rigging and in armament that confronted Venice in the competition with the rising western nations were also partly responsible for the decline of Venetian commerce.[1]

Portugal, favored by her position on the Atlantic, possessed a mountainous country not well suited for agriculture; with Spanish enemies on land, and desirous of competing for European trade, she was the first to engage in long sea expeditions. Her harbors had become shelterports for the growing commerce between the Mediterranean and the north of Europe. Learning from the proficient Italian seamen who had introduced the mariner's compass into Europe in the thirteenth century, using the astrolabe for determining a ship's position at sea, developing the art of making sailing charts and maps, and introducing many improvements in sailing, Portugal sent her mariners down the African coast seeking commerce and trade. After the middle of the fifteenth century, each captain tried to push farther south than his predecessor. Every fleet carried the banner of Christianity to the islands off the African coast, and the trade that developed, strangely enough, brought back Negro slaves, reintroducing into Europe slavery which had come to an end with Rome's downfall.

After Portuguese sailors had crossed the Equator, they discovered that the north star disappeared and that a southern constellation of stars appeared. New charts of the sky had to be devised and much superstition about unknown areas had to be overcome. Finally, in 1486, Bartholomew Diaz rounded the Cape of Storms and even sailed a few hundred miles beyond; but it was not until ten years later that

[1] F. C. Lane, *Venetian Ships and Shipbuilders of the Renaissance* (Baltimore, 1934), pp. 217 ff.

this point, renamed the Cape of Good Hope, was not only rounded, but the adventurous Vasco da Gama reached the coveted land of India. Two and a half years later, after much trouble with the native Mohammedans whom he found there, he returned home with a cargo worth sixty times what his expedition cost. The king of Portugal, after knighting the victorious explorer, assumed for himself the title "Lord of the Conquest, Navigation, and Commerce of Ethiopia, Arabia, Persia and China." The discovery of the new route to the Indies was a decisive blow to Venice and the other declining Italian cities. Spain soon followed Portugal in sending explorers to distant parts of the world. Commerce and seafaring were no longer confined to the Mediterranean as mariners sailed eastward and westward. This change from the Mediterranean as the chief scene of commerce to the Seven Seas, together with the tremendous economic results that followed, has been called the commercial revolution.

THE PORTUGUESE EMPIRE

A long line of explorers and discoverers built Portugal's commercial empire. It was based on a monopoly of trade in the East Indies and parts of India. The spice trade to Europe, controlled heretofore in the Mediterranean largely by Venice, now passed to her rising competitor, and the old monopolies of the Italian cities over all types of Eastern goods were broken. Trade was also extended to parts of China and Japan. The Portuguese established a colonial and commercial empire which embraced the western and eastern coasts of Africa from Guinea to the Red Sea and extended along the shores of southern and eastern Asia to China. This great expanse of territory was linked by chains of fortresses and factories. In the New World, Brazil was claimed by Portuguese explorers and a profitable trade in dyewood and other products of that region developed as colonization was encouraged. For a time, Lisbon, the capital of Portugal, became the center of the world's commerce.

The Portuguese Empire was a warlike one, ruled over by viceroys, admirals, and generals, who delighted to fight the "infidel" and despoil the "heathen." At its height, it boasted of an area containing thirty-two foreign kingdoms and 400 fortresses, but the home government exercised little control over these far-off officials. This great empire had but a brief existence. Incompetent monarchs and corrupt governments led to its decline. Within a century, Portugal had come under the power of Spain and a generation later most of her possessions passed to the Dutch.

THE SPANISH EMPIRE IN THE NEW WORLD

While Portuguese explorers were seeking distant lands, Spain became active. After offering his services to the king of England and the monarch of Portugal without result, the Italian navigator, Cristobal Colon, whom we call Christopher Columbus, sailed westward under the flags of a united Spain with the financial aid and the blessing of Ferdinand and Isabella. Obstinate and ambitious, he had waited for years until the conditions he laid down should be accepted. Among these, his demands that he be made viceroy of all lands he discovered and that he be granted one-tenth of all their produce were finally accepted with some reluctance. On August 3, 1492, his epochal first voyage began at Palos as the three little caravels slowly sailed out of the harbor.

Whether Columbus left Spain to discover a new route to India and Cathay, or to find islands and lands which could be Christianized and bring honor and wealth to the Spanish monarchs and to himself, we do not know. In spite of a mutinous crew, the failure of the compass when the line of "no variation" was crossed, and gross miscalculations as to distance, the expedition reached San Salvador (Watling Island in the Bahamas) on October 12, 1492. Clad in armor covered with a cloak of scarlet, Columbus was rowed to shore and unfurled the royal banners of Aragon and Castile. He found the peaceful inhabitants in a lowly stage of culture, for they pointed their javelins with fishbones and their darts with the teeth of fish. They brought to the explorers parrots, cotton threads in balls, and darts, for which they received in exchange red caps, small bells, strings of glass beads, and other trinkets. Columbus seemed sure that he was near the Indies. In his travels to the various islands he sought to verify this belief. He had with him an interpreter "who had been a Jew, knowing Hebrew, Chaldee, and even some Arabic," and together they tried to persuade themselves when they heard the natives talk of Cuba that Cipango (Japan) was meant. He refused to believe that he had not reached the Orient, an attitude that was shared by the Spanish rulers and officials for many years. On the return voyage, marked by mistakes and catastrophes entailing the loss of two vessels, he reached Portugal and then arrived in Spain, when he experienced the moments of his greatest glory. He was now Lord Don Cristobal Colon, Grand Admiral of the Ocean Sea.

In his later voyages, Columbus sought feverishly for gold and other riches on many islands of the West Indies as well as for a passage to the Orient. The fourth voyage, begun in 1502, was a pathetic attempt to remove the ignominy that had fallen upon him. On this trip, Columbus and his men, with their rotting ships, were marooned at Jamaica, until, after horrible hardships and mutiny, they were finally rescued and reached Spain toward the end of 1504. Two years later, after a life of trials and vicissitudes, the great navigator died. Columbus was not the first European to come to these shores. But all his forerunners failed to leave records which could be pieced together to form an intelligent picture of their activities. It was Columbus who led the way in bringing to the Western Hemisphere permanent occupation by the Christian faith and by European civilization.

Spain lost little time in exploiting the resources of the New World. The Spaniards found that the Incas of Peru, the Mayas of Central America, and the Aztecs of Mexico were well advanced in the arts of civilization. Although unskilled in the use of firearms and steel weapons, certain types of handicrafts and trades were relatively well developed. While agriculture was the main occupation of the natives of the southern lands, there was some specialization in industry and various regions became noted for certain products. Markets under government supervision were held regularly in specified places. Silver, lead, and tin were mined at Tasco and copper was taken from the mountain of Zacotollan. Gold, found in many places near the surface of the earth, in the beds of rivers and even in mines, was cast into bars. Vessels of gold and silver were made and often carved with great skill as can be attested by recent finds in ruined and moldering temples. The two Indian kingdoms, Mexico and Peru, conquered by Cortez and Pizarro, respectively, were the richest and most important provinces of Spain in the New World, and like all the Spanish provinces in America were administered by viceroys.

Under the rule of the Spaniards, mining of precious metals continued and European methods of securing the riches were adopted. Of the thousands of mines which were opened and exploited, many became famous. Indian and Negro workers produced great wealth for their masters. Vast quantities of gold and silver were sent to Spain, which were wasted by the Spanish monarchs in wars and politics. The great increase in the supply of gold and silver in Europe speeded up the change from a barter to a money economy and brought about a startling rise in prices. Spanish America fell prey to plunder first; then trade and colonization developed. A land system was established which included peonage. The conquistadores vigorously explored much of America and made known to the world the flora, fauna, tribes, and geography of a large part of the American hemisphere.

Spain made contributions to the New World in the form of her distinctive culture. Mexico City and Lima became the capitals and the centers from which Spanish-American civilization radiated. In these cities were the palaces of the viceroys and archbishops, cathedrals, and the first universities in America. In the wake of administrators and clergy, Spain sent to her overseas empire many craftsmen, artists, and architects, who taught the Indian workers to build splendid churches, monasteries, and homes of Spanish design. Teachers brought across the ocean the learning of the Old World, and Spanish customs as well as language were established wherever there was a settlement. The *fiestas* of the Church and of patron saints were celebrated and also Indian ceremonies. From the beginning there was intermarriage between the Spaniards and the Indians so that in time their offspring of mixed blood, called *mestizos,* made up a large part of the population.

Throughout the history of Spanish America the Church was a great civilizing and inspiring influence. Missionaries and priests accompanied soldiers on expeditions of conquest to save the souls of those who were often plundered and enslaved. After Spanish culture was well established in Mexico and Peru, these missionaries pushed to the outposts of Spanish settlement. They were not afraid of manual work, for ancient buildings in northern Mexico and California still stand as a record to their genius, labor, and devotion. Out of homesick memories of great churches and monasteries of the homeland they designed mission houses with thick walls and beautiful bell towers and built them with the help of their Indian charges.

Great estates, called *haciendas,* were established in Spain's American colonies. The master, overseers, managers, and Indian workers lived together in self-sufficient communities, frequently many miles from any town. On these large plantations corn was grown and also wheat, rice, and sugar cane. Groves of oranges, lemons, and other semi-tropical fruits flourished. Later, coffee trees brought to Martinique in the West Indies by the French were transplanted in Central and South America by the Spanish and the Portuguese. Great coffee and cacao plantations brought wealth to their owners. Cattle were also raised on huge ranches. The home government encouraged agricultural development in the colonies, but was chiefly interested in the precious metals which were used for the gain and glory of Spain.

Several times a year the galleons sailed for Spain from Vera Cruz in Mexico and from Nombre de Dios or Porto Bello on the isthmus of Panama. Gold and silver were taken by ship from Peru to Panama and then carried on the backs of slaves or mules through jungles to the port of shipment. Spanish commercial policy was highly restrictive and trade was limited to a group of select merchants. From the seat of government in Spain, all the trade of the empire was regulated.

Colonial New Spain's farthest outpost was the Philippines. From 1565 to 1815, the Manila galleon plied its way annually from Acapulco, Mexico, to Manila, returning with Oriental goods to enrich the life of Spanish America. To Manila harbor came Far Eastern traders, largely Chinese, but also Japanese, Portuguese, and others. Here they sold their silks, spices, porcelains, and other wares to Spanish merchants who sent part of them on the long and perilous trip to Mexico. On the journeys across the Pacific, occasional conflicts occurred with the Dutch and English for the domination of the region or more often

THE WESTERN HEMISPHERE IN 1600

for booty. Drake, Cavendish, Dampier, and Rogers sought to capture the richest of all prizes ever sought by buccaneers—the Manila galleon. These voyages made and lost the fortune of many a Spanish grandee of Manila, but the commerce did not expand much, for it was carried on against the background of the restricted Spanish colonial and economic policy.

During the Spanish settlement of America the question of the sphericity of the world was settled in one of the most amazing journeys on record. Five antiquated, but well-calked and well-repaired vessels under the command of Magellan, a Portuguese in the service of Spain, left Seville in 1519, seeking a new way to the Far East. The largest ship, the *San Antonia* had a displacement of only 120 tons, but the mariners looked forward to a long voyage as is evident by the large stores of sea biscuit, cheeses, anchovies, honey, raisins, and wines as well as the seven cows that they took along. In spite of this, the crew was driven to cook and eat the leather housings of the riggings and the voyage was fraught with peril including mutiny.

After poking into the La Plata estuary, wintering in the desolate bay of San Julian, and sailing through the strait that now bears his name, Magellan courageously pushed across the Pacific. His men who had been lucky enough to live through the terrors of the voyage were walking skeletons when they landed on the Philippines, but Magellan knew what he had accomplished when he discovered islanders speaking the Malay tongue. While exploring the islands, the great navigator took sides in a petty and unnecessary skirmish between natives and lost his life. In September, 1522, one vessel instead of five, and eighteen men of the original 265 got back to Cadiz. The globe had been circumnavigated. It was proved that the westward route to the wealth of the Indies lay across the Pacific which in itself was a voyage covering almost half the globe. The money, power, and prestige that Magellan had looked forward to on his return had been denied him through his tragic death. The merchants who financed the voyage made a profit over and above their investment and the loss of their ships, from the spices brought home in the eighty-five ton *Victoria*.

FRANCE AND THE NEW WORLD

French fishermen visited the Grand Banks off Newfoundland as early as 1504 and within a century they had built up an industry there and in the Gulf of St. Lawrence that employed hundreds of vessels annually. Long before the close of the century the French, in connection with their fisheries, carried on barter for furs with the

Indians. In the 1580's merchants of St. Malo used some of their vessels for the fur trade alone and made large profits. Keen competition followed. Privileged companies were organized, but because of the hazards of the trade they usually combined fishing with the fur trade to lessen the expenses of the distant voyages. Long before the establishment of New France a profitable trade in fish and furs had been established.

In the meantime, French explorers sailed westward in the name of France. Verrazano, a Florentine seaman, in 1524 provided a French paper claim to much of North America. Jacques Cartier of St. Malo sailed up the St. Lawrence River and explored it as far as the site of the present Montreal. His three expeditions (1534–1542) served to fix attention for the time being on the region near the Gulf of St. Lawrence. In 1562, Jean Ribaut explored the coast of Florida seeking a place of settlement for French Huguenots, but without success. Two years later, Huguenot colonists built Fort Carolina on the St. John's River, Florida, but the Spaniards put a quick end to it, blotting it out entirely. Before the end of the century a number of groups attempted to establish small colonies. None was permanent until Champlain, after several years of exploration, made possible the first permanent French settlement at Quebec (1608).

In spite of the devotion of Champlain, the "Father of New France," to the colony, its growth was slow. He had visions of a future nation with its capital at Quebec, but the French authorities, whose imagination was restricted to nomadic trading and trapping, granted monopolies to commercial companies. The colony on the St. Lawrence therefore expanded slowly. Priests, explorers, and traders blazed a trail along the Great Lakes and down the Mississippi, preparing the way for scattered settlements in the heart of the continent. French posts finally extended from Nova Scotia to New Orleans. The expanding fur trade of New France as well as the harsh climate of the more settled regions in the north handicapped the production of agricultural products and made the French settlements dependent to some extent on the French West Indies, and the French fishing industry dependent on the English mainland colonies for supplies. Government policy, especially the principle of commercial monopoly and the seignioral system, together with the dominance of the Roman Catholic Church, strengthened control over the fur trade, but seriously restricted population and growth, which in the course of time led to the fall of New France as the English along the seaboard grew in numbers and power.

THE ENGLISH BACKGROUND

England was much later than Portugal and Spain in developing a passion for colonization. The change in the map of the world following the discovery of America and the Cape route to the East placed that country closer to the center of world affairs. Yet she did little in this respect until the middle of the sixteenth century. It is true that a few years after Columbus' discovery, John Cabot, a Venetian by birth, a Genoese by legal adoption, and a merchant of Bristol at the time, sailed westward under the English flag. Like others of his period, he looked across the sea to lands unexplored and unknown. In 1497, with his son, Sebastian, he left Bristol and finally reached some of the islands and the mainland coast of North America. After an absence of about three months he was back in England. The voyage caused much enthusiasm in English seaports and led to a second expedition the next year under Sebastian Cabot to explore what was believed to be the coast line of northern Asia. The expeditions noted among other things the importance of the cod-fisheries of Newfoundland, but they were devoid of real results. Merchants and businessmen were thinking in terms of rich Oriental products and gold, not of fish, and as a result more than a hundred years passed before the first English colonies were established, although within a decade English fishing fleets were venturing to the New World. In closing this brief attempt at English exploration, Henry VII wrote in his account book: "To hym that found the new Isle, £10," and he granted John Cabot a pension of £20 annually which he did not live long to enjoy.

Many reasons can be given for the lack of British interest in exploration and colonization during the first half of the sixteenth century. While the modern period of English history may be dated from 1485 when the first Tudor, Henry VII, emerged the victor from the long and disastrous Wars of the Roses, England did not possess the energy to turn westward, largely because internal problems and concentration on domestic development absorbed her energies. As the island kingdom emerged from feudalism, she had little surplus capital to spare in expensive and hazardous ventures; land was still the principal form of wealth, although mercantile pursuits were developing; her vessels were poor and her merchant marine was small; her enemies, particularly Spain, were powerful and controlled the sea lanes. During the reign of Henry VIII, the religious and political scene was unsettled and remained so until Elizabeth came to the throne. The geography of exploration was also against Britain, for the parallel lines of latitude and ill-favored winds directed the course of its tiny vessels, in days when tacking was undeveloped, to harsh climates and bleak coasts and not to the mild sunny regions.

But England had many advantages which in the course of time were to make her the greatest of all colonizing powers. These included a long coastline and abundant harbor facilities; an insular isolation which in this period saved her from invasion and the devastation of wars; a sturdy population made up of Anglo-Saxons, Celts, Danes, and Norman-French elements; a temperate climate; a rapidly increasing middle class of merchants and manufacturers; and, a surplus of agricultural workers.

While earlier monarchs had worked to move England from a passive to an active economic role, it was the first Tudor who adopted a positive policy of expanding England's influence on the seas. In addition to having considered the financing of Columbus and having encouraged the activities of the Cabots, Henry VII did much to develop regular war fleets instead of the haphazard gathering of armed merchant vessels from the Cinque Ports and other places in times of emergency and during wars. He was responsible for the early elementary form of navigation legislation; while through diplomacy and alliances, he did everything possible to increase England's commerce, trade, and manufactures.

Henry VIII continued the policy of his father. He expanded the British navy and even interested himself in problems of naval construction, as can be seen in the part he took in designing the *Great Harry,* a remarkably large ship for her day. Throughout his life and during the reigns of Edward VI and Mary Tudor, English seamanship steadily developed and the art of navigation advanced. Fishing fleets sailed regularly to Icelandic waters, while fishing in home waters increased. British seamen were also furnished with letters of marque, giving them authority to attack the Spaniards and others who could be considered enemies and not friends. By Elizabeth's reign, those privateering fleets had gradually grown into the navy of Hawkins, Howard, and Sir Francis Drake.

During this transitional period in English history, practices were begun which, while causing suffering to many groups and interests, were to result in greater glory to the nation and were to furnish wealth for new ventures in colonization and trade. The system of enclosures, enforced by law for the benefit of important landowners, brought together large tracts of land chiefly for the purpose of sheep raising. The enclosure of lands resulted in higher rents and greatly increased profits from wool for the landowners, but ousted peasants from plots which they had held by right, custom, or tenantry, bringing widespread unemployment. The seizure and confiscation of much of the wealth of the Church during the English Reformation enriched the government, but the spoils found their way into the hands of favorites and courtiers, furnishing much capital that was used in commercial undertakings. The beginning of the English slave trade also was an important factor in the expansion of British commerce. As early as 1562, John Hawkins carried African slaves from the Guinea coast to Spanish possessions, although many years were to elapse before Britain broke the Spanish and Dutch slave-carrying monopolies. But by the time of Elizabeth the stage was set for expansion and for the beginnings of English imperialism.

CHAPTER 2

The Beginning of a New Society

The first important English explorations and the earliest attempts at colonization began during the reign of Elizabeth. That age, like the works of Shakespeare, its literary crown, did not spring spontaneously into existence. In all its aspects—social, economic, cultural, and political—it was the culmination of all that had gone before. The Renaissance in England, like that on the continent which had preceded it, was of slow growth and was rooted in medieval soil. Centering in Elizabeth's court, it burst into bloom like an unfolding rose. But even during this period of splendor, England was a turbulent and brawling country, where men defended their lives and property by their wits and swords, where political intrigue ran high and was fanned by religious differences, and where piracy and patriotism were closely related. During Elizabeth's long reign of forty-five years, however, the English people achieved relative prosperity, international prestige, and much fame—and ill-fame—on the high seas.

The most spectacular features of Elizabeth's "glorious age," which have cast a colorful glamour over that period, were the attacks of bold English buccaneers on the treasure cities of the Spanish Main and the plundering of Spanish galleons returning to the Old World laden with gold and silver from America. John Hawkins, Martin Frobisher, Sir

Francis Drake, and other "sea dogs" sailed the Seven Seas, exploring barren Arctic wastes and luxurious tropical climes. They took great pride in daring adventures, especially against the Spaniards, who were forced to defend their possessions in America, as well as their right to sail the sea. The figure of Sir Francis Drake is one of the world's romantic characters, whose exploits included the circumnavigation of the globe, and were to culminate in the Channel fight against the Armada when the fleet under Lord Admiral Howard broke the might of Spain. But many others also played a most important part in building up England's prosperity during this period.

At the time that Elizabeth ascended the throne, England was not a rich country, while Spain was at the height of her power. How desperately poor England actually was can be sensed by the fact that the treasure of a single captured galleon was almost equal to one-fourth of the government's annual income. It is no wonder that the island kingdom with the connivance of Queen Elizabeth herself turned to such activities as privateering in which she participated. However, her ministers were at pains to keep her actions in this respect well concealed.

Among the earliest English explorers who sought the northwest passage and blazed the trail of discovery for England's glory was Martin Frobisher, who was financed by the Cathay Company. On his first westward voyage in 1576 he explored the bay that now bears his name and discovered Baffin Land. He returned with an Eskimo and with a small sample of what he thought was gold. On his third expedition, believing he had found vast stores of the precious metal, he returned home with a cargo of worthless pyrites or "fool's gold," to his own disappointed astonishment, the amusement of his friends, and the jeers of his enemies. Following the path of Frobisher, between 1585 and 1587, John Davis led three expeditions into Davis Strait and Baffin Bay in an unsuccessful attempt to find a passage through the intricate network of seas, inlets, and bays. But out of the dreams of Sir Humphrey Gilbert to discover the northwest route to the East came the first real though futile attempts at English colonization.

FUTILE ATTEMPTS AT COLONIZATION

Sir Humphrey Gilbert, a member of the Muscovy Company, who wrote a *Discourse of a Discovery for a New Passage to Cataia* to prove the feasibility and desirability of seeking the northwest passage, secured from Elizabeth a patent for establishing a colony which he was to rule, reserving to the Crown one-fifth of all the profits from the venture. A settlement at Newfoundland was planned which would provide Sir Humphrey with a great estate, aid the English fisheries, and afford a station on the route to the Indies. Lands were sold, especially to wealthy English Catholics. Gilbert's friend, Richard Hakluyt, the geographer, gave the project publicity in his book, *Divers Voyages.* In 1583, with 260 men of all ranks and occupations, the colony was established; but the bleakness of the environment, the rigors of the winter climate, sickness, the thwarted desire to find gold, and serious mutiny brought about its failure. While attempting to reorganize his project, Gilbert was lost in a storm at sea and his colonizing mantle descended on his half brother, Sir Walter Raleigh.

English seagoing activities began to take on a more constructive form under Gilbert and Raleigh as these men promoted colonization. Raleigh was a navigator, warrior, statesman, writer, and a favorite at Elizabeth's court. Following the tragic death of Gilbert, Raleigh received a royal grant almost identical with that of his predecessor. He sponsored three expeditions to the Albemarle region of present North Carolina, a region then vaguely known as Virginia, in honor of the Virgin Queen. The first expedition, in 1584, was one of exploration. After two months, the party returned to England with reports of a beautiful country, vast forests, an abundance of game and fish, a fertile soil, and friendly Indians. Queen Elizabeth was pleased; she formally named the land Virginia; and she rewarded Raleigh by knighting him.

Now the project of founding a colony was seriously undertaken, but with no adequate conception of the economic problems involved. For the next century optimistic colonizers, dreaming of an overseas empire and personal prestige and profits, failed realistically to assess the amount of capital needed to plant a successful overseas colony. The colony placed on Roanoke Island in 1585 with Sir Richard Grenville in charge of the supply fleet was no exception. While Thomas Hariot, the publicist of the group, pointed out correctly that the manufacture of iron in the New World would be advantageous to the mother country, and noted the presumed abundance of ores, together with an infinite supply of wood from the vast forests—a suggestion of importance in view of the shortage of wood in England which affected shipbuilding—the colony failed. Inadequate supplies, the increasing unfriendliness of the Indians, and a vain quest for gold brought unrest and distress. When Drake's fleet appeared on the coast, the colonists returned to England after an experiment of only ten months. Grenville returned with supplies, but found the colonists gone; he left fifteen men to maintain possession. But when Raleigh's third expedition reached Roanoke in 1587, headed by Captain John White, only the bones of one of Grenville's men were found. The fort and houses were in ruins.

The third expedition also failed from a lack of adequate investment. The settlement, usually known as the Lost Colony, was incorporated as "the Governor and Assistants of the Cities of Raleigh in Virginia." Three small ships left Plymouth on May 5, 1587 carrying 117 persons for the new colony. Although not by intention, Roanoke Island was once again the scene of colonization. Here the daughter of Governor White and wife of Ananias Dare gave birth to the first English child born in America. White returned to England to find that excitement and danger from the threatened Spanish Armada overshadowed everything else. He did not return to the colony until 1591 and when he reached the spot with new supplies, he found no trace of the colony except the letters CRO carved on a tree and the word Croatoan cut into the doorpost of the palisade. The fate of the colony remained a mystery. It has been assumed that the colonists went to the Indians on the island of Croatan to the southward; some have thought that they were victims of the Spanish or possibly of unfriendly Indians.

While English sea power developed by leaps and bounds and English commerce was spreading to distant parts of the world, it became apparent that it would take more than individual initiative to establish permanent colonies. Out of British commercial enterprises the first successful colony was established. But this was not accomplished until after the death of Elizabeth and during the reign of her successor, the headstrong son of the tragic Mary, Queen of Scots, James I of England.

THE FIRST SUCCESSFUL ENGLISH COLONY

The growth of the sea power of England and of Holland challenged Spanish control of the sea lanes. The English defeat of the "Invincible Armada" in 1588, with the help of storms and favorable winds, was an important event in the beginning of the decline of Spain's power. That country's fall was brought about not only by the increasing power of her enemies, but through attempts to accomplish too much. While colonizing, developing, and defending America and the Philippines, and after 1580, all of Portugal's empire, Spain was waging war on the Mohammedans in North Africa, the eastern Mediterranean and eastern Europe; intermittently fighting France and England; attempting to dominate Italy and the Papacy; trying to secure

EARLY SETTLEMENTS IN THE ENGLISH COLONIES

some control of Germany; seeking to uphold Catholicism and crush heresy throughout Europe; and, trying to retain mastery over the revolting Netherlands. As a result, the doom of Spanish power was sealed and as a gradual decline set in, nations that had directed more of their energies to domestic economic growth assumed world leadership.

By the beginning of the seventeenth century, in spite of the failure of colonial projects, there developed an increasing desire in England for expansion. In the words of a prominent man of the time, many had come to believe that "Nothing adds more glorie and greatness to anie nation, than the enlargement of theire territories, and multiplyinge of theire subjects." Many factors were responsible for this outlook. The successes against Spain; the hope of quick wealth; the need for such raw materials as lumber, naval stores, and iron; the desire for more land for what was considered a surplus population; the hope of solving the problem of widespread unemployment brought about partly by the enclosures of land for the purpose of sheep-raising; and, the necessity for finding markets for an increasing supply of manufactured goods, all these created an enthusiasm for expansion.

In establishing the first successful colony, English entrepreneurs made use of the chartered stock company. Although they appeared in the reign of Mary, it was during the age of Elizabeth that many regulated and joint-stock companies were chartered by the Crown. They were given economic concessions and a considerable degree of power in the regions specified in the patent or charter. The Eastland Company was granted a commercial monopoly in the Baltic Sea region; the Muscovy Company in Russia; the Levant Company in the eastern Mediterranean; and, the greatest of them all, in 1600, the East India Company in the Oriental trade. The last-named company, long-lived, and the richest of the trading companies, exercised an influence on British colonial policy and was instrumental in building up Britain's empire in India. Its charters gave it a monopoly of trade with India, China, and the East Indies. The company, at the height of its power, was given authority to appoint governors, to administer justice, and to fortify and command fortresses; it could equip war vessels, maintain troops, and was granted broad political and diplomatic powers. In 1858, as a result of the Sepoy mutiny, sovereignty of India and the powers of government vested in the company were transferred to the British Crown. In various parts of Europe, many trading companies were established during this age of commercial activity. By 1700, there were more than fifty in England, Holland, France, Sweden, and

Denmark. No doubt the success of these companies operating in old thickly populated areas gave a false impression of the costs and problems of pioneer settlement.

In 1606 two groups of promoters succeeded in getting colonial charters from James I. Called the London and Plymouth Companies, both received similar rights and both were to be under the jurisdiction of the Royal Council for Virginia in London. The Plymouth Company sent out its first expedition in the summer of 1606 to seek a place for a plantation, but the vessel was captured by the Spaniards near Puerto Rico where it was driven by adverse winds. The members of the crew were taken as prisoners to Spain. A second vessel dispatched in the autumn of 1606 reached the coast of Maine and returned with such glowing accounts of the land that two ships were sent out early the next year carrying settlers. Spurred on by the hope of utilizing the rich resources of fish, lumber, furs, minerals, and farming lands, which explorers had mentioned, Sir John Popham organized a venture that sent about 120 settlers to the mouth of the Kennebec River; on the west bank they built a fort named St. George, a church, storehouse, and fifty houses. The difficulties of getting started, constant quarrels among many who had spent earlier days in English jails, the death of the sponsor of the venture, Sir John Popham, in England, and a savage Maine winter brought an end to the new colony. Most of the settlers sailed for home and a few joined the temporary fishing colonies which flourished in that region from time to time.

The London Company was more successful in founding a colony, but also failed to achieve the corporate purpose of profit for the stockholders. In the spring of 1607, the first settlers—120 men and boys, representing a cross section of English contemporary life from the high-born Captain George Percy to the lowest laborer and including the imaginative Captain John Smith—disembarked and settled on a site which they named James Fort, or Jamestown. On an enclosure of about an acre they erected rude huts and tents and made dugouts in the ground. A small fort was built and wheat sown. The settlement began happily, but was continually confronted with dangers—from disease, Indians, and Spaniards. For a few years a "comunitie" plan of society was tried, in which all production beyond subsistence would accrue to the company. The circumstances of frontier life, distance from the company headquarters and weak local management, led to failure and deficit instead of profits. Governor Thomas Dale (1611–1616) admitted defeat for the stockholders and introduced individual production and ownership. Because of the early difficulties the London

Company secured charters in 1609 and 1612 which transferred matters of colonial government from the Crown to the company. Under the charter of 1612 the London Company became a self-governing corporation and from this time was commonly known as the Virginia Company.

The Virginia Company planned to establish lumber industries, ironworks, and glass works, and to engage in silk production; but it also hoped that gold and silver would be found. The early broadsides issued by the company helped to entice to the new settlement "blacksmiths, coopers, carpenters, shipwrights, turners, all who work any kind of metal, men who make bricks, architects, bakers, weavers, shoemakers, sawyers, and those who spin wool." Even skilled workmen from foreign countries were encouraged to migrate to Virginia. Within a short time after settlement, naval stores were sent to England and also a cargo of iron ore which found its way to the East India Company. A group of men, known as the Southampton Adventurers, under rights granted by the Virginia Company, began to erect ironworks on the west side of Falling Creek, sixty-six miles above Jamestown. By 1621, the furnaces were well under way. The lighting of the fires was the signal for the terrible Indian massacre of 1622. The workmen were killed and the plant destroyed; no iron was produced in Virginia thereafter for a hundred years. Before the Virginia Company had time to recover from the blow, its political troubles with the English king increased, and in 1624 its charter was revoked. Virginia was transformed into a royal colony, becoming the model for others that were to follow. In the meantime, while the settlers were in a pre-

Transportation to the New World

NOVA BRITANNIA.

OFFERING MOST

Excellent fruites by Planting in
VIRGINIA.

Exciting all such as be well affected
to further the same.

LONDON
Printed for SAMVEL MACHAM, and are to besold at
his Shop in Pauls Church-yard, at the
Signe of the Bul-head.
1 6 0 9.

carious position, John Rolfe gave the colony new economic life in 1612 by introducing the culture of tobacco—learned from the Indians. Tobacco became a "staple" crop in the sense that there was a large and steady demand for it in Europe. Thus its export provided a reliable source of income, or payments from the colonies. Manufactures in Virginia were forgotten and tobacco growing became a passion. When Maryland and the Carolinas were established later, the culture of tobacco spread also to those regions.

The relatively short career of the Virginia Company resulted in the beginning of succesful British colonization. But the company had been formed for the purpose of making profits from its colony or plantation. Its stockholders who lived in England sent out workmen to labor in its interests. In its efforts, the company spent altogether £200,000 and sent to the New World many thousands of emigrants, but partly from the unexpected factor of Indian attacks, from a lack, that is, of government protection for the investment, the commercial venture very definitely failed. However, as a result of its activities the company laid a part of the foundation of a great empire that was to arise with astonishing rapidity.

THE NEW ENGLAND COLONIES

The second English colony to be established was New Plymouth. By the time the *Mayflower* sailed, men could be found in almost every important fishing port of western Europe who could tell much about the Massachusetts coast, for those who fished at the Grand Banks, the submerged tableland between Newfoundland and deep water where Arctic currents and the Gulf Stream produce almost constant fog, often found shelter and succor there. Many explorers had sailed in that region. In 1602, Bartholomew Gosnold visited Cape Cod and gave it its name. Two years later, Champlain made a chart of the harbor of Gloucester. In 1614, Captain John Smith examined the Massachusetts coast and named the region, while he designated many Indian villages by English names.[1]

The Plymouth Company of 1606, after its failure on the Kennebec, was unsuccessful in financing further ventures. In 1620, its leading members secured a new charter which created the Council for New England. While the company was still engaged in making plans for

---

[1] *Description of New England.* When Smith returned to England, he took with him a map he had made of the region. He persuaded Prince Charles to change the "barbarous" Indian names to "good English names." Accordingly, the Indian village of Accomack was renamed "Plimouth" as Smith's map shows. This was six years before the Pilgrims reached there.

colonization on a commercial basis, chance directed a band of Pilgrims to its shores. The group of English emigrants, who came in 1620, had planned to settle somewhere in Virginia and had received permission from the London Company to do so. But after five weeks spent in exploring Cape Cod, the *Mayflower* anchored in the harbor of what came to be Plymouth, and made the famous pact which provided that all should make and keep the laws. After they had established the colony, they secured a new patent from the Council for New England.

The group that came to Plymouth was made up in part of Separatists, who had come from Leyden in the Netherlands where they had been living for more than a decade. They had abandoned their homes in northern England to escape religious persecution. While enjoying religious freedom in Holland, they became dissatisfied under a foreign flag; they were unused to the Dutch language and customs; they were having difficulty in plying their trades because of the guild regulations; and, they were disturbed because of the dangers of worldliness and immorality that confronted their children. A number of them decided to go to the New World when they heard of the Jamestown settlement. In England they were joined by a few other Separatists and by a number who did not belong to their religious group. Only thirty-five of the 102 were really Pilgrims. From time to time the group was augmented by others sent from England, some of whom were of their faith and some who were not.

Those who set sail on the *Mayflower* were financed by a group of London merchants. A total of £7,000 was subscribed for the venture. An agreement was made between these "adventurers" and the "planters." The latter came to the colony both as servants and members of the joint-stock company. Each emigrant received one share of stock for "adventuring" and for every £10 of property he took with him he was given an additional share. It was agreed that the group should live in a communal fashion, all wealth produced going into the "common stock." At the end of seven years there was to be a "division" of both capital and profits. The plan proved unsatisfactory to all concerned. The hardships of settlement, dissatisfaction with working for the company, shipwrecks, dishonesty, and consequent slow economic progress, resulted in much discontent within the new colony. In 1627, the London merchants, desiring to retrieve at least a part of their investment, sold their interests to the colonists for £1,800, which was paid largely through profits in furs. From this time on the settlers became the stockholders of the corporation. After the first decade, other villages were established and the town of Plymouth broadened into the colony of New Plymouth, which in the course of time was absorbed by the Massachusetts Bay Colony.

The religious note was especially dominant in the settlement of Massachusetts Bay Colony, although colonization was carried out at first through the medium of a commercial company. A royal charter of 1629 confirmed to a group of merchants and other investors lands that had been granted to them by the Council for New England the year before, with rights to trade and colonize between the Merrimac and Charles Rivers. In its beginnings, the company resembled others operating in the New World, but after receiving its royal charter, the emphasis of its interest changed from trade to religion. A number of Puritan stockholders who felt that the religious reforms they desired within the Anglican Church were hopeless, as Charles I began his "personal government" and Archbishop Laud enforced uniformity in the Church, looked across the seas to the new continent where they could establish a reformed Church free from what they considered to be Roman Catholic practices. The Cambridge Agreement was made by the leading Puritan members of the Massachusetts Bay Company, who bound themselves to embark for America. They decided to take their charter with them. Compromises had to be made with the merchants left behind concerning the business administration, but control of the enterprise in the future was with those who left England in the "Great Migration" of 1630, although a part of the joint-stock remained for a time in the hands of English businessmen. The arrangements distinguish the Bay Colony from the others, and go far to explain its success. With able men risking their lives as well as their fortunes the company became a sound colonizing enterprise. The charter of 1629 included provisions for a form of government with a governor, assistants, and General Court of the stockholders. No clause, however, was included requiring the company to conduct its meetings in England and as a result the company became practically independent of the Crown and developed into a strong theocracy. The Puritans, in the strict sense of their name, did not wish to separate from the Church as did the Pilgrims. They wanted to purify it of what they termed the "trappings of popery." But after arriving in America, they did separate and accepted many of the doctrines of the Separatists.

With both capital and management supplied by their own leaders the Puritan colony was relatively prosperous, in contrast to the early struggles at Jamestown and Plymouth. Quite soon the characteristic maritime activities of Massachusetts—fishing, shipping, and trading with the West Indies—appeared. During the decade of the thirties about

14,000 people emigrated to the Bay Colony. Not all, of course, were Puritans. Depression in English agriculture and in the cloth trade led many to the Bible Commonwealth for economic betterment. Among these were some who became discontented and quite troublesome.

While the Puritans sought toleration in the New World, they demonstrated that they in turn could not be tolerant. Differences and controversies arose within the settled community and especially between the east and west settlements. Many of these disputes found their way to the General Court. The strife over doctrine and polity resulted in the scattering of many groups to different regions of New England. Roger Williams, the brilliant minister of the church at Salem, who believed in religious freedom and a separation of church and state, came into conflict with the authorities and in 1636 was banished to England. To escape this, he made his way in midwinter to Narragansett Bay where he bought a tract of land from the Indians and founded Providence. Portsmouth was established by Mistress Anne Hutchinson and a number of followers who left Massachusetts during the Antinomian controversy. Newport was founded the next year as an offshoot of Portsmouth and later Warwick came into existence. These settlements laid the basis for the colony of Rhode Island which was founded on the principle of religious freedom and became a refuge for sects that encountered persecution and discrimination elsewhere in America.

The story of the origin of Connecticut begins in the same period as that of Rhode Island. At the time of the Puritan migration the land from Narragansett Bay to the Pacific was granted to Lord Saye and Sele, who some years later founded Saybrook. During 1635 and 1636, groups from the Bay Colony, under the leadership of Thomas Hooker and others, tired of controversy and seeking more fertile lands, settled the three river towns of Windsor, Hartford, and Wethersfield. Other settlers from England established themselves independently on the shores of Long Island Sound. A group under Theophilus Eaton and the Reverend John Davenport located at New Haven with the purpose of establishing a trading town. Round about, other settlements grew up to form the New Haven Colony. All of these settlements in time became part of Connecticut.

Many from turbulent Massachusetts fled to the wild Maine region. Explorers had touched this coast long before any permanent English settlements were attempted. Verrazano, Hawkins, Gilbert, Gosnold, Champlain, Weymouth, and John Smith had visited its shores. Long before Plymouth was established lusty English, Dutch, French, and

Spanish settlements had appeared and disappeared along the Kennebec as fishermen and hunters moved from place to place. In the early days of the Pilgrim colony, settlers on the rocky island of Monhegan just off the Maine coast gave aid to the Pilgrims in their dire distress and "fed them fat, loading them down with fish," but refused to take any kind of pay for their assistance. Attempts by Captain John Mason and Sir Ferdinando Gorges, who were given proprietary grants, failed to establish a permanent colony in Maine. But after 1630, a number of dissenters fled from the strait-laced Puritan colony to join the sturdy fishers and hunters whom they found there. Massachusetts claimed jurisdiction over the region and later was able to exercise authority over it.

The territory granted to Mason and Gorges also included the region that later became New Hampshire. In 1629, Mason alone held the area. Like Maine, the brief New Hampshire coast and the Isle of Shoals near it were visited by fishermen in the sixteenth century. Later, following persecution in Massachusetts Bay Colony, religious dissenters fled there, especially those of strong Anglican and Antinomian tendencies. For a time Massachusetts was able to assume control until finally royal authority was extended there and New Hampshire became a Crown colony (1679). Farming, lumbering, fishing, shipbuilding, and fur trading were the chief occupations in the northern outposts of the parent colony.

From the earliest years of the settlement of Massachusetts Bay Colony, groups scattered to various surrounding regions. Religious differences account largely for the centrifugal movement that forced many from the original settlement. While New England in time would have developed and expanded naturally, the intolerant attitude and actions of the rulers of Massachusetts resulted in forcing from the colony those who would not conform to Puritan ideals and practices.

THE FIRST PERMANENT PROPRIETARY COLONY

In spite of the failure of colonization companies to pay any dividends, colonial investment remained attractive to wealthy Englishmen. In a society where prestige was based on landownership, men were willing to risk fortunes to become lords or proprietors of millions of colonial acres. Throughout the seventeenth century wealthy gentlemen petitioned, and the Crown granted, vast proprietary estates in North America. The right to govern these areas subject to certain restrictions was included in the grants.

Whereas the colonizing corporations had hoped to make money from production and trade, the proprietors based their hopes on land sales and taxes. But generally the costs of settlement and administration outran returns during the lifetime of all the original proprietors. Lord Baltimore and William Penn, the greatest proprietors, each claimed to have sunk over £30,000 in their colonies before receiving any annual net return. Yet the investment made these men great figures in the English world of their day, as well as in history, and perhaps this was their anticipated reward.

Maryland was the first permanent English proprietary colony. Like Plymouth and Massachusetts Bay Colony, the religious motive was prominent, although it was established by Catholics rather than dissatisfied or dissident Anglicans. Sir George Calvert, who had connections with the Virginia Company and the Council for New England, had in 1623 planned to colonize the Peninsula of Avalon in Newfoundland. The difficulties of settlement on its bleak shores convinced him that he should look farther south. He maintained the friendship of Charles I and secured from him a grant of land which became known as the Province or Palatinate of Maryland. It was not until 1632 that the right was granted. George Calvert died before the patent was completed and the charter was issued to his son Cecil, the second Lord Baltimore. The charter of Maryland was modeled after the earlier one to the Avalon plantation which in turn was patterned after the County Palatine of Durham, a Crown fief, the powers of whose bishop and ruler were second only to those of the king. The grant was carved out of the region known as Virginia, but the boundaries were very indefinitely stated. The proprietor was given the land outright together with extensive powers of government, including the collecting of taxes. He was an overlord with the right to select lords under his authority and was given the right to create manors in his province. In return he was to reserve for the Crown one-fifth of all the precious metals found within his domain and deliver two Indian arrows to the sovereign at Windsor Castle each year.

In March, 1634, the first settlers landed on Maryland soil. A cross was erected on St. Clement's Island in the Potomac and some distance down the river a permanent settlement was established centering in St. Mary's City. Lord Baltimore induced men of wealth to accept grants of land in return for aiding in colonization. He provided a refuge for Catholics, but welcomed without distinction all who cared to unite with him. The early history of Maryland was disturbed by conflicts between the proprietary party and Virginia traders, but economically, from the local point of view, as opposed to profits for the proprietor, the colony was successful from the beginning. Copying the Virginia pattern, tobacco became the chief staple of production and the important commodity for export. During the eighteenth century, the dependence on tobacco began to give way to the diversification of crops as settlement moved inland. Food products, shipbuilding, the importation of indentured servants and slaves, and a diversified commerce increased throughout the period.

THE COLONIES IN THE MID-SEVENTEENTH CENTURY

By 1640, there were about 25,000 settlers in Plymouth, Massachusetts, Connecticut, Rhode Island, New Haven, New Hampshire, Maine, Virginia, and Maryland. Within the period of a generation, several successful mainland colonies had been established. The West Indies were also being settled but at this time at a more rapid rate than the mainland colonies. By the same date, 40,000 had left England for the Sugar Islands, as they were called. Of the colonies along the seaboard, Massachusetts led with 14,000 while Virginia claimed about 8,000.

The years 1640 to 1660 in England were marked by the struggle between Parliament and the king, the Civil War, the Puritan Revolution, the beheading of Charles I, the dictatorship of Cromwell, the decline of the Commonwealth, the dissatisfaction with drab Puritan rule, and finally the return of the Stuarts to power. The tide of migration to the colonies did not cease during the period but it changed somewhat in character. The Puritans lost interest in migrating to America, although Massachusetts had now become especially independent of the Crown. Some royal sympathizers left England for the southern colonies, but the number was not large. A few businessmen, tired of Puritan rule, came to the New World. Increasing numbers of unemployed and political prisoners and criminals sold, or "indentured," their labor for terms up to seven years in return for transportation to the colonies.

THE ENTERPRISES OF THE RESTORATION

The return of Charles II from the continent to rule as king signaled a revival in England. As the king rode into London, the city became madly exuberant. A new era in English history had begun and a new phase of colonization had opened. The king was surrounded by royal favorites who imposed upon England an aristocratic rule. All gladly accepted the numerous titles, honors, and presents conferred upon them. Most were interested in the great monopolistic companies and therefore in commerce and colonies. In their desire to secure money and avoid the pitfalls of Charles I, the new monarch and his courtiers looked to the colonies as means of securing revenue and enlarging English trade. During the early years of the Restoration several charters were granted and the growing commercial spurt led to the founding of new colonies. Important navigation acts were passed in an attempt to control the economic activities of British possessions over the seas; and definite attempts were made to put the mercantile theory into practice.

In 1663, with characteristic generosity and the encouragement of the commercialists, Charles II gave the Carolinas to eight English nobles. By a second charter two years later they received the southern half of the present United States. The grant was a proprietary one. A plan of government was prepared by the English philosopher, John Locke, in the elaborate and unworkable *Fundamental Constitutions*. This form of government provided for control by an hereditary nobility whose estates should be inalienable and indivisible. Agreeable to Charles II it was designed as a safeguard against a "numerous democracy." Although practiced to some extent, the plan soon failed.

The first permanent settlement in the Carolinas was made on the northern shore of Albemarle Sound where some disgruntled Virginians had settled as early as 1650. This was not far from Roanoke Island, the scene of the tragedy of Sir Walter Raleigh's attempts at colonization. The proprietors offered land grants, tax exemption, and other inducements to settlers in this region which became the nucleus of the colony of North Carolina. A settlement was made in the south also, at the present site of Charleston. Promotional ingenuity by the proprietors helped the colony to prosper, but consumed all the potential profit. The excellent harbor, and the influx of various groups including English dissenters, Scottish Highlanders, and French Huguenots, soon created a settlement that was the beginning of South Carolina. Until the early part of the eighteenth century, things went fairly well with the settlers at Albemarle and Charleston, except for struggles against the proprietary system of control, both economic and political. Then, Indian and Spanish attacks, pirate raids, the loss of settlers to other colonies, difficulties in collecting quitrents, and other problems resulted in the sale of the proprietary rights to the Crown. In 1719, when a Spanish invasion threatened, the colonists used the occasion to march on Charleston and seize control. A revo-

lutionary convention took over the province in the name of the king
and later the proprietors received remuneration for it. In 1729, they
surrendered to the Crown their rights to the region in the north. The
two groups of settlements clustering in Albemarle and Charleston
became the separately governed royal provinces of North Carolina
and South Carolina.

During the early years of the Restoration, the English wrested
from the Dutch the province of New Netherland, which separated the
New England and southern British colonies. The story of Dutch settlement goes back some decades. By the beginning of the seventeenth
century, Holland had developed into one of the leading commercial
and industrial nations in Europe, especially through its trade with the
Far East. Like its competitors, it was anxious to find a new route to
the Orient other than around Africa. About the time that Jamestown
was first being settled, an English captain, Henry Hudson, sailed
from London with only ten men and a boy in search of a probable
northeast passage and proceeded beyond the eightieth degree of latitude. A daring and ambitious sailor, he made repeated attempts to
find an all-water route to India and China. Sailing in the far North,
he forced his ship into unknown waters, but ice packs barred his way.
During the summer of 1609 he sailed for the Dutch East India Company in quest of a northwest passage. From Newfoundland, he moved
southward and reached the coasts of what are now Virginia, Maryland,
Delaware, and New Jersey. On September 2, 1609, the *Halve Maene*
or "Half Moon," a clumsy Dutch vessel of eighty tons, sailed into a
silent bay into which flowed a great river. Henry Hudson continued
up the river to the head of navigation, but found no northwest passage.
Instead, he gave the Netherlands a seat of settlement in America and
brought Dutch influence to the New World.

Fifteen years later, the Dutch began the settlement of New Amsterdam and Fort Orange, but colonists were few. In order to secure
increased immigration, a new Dutch West India Company began to
grant large domains which seated the patroons on the river which
Hudson called the "Great River of the Mountains." The patroon
held his land as a "perpetual fief of inheritance" and swore fealty to
the company, whereupon he was given complete jurisdiction over the
settlers he was required to bring from the Old World. The plan was
not very successful. A few patroons secured control of most of the land
along the Hudson. But Dutch colonization continued at a slow pace,
held back by the same problem that had defeated English companies:
the large cost of establishing a permanent settler who could return

an income. As in the case of the English companies there were also the difficulties of managing affairs across the ocean and Indian troubles. In addition there were conflicts with the English settlers to the North, and threats from the attempted Swedish occupation of the Delaware. Moreover, there was no great surplus population in Holland and no driving political, religious, or economic discontent to induce any considerable number of people to try their fortunes in a new land. The quasi-feudal patroonships along the Hudson did not attract many colonists from other countries in Europe, although New Amsterdam early became quite cosmopolitan. The preoccupation of the Dutch at home contributed to the precariousness with which they held on to their possessions in America.

The new nationalism of the Restoration period, including the program of drawing the colonies into closer relation with the mother country in the interests of mercantilism, demanded the elimination of the Dutch as competitors on the American continent. In 1664, an English fleet under the command of Richard Nicholls sailed into the harbor of New Amsterdam and demanded the colony. Old peg-legged Peter Stuyvesant, the governor, made frantic appeals to the people to fight, but the settlers—a cosmopolitan crowd—not wanting the town destroyed, refused. Many of them welcomed English rule. Without a blow, the entire possessions of the Dutch on the continent of North America passed to the English. New York, New Jersey, and Delaware were granted to the Duke of York, brother of the king. The change from New Netherland to New York marked the beginning of a new government. The Duke's charter made him lord proprietor with complete authority to rule in his province, unchecked by a representative assembly. The "Duke of York's Laws," compiled largely from the existing codes of Massachusetts and New Haven, were gradually extended over the whole province. When the Duke became James II in 1685 after the death of his brother, the colony was added to the growing list of royal colonies.

Not long after the Duke of York received New Netherland, he conveyed by deed the part of it located between the Hudson and Delaware Rivers to Lord John Berkeley and Sir George Carteret as joint proprietors. By terms of the conveyance the province was to be called New Caesarea or New Jersey. The proprietors assumed powers of government and established the usual form. To the small Dutch and Swedish population were added settlers from New England and Old England, especially after Quaker interests headed by William Penn secured the western portion. At this time the province was divided into East and West Jersey (1676). The latter became a refuge for persecuted Quakers who established the towns of Salem and Burlington. East Jersey was offered at auction by Carteret's heirs and was purchased by Penn and a number of associates in 1682. Puritans, Quakers, and Baptists from Long Island and New England first settled in this region. Many problems arose and proprietary authority disintegrated. As a result, the proprietors surrendered the government to the Crown in 1702 and the two divisions were reunited under royal rule.

Pennsylvania was also settled in the period of the Restoration. Early in the century, the territory on the Delaware was claimed by the Dutch and English. But it was the Swedes who made the first definite attempt to colonize the region. In the spring of 1638, a company of Swedes, Finns, and Dutch under the leadership of the doughty Dutch cosmopolitan, Peter Minuit, established a Swedish colony on the banks of the Delaware, made peace with the Indians, purchased land from them, and called the new outpost New Sweden. They laid out farms in scattered settlements, began trading with the red men for furs and established Fort Christina (now Wilmington). A few years later, Colonel Johan Printz, a soldier schooled in the Thirty Years' War, was appointed by the Royal Chancellor of Queen Christina as the third governor of New Sweden. The weighty Printz made Old Tinicum Island the new site of his fort, settlement, and mansion because the island gave him excellent command of the river. Although Old Sweden was rapidly developing industries, especially the production of iron, and many Swedes were fired with the desire to emulate the mother country in this respect, they faced too many difficulties in the New World in establishing settlements to make much progress in manufactures. New Sweden maintained its independence only seventeen years, for in 1655 it was taken under the control of the Dutch who had claimed this territory long before the Swedish settlement but who held New Netherland only until 1664.

Although Swedish control on the Delaware was brief, these early Swedish pioneers affected American life. They contributed the log cabin to America's frontier culture; they set an example of peaceful dealings with the Indians; and they blazed the trail for the large number of Swedes who two hundred years later became a dominant factor in the settlement and civilization of several territories and states in the northern part of the United States.

While small colonies of Swedes, Finns, Germans, and Dutch were living along the Delaware, William Penn, the distinguished convert to

Quakerism, received from Charles II a proprietary grant of the province which became known as Pennsylvania. It was presented to him to extinguish a debt owed by the Crown to his father, Admiral Penn, who had been active in helping to bring about the restoration of the Stuarts. It was given also to advance the commercial interests of the mercantilists. Penn's dream was to make it a haven for Quakers and all other persecuted groups. As proprietor, in 1682 he drew up his first Frame of Government, thus initiating his Holy Experiment, guaranteeing civil liberty, religious freedom, and economic opportunity to all who would settle in his province. His plans for government were based on extreme pacific principles that seemed fantastic to his critics as he established complete freedom of worship for all creeds. In 1682, he granted a liberal charter to the Free Society of Traders, including large tracts of land and the privilege of carrying on manufactures and trade. In order to have direct access from his province to the ocean William Penn secured from the Duke of York the Lower Counties on the Delaware which became Delaware. With the permission of Penn, these three counties set up a separate assembly in 1704, but remained under the same governor until the Revolution. Although late in getting started, Pennsylvania made rapid economic progress. Skillful advertising by Penn, especially in England and in the German Palatinate, and the freedom afforded within the province together with its location and resources brought increasing numbers of settlers and made it one of the leading colonies within a few decades. Philadelphia, its capital, became the chief city of all the colonies and the center of commerce, trade, handicrafts, science, and culture. Yet William Penn failed to recover the large sums he invested. To avoid debtor's prison he had to assign the proprietary revenues to his creditors. In later decades, however, his heirs drew a net income from the colony.

THE FOUNDING OF GEORGIA

Georgia was the last of the mainland colonies to be established. Motives for its founding varied with the different groups who were active in its creation. To erect a barrier against the Spanish to the south and the French in Louisiana, to produce silk and other raw material, to rehabilitate English debtors unfortunate enough to be jailed, and to offer a refuge for persecuted Protestants were the reasons for its founding. James Edward Oglethorpe and Lord John Percival led in securing its charter in 1732 from George II. It provided that a board of trustees should govern the colony for twenty-one years, after which control was to revert to the Crown. In 1733, the first colonists settled at Savannah. In addition to English settlers, other unfortunate victims of hardship and oppression from Germany and Switzerland were welcomed to Georgia by the trustees. Although various groups came to the new colony, it did not prosper, partly because of certain rules formulated by the trustees, such as the exclusion of Negroes, prohibitions against rum, and a restricted land system. In 1752, after twenty years of control, the trustees surrendered their charter, and Georgia became a royal province.

THE VARIOUS ETHNIC GROUPS

The early colonists were faced with a people new and strange to them, to whom the name of Indian had been mistakenly given by early explorers. According to the generally accepted theory today, the Indians are descendants of early Mongoloid peoples who reached northern America from Asia by way of the Bering Strait thousands of years before the white man came, possibly before the mammoth, the wild horse, and the ground sloth became extinct on the continent. Those who got into Central and South America developed relatively high cultures, while those of the North made little cultural advancement. As the ancestors of the American Indian scattered into various types of environment, they developed different methods of warfare and hunting, religious practices, family life, and legal codes. They remained primarily hunters and gatherers of wild foods, but they sporadically engaged in agriculture—corn being their chief crop. Tobacco was grown largely for ceremonial uses. Through Indian languages and dialects modern scholarship has been able to classify them and to show that all the widely dispersed groups and tribes belonged to one original stock. The emigrants from Europe found the Indians of the eastern coast friendly and very helpful at times, but also fiercely warlike and cruel at other times.

Economically the Indian was valuable for his agricultural knowledge of crops like corn and tobacco, and most of all as a gatherer of furs for trade. He did not readily accept the discipline of wage labor and was driven back rather than employed or "civilized" by the colonists.

If the Indian and his ways appeared strange to the Englishman, the white man puzzled the Indian, especially by his settled mode of living, his peculiar customs, his sacred right for individual holdings, and the rights of property. The European not only crowded the Indian westward, but gave him his diseases, often more fatal to the savage than the white man's greed, treachery, and anger; he furnished the Indian with firearms which increased the deadliness of inter-tribal warfare and also the danger to the colonists themselves; and he gave him liquor which debauched and demoralized him. The Indian, on the other hand, when aroused or opposed, became hostile and savage. At times, when on the warpath, he attacked and slew innocent colonists living in peaceful settlements. He could be extremely cruel, scalping the living as well as the dead and putting captives to death by means of the most terrifying and brutal forms of torture.

As they were never considered to be inhabitants of the colonies, it is impossible to know how many Indians there were in the east coast and Appalachian Mountain regions in the seventeenth century. A hundred thousand would probably be a high estimate. By 1700 in man power alone they were no longer a match for the 250,000 colonists along the coast. Driven inland beyond the settled area of the colonies the Indians met the later settlers only along the frontier.

The other non-European ethnic group, the Negroes, who by 1750 were probably more numerous than the Indians east of the Mississippi River, came to live chiefly as slaves and servants in the older and wealthier part of the colonies. From the early eighteenth century on the Negroes always far outnumbered any other non-British ethnic group in the colonies. By 1770 the 460,000 Negroes were over 20 per cent of the total population.

As we have seen, in the mid-seventeenth century Dutch, Swedes, and other European groups added to the non-British minority. By 1700 there were many Germans, chiefly from the Rhinish Palatinate and Württemberg, where political and religious persecution, endless wars, and economic disorders, and destruction prevailed. Many victims of the Thirty Years' War and the wars of Louis XIV left their devastated homelands and came to the New World. The advertising of

ESTIMATED POPULATION OF THE AMERICAN COLONIES, 1650 – 1770

	1650	1700	1750	1770
New England	22,832	92,763	360,011	581,038
Middle Colonies	8,805	83,141	437,532	758,503
Southern Colonies	18,731	74,984	373,217	808,535
Total	50,368	250,888	1,170,760	2,148,076

Source: U.S. Bureau of the Census, *Historical Statistics of the United States, Colonial Times to 1957*, Washington, D.C., 1960, p. 756.

the Carolina proprietors and the efforts of William Penn to induce settlers to leave their old homes bore results. In the first half of the eighteenth century, increasing numbers, especially Moravians, Mennonites, Dunkards, Lutherans, and Reformed Germans settled in Pennsylvania, New York, New Jersey, Delaware, Maryland, Virginia, the Carolinas, and Georgia. Most of them took up the best lands just west of the settled regions. The different groups were clannish, but proved to be hard-working, careful, thrifty farmers, whose traits survive today in the "Pennsylvania Dutch." On the eve of the Revolution, there were about 225,000 people of German blood in the United States, making up almost one-tenth of the total population. One-third of those of German stock lived in Pennsylvania.

New types of British immigrants also appeared. The Scotch-Irish came to America from northern Ireland. Their history in that country goes back to the reign of James I. That monarch, a Scotsman by birth, decided to put down the troublesome and long-rebellious Irish by replacing certain sections of their country with English and Scotch colonists. Irish estates in northern Ireland were confiscated and given to British landowners, who encouraged English and Scotch colonists to settle on their lands. The migration from Scotland to Ulster, begun in 1607, continued intermittently in the decades that followed, so that more than a million Scotch Presbyterians were living in Ireland by 1700.

Although the new settlers frequently fought Catholic neighbors and were often involved in controversies with the English government, these thrifty farmers and businessmen prospered for a time as they adjusted themselves to new conditions and modified their Scotch customs. During the latter part of the seventeenth century, however, they faced many difficulties. Parliament passed laws prohibiting the importation into England of cattle, meat, butter, or cheese from Ireland; the export of Irish woolen manufactures was also forbidden to any country except England, and these goods were burdened with such heavy duties when exported to England that the Irish cloth industry was slowly destroyed. The Woolens Act of 1699 forbade the exportation of wool from Ireland, rendering sheep-raising unprofitable. These laws were passed to protect English interests and prosperity; they had the effect of seriously injuring the Scotch-Irish. By the Test Act of 1704 they were excluded from holding civil and military offices, denied a voice in government, and required to pay taxes to support the Anglican Church. Because of these restrictions, many left Ulster for America.

Scotch-Irish Presbyterians came to the English mainland colonies in America as early as the middle of the seventeenth century. Their numbers were not large until the opening of the eighteenth century. The movement was then accelerated when absentee English landlords began to increase rentals on farms held by them under long-term leases which were expiring. A steady stream of Scotch-Irish immigrants poured into American ports. The total number has not been definitely ascertained, but it is estimated that nearly 200,000, about 8 per cent of the population, were of Scotch-Irish extraction at the time of the Revolution. They established clusters of settlements in all the colonies, especially in Pennsylvania, Virginia, Maryland, and the Carolinas, but were most numerous in the back country.

Other peoples in smaller numbers came to the seaboard colonies. During the religious troubles in France, Huguenots—whose religion was Calvinistic in theology, ritualistic in form, Presbyterian in government, and tolerant in principle—fled to different parts of the world. During Dutch control, small groups of Huguenots, chiefly French-speaking Walloons, settled in New Netherland. After the dragonnades of Louis XIV, several hundred French Protestant families reached Boston and from 1670 Huguenots played an important part in the settlement of Charleston, South Carolina, where sections of the city became largely or entirely French. After Louis XIV revoked the tolerant Edict of Nantes in 1685, a number settled in Rhode Island, Connecticut, New York, Delaware, Maryland, and Pennsylvania, as well as in South Carolina.

Swiss immigrants came singly and in small groups, making settlements especially in Pennsylvania, North Carolina, and South Carolina. The Welsh were among the early settlers in many colonies and were firm advocates of political and religious liberty. Some of them were Quakers and groups settled outside Philadelphia on the tract provided them by William Penn, where Celtic place names still remain. Others, representing different types of dissenters, settled elsewhere in Pennsylvania, the Carolinas, and even in sections of New England. Scotch Presbyterians settled in New Jersey, New England, and South Carolina, while thousands of Irish Catholics sought freedom in the various settlements along the coast. Jews in small numbers came during the earliest days in spite of British restrictions against them. By the close of the colonial period, they could be found in all the important commercial towns. Most were of Spanish and Portuguese origin, although many came from Holland and a few from other European countries.

Regardless of national origins, all of the people who came to America necessarily shared characteristics common to migrants. For example, there is a higher percentage of young males in groups deciding to migrate than in the old settled population. Since these young men are in general the most vigorous workers and innovators, they give an area of in-migration an economically lively atmosphere. Later studies suggest that in addition to a large percentage of young adults, migrant groups probably have slightly higher I.Q.'s than stay-at-homes. The very decision to leave is a sign of thoughtful weighing of opportunities rather than unquestioning acceptance of familiar ways of life. In addition, migrants leave behind them whatever benefits family and community connections can confer, and generally have to make their own way unaided in a new society. This situation no doubt breeds regard for equality and democratic opportunity. In the 1890's an historian, Frederick Jackson Turner, ascribed these desirable qualities to the conditioning of the frontier. More recent studies by demographers (students of population) ascribe the qualities to participation in the *process* of migration, rather than to any particular type of area.

THE COLONIES AND THE EMPIRE

While colonies were established by various agencies—commercial or trading companies, proprietors, independent groups, or directly by the king—there was a tendency to bring them all under the direct control of the Crown. This can be seen in the unsuccessful attempt of James II who made Sir Edmund Andros governor-general of all the New England colonies, New York, East Jersey, and West Jersey. Although the plan failed when the king was banished and William and Mary became England's rulers as a result of the Glorious Revolution of 1688, the trend continued. In 1775, there were only three proprietary provinces—Maryland, Pennsylvania, and Delaware; and two independent colonies—Connecticut and Rhode Island—virtually independent under their charters. All the rest were royal colonies, although Massachusetts had a charter which granted certain privileges denied to the other royal possessions.

England's colonial activity benefited from a large scale emigration from the mother country. This was due partly to a relative overpopulation at certain times, to agricultural and industrial depression and to political and religious quarrels. The Catholic nations believed it to be a religious duty to keep their colonies pure in Catholic orthodoxy. Not so the English. Different religious, political, and social groups from foreign countries as well as from Britain were not only permitted but were encouraged to settle in the English possessions. The result by

1775 was the establishment of a new nation, bound by various bonds, fretting over imperial regulations, and having a population somewhat different in origin and customs from that of the mother country. At the outbreak of the Revolution, the population of England and Wales was about 7,500,000 compared to 2,500,000 in the seaboard colonies.

In considering the rise of the scattered settlements along the Atlantic seaboard, it should be kept in mind that by the middle of the eighteenth century, England had established a far-flung empire of great extent, possessing remarkable diversity and much material wealth. By this time, the "British flag was flying from outposts scattered from the Arctic to the equatorial belt, from the Great Lakes of North America to Borneo in the Far East." It had come into existence as a result of wars of conquest, by treaties of cession, and through overseas trade as well as colonization. Its 15,000,000 people included white, bronze, black, and brown subjects. All together thirty-one governments were subordinate to Great Britain, ranging from the practically autonomous charter colonies of Connecticut and Rhode Island to the Crown possessions and the factories of the East India Company.[2] Diversity is seen not only in peoples and institutions, but also in economic life. Wool, coal, iron manufactures, and wheat from England, flax and farm products from Ireland, ships and timber from New England, articles of food and iron from the middle colonies, tobacco from the Chesapeake Bay region, rice and indigo from South Carolina, logwood from Honduras Bay, sugar and molasses from the West Indies, fish from the regions of Newfoundland, furs and skins from Hudson Bay and the back country, slaves and ivory from the West African coast, and a variety of desirable articles from the East India posts attest to the material wealth of a great empire built up in a period of a century and a half.

[2] L. H. Gipson, *The British Empire Before the American Revolution,* Vol. I: *Great Britain and Ireland* (Caldwell, Idaho, 1936), pp. 3 ff.

CHAPTER 3

Agriculture in the Colonies

The early immigrants who reached the Atlantic coastal plain after crossing a broad expanse of ocean in small, sturdy, ill-smelling vessels —crowded with man and beast—surviving disease, storms, pirates, and enemy privateers saw a land covered with great primeval forests. From Maine to Georgia the forests offered the settlers almost limitless lumber for their homes, barns, furniture, and tools as well as an abundance of cheap fuel and a product for export. Settlement was made just beyond the sandy beaches or the rocky shores of the coast, frequently in open spaces that had been cleared at some earlier time by the nomadic Indians, or in areas where the trees were less dense, or even within the forest shade.

North America was a country rich in food and in material resources. The forests of the Atlantic region were full of deer and other game, while the rivers and creeks teemed with fish. Wild ducks and other birds frequented the marshlands in vast numbers and wild fruits, berries, and nuts were plentiful in most sections. Yet some of the earliest settlers faced starvation at times because they knew little or nothing about hunting or fishing or because of harsh and severe weather. In all colonies, after the trying period of getting started was

49

over, the settlers were able to raise sufficient food for their own use, and in time they produced a surplus to be sold locally and even for export.

The string of settlements that was established by the English remained bound to the coastal plain throughout the colonial era. This was due primarily to the Appalachian barrier and to the fact that no great river or mighty waterway led directly into the lands of the interior. The French settlements were dominated by two great rivers, the St. Lawrence and the Mississippi; as a result New France developed as a series of scattered settlements, whose inhabitants traveled far and wide in search of furs. Throughout the early period, the English settlers were influenced by the large and small indentations of the coast and by the streams and rivers draining into them. The mountains restricted their horizon, took away the temptation to immediate broad expansion, and made agriculture their dominant occupation. At the one place where penetration was possible—by way of the Hudson and the great Mohawk Valley gateway to the West—the Iroquois Confederacy prevented migration.

THE ENGLISH HERITAGE

Seventeenth-century England where the first settlers originated was essentially an agricultural country. There were towns, of course, including the metropolis of London, but English wealth was largely secured by the ownership of land, and most English workers labored on farms. England was concerned chiefly in the raising of wheat, called corn, and livestock. The eastern and southern parts of the country supplied a surplus of wheat, while the western and northern parts were devoted to grazing and stock raising. But such activities were not confined to these regions alone. Grain was grown in almost all sections. About half the land was under cultivation, the remainder being pasture, woodland, moor, or fen. The forests which had once covered the island had been largely cut down and laws were in force, attempting to save what remained of them. Agricultural progress, which became apparent during Elizabeth's reign, continued until checked by the wars between the Cavaliers and the Puritans in the reign of Charles I.

Under the first two Stuarts, James I and Charles I, the rise in prices, brought about chiefly by the influx of precious metals from the New World to the Old, and an increasing demand for foodstuffs as population grew, resulted in slowing up the enclosure of lands for sheep raising and stimulated an interest in more scientific methods of farming, improvements in conditions of tillage, and even in the reclamation of waste lands. Larger profits in grain and meat sped production of those commodities. Agricultural books appeared and were read; Italian methods of irrigation were tried; attempts were made to drain the fens; experiments were carried out in growing turnips and clover as a substitute for letting the land lie fallow; new vegetable crops such as potatoes and carrots were introduced; and more attention was paid to orchards and gardens. But the difficulties of the Civil War and the problems of the Restoration held back advancement, and improvements in farming did not get under way until the eighteenth century, when the so-called agricultural revolution occurred.

Although the enclosures continued, a large part of the English countryside in the seventeenth century was still in unfenced open fields. This was chiefly because the holdings of many individuals were scattered among the lands of others, a heritage from feudal days. The enclosures largely benefited great landlords. Under the authority of the law they ejected peasants who had inherited the right to squat, cut turf, hunt, fish, and pasture a cow or two. The movement also resulted in the enclosure of much of the "commons" and the strips of the villages. Such village lands were divided into as many sections as there were landholders according to their rights. Each then could use his individual holding as he saw fit. But in spite of these changes and the experiments for better farming, the three-field system was still widely used. Under this medieval plan, jointly-held plowlands were divided into three parts, one cultivated for a winter grain, such as wheat or rye sowed in the fall, one for a cereal sowed in early spring, and the third left fallow.

By the seventeenth century, industry was extending into the English country districts. As the merchant and craft guilds declined, merchants distributed wool to farmers and villagers to be worked into cloth. This "domestic system" had the advantages of extending the production of woolen cloth and of opening up a new field of occupation to agricultural laborers and small farmers. Under this system fine cloths, coarse weaves, long ells, serges, crepes, and linsey cloth, as well as a variety of other goods were produced. In many sections, this plan of industry was extended to iron and brass manufactures, including the making of tools. Rustics had small forges at which they hammered out nails or fashioned implements of iron and brass when not employed in the fields, especially during winter months.

Except for the great city of London which had a population of almost half a million (one-tenth of England's inhabitants) only four towns had more than ten thousand people in the seventeenth century. Bristol, a busy seaport on the southwest coast, important in American trade, Norwich, the center of the East Anglian woolen industry, York, the "capital" of the north, and Exeter, the "capital" of the west led a number of smaller towns in size. The places that were to become important in the next century as the industrial revolution got under way were small. Manchester, Leeds, Birmingham, and Sheffield had only a few thousand inhabitants each. But the provincial towns were important especially for their industry, commerce, and trade. Here the courts, markets, and fairs were held and in these urban centers gay balls and all sorts of social activities attracted the important country families for miles around.

The gradations of social classes stand out in seventeenth century rural England. English society was composed of the nobility and gentry with their broad acres; the clergy varying from the bishops and town clergy to the poorly supported country parsons; the yeomen freeholders who tilled their lands with the help of a few laborers; the townsfolk who engaged in trade and industry; the tenant farmers who rented holdings that averaged forty to fifty acres; small tenants called cotters; and, the mass of agricultural laborers. From the small number of hereditary landlords, at the top of the social scale, each group increased greatly in number, so that the lowest stratum of society, the agricultural laborers, including their families, made up almost one-half of England's five million inhabitants. While class distinctions were well-rooted and deeply respected, and most people lived and died in the social group into which they were born, there was some degree of friendly association among various classes. This could be seen especially between those of different rank who often mingled in the village and grammar schools of the provincial towns, although at the universities there were marked distinctions. It could be sensed in the condescending spirit of concern and good will on the part of the landlords, or squires, for their tenants and others beneath them in rank. It could also be observed in the links forged by marriage between many of the landed gentry and the rising trading classes.

INFLUENCES THAT SHAPED COLONIAL AGRICULTURE

The early colonists brought with them a knowledge of English rural life and customs. But regardless of European cultural backgrounds the first type of American farming was, of necessity, governed

by the stern law of assuring subsistence. Thrown upon their own resources, with an abundance of cheap lands and in most places fertile
soil, the early settlers cleared and cultivated the land, kept livestock
on natural grasses, roots, nuts, and acorns, and carried on household
industries. They were forced to live much more primitively than they
were accustomed to in Europe. With them they brought not only the
earliest tools (the plow, harrow, hoe, rake, spade, sickle, axe, and flail)
but also the seeds of such grains as wheat, barley, rye, and oats; vegetables such as cabbage, beans, peas, and onions; fruits, especially apples,
plums, pears, and several kinds of berries; farm animals such as
cattle, oxen, horses, sheep, swine, goats, and poultry of different
kinds. The early colonists found many plants that were unfamiliar:
maize or corn, tobacco, white and sweet potatoes, pumpkins, squash,
tomatoes, and strawberries. Corn, adopted from Indian agriculture,
became an all-important crop in every colony; the growing of tobacco,
also learned from the Indians, became the economic basis of existence
in the South.

       While the earlier settlers understood European farming, the stone-
tool-using Indians taught them much. They showed the first English
pioneers how to kill trees by girdling them—making a circular cut
through the bark; how to fell and burn them; how to clear the under-
brush; how to fertilize corn and other crops with fish; how to cultivate
their virgin fields to the best advantage; and, how to preserve corn
and other vegetables and fruits by drying and storing them away in
caves or pits lined with bark. The row culture of agriculture was
first adopted from the Indian; the field system of Europe came with
more mature development.

       Methods of agriculture throughout the colonial period were, in
general, crude. European visitors and observers in the eighteenth century condemned the colonists for their "land butchery," that is, cultivating land year after year until it had become exhausted, without
attempting to let it lie fallow or fertilizing it. Instead, new land was
taken up where the process of exhaustion was repeated. This was
not due to ignorance as many foreign travelers charged, but was natural in a country where land was cheap and labor scarce and dear.
The two- or three-field system of rotation was not used because it
meant that large tracts would have to be cleared at one time. The
efforts of the first settlers to clear the ground literally of every stump
and to provide several fields where a part could lie fallow would have
been a misapplication of energy, needed for more urgent tasks. Fertilizers were not used to any great extent, partly through ignorance

and partly through indifference. The butchery of the land, however, led to bad agricultural habits and robbed later generations of the wealth of the soil.

Primitive methods of agriculture continued in general use throughout the eighteenth century. The land was broken with a crude wooden plow drawn by oxen or horses. The harrow used to break and level the upturned clods was roughly made of wood in the shape of a V, containing wooden teeth. Grain was sown by hand, cultivated laboriously with crude tools, reaped with a sickle, and threshed with a flail or trod by horses. While attempts were made even as early as the middle of the eighteenth century by plantation owners, ironmasters, prosperous farmers, and a few others to apply scientific principles to crop production and to the breeding of livestock, such instances were chiefly confined to wealthy and highly intelligent men who were familiar with European developments and tried to apply such techniques.

NEW ENGLAND FARMING

The importance of geography in shaping human activities is well illustrated in the settlement of America, especially in the three main regions of the coastal plain—New England, the middle colonies, and the South. The coastal belt of New England is comparatively narrow. This region suffered from the prehistoric Ice Age. In many places it was covered with a deposit of boulders and smaller stones which had to be removed before the land could be cultivated. The soil, not too fertile in many places, and the climate were also factors of importance. Short summers and severe winters prevented the growth of certain crops. Indian corn was the most easily grown and therefore became an important food for man and for beast. The attempts to grow wheat in New England were not very successful, and were given up during this period, except in parts of the Connecticut Valley and the Narragansett region. Barley, oats, rye, and buckwheat were successfully raised. English and Indian vegetables and fruits were grown and English grasses, after 1700. Potatoes which had reached Ireland from the West Indies before English colonization had begun were seldom used by New Englanders during the colonial period.

Cattle raising in New England developed slowly. To the English breeds were added Dutch strains from New York, Spanish from Virginia, and Danish which were imported into New Hampshire. Oxen were preferred to horses for plowing the stony ground, although horses, which multiplied rapidly, provided a profitable trade with the West Indies. By the time of the Revolution, dairying had become important. Swine adapted themselves rather well to their new environment and multiplied rapidly, resulting in an export trade in barreled pork to the West Indies. Goats were raised largely because of their yield of milk; sheep, although menaced by a harsh climate, wild animals, and Indian raiders, produced sufficient wool to supply local needs in addition to a very poor brand of mutton.

New England farming can be understood only in relation to its land system which was based upon a division known as the town. While the original land-holdings were made individually, later, groups or congregations also secured grants, generally thirty-six square miles in area. Originating in Massachusetts, this plan was applied to many parts of New England as population expanded. The idea of the nucleated village with its meeting house, school, common, and homes in the center of the town, together with the small tracts or strips allotted individually, and the common pasture surrounding the village was transplanted from the Old World and was the basis for New England's early economic life. The town system was economically inefficient, for a man's holdings were scattered, his cattle kept with the common herd, and he was required to join his neighbors in cultivating crops in the common fields decided upon at the town meeting. In the course of time, as population in the towns increased and the fear of Indians disappeared, the proprietors of the towns divided the lands held in common, and individual holdings or small farms of one piece took the place of the medieval plan. As a result of this early system, New England farms were usually not very large.

Exceptions to the general pattern of land organization could be found at all times and in many places. The outstanding exception to the general scheme in New England was along Narragansett Bay. The Narragansett planters were stock and dairy farmers who lived in the southern portion of Rhode Island. Enriched by their trade with the other colonies and with the West Indies, they established large estates. They owned many slaves, built beautiful houses, and exerted a social, financial, political, and cultural influence similar to the planters of the South. After the Revolution, they declined in power and were remembered in later years chiefly by their production, through careful breeding, of the Narragansett pacer, a champion on European as well as on colonial race tracks.

FARMING IN THE MIDDLE COLONIES

The land system of the middle colonies played an important part in the development of agriculture of that region. With the exceptions of the large holdings of the Dutch along the Hudson, the estates given by the English kings to their favorites in New York, the gifts of the proprietors in New Jersey and Pennsylvania to their friends, and the plantations of the ironmasters, farms were relatively small. Although at first, William Penn offered 500 acres to each person who would bring his family to Pennsylvania, and was willing to sell 5,000 acre tracts for $100 and give fifty acres for each servant brought across the ocean, farms in Pennsylvania were not large. The same was true in other sections of the middle colonies.

As a result, also, of a more temperate climate, a more fertile soil—except in certain places as the pine regions of New Jersey—and a heterogeneous population, agriculture was superior in the middle colonies to New England. The various settlers—Dutch, English, Welsh, Swedish, German, and Scotch-Irish—introduced their own methods, plants, and livestock. The thrifty Germans led the other groups in their more thorough and skillful ways of farming. Today, the well-kept and profitable farms of their descendants in Lancaster County, Pennsylvania, and elsewhere attest to the industry of generations of careful farming.

By the middle of the eighteenth century in these colonies, many farms between the coast and the frontier were fenced, and even meadows, wheat fields, and orchards were often enclosed because the livestock were allowed to run at large. Some fences were built of rails, split in halves, quarters or eighths, laid one above the other in zigzag fashion, the so-called "worm fence"; some were of live hedge, and occasionally some were of stone taken from the fields during clearing. By this period, the "spring house" or "milk house" became a familiar sight in the region. Built usually of stone over a flowing brook or running stream, it was used to preserve milk, vegetables, and fruits and was the forerunner of modern refrigeration. The smokehouse, found on many farms, was a place for smoking meat after butchering. Not far from the dwelling house, which varied from the fairly large stone house to the log and stone cabin, was the barn. Important for the storing of grains, it was also used for milking cows and threshing grain.

While methods were largely primitive, some improvements took place. One practice borrowed from Europe, and more highly developed in Pennsylvania than in any other colony, was that of watering the meadows by conducting streams of water through canals dug along the sides of hills and, wherever needed, allowing the water to run into the fields through small troughs cut into the sides of the hills. Before the Revolution, the horse-drawn seed drill, invented by Jethro Tull in

England in the early years of the eighteenth century, was used in this region by advanced farmers, and many ironmasters attempted to apply the crop rotation, horse-hoeing and other improvements that were taking place in England.

The crops of the middle colonies were in general similar to those of New England except that a little less attention was given to corn, and large quantities of wheat were grown. This region became known as the "bread colonies," as wheat, bread, and biscuit were shipped to other colonies, Europe, and the West Indies. In 1775, more than 350,000 barrels of flour were exported from Pennsylvania alone. Among other crops grown were rye, oats, barley, buckwheat, peas, beans, hemp, flax, turnips, and potatoes. Tobacco was cultivated in the early years of Penn's colony and at that time became an important article of export, but the growing trade in wheat and flour soon overshadowed it. Varieties of fruit were grown all over the region, but New York became noted for its apples and New Jersey and Delaware for their peaches. Brandy was distilled from peaches, plums, cherries, and grapes; apple-jack and cider became common. Native fruits which grew wild included strawberries, raspberries, dewberries, mulberries, plums, grapes, and whortleberries.

Among the livestock raised in the middle colonies were cattle, horses, sheep, hogs, and goats. They were introduced from England, Holland, and Denmark, as well as from other colonies. On an average farm in 1750, the cattle numbered four or five although twenty to forty were not uncommon, and a few herds exceeded 100. At this time, each farm usually had two or three horses. On some farms they were bred in large numbers for the West Indies. Beef cattle were also raised for the export trade in meat. During most of the colonial period, cattle suffered from a lack of attention. They were allowed to roam at large to find most of their own food and were rounded up only long enough to be milked. Even in cold weather, they were not kept under shelter, although the best farmers had sheds built near the barn for cattle and sheep as well as slightly constructed barns for horses. One of the most harmful results of the practice of permitting cattle to wander afar was the neglect of the dung which might have been used for fertilizing lands under cultivation. By the time of the Revolution, however, the more enterprising farmers of this region were using stable manure and potash, and also leaf mold and muck from the swamps to fertilize their lands. Lime was introduced as a corrective of soil acidity about the middle of the eighteenth century and gypsum came into use for the same purpose soon afterward.

FARMING IN THE SOUTHERN COLONIES

The first settlers at Jamestown were not very successful in reproducing the English form of agriculture. Wheat and other seeds that they brought with them grew with amazing rapidity, but failed to germinate into hard kernels. With the aid and knowledge of the Indians, corn became the first basic food crop. While the settlers were making successful attempts to develop a variety of edible products and to engage in manufacturing and industries as they were instructed by the company, they found that tobacco, grown in the Indian way, would bring immediate returns. Encouraged by John Rolfe's experiments with tobacco suitable for commerce, an increasing number of Virginians turned their attention to its culture.

Tobacco was used in Spain soon after early explorers returned with small quantities of it to the Old World. It was introduced into England as early as the year 1565, and in time a demand for it was created there. When Rolfe planted his first crop at Jamestown in 1612 the English people were already expending £200,000 a year for tobacco from the West Indies in spite of the objections of James I to the "black stinking fume resembling the horrible Stygian smoke of the pit that is bottomless." However, James issued proclamations to regulate its trade, and showed no aversion to an income derived from its duties. Small quantities from Jamestown were sent to England during the early years of tobacco growing. In 1619, the first large shipment of 20,000 pounds was made. Within a decade, Virginia was exporting more than 500,000 pounds annually. Its use spread all over Europe as an increasing number of people came to smoke, snuff, and chew it, and to use it for its alleged medicinal and curative properties.

Throughout the period many problems in the production of tobacco arose in the South. Inspection systems to guarantee the quality of the exported commodity were evolved; large crops from time to time drove prices down and, in one period after 1680, attempts were made to control production; tobacco had to be sent only to England or to other colonies as it was on the enumerated list and most of it destined for the continent reached there through the mother country. By the end of the colonial period many planters through extravagant spending were seriously indebted to British merchants. The exportation of tobacco suffered throughout the Revolution. Partly as a result of this, a new rival appeared—cotton. The demand caused by the industrial revolution for cotton provided a new and more important economic crop for the South. Not until after the War of 1812 did the production of tobacco reach old levels.

Tobacco brought about the plantation system of production. By the beginning of the eighteenth century, large plantations worked by Negro slaves from Africa covered the coastal areas of Virginia. A liberal system of land distribution together with the profits from decades of agricultural exports provided the wealth necessary to build beautiful houses, to secure the best imported furniture, to hire managers and overseers for slave labor, and to organize almost self-sufficient communities. But it must not be imagined that the South at any time was a land made up entirely of large plantations. There were many farms, large and small, where methods and crops were similar to those of northern farms. The production of rice and indigo was concentrated along the Carolina coast. There was much woodland all over the South and, by the eighteenth century, there were tracts of worn-out land lying idle and barren. As the plantation system tended to concentrate wealth in the hands of a small group, class distinctions evolved among the planters, farmers, professional classes of the cities and towns, the artisans, the poor whites, and the Negro slaves.

From the time that the London Company sent a few sheep with the first colonists to Jamestown, there was an interest in sheep raising, especially for their wool. By the end of the seventeenth century, it was common for a planter to have fifty to a hundred sheep. Later, Washington did much to encourage the industry. He owned a flock of 700 to 800. On plantations and farms throughout the South could also be found cattle, hogs, oxen, horses, and other farm animals. That section produced much, but not all, of the meat it consumed.

Before the middle of the seventeenth century attempts were made without success to grow rice in the South, particularly in Virginia. In the latter part of the century a brigantine from Madagascar put into Charles Town Harbor with seed rice, which was cultivated in the warm moist lands of South Carolina. From this humble beginning an agriculture grew which exported 1,150,000 pounds in 1775 and produced 160,000,000 pounds of rice in 1850. Rice culture was begun in Louisiana as early as 1718, and was confined to the lower delta of the Mississippi. However, it was not very important in this region until after the Civil War.

During the colonial period, rice cultivation was carried on along the southern coast by impounding rain water and brooks above the inland swamps. After the Revolution, the system of tidal-flowing was introduced. It was in this later period that the sea-island beaches of sea marshes and the back waters of cypress swamps formed the basis for the great rice plantations of South Carolina and Georgia. These will be discussed in a later chapter.

The culture of indigo was introduced into South Carolina early in the history of that colony. In 1723, the legislature encouraged its production by granting a bounty on the commodity. In 1744, Eliza Lucas, of St. Andrew's Parish, proved that indigo could be produced profitably with slave labor. Others adopted the idea, often combining the production of rice and indigo. The production of indigo was further stimulated by the grant of the British government of a bounty of sixpence a pound on all indigo shipped to England. Next to rice, it became South Carolina's chief crop. Late in the eighteenth century the production of indigo declined rapidly. The loss of the British bounty and the development of cotton culture brought about its end, although some was produced for local consumption until the close of the Civil War.

LAND SYSTEMS

The land system of early New England was based largely upon the rectangular town with the semi-communal village in its center. Individual holdings of land had been granted from the earliest years of settlement, but grants were also made to groups or congregations. In time the common holdings of the proprietors were apportioned among them. Land was also consolidated by purchase and exchange. This movement, together with the direct parceling of land, resulted in individually owned farms and tracts of land. But New England farms were generally small. The town, however, remained the unit of local administration and provided an excellent illustration of the functioning of a pure democracy. At the town meetings, town officers were elected, provisions were made for new schools, decisions regarding roads and local improvements reached, and other questions of public policy determined. The larger territorial division, the county, was unimportant in local administration. The chief county functions were judicial and military.

In the middle colonies, with the exception of some large estates in New York and in Pennsylvania (p. 56), land holdings were not of great size, averaging in 1775 not more than 175 acres. Larger than the ordinary New England farms, they were much smaller than the great plantations that developed in the South. The political organization of land in the middle colonies was extremely varied. The town form of organization characteristic of New England appeared also in New York and was the basis for the township in Pennsylvania, which lacked, however, many of the democratic practices of New England. But the county played a much more important part politically and economically in the middle colonies.

In the South, great tracts of land were granted throughout the colonial period for meritorious work done in England or through favoritism. After the failure of company farming in early Jamestown, land was parceled out and granted in fee simple. At first most holdings were small, but attempts to keep them small failed. From the early days planters were permitted to add to their holdings by buying lands at fixed prices and many took advantage of the opportunity to create large estates in this way. There were times when southern colonies refused to sell land because of the fear of speculation. The "head-right" system became important in land distribution in the South although it was used in most of the colonies. It was intended to parcel out small units, but resulted often in adding to the possessions of the wealthy planters. In the South, it permitted a "headright"—usually fifty acres of land—for each person brought from Europe. Indentured servants and others transported proved profitable in this way to the planter. The plan was abused at times. Headrights were bought and sold; false lists of immigrants were compiled; and other forms of fraud added large holdings to a number of colonial plantations. The acquisition of great tracts of land was necessary for the production of tobacco as its culture quickly exhausted the soil, necessitating the frequent use of new land. The political organization of the southern colonies followed the plan of the mother country very closely. The county was the all-important unit; it was divided into parishes that had few governmental powers.

A number of legal practices and customs, whose origin goes back to medieval times, developed in connection with colonial landholding. The quitrent originated in Europe and at first was a commutation into a money payment of food and labor due the lord of the medieval manor. By the beginning of colonization quitrents were firmly established in England. It was natural therefore that such a system should be transplanted to the colonies. Companies and proprietors were permitted, through rights in their early charters, to require a small amount of money paid annually from all freeholders. Quitrents were also collected in the royal colonies. Because of the system of land-holding in New England the quitrent system did not take hold in that region, but quitrents were nominally due in all other colonies. They were more effectively enforced in Pennsylvania and the southern colonies than anywhere else. The annual amount required varied from place to place and from time to time, but generally was from two to four shillings per hundred acres of land. Because the quitrent was a feudal inheritance and also because of objections to an annual payment—even though nominal—on lands held in fee simple, it was difficult to collect and it became a frequent source of irritation as well as a constant problem in the colonial assemblies.

Primogeniture, the exclusive right of inheritance by the eldest son, existed in some form at different times in all the colonies. In New England, except Rhode Island, opposition reduced this practice, so that by the Revolution it had practically disappeared in that region. In Massachusetts, for example, a law of 1641 provided that all children should share equally in an estate, except that the eldest son should receive double portion. In the southern colonies and to a certain extent in New York, where economic and social forces favored the holding together of large estates, primogeniture prevailed, but even here, in order to defeat the law, occasionally subsidiary plantations or estates were provided for younger sons. In all the other colonies, it was the general practice but in the middle colonies, as in New England, it was widely regarded as alien and undesirable, and plans were often used to defeat it.

The law of entail, which vested the title to an estate or property in a future heir so as to prevent its sale or disposal, became fairly common in the southern and middle colonies. At the same time, opposition was constant on the ground that it perpetuated in America a landed aristocracy. As might be expected, the practice was weak in New England and strong in the South. Virginia abolished entail in 1776, and the other states followed. These practices—quitrents, primogeniture, and entail—an inheritance of feudalism, came to an end with the Revolution or in the years that followed. In more recent times entail has reappeared in a few states.

LABOR

The need for labor is great in any new country where forests must be cleared, dwellings and barns erected, roads and bridges built, fields cultivated, and commerce and fishing expanded. This was true throughout the colonial period and labor—both common and skilled—was always scarce since workers, seeking independence, took up lands of their own. Colonial labor consisted of the family itself, free laborers and artisans, indentured servants, and slaves.

The family was the chief source of labor supply and the needs of colonial economy required large families. Early marriages and many

A colonial loom

children were the rule, although infant mortality, disease, and medical ignorance and superstition resulted in a heavy toll of life among women and children which offset somewhat the exceedingly high birth rate. From ten to twelve children in one family was not unusual. Of necessity the death of the mother meant a quick remarriage for the father. Colonial life centered in the family and each member had his tasks to do. In addition to accomplishing necessary work, boys and girls from an early age were given a valuable training in diligence, perseverance, skill, and self-reliance. Educational programs today which include manual training, domestic science, household arts, and shop courses are attempting to supply training that was given in the home in an earlier epoch.

A second source of labor supply was indentured servants. They were used in all colonies during the first half century. In the South they were displaced by Negro slaves but in the North, Negroes were generally used only for household servants, porters, or loaders. White indentured servants were chiefly bought in the North where they were employed as agricultural workers, household servants, shop workers, and even in the production and manufacture of iron. Indentured servants were of two classes—voluntary and involuntary. The former, poor emigrants who came of their own free will, bound themselves for a term of years to merchants, planters, and farmers, who imported them. Sea captains and speculators also brought indentured servants to the colonies in return for their passage across the ocean. On arrival at a colonial port, the servants were "sold" to the highest bidder by the captain or speculator who was thus reimbursed. An indenture was then made between master and servant. The term "redemptioner," although used loosely, usually meant those indentured servants who did not bind themselves beforehand, but were given transportation with the understanding that on arrival they would be "sold" to someone who would pay their passage. At first most servants were English, but in the eighteenth century large numbers of Germans and Scotch-Irish entered the country in this way.

Involuntary indentured servants included kidnapped persons, political and religious offenders, and criminals. Many boys and young men, shanghaied and rounded up in the taverns of Bristol and other seaports, were spirited away on ships bound for America and forced into this limited form of slavery. In this way, during the political and religious struggles in England, political offenders were banished for a term of years. Counterfeiters, robbers, and murderers were often sentenced to "His Majesty's plantations" in America and were a menace to the colonists; many, of course, began life anew and in their new environment made good citizens. Although these servants were shipped to all the middle and southern colonies, Maryland received more than its share.

The terms of service as specified in indentures made between master and servant varied from three to seven years. For political and religious offenders as well as criminals the term was often extended to fourteen years. A body of colonial laws regulated the treatment of indentured servants and set forth the duties and responsibilities of both master and servant. In most cases, the servant had to be provided with clothing and equipment, and at the end of his term of service was often given land grants or warrants, and sometimes tools or supplies to begin farming.

Free laborers and artisans were a third type of labor. Although relatively small compared with the other groups, this class was extremely important, for it included the skilled workers as well as the unskilled. From the beginning of settlement, mechanics and workers, such as tanners, carpenters, masons, and weavers, came to the colonies. Many became farmers, but others plied their trades in the rising commercial towns and in the boroughs and villages. Throughout the period, artisans were attracted from Europe by the relatively high rate of wages. Others were brought over by planters, ironmasters, and by the proprietors of colonies.

After the middle of the seventeenth century, Negro labor slowly became all-important on the expanding southern tobacco plantations, but slaves were used in all the northern colonies as well. Slavery, which had died out after the decline of the Roman Empire, was reintroduced into Europe by the Portuguese at the time they were pushing their sailing craft southward among the islands off the African coast. During the sixteenth and seventeenth centuries, as distant lands were colonized, the slave trade flowed westward in ever-increasing proportions to reach its height in the late eighteenth century, when overcrowded markets, decreasing profits, and the rising philosophy of the rights of man brought about philanthropic efforts to check it. But not until the nineteenth century did these factors become effective enough to wipe out entirely the trade in slaves and finally slavery itself.

The history of the Negro in what is now the United States began in Virginia in 1619 when a Dutch vessel, manned chiefly by Englishmen, stopped at Jamestown and sold the colonists twenty Negroes captured from a Spanish frigate. At first, they were used as servants—not slaves—and the number increased very slowly. In 1648, there were only 300 Negroes in Virginia and as late as 1671 there were but 2,000 slaves compared with 6,000 indentured servants in that colony. Ten years earlier, in 1661, slavery was made an established institution by act of council in Virginia, which set the pattern for servitude in the other southern colonies.

Slavery did not develop very rapidly in the mainland colonies because of the lack of a supply of slaves. During most of the seventeenth century, the Spanish, Portuguese, and especially the Dutch monopolized the trade and did everything possible to keep the British from the African trading stations. The English slave trade grew very slowly. The high cost of slaves also prevented the immediate adoption of slavery in the seaboard colonies. In spite of these difficulties, as early as 1637, the first American slave ship sailed from Marblehead, Massachusetts, and in the years that followed a few New England vessels engaged directly in the slave trade. The victories of England over the Dutch early in the period of the Restoration had important results for all types of British commerce. The monopoly granted by the Crown in 1672 to the Royal African Company to carry slaves between the African Gold Coast and the British colonies put a legal end for a time to colonial ventures, although there were colonial violations. When the company lost its privileged position toward the end of the seventeenth century, American and English shipowners entered the trade, which brought large profits to the New Englanders and increasing prosperity to shipowners and merchants in Bristol, Liverpool, and other English seaports.

The Puritans, after many unsuccessful attempts to put the northern Indians to work for them, turned to the Negro. Slavery was legalized in New England as early as 1641; other colonies followed within a few years. In all the colonies such labor was used. But it was in connection with the plantation system of the South that large numbers of slaves were necessary and also highly profitable. In the North, they were put to work as household servants and could also be found in the craft shops of the towns and boroughs, and even in many ironworks. The exact number of slaves imported into the American colonies can never be known. However, it has been estimated that in 1775 there were more than 500,000 who lived along the Atlantic seaboard, distributed as follows: 15,000 in New England; 40,000 in the middle colonies; and, the rest in the South: 200,000 in Virginia; 90,000 in South Carolina; 80,000 in North Carolina; 70,000 in Maryland; 16,000 in Georgia and small numbers in the area beyond the mountains.

CHAPTER 4

Colonial Industries and Manufactures

The history of industry during the first two centuries of American development centers around the problems of adapting European technology to a new environment. Some of the raw materials differed from those of Europe, local transportation costs were higher, and both labor and capital were more scarce. Demand was generally for more cheaply and crudely made goods than in older societies. Such changes in conditions are a major source of technological innovation, but no American innovations or inventions prior to the Revolution changed the basic character of these hand labor processes.

Before developing local industry a pioneer settlement needed several kinds of public facilities. Wharves, streets, roads, and public buildings marked the beginning of investment in what economists call "social overhead capital." In the private promotion of colonies these initial costs had to be borne by the company or proprietor and were among the many expenses that were underestimated.

HOUSES AND PUBLIC BUILDINGS

Continuous movement to new areas, even in the twentieth century, deprived Americans of the heritage of old buildings so useful in more settled countries. Although early statistics are lacking, it seems certain that houses and other buildings have always been the most important type of American investment. Many of the first houses were temporary—caves and hillside shelters, and even tents of sailcloth or canvas. Some cone-shaped huts of branches covered with rush, sod, bark, clay, or mud were built cooperatively. The Indian term "wigwam" caught the imagination of the English and they applied it to their huts, many of which were patterned after those of European shepherds and charcoal burners. A few, however, were similar to Indian wigwams, covered with bark, rush mats, or hides obtained from the red man.

Temporary habitations soon gave way to frame houses and to houses of brick and stone. These were crudely patterned after those of the homeland. Dwellings of hewn oak timber and thick sawn planks were well established in medieval England, although many Elizabethan houses were partly covered with plaster. But as English forests were depleted, more and more English houses were built of brick and of stone. Early in Jamestown and Massachusetts, following the English pattern of timbered dwellings, "well framed houses" were erected, although the first ones were built of split clapboards, nailed directly to the hewn oak studding. Roofs were first made of straw-thatch or plain wood; windows were usually of oiled or greased paper; the earliest chimneys were of wood daubed with clay. Chimney bricks were made in Virginia as early as 1612 and a kiln was erected in Salem in 1629. Bricks were also brought across the ocean, and used in the beginning for chimneys and fireplaces, later for building homes. Lime for making mortar was obtained from limestone beds, as in Rhode Island where Roger Williams made lime a trade commodity; it was also obtained from oyster shells along the shores of many settlements. By the eighteenth century an increasing number of brick houses appeared. As a result, brick making thrived and bricks became a commodity in intercolonial trade.

Stone houses appeared in sections where good limestone was available, as in the middle colonies, especially in Pennsylvania. The Dutch, German, and English settlers used much stone so that today eastern and southern New York, New Jersey, and eastern Pennsylvania are still dotted with sturdy colonial stone dwellings and barns. At first, rubble, or rough, unhewn stones, was the only form of masonry, but in time, ashlar, or squared and evenly cut stone, was also used in building.

Log cabins were first built by the Swedes who made an unsuccessful attempt to found a New Sweden on the shores of the Delaware. This form of dwelling was of Swedish and German origin and was used by some Germans in the middle colonies in the late seventeenth and eighteenth centuries. Its use spread slowly throughout the back country. By the time of the Revolution and in the period that followed as the westward movement got under way, the log cabin became the typical dwelling of the frontier and a symbol of the struggle with the wilderness, of the individualism of the frontiersman, of a rising democracy, and of limitless opportunities.

Naturally the Dutch, Swedish, German, and English settlers sought to reproduce the architecture of their homelands. The low Dutch stone houses, with their double-pitch steep roofs of shingles, and exaggerated overhang of eaves, often curving slightly upward to prevent an appearance of top-heaviness; the steep roofs, clustered chimney stacks, second story over-hang, and exposed beams of frame houses in New England; the early gabled houses in the South; and the plain stone cabins or stone houses of the Germans, were based on ideas brought from regions where the settlers had lived in the Old World. All these designs were modified in America by a lack of money, a dearth of professional architects, and by other conditions of a new environment. As the merchants of the commercial towns, the southern planters, and the ironmasters of the North became more prosperous, the more informal type of house gave way to the spacious Georgian or colonial mansion, varied in detail to meet local ideas and needs. Compared to the capital used for business purposes, that in homes appears to have been large, a relationship usual in underdeveloped areas.

The Georgian mansion reached a height of splendor in relatively poor eighteenth-century America. Beautifully carved doorways and many-paned windows were characteristics. Within, magnificent staircases, decorated mantels, carved wainscoting, and detailed paneling bore witness to the skill of colonial workmen. In the South, many mansions were adapted to warm weather. The wide transverse hall with doors opening at both ends, the detached buildings for kitchen, laundries, and office, planned as a symmetrical whole, made for greater comfort, privacy, and convenience. In the North, the broad halls and spacious rooms were built more compactly because of the need for heat in winter. The kitchens and laundries, therefore, were usually in the main house. In all types of homes, the broad, open fireplace provided facilities for cooking and spread warmth in winter to the family group gathered about its cheerful glow.

In the erection of such public buildings as capitols, court houses, market places, and churches, European influences were strong in both architecture and large expenditure. In Williamsburg, the robust Renaissance architecture of Sir Christopher Wren was followed; in the Pennsylvania State House (later Independence Hall), and in Christ Church, Philadelphia, the simpler dignity of the early Georgian period stands out; in New England, the tall-spired meeting house, and in the South, Anglican churches were patterned after English models. As there were few professional architects in the colonies, designing was done by master carpenters or carpenter-architects. Many gentlemen, like Andrew Hamilton, the distinguished lawyer who planned the building where the Declaration of Independence was later adopted and signed, became proficient in architecture, studied as an avocation. Their libraries contained books by the English architects, Wren and Jones, and by the Italian, Palladio. In the later period one of the most influential books was William Halfpenny's *Modern Builder's Assistant* (1747).

LUMBERING INDUSTRIES

As in the case of building construction, familiar European technology was applied to the American scene. For the first two centuries of American experience, there was little change in these machines and processes. Those changes that did occur were generally the direct result of adapting the European model to the American environment.

Vast forests, providing timber and lumber for building and many other industries led to an early milling industry. New England was rich in white pine, cedar, and spruce; the middle colonies in white pine, spruce, fir, hemlock, and in such hardwoods as beech, birch, cherry, walnut, and chestnut; the southern colonies in yellow pine and cypress. In various regions white and red oaks and maples flourished.

Sawmills were introduced early in Maine and then in other settlements. By 1706, there were about seventy operating along the Piscataqua River alone. At first they were used for soft timber of moderate dimensions. A straight saw, moved up and down by a crank attached to a water wheel, was the first type. Improvement came with "gang saws," where several parallel saws were set in one frame designed to cut a tree trunk or a piece of timber into several boards at one time. (The circular saw was not used until the nineteenth century.) Hundreds of sawmills were established during the colonial period, the large ones at the fall line of the rivers. Water wheels were made larger and saws stronger but no further improvements in technique were made at this time.

An eighteenth century lumber mill

The lumber industry was relatively free from imperial restrictions throughout most of the period, although English laws provided penalties in New England, New York, and New Jersey for felling trees which had been marked with a broad arrow by the surveyors of the "King's Woods," and were intended for masts for the royal navy. Because these laws, the subject of controversy from time to time between British officials and the colonists, were not well enforced, they interfered little with the industry in a country where timber abounded. However, in 1766, lumber and timber were enumerated and had to be shipped only to England, thus destroying the profitable market in southern Europe.

Shop industries in cities and towns utilized many different kinds of wood. Coopers flourished during the period, for there was a constant demand for wooden barrels for flour, biscuit, meat, fish, cod oil, whale oil, molasses, rum, turpentine, tar, and pitch. Hogsheads, casks, and pipes were used as containers for wines. Barrel staves, barrel heads, and hoops became important articles of commerce. White pine, spruce, cedar, oak, and fir were cut for use in building ships and houses. Cherry, birch, and walnut provided much of the wood for furniture and gunstocks; red maple for spinning wheels, handles, and wooden tools.

Simple lumbering operations were carried on by farmers in all sections, especially during the winter months. The larger sawmills were owned and operated by a number of partners who engaged in no other work and often employed laborers to work for them. Like ship-building, lumbering was financed partly by British capital advanced in the form of goods or credit in return for lumber. By the last half of the colonial period, merchants and land speculators turned their attention to this profitable industry. Men like Mark H. Wentworth and Elisha Cooke were the progenitors of the lumber kings who appeared in a later period of American history.

SHIPBUILDING

The building of ships became an exceedingly profitable industry. While vessels were built in all the colonies, New England and the middle colonies were heavy producers of all types of seacraft. The southern colonies attempted to stimulate the industry by the payment of bounties, but not with any great success.

As early as 1614 Captain John Smith and his companions built several small fishing vessels on the coast of Maine. With the coming of the Puritans to Massachusetts Bay Colony, shipyards quickly arose, the chief impetus coming at first from the fisheries, but very soon from a thriving commerce. In the middle colonies the industry was begun by the Dutch in New Netherland and after English occupation, shipbuilding, centering in the city of New York, grew rapidly. After Penn's province was established, Philadelphia became the chief scene of shipbuilding activity in that region, although ship-yards could be found all along the Delaware River.

Colonial shipyards were usually established on a conveniently sloping shore or beach. Each had its rough shipways with ample space to pile lumber. A few crude sheds provided the necessary shelter for drawings, plans, tools, and other materials. The noise of nails and spikes being driven into the hulk of a new vessel along with the incessant hammering of the caulkers' mallets often gave the name of "Kockers' Hole" or "Bedlam" to the shipyard sections of the towns. In the early days small vessels were built in the forests and were rolled on tree trunks to the water's edge. In the late colonial period boats were even built in inland cities like Reading, Pennsylvania, and sent down the rivers to the sea. Vessels varied in size from ten to 400 tons and were of such differing types as ships, schooners, sloops, brigantines, and brigs.

Materials other than lumber were used in shipbuilding and various dependent industries accordingly sprang up. To a considerable extent the shipyard became an assembly point for prefabricated parts. Iron in quantity was necessary for spikes, nails, chain plates, rudder iron, and anchors. This work was done by blacksmiths and other ironworkers, who found permanent work near, or in direct connection with, the shipyards. Anchors were often produced separately at anchor forges.

Sailmaking was carried on at first by journeymen workers for ship-builders or merchants. However, as governmental bounties and pre-miums encouraged the raising of flax and the production of duck, sailmaking developed as a separate industry before the eighteenth century. In the huge old sail lofts, with their smooth surfaced floors, sail patterns were drawn with chalk and yards of canvas were cut and sewn. At the large shipyards, sailmakers and riggers worked in unison to add the sails and ropes as soon as the hulk and masts were ready for them.

Vast quantities of rope for the ships were made first at the open-air ropewalks and later in crude sheds. These long, drafty sheds, sheltering wooden wheels, cranks, and cordage in various stages of manufacture, were relegated to places outside of the town because of the danger from fire. Generally, hemp and flax were used in ropemak-ing, although experiments were carried on with all sorts of long grasses. The products of the ropewalk, all made of twisted fibers—string, cord, rope, hausers, and cables—were classified and graded.

Jumbled around the shipyards and wharves of colonial seaport towns were little shops where hardware and other supplies could be bought. From these developed the ship chandler's store where marine equipment of all kinds could be obtained, including anchors, oars, pulleys, blocks and tackle, casks, buckets, capstans, pumps, lanterns, rope, and helms.

By 1676, a total of 730 vessels had been built in Massachusetts and hundreds of others elsewhere in New England. On the eve of the Revolution, New Englanders owned 2,000 vessels exclusive of fishing craft and at the same time almost one-third of the vessels engaged in the commerce of Great Britain had been built in the colonies. The shipowners were largely merchants and fishermen. Many captains became owners or part owners of vessels, but the cleverest retired and conducted their mercantile activities from the towns. In the middle colonies, shipbuilding was second to that of New England and many vessels were sold abroad. In the South, shipbuilding did not thrive. A survey of 1769 revealed that only twenty-two three-masted or square-rigged vessels and fifty-one two-masted and one-masted vessels were built there in that year and that the total tonnage was but 4,059 tons.

NAVAL STORES AND FOREST BY-PRODUCTS

Closely allied to colonial shipbuilding was the production of naval stores for England. One motive for founding and maintaining colonies was to free the mother country from dependence upon the Baltic countries for materials needed in building her navy and mercantile fleets. Timbers for masts, yards, and bowsprits, together with such naval stores as tar, pitch, rosin, and turpentine were included in the cargoes of many vessels sailing to England.

Beginning with early Jamestown, all colonies contributed naval stores to the mother country, but by 1720 the long leaf pine section of North Carolina became the chief producer of these materials. In 1705, when the danger of English dependence upon Sweden and other northern countries for naval supplies became more obvious and threatening, England granted bounties on American naval stores. The law provided a bounty of £1 a ton on masts; £4 a ton on pitch; £6 a ton on hemp; and £3 a ton each on turpentine and rosin. The act, although modified somewhat in the reign of George II, greatly stimulated the production and export of naval stores especially from the southern colonies. In the northern colonies, more would have been sent to England had not the colonists themselves used such material in shipbuilding.

The naval stores industries were based largely on the pine forests. Tar was obtained from dead pines, especially from the protruding knots of rotting logs. Different methods were employed in various regions, but whether pots, kettles, sloping clay floors, or kilns were used, the principle was the same—the tar was sweated out and was run into barrels. The heavy residue that remained was pitch, also an important commodity. Turpentine was easily secured in quantities from pines. Hard rosin, amber-colored to almost black, was left after distilling the volatile oil of turpentine.

From the forests other products were obtained that have been since largely forgotten in the march of progress. In the hardwood areas, the manufacture of potash and pearlash proved profitable. Potash was obtained by burning the wood, then leaching or running water through the remaining ash, and finally, by boiling the water away until a powder remained in the form of lye. When potash was baked again to burn out the carbon, it became the more refined pearlash. Both of these products were in demand in England as well as in the colonies for bleaching cloth, making soap and glass, and for fertilizer.

In many places in New England and the middle colonies, the potash industry centered in village shops, which bought wood ashes from neighboring farmers. From the earliest days, farmers thus obtained a small income from clearing their lands. The amount of potash exported annually from New England alone in the year preceding the Revolution was estimated at 14,000 barrels, at £2–10 a barrel or about one-third of the total value of this area's exports to England. Much of course, was also used in this country. The bark of oak and other trees—another forest by-product—used in the tanning of leather, became increasingly important as leather making developed.

THE FISHERIES

More than a hundred years before permanent English settlements were made, European fishermen—especially Spanish, French, Portuguese, and a little later English—crossed the Atlantic regularly to fish off the Newfoundland Grand Banks. All the early explorers to this region noted the presence of cod and other fish in the waters of Newfoundland, Labrador, and New England. On islands and along the coast line of the mainland early fishermen set up fish "stages," the platform on which the curing was done; and "drying flakes," the wooden frames for drying the fish in sun and air after the cleaning process. They established temporary settlements to which they returned from time to time; and in the pursuit of their difficult tasks, they became familiar with a part of the New World and prepared the way for the settlement of New England.

While the Pilgrims sailed with high hopes and a burning faith, they had a few definite ideas of how they were to make a living. After sad experiences, they learned the secrets of fur trading and fishing in addition to planting fields of corn. Many leaders of the early Puritans, who came in much larger numbers than the Pilgrims, first attempted to develop landed estates, tilled by tenants and hired labor. They soon failed and free villages and the town system sprang up instead. From the beginning many in the Puritan colony were attracted to pursuits of the sea. In 1639, Massachusetts Bay Colony exempted from taxation for a period of time all vessels and property used in the fisheries; shipbuilders and fishermen were relieved from military duty. Fishing and commercial activities became the chief sources of wealth in Massachusetts and within a short time in other parts of New England as well.

The early catches of fish in this area were vast quantities of cod, haddock, hake, mackerel and pollack. Cod was valuable not only for its direct food value but also for its oil. Fishing was done by groups of men in small vessels. Each member of the crew—master or steersman, midshipman, shore man, and fisherman—had his own particular duties. Salem, Gloucester, and Marblehead became important fishing centers, but fishing villages could be found all along the coast. At first, capital for the industry came from English merchants, but, as New Englanders grew prosperous, they invested their profits obtained in commerce and trade. By the eighteenth century small groups of merchants and others who had accumulated capital owned a large part of the fishing fleets, wharves, stages, and supplies. In many villages groups of fishermen jointly owned their vessels and equipment.

In spite of rivalries with the French, intermittent warfare, and problems within the industry, the fisheries made rapid progress. In 1700, about 10,000,000 pounds of fish were exported from New England. By 1765, many thousands of men were employed in the industry which yielded $2,000,000 a year, while more than 350 vessels were engaged in the export of fish to the West Indies and Europe.

As was the case with the fur trade, the fisheries played an important part in international intrigue and diplomacy. England continually exasperated the colonists by failing to consider the importance of the American fisheries in treaties made with France. From St. Germain (1632) to Ryswick (1697), colonial interests were not well protected and the French benefited. The colonists were particularly bitter in 1697 when Acadia (Nova Scotia), although captured by the Americans, was returned to France. The Treaty of Utrecht (1713) gave Nova Scotia and Newfoundland (as well as the Hudson's Bay region) to England, but France retained the island of Cape Breton and certain fishing privileges. As a result of the defeat of France in 1763, the only fishing islands left to that nation were St. Pierre and Miquelon in the St. Lawrence. She also retained her islands in the West Indies. The victory of the colonists, however, was dampened in respect to the fisheries, for the enforcement of the British Sugar Act of 1764 threatened to ruin the profitable trade with the French and other foreign West Indies, which was partly based on an exchange of fish for sugar and molasses. After strong protests, the duties on sugar and molasses were reduced, and the threat to the fisheries was removed. In the Treaty of Peace, 1783, granting American independence, was a clause pertaining to the Newfoundland fisheries. John Adams, loyal son of New England, insisted at the peace table that "the people of the United States shall continue to enjoy unmolested the right to take fish of every kind on the Grand Banks, and on all the other banks of Newfoundland," and also in the Gulf of St. Lawrence. But the immediate period that followed was not a prosperous one. The exclusion of American vessels from trade with the British West Indies, the enforcement from time to time of restrictions in the Spanish, French, and Dutch West Indies, the contraction of the European market, and the general depression that followed the Revolution brought economic difficulties and distress for some time.

While the New England fisheries have been emphasized because of their importance, it should be noted that there was much fishing along the coast of the middle and southern colonies, as well as in their tidal rivers. For example, the sturgeon and shad fisheries of the Delaware were important, while rockfish, perch, herring, and also oysters and crabs were obtained in abundance in the Potomac and other rivers. In the fresh water rivers and creeks in all the settlements, quantities of many different types of fish were secured, which were sold chiefly in local markets.

WHALING

Closely related in many ways to the fisheries was the whaling industry. Whaling began as a shore pursuit. When the first settlers built their homes, whales abounded up and down the northern Atlantic seaboard and even the Indians who lived along the coast captured and used them. At Nantucket, which became the great whaling center, they were often stranded on the beach, drifting into shallow water at low tide.

Whales were sought for their products of sperm oil, whalebone, spermaceti, and ambergris. By the first part of the eighteenth century, it became necessary to pursue the monster creatures into the ocean and much later, as they grew scarcer, to seek them in the icy-cold waters of the distant arctic and antarctic regions. As the distance of whale hunts increased, it became necessary to extract the oil on shipboard. Beginning about 1730, "try works" or furnaces were built on the whalers and, after the oil was boiled down, it was stowed away at sea, permitting longer voyages.

The life of the whalers was exciting and dangerous. After the seas were scoured and a whale sighted from the mast-head of the vessel, the eager cry: "Thar she blows!" was given. The ship became a hive of activity. Boats were put overside and manned. To hurl the harpoon by hand meant coming very close to the giant. A crew had to be expert in getting away and in paying out the line or the boat would be smashed by a blow from the creature's mighty flukes. Frequently a harpooned whale would tow a boat for miles before being subdued and killed.

Whaling was difficult, for after a whale was captured, killed, and "brought alongside," it had to be cut up a little distance above the water. This was done from a platform swung out from the vessel's side, and was extremely dangerous in rough weather. As the parts were hoisted on board, the deck ran with oil and blood. The blubber produced oil used in soap making, and for lighting and lubricating; the cavities of the head and the blubber yielded a waxy solid substance called spermaceti, which was made into candles and ointments; the jaws produced the strong, light and flexible whalebone, used for corset stays, whip handles, and many articles. Another valuable product obtained from the sperm whale was ambergris, important in making perfumes.

The giant whales were dangerous to hunt and difficult to handle, yet Yankee courage and endurance made the task possible. The longboat might be crushed by a blow from the leviathan's tail; scurvy was certain to set in after the vegetables had been consumed, for trips were often long, sometimes as much as two years; and occasionally a crew grew dissatisfied and mutinied. However, mutinies were not frequent because a whaling expedition was usually a community enterprise, each member of the crew from captain to cabin boy sharing in the profits.

The industry rapidly expanded after the early years of the eighteenth century when whaling vessels first put out to sea on distant voyages. By the outbreak of the Revolution 360 colonial vessels were engaged in the perilous work. Nantucket, New Bedford, Marblehead, and Provincetown in Massachusetts, and Sag Harbor on Long Island were the important whaling ports. There were many other towns and villages along the northern coast dependent upon the industry.

Whaling reached its height about the middle of the nineteenth century during the era of the clipper ship. The Civil War, the loss of a great fleet caught in the arctic ice floes in 1871, the increasing use of kerosene instead of whale oil for lighting, and the use of other substitutes for whale products brought about the decline. The old whaling wharves disappeared and only stories and memories remain. Modern whaling operations are conducted in swift vessels and the whale is killed by harpoons shot from guns.

THE FLOUR MILLING INDUSTRY

The production of flour became a most important industry. Colonial flour mills were of two kinds. First, the country grist mill for a small fee ground grain brought by neighboring farmers. Such mills were scattered all over the settlements and were simple affairs consisting mainly of a set of crude mill stones operated by a large water wheel, usually dark and green with slimy moss, which was slowly turned by a stream of water. The machinery was made of wood. A few, in Rhode Island, along the Hudson River, and in one or two other sections of the country depended upon the wind for power. The second type of grist mill was the much larger and more complicated merchant mill, which prepared flour to be sold in the stores of the towns and also prepared flour for export.

The merchant mill possessed a series of mill stones, screens for cleaning the grain, and bolting machinery, all run by water power. This type of mill also possessed warehouses or elevators.[1] In most of these plants, coopers' shops provided the barrels for holding the flour and occasionally bakehouses were attached. While these larger mills often did custom work, their chief business was preparing flour for export. They were most numerous and largest in the middle colonies, especially in the vicinities of New York and Philadelphia, although some of the Virginia mills on the James River and at Petersburg could each grind 75,000 bushels of wheat into flour a year. By the late colonial period, the mills on the Delaware, the Brandywine, and the Chesapeake could be compared favorably with the largest and finest in the world.

Manufacturers of flour embarked in speculative practices to a certain degree even in the eighteenth century. Companies of millers—always partnerships in the colonial period—at times held off purchasing surplus grain from farmers while awaiting a lower market; they kept flour in their warehouses for higher prices; and there are instances when they formed corners in the commodity in different localities by buying the available supply in order to control the price.

HOUSEHOLD INDUSTRIES

Pioneer conditions forced the early settlers to provide for their own needs, including the production of food and the making of clothing, furniture, utensils, and tools. The primitive way of life required

[1] The term "elevator" was used in connection with milling before the middle of the eighteenth century.

all members of the family to contribute to its support in an age when self-sufficiency was not only desirable but absolutely necessary. Men women and children had their tasks in producing the necessities of life and a variety of household industries resulted.

In the production of food all participated. The men worked long hours in the fields, but were often helped during busy seasons by the women. Women's tasks included the making of butter and cheese, the rendering of lard, the pickling of pork, the chopping of head-cheese and sausage meat, the preserving of foods for the winter, and an endless variety of similar tasks. Meal, hominy, maple sugar, dried fruits, candles, lye, and soap were produced in the homes.

The production of textiles was largely a household industry. Imported clothes were expensive and a suit of such material was usually worn only for best. Therefore almost every home had its spinning wheel and hand loom to produce homespun. Rough serges, kerseys, and broadcloth and other woolen fabrics were made into clothes. More important in the later colonial period was linsey-woolsey, a cloth having a wool weft and a flax warp, although hemp or cotton were sometimes substituted for the flax. Of flax fabrics, osnaburgs—coarse cloth for outer garments—were most common, while calico and linens were also made. In addition to garments, other textile goods such as bed linen, tablecloths, and towels were produced in the home. In making woolen cloth the processes of carding, spinning, weaving, fulling, dyeing, and dressing were employed; for linen, which was made from the blue-flowered flax, such processes as braking, swingling, combing or hatcheling, spinning, reeling, weaving, bleaching, and coloring were necessary. Almost all of these processes were carried on by the women and children, with the men helping at times with the harder work of weaving and fulling. A finer fabric was produced by pounding the woolen cloth with large wooden mallets while it was kept wet with warm, soapy water to shrink the fibers. This process was called fulling. In addition to being a household industry, it also became a shop industry. Home weavers took their cloth to the fulling mill just as they took their grain to the grist mill, for one mill could serve the countryside. In the dyeing process, indigo, which produced a variety of shades, was often used. Flowers, such as iris and the goldenrod, were also employed in the making of beautiful dyes, as were berries of different kinds and the bark of red oak, hickory, and other woods. Thus the laborious industry of cloth making was largely carried on in the home. On the southern plantations, as well as on the large estates and manors of the North, slaves and indentured servants were commonly employed to do such household tasks.

The men on the farms, like the women, engaged in a variety of tasks. In addition to farm work, including the raising of livestock, butchering and smoking meats, they built and repaired fences and small bridges, erected barns and other buildings, opened roads, and did many other things, often cooperatively with neighbors. Among the home manufactures on colonial farms must be included the making of crude furniture, tools, implements, wagons, leather, harness, shoes, and even nails, which were hammered out at small forges.

SHOP INDUSTRIES

While farm families could make the necessities of life in crude forms, well-finished products required skilled specialists. To take advantage of the rising demand for necessities and luxuries in the growing American cities, craftsmen from the Old World set up shops and advertised their foreign skills. The simple hand-run machinery needed for most of these shops was not expensive; the average investment in equipment may have been about £50. But this sum was beyond the reach of an ordinary workingman and hence the control of these businesses tended to be hereditary.

Within the towns and boroughs a plan faintly resembling the guild system of Europe slowly took form in many trades. Apprentices and journeymen were to be found in most trades and manufactures. In the case of apprenticeship an indenture, drawn up before a magistrate, specified the duties of the boy and the obligations of the master. The latter usually promised to feed his charge, teach him the specified trade under the direction of a competent journeyman, and have him instructed in reading, writing, and arithmetic. When the apprentice became of age or finished his work he was to receive a new suit of clothes and a small sum of money to buy a set of tools. The apprentice then stepped into the ranks of journeymen and joined the artisans of his trade.

The master craftsman's combined workshop and store was usually in his own house. Apprentices, who received room and board while learning the craft, were hard to attract although the English rule of seven years had been relaxed to three or four. Most of the apprentices were relatives who hoped for a share in the business or sons of friends in the trade sent away from home for more rigorous training. Journeymen, mature skilled workers, were even harder to secure. The manifold opportunities for skilled workers in colonial life left mainly the less competent or reliable as wage laborers. Hence most business was by necessity a family affair, often conducted by widows when husbands died, and passed on to sons and nephews. The small scale of operations matched the small size of the markets. Customers were usually limited to people living within walking distance. Local newspaper advertising might bring buyers from the metropolitan area, but only a few entrepreneurs with special abilities were able to sell to customers in other colonies.

Among the craftsmen able to command wide markets were the able and enterprising cabinetmakers. From John Alden of Plymouth in the early period to William Savery of Philadelphia in the later, these excellent craftsmen-artists produced chairs, tables, chests of drawers, highboys, lowboys, and other types of furniture equal in most respects to imported articles. American "joiners" or cabinetmakers were influenced in the later part of the colonial period by English pattern books, especially *The Gentleman and Cabinet-Maker's Guide* by Thomas Chippendale. But colonial artisans injected their personalities and tastes into their work which together with local characteristics produced many distinctions between American and English furniture. Examples of localized styles can be seen especially in the heavy furniture of the Dutch and the gaily painted pieces of the Pennsylvania Germans, but basic and artistic differences could be found in the work of the cabinetmakers of Boston, New York, Philadelphia, Baltimore, Annapolis, Charlestown, and elsewhere.

The production of leather and leather goods became important colonial shop industries of the towns, although such activities were also carried on in rural sections. From the earliest days of settlement the tanning of hides and the making of leather products were very necessary occupations in all the scattered communities along the Atlantic seaboard. Tanners were among the first arrivals in many colonies, for they were quick to perceive the unusual opportunities afforded by a new country where all the materials needed in their craft were plentiful, where restrictions on their activities would be few, and where increasing populations would provide an ever-expanding market for their goods. For example, by 1650, in the Puritan colony of Massachusetts Bay there were fifty-one tanners and a lesser number in each of the other colonies that had been settled by that time.

The basic techniques were essentially the same as those used by countless generations of American Indians. But the more highly developed tanneries of the colonist contained vats, limes, water pools, bark houses, currying shops, skin dressing shops, and often facilities for making certain types of leather goods. Leather "fulling" or "beating" where material for garments was made pliable and surfaced was usually carried on in separate shops.

The tanning of leather was no idyllic occupation. Among the malodorous odors of colonial cities, towns, villages, and boroughs can be counted the noxious and sickening smells of thriving tanneries. In some places, tanyards were restricted by law or ordinance to certain parts or sections of a community and in a few were banished beyond the town limits. But they could be found in all the colonies.

Many colonial laws were applied to the industry. In the latter part of the seventeenth and the early eighteenth centuries, largely through the pleas of shoemakers and other leather workers, several colonial legislatures prohibited the exportation of raw hides and calfskins, while a few placed heavy duties on the exportation of leather at different times. Laws requiring the inspection of leather and prescribing standards in processing were adopted by most colonies. With varying success, attempts were also made by law to maintain tanning, currying, finishing, beating, shoemaking, and garment making as separate trades. English precedents were adopted in establishing these policies. Such laws, however, were difficult to enforce in the New World. By the latter part of the period, small quantities of leather were exported from one colony to another and even to parts of Spanish America.

The making of leather goods was a widespread occupation. The prepared skins of deer and other animals of the forests as well as those of domestic cattle, sheep, and goats were made into various articles. Cowhides and calfhides were used for making boots, shoes, and saddlery; bearskins for bedding, robes, blankets, and wraps; deerskins for hunting shirts, pantaloons, coats and waitscoats, leggings, moccasins, and petticoats; the skins of squirrels and beavers for gloves and mittens; and the skins of raccoons, bears, foxes, wildcats, rabbits, and woodchucks for caps and hats.

Bootmakers and shoemakers, saddle makers, and harness makers established themselves as artisans early in the settlement of the colonies and in all important communities members of these crafts carried on their trade. A few short-lived groups organized themselves as guilds. Shoemaking attained relatively large proportions as shops turned out shoes for export as well as for the local market. Lynn, New Haven, Newark, and Philadelphia became centers of the leather goods trade. In 1767, about 80,000 pairs of shoes were made in the shops of Lynn, Massachusetts; and statistics for the next year show that 13,000 pairs were included in all intercolonial commerce.

Shoemaking was also a household occupation on a large number of farms, and shoes were made by itinerant shoemakers who at certain times of the year traveled from place to place. The making of saddles and harness, and all sorts of leather wearing apparel was not confined to the cities, towns, and boroughs alone, but was also carried on in lonely farmhouses, especially during winter months.

Although colonial tanners even imported skins and exported small quantities of leather, the industry centered in local markets and grew because of local needs. No attempts were made to invest large amounts of British capital in the industry or to foster it by special privilege. Yet it played an important part in early American life.

The manufacture of beaver, raccoon, woolen and other hats, at first largely a household task, soon became a shop industry. By the first part of the eighteenth century, American-made hats were worn by all the colonists except the wealthy who could afford imported hats, although the latter were not of better quality or workmanship than the best hats made in American shops. In 1731, the London hatmakers in petitions to Parliament complained that the shops of New England and New York were ruining their export business to the colonies and were exporting quantities of hats. Parliament adopted restrictive legislation. The Hat Act of 1732 forbade the exportation of hats from one colony to another or to any other country; apprentices were required to serve seven years in the industry; and, Negroes were forbidden to work at the trade. The law was largely ignored by the colonists.

Candles were largely made in the homes, but itinerant candlemakers and professional chandlers also engaged in the industry. Tallow dip, made from well-rendered mutton fat, was the most common candle, but bear grease, deer suet, bayberry, spermaceti, and beeswax were also used. The last named type of candle was used largely for lighting public buildings, while the sweet-smelling bayberry was generally reserved for special occasions in the home. The task of dipping or molding the household supply in winter months was tedious at best. The wick was fashioned from rough hemp, milkweed, or cotton. During the last decades of the colonial period, many shops in the towns produced candles, but candlemaking continued to be a household industry to a certain extent well into the ninetenth century.

About 1750, the manufacture of sperm candles was begun in Rhode Island. In 1761, the chief spermaceti chandlers in the colonies, under the leadership of Richard Cranch and Company, attempted a monopoly by keeping their processes a secret. Through detailed trade agreements they set maximum buying prices for spermaceti, fixed prices at which sperm candles should be sold, permitted no new members without the consent of all, and prevented any competition "by fair and honorable means." They also began to build up a whaling fleet of their own. Their processes in time were learned by others and competition broke the power of this early "trust."

Silverware and ornaments were important signs of social prestige in the seventeenth and eightenth centuries. Hence this luxury industry began earlier than might be expected on the basis of general colonial development. Disciples of the ancient craft left the cities of the Old World to carry on their highly advanced skills in the New. During the colonial period a long line of skillful artisans from John Hull, Robert Sanderson, and Jeremiah Dummer to Jonathan Otis, Paul Revere, and the notorious Samuel Casey fashioned silverware that graced the sideboards and tables of early Americans.

It may seem strange that the malleable and ductile silver was worked into objects of shining beauty and intricate design in a pioneer country possessing no silver mines. Some of the silver plate owned by colonists who could afford it came from England, but most of what was produced in this country came from English, Spanish, and Portuguese coins obtained largely in the West Indian trade.

This calls attention to economic motives in acquiring silverware. The balance of trade with England was continually against the colonists and drained the country of much of its money. Americans did everything to prevent coins from leaving the colonies. One way to achieve this was to convert silver coin into silverware. There were no banks in which to deposit money and it became convenient to have it made into plate to be displayed for the admiration of friends and visitors. Plate did not lose its value and, if stolen, could be easily identified provided it were not melted. Furthermore, it could be reconverted into the equivalent of money if necessary. Silversmiths gathered in the commercial towns where wealth was beginning to develop, and some could be found in the provincial boroughs and villages. With the introduction of banks and the advent of Sheffield plate, the art of the individual silversmith declined in the nineteenth century.

Pewterers increased in number as the wooden dishes of early days gave way to pewter ware, which at first had been imported. Not until 1750 were large amounts of pewter ware made in the colonies, because tin, the basic metal in its production, had to be imported. Colonial pewter was about 80 per cent tin and 20 per cent copper. Often lead was used as the alloy instead of copper. Sad ware was produced by hammering out the metal into platters and trays; hollow ware, such as tankards, bowls, and even small plates and spoons, was cast in molds of gun metal. Philadelphia, New York, and Boston were the centers where pewter was made. The Revolution brought a demand for metals of all kinds, especially lead, for making munitions and as a result the pewter trade languished. In the period that followed, the use of chinaware and porcelain increased, as changes in the English potteries during the industrial revolution resulted in lower prices and in new types of commodities.

Printing shops arose in most of the colonial towns. The art of printing slowly developed in the seventeenth century. The press of Stephen Daye was set up early in Massachusetts Bay Colony and others slowly appeared in the colonies. The books and pamphlets produced by the early American printers were chiefly religious in nature. By the eighteenth century all colonies had printing shops which issued almanacs, broadsides, tracts, and sermons. Newspapers and documents were also their products. Among the outstanding printers besides Daye might be mentioned William Nuthead whose shop was suppressed by Governor William Berkeley of Virginia, and who then moved to Maryland to carry on his activities; William Bradford, who established a printing office in early Philadelphia and, wearied by religious and civil interference, moved to New York; and, the famous Benjamin Franklin, whose large shop printed the *Pennsylvania Gazette* and *Poor Richard's Almanac.*

In 1690, William Bradford, the printer, joined David Rittenhouse, a Dutch paper maker, in erecting the first paper mill in America on the Wissahickon Creek near Philadelphia. Others followed closely. In 1756, the first pulp engine was introduced from Holland; then the number of paper mills increased rapidly. Colonial paper making entailed the reduction of rags to a pulp, which was then pressed and molded in a variety of fine-meshed wire molds from which the paper derived its texture. The use of wood pulp in paper making came much later.

Bookbinding, "the art of arranging the pages of a book in proper order and confining them there by means of thread, glue, paste, pasteboard, and leather," became a relatively important shop industry. Stamps, dies, and other tools, as well as presses were used by skillful bookbinders. From the time of John Sanders in the early Puritan colony, many professional bookbinders engaged in this work, although printers and booksellers also developed the art of bookmaking.

Among other shop industries, the production of watches and clocks should be noted. Belfry clocks and household timepieces were at first made to order. By the latter part of the eighteenth century, chronometers and watches were produced in quantity and were sold in the shops of the towns and by traveling peddlers throughout rural areas. During the colonial period most common folk had to get along with sundials and hourglasses, as watches and clocks were expensive. The manufacture of rifles became important after 1730, especially in the regions settled by the Pennsylvania Germans, many of whom were expert rifle makers. The production of wallpaper was begun late in the colonial period by Plunket Fleeson, although "painted papers" had been imported in small quantities from an early date. The origins of the manufacture of floor coverings will also be found in the colonial period. A meager domestic supply was produced in the homes or in small craft shops, some of which operated under a "putting-out" system. In 1791, William P. Sprague of Philadelphia established the first factory for manufacturing carpets. Slowly other plants appeared, but for many years homemade floor coverings remained important. Altogether many different types of shops in the urban centers turned out products of all kinds to supply local needs and for intercolonial trade.

The spinning school movement aided the shop production of textiles. Instances of providing instruction for poor children in carding, spinning, weaving, and knitting can be found in the seventeenth century in Massachusetts, Virginia, and Maryland. During the latter part of the colonial period many communities possessed such schools, philanthropic in nature and intended to give employment to the poor of the urban regions. They were supported by general contributions or by private societies. One of the best examples was the Society for Encouraging Industry and Employing the Poor, established in Boston in 1751. By the time of the Revolution, spinning schools sponsored by such societies were developing into textile shops which contained the germ of the factory.

IRON MANUFACTURES

Attempts were made to establish an iron industry from the very beginning of settlement. When Virginia was under the jurisdiction of the London Company, blast furnaces were built, but before production got under way the works were demolished and the ironworkers slain in the Indian massacre of 1622. The Puritans under the leadership of John Winthrop built furnaces and forges among the bog ores of the Bay Colony at Lynn and Braintree. These operated for more than fifty years, but lawsuits, technical difficulties, and other problems constantly interfered with the production of iron. A few other ironworks, chiefly bloomeries, were established in New England in the seventeenth century and one in Shrewsbury, New Jersey. But not much real progress was made until the eighteenth century. Most iron articles and ironmongery together with bar iron were imported from England.

From the second decade of the eighteenth century cheap fuel and ore close to the surface of the ground stimulated the colonial iron industry in spite of high costs of transportation. Before the Revolution, ironworks had been built in every colony except Georgia. In 1775 there were more blast furnaces and forges in the colonies than in both England and Wales, and the colonies produced more pig and bar iron than the mother country.[2] In 1700 the seaboard colonies made about one-seventieth of the world's supply of iron; in 1775 they produced almost one-seventh. Although the industry was scattered, it was most highly concentrated in southeastern Pennsylvania. An adequate supply of ore was, of course, a most important factor in determining the location of a blast furnace and water power was also necessary. Accessibility to markets was not as important as nearness to ore and fuel, and hence transportation costs from these inland locations to the port towns were generally high.

Establishing a furnace, a bloomery, and a forge near iron deposits with water power together with the thousands of acres of woodland necessary for fuel required a larger capital investment than any other business activity. At the end of the colonial period, an iron plantation, including the land, blast furnace, forges, houses, grist mill, sawmill, and all equipment cost from £7,000 to £12,000. Plantations having only forges and the other equipment, but no blast furnace, were valued at £5,000 to £7,000. The smaller ironworks, usually located in towns or boroughs, varied in cost. A slitting mill could be built for £1,200, a steel furnace for £700, a plating mill for £300, a blacksmith shop for £150, and a nailery for about the same figure, all exclusive of land. An air furnace was worth about £200.

Most of the capital for industry came from merchants who formed partnerships with ironmasters who lived at the works and conducted operations. The earliest ironmasters were English, but as time went on they came from many countries including Germany, France, Switzerland, Scotland, and Wales. By the time of the Revolution, many men of importance were ironmasters or had investments in the manufacture of iron.

With the exception of the primitive bloomeries in regions of New England and a few other places where the iron was crudely made by

[2] England produced large quantities of manufactured iron products at this time, but was largely dependent upon Sweden for the bar iron from which they were made.

heating and hammering bog and other types of ores, pig iron and bar iron were produced on "iron plantations." The mansion house, built on a hill or elevation overlooking the blast furnace, where the iron-master could keep his eye on its activities day and night, the refinery forge not far distant, often found in connection with the blast furnace or on separate plantations, the ironmaster's store where all the necessities of life could be obtained, the clustered dwellings of the workers in the village, and, some distance away, the mines, the woodlands, the farmlands, the gristmill, the sawmill, and the blacksmith shop—all made up an almost self-sufficient community.

The furnace, a truncated pyramid of stone, built into the side of a small hill in order that the ore, limestone flux, and charcoal could be put into the furnace at the top, was an impressive sight when in blast. The intermittent roar of the forced blast could be heard a long distance away. From the top of the furnace stack a stream of sparks was occasionally emitted as the flames rose and fell—pulsating with the blast. At night the almost smokeless flames cast a lurid glare upon the sky, visible for miles around, which illuminated the surrounding buildings. Within the main casting house or casting shed as it was called, which was built directly in front of the furnace, the "mysteries"

The furnace at the
Hopewell Ironworks
in Pennsylvania

of casting were carried on. Here the molten metal was run from the hearth into the waiting molds of scorched and blackened sand. Creaking wagons drawn by teams of horses hauled the iron ore up the furnace road. From the "bank," the fillers carried their baskets of ore, limestone, and charcoal across the bridge to the furnace top. Pig iron was the chief product of the blast furnace, although pots, pans, kettles, stove-plates, and fire-backs were also cast.

The forge, where the pig iron was refined and hammered into blooms, or bars of wrought iron, was generally not far distant. The dull, unvaried turning of the water wheel, the irregular splash of falling water, the rhythmic thump of the hammer, and the droning sound of the anvil, were a part of life on the plantation. Within the forge strong half-naked men swung the white-hot pasty metal from the hearths to the great hammers by means of wide-jawed tongs. Under the steady strokes of the hammers, amid showers of scintillating sparks, the forgemen drew the bar to given sizes. Bar iron from the forges was used by blacksmiths to make tools, implements, and ironware of different sorts.

The problem of obtaining a sufficient supply of skilled labor faced the ironmasters continually. Many skilled workers, including iron-workers, miners, and charcoal burners, were imported from Europe. Most remarkable was the importation of 535 men and their families from England and Germany in 1765 for the New York and New Jersey enterprises of Peter Hasenclever, which included ironmaking, the manufacture of potash, and the production of hemp, flax, and madder. Although brought under contract, Hasenclever's workers were not indentured servants, for they were free and were paid daily wages. In the manufacture of iron, free artisans usually performed the work of founding, casting, and "drawing" the iron, although indentured servants were sometimes employed, and even Negro slaves were used, many of whom became very proficient in "drawing" the iron under the large hammers at the forges.

In addition to bloomeries, furnaces, and forges, other types of iron-works developed in the colonies but were usually found in towns or boroughs. At the rolling and slitting mills, the bars from the forge were heated and slit into small strips called slit iron, used for making nails. Small amounts of "blister" steel were produced in small furnaces by the trial and error method. Bars were stacked in pots or ovens, and carbon in the form of charcoal dust, bone, or other material was scattered between them. After the pots were sealed, heat was applied for seven to eleven days. If the process was successful, the carbon from the charcoal and other substances was absorbed by the bars and they were transformed into steel. In the plating mill, bars were hammered out into thin sheets by powerful hammers driven by water wheels. The sheets were usually given a coating of tin after being annealed, thus producing tin plate. An increasing number of works of these types was established and the colonists began to supply themselves with nails, steel, and tin plate. The production brought opposition from the mother country and the passage of restrictive legislation. Still another type of plant appeared late in the colonial period—the air furnace. It had a capacity of about five tons for making castings from pig iron and was the progenitor of the modern cupola.

The Iron Act of 1750 encouraged the making of colonial pig and bar iron but regulated the production of the more refined types of iron. It provided that colonial pig iron could enter Great Britain free of duties and that colonial bar iron could be imported into London duty-free (extended in 1757 to include all English ports). The law specified that slitting mills, steel furnaces, and plating mills could not be erected in the colonies, although those already in operation were permitted to continue. The legislation was in no way successful. Increasing amounts of iron were sent to the mother country but not in such quantities as to reduce the amount imported into England from Sweden and Russia to be manufactured into tools and implements for exportation and domestic use. The colonists worked up most of the iron they produced into articles needed by themselves, thus defeating the plan of sending pig and bar iron and receiving the finished iron products from the homeland—at a great profit, of course, to English manufacturers. The restrictive aspects of the law, also, were not observed and many forbidden ironworks were erected all over the colonies—even in the capital city of Philadelphia under the eyes of the governor who was charged with the duty of putting the law into effect.

The blacksmith, as a skilled artisan in iron, occupied an important position in colonial economy. His activities were not confined to repair work, for he shaped bars of iron into axe-heads, hoes, shovels, chains, bolts, latches, scythes, and other needed articles. There were hundreds of blacksmith shops scattered throughout the colonies and the most highly proficient blacksmiths were skilled craftsmen as can be seen in their handiwork that still survives in the form of artistic hinges, weather vanes, iron gates, railings, and balconies.

NON-FERROUS METALS AND GLASS

Whitesmiths, workers in tin plate, could be found in some of the towns and boroughs during the latter part of the colonial period. At their shops, some of which employed twenty or more workers, a variety of utensils was made, such as kettles, coffee pots, saucepans, stewpans, fish kettles, lanterns, sand-shakers, boxes, and Dutch ovens, for which there was a constant demand. The whitesmiths secured tinned plates, chiefly from South Wales, and often imported block tin with which they tinned iron sheets hammered out at American plating mills.

Articles of brass manufactured at small foundries, and large quantities of brass buttons produced by merchant-manufacturers in the towns were made from old English brass ware, often obtained by itinerant peddlers in part payment for their goods which they in turn sold to the brassworkers. Some warming pans were made from copper and brass but most were imported. Cast lead was also used for making urns and other articles, although most of this metal provided part of the material necessary for pewter. Metal industries other than iron did not flourish in the colonial period. Though small copper and lead mines were opened up from time to time, these industries did not make much progress. The production of brass—an alloy of copper and zinc—was not considerable, in spite of many attempts to produce the metal, because zinc had to be entirely imported.

Attempts to produce glass, badly needed for windows as well as for bottles, and other utensils, were made early. At Jamestown in 1609 and 1621, and in Salem in 1639, glass was made but chiefly for beads for the purpose of trading with the Indians, although some other forms of glass were produced. In New Amsterdam, Jan Smeedes in 1654 and Evert Duyckingk the following year began glassmaking. The street on which they lived and worked became Glass-Makers' Street (later William Street). Several other attempts were made in the seventeenth century, but without much success. In the eighteenth century, Caspar Wistar and Heinrich Wilhelm Stiegel laid the foundations for American glass manufacture.

In 1739, Caspar Wistar started his works at Wistarburg on the Jersey side of the Delaware River across from Philadelphia. He imported expert glassworkers from Rotterdam and together with his son, Richard Wistar, established a business that continued for forty-two years. Window glass, bottles, pitchers, bowls, phials, tubes, and other glass products were made from silica (sand), soda or potash, and lime.

The Wistars were the first in America to make flint glass successfully by substituting oxide of lead for lime in the composition. The Revolution bore heavily on the affairs of the Wistars, who were engaged in many mercantile projects in addition to glassmaking, and their enterprise finally came to an end. Their skilled workmen scattered and aided in establishing glass factories in different regions, and so caused the beginning of a rapid expansion in the industry.

Heinrich Wilhelm Stiegel came from Germany about the middle of the eighteenth century and first turned his attention to iron manufacture. Beginning in 1763 he erected glass houses at the village of Manheim, near Lancaster, Pennsylvania, which he planned and built. He secured skilled labor from Germany and produced window glass, bottles, glasses, flasks, retorts, tableware, vases, dishes, snuff bottles, scent bottles, and toys. He produced not only "white" (transparent) glass but colored glass of exquisite quality—deep blue, amethyst, wine-colored, and green, all much sought after by collectors today. A love of ostentatious display and speculation of different kinds, especially in land, brought about his downfall and the self-styled "Baron" Stiegel died in poverty in 1785. But together with the Wistars, he played an important part in an industry that was to flourish in the next century.

THE POTTERIES

Potteries were established during the early days of settlement in Virginia and New Netherland. The clays of different sections of most colonies were baked in kilns in attempts to produce tiles and the coarser sorts of stoneware. In 1684, Dr. Daniel Coxe of London, a proprietor of West Jersey, made the first white ware produced in the colonies. The early pottery industry was characterized by many small plants scattered over the colonies, some flourishing for a time only to disappear, usually because of financial failure. New York became important for stoneware, especially after John Remmey and William Crolius started their plant about 1735 in New York City. But important potteries were also established in Salem, Braintree, Boston, and Peabody in Massachusetts, Litchfield in Connecticut, East Greenwich in Rhode Island, as well as in many places in southeastern Pennsylvania.

Before 1765, English manufacturers of pottery and earthenware became alarmed at the number of potteries in the colonies. Josiah Wedgwood expressed fear for England's earthenware and stoneware trade with America and prophesied that the young country would prove a rival since "it has every material there equal, if not superior, to our own for the manufacture." Before the Revolution, porcelain was made in the colonies and potteries like the Southwark China Works in Philadelphia were advertising for "skillful painters and enamellers in blue," and offering premiums for the production of zaffer, a compound of cobalt.

The methods of making pottery, like those of other industries, were improved throughout the period. Originally each piece was shaped separately by hand on the potter's wheel but in the eighteenth century, molds of porous hard clay, and later of plaster of Paris, were used. Into these molds the clay was run or pressed. Some changes came in connection with the decoration of the surface as well as with the body and the glaze. Slip ware or pottery upon which color designs were imposed was especially popular among the Pennsylvania Germans. Other types of pottery included designs baked into the clay.

THE DISTILLERIES

The manufacture of rum became an important New England industry after the latter part of the seventeenth century. Molasses, the chief ingredient in making rum, was obtained from the West Indies in return for lumber, fish, and other products. Much rum was drunk in all colonies for it was generally believed that men could not stand the hardships of their employment or the rigors of the weather without it. Rum became a basis for trade with all the colonies and with the West Indies, although West Indian and other important rums had been largely used in the seventeenth century. By 1750, Massachusetts was exporting 2,000,000 gallons annually and on the eve of the Revolution there were sixty-three distilleries in that colony and large numbers in Connecticut and the other New England colonies. The distilling of whiskey and gin were also begun at this time. Attempts were made in the middle colonies to distill rum for commercial purposes, but in general they failed, except in New York. On the larger plantations of the southern colonies liquors were manufactured for home consumption, the distillery being a part of every large plantation. On northern farms, also, liquors were distilled and wines of different sorts were made almost entirely for home consumption.

ATTEMPTS TO PRODUCE SILK

England developed a vital interest in silk culture in the colonies because, following mercantile reasoning, if raw silk could be produced in sufficient quantities the mother country would be free from dependence on foreign countries for the commodity; the export of specie for such material would cease; and colonial silk could be obtained in exchange for English manufactures. Early in its history silkworm eggs, mulberry-tree seed, printed instructions, and skilled silk workers were sent to Virginia. The production of silk was attempted in most colonies at various times. Several colonial assemblies offered bounties for growing mulberry trees, raising cocoons, and for reeling the silk thread. In 1750, Parliament removed the duties on raw silk imported from the plantations and in 1769, granted a bounty, while direct appropriations were made from time to time to Georgia. Several English learned societies promoted the production of silk in the colonies and the American Philosophical Society in Philadelphia encouraged it. Although Georgia exported some silk to England including a quantity which was made into a dress for Queen Caroline, all efforts failed to establish a permanent silk industry in the colonies. The cheap labor and high skill necessary to its success were not to be found. The colonists were too busy subduing the wilderness. England refused to consider the difficulties and continued to encourage silk culture until the Revolution.

CHAPTER 5

Trade and Public Policy

The seaboard colonies as an area were able to continue to attract the capital needed for settlement and expanding industry because they could produce surpluses of commodities for which there was an international demand. From the proceeds of exports of iron, sailing ships, whale oil, rum, fish, lumber, wheat, tobacco, rice, indigo, and other lesser products, the colonists bought slaves, indentured servants, contract laborers, and manufactured articles needed to develop home enterprise. Markets for colonial products developed in the West Indies, northern Africa, southern Europe, and elsewhere, as well as with the mother country. Commerce laid the basis for seaport towns and brought wealth to their merchant classes and to the planters of the South. It resulted in continually increased activities in the ports as ships were built larger, wharves extended, warehouses expanded, insurance developed, and reliable maritime news became more and more necessary.

COLONIAL MARKETING

The business community reflected the critical importance of foreign trade. The key figure was the importer-exporter who came to be dignified by the term "merchant" as distinct from retail "shopkeeper." The merchant, to be sure, generally sold retail as well as wholesale, but he was the source of the imported goods that found their way to town and country stores, and he routed the local exports to other colonial or foreign markets. The merchants' control of the trade came from having the capital or commanding the credit necessary to carry accounts for months or years. Colonial merchants varied in rank from the important and wealthy who lived in houses as "handsomely furnished as most in London" to the smaller operators whose capital was only a few thousand pounds. In a few cases the business descended from one generation to another as famous mercantile houses were established. In the seventeenth century some of the southern trade was in the hands of British merchants who kept factors in the South, but in the eighteenth century, commercial activities were carried on largely by a merchant class similar to that of the North. The great merchants guided and directed mercantile enterprise through prosperous periods, depressions, shortages in currency, crop failures, and restrictions on trading activities, as well as during the embargoes and nonimportation agreements of the later period.

Many merchants maintained or were part owners of shipyards, warehouses, and wharves as well as the vessels that carried their goods. As a group they were undoubtedly the largest employers of labor. Some invested a part of their money in breweries, distilleries, ironworks, grist mills, sawmills, fulling mills, and other industrial enterprises, and thereby provided most of the early capital needed in manufacturing. There are records to show that colonial merchants "put out" flax, wool, and cotton to be spun and woven in rural sections. The influence of merchants on the management and operation of the handicraft shops was not great, although merchants often contracted with the artisans for a part of their wares and products.

By means of correspondence and travel, merchants of different towns maintained business and even social connections with other merchants in the colonies, Great Britain, the West Indies and in other parts of the world. In various seaport towns of the mainland colonies, commercial connections were frequently cemented by intermarriages as kinsmen maintained trading relations in different regions. Jewish families, such as the Franks, Lopezes, and Harts of Newport, New York, and Philadelphia, developed close trading bonds. Within each of the commercial towns, exchanges were established where merchants met daily at a coffeehouse or an office where they made contracts, discussed business conditions, and secured news of world affairs.

Merchants took care of banking, investment, and insurance. They ran "book" accounts for their customers who might settle once a year, or if unable to pay in cash might transfer goods or a mortgage to their property. The merchant bought British government bonds for conservative investors or invited the more venturesome to share in the risks of foreign trade. Until the middle of the eighteenth century insurance was generally underwritten by groups of merchants meeting in certain coffeehouses. Active in all types of local affairs the merchants guided the social, religious, educational, and political life of the cities.

THE SEAPORT TOWNS

In accordance with the nearly universal pattern of agricultural countries exporting staple products, seaborne commerce centered in a few towns, or "cities," favorably located by geography. As these ports grew, they became seats of commerce and trade, the chief places of culture and fashion, and political and financial centers as well. For many years Boston was the largest town, the population rising from 7,000 in 1690 to 18,000 in 1750. By the middle of the eighteenth century, Philadelphia, whose career began later than that of the other cities, forged ahead to become the metropolis of British America, having in 1774 an estimated population of 40,000, about double that of Boston at the same time. New York also grew rapidly in the eighteenth century and on the eve of the Revolution had 30,000 people. At this time, Newport, Rhode Island, numbered about 12,000 and was known throughout the country as a famous summer resort. Planters from the South and merchants from the cities vacationed there. The chief commercial town in the South was Charleston. A thriving port and a dominant political and social center, it possessed a distinguished culture. Many southern planters had town homes there. Communities of less than 12,000 inhabitants included Salem, Providence, and New Haven in New England; and Baltimore and Savannah in the South. While the figures of population seem small compared with those of the great urban centers of the present, it should be remembered that they compared favorably with the English towns—excluding the great metropolis of London—before the industrial revolution.

Each American seaport town had its own characteristics and atmosphere, but all had certain similarities. The wharves, warehouses, and merchants' offices, called counting houses, together with the nearby shipyards and maritime shops, were the busiest parts of a town. Cargoes were brought ashore to the accompanying noises of hand-turned windlasses and capstans. Nearby, bundles, boxes, and barrels were loaded on tall-masted vessels awaiting their turn to leave for some distant port. The detail of imports and exports was faithfully recorded in ponderous ledgers at the counting houses. Not far away the officials of the customs in their offices checked and noted the duties levied on goods that had just been landed.

Near the noisy wharves were the retail shops of the town, where almost anything one desired could be obtained. Their many-paned windows did not display wares as enticingly as the stores of today. Many were general shops stocked with a variety of commodities. Others made an attempt to specialize in such high-priced luxuries as crimson breeches, silks, fancy handkerchiefs, rings, and necklaces. In some, tools, meat-jacks, fishhooks, nails, gooseshot, Philadelphia bar iron, and Bristol crown glass could be purchased as well as bohea tea, French indigo, Poland starch, and West Indian brown sugar. A few merchants restricted themselves to imported English goods. The goldsmith usually specialized in jewelry, and bookshops offered anything made of paper. One type of shop, the apothecary's, was even more highly specialized than its descendant, the drugstore of today. Within its field it offered a variety of articles: all kinds of balsams of life, female medicines, purges, and vomits, as well as smelling salts, spices, white sugar candy, saltpetre, "anodyne necklaces for the easy breeding of children's teeth," "blood stones," "teeth drawers," and different types of medical apparatus. The faint beginnings of the chain store system can be observed in the colonial period as a few of the larger merchants, dealing in many commodities, extended their stores to two or more towns.

Jumbled among the retail shops were wholesale and craftsmen's shops. Cabinetmakers, coopers, anchor smiths, chaisemakers, leather workers, chairmakers, silversmiths, and other craftsmen had their shops in the main part of the towns. After the fashion of medieval European towns, there were attempts to group in one area, those of a single craft, such as the cabinetmakers or silversmiths. Each shop, whether that of a merchant or a craftsman, had its own picturesque and informing sign, marking its location and representing its business.

Taverns, inns, alehouses, and coffeehouses could be found in all the eighteenth-century towns and boroughs. They varied from the well-equipped taverns of the commercial centers to the wretched, dirty, verminous inns of the back country. In the larger towns, the tavern was especially important. It was the meeting place of its day—the club, the bourse, the casino, political headquarters, and the place to hear the news important or trivial. Here cargoes were bought and sold, and slaves and goods were auctioned by merchants and traders. Here travelers, wearied and worn from long journeys by stagecoach, sought refreshment and rest in its hospitable atmosphere. A signboard set forth the name of the hostelry: the Three Crowns, the Bunch of Grapes, the London Tavern, the Dog's Head, the Black Horse, the Unicorn, the Indian Queen, and the Swan were some. During the Revolution the Union Jack became the Flag of the United States of America—while to save the cost of repainting, perhaps, the Golden Lion became the Yellow Cat.

THE FUR TRADE

The trade in furs and skins along the coast of North America began when the first explorers and fishermen made contacts with Indians, long before the English colonies were established. A realization of the importance of the trade gave some impetus to colonization. As permanent settlements were made, the pelts of the beaver, otter, fox, raccoon, mink, muskrat, and other fur-bearing animals provided the needy colonists with an income. In early Plymouth, the fur trade was largely the means of existence for some years, while in New Netherland, the Dutch West India Company enjoyed a monopoly of the trade. The settlements of New France in the interior depended on the fur trade and the French-Canadian *voyageurs* or *coureurs de bois,* the unlicensed traders, added a most colorful romantic touch to the industry.

As the coastal plains became more populated, fur-bearing animals became more scarce in that area, and trappers and traders began their long treks across the mountains into the West, blazing the way for the missionaries and explorers. In return for knives, firearms, axes, hatchets, fish hooks, kettles, trinkets, blankets, munitions, English rum, and French brandy, they secured valuable furs from the Indians. Rivalries between the French and English traders were intense. The traders suffered from cold and hunger, the dangers of the forests, and torture and death if captured by hostile Indians. Small firms and partnerships formed at important trade centers in the East provided the traders with exchange commodities for the Indians and markets for the furs. By the end of the colonial period the annual exports of furs from North America to England was reaching £50,000, but four-fifths of the total was from Canada.

While many individuals and partners participated in the trade during the colonial period, one great monopolistic English company stood out in the North—the Hudson's Bay Company, which came into being as a result of the western explorations of the imaginative Radisson and his brother-in-law, Sieur des Groseilliers. Chartered in 1670, this company established many posts in what is now Canada. In time it extended its authority into the northern regions of the present United States.

In the constant rivalry between the English, Dutch, Spanish, and French, the fur trade played many roles, diplomacy not being the least. In the great duels of the colonial period between England and France, which in 1763 finally gave England North America and ousted the French to a few Atlantic islands, the fur trade, together with the fisheries and the question of land ownership, were important subjects of dispute. In this struggle during two centuries for colonial and commercial supremacy four wars were fought: King William's War (1689–1697), ended by the Treaty of Ryswick; Queen Anne's War (1701–1713), known in Europe as the War of the Spanish Succession, which was concluded with the Treaty of Utrecht, giving England among other things Newfoundland, Nova Scotia, and the Hudson's Bay Region; King George's War (1744–1748), having a counterpart in Europe known as the War of the Austrian Succession; and the French and Indian War. The last named war, begun in the colonies, led to a world war—the Seven Years' War (1756–1763), which resulted in the downfall of the French Empire and the supremacy of England in North America.

TRADE WITH GREAT BRITAIN

It has already been noted that long before the English established permanent settlements, many Europeans steered their craft to the fishing banks and returned home with their catch. As some of these mariners were English, the first commercial commodity of the New World to reach the mother country was fish, although the wealth plundered from Spanish galleons must also be considered an early American product to reach England. As colonies were established and New England became essentially maritime, fish was exported to the homeland, but the market in England for the fish of the Puritans did not grow materially. Great Britain was supplied by her own fleets which sailed annually to the Newfoundland banks, and later in the colonial period from the settlements on the island of Newfoundland. Baltic fleets also carried fish to English shores. The New Englanders, forced to find other markets, secured these quickly in the West Indies and southern Europe.

The earliest exports from Jamestown and Massachusetts Bay Colony included lumber, naval stores, and furs exchanged for English manufactured goods. As southern colonies increased in population, it was fortunate that tobacco with a ready market in Europe could be grown, for its culture and exchange for English goods fitted perfectly into the mercantile scheme. By the middle of the eighteenth century, hundreds of vessels, each carrying from 200 to 400 tons, the property of English and American shipowners, were used in the trade. As early as 1621, a royal proclamation required that Virginia tobacco be sent only to England. This was done to keep colonial trade in the hands of English merchants who would pay for the tobacco in English goods and distribute it profitably within England and to foreign countries. The Navigation Act of 1660 (p. 118) required that tobacco exported from all the colonies be first landed in England where duties would be paid and where it would be handled by English merchants. To evade the duties some tobacco was smuggled into Scotland and also landed along remote sections of the English coast. Just how much entered in this manner is impossible to state because of the nature of the activity, but from parliamentary investigations and reports, it is evident that at times it was fairly large and that some was sent in violation of the law direct to foreign countries.

Most tobacco, however, was sent through the prescribed channels. At first, the merchants of Bristol, Liverpool, Southampton, and Plymouth competed with London merchants for the American tobacco trade. By the eighteenth century, the merchants of London had captured most of it. The merchants there usually acted as commission agents for the planters. In accord with instructions, they sold the tobacco at a fixed commission and bought and returned to the planters the merchandise that they desired. The merchants of the other ports where tobacco entered usually sent commodities needed in America in their own vessels, selling them to the planters at a profit and buying tobacco and furs with the proceeds. Southerners who owned their own vessels were in a much better position to trade with English merchants than were the majority dependent on English or northern shipping.

In the eighteenth century, rice and indigo together with increasing quantities of naval stores from the Carolinas were added to tobacco, the chief southern export. Rice had to be shipped exclusively to England after 1704, and the next year bounties were granted on naval stores. The exportation of indigo to the mother country was also encouraged in 1748 when a bounty of sixpence was offered for each pound reaching the mother country. Among other products exported by the South to England were peltries and grain. In return were sent manufactured goods, clothing, wine, seed, and other commodities.

Despite the fact that the southern trade with England fitted far better into the mercantile system than the trade of the northern colonies, there was, in reality, a continual unfavorable balance of trade against the South. Although official statistics usually show a trade balance in favor of the southern colonies, the opposite is true when duties, commissions, damages, and charges for transportation, handling, inspection, and storage are taken into account. The unfavorable balance was due to the fact that the planters obtained more commodities in England than their products brought. In 1769, the total imports into the southern colonies amounted to approximately £1,247,246 while total exports to England were about £1,100,369. In analyzing such statistics allowance must be made for the importation of slaves. Because of the reliance upon a few staple crops and a lack of manufactures, the South was dependent to a considerable degree upon England throughout the entire period. There were times, therefore, when English and even northern goods were scarce in the South. On the other hand, the plantation system was being expanded with the aid of English capital sent to the South through commercial lending. By the time of the Revolution, largely because of the cultivated tastes of the planters, they were greatly indebted to English merchants.

The developing northern colonies did not adapt as well to the English trade. Aside from naval stores, furs, and peltries, they produced commodities similar to English goods and in many ways competed with the farmers, fishermen, shipbuilders, and manufacturers of the mother country. This was clearly brought out by Sir Josiah Child, in his *Discourse on Trade* as early as 1680: "New England is the most prejudicial Plantation to this Kingdom." This charge applied

AMERICAN COLONIAL TRADE WITH ENGLAND, 1700 – 1774
(In pounds sterling)

Year	Exports	Imports
1700	£395,021	£344,341
1725	£415,650	£549,693
1750	£814,768	£1,313,083
1774	£1,373,846	£2,590,437

Source: U.S. Bureau of the Census, *Historical Statistics of the United States, Colonial Times to 1957*, Washington, D.C., 1960, p. 757.

not only to Massachusetts and her neighboring settlements but to the middle colonies as well.

As the eighteenth century opened, however, and England was becoming more and more industrialized, the attitude of the Lords of Trade changed somewhat in this respect. With their increasing populations and growing wealth the northern colonies came to be regarded as valuable markets for the manufactured goods of England, especially because the climate required woolen goods and other fabrics, which the colonists could not entirely produce themselves. The West Indies— important in British economy because of their sugar and other semitropical products—only slowly increased in population and were less valuable as markets because of the large proportion of non-purchasing slaves. The growing importance of the northern colonies as markets for English goods was reflected in such laws as the Woolen Act, Hat Act, and Iron Act and many adjustments on duties.

New England exported to the mother country small quantities of fish and such products as masts, lumber, potash, livestock, and provisions. In the eighteenth century whale oil, fish oil, and whalebone became of increasing importance. Especially profitable was the sale of ready-built vessels. In the growing competition in shipbuilding with England, the Americans could build vessels much cheaper, while the English shipbuilders were especially handicapped by lack of timber, depending upon other countries for it. In New England plentiful supplies of timber and naval stores more than offset the higher cost of labor. In competition with Europe, therefore, American shipbuilders were at a great advantage and, during the first half of the eighteenth century, New England vessels were sold in all parts of the Atlantic world. Ships were sent to England loaded with lumber and other forest products in return for English manufactured goods. As a result, a large part of the merchant marine of Great Britain was built in America. For most of their fish products, rum, and other commodities, New England had to seek other than English markets.

The trade of the middle colonies with England was fraught with difficulties because its commodities, like New England's, competed with those of the homeland. In the eighteenth century, most of its commerce was carried on from Philadelphia and New York. Through these ports the products of the "bread colonies" were distributed. Among the exports to the mother country were wheat and other grains, ships, lumber, skins, furs, flax seed (chiefly to Ireland) and toward the end of the period, pig and bar iron. Some goods, secured in trade with other countries and colonies, such as logwood, sugar, rum, and tobacco, were sent to Britain. As was true of New England much of the region's commerce was carried on with the West Indies.

From 1700 to the eve of the Revolution, the commerce of the southern colonies with the mother country was more than double that of the northern colonies with Britain. In the decade before the Revolution five-sixths of all the exports from the South went to England and in return Virginia, Maryland, the Carolinas, and Georgia received most of their manufactured goods. On the other hand, only one-fourth of New England's exports went to the homeland and less than one-half of the total exports from the middle colonies. The striking difference in the commercial relations of the northern and southern colonies with Great Britain was due to the nature of the products of the different regions—tobacco, rice, and indigo together with naval stores and skins from the South supplied English needs rather than competed with English products as did the products of the North.

TRADE WITH THE CONTINENT OF EUROPE

Although restricted as to the character of goods by the Navigation Acts, trade developed between New England and Portugal, Spain, and southern France. Dun fish—the best grades of fish—together with barrel staves, pipe staves, and shingles were exchanged for Cadiz salt, domestic wines, Malaga grapes, Bilbao iron, pieces of eight, Valencia oranges, and, after 1690, for ship timber. This Mediterranean traffic was permitted because it did not interfere with English commerce. The northern colonies also sent fish, lumber, and provisions to the Canary Islands, Madeira, and Fayal in exchange for a variety of wines. Some of the wine was carried to England in American vessels to obtain credit for English goods.

Much colonial commerce was not a two-way trade but a triangular one. It might involve a colony, a European country, and England. For example, Massachusetts might send fish to Spain; the vessel would return to England with wines; and, some of the wines might be exchanged for English manufactured goods for the colony. Newfoundland or a West Indian island and the mother country might be associated in a colony's trade. A northern colony, a southern colony, and England might be involved in shipping provisions from the North to a southern port, tobacco or rice from the South to England, and manufactured goods to the original place of departure. Quite lucrative was the New England triangular trade with the northern coast of Africa and the West Indies; the two-way trade to the Sugar Islands was also relatively large.

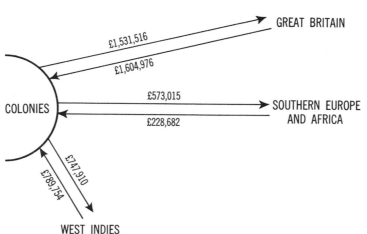

RELATIVE IMPORTANCE OF TRADE, 1769
(In pounds sterling)

Source: U.S. Bureau of the Census, *Historical Statistics of the United States, Colonial Times to 1957*, Washington, D.C., 1960, p. 758.

THE WEST INDIAN TRADE

The northern colonies traded most profitably with the British islands of the Caribbean: Jamaica, Barbados, Antigua, Montserrat, Nevis, and St. Kitts. Here much of the world's supply of sugar was produced by slave labor and the islands were dependent upon the outside world for most necessities. From New England they secured lumber for their houses, the poorest varieties of fish for the slaves, much packed beef and pork, dairy products, horses, candles, whale oil, and Yankee manufactures. In exchange, cargoes of sugar and molasses for the New England distilleries, coin, coffee, cotton, ginger, pimento, and bills of exchange were returned. From the "bread colonies" of Pennsylvania and New York, wheat and other grains, flour, bread, biscuit, packed meat, vegetables, potatoes, barrels, staves, candles, and lumber were exchanged for West Indian products. The southern colonies exported much less to the Caribbean area, but shipments included foods, casks, staves, and cypress shingles.

Out of the New England trade with the West Indies developed the lucrative triangular traffic in slaves with the western coast of Africa. From Boston, Newport, and other northern towns, vessels sailed to the Gold Coast of Africa with rum, pots, manufactured goods, provisions, shirts, shackles, and "African iron" (short bars used as currency in

Africa). These cargoes were exchanged for slaves, gold dust, ivory, and pepper, obtained from African traders and Negro chieftains. The slaves and much of the rest of the cargo were sold in the West Indies for molasses, sugar, and bills of exchange drawn on London, Liverpool, or Bristol. Landed at the original port of departure in New England, the molasses was the basis for rum to be used in the African trade and sold for home consumption. While cargoes, routes, and ports varied, this trade was built largely on the never-ending cycle of rum, slaves, and molasses. Stories of the journey from Africa to the West Indies by way of the terrible "middle passage," the second leg of the triangular voyage of a slave ship, have been embodied in the world's literature. Unbelievable tales have been told, without exaggeration, for the horrors of the trip were attended by brutality and by a high mortality. The shackled slaves were laid side by side on the decks of the slave ships or were callously packed into holds. Slaves taken ill were often thrown into the sea that the rest might not be contaminated by fever or pestilence. Those who survived were sold in the West Indian markets to all the British colonies. By means of the two-way trade, a relatively small number were brought direct from Africa to the southern colonies and were paid for with rice, tobacco, indigo, and provisions.

INTERCOLONIAL TRADE

Most of the trade between the mainland colonies themselves was coastwise. It was largely in the hands of Americans—especially northerners—with very little competition from English shipowners and captains. This monopoly played a most important part in the growth and prosperity of the seaport towns, for they became the commercial centers for most of the trade of the colonies. In addition to the exchange of goods, the sea lanes of intercolonial commerce linked the different settlements in an era when good roads were scarce and other means of communication lacking.

Tobacco was sent from Virginia to New England in return for fish at a very early date. All types of vessels were used in the trade. As might be expected this commerce was small in volume at first. After 1700, however, it broadened and became important, although it never equalled in value the trade with England or the West Indies. Intercolonial trade consisted not only of a supplementary trade of one colony with another, but also of a redistribution of goods from England, the West Indies, and foreign countries. Imported wines, spices, and sugar, for instance, were sent from Boston to the colonies to the south in exchange for their products.

New England shipped to the middle and southern colonies such commodities as packed meats, salted fish, cider, rum, and candles. From New York, Philadelphia, and the Chesapeake area flour, bread, biscuit, bar iron, and stoves were sent both north and south. Tobacco, rice, indigo, and naval stores were exported northward from the South. All sorts of manufactured articles were shipped from one colony to another. These included the products of the cabinetmakers, silversmiths, and others—and such industrial by-products of northern farmers as hewn lumber, buckets, brooms, ox-tows, and ax-helves.

LOCAL TRADE AND TRANSPORTATION

The important centers of local trade were the commercial towns, located near the coast where there was a relative density of population. In them commodities from surrounding regions and imports from across the sea were sold. In addition, the shops and country stores of hundreds of scattered boroughs, villages, and plantation towns provided for the needs of those who lived in isolated localities. In the larger towns of all the northern colonies, markets and fairs—similar in many respects to those of the Old World—were important agencies for distributing goods. In some places, markets were held frequently; in others only once a week. The town or borough charter usually included such provisions and permitted fairs to be held, generally, twice a year. The fairs brought visitors from miles around. Merchandise, provisions, tools, supplies, and livestock were sold and exchanged. Many people came for excitement and pleasure as well. Young people attended, seeking romance; and some who had passed the age of romance planned a wild frolic. Horse racing, drinking, and gambling were often prominent. Largely because they degenerated into licentiousness, but also because of opposition from shopkeepers, most of the fairs were abolished toward the end of the eighteenth century.

The earliest travelers of the colonial period went from place to place over age-old Indian trails. These led beside streams, wound among rocks, ran by the easiest grades over hills, and followed animal tracks through the woods and forests. They were rough and narrow, but useful as foot trails and horse trails. As they were cleared and widened, many of them became the basis for early colonial highways and roads between the settled regions.

The first local "ways" or streets, developed from paths through cleared fields, in time were legalized as rights of way from which fences and other obstructions were removed. The public road was the other type of thoroughfare and much colonial legislation was devoted to its building and upkeep. It became the custom in many colonies to require a certain number of days' work each year from all able-bodied male inhabitants to keep the roads in repair and to build new ones.

Before the end of the seventeenth century there were some fairly good cleared roads in the more settled communities and cobbled streets in the older towns. Outside the settled areas, rough highways linked the colonies, permitting horseback riders and heavily freighted wagons to pass over them without great difficulty. Compared with modern roads, these clay and dirt highways were crude indeed, dusty in summer and muddy in winter. During bad weather, mudholes, roots, rocks, and fallen trees frequently interfered with traffic, overturning vehicles and breaking axles or wheels. Between 1700 and 1750, these roads were as good as most contemporary highways in England and France which were characterized by a writer of that period as notoriously "bad for the rider and good for the abider." But in the colonies more difficulties of travel were encountered because of a lack of bridges across rivers and streams. Rivers were often crossed by fording them or by ferries propelled by ropes or oars. In spite of hazards, intercolonial travel and freight traffic over these roads increased. For the convenience of those who used the highways of the country, Daniel Henchman and T. Hancock of Boston in 1732 issued a guidebook, *The Vade-Mecum for America: Or, a Companion for Traders and Travelers,* which included a description of the roads, inns, and taverns from Maine to Virginia as well as a directory of Boston streets. Among the most important roads of the colonial period were the "King's Highways" in many of the colonies, the early "Post Roads," and the two famous roads to the West, built during the exciting times of the French and Indian War—Braddock's Road and Forbes' Road.

By the middle of the eighteenth century, as settlement increased and inland trade began to spread, the important highways and post roads of the country were improved by scraping, patching, and filling the holes with stone. Country roads multiplied, especially in the regions of the seaport cities, and the cobblestone and semi-paved roads of the larger towns served their purposes with increasing efficiency. Stagecoaches had appeared by the beginning of the eighteenth century, especially in New England, but it was not until near the middle of the century that regular stagecoach "lines" were operated chiefly between Boston and Providence, New York and Philadelphia, and Philadelphia and Baltimore. There was intermittent stagecoach service to the smaller towns as well.

On the highways, increasing numbers of various types of freight wagons were used. By 1750, more than 7,000 Conestoga wagons were carrying goods in many regions throughout the colonies. This "vehicle of empire" originated in the Conestoga Valley, Pennsylvania, among the Pennsylvania Germans. Large and strongly built, with broad wheels, the body curved upward at each end, and covered with a coarse cloth stretched over hoops, the Conestoga wagon played an important part in economic development during the last decades of the colonial period. After the Revolution it became a general means of transportation on the overland routes across the Alleghenies to the western country and in time evolved into the prairie schooner that plied the regions of the Middle West and beyond.

Travel, however, was exceedingly slow, during the colonial period. For example, it took days to go from Philadelphia to New York or from New York to Boston. Because of the hazards of travel, it became customary for businessmen and other travelers, before a trip was begun, to be sure that their wills were in good order, or to write one if none existed. Plans were made to speed up travel, especially by the postal service during the last decades of the colonial period. When, in 1771, the new stagecoach "Flying Machine" made the trip between Philadelphia and New York in the record time of one day and a half, the achievement was hailed as the beginning of a new era in transportation.

Because of the poor condition of most roads, the cost of transportation was very high. For example, the cost of transporting iron from the furnaces near Reading, Pennsylvania, to Philadelphia, a distance of about fifty miles, averaged £2 a ton throughout the period although the price of iron at the furnace was but £3 a ton. The importance of the roads for travel and trade, however, cannot be minimized in the decades preceding the Revolution. When stagecoach service increased, and as taverns and inns sprang up throughout the countryside, the roads became increasingly a tie to bind the colonies and were a means of dissipating isolation and provincialism.

Over colonial roads traveled "merchants and inland traders in carts" with their loads of coats, breeches, shoes, buckles, shirts, neck-cloths, gloves, salt, spices, and other goods for stocking the shelves of country stores. Itinerant peddlers, chapmen, and hawkers with their mysterious packs, increased in number after 1700. Traveling on horseback or by boat or carriage, they carried with them a surprisingly large number of articles, such as brooms, kettles, pans, ovens, tinware, books, spinning wheels, shuttles, wooden bowls, plates, needles, and many other types of merchandise and "Yankee notions" produced in the shops and homes of New England, but some of these wares were made in the middle colonies and even in the South. These itinerant merchants were popular in the back country, for they distributed news and gossip as well as their wares. In the more settled communities, they were opposed by the merchants when competition increased and in a few localities, peddling was prohibited under penalty of fines. Such laws and ordinances were difficult to enforce and they usually had little effect on the itinerant merchants.

PIRATES, PRIVATEERS, AND SMUGGLERS

Throughout much of the colonial period, pirates who preyed upon shipping had their headquarters in many places along the Atlantic and Gulf coasts and on many coastal islands. The attacks of the Elizabethan sea dogs against the Spaniards had led easily into piracy and from New England's earliest settlement, its shipping suffered by being plundered just off the coast. Early in the colonial period, Massachusetts Bay Colony made piracy punishable by death and sent armed ships to attack the marauders offshore. But as time went on, pirates were welcomed in several of the colonies as they exchanged their gold for the commodities and supplies that they needed. Toward the close of the seventeenth century the Earl of Bellomont was sent from England to North America to suppress piracy. He reported to the home government in 1697 that there was general connivance with pirates on the part of officials and merchants, especially in sections of Rhode Island, in New York, and in Philadelphia, "where they not only wink at, but Imbrace Pirats, men and shippers." Increasing complaints to Parliament led to the passage of an act in 1699, suppressing piracy and making it a capital offense. Although Captain Kidd and other pirates were executed under this law, it brought little relief and there followed a period of terrorism all along the coast. As piracy reached its height about 1720, English men-of-war destroyed many groups of buccaneers, reducing the peril considerably. Condemned seamen were hanged and set up high in chains on an island or along a prominent part of the coast as deterrents to passing sailors.

Many pirates regarded themselves as men following a calling much as any tradesman might. Certain groups were well organized and operated according to accepted rules and laws. For instance, a few outlawed gambling and prohibited women or boys on shipboard, even imposing the death penalty for seducing women at sea. That pirates possessed hoards of buried gold is unfounded and the idea may be credited to the imaginative tales embodied in literature. Pirates quickly spent their plunder and few ever possessed much wealth.

Privateering, though closely related to piracy, was carried on under the legal sanction of a government against enemy vessels. In the colonies, letters of marque and reprisal were granted by the governors under royal warrants to shipowners, authorizing them to send their ships against enemy commerce. The legality of captures was decided in prize courts and profits were divided among the owners of a ship, the officers and the crew, and the government in time of war commissioning it as well. During the intercolonial wars privateering, especially against the French, was widely practiced and was highly profitable. In the French and Indian War, 11,000 Americans were so engaged.

Since privateers carried cannon and usually a large crew, it was difficult to distinguish them from war vessels. On the return of peace, it seemed easy to many shipowners and mariners to continue their activities, thus becoming pirates.

British or colonial laws prohibiting certain trades or levying high import duties led to smuggling. The indented coastline of the Carolinas with its shallow approaches, and the small islands off Florida, were ideal for nests of smugglers. Up and down the coast smuggling was carried on by buccaneers and at times independently under the direction of respectable merchants who felt that the violation of the English navigation acts was no serious sin against God or man. Small boats, under the cover of darkness, landed goods in bays, inlets, streams, and tidal creeks, eluding English officials when supervision or suppression was attempted. Smuggling continued not only throughout the colonial period but for many years afterwards.

THE RISE OF INSURANCE

Although the earliest form of indemnity on vessels can be traced to Roman days, marine insurance as we know it today originated in Italy during the Renaissance. It spread to Spain, Portugal, Flanders, and other countries and was adopted in England in the sixteenth century. By the next century it was fairly well developed in Europe, and London was one of the chief centers. With the introduction of the insurance exchange at the end of the seventeenth century in that metropolis, brokers and underwriters met daily and insured maritime "ventures."

During the first part of the colonial period, American shipowners had to secure the desired protection from their correspondents in London. Often, when a vessel sailed, conditions might have changed and the insurance was refused or voided so that a merchant rarely knew whether his vessel was actually covered or not. In 1721, John Copson opened a marine insurance agency in Philadelphia. A few years later Francis Rawle of Pennsylvania unsuccessfully advocated the establishment of an office for insurance under legislative sanction. Attempts were made in Boston and elsewhere to underwrite marine policies. After the middle of the eighteenth century the business expanded under the leadership of such men as Joseph Saunders, John Smith, William Shee, Thomas Willing, Thomas Wharton, and others.

Early methods of insuring a vessel and its cargo were simple. At the broker's office a policy was made out and the amount of coverage together with the rate of the premium determined. The policy was left with the broker and those individuals, usually merchants, who wished to speculate as to whether the vessel would ever reach its destination, each noted after his signature the amount for which he would be responsible. When the total amount of insurance was finally subscribed, the shipper was given a copy of the policy and another copy was filed in the broker's office. If the vessel reached its destination safely, the premium was divided among the underwriters pro rata according to the amount they had underwritten. In case of loss, the broker collected the various amounts from the underwriters for the insured. The broker's fee was about two per cent. The underwriters assumed their risk for a premium that varied from ten to eighteen per cent.

In the policies of that period, there was the usual stipulation that the assurers were willing to bear the "adventures of peril" including those of the "Seas, Men of War, Fires, Enemies, Pirates, Rivers, Thieves, Jettesons, Letters of Mart and Counter Mart, Surprisals, Taking at Sea, Arrests, Restraints and Detainments of Kings, Princes, or Peoples of what Nation, Condition, or Quality forever, and Barratry of the Masters and Mariners." In order to give legal sanction to the document most policies further provided that they should "be of as much force and effect as the Surest Writing or Policy of Assurance heretofore made in Lombard Street or elsewhere in London." It was not until insurance companies were chartered in the latter part of the eighteenth century that marine insurance became increasingly stable, less speculative, and more businesslike.

In the colonial period life insurance was never organized as a regular business, but a fire insurance company was started in Philadelphia. Before 1750 efforts to launch this type of business had failed in Boston and Charleston. Perhaps because of the prestige and acumen of one of its founders, Benjamin Franklin, the Philadelphia Contributorship for the Insurance of Homes from Loss of Fire organized in 1752 had a continuously successful history.

PUBLIC POLICY: CURRENCY

One great hindrance to trade and commerce—both domestic and foreign—was the lack of a convenient medium of exchange which prevailed throughout the entire colonial period and even continued well into the nineteenth century. As trade expanded, the problem became more acute. Barter was common from the first, but many plans were attempted from time to time to provide a satisfactory currency. Most of these were not very successful.

Wampum—a string of shell beads—was a medium of exchange used by the Indians long before the white man came, and was often exacted as tribute from conquered tribes. Its values were so well established by the Indians that the first settlers used it in dealing with the red men and among themselves. The wampum belt, in addition, was an Indian symbol of a message of good will, peace, or war between individuals and sometimes between tribes. As a medium of exchange, wampum was widely used in the seventeenth century. The colonists manufactured it and often substituted colored glass beads and imitation substances for the shells. Glass furnaces were built in early Virginia chiefly for this purpose. These adulterations caused fluctuations in value and made the "genuine" wampum more desirable. In 1640, Massachusetts made it legal tender. The use of wampum began to decline toward the end of the seventeenth century as beaver skins came to rival it and took its place as legal tender and in Indian trade.

During the colonial period many different commodity currencies were used because of the scarcity of coin and other suitable forms of exchange. In addition to beaver skins, used as legal tender in most colonies at different times, wool, cattle, and corn were authorized as currency in New England; lumber and tobacco in New York; rice, pitch, and corn in the Carolinas; and tobacco in Virginia and Maryland. By 1750, tobacco certificates were the chief medium of exchange within Virginia and debts, contracts, and financial transactions were stated in terms of pounds of tobacco. This form of currency, however, was not satisfactory, for tobacco prices fluctuated, with resulting hardships for debtors or for creditors, depending on the direction of fluctu-

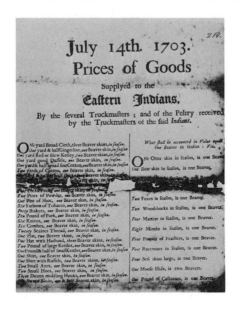

Indian trade — a facsimile
of a broadside

ation. At different times, in various colonies, wheat, rye, barley, oats, hemp, flax, corn, butter, tallow, pork, and feathers became legal tender.

With the exception of the coinage of the pine tree shillings, together with sixpences and threepences, in Massachusetts (1652–1684), the British government permitted no coins to be minted in the colonies. The Americans clung tenaciously to the British system of pounds, shillings, and pence in their transactions and in their bookkeeping in spite of the fact that relatively few English coins were in circulation. Gold, silver, and copper coins were brought across the ocean by new settlers; pirates and traders spent English, French, German, Dutch, Spanish, Portuguese, and Arabian gold on their occasional visits to the commercial towns; and the silver pieces of Spain, Mexico, and Peru found their way into the colonies through the channels of trade. Most coins, however, were obtained in the West Indies trade, as barrels of coins were shipped with other goods in exchange for commodities from the mainland. The unfavorable balance of trade against the northern colonists in their commercial relations with the mother country tended to drain most of the specie from the country in the direction of England.

The use of a variety of foreign coins presented many problems. It was especially difficult to fix the values for the different gold and silver pieces. The Board of Trade in London made several attempts to fix rates for foreign coins circulating in the colonies but without much success. In the last decades of the colonial period merchants in various commercial towns made agreements whereby gold and silver coins were to be received at a definite and fixed value. The agreements were published in the newspapers as occasional changes were made from time to time. Among other problems, the "clipping" and "sweating" of coins impaired their value. "Clipping" was accomplished by cutting from the edge of a coin small pieces which could be sold to the goldsmith or silversmith when enough was obtained. "Sweating" meant the securing of small particles by shaking the coins violently in a bag or other receptacle in the attempt to accumulate the valuable dust. In a later period, milling of coins—providing fine grooves around the edge—put an end to the widespread practice of clipping.

The colonies made pioneer experiments in the use of paper money. In 1690, Masachusetts issued bills of credit to meet the expenses of the unfortunate expedition against Quebec during King William's War. This example was in time followed by other colonies. Bills of credit were often issued on loans, land, silver, or gold plate, or on no tangible security to meet a sudden emergency, to furnish money for the ordinary operations of governments or to provide an adequate currency. All colonies except North Carolina finally adopted these modern methods of increasing the currency. Some issues bore interest; others did not. Some were made complete legal tender; others were restricted in various ways in the payment of debts. Some were payable on demand; others were irredeemable. As most of them depreciated, creditors forced to take them for debts and all salaried persons suffered. As notes declined in value, they tended to drive out of circulation whatever silver and gold there was in a colony. Only a few issues, such as the Pennsylvania issue of 1723, were fairly well managed. Most notes failed to provide a satisfactory currency. In response to the loud complaints of English creditors, Parliament passed a law in 1751 forbidding any New England government to issue additional legal tender bills of credit. In 1764, the law was extended and applied to all colonies (p. 126). This act led to vigorous protest and much discontent. It was one of the grievances that was aired prior to the Revolution.

The usual method of trading with England and of engaging in large transactions within the colonies was by means of bills of exchange. Such instruments were commonly drawn by American merchants, traders, planters, and sea captains on English merchants with whom they had established credit by reliable shipment of goods. In order to secure and hold American trade, English merchants extended credit in large amounts. In this way the London and Liverpool merchants served as bankers to facilitate trade. They profited from interest charges on bills and brokerage fees.

Bills of exchange were drawn on the security of tobacco and other commodities sent or to be sent to England. Northern colonies became markets for the sale of bills drawn in the South and of course bills were drawn directly by northern merchants on English correspondents for goods exported or to be forwarded in the future. In the triangular trade involving three or even more ports, bills of exchange drawn on London merchants were of much importance. The usual term of credit was nine months, within which time a "covering remittance" was expected by the English merchant. If the drawer of the bill was unable to deliver goods or money to the merchant, the latter might take a mortgage on the debtor's property. Through such overdue bills the Virginians came to owe debts of millions of dollars to English merchants. The system worked fairly well, although there were continual difficulties due to the circuitous journeys of the bills, the long intervals before they were presented for redemption, the problem of securing bills for small amounts, the fluctuation of rates of exchange, the overdrawing of credit, and the length of time that elapsed after a bill was protested.

PUBLIC POLICY: TRADE

Many early American historians believed that commercial relations between the mother country and the colonies were based on injustice. They painted dark pictures of a tyrannical England and a suffering infant offspring, as the former developed policies that appeared selfish and injurious to the latter. More recent research, however, presents a different perspective and approaches the problem from the point of view that the colonies were but a part of greater England and that regulative and restrictive legislation and orders were an attempt to work out an intelligently conceived plan—notwithstanding weaknesses and contradictions—to build up a self-sufficing empire. Contrary to popular understanding even at the present time, the British mercantile system as embodied in various acts of Parliament, Orders in Council, royal instructions to the governors and in other ways was evolved not to levy tribute upon the colonies, but to provide a system of protection along imperial lines for all those great interests that aided in building material power and wealth.

Many influences and impulses, varying with each settlement, went into the founding of the individual colonies. Some were for corporate or private profit; others were for the oppressed and dissatisfied. But long before all of them were safely organized, statesmen in London agreed more or less upon the reason for their being and upon their place in the national system. This can be seen in the prevailing philosophy of the times—British mercantilism.

During the early years of the American experiments, English policy toward the colonies was defined and put into effect by the king and Privy Council. After the Civil War and under Cromwell's Commonwealth, Parliament sought to control the colonies. With the return of the Stuarts, the stage was set for the formal pronouncement of the prevailing mercantile theory and the attempt to work it out in some detail.

Laws had been passed as early as the fourteenth century encouraging the use of English vessels in English commerce. The first important commercial laws affecting the colonies were enacted by Parliament in 1649 and 1651. These constituted the legal formulation of a comprehensive system and were adopted by the government of Cromwell, supported by the merchants and shipowners of London. Directed at the Dutch, who at this time were superior to the English in finance, shipbuilding, commerce, and the carrying trade, this legislation provided that goods could be carried to or from any English colony only in British vessels with crews at least three-fourths British. Other clauses required that any products from Asia, Africa, or America enter England only in British vessels and that goods from European countries be imported into England in ships of the country where the goods were produced or in British vessels. These monopolies were granted not only to Englishmen living in England, but to all who were British, including those who lived in the colonies.

The navigation legislation of the English Puritan regime was re-enacted, consolidated, and expanded in the laws of 1660 and 1663. In addition to restricting most of the commerce of the growing empire to British ships carrying crews that were at least three-fourths British, a system of enumeration of goods was adopted (1660). Certain important colonial commodities could be exported from the place of production only to another British colony or to England. The enumerated list at first included tobacco, sugar, raw cotton, indigo, ginger, and fustic and other dyewoods. Later, naval stores, hemp, rice, molasses, beaver skins, furs, copper ore, iron, and lumber were added to the expanding list. Another aspect of the system provided that all European and Asiatic goods and manufactures would have to pass through English ports before being sent to the colonies (1663).

A few exceptions were made, such as salt and wines from southwestern Europe and the Wine Islands and food products from Ireland and Scotland. The Navigation Act of 1696 codified the earlier laws. It provided also that all British vessels be registered, that colonial laws at variance with the acts of trade were null and void; it authorized writs of search, and provided for vice-admiralty courts to enforce the law. An attempt was made to make the colonists strictly obey the acts of trade, but after a few years the efforts were relaxed.

Laws were also enacted applying specifically to the seaboard colonies. The act of 1699 forbade the export of wool, raw or manufactured, from one colony to another "or to any other place whatsoever"; the Hat Act of 1732 provided that no American-made hats could be exported from any colony; and a section of the Iron Act of 1750 encouraged the production of colonial pig iron and bar iron by relaxing the duties when imported into England. Another type of commercial legislation applied to the bounties paid by the British government on naval stores and other commodities. This has already been discussed (p. 74). It should be emphasized that such laws encouraged certain industries and also aided in expanding commerce, which benefited the colonists.

The conflicting economic interests of the American seaboard and the island colonies resulted in the passage of the Molasses Act of 1733. It directly benefited the British planters of the West Indies who had petitioned Parliament that the "Bread Colonies" be prohibited from exchanging provisions for sugar products from the Spanish, French, and Dutch West Indies. It laid a prohibitive duty of ninepence on each gallon of rum, sixpence on every gallon of molasses, and five shillings a hundredweight on sugar imported from foreign colonies to the British plantations. Through smuggling and conniving with officials, the effect of the act was minimized, but it did serve as a mild protective tariff until superseded by the less drastic Sugar Act of 1764.

The Board of Trade and Plantations attempted to supervise colonial administration. The Board, the growth of an earlier seventeenth century committee of the Privy Council, functioned from its organization in 1696 as the chief British colonial office. It had jurisdiction over poor relief in England and ordinary commercial relations with other nations, but it was especially charged with the enforcement of the trade and navigation acts. It was required to be posted about colonial affairs including economic conditions, progress of settlement, statistics of population, actions of the Assemblies, details of revenue, dangers from Indians and foreign colonies, and many other phases of colonial life and activity. It heard and investigated the complaints of colonial merchants and recommended to Parliament the passage of legislation within its field. Its voluminous records attest to its varied activities.

The administration of parliamentary legislation pertaining to the colonies was largely in the hands of the governors who were also required to enforce the regulations of the Board of Trade. The impossibility of the task and the indifference of many governors—whose authority varied in the different types of colonies—resulted in a laxness in enforcing policies and in exercising control over the colonists. Then, too, the overlapping jurisdiction of many imperial agencies resulted in inefficiency and often in neglect. There was no clear-cut authority in colonial administration, for the Crown, Privy Council, Parliament, Board of Trade, Commissioners of Customs, Treasury, Admiralty, War Office, and quite late in the colonial period, the Secretary of State for Colonial Affairs, all had a part in imperial control. The attempt to administer the colonies strictly and to enforce laws, orders, and regulations after 1763 led finally to the Revolution and to the loss of the mainland colonies.

As was customary in England, colonial assemblies adopted legislation to safeguard and protect the consumer. Derived from early British market laws and the regulations enforced by the European guilds, they fixed maximum wages, regulated the weight, quality, and price of bread, set standards for the different grades of flour, provided the conditions for packing meats, prescribed the size and type of barrels for certain commodities, and forbade the adulteration of a variety of products. From time to time, inspectors, sealers, and other officials attempted with varying success to enforce these laws.

PUBLIC POLICY: INDUSTRY

The Iron Act of 1750 is an excellent example of an attempt to make the principles of British mercantilism practical. On the one hand, it encouraged the exportation of unfinished colonial iron to England by relaxing the duties; on the other, it forbade the further erection of mills where semi-finished materials such as slit iron, steel, and tin plate could be produced and which would lead the colonists to manufacture for themselves. The earlier law of 1699 forbidding the export of wool and woolen goods from any colony was intended to benefit English woolen manufacturers. Likewise, the restrictive clauses of the Hat Act of 1732 were passed at the request of English hatmakers who were losing a part of their markets because of the activities of colonial hatmakers.

Restrictions, however, were attempted not only through the passage of laws but also by administrative action. In its inquiries and reports, the Board of Trade was constantly concerned with the problem. It frequently emphasized in its instructions to the governors that the restriction of manufacturing was one of their important duties. Only in a few cases were such orders taken seriously. Especially after 1763 was the Board active in this respect, but the governors were too busy, too unconcerned, too ignorant of conditions, or too apprehensive to make accurate reports and those forwarded to the official bodies in England were written to please English eyes rather than give a true account of actual conditions. The Privy Council was also concerned in restricting colonial manufactures and it had occasion to order the colonists to refrain from imposing tariffs on English goods.

The colonial assemblies viewed their economic needs quite differently. Throughout the period before 1775 there are innumerable examples of local colonial bounties, premiums, and subsidies paid for the production of raw materials. In some cases bounties were paid in cooperation with the English acts that subsidized such commodities as naval stores and hemp. But most colonial bounties—even on raw materials—were given to encourage manufactures. Woolen cloth received bounties from many assemblies until the British Woolen Act of 1699 was passed. After this date and until 1775 only Rhode Island ventured to give direct encouragement to woolen manufacture. Bounties were paid on the production of linen, duck, potash, stoneware, wool cards, and other commodities. In 1759, Virginia established a corporation to encourage arts and manufactures by means of premiums. Other means of aiding manufactures were provided through land grants, the authorization of lotteries, the granting of loans, and the exemption of workers from military, road, or other services. A mass of legislation was adopted which aided the establishment of many industries.

COLONIAL ECONOMY: AN OVER-ALL VIEW

By standards of either the eighteenth or the twentieth centuries, the colonies were an underdeveloped agricultural area. Their imports of tools, equipment, and workers (indentured servants and slaves) were paid for mainly by exports of rice, indigo, and tobacco from the South, grain and lumber from the middle colonies, and fish and ships from New England. From 1700 to 1750 the exports more than paid for the imports, prices were relatively stable and a surplus of specie accumulated in the colonies. But in the later colonial years, more severe restrictions on the profitable West Indian trade and increasing demand for capital and consumer goods in the colonies caused an adverse balance of payments and inflation. Carried largely by credit on the books of English merchants, these colonial debts represented an involuntary British investment in American economic growth. The hope of at least temporary relief from this burden of English debt was one of the factors working in favor of independence.

In a society dependent on foreign trade for prosperity and growth, the importing and exporting merchant was the key business figure. He performed: the financial operations now cared for by bankers, mortgage lenders, and insurance companies; the marketing operations later carried on by wholesalers, jobbers, and retailers; and, the transportation services ultimately supplied by many types of common carriers. With his profits the merchant helped to finance iron manufacture, shipbuilding, and the few other large-scale local enterprises. A man of wealth and international connections, he occupied a position in colonial life much superior to the small retailer or artisan.

In contrast to the aristocratic societies of Europe in which hereditary, feudal land tenure was the basis for prestige, the colonies were a democratic, businesslike society. Commercial activity was respected and the sons of successful merchants could mingle with those of planters and landlords, while the latter did not hesitate to go into trade. The possibility of rapid advancement through business, coupled with great resources and a supply of aspiring immigrants continually bringing new skills and new ideas, made for economic change and growth. Over three hundred and fifty years of history the absence of feudal origins, and fluidity of population in both geographical and social movement have continued to differentiate America from Europe.

CHAPTER 6

A New Nation

In the years from 1763 to 1790 economic welfare and growth were closely related to revolutionary changes in government. In contrast to England, where the industrial revolution was going through its early stage, technological change in America was slight. Until the end of the Revolution, Americans paid little attention to the fragmentary information about new industrial and agricultural developments in Great Britain. The first Agricultural Society to spread information to the farmer appeared in Philadelphia in 1785, and at the same time and place John Fitch started experimenting with a steam engine for navigation. But these were only symbolic beginnings. Public attention was still on problems of currency, taxation, and other policies of the newly-created goverments. Therefore, it seems best even in an economic history to treat this quarter century as a separate period with major attention focused on changes in public policy.

THE PROBLEM OF IMPERIAL ORGANIZATION

The causes of the struggle for American independence were multifold and complex. They cannot be described on the basis of one or two generalizations, as for example, "taxation without representation." Such statements made excellent rallying cries, but fundamentally the struggle lay much deeper. The clash was inevitable as forces beginning early in the colonial period grew. Revolutions are not brewed overnight; they come from accumulating, deep-lying causes. The common experiences developed on a distant frontier of the British Empire; receding memories of a British past; the presence of alien groups having no bonds with England; the growing feeling of local strength, and a new feeling of security brought about by removal of the French from Canada were also important factors. The Revolution came after English statesmen made their first serious attempts to administer the Empire in an efficient manner, incidently requiring the Americans to help in supporting it financially.

The Treaty of Paris, 1763, which ended the French and Indian War, or the Seven Years' War as it was known in Europe, removed the constant threat of the French in the very heart of the continent and decided that North America should be British. France lost her colonial empire. Only the islands of Martinique, Guadeloupe, and St. Dominique in the West Indies and two small fishing islands in the Gulf of St. Lawrence were left in the New World to that great nation. The treaty, which followed a world war fought in America, Europe, and Asia, and on the seven seas by peoples of different races confirmed many of England's claims that heretofore had been ambiguous or contested; it even added to these claims. It applied to far-off India as well as to the Spanish possession of Florida in America. The Peace of 1763 was most significant and marked an epoch in imperial history.

The question of administering the Empire in a more efficient manner was discussed before the Seven Years' War began. The policy developed in the first half of the eighteenth century to "let sleeping dogs lie" was being increasingly condemned by London statesmen, who about 1750 became outspoken in their demands for more logical practices, especially regarding Indian relations and land speculation in America. As the result of such considerations the English government issued the Proclamation of 1763. By its terms, parts of the territory acquired by the Treaty of Paris were organized as the provinces of Quebec, East Florida, and West Florida. But the section of the Proclamation that became more and more irritating to the colonies and aroused their ire was the provision aimed at conciliating the Indians. Governors were forbidden to grant lands beyond the crest of the Appalachian Mountains. While this policy of limiting the western boundaries of the colonies to the Appalachians had been endorsed by a Congress of colonial representatives in 1754, it came as a surprise—especially to Virginians who had not been represented at the Congress. For at one stroke of the pen, trans-Appalachian migration had been prohibited at a time when settlement was drawing near to the mountains, and Americans were looking beyond them. Indian traders were strictly licensed and were bound to observe all regulations that applied to them. Many colonists voiced their objections to the restriction and several colonies protested on the ground that they had prior claims to the lands involved. In the decade that followed, the restriction became the cause of increasing bitterness against the British government although many settlers paid little attention to the edict and moved into the forbidden territory.

George Grenville, who became prime minister of England in 1763, stressed the need for imperial unity. But imperial re-organization, vital as it was to Great Britain, was of little concern to most of the colonists. In the same way, the financial burden left by the Seven Years' War—brought about largely by William Pitt's lavish system of subsidies to European allies and even to the American colonies to bring them fully into the struggle—troubled them but little. The announcement that 10,000 troops were to be stationed on the American outposts of the Empire for defense against foreign enemies did bring apprehension, especially when it became clear that the colonists would have to help in supporting them. The acts, passed in the years that followed, requiring the local governments to pay for quartering the troops, brought the new imperial plans close to home.

The new policy of requiring the colonies to give more definite financial support to the Empire raised objections in 1764 when the Sugar (or Revenue) Act was passed by Parliament. The law undertook to stamp out colonial smuggling in the foreign West Indian trade and at the same time raise a revenue. It cut in half the duties of the Molasses Act of 1733 in the expectation that the lower rates would put an end to the evasion of the law and that merchants would pay the duties on molasses and sugar. The law also placed or increased duties on indigo, coffee, wines, silks, and calicoes; at the same time it expanded the list of enumerated commodities. In addition, the policy of permitting the colonists drawbacks or a remittance of duties on goods imported from foreign countries through England was abandoned. The law also attempted to provide for the enforcement of the payment of duties in the colonies by requiring heavy bonds from shipmasters, ordering governors to be strict in supervising customs and commerce, imposing heavy fines for violations, offering inducements for information against violators, and providing many patrols to suppress smuggling.

The administration of the American customs was unsatisfactory and was partly in the hands of absentee officials living in England on choice sinecures. It was evident that the navigation laws were often violated and that this was largely due to the laxity, inefficiency, and corruption of the home government. Thus, in order to aid in enforcing the Sugar Act, writs of assistance or general search warrants issued by the superior courts of the various colonies came again into increasing use. Authorized as early as 1696 by the Navigation Act of that year and used in Massachusetts especially after 1751, they began to excite controversy about 1761, when opposed by merchants like John Hancock and lawyers like James Otis who unsuccessfully raised the question of their legality.

Also in 1764 the Currency Act was passed by Parliament at the solicitation of British creditors. Applied to New England in 1751, the law now was extended to all the colonies. It forbade further issues of paper money except with special safeguards and prevented colonial debtors from settling their sterling accounts in terms of depreciated currency. Coming during the depression that followed the French and Indian War and when attempts were made to enforce the navigation acts, it resulted in bitter complaint from the debtor groups and added to the discontent. It must be considered another grievance which stirred up opposition to the British government.

The new British policies were discussed in taverns, inns, and on the streets. Merchants, legislatures, and town meetings protested against the Sugar Act. Lawyers like Samuel Adams coined the slogan "taxation without representation." The opposition, while loud, was unorganized, but soon crystallized over another fateful act which aroused most of the colonists.

Further to increase inadequate revenues the Stamp Act was applied to the colonies. The act required stamps on all legal and commercial papers, pamphlets, newspapers, licenses, almanacs, broadsides, notes, bonds, cards, and dice, the cost depending on the type and value of the article taxed. It provided for a Stamp Office in London, an inspector for each colonial district, and a stamp distributor for each colony. It was estimated that the stamps would produce in the mainland colonies and in the West Indies from £60,000 to £100,000. The combined revenues of the Sugar and the Stamp Acts were expected to produce £105,000 to £145,000, about half the cost of providing for the garrisoned forces in America.

RESISTANCE TO ENGLISH POLICY

Out of well-intentioned fairness Grenville deferred the plan for a year (to 1765) to give the colonists an opportunity to suggest means more to their liking. Edmund Burke, with keener perception than Grenville, scathingly stated that the delay allowed time "for all the discontents (of the colonies) to fester and come to a head, and for all the arrangements which factious men could make toward an opposition to the law." Aided by the depression, anti-Brititsh leaders were able to get merchants to sign agreements not to import British goods. The most radical elements organized the Sons of Liberty, lower-class city groups that smashed the stamp offices and prevented the operation of the law. Alarmed by this sudden outburst of mob violence, the more conservative merchants and landowners had their provincial assemblies call a Stamp Act Congress in 1765 to offer an orderly form of protest.

English manufacturers, merchants, and shipowners did not welcome the interruption to trade caused by nonimportation. Many petitioned Parliament for repeal or modification of the Stamp Act. They finally triumphed as Parliament repealed the Stamp Act, cut the duties on foreign molasses to one penny per gallon, and reduced them on a number of commodities. In order to appease the opposition in England and safeguard its authority, Parliament passed a Declaratory Act, setting forth its right to tax the colonies as well as to annul colonial legislation. The repeal of the Stamp Act brought rejoicing to America. The embargoes ceased; British goods again began to flow into the colonies; dinners were held in honor of George III and toasts were drunk to his health. The real significance of the Declaratory Act was lost in the excitement as all groups, except some of the merchant class, celebrated. The victory, however, was shortlived for the British budget was still unbalanced and provisions for a unified Empire were still unsolved. Quite evident from the viewpoint of the present—but apparently not so obvious then—was the fact that, if America was to be fitted into the mold of imperial organization, the plans would have to consider American conditions.

When Lord Charles Townshend became Chancellor of the Exchequer, he examined the American arguments—set forth by many legal pens—regarding direct and indirect taxation and suggested to Parliament a series of laws designed to raise the needed revenue. As finally passed, they required duties to be paid at American ports on white and red lead, paints, paper, glass, and tea. Under the provisions of the navigation acts, all these commodities had to be brought from Great Britain, regardless of their place of origin. The revenue so derived was to be used first, for the cost of collecting the taxes and then, to pay governors, judges, and other Crown employees who would thus become independent of appropriations from local assemblies. The legislation also established a Board of Customs Commissioners at Boston which was given complete control over American customs. It could revise and reorganize the system, establish ports of entry, appoint officers and spies, send out vessels provided with search warrants, and do whatever else was necessary.

As the colonists once again became embittered, many things showed their discontent. The New York assembly was disbanded because it would not bear part of the expenses of supporting British troops within the colony. The Circular Letter of Massachusetts suggested protest and argument to the other colonies and nonimportation agreements were revived. The agreements brought less pressure on England than before, as new markets for English goods were being found in Europe and the East. But in the colonies the embargoes gave a renewed impetus to colonial manufactures in an attempt to supplant English goods.

When Lord North became prime minister in 1770, he adopted a more conciliatory attitude toward the colonies. Parliament repealed the Townshend duties, except those on tea. As a result, with the exception of one or two untoward incidents, such as the burning of the British revenue cutter, *Gaspee,* the early seventies were comparatively quiet. Better times increased the desire on the part of the merchant and propertied classes for peace and stability. In spite of the activities of leaders like Samuel Adams to keep opposition to British oppression alive, peace was making headway when North's ministry committed a blunder which set in motion a series of events that led directly and inevitably to war.

CLIMAX OF THE DISPUTE

The Tea Act of 1773 permitted the East India Company to export tea directly to America and to set up wholesale markets in the colonies. The saving in duties and other charges would allow company agents to undersell those securing tea elsewhere. The Sons of Liberty and the radical leaders were determined to resist the "monopoly." In New York, citizens persuaded the consignees to refuse the East India Company cargo, and it was turned back. At Portsmouth, N. H., and Philadelphia, the ships were turned away and the captains sailed back home. At Annapolis, the vessel was burned. This incident was called the "Peggy Stewart Tea Party" after the name of the ship. At Charleston the tea was landed, but kept sealed in warehouses. Later, it was sold and the funds used to promote the cause of independence. The spectacular

Boston Tea Party brought more serious consequences. Sons of Liberty there, dressed like Indians, and shouting "Boston harbor a tea-pot this night" swooped down on the three vessels and destroyed 342 chests of tea. This marked a crisis. While Franklin and others were condemning the loss of the tea "as an act of violent Injustice" and were seeking other means of attacking the East India Company's privilege, Parliament rashly singled out Massuchusetts for punishment.

The series of punitive laws in 1774 directed at Massachusetts became known as the Intolerable or Coercive Acts. The port of Boston was closed until the East India Company should be reimbursed for the tea destroyed and the future loyalty of the citizens assured; the government of Massachusetts was brought more fully under the Crown; British soldiers and officials charged with capital crimes were to be taken to England for trial; and more troops were to be quartered in Massachusetts. A fifth law—the Quebec Act extending the boundaries of Catholic Canada to the Ohio and Mississippi Rivers—although not punitive, was used by colonial propagandists to make it appear a menace to the religious as well as civil liberties of the colonists. To Lord North's surprise, these laws, intended to restore order in America, brought about strong and unrelenting opposition in all sections and achieved the ends sought by the radicals.

While the opposition to England was surprisingly well organized and vocal, it represented a minority of the population. In the North, aside from Boston, the substantial landowners and merchants wanted no trouble. In the South there were some planters interested in western lands, such as George Washington, who resented the restriction placed on westward expansion by the Proclamation of 1763, and other planters and merchants who were almost hopelessly in debt to their English correspondents—their aggregate indebtedness has been estimated as high as $10,000,000—but there were many others who had no more desire for revolution and violence than their counterparts in the North. In general the revolution was a movement of small farmers, workers, and shopkeepers who hoped to better their status. Enough of the wealthier groups were willing, for various reasons, to participate in the movement to supply the normal upper-class leadership.

But at first all but a handful of these upper-class leaders hoped for compromise. Following the formula that had cured the Stamp Act trouble, the middle-of-the-road Whigs supported a Continental Congress. Town meetings and "Committees of Safety" first suggested the move, which was made concrete by the calls of the Massachusetts Assembly under the leadership of Samuel Adams and by the Burgesses of Virginia. "The Congress," as it was known, was for "the restoration of union and harmony between Great Britain and the colonies most ardently desired by all good men." The delegates, including those who might be classed as moderates as well as many radicals, were chosen largely through the agency of committees of correspondence. The gathering was not representative of the colonial governments, but chiefly represented the dissatisfied elements who had the initiative to act in spite of much opposition from the conservative minority and the disfavor or condemnation of the governors.

THE CONTINENTAL CONGRESS

Among the fifty-six delegates who met in Philadelphia in September, 1774, the agricultural interests were well represented, but the majority were lawyers. Only eleven merchants were present. The spirit of the Congress soon became evident in the opposition to the abuses of parliamentary authority and in the desire to retain the constitutional rights claimed on the basis of "the laws of nature," the colonial charters, and the English unwritten constitution.

The moderate element in the Congress, under the leadership of Joseph Galloway, a Pennsylvania political leader, student of law, and ironmaster, presented a plan of union to settle the conflict between England and the colonies. It proposed the establishment of a colonial legislature as a branch of the British Parliament. The assent of both bodies would be necessary to make valid laws relating to the colonies. Although favorably received at first, Galloway's plan was finally defeated by the vote of one colony. The proposal was subsequently expunged from the journal of the Congress. The attempt at compromise had failed.

The Congress led by the more radical John Adams then agreed to a "Declaration of Rights." The document declared that the Intolerable Acts were "impolitic, unjust, cruel, as well as unconstitutional, and most dangerous and destructive of American rights." In order to restore harmony between Great Britain and the colonies, the repeal of a number of the acts of Parliament, specified in the document, was asked. The Congress also decided to prepare an address to the people of Great Britain, a memorial to the inhabitants of North America, and a "loyal address to his Majesty, agreeable to resolutions already entered into."

One of the most important steps taken was the Association—a nonimportation, nonconsumption, nonexportation agreement. Its provisions were to be carried out by committees in every county, city, and town. Committees of correspondence were required to supervise the work, and enforcement was to be secured by boycotting violators. Among other provisions, the discontinuance of the slave trade was important. The Congress then completed its work and a final resolution voiced the opinion that if the grievances were not redressed another Congress should meet on May 10 of the following year.

The Association went into effect immediately. Within a few months, the import trade from Great Britain declined 95 per cent. Some English merchants petitioned Parliament, asking "a full and immediate examination of that system of commercial policy, which was formerly adopted and uniformly maintained to the happiness and advantage of both countries" and the application of "such healing remedies as can alone restore and establish the commerce between Great Britain and her colonies on a permanent foundation." In addition to the loss of markets, English merchants were also seriously concerned with the collection of large debts owed them by Americans, especially by southern planters. At the same time, Edmund Burke urged the repeal of the Intolerable Acts, William Pitt warned of foreign aggression if the colonies should revolt, and others also raised their voices on behalf of the colonies.

When the Second Continental Congress met in Philadelphia on May 10, 1775, fighting had already occurred at Lexington and Concord, and colonial militia were gathered near Boston ready for battle with the British. The Congress itself had no legal or constitutional basis, but by necessity it became a *de facto* central government. As time went on and colonial governments were replaced by state governments, its members were backed by the authority of the state legislatures that chose them. But the actions of Congress at all times rested on the power of the states. From 1775 to 1781 when the Articles of Confederation went into effect, the Continental Congress exercised legislative and executive functions of a central government.

An army was organized and Washington appointed commander in chief, partly because of his military experience in the French and Indian War and partly because of the leadership of Virginia in the American cause. Lord North's Conciliatory Resolution came too late and was rejected. In August, George III issued a Proclamation of Rebellion. This meant that the leaders of Congress and of the American cause might be tried for treason and put to death. The war was on! In the fall of 1775, Congress authorized the creation of a navy. Letters of marque were issued to shipowners authorizing them to prey on British commerce. Congress also took over the direction of Indian affairs and assumed charge of the post office. Franklin was again made postmaster general. In the spring of 1776, commerce and trade were opened with the whole world except Britain.

The most important accomplishment of the Second Continental Congress in its seven sessions was the Declaration of Independence. Even after the war began, from September, 1775 to January, 1776, one-half of the colonial provisional governments went on record as opposing independence. At the same time a series of new grievances created sentiment strong enough for independence. The Proclamation of the king calling attention to the "rebellion"; the acts of Parliament prohibiting commerce with the colonies; the employment of Hessians to supplement English troops in fighting the Americans; and Thomas Paine's *Common Sense,* were factors that prepared the way for separation. Paine's pamphlet, which sold by the thousands, emphasized the economic advantages of independence and pointed out the unprofitableness of remaining within the Empire. Complete independence was the only remedy and, with patriotic fervor, he concluded: "The blood of the slain and the weeping voice of Nature cries, 'Tis time to part.'" Action in Congress was initiated by Richard Henry Lee, who was instructed by Virginia to introduce resolutions declaring "That these united colonies are, and of right ought to be, free and independent states," and proposing foreign alliances and the formation of a confederation. The resolutions were introduced on June 7, and on July 1, the one declaring independence was discussed and debated. In the meantime Jefferson's committee was appointed to draft the Declaration of Independence. On July 4, it was adopted by the vote of the twelve states which shortly before had adopted Lee's resolution. The New York delegation refrained from voting.

The Declaration was made public on July 6, but it was some time before people in distant regions heard about it. Although containing ideas that were well known, Jefferson set forth the American stand in a succinct manner and in happily combined words and phrases which have lived on. The document embodies the philosophy of the Revolution, the charges against George III, a complaint against the British people for failure to heed American appeals, and the assertion of independence. The adoption of the document meant the parting of the ways between the Patriots and the Loyalists. Many of the latter who refused to join the American cause had to leave the country. Independence also made necessary permanent state governments. But to make valid the Declaration of Independence it was necessary to wage the war to a successful conclusion.

FINANCING THE WAR

Needing money immediately to pay soldiers and lacking authority to levy taxes, Congress was forced to issue paper money. During 1776 the bills helped to compensate for lack of other circulating currency. But the relative failure of loans and requisitions for money from the states forced Congress to print paper in increasingly larger quantities, $240,000,000 in all. By early 1780 the notes were passing at less than a cent on the dollar and conservative leaders demanded the end of note issue. Congress converted the outstanding bills into interest-bearing certificates at the ratio of $40 in currency for one dollar in a certificate. The latter, in turn, also failed to bring their face value in relation to specie. Meanwhile, several states, especially Virginia, North Carolina, and South Carolina, had added $210,000,000 to the fiat money, making a total of more than $450,000,000. In addition to the problem of rapid depreciation, continental and state notes were counterfeited by the British forces and by individual Americans in spite of the threat of death to counterfeiters printed on the back of many bills. Disruptive as these methods of finance were to many economic relations, such as those of debtor and creditor, paper currency was the major source of government funds; without such paper the war could not have been supported.

Another means of financing the war was a system of direct requisitions on the states. This method had been used by Great Britain in securing colonial aid, especially during the intercolonial wars, but not always with success. Now, application was still more difficult. The newly-created governments, gaining their power from uncertain, often minority, popular support, were hesitant to vote large taxes. Furthermore, collection was generally in the hands of locally elected officials who refused to risk their popularity by vigorous enforcement of the levies. As a result, state tax programs were a failure locally, and only part of the requisitions of Congress could be met. Four requisitions were made between 1777 and 1779 for a total of $95,000,000 in paper money. Only $55,000,000 was forthcoming which equalled less than $2,000,000 in actual specie. By the end of the Revolution the equivalent of only $6,000,000 in specie had been obtained from the states. In 1780, direct requisitions for corn, pork, beef, and other provisions were made on the states, but the results were discouraging, as this way of securing supplies lacked an efficient means of assessment, collection, and record.

The domestic loan program was a failure for at least two reasons:

the risk that Congress might cease to exist; and interest rates that failed to reflect this risk. Still influenced by the idea that high rates were usury, Congress tried to float 4 to 6 per cent bonds. In all the equivalent of about $7,500,000 in specie was subscribed by patriotic citizens. In addition interest-bearing bonds, quartermaster, commissary, and purchasing agent certificates were issued to pay for supplies bought or taken from farmers or manufacturers.

Foreign loans were secured from France, Spain, and Holland largely because of the influence of Franklin and John Adams. In the early part of the war, the gifts of munitions, supplies, and money made by France through their secret agent, Beaumarchais by means of the fictitious commercial company, Roderique Hortalez et Cie enabled the revolting colonies to carry on the war and to win the important victory of Saratoga. After the French alliance of 1778, France openly aided the Americans although the dummy company continued throughout the war. French loans from 1777 to 1783 amounted to $6,352,500, Spanish loans to $174,017, and Dutch loans to $1,304,000, a total of $7,830,517. Most of this money, but not all, was used to buy supplies in Europe.

THE END OF THE WAR

On October 19, 1781, General Cornwallis surrendered at Yorktown, Virginia, where his army had been trapped by French and American troops. This really marked the end of the war, although military operations of an insignificant nature continued on land, and naval operations that were more significant were carried on in the waters of the West Indies. But it was almost two years from Cornwallis' surrender before the definitive treaty of peace was signed.

In spite of a divided people, a Congress with uncertain powers, questionable tenure, and little unity; armies that were ill-armed, poorly clothed, and badly fed, where desertion was common and discipline for the most part never good; and a lack of sufficient supplies, equipment, and money to carry on efficiently, the war was brought to a successful conclusion. Speculation as to the chief cause of victory is futile for many factors were involved. The ability and genius of Washington who kept the armies from complete disintegration and destruction; the spirit of Washington and other leaders which permeated to a greater or lesser degree a part of the military and civilian populations; the bungling of English governmental officials as they planned campaigns in London; the general incompetency of most of the British military officers; foreign aid, especially from the French, who, from the beginning, sent supplies, money, and troops; the state to which manufactures and commerce had risen by 1775; and the success of the privateers in the capture of ships laden with merchandise must all be considered. At the close of 1781, England recognized that she was surrounded by enemies—Spain, France, and Holland, while no ally gave her assistance or even encouragement.

In 1783 a treaty between the United States and Great Britain was signed at Paris. The recognition of complete independence, the generous boundaries to the Mississippi, and the right of Americans to fish off Newfoundland together with permission to dry and cure their fish in certain uninhabited places of British Canada were the chief provisions of the treaty which brought into existence a new nation.

THE RISE OF A NATIONAL ECONOMY

Wide and fairly uniformly distributed natural resources permitted a remarkable spread of small-scale manufacturing. Even before British goods were cut off at the beginning of hostilities, colonial assemblies formulated policies for encouraging and expanding manufactures. Premiums and bounties were offered for the best specimens of linen, woolens, ironware, woolen cards, gunpowder, saltpetre, and other commodities. Subsidies were given to those erecting slitting mills and steel mills. Loans were made to those engaging especially in the manufacture of munitions and materials of war. In the fateful year 1776, the Continental Congress recommended to the assemblies, conventions, and councils of safety, the establishment of societies for the improvement of "agricultural arts, manufactures, and commerce as soon as possible." In a variety of ways manufactures of all sorts were encouraged and the results were gratifying.

Iron manufacture was highly prosperous throughout the war. Scattered from New England to the Carolinas and westward to the silent frontier, flaming blast furnaces turned out cannon and shot, as well as cast-iron kettles, salt pans, ovens, and boilers for the armies. The bar iron from the refinery forges and from bloomeries was shaped into many products as, in villages and towns, blacksmiths and workers in iron were busy making weapons of war, as well as tools and implements. If the iron industry had not reached a relatively high stage prior to 1775, it is doubtful whether the colonists could have defended themselves against the British army or could have provided themselves with necessary war manufactures. It should be noted, of course, that French aid was also extremely important, especially in regard to munitions and military supplies as well as men and money.

The progress made in manufacturing rifles was an important factor in winning the Revolution. In the first part of the eighteenth century, many Palatine and Swiss immigrants brought with them to Pennsylvania a knowledge of gunmaking. Lancaster County became a center for gun manufacture, and from this region guns and parts of guns were sent to all the colonies. The American gunsmiths made many improvements. By 1775, there had evolved the Pennsylvania long-barreled, small-bore piece, effective at long range in contrast to the large-bore, short-range muskets of the British. Various types of American muskets, of course, were produced, even the older type of firearms including blunderbusses and flintlocks or firelocks. In other colonies also, expert gunsmiths could be found. As the Revolution began, many new gunshops were quickly established in various sections of the country. A complete gunshop of the period contained several barrel forges, a water-powered mill for grinding and polishing barrels, a lock shop with a number of small forges, a foundry for mountings, a shop for forging bayonets and ramrods as well as a mill for grinding and polishing them, together with a fitting and assembly shop. Such a plant represented a considerable degree of specialization in labor and in tools, and also a continuous process of production.

Although the British armies made many attempts, often successful, to destroy shops, mills, forges, furnaces, and other places where manufactures were carried on, the comparative tranquillity of most sections in the North permitted industrial activities, which had been developed before the war, to continue and expand. In the South, which was less organized for the conflict, more subject to local conflict, and the chief battleground during the last years of the war, the tobacco plantations increasingly engaged in household manufactures. The tidewater South was changed from a region depending largely upon the outside world for most manufactured commodities to one in which clothes and even shoes and stockings were made on the plantations, the planters using their slaves and employing their poorer white neighbors for the purpose.

The boycott on English goods, especially textiles, during the troublesome decade of the sixties prepared the way for colonial self-sufficiency during the Revolution. The supply of homespun and other types of homemade wearing apparel had become an important factor on the farms of New England, of the middle colonies and in the back country of the South long before hostilities were thought of. Such manufactures greatly increased during the war. In addition to supplying their own immediate needs, household industries were called upon to aid in furnishing supplies for the army. In June, 1776, each state was asked by the Continental Congress to furnish a suit of clothes, two shirts, two pairs of hose, two pairs of shoes, and a felt hat for each of its enlisted soldiers. Other calls for military materials were issued from time to time. The general supervision of collecting these was in the hands of agents of the states, working under the direction of the clothier-general.

While British mercantile relations were quickly resumed and immense quantities of English goods were dumped on the American market in 1783 and 1784, the effect on local manufacturing was less than might be expected. Much of the goods was bought by residents of the coastal cities where there was stored-up specie and pent-up demand. The high cost of inland transportation operated as a powerful protection for industry beyond tidewater navigation. Once the postwar buying spree was over and a recession began, in 1785, local heavy goods such as iron and steel products, wagons, and furniture regained much of the coastal market. Local activity was aided in New England and Pennsylvania by higher state tariffs. In all, the new states tended to become more self-sufficient in relation to this hand labor manufacture than they were to be in the early age of machine production.

General farming, as distinct from the export staples such as tobacco and rice, prospered during the war. In regions where armies were operating, there was a great demand for food and supplies not only for American troops, but for the French and the opposing British armies as well. In these districts high prices were paid and foreigners frequently had the advantage in securing commodities as they gave gold for what they bought while the Continental officers paid in currency. In these commercial farming areas the increased demand seems to have stimulated the use of gypsum and other fertilizers. A number of Hessian officers, deserting from the British service, brought improved agricultural knowledge to New Jersey and Pennsylvania. Starting with the Philadelphia Society for Promoting Agriculture in 1785, leading citizens tried to transmit new English and European knowledge to the American farmer.

Throughout the Revolution commerce continued. In the British-held areas, especially in New York, there was a great traffic in military goods, and many loyalist merchants prospered for a time. In all other seaport regions, trade was carried on, despite British vigilance, with the different colonies. Tobacco was exchanged for needed commodities in friendly ports in the West Indies. The Dutch island of St. Eustatius was notoriously open to American commerce until captured by Rodney in 1781 when the Danish islands of St. Thomas and St. Croix took its place. France, friendly to the American cause from the beginning of the war, was extremely liberal in furnishing materials and opening her ports to American vessels, especially her West Indian islands. As Spain joined France on the American side, that country offered the Americans lucrative markets for lumber and provisions in her West Indian colonies.

Foreign trade changed as the navigation acts were broken and American commerce was opened to the world. Most of the old colonial import duties were abolished for the time being, and many ports that had held commercial power because they were the only legal ports of entry were now forced to share a part of their trade with rivals. Newport in Rhode Island, and Annapolis in Maryland, now had to share their foreign commerce with the rapidly rising ports of Providence and Baltimore. Some of the new commerce was with northern Europe. Sweden slowly admitted American vessels and in 1780 established direct trade relations. Through that country a new trade was begun with Russia. Commerce with France also grew as the French commercial treaty of 1778, which granted privileges on both sides, went into effect. From January, 1777, to March, 1778, ninety-five vessels cleared from Bordeaux for the new American states and promising relations developed with many other French ports. French commercial houses opened branches in America, and Americans set up branches in France. Dutch firms also dealt with the Americans. Like the French and Spanish they invested in American privateers. Thus, during the Revolution, there developed a promise for a new and prosperous commerce with the rest of the world.

Privateering played an important part during the Revolution. In 1775, most of the colonies issued letters of marque and reprisal to shipowners and the next year the Continental Congress sanctioned privateering and commissioned many vessels. The 1,150 privateers authorized during the Revolution captured a number of British vessels, including sixteen men-of-war. Almost one-half of the privateers were from Massachusetts, and Rhode Island had nearly 200. American privateers swarmed the West Indies and even sought British merchantmen in different parts of the Atlantic, the British Channel, and the North Sea. Risks were great and captures by the enemy frequent, but many loved the adventure that privateering entailed and were attracted also by the enormous profits which were divided among the owners and crew. Many shipowners, especially in Massachusetts, made fortunes through privateering activities.

While an American navy, consisting of vessels of all descriptions, was developed during the last three years of the war, privateers had to carry on the brunt of sea operations against the British, for only three public cruisers remained in 1781. The naval vessels were used chiefly for seizing British supply ships and merchantmen, the transport of munitions from France, and the carriage of diplomatic agents and dispatches to and from Europe. The operations of the privateers were financially profitable and also an invaluable aid to the navy.

In establishing independence, many in the United States looked forward to a profitable era of trade expansion, free from the burdensome restrictions of the English navigation acts. But only slowly were trade relations established with the rest of the civilized world. The mercantile systems of the various European nations in general operated against the Americans. By achieving independence, the United States had forfeited part of the commerce carried on previously with the mother country and with the British colonies, especially the lucrative trade with the British West Indies. After the conclusion of peace, Great Britain would not permit American vessels to enter her colonial ports, and her refusal to embody any commercial clauses in the peace treaty was a bitter disappointment to the peace commissioners and to Congress. All proposals for commercial agreements were rejected until Jay's treaty was negotiated in 1795, and few commercial benefits were secured from that unsatisfactory treaty.

Certain Orders in Council, however, did permit English vessels to carry timber, naval stores, provisions, and breadstuffs produced in the United States to the British West Indies. They also allowed naval stores, pig and bar iron, and most raw materials to be imported into England under practically the same conditions as had existed prior to the Revolution—even in American vessels—upon the payment of the same duties as on the same kind of goods imported from any British possession in North America. American manufactured goods, whale oil, and fish oil, however, could not be admitted into England. Regardless of this, American exports of raw and semi-finished material to England and Scotland averaged in 1784–1788 about two-thirds of that of the years 1770–1775. In 1790, the first year that accurate records were kept, over 75 per cent of all the foreign commerce of the United States was with Great Britain, but British ships carried more than half of it. About 90 per cent of American imports came from Great Britain, chiefly in the form of manufactured goods. The hope of many merchants and diplomats during the Revolution to develop trade with France instead of England failed. The old ties with Great Britain were too strong and the Americans, preferring English goods, business methods, and long-term credit again took up commercial relations with England and forgot the hopes and pledges made to France during the struggles and dangers of the Revolutionary conflict.

Although no commercial treaty could be obtained with England, treaties were made with several European countries. By the treaty of 1782 with the Netherlands, Americans were granted most-favored-nation privileges and American vessels were admitted to the Dutch West Indies. High Dutch duties held back to some extent the development of such commerce. Treaties with Sweden (1783) and Prussia (1785) extended the most-favored-nation treatment but little trade resulted. Attempts to build up commerce with Mediterranean countries were thwarted largely through the raids of the Barbary pirates of Morocco, Algiers, Tunis, and Tripoli. Immunity from attack was purchased from Morocco, but the other pirates continued their raids. Except for a somewhat restricted commerce with Spain and Portugal, little trade developed in this region.

American trade with the Orient had its beginnings at this time. In 1784, the *Empress of China* left New York for the China Sea and Canton by way of the Cape of Good Hope. Merchants of Philadelphia, Boston, Baltimore, Providence, and Salem quickly grasped the new possibilities and vessels were fitted out to tap the China trade. The early cargoes were made up chiefly of ginseng, a plant believed by the Chinese to possess high curative properties, and also of Yankee notions, and clothing. American vessels carried cargoes of naval stores and certain raw products to England and Holland on their way to the Orient and were able to engage to some extent in trade with the Dutch East Indies and other ports of the South Seas. Returning home from the Far East, Yankee skippers brought tea, China, enameled ware, nankeens, and silks. Another aspect of the China trade had its beginning when Captain Robert Gray sailed to the Pacific Northwest in 1787 with Yankee manufactures which he exchanged with the Indians for sea otter peltries and other furs and then continued to Canton, where the furs found a ready sale. A three-cornered trade route developed; American hardware, knickknacks, and clothing were exchanged for peltries and furs of the far Northwest, which in turn were taken to China and exchanged for Oriental goods.

AN AMERICAN BUSINESS COMMUNITY

While from 1775 to 1783 British trade was very restricted, the war offered unusual opportunities to merchants willing to assume new and unknown risks. Chief among the wartime venturers was Robert

Morris, a member of the important Philadelphia firm of Willing and Morris. Importing British goods through agents in the West Indies, Morris sold them, in terms of specie, for four to five times the cost in London. Through his friend, Silas Deane of Hartford, a member of Congress and the earliest envoy to France, Morris participated in army supply and French trade. More than any other American merchant he invested in privateers and, in spite of losing 150 ships, made large profits. He was also a leader in buying the lands of those loyal to Britain, which were confiscated by the states and sold at public auction.

As might be expected, the radical leaders blamed the merchants for high prices and inflation. State price-and-wage-fixing laws were opposed by the merchants, and generally evaded by black market operations. But by 1779 the force of events was bringing the conservative business group back into power. The currencies had depreciated to points that made price-fixing laws useless; furthermore, the country was prosperous. In 1780, the conservatives, now in control of Congress, stopped the issue of currency, and made long-term contracts with the merchants for supplying the army.

The administration of congressional finances was in a sad state during most of the period. Jealousies in Congress, differences among

Continental currency, 1778

The coins shown here were minted by different state governments; the bill was printed by the Federal government.

the states, and the radicals' fear of over-centralization prevented the establishment of efficient machinery. The two treasurers—one to receive and the other to pay out public funds—soon gave way to a committee of thirteen which was replaced by a treasury board of five. Not until the beginning of 1781 was the new office of Superintendent of Finance created, and Robert Morris appointed to fill it. In this position Morris was able to give to the government the confidence of businessmen, and in return he used his position to reinforce his leadership in the new American business community.

With paper currencies virtually repudiated and specie drawing away because of lack of staple exports, some other type of acceptable notes was needed. British regulations could no longer prohibit banks, and they were the obvious solution. In 1780, the merchants of Philadelphia secured a charter for the Bank of Pennsylvania. The following year Morris merged this with the new Bank of North America, particularly designed to facilitate government finance.

The new American financial community was reinforced in 1784 by banks in New York and Boston. With the population of these three major cities less than 100,000 in all, this was a tightly knit business group. Allied by intermarriage, and stockholding in all three banks, the chief merchants began to think in American terms. Local banks were a partial substitute for credit in London, and ventures in internal development, chiefly in the form of transportation and land companies, took their place alongside new foreign developments such as the China trade.

When British control was broken, the state legislatures assumed the function of incorporation that originally had its authority in the Crown and the colonial assemblies. American capital slowly began to organize systematically as the states issued charters through special acts for business purposes. From 1781 to 1789 about thirty companies were incorporated for building and maintaining roads, canals, and bridges, and for river improvement projects, banking, and insurance. At least three charters were granted for the purpose of manufacturing. During these years many efforts were made, also, to extend stagecoach and stage wagon routes and facilities into various regions, marking the beginning of the revolution in transportation.

A STRONGER GOVERNMENT

During the period of the Confederation (1781–1789), the United States existed under its first constitution—the Articles of Confederation. The American federal system was largely accidental, a result of there being thirteen mainland colonies instead of one. A few weeks after the victory at Saratoga, Congress approved a draft of the Articles and sent it to the states for ratification. Accompanying it was a circular letter which declared that the document "is proposed as the best which could be adapted to the circumstances of all; and as that alone which affords any tolerable prospect of a general ratification."

Nine states ratified the Articles of July, 1778, but the new frame of government did not go into effect until March 1, 1781. This was because several of the states, especially the smaller ones, whose boundaries were limited, demanded that the western lands be regarded as the common property of all. When the thirteen colonies declared their independence, seven of them had overlapping and conflicting claims to lands in the West, based on royal grants and charters. New York's claim was based on Indian treaties rather than a royal grant. Presumably, all these claims had been eliminated by the Proclamation of 1763 and the Quebec Act of 1774. But after independence was declared, they were revived. Virginia's claim included much of the West and overlapped those of Massachusetts, Connecticut, and New York. South of Virginia were the claims of North Carolina, South Carolina, and Georgia which included lands between their present northern and southern boundaries to the Mississippi River. The smaller states possessing no western territory feared the strength of the larger ones in the Confederacy. The lands were important from the point of view of the fur trade, of their sales value, and as bonuses to veterans of the Revolution. With such land, mighty commonwealths could be established. Maryland held out until convinced that the landowning states would give up their western claims, and when assured of this, ratified the Articles which went into effect. It took several years for the states to cede their lands. Virginia reserved territory in Ohio to satisfy military grants made during the Revolution. Connecticut also retained the Western Reserve area in Ohio which was used for the relief of Connecticut citizens whose property had been destroyed by the British; the remainder was sold to the Connecticut Land Company. Not until 1802, when Georgia transferred her territory in the West, was the last cession of lands made. The cessions gave the Confederation a vast public domain, the basis of wealth and power. Moreover, the quarter of a million square miles of land became a common bond of union.

The Articles of Confederation established a single house in which each state had one vote. This body had all executive, legislative,

LAND CLAIMS OF THE THIRTEEN STATES

and judicial functions. Congress carried out its executive functions
through committees or offices. The "president of the United States
in Congress Assembled" was the presiding officer and not an executive.
No system of national judiciary was provided except that Congress
was authorized to establish special courts "for the trial of piracies and
felonies committed on the high seas," prize courts "for receiving and
determining final appeals in all cases of captures," and was itself to
be the last resort on appeal in disputes between two or more states

regarding "boundaries, jurisdiction, or any other cause whatever." But the complicated process of setting up commissions described in the Articles resulted in few actual accomplishments in settling boundary and other disputes.

In its legislative aspects, Congress had the power to declare and wage war, to make peace, to negotiate treaties, to emit bills of credit and coin money, to manage Indian affairs, to establish post offices, and to carry out a number of less important duties. It lacked power, however, to tax, to regulate commerce, and to enforce treaties. All national expenses were to be paid out of a common treasury, but such money was to be secured by making requisitions on the states "in proportion to the value of all land within each State, granted to or surveyed for any person" together with the buildings and improvements on such land. Each state was to raise its quota through taxes levied by its own legislature. In practice, the plan of apportionment was difficult to work out and, after a requisition was made, the states paid what they pleased and sometimes nothing at all. The inability of the government to tax rendered it weak, for there was no provision to coerce the states to pay their requisitions. During the years 1782 and 1783 Congress asked the states for $10,000,000 but received only 15 per cent of it. Throughout the period it was impossible to provide for interest on the public debt. Relief through the issuance of more paper money was impossible as the Second Continental Congress had exhausted the possibilities in that direction. Money was borrowed from the newly-chartered Bank of North America and $2,296,000 was obtained from Holland. To avert trouble with the officers of the Continental army, who were clamoring for their pay, Congress issued certificates of indebtedness, which immediately depreciated. Attempts to amend the Articles to permit Congress a revenue through duties on imports failed because amendments to the Articles had to be ratified by all the states.

The postwar deflation brought new demands by the agrarian and debtor groups for currency expansion. Paper money parties appeared and sought political control in state legislatures. The advocates of paper currency were successful in Rhode Island, New York, New Jersey, Pennsylvania, North Carolina, South Carolina, and Georgia. Not only did legislatures authorize large amounts of money which immediately depreciated but such currency was made legal tender, requiring the acceptance of the paper by creditors in payment of debts. Stay laws were also passed which provided for a moratorium or extension of time in paying debts.

In Massachusetts where the paper money advocates failed to get control of the legislature, a serious situation developed. Here, many small property holders, who were losing their possessions through seizure for overdue debts or were facing imprisonment for debt, sought stay laws, the issuance of paper money, and lower taxes. At Northampton in 1786, debtors resorted to massed efforts to intimidate and close the courts to prevent action against them. Then followed an uprising at Springfield under the leadership of Daniel Shays, a veteran of Bunker Hill, demanding that the Massachusetts Supreme Court refrain from indictments against them for treason or sedition. A clash with the militia was avoided when the rebels dispersed and the leaders fled the state.

Shays' Rebellion was profoundly shocking to conservatives who feared the lasting effects of the Revolution upon the lower classes. Had Congress the strength to protect property if such rebellion should become general? But there were other failings of Congress which also bothered men of property. England refused to negotiate a commercial treaty with the weak central government, and occupied forts on the American side of the Great Lakes that controlled the western fur trade. Merchants were also dissatisfied because states dominated by back country interests, like New York and Rhode Island, raised most of their revenue from burdensome duties on trade.

As a result of all these difficulties a movement for a stronger government, present ever since the signing of the Articles, erupted into action. At Annapolis in 1786 representatives of six states called for a convention of all the states to devise such "provisions as shall appear to them necessary to render the Constitution of the federal government adequate to the exigencies of the Union." By endorsing the call Congress legalized the convention which met in Philadelphia on May 25, 1787.

The fifty-five members who attended the Convention during the summer of 1787 varied from strong nationalists like Alexander Hamilton and James Madison, who desired a new Constitution that would establish a strong central government, to those who desired to retain the Confederation, but in a stronger form. The New Jersey plan, representing this view, was presented as a direct challenge to the large states. However, the Virginia plan became the chief basis of discussion. The Constitution that resulted after a very hot and humid summer's work in Philadelphia was the result of much argument, compromise, and agreement.

The document was based upon ideas represented in the unwritten

English constitution and common law in the light of American experience. Its sources can also be traced to the colonial charters, state constitutions, and Articles of Confederation as well as to the teachings of the great political writers including Hobbes, Locke, Milton, Montesquieu, Harrington, Halifax, and Blackstone. The founding fathers had framed a brief and concise document that set forth a constitutional form of government based on grants and prohibitions of power and on a system of checks and balances. They produced a Constitution suited not only to the needs of an agrarian society, but also to a great industrial nation, for it proved to be elastic enough to be modified by amendment, judicial interpretation, legislative expansion, executive order, custom, and tradition as the country expanded tremendously in size, population, and economic development. As originally adopted, it provided for little that was democratic, beyond the principle of representative government.

The most serious defect of the Articles was remedied by granting Congress power to levy taxes and also duties on imports as well as excise duties on manufactures, sales, consumption, business transactions, vocations, occupations, and privileges. All direct taxes, however, were to be levied in proportion to the population, determined by census enumeration every ten years, and counting slaves at three-fifths of their number. It was also provided that all revenue bills should originate in the House of Representatives, although the Senate could amend bills for raising revenue.

Hardly less important than the right to tax was the power granted Congress to regulate foreign and interstate commerce. The problems, ill feeling, and economic losses which grew out of the trade limitations and discriminations in the earlier period came to an end when the Constitution went into effect. This clause together with the prohibition on the states from levying import or export duties gave Congress the complete right to regulate commerce. The broad meaning of interstate commerce, however, gradually evolved over a period of decades, through court decisions, as new problems arose.

To help remedy the existing monetary confusion Congress was given the sole power to coin money and to determine its value, and also to fix a uniform value for foreign coins which continued to circulate until United States coins were issued in sufficient quantities to supply commercial needs. Nothing was stated about authority to issue paper currency by Congress. States were forbidden to coin money or emit bills of credit (paper money). The states, however, avoided this provision by chartering state banks with the power to issue notes.

The so-called "elastic clause" became important in time, as the Supreme Court interpreted it more and more liberally. It granted Congress the power:

To make all Laws which shall be necessary and proper for carrying into Execution the foregoing Powers, and all other Powers vested by this Constitution in the Government of the United States or in any Department or Office thereof.

This clause has permitted the passage of many laws by which the power of the Federal government has been greatly expanded. Examples can be found in the right to establish and supervise national banks as implied in the power to collect taxes and borrow money, the power to improve rivers and harbors as implied in the power to regulate foreign and interstate commerce, and maintain a navy.

Property rights were safeguarded in several different ways. Congress was given the power to use the militia to suppress insurrections and to send armed forces into a state upon request of a state government for protection against domestic violence. No state could pass a law impairing the obligation of contracts; copyright and patent laws were authorized; fugitive slaves escaping into another state were not free, but should be delivered up on claim to the owner; and the foreign slave trade could not be prohibited before 1808. The apprehension of the southerners relating to the northern attitude toward the southern slave trade was well founded for Congress promptly imposed the maximum (ten dollars) tax allowed by the Constitution on imported slaves. By 1808 southern legislatures had abolished the foreign slave trade, and action by Congress was merely an added protection against smuggling.

The submission of the Constitution by Congress to the states for ratification resulted in a lively campaign. Opinions at first were favorable to the Constitution, but as groups in different parts of the country studied the document, they detected dangers to liberty. In fact, two national parties arose—for the first time in the history of the United States—for earlier parties, whether Whig, Tory, paper money, or others, were local and not national in scope. Now, within the country from north to south were two general groups—the Federalists, led by the signers of the Constitution, and the Anti-Federalists, led by those who insisted on states' rights. The Anti-Federalists opposed the Constitution on the ground that it provided too strong a central government, that it imperiled the rights of the states, and that it was too aristocratic in safeguarding the rights of property and not the rights of man. The lack of a bill of rights was greatly emphasized.

Generally speaking, the chief strength of the Federalists lay in the cities and the regions near the coast, while the Anti-Federalists were stronger in the back country. The former were the wealthy and conservative interests of the country—the business and propertied groups; the latter were for the most part, the debtor and agricultural classes, although some of their leaders were outstanding men. Whether the majority of the people as a whole favored or opposed the Constitution cannot be determined, for the ballot was restricted at the time and was in the hands of the same groups or classes who had chosen the delegates to the Constitutional Convention.

The Constitution provided that the new government should go into effect as soon as nine states should ratify it. The states generally acted through specially elected conventions. In June, 1788, New Hampshire, the ninth state, accepted the Constitution. Several states like New York made ratification conditional on a bill of rights which should be added to the Constitution as soon as the first Congress was elected. When the new government went into operation in the spring of 1789, two states controlled by back country elements were outside the Union. Under threats of trade barriers North Carolina ratified the Constitution in November, 1789, and Rhode Island in May, 1790.

CHAPTER 7

Westward Migration

By 1750, the frontier was moving slowly toward the Appalachian Mountains, although the westward spread and dispersion of population was greater in the settlements to the south. The lowland regions in New England are relatively narrow, but broaden so as they continue southward that the mountains in the Carolinas are about 250 miles from the sea. Westward settlement thus became more extensive and scattered in the middle and southern colonies and lands were taken up in the back country of these sections by German, Scotch-Irish, Dutch, English, and other settlers.

CROSSING THE MOUNTAINS

The first move of population west of the mountains surged into the region that became known as Tennessee. Attracted by the stories of traders, trappers, and agents of early land companies, the first permanent settlers as early as 1769 pushed into the Tennessee region from the back country of Virginia and the Carolinas. In spite of warlike Indians to the west and the Proclamation of 1763 which prohibited going beyond the crest of the mountains, settlements took form along the Watauga River in western North Carolina.

As population increased, the pioneers discovered in their midst a number of criminals who had fled to the frontier to escape eastern

150

justice. Cut off from the reach of the arm of colonial authority by forest and mountain, the settlers established a government under written articles known as the Watauga Association, in effect from 1772 to 1777. Under this form of government, patterned to some extent after that of Virginia, they established manhood suffrage, organized a militia, recorded deeds of lands, issued marriage licenses, tried and punished offenders, and carried on negotiations with the Indians. This Association became the model for many later miniature republics created under similar circumstances as people moved ever westward.

Other groups settled in this area which became Washington County within the state of North Carolina during the Revolution. When that state ceded her western lands to the United States in 1784, the settlers organized the "State of Franklin," in order to secure an orderly government. Although the cession act was quickly repealed, the state of Franklin, with John Sevier as governor, maintained a

THE APPALACHIAN FRONTIER

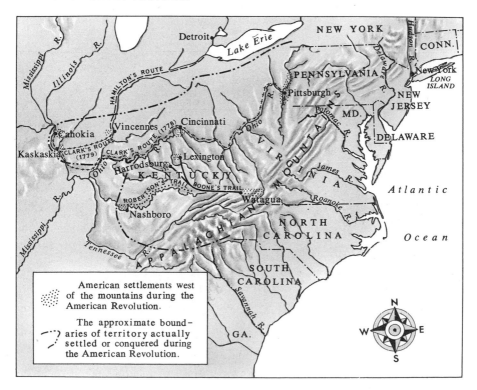

precarious existence for four years, marked by difficulties with the Indians, intrigues with the Spanish, and ineffective efforts to obtain recognition from Congress and North Carolina. The latter re-established jurisdiction over the region by 1789. After a second cession of its western lands was made by North Carolina in 1790, they were organized as the "Territory South of the Ohio River." In 1796, Tennessee was admitted to statehood.

About the same time, settlements were being made in the Kentucky region. The earliest important leader of this movement was Daniel Boone who gained an interest in the trans-Allegheny West while serving in the ill-fated Braddock campaign against the French and Indians. Typifying the popular concept of frontiersman and backwoodsman, Boone has become America's classic pioneer, a figure almost legendary in history. Lord Byron, John Filson, Timothy Flint and a host of later writers have built around him an aura of legend, myth, and rumor through extravagant statement that has mingled fact and fiction without distinction. The first permanent settlements in Kentucky had their beginnings in 1775 at Harrodstown, Boonesborough, McGary's Fort, and St. Asaph, under the leadership of James Harrod, Daniel Boone, and Judge Richard Henderson of the Transylvania Company.

For a decade after the first settlements, frequent and sometimes bloody Indian attacks occurred. Yet people poured into the Kentucky country through the Cumberland Gap and also by way of Pittsburgh and down the Ohio. Between 1784 and 1792, ten conventions were held in the interests of statehood and in 1792, Kentucky was admitted as a state in the Union.

Pioneers also moved into the region of Pittsburgh. During the French and Indian War, Fort Pitt was established in 1758, giving the English control of a strategic point in the Ohio Valley. Two military roads, Braddock's Road and Forbes' Road, had been cut through the wilderness and connected it with the eastern settlements. A village with 146 houses and thirty-six huts in 1760 slowly grew under the protection of the fort. Traders, trappers, mule drivers, fugitives from the east, pioneer farmers, and Indians made up its earliest population. The region became a bustling frontier community with sawmills, tan yards, lime kilns, trading houses, coal mines, and fields of corn, hay, and vegetables.

During the Revolution, stories of green valleys, clear streams, and abundant game lured many to the region where the Allegheny and Monongahela Rivers meet to form the Ohio. After the war emigrants

in increasing numbers sought the newly opened West. The Monongahela region became one of the great highways over which stalwart
pioneers and their families passed on their arduous and difficult trek
westward—pioneers who looked forward to making homes for themselves in the fertile wilderness, staking their strength, courage, and
ambitions against isolation, privation, and hardship. Among the factors that brought settlers to the western country after 1783, the most
important were the removal of British restrictions on westward migration, a high birth rate producing large families that had to seek new
land, the encouragement given by agents of land companies, the land
hunger of veterans of Washington's armies, and the passage of the
Northwest Ordinance (p. 154).

A FEDERAL LAND POLICY

By 1784 the state cessions (p. 143) had given Congress a public
domain of over 200 million acres stretching from the western boundary
of Pennsylvania down the Ohio River and westward to the Mississippi.
South of the river the states still controlled their western lands. Congress inevitably became the focus of contending land interests. Virginia
was selling land in her western territory that was to be Kentucky.
Pennsylvania and New York both had extensive areas in the western
parts of the state that they were selling in both large and small tracts.
Connecticut, North Carolina, and Georgia also had western lands.
The interest of these governments was to keep Congress from becoming a strong competitor until the states had disposed of their
land. Furthermore, New York, Pennsylvania, and Virginia, particularly
the latter, had already conveyed immense acreages to private companies
that desired to prevent competition from the sale of Federal land.

In seeking to prevent retail sale by Congress the state interests
were reinforced by additional company agents, some of whom were
also members of Congress, who wanted the national land sold to their
companies at low prices in wholesale quantities, but its resale protected
by keeping the Federal government out of the retail land market. As
bonuses for military service, both the states and Congress had issued
warrants entitling the holder to so many acres of land. Soldiers sold
these warrants at low prices to land operators who accumulated them
in large quantities. The holders of such warrants were opposed to
any government competition in land sales. Under the combined pressures of land-selling states, business companies, and warrant holders,
Congress passed a land sale ordinance that was a model of systematic

precision regarding surveys, but practically withdrew Federal land from the retail market.

The Ordinance of 1785 adopted the rectangular town system used in New England. It provided that the unit of survey should be the township of thirty-six square miles, based on meridians of longitude and parallels of latitude. Every township was to be subdivided into thirty-six sections each of 640 acres. This plan of survey was used throughout American history as new lands were added to the national domain and were opened up for settlement all the way to the Pacific. In addition to providing an efficient survey system, the Ordinance set forth the terms on which the lands were to be sold. In general, following the precedent established by the New England colonies, one section of each township was reserved for the support of schools. The rest of the surveyed land was to be offered at auctions, held only at the capital, in whole sections, at a minimum price of one dollar an acre. Since no farm family could cultivate 640 acres, and good state lands were selling in farm-size tracts for less than half as much per acre, Congress had effectively removed Federal competition.

The first surveys under the Ordinance ran due west from a point where the Pennsylvania boundary intersected the Ohio River. The survey was begun in 1785 by Thomas Hutchins, geographer of the United States, but hostile Indians, disease, and bad weather delayed the work and inaccuracies occurred in the surveys. Land was placed on sale two years later.

Having won a measure of insurance against Federal competition, the big land interests were prepared to make wholesale purchases from Congress if they could be assured of a responsible, practical form of government in the new territory. Skillful lobbying in a moribund Congress in 1786 and 1787 by the Reverend Manasseh Cutler, Samuel Parsons, and General Rufus Putnam, representing the land companies, resulted in a system of government for the West.

By the Northwest Ordinance the region north of the Ohio and east of the Mississippi was to be divided into not less than three nor more than five states. There was to be a temporary government consisting of a governor, a secretary, and three judges, appointed by Congress. As soon as there were 5,000 free adult males in the territory, a representative legislature was to be established, and when the population in a territory reached 60,000, its inhabitants could apply to Congress for statehood. A bill of rights which established religious freedom, prohibited slavery, guaranteed the fundamental rights of English liberty, provided for a just treatment of the Indians, encouraged education, and safeguarded the rights of the future inhabitants of the territory was included in the Northwest Ordinance. The Ordinance of 1787 laid down principles of government and fundamental rights, most of which were re-enacted over and over again as the country expanded.

The largest land company purchases were those of the Ohio Company which contracted for 1,500,000 acres, and the Scioto Company which took 5,000,000 acres. Both depended on New England capital for the down payment, but the Scioto Company also included many of the members of Congress. Another large purchaser, the Symmes Company, represented New Jersey and Pennsylvania capital. The great Virginia land operators had been served by special grants made in return for the state cession of its claim.

The companies that contracted to purchase these vast acreages became the victims of changing circumstances and were no more successful than the early English colonization companies. To begin with, they agreed to a series of time payments running half a dozen years or more to be made in the depreciated certificates of Congress. At the rates current in 1787 the prices were only a few cents an acre. But the creation of a strong central government with revolutionary rapidity put the price of government paper close to par, and the companies were called upon for amounts of real money that had never been anticipated. Even these sums, however, might have been met if retail sale and settlement had gone forward rapidly. But again, fate was against the promoters. Efforts to tap the European market were badly mismanaged in America. Half of a French settlement of the Scioto Company died from lack of supplies during the first winter. Before the discouraging effects of this failure could be counteracted, the French Revolutionary wars cut off the supply of European immigrants.

As a result of these problems and generally lax management the Scioto Company failed, the Ohio Company had to surrender most of its land in order to keep a part of it, and the Symmes Company survived by the same type of arrangement plus John Cleves Symmes' hard work at raising money and influencing Congress.

By 1796 prices had advanced and both state groups and the Federal grantees could foresee potential competition from Federal lands at a dollar an acre. Furthermore, a depression in that year put pressure on land operators, a pressure that ultimately bankrupted Robert Morris. Congress came to the aid of the private interests by advancing its price to two dollars an acre. A provision allowing one year for payment may also have been a reflection of temporary hard times in the midst of a boom period.

The first law partially designed to sell Federal land directly to settlers was enacted in 1800. Introduced by William Henry Harrison, delegate from Ohio Territory and son-in-law of John Cleves Symmes, it represented a compromise between private company and settler interests. The two-dollar price was retained, but the minimum acreage was cut in half, still three to four times the size really required. Land offices were opened in Ohio, an essential for sale to actual settlers, and four years' credit was allowed. The latter turned out to be the true concession. Young settlers full of optimism readily took on obligations due in three or four years. Furthermore the government soon demonstrated that it was afraid to foreclose on delinquents, and some settlers ceased worrying about their installment payments. Under the pressure of accumulating unpaid obligations Congress reduced the minimum to a more realistic 160 acres in 1804.

By 1820, even with considerably higher private land prices, it was evident that the federal policy was not a success. Large areas of land were sold, but many settlers found it both burdensome and unnecessary to meet the deferred payments on their farms until they were ready to resell. The Panic of 1819, partly caused by overspeculation in land, revealed the debtor position of many westerners. Faced with the problem of taking back about one-third of the land contracted for, valued at $20,000,000, Congress was forced to pass laws for the relief of the settlers. After much agitation an act in 1820 abolished the credit system; reduced the minimum price at public sale to $1.25 an acre; and, provided for the sale of tracts as small as an eighth of a section. Thus, after 1820, anyone with $100 could buy eighty acres of land. In 1832, the minimum was reduced to 40 acres, which remained the rule until 1862, when the Homestead Act provided grants of 160 acres free if certain conditions were met (p. 348).

Many who went to the frontier after 1820 lacked even the $100 with which eighty acres could be bought. Their only solution was "squatting" on land without possessing title to it, a practice that began in Virginia, Pennsylvania, and elsewhere in colonial times. As waves of migration sped past the crude log cabins and small clearings of squatters, they frequently found that their lands were put up for sale and sold to others, forcing them to move from homes that they had often struggled years to establish. Squatters early besought Congress by petition and otherwise to grant them the right to pre-empt their claims in advance of the land sales so that they would not be required to bid for them against speculators, if they had the money to bid at all. Pre-emption rights were granted to sixteen special groups before 1830 and to others in the years that followed. In 1841, a general pre-emption measure was passed, which for the first time legalized squatting on surveyed lands. Squatters received the right to purchase forty acres at a minimum price before speculators could purchase them at higher prices. The act was a victory for the westerners but it did not satisfy them completely. It did not apply to unsurveyed lands, and it did not provide free grants to settlers. The law was in effect until 1891. By this time it was seriously abused as powerful interests hired "floaters" to pre-empt valuable land for them. Bribery of land officers and laxity of supervision resulted in much corruption. When public sentiment was aroused, the law was repealed. However, during the early years of its operation, it did protect the squatter and was an important part of the early land system.

As settlers moved westward the government opened additional tracts of land for sale. The original offering was at an advertised public auction at the nearest land office. The auction system often worked badly for the poor man trying to buy a farm. In areas where land was unusually valuable the representatives of land companies, who had been over the ground, bid for the best tracts such as those on rivers or in fertile, level valleys. These choice locations were worth far more than two dollars an acre, above six dollars even before 1800, and hence were attractive to investors. Often the large interests combined to keep the bids of the individual settler from being heard, and often the auctioneer had been bribed. The land laws offered loopholes for the experienced operator. As a net result the government, even in years of the most frenzied land booms, never averaged more than a few cents per acre above the minimum price for land, and up to 1832 the costs of administration exceeded the revenue.

Prior to 1841, if there were many squatters on a tract by the time the land was put up for auction they would form an "honor" or "claim" association to respect and protect each other's holdings. Armed with bowie knives and rifles, the association would attend the auction, and company agents seldom chose to bid against them. In this way squatters strong enough to protect their claims, and land companies often had the first choice. Since squatters usually lacked any ready cash, "loan sharks" made as much money by lending at 10 or 12 per cent as by buying land.

There was so much land in the West that up to 1835 three-quarters of the land offered was unsold at auctions, and later comers could usually buy the less desirable land at the minimum price. In fact, large acreages remained for decades unsold at $1.25 an acre and there was continual agaitation in the West for disposal of unsold land at bargain rates. For sixty years eastern votes in Congress prevented a graduation in price, but by the 1850's the West, both north and south, was too strong to be denied. The eleven states of the Mississippi Valley still had 71,000,000 acres of unsold land.

The Graduation Act of 1854, passed by both Democratic and Whig votes, provided that after land was on the market more than ten years its price should be reduced to a dollar, after fifteen years to 75 cents, after twenty years to 50 cents, after twenty-five years to 25 cents, after thirty years to 12½ cents, and all land unsold at the latter price should revert to the states. There were no limitations on the quantity that could be bought by a single purchaser. This law rapidly disposed of the land in the older public-land states, largely no doubt to investment or speculative interests.

In appraising the history of United States land policy, it must be remembered that in a period when there were few reliable securities, land was the common form of investment for all who had savings. The ordinary settler could not afford to go out, map in hand, in advance of the auction to explore and locate land. The investors operating through expert agents acted as middlemen profiting from the difference between government minimum prices and either the current market value or the value at some later time. The government certainly received less that a truly competitive market price, but whether the settler paid more is impossible to determine. One unquestionably bad feature of large-scale buying for investment was that land was held off the market, and farmers had to go still further west to find cheap land.

THE NORTHWEST TERRITORY

The region beyond the Appalachians, north of the Ohio, east of the Mississippi, and south of the Great Lakes became known as the "Old Northwest." Scattered over this region in 1787 were some 45,000 Indians, 2,000 French, some Englishmen, and a number of Negroes. Settlement was slow partly because of the presence and menace of the Indians. In spite of the efforts of the land companies to open up new regions in the Ohio country, the earliest settlements beginning with Marietta made little progress until Anthony Wayne's decisive victory over the Indians at Fallen Timbers in 1794. By the subsequent Treaty of Greenville (1795), the Indians surrendered their claims to most of southern Ohio and agreed to move westward. The treaty established a definite boundary between Indian lands and those open to settlement. Much of Ohio then was opened up to settlement and increasing numbers pushed into the region. A territorial form of government was established in 1799, followed in four years by statehood.

To some extent the Indian war in Ohio had been incited by British officers occupying forts along the Great Lakes at such key locations as Oswego, Niagara, and Detroit. The treaty of 1783 specified no definite time for the withdrawal of the troops, but stated that it should take place "with all convenient speed." English statesmen excused their failure to withdraw the troops on the ground that the Americans had not fulfilled their obligations set forth in the peace treaty to place no obstacles in the collection of the debts owing English merchants, and of Congress to recommend to the legislatures of the states that they make restitution to Loyalists whose estates had been confiscated during the Revolution. Congress had done its duty in these respects, but English debts remained unpaid, and the Loyalists had received no recompense. The real reasons why English troops still remained on American soil in the Northwest were: (1) to command the valuable fur trade of the northern regions, and (2) because of the fear that the withdrawal of the troops would leave the Indians uncontrolled, which would bring serious problems regarding the Indians living in Canada. In 1794, the year of Fallen Timbers, Jay's Treaty led to British withdrawal.

After the Treaty of Greenville, the Indians steadily fell back across Ohio and Indiana. Nine treaties of cession were forced upon them between 1795 and 1809. On the banks of the Wabash an unusually able chief, Tecumseh, tried to rally the tribes for organized resistance, but American armies in the War of 1812 broke the Indian power both north and south. Shortly after the war was over the northwest, below the Great Lakes, was clear of Indian claims as far as the Mississippi River. And many of the Indians had learned the futility of resistance.

A stream of hopeful pioneers continued westward. During the War of 1812 settlements grew rapidly and a territorial census of 1815 showed Indiana to have a population of more than 60,000. When the state government was set up in 1816, most of its people lived along the southern edge, along the Ohio boundary line and along the Wabash to Terre Haute. Before other parts of the state were populated, the adjoining territory of Illinois was experiencing waves of migration. In 1818, Illinois was admitted to the Union with a popula-

POPULATION BY GEOGRAPHICAL DIVISIONS, 1790–1860

	1790	1800	1810	1820	1830	1840	1850	1860
New England	1,009,408	1,233,011	1,471,973	1,660,071	1,954,717	2,234,822	2,728,116	3,135,283
Middle Atlantic	958,632	1,402,565	2,014,702	2,699,845	3,587,664	4,526,260	5,898,735	7,458,985
East North Central		51,006	272,324	792,719	1,470,018	2,924,728	4,523,260	6,926,884
West North Central			19,783	66,586	140,455	426,814	880,335	2,169,832
South Atlantic	1,851,806	2,286,494	2,674,891	3,061,063	3,645,752	3,925,299	4,679,090	5,364,703
East South Central	109,368	335,407	708,590	1,190,489	1,815,969	2,575,445	3,363,271	4,020,991
West South Central			77,618	167,680	246,127	449,985	940,251	1,747,667
Mountain							72,927	174,923
Pacific							105,891	444,053
United States	3,929,214	5,308,483	7,239,881	9,638,453	12,866,020	17,069,453	23,191,876	31,443,321

Source: U.S. Bureau of the Census, *Population Volume of the 1930 Census*, p. 11.

tion of 40,000. The rapidity of settlement can be seen in the population statistics as thousands swarmed into one region after another.

The northern portion of the Old Northwest was neglected as the pioneers pushed into Ohio, Indiana, and Illinois. The French had played a role in the early history of the northern region which became Michigan. For 200 years, from the early seventeenth century, it remained a wilderness outpost successively of New France, Great Britain, and the United States. Until the end of French control (1763) it was a center of Indian trade; by the Proclamation of 1763, the British made it an Indian reserve; and, in 1774 it was brought within the limits of the newly-created province of Quebec. While it was a part of the area obtained by the United States under the terms of the treaty of 1783, it remained under British rule during the period when England refused to give up the western posts. Not until 1796 was the American flag raised at Detroit. The territorial area of Michigan was enlarged and contracted from time to time. After the War of 1812 there was much interest in this region on the part of American settlers. Then, as Indian titles were extinguished, knowledge of the fertility of the lands made known, and the Erie Canal opened, Michigan came within the sweep of the westward movement and as the tide of both American and Canadian migration rose, the territory became eligible for statehood. Prior to its admission to the Union, a long controversy ensued over the boundary with Ohio, reaching a climax in the bloodless "Toledo War" of 1833–1836. To settle the question, Congress offered to admit Michigan on condition that a tract of land of 9,000 square miles on the Upper Peninsula be accepted in lieu of the disputed Toledo strip. A convention rejected the proposal, for the land seemed a barren waste, but an unofficial convention of citizens, irritated by the delay, voted to accept the compromise and Congress, without waiting to examine the status of the new convention, admitted Michigan to statehood in 1837. Not long afterwards it was discovered that the Upper Peninsula contained amazing wealth in the form of large copper and iron deposits.

Wisconsin, to the west of Lake Michigan, possessed an early history similar to that of Michigan. French explorers, missionaries, and trappers for almost two centuries were the only white men in the region. Under American control it became a part of the Northwest Territory. During the War of 1812, the Indians and its few settlers sided with the British, but the first American flag flew over Fort Shelby at Prairie du Chien in 1814. After the war, when the British evacuated the region in accord with the terms of the treaty of peace,

forts were built and the military controlled the area until Wisconsin
became a formal territory in 1836. During this period, agents of the
American Fur Company as well as independent American fur traders,
and lead miners from Virginia, Kentucky, and Tennessee led the van-
guard of pioneers. Many difficulties arose with the Indians who objected especially to trespass by the miners, for the Indians themselves
for years had smelted quantities of lead which they exchanged for
goods from American and Canadian traders. The Winnebago War
(1827) was followed by the Black Hawk War (1832), and resulted
in the cession of the Indian lands. Immigration increased rapidly,
the territorial census for 1840 showing 30,000. In addition to those
from the older states, Germans, Norwegians, Belgians, Swiss, Irish,
and Poles took up lands in this region. When Wisconsin became a state
in 1848, it had a population of more than 200,000.

THE OLD SOUTHWEST

The term, "Old Southwest," in general, came to be applied to
the region south of the Ohio and as far westward as the Mississippi
River, although the historical concepts of the territorial limits were
never so exact as those of the Old Northwest. After the Revolution
there were difficulties with Spain in this area. American settlements
in the Tennessee and Kentucky country depended on the Ohio and
Mississippi Rivers for contact with the outside world. While Great
Britain and the new United States agreed in the peace treaty to
guarantee mutual navigation of the Mississippi, Spain controlled the
mouth of the river and therefore was in a position to retard American
settlement by closing the river to foreign navigation. Another problem
related to a dispute over the boundary of West Florida, which together
with East Florida had been returned by England to Spain in 1783.
Attempts to negotiate a commercial treaty with Spain failed. Not until
1795 were these problems solved, when the Pinckney (San Lorenzo)
Treaty established the free navigation of the Mississippi by the United
States, and also gained the "right of deposit," or the privilege of
landing goods at New Orleans for reloading on ocean-going vessels.
The West Florida boundary was settled at the same time in favor of
the American contention, and certain minor commercial privileges
were also obtained. American commerce on the Mississippi grew as
the western states sent their produce to New Orleans where most of
it was transshipped to the Atlantic ports, the West Indies, and the
outside world.

In the Mississippi Valley, the Tennessee and Kentucky regions, the first to be settled by Americans, were admitted to statehood before the end of the eighteenth century. Soon afterwards planters and farmers from the Old South moved westward to the fertile lands of Alabama, Mississippi, and Louisiana as cotton quickly succeeded tobacco as the leading staple crop of the South.

The beginnings of Alabama's history, however, reach back to the Spanish occupation of North America. The region was owned successively by the Spanish, French, British, and finally by the Americans. Early in the nineteenth century, planters came from the exhausted lands of the seaboard accompanied by their slaves. The demand for raw cotton from England and the rising factories in the North opened up a market that for a time seemed insatiable. It should be noted that while small farmers, professional men, and others moved into the lower southwest, migration in this region was a little different from that of other sections of the West, in that it included a few of the old and aristocratic families of the seaboard South. Alabama attained statehood in 1819.

The migration into Mississippi and its early history was similar in character. During the beginning of the nineteenth century, after the Louisiana Purchase (p. 164), a part of this region, like a part of Alabama, was plagued by boundary disputes and questionable land titles. In 1795, the legislature of Georgia before giving up Georgia's public lands to the Federal government, as agreed at the time the Articles of Confederation went into effect, sold the greater part of what is now Alabama and Mississippi for the sum of $500,000 to four land companies made up of stockholders from different parts of the country. Some of the legislators who passed the law were represented in the companies and the "Yazoo land frauds" brought nation-wide attention and criticism. As a result, a new legislature the next year rescinded the act and burned all papers connected with it. Yazoo claimants appealed to Congress as well as to the courts. After years of debate a case reached the Supreme Court (Fletcher *vs.* Peck, 1810) which decided that the state grant was an implied contract and hence the rescinding law was unconstitutional. Finally, Congress paid the claimants more than $4,000,000. In the meantime, parts of Mississippi were settled chiefly by cotton growers. Statehood was achieved in 1817, almost two years before Alabama. In 1830 and 1832, the opening to settlement of the Indian lands within the state brought another rush of immigration to this and the adjoining fertile regions of the Southwest.

THE ACQUISITION OF NEW TERRITORIES

One of the most spectacular aspects of nineteenth-century American development was the acquisition of new territories. To the original area between the Atlantic Ocean and Mississippi River were added in quick succession new regions in the West to which land-hungry settlers quickly moved. By the middle of the nineteenth century, the American flag had been carried all the way to the Pacific, and while vast areas remained unsettled, the older western frontier was pushing farther and farther westward. A new eastward-looking frontier in the far West was in the process of development as men sought gold on the Pacific coast and began to move eastward toward the Rocky Mountains.

The first acquisition of land by the new nation was Louisiana in 1803. For more than a generation, that region had been a pawn in European diplomacy. In the secret treaty of San Ildefonso (1800), Napoleon forced the Spanish King to cede the province. France dreamed once again of the control of the Mississippi Valley and the establishment of a colonial empire in America, a granary for the new European state planned by Napoleon. President Jefferson, alarmed by the danger to American expansion offered $10 million for the Isle of Orleans and the Floridas, mistakenly believed to be French. If France refused, the ministers were to seek a small piece of land at the mouth of the Mississippi or the permanent right of deposit at New Orleans. At this time rumors of an Anglo-American alliance reached France. Napoleon decided to sell all of Louisiana to the United States for $15 million in order to secure some of the finances necessary to continue the war against England. In spite of Spanish resentment and threats— because Napoleon had promised never to dispose of Louisiana to another power—Louisiana was formally transferred to France in November, 1803 and the next month by France to the United States. The extent of the territory was 1,172,000 square miles and included almost all the area that now constitutes fourteen states.

The boundaries of the new acquisition were vague because they had varied under Spanish and French control. In the years that followed, West Florida was occupied by the United States as a part of the Louisiana Purchase. Controversies with Spain continued not only over this question but also over East Florida, for with the relaxation of Spanish power in America because of the European wars, the Floridas became a scene of Indian disturbances, filibustering expeditions, and land speculations. Beset by rebellions all over her empire Spain decided that it would be better to sell the Floridas than to have them seized. The treaty ratified in 1821, transferred them to the United States. Spain obtained no money for the deal because the $5,000,000 agreed on was used to satisfy the claims that Americans had against Spain. In spite of opposition from many Americans the United States agreed to the undisputed possession of Texas by the Spanish, thus giving up a claim arising out of the indefinite provisions of the Louisiana Purchase treaty. A zigzag line was drawn from the Sabine River in the south, and westerly to the forty-second parallel at the Pacific. Thus Spain also gave up whatever claims she had to the Oregon territory in the north. A definite western boundary had been marked for the United States and controversies with Spain over shadowy claims were ended. In the same year that the line was drawn Mexico revolted and became independent of Spain. The boundary, however, was accepted by the new Mexican government.

In the year 1821, a few Americans began their trek into Texas. Moses Austin, a land-hungry Yankee pioneer, who had migrated to many places and finally reached Missouri, received permission from the Spanish authorities in Mexico to settle in Texas. He died before he could carry out his project, and his son, Stephen F. Austin, led the group to the southlands, establishing a colony on the lower Brazos River. The American settlements grew from 15,000 in 1827 to 30,000 in 1836. Most Americans were from the South, although there was a sprinkling of settlers from all the states. Many Southerners took their slaves with them in spite of the prohibition of slavery by the Mexican constitution and laws. For a time, the laws were waived in favor of the Americans, but later, slaves were brought into Texas on the master-and-servant contract basis. The Americans did not comply completely with the colonization laws, as they did not adopt the Spanish language officially and few became Roman Catholics.

Growing difficulties with the Americans led the Mexican government to reaffirm the laws against slavery, forbid further immigration from the United States, send Mexican troops to the American settlements, impose heavier customs duties, and establish additional custom houses. American protests brought no results and a struggle for liberty ensued. A new Republic of Texas emerged, but Mexico did not recognize its independence. The Texans had received aid in both money and volunteers from their former countrymen and most Texans desired annexation to the United States.

The United States recognized the new republic, but when the proffer of annexation was made to President Van Buren, he declined because he believed it would involve the United States in a war with

Mexico. Assuming this risk, Democratic President Polk encouraged Congress to annex Texas, with the latter's consent, in 1845.

By the time that Texas was annexed, the term "Manifest Destiny" was in use. It was applied first to the acquisition of Texas by the editor of the *Democratic Review,* who wrote that it was "our manifest destiny to overspread the continent allotted by Providence for the free development for our yearly multiplying millions." The expansionists applied the idea also to Oregon. When Polk became President he was pledged to acquire Oregon and he was determined to have the problem settled as soon as possible. At this time the region was held in joint occupation by Great Britain and the United States, but claims to the area went back into the past.

At the beginning of the nineteenth century, four nations were interested in the Oregon country: Spain, Russia, Great Britain, and the United States. Spain gave up her claims in the Florida treaty (1819–1821). Russian fur traders from Alaska, employees of the Russian American Fur Company, had pushed down to California and in 1811 established a colony north of San Francisco Bay, which became a base for an extensive sea otter trade all along the coast. These activities brought forth a clause in Monroe's famous "doctrine" of 1823 that "the American continents . . . are henceforth not to be considered as subjects for future colonization by any European powers." The next year, Russia yielded all territorial claims south of 54° 40′. This left the problem of ownership of the Oregon territory to Great Britain and the United States.

Great Britain claimed the territory chiefly on the basis of the exploration and discoveries of Sir Francis Drake in the sixteenth century, Captains Cook and Vancouver in the eighteenth, and the activities of British fur traders of the Hudson's Bay Company. American claims were based on the voyages of Captain Robert Gray to the region and especially his discoveries in the Columbia River in the latter part of the eighteenth century, on the Yankee coastal fur trade with the northwest Indians, on the explorations of Lewis and Clark in 1805–1806, and on the establishment of John Jacob Astor's fur trading post, Astoria, in 1811. During the War of 1812, British interests supplanted American in this region, but the Treaty of Ghent provided a return of all conquered territory. In the settlement after the war, both nations agreed that this country west of the Rockies should be held in joint occupation and be free and open to the citizens of both powers (1818). This convention was extended in 1827 indefinitely, but either nation had the right to give one year's notice of withdrawal. Several attempts

The "Columbia" — Captain Robert Gray's ship at Gray's Harbor, 1792

were made from time to time to settle the question amicably, but all failed. In the thirties, Americans, led by missionaries from the East, moved to the region, and a settlement of the question was necessary because land titles and government were involved.

The slogans used in the campaign of 1844 that related to Oregon—"Reoccupation of Oregon" and "Fifty-four forty or fight," were excellent for campaign purposes at a time when many Americans were contracting the expansionist fever. But political leaders had no desire to go to war with Great Britain for the whole territory. After making a demand for all of Oregon, President Polk ultimately sent to the Senate a British compromise that drew the boundary at the forty-ninth parallel, but retained all Vancouver Island for Great Britain. He threw upon the upper house entire responsibility for acceptance or rejection. The proposal was accepted and the treaty consummated.

On the promise of the Mexican government to receive him, President Polk sent a special envoy to Mexico on a secret mission to secure the purchase of New Mexico and California and to solve the other problems as well. He was authorized to offer assumption by the United States of the American claims against Mexico if the Rio Grande were accepted as the western boundary of Texas; $5,000,000 in addition for New Mexico; and $25,000,000 as well as the assumption of claims if California were added. A new revolution in Mexico prevented negotiation. To Polk, the refusal of Mexico to negotiate a settlement, the upholding of national honor, and the threat of a Mexican attack on Texas at the same time, justified war. Believing that a conflict was inevitable and that the United States should strike first, he began writing a war message. A few days before it was delivered to Congress, word came from the disputed boundary strip between the Rio Grande and the Nueces River, to which American troops had been sent, that a Mexican force had crossed the Rio Grande, engaged in a skirmish with United States dragoons, killed a number of troops, and had captured the rest. The news came in time for Polk to add to his message: "The cup of forbearance has been exhausted. After reiterated menaces, Mexico has passed the boundary of the United States, has invaded our territory, and shed American blood upon the American soil." Two days later, although the United States was entirely unprepared for it, Congress declared that a state of war existed between the two countries.

The Mexican war was a relatively short one and complete victory was assured when General Winfield Scott reached the heart of Mexico. Zachary Taylor had struck in the northern sections and Commodore Sloat and Colonel Kearny had occupied California, their main objective. The Treaty of Guadalupe Hidalgo, made early in 1848, provided that the completely vanquished Mexico relinquish to the United States the immense territories of upper California and New Mexico. In return the United States agreed to pay Mexico $15,000,000 and to assume the claims of United States citizens to the sum of $3,200,000. It was felt in many parts of the country that too much leniency had been shown Mexico and that even more territory should be demanded. Manifest Destiny became rampant. Much was said and written about saving Mexico from anarchy and about spreading enlightened American institutions over the New World. In Congress members from the South and West demanded more territory; but many northerners, especially New Englanders, felt that too much territory had been secured in that part of the country, for they feared the growing influence of the South and the acquisition of land that might become slave territory. The treaty was ratified after the usual bitter debates. But the acquisition opened up the slavery question which was finally to rend the country in two.

By the treaty of 1848, the United States rounded out her continental possessions to the Pacific. To complete the present southwestern boundary, the Gila River Valley in southern Arizona was purchased in 1853 from Mexico for the sum of $10,000,000. The Gadsden Purchase, as it became known, comprised 45,535 square miles of territory and was obtained largely for the purpose of securing a convenient location for the proposed southern railroad route, although problems relating to the inroads of American Indians were also involved. Southern expansionists continued to demand more territory, even Cuba, but the events leading to the Civil War obscured all other issues.

THE PATHFINDERS IN THE TRANS-MISSISSIPPI WEST

Long before the acquisition of Louisiana, many Americans had shown a curiosity about the area beyond the Mississippi. After becoming President, Jefferson secretly asked Congress for an appropriation of $2,500 to equip a party that would explore the country in the region of the Missouri River in the interest of the Indian trade, then controlled by British and French half-breed traders and trappers. Congress granted the request and Captain Meriwether Lewis, Jefferson's private secretary, and Lieutenant William Clark, younger brother of General George Rogers Clark, were given command of the expedition. They were instructed to explore the Missouri and the principal water communications to the Pacific. They were required to note all that they saw and were given elaborate orders regarding careful treatment of the Indians. Jefferson's interest was two-fold: (1) scientific, and (2) development of the American fur trade. As the expedition began its preparations, news came of the proposed purchase of Louisiana.

Late in 1803, the party was assembled near St. Louis, ready for the start up the Missouri. In the spring of 1804, the expedition ascended the river, wintered among the Mandan Indians, set out again the next spring, crossed the Rocky Mountains, and late in 1805 traveled along the Columbia River to the Pacific Ocean. The return trip was begun in March, 1806, and the explorers reached St. Louis in November of that year. Valuable information concerning the geography, climate, natural products, and animal life of the region had been obtained; many councils had been held with the Indians; and, impulse had been given to the westward extension of American trade, commerce, and settlement.

Other expeditions were undertaken in parts of the vast region beyond the Mississippi. Most notable among the explorations of this period were those of Lieutenant Zebulon M. Pike, who left in August, 1805, with twenty soldiers on a seventy-foot keelboat to explore the sources of the Mississippi, to assert the authority of the United States against the British in that region, and to find suitable sites for military posts. His achievement led to his appointment to lead a southwestern expedition. In the summer of 1806 he ascended the Missouri and the Osage Rivers into the present state of Kansas, then went southward to the region of Colorado, where he discovered the peak that now bears his name. Traveling home across northern Texas, Pike obtained much information about that region.

Most of the early explorers published the results of their expeditions, stimulating the interest of readers in the older sections of the country and furnishing useful information for the adventurer, trader, merchant, and settler seized with the urge to go west. Patrick Gass, a member of the Lewis and Clark expedition, kept a journal which was published in 1811, and three years later Nicholas Biddle edited the journals of the members of the party, which became the most popular of all the accounts of the expedition. Even earlier, Pike had

TRAILS TO THE WEST

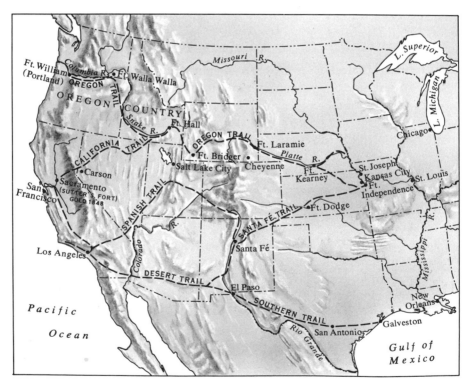

published his narrative of human daring and courage, affording his countrymen the first description of the Southwest, stimulating interest in old Santa Fé, and laying the groundwork for the myth of the Great American Desert.

Other explorations followed these famous ones. Fur traders, like Jedidiah Smith, explored the Rocky Mountain region and beyond, to the Pacific coast. The growth of interest in the Oregon country by the early 1840's led the government to select the famous pathfinder, John C. Frémont, to lead many expeditions in the far West. By this time much information, real and fanciful, had been disseminated all over the East about the distant western regions.

THE WESTERN FUR TRADE

Fur traders and trappers played a most important part in western exploration. They were the advance guard of civilization, always keeping far ahead of settlement where game was plentiful. During the colonial period the American fur trade was in the hands of private individuals or groups. Great Britain chartered but one great company in that period—the Hudson's Bay Company in 1670, whose activities were confined to the northlands. After the fall of New France, British merchants and many Scotch gradually took over the system built up by the French in Canada and the region of the Great Lakes, but the system of government monopoly, characteristic of the French, entirely disappeared. Monopoly in the fur trade continued as a few great British companies dominated the trade. The North West Company, chief of these, was not an incorporated company, but was similar to a modern holding company, the parts of which were chiefly Montreal firms and partnerships engaged in the fur trade. Another was the Mackinac Company, with headquarters at Montreal and with activities extending throughout the regions of Wisconsin and Minnesota.

At the outset of the American Revolution, the First Continental Congress appointed a committee to devise a factory or government trading system, but it was not until 1795 that the United States inaugurated a plan of government-owned and operated trading posts. They were established at Detroit, Chicago, Fort Wayne, Green Bay, Sandusky, Chickasaw Bluffs, and elsewhere. The purposes of the system were to promote peace among the Indians, to protect them from exploitation by private traders, to offset the influence of the British and Spanish on the Indians, and to strengthen military policy. The government agents at the factories sold all kinds of goods to the Indians in return for furs, skins, animal oils, beeswax, and other products, which were sent eastward to the superintendent of Indian trade for sale at auction or in foreign markets. Many problems arose as private traders, companies, Indian agents, and designing Indians opposed government control. The great trader, John Jacob Astor, with the aid of lawmakers like Lewis Cass and Thomas Hart Benton waged campaigns against the system, and Congress abolished it in 1822.

The American Fur Company became the greatest of all the fur trading companies. It was established by John Jacob Astor, who arrived in New York in 1784, a poor German boy, and immediately became a trader in furs. By 1808, when he organized the American Fur Company, he was a rival of the older British companies in Canada and envisioned control of the entire American fur trade as he planned a series of posts from St. Louis to the Columbia River, as well as a large share of the China trade from the Pacific Northwest. By 1811 he had established Astoria in the Oregon country, seized by the British during the War of 1812, but returned after the war. He gave up his project beyond the Rockies and concentrated on the region to the east of those mountains. By 1830, the American Fur Company had a virtual monopoly of the fur trade of the United States. This had been accomplished in devious ways. Rival companies were fought, suppressed, and absorbed, by fair means and foul; private traders were forced out of business by ruthless competition; agents of the company were not averse to violence in competing for the wealth of new areas; and, Congress was influenced to pass laws excluding foreigners from the trade as well as ending the government factory system. In 1834, a visit to London convinced Astor that silk and other fabrics were displacing beaver in the manufacture of hats and at the same time it became evident that fabulous profits could no longer be made, for in many areas the fur-bearing animals were getting scarce. The fur trade had reached its height and was on the verge of a downward trend. Astor sold his interests to his associates and turned his attention largely to real estate in and near the rapidly developing city of New York. He died in 1848, leaving about $30,000,000, the first American fortune to approach such size.

SETTLEMENT OF THE MISSISSIPPI REGIONS

Before the Louisiana Purchase, many American merchants in the East had agents and factors in New Orleans, the center of French and Spanish settlement at the mouth of the Mississippi. In 1803, with a population of 8,000 New Orleans was similar in many respects to European towns and had a very cosmopolitan population. Under

American control, increasing numbers of settlers and traders moved there from the United States and from Europe. Prior to the Civil War it was the second port of the United States and the great commercial and financial emporium of the Mississippi Valley. By the beginning of the nineteenth century, American planters, moving from the older states with their slaves to the region surrounding New Orleans, crossed the river to the west side and joined French and Spanish plantation owners in developing rich sugar, cotton, and fruit lands. This nucleus of settlement expanded rapidly so that by 1810, the territory of Orleans, as this part of the Louisiana Purchase was named, had a population of more than 76,000. Two years later, in accord with the promise made in the treaty of 1803, this region with its French and Spanish as well as American peoples, became a state, although strong protests were made by New Englanders, who feared the increasing ascendency of the South and the growth of western power.

Also on the western side of the Mississippi, centering in the growing village of St. Louis, Frenchmen and Americans established plantations during the latter part of the eighteenth century. After the turn of the century, fur traders, slaveholders, farmers, lead miners, and businessmen moved into this region, largely from the Old South. As the western fur trade expanded during the first decades of the nineteenth century, St. Louis, situated midway between the fur regions of the West and the markets of the East, increased in size. Its wharves were continually extended as trade increased, and its merchants equipped traders and trappers as they prepared to go into the western wilds. The advent of the steamboat contributed to its increase of population and wealth, as it did to most of the Mississippi towns. By 1818, more than 60,000 lived in the Missouri area. Application for statehood brought out the serious controversy over slavery there and a sectional struggle for the control of the region beyond the Mississippi was begun. The Compromise, admitting Missouri as a slave state, Maine as a free state, and the prohibition of slavery north of the 36° 30′ parallel in all the territory of the Louisiana Purchase, except Missouri, settled the question for the time being, but marked the beginning of a struggle between the North and South, which was to end in a tragic, bloody civil war. With keen insight, John Quincy Adams wrote in his diary of the Missouri Compromise: "I take it for granted that the present question is a mere preamble—a title-page to a great tragic volume."

Before Missouri was granted statehood, American settlers were moving into the region of Arkansas. This part of the Mississippi area had been neglected by settlers because of the vast swamps along the western banks of the river. In 1810, about 1,000 people lived there; by 1820, population had increased to 14,000. In the years that followed, slaveholders in increasing numbers from the Old South took up lands in the rich regions of the White, Washita, Arkansas, and Red Rivers, cultivating cotton, tobacco, and corn. The planter classes dominated the entire economic life of the area and were able to rush the territory into statehood (1836) ahead of time as measured by population, partly in order to establish state banks as the life of the Second United States Bank ended, and also to get other benefits conferred by statehood.

The surge of population was also affecting the upper Mississippi Valley. As Wisconsin was being settled, it was natural that pioneers should push across the Mississippi into the region of Iowa and Minnesota. The Black Hawk War of 1832 resulted in the first Indian cession of Iowa land and in the years that followed, the Indians gave up their lands for less than ten cents an acre. Frontiersmen, land speculators, and miners moved into the eastern region and then settlement pushed westward. European immigrants were among them. Farmers grew corn, wheat, oats, rye, and vegetables. Towns were quickly established. Many were attracted to Dubuque by lead-mining. Burlington, Davenport, and other river towns began to thrive. When Iowa was admitted to statehood in 1846, Iowa City, 100 miles west of the Mississippi, had been established.

Further north, Minnesota—a Sioux name, meaning sky-blue water—received its first real settlement in the region of St. Paul, after Indian treaties had been made and hardy lumbermen, hopeful farmers, and town-builders began to arrive in the years just prior to the mid-century. After 1851, the year that treaties were made with the Sioux Indians, southeastern Minnesota was rapidly settled. Many Germans, Scandinavians, Irish, and English joined the native American pioneers. The migratory movement at first was largely by way of the Mississippi. The building of the Chicago and Rock Island Railroad in 1854 aided settlement in Minnesota as it made the journey easier and less expensive. Population jumped from 6,000 in 1850 to 157,000 in 1857, when application was made for statehood. The Kansas question delayed admission, but the next year Minnesota took its place among the states. Immigration continued, most settlers coming from the middle states, especially New York, although New Englanders, many from the older central western areas, and newly-arrived immigrants from Europe swelled the stream of settlers.

KANSAS AND NEBRASKA

In the 1850's Kansas and Nebraska were also opened up for settlement. Land-hungry settlers, profit-seeking land speculators, northern capitalists anxious to build a transcontinental railroad from the Mississippi Valley to the Pacific, and southerners seeking more slave territory were all partly responsible for the law which opened up this vast area that earlier had been dedicated to the Indians forever. The Kansas-Nebraska Act of 1854, opening both territories to slavery, also put an end to the Missouri Compromise line; it brought the struggle between the North and the South over the expansion of slavery to a white heat; it led to a general realignment in American politics; and it swept the country nearer to the Civil War. The struggle for Kansas resulted in a bloody war on its broad plains as settlers from the North and South sought control. As the preponderance of northerners in Kansas increased, their control of the region was assured, thereby substantiating the contention of Stephen A. Douglas, who had written the doctrine of "popular sovereignty" into the Kansas-Nebraska Act, that free states actually became such by self-determination rather than by Federal law. But it took several years to settle the issue and it cost 200 lives and $2,000,000 in property that was destroyed in the new settlements. In January, 1861, after secession had begun, Kansas became a state. The settlement of Nebraska was more peaceful and this region of the Platte watershed was sufficiently populated by the close of the Civil War to consider statehood which came in 1867.

SETTLEMENT ON THE PACIFIC COAST

Increased interest in the far West developed with the early migration of Americans to Oregon and California in the 1830's. Following on the heels of fur traders, missionaries to the Indians led the way to Oregon. In 1834 the Oregon Mission of the Methodist Church was established in the Willamette Valley. Two years later, the American Board Mission, a Congregational organization, sent a doctor and a Presbyterian minister to Oregon. The missionaries attracted pioneers who traveled in their covered wagons by way of the deeply rutted Oregon trail. As long as the country was held jointly by Great Britain and the United States no legal title to land was possible, and the settlers held their lands simply by "squatters' rights." Far away from American civilization, they established their own provisional government. The settlement of the Oregon boundary dispute (p. 167) encouraged increased migration and, in 1859, Oregon became a state.

In the meantime a most interesting experiment was being carried out in Salt Lake Valley by the Mormons. The Church of Jesus Christ of Latter-Day Saints, or the Mormon Church, was founded by Joseph Smith in the state of New York in 1827. In many respects the organization was similar to the many new sects of that period, but was subject to more persecution than most, partly because of the practice of polygamy. In 1846, about 12,000 Mormons from Illinois moved westward. They migrated with their wagons, cattle, sheep, hogs, poultry, tools, and furniture to Council Bluffs, Iowa, and then proceeded in several divisions to Great Salt Lake which their leader, Brigham Young, selected as "the place." Through irrigation the Mormons soon transformed the desert into a fertile region. Plans were worked out by which all had to cooperate and industries of different sorts were encouraged. Many persons converted to Mormonism in Europe had joined the colony in its earlier locations. Now thousands arrived at the new Zion in the wilderness, encouraged by Mormon missionaries in the Old World. The Mormons were soon aided by supplying the gold seekers on their way to California. Fresh horses, mules, and supplies were sold to those who went to the diggings by way of Great Salt Lake, and profits were high. In 1849, a constitution was adopted for the "State of Deseret," but Congress refused admission of the new state and organized the territory of Utah, a part of the Compromise of 1850. The practice of plural marriages prevented statehood until 1896. Laws passed in the meantime to suppress polygamy could not be enforced, but in 1890 the Mormon church at last declared that it no longer countenanced the practice.

California was also settled by Americans about this time. Early in the nineteenth century, the few Americans in Spanish California were deserters from New England trading ships calling along the coast, factors representing eastern shipping interests, and itinerant fur traders. Beginning in 1840 small groups on the westward moving frontier, especially in Missouri and Arkansas, began to make plans to cross the plains and mountains to the Pacific coast. During the next few years several large expeditions crossed the Rockies bound for California. Soldiers and sailors went there during the Mexican war and many remained. The Treaty of Guadalupe Hidalgo made California American territory. Before the treaty was signed gold was discovered at Sutter's Fort (Sacramento), in January, 1848.

As more gold was discovered in scattered places along the Sacramento and San Joaquin Rivers and in the streams and creeks of that region, miners with picks, shovels, and tin pans feverishly sought the coveted metal. Thousands crossed the prairies from the East. Most of the early groups and companies organized for the westward trek at Fort Smith, Arkansas. During the years of the gold rush many thrilling and tragic stories were enacted on the way to the land of opportunity. Terrible desert heat, choking prairie dust, violent rains, tragic accidents, Indian attacks, hasty funerals and unmarked graves, fighting among the emigrants, abandoned property along the way, and singing and crude amusements at night around camp fires must be woven into the story of the overland trail to California. Farmers and businessmen from Oregon flocked southward, and the Oregon migration was deflected to California.

A second route from the East to California, preferred by those who did not wish to face the dangers and terrors of the overland trip and had the money to pay their passage, was the long sea voyage around Cape Horn in clippers or in slower ships. Other routes were those by steamer to Panama, across the deadly isthmus by foot or on horseback, later by railroad, and then by ship to California, or the same combination by way of the isthmus of Nicaragua. Soon the population grew so large that California became a state as a part of the Compromise of 1850.

CHAPTER 8

The Corporation and Transportation

The central feature of industrialism is mass production, and this, in turn, requires large markets for the goods. In some regions, particularly the Far East, potential customers are tightly packed together, but they lack the money with which to buy. In contrast, in the United States the customers could afford to buy; they had a surplus to exchange, but they were widely scattered. Economical inland transportation, therefore, was essential to the development of the United States as an industrial nation.

Economists call the devices that facilitate production and distribution, such as schools, port facilities, roads, bridges, canals, railroads, telegraph, and later, electric power and light "social overhead capital." It is the investment necessary to allow the industrial machine to function. The general geography of the United States, and particularly the Appalachian Mountains, required a relatively large investment in social overhead facilities, one that, aside from building construction, was the chief consumer of capital during the nineteenth century.

Some forms of social overhead capital, such as improvement of harbor facilities, were regarded as suitable only for government investment. Small-scale operations of the social overhead type, such as schools, could be easily supplied by either private or public funds, but the really large works needed for long distance inland transportation have in most nations appeared too risky and slow in return to be undertaken by private capital alone. There is a paradox that at the stage of development when such works are most needed capital is scarce and commands high rates. When one can invest in trade, real estate, or finance and get reasonably sure returns of 8 or 10 per cent, there is small incentive to invest in transportation that will take years to complete and may never pay large returns. In fact, most of the economic gain from an improvement in transportation comes in such forms as increased land values in which the transport company does not share. Hence the state is almost always called upon to assist in constructing the costlier additions to social overhead capital.

THE CORPORATION

In 1792 no single American would have considered investing the half million dollars necessary to complete the Philadelphia and Lancaster turnpike, a toll road only 66 miles long. Few Americans could have produced that much money for any purpose. The private side of such investments in transportation had to be organized through use of the corporation.

While the earliest colonizing efforts were by British corporations, the form was little used for routine business ventures. Parliament was opposed to granting power to corporations except for government, as in the case of towns and cities, or semi-public purposes. It was never altogether certain that the colonial assemblies had the power to grant charters for business purposes, and in that period the demand for large capital was rare. In a few instances the assemblies established corporations for nonprofit institutions, and for water, insurance, and wharves. Most colonial "companies" were not corporations, but joint-stock associations. While these were prohibited in England, no one interfered with groups of colonists contributing capital to a common fund and operating such an enterprise. Shares were saleable, but there was no charter or recognition by the state. If the enterprise failed, all participants were liable for all the debts.

Most of the thirteen new states readily granted corporate charters for developmental and nonprofit purposes. By 1800 over 300 corporations had been created, chiefly for providing social overhead capital, but including some 30 banks and about the same number of insurance

companies. Meanwhile, England and France the leading business nations had each only a score or so of corporations. Obviously the corporate form particularly suited the United States.

What factors had led to this rapid and continued rise of the corporation? To begin with, it was easier to get a charter from a small
state legislature than from the British Parliament or the French
bureaus. Since each state felt itself to be in economic competition
with its neighbors, granting charters to develop the back country and
subscribing to the corporate shares were matters of local patriotism.
Perhaps Americans are, as foreign observers have said, natural "joiners"
who like to associate themselves in community causes. The chance
for increasing returns in a rapidly growing country gave Americans
a well-founded optimism regarding investment. While no prosperous
citizen would risk most of his fortune in a turnpike or canal, many
would gamble the price of a few shares of stock, especially if the
investor also owned land or business properties that would be benefited.

Between 1783 and 1850 most characteristics of the twentieth century corporation appeared in, at least, primitive form. Gradually limited liability was written into charters and upheld by the courts—no
one could lose more than his stock. General laws were passed in the
leading industrial states making it unnecessary to have legislative
action on certain types of charters. Massachusetts led with a general
law for chartering water companies in 1799, New York for manufacturing in 1817, and Michigan for banking in 1837, but general incorporation did not spread to most of the states until the period from
1850 to 1875. Meanwhile, the Supreme Court had ruled: that a
charter was a contract with the state (Dartmouth College *vs.* Woodward, 1819); that unless specifically prohibited by law, corporations
could do business in other states (Bank of Augusta *vs.* Earl, 1839);
and in later years that corporations were "persons" within the
equal privileges and immunity clause of the Fourteenth Amendment (Paul *vs.* Virginia, 1869); and, that corporations could not be
deprived of property by state law without having the action reviewed
as to its substantial justice by the Federal courts (Southern Pacific
Railroad *vs.* San Mateo County, 1883).

Initially the corporation was conceived of as a democratic body
in which the shareholders annually elected directors who, in turn,
hired the necessary managers. To emphasize the importance of the
individual owner some charters provided for one vote for each share
up to a certain number, such as five, and less votes per share for

larger holders. This practice was soon given up, however, in favor of a uniform one vote per share. In any case, democracy proved unworkable. Small stockholders were uninformed regarding company affairs, busy with other matters, and often some distance from the place of meeting. From the earliest days the boards of directors of big companies tended to be self-perpetuating. The stockholders cast their ballots for the slate nominated by the existing leaders. If stockholders did not like the management their best recourse was to sell their shares.

The power of corporate directors over the management of other peoples' money opened the door to many abuses. Since the directors of large canal or railroad companies might own little stock in the enterprise they were directing, they could often profit by selling it properties at exorbitant prices, charging the corporation high rents for the use of personally owned land, buildings, or bridges, or contracting for new construction. Insiders could also speculate in the company stock on the basis of advance information. In all these ways fortunes could be made by ruining large corporations as well as by building them up. It took most of the nineteenth century even for conscientious directors to agree upon what was proper regard for the interests of the stockholders.

TURNPIKES AND IMPROVED HIGHWAYS

As the new nation arose, many stressed the importance of good roads as a means of binding the settlements together and as a necessity for national economic advancement. A few road companies received state charters for building and operating improved roads. However, it was an eastern Pennsylvania road that introduced the era of turnpike building and the improvement of roads. In 1791, a number of prominent Philadelphians organized the Society for the Improvement of Inland Navigation to rival the Potomac Company. Promoted by George Washington in 1785, the Society proposed to develop a system of transportation between the Potomac and the Ohio Rivers. As a result of the labors of the Pennsylvania group, the Philadelphia and Lancaster Turnpike Company was chartered by the state to build a sixty-six mile road connecting Lancaster with Philadelphia. It was completed during the years 1792–1794 at a cost of $465,000. At first, stones of all sizes were used in paving the road, but when it was found that "drivers kept biting their tongues and bobbing up and down like jumping jacks," stones that would pass through a two-inch ring were used and the entire road was overlaid with gravel. Travelers called it a masterpiece of engineering. The road was built on a plan similar to the roads of the Scotch engineer, MacAdam, and had excellent drainage. In the "macadamized" roads of that period a tar binder was not used; this method was a much later development. A number of tollgates were distributed along the course of the Lancaster turnpike and all vehicles using it were required to pay a fee at every gate. Almost immediately, as freight wagons, stagecoaches, and ordinary vehicles used the road, the company made excellent profits on its investment and encouraged similar projects in other regions.

A mania for building turnpikes followed the opening of the Philadelphia and Lancaster turnpike. By 1811, New York had granted charters to 137 companies whose capital totaled $7,500,000. New England states, by the same year, had chartered about 200 companies, having a capitalization of $5,000,000. By the 1820's so many eastern turnpikes had been built that competition was ruining profits and the companies started selling the roads to the states. For some years states such as Pennsylvania, which had spent $37,000,000 for 2,500 miles of turnpike by 1838, continued to build, but the depression following the panic of 1837 generally ended turnpike construction. In the southern and western states, also, many turnpike companies were granted charters, although throughout this period the development of the West was continually hampered by a lack of good roads. The increase in turnpikes required the building of a large number of bridges. Some of the new companies built their own, but separate companies were often organized to build and keep up bridges, from which they derived a revenue by charging tolls. Many ferry companies were also formed as the necessity for them increased.

About the middle of the nineteenth century plank roads were built. Between 1848–1850, twenty-four companies in Alabama alone were chartered for building such roads. Although most were built by private companies, some states undertook to build their own, collecting tolls as did the companies. The chief purpose of plank roads was to connect villages and towns with the nearest railroad centers, although in some regions, especially the South, they were designed to compete with the railroads. When in good repair, these roads, constructed of planks about ten feet long and three or four inches thick, were excellent, but when the planks were worn or warped, the roads were rough. They were always expensive to maintain. While a few plank roads persisted down to the beginning of the twentieth century, railroad development gradually crowded them out of existence. Another type of road, found especially in the rising West, was the corduroy road, so called because it was ribbed and rough. This road was built over low or boggy ground, especially where the ordinary filling of earth would not stand up. Logs were laid side by side and, above these, another layer was laid crosswise, the interstices usually filled with dirt and gravel. A few corduroy roads still exist in remote sections of the country, bearing witness to a bygone age.

As turnpikes and new roads were built by both private and public capital in the early nineteenth century, many improvements took place in the mode of travel. Coach service grew more rapid and frequent, as additional routes were established. Rival transportation companies not only sought to outdo each other in speed, but also in accommodations. Stagecoaches were made larger and more comfortable. These reached their height in the Concord coach, with its brilliant decorations and silk upholstery, accommodating as many as nine passengers inside and one or two beside the driver on the very high seat outside. These famous American coaches were manufactured by Abbot, Downing and Company, of Concord, New Hampshire, who began business in 1813, and by 1860 had the largest factory of its kind in America, supplying Mexico, South America, Australia, and other foreign countries, as well as all parts of the United States. There were also many similar, though smaller, factories in the United States.

Many stagecoach lines became important, and to a certain extent monopolistic, because of their better service and greater comfort. Among the outstanding companies of the period were the National Road Stage, June Bug, Good Intent, Pioneer, and Stockton lines. On the most important highways, the larger companies ran both the rapid "limited" coaches carrying mail and a few passengers at high fares, and also "accommodation" coaches, which stopped more frequently and permitted stopovers at taverns for the night. As travel increased, hostelries along the highways also offered improved accommodations. Many landlords were partners in transportation companies or had an interest in them. By the middle of the century, stagecoach travel was declining in the older states of the East as the spreading network of railways connecting the towns and cities broadened, and the lines became more closely knit. In the West, however, the stagecoach served for many more decades, but the transcontinental railroads marked the beginning of the end of this mode of travel.

THE GOVERNMENT AND
INTERNAL IMPROVEMENTS

As the turnpike movement got under way early in the nineteenth century, a demand developed for road improvements planned and financed by the Federal government, but the question of the constitutional right of Congress to appropriate money for such internal improvements prevented much help. In addition to aiding the construction of some smaller roads, Congress did build one important road during this period, the Cumberland Road, often called the United States or National Road. At the beginning of the century, the deteriorating Braddock's Road, from the Potomac to the Monongahela, and the overburdened Forbes' Road, from Philadelphia to Pittsburgh, were used by streams of emigrants on their westward trek. It was evident that better roads to the West were essential.

When Ohio was admitted as a state, it was agreed between the new state and the Federal government that a small percentage of the proceeds from the sales of public lands within Ohio should be used for building a highway from the Atlantic to the state of Ohio. In 1806, Congress passed a law for the necessary appropriation and for the marking and construction of the road which was to begin at Cumberland, Maryland, since there were roads from the coast to that point. It took some time to make surveys and secure rights of way. Pennsylvania was slow to grant permission chiefly because Philadelphians were afraid that Baltimore would get much of the western trade then passing through Philadelphia. The way was clear by 1811, and construction was begun. By the close of the War of 1812, only twenty miles had been completed. Then rapid progress was made; in 1818, the road was opened as far as Wheeling, Virginia. The route in most places followed many older trails and roads, including Braddock's Road. Congress voted funds for the continuance of the road through Ohio, Indiana, and Illinois, but it was completed through the last two states after the Federal government had relinquished its control. The last important Federal appropriation for it was made in 1838, although a small sum to survey the road to Jefferson City, Missouri, was provided in 1844.

The Federal government gave up its control of the road because of the constitutional argument in Congress. A few years after the road had been completed to Wheeling, Congress passed a bill for the establishment of tollhouses along the route to provide for the collection of revenue to keep the road in repair. President Monroe vetoed the measure (1822). Like his predecessors in office, he recommended an amendment to the Constitution granting Congress the power to build and maintain roads (p. 187). Later, money was appropriated for repairs and even for extending the road. After it was turned over to the states through which it passed—Maryland, Pennsylvania, Virginia, and Ohio, tollhouses in some cases were erected by the states. The road from Cumberland to Vandalia, Illinois, a total length of 600 miles, was completed about the middle of the century. The Federal government had appropriated altogether $7,000,000 for its building and for repairs.

The Cumberland Road for most of its length was from sixty-eight to eighty feet wide and was macadamized in the center to a width of thirty feet. Its foundation consisted of about a foot or more of crushed rock, with gravel laid on the surface. The center of the road was raised to bring it well above each side, where a shallow trench of large flat stones set on end provided drainage. Stone culverts and bridges carried the road across gullies, creeks, and streams. Much of the work was done by Irish immigrants. The cost of building the road from Cumberland to Wheeling was about $13,000 a mile, a high price for that period.

The importance of the Cumberland Road during the first half of the nineteenth century cannot be overestimated. It operated as a powerful factor in westward migration and in the establishment of new settlements, as well as aiding the growth of Wheeling and other towns. By the middle of the century no other post road did so much business. A constant procession of Conestoga wagons drawn by four, six, or eight horses carried large quantities of supplies westward and brought agricultural and other products to the Atlantic coast. As freight traffic increased, rates dropped. Travelers marvelled at the large number of four-horse stagecoaches that traveled over the road. The time of travel from Baltimore to Wheeling was reduced from eight to three days. As taverns along the road increased in number and improved in accommodations, many became the nucleus for villages and future towns. These taverns at night housed farmers, businessmen, travelers, and wayfarers, and their adjoining yards and pens cared for horses, mules, cattle, hogs, and sheep, which were on their way to western farms or to eastern markets. The road was a veritable stream of life. In addition to stimulating the economic development of the country, it contributed greatly to the growth of population in the West as the Monongahela gateway for a time became the most important of the westward routes.

During the first three decades of the nineteenth century, the insistent demand, especially from the West, that the Federal government develop systems of roads and canals and appropriate large sums of money for all sorts of internal improvements, resulted in a continual controversy in Congress. The first comprehensive plans were projected during the Presidency of Jefferson at the time of the beginnings of the Cumberland Road. The opposition, largely but not entirely from members of Congress from the Old South, prevented many programs from being projected and held back Federal aid.

In 1806, Jefferson, apprehensive because a government surplus was increasing, suggested to Congress that money from the "overflowing treasury" could "be applied in time of peace to rivers, canals, roads, arts, manufactures, education, and other great objects within each state." He stressed, however, his belief that an amendment to the Constitution was necessary to authorize the expenditure of money for purposes which were not enumerated in the grant of powers. The recommendation was followed, not by an amendment but by a Senate resolution requesting Albert Gallatin, Secretary of the Treasury, to make a survey for the consideration of Congress. In 1808, Gallatin made his report in which he outlined a comprehensive system of canals and roads for construction by the Federal government. His able program suggested a series of Atlantic coastal canals from Massachusetts to the Carolinas; roads and improved waterways between the eastern coast and the midwestern rivers, as well as communication with the St. Lawrence and the Great Lakes; and interior roads and canals. Although the plan was both highly praised and bitterly denounced, nothing was done to carry out the proposals; the embargo and the non-intercourse acts had cut down Federal income and dissipated the surplus. Not until the close of the War of 1812 was the question of Federal aid for internal improvements seriously considered again in Congress.

The War of 1812 demonstrated the need for better communications, especially in the West and the outlying regions of the North. In his first annual message after the war, Madison advocated the necessity for Federal activity in this realm. He pointed out that the prosecution of the war was hampered by a lack of good roads and that the development of the West laid a new stress on communication and transportation as bonds of union. However, like Jefferson, he reminded Congress of the necessity for an amendment. Congress did not respond immediately, and Madison found it necessary to repeat his recommendation the next year. Late in December, 1816, John C. Calhoun, as chairman of a committee appointed for the purpose, introduced a bill to set apart as a permanent Federal fund for internal improvements, the $1,500,000 bonus exacted from the newly-chartered Second Bank of the United States as the price of its charter, together with all dividends and profits the United States would receive from the $7,000,000 of the bank's stock owned by the government. The bill became known as the "Bonus Bill." In the debates in Congress, those who favored the proposal argued that the clauses in the Constitution giving Congress the right to establish post roads, to support armies, and to regulate commerce, as well as the general welfare clause, justified such an act. While the strict constructionists objected strenuously, a majority vote was obtained in both houses. But Madison, familiar with the intentions of the framers of the Constitution, was not moved by the eloquent arguments of Calhoun and others, and vetoed the bill at the close of his administration, still insisting that an amendment to the Constitution was necessary.

James Monroe, who succeeded Madison to the Presidency, was in harmony with the views of his two predecessors. In his first inaugural address he referred to roads and canals as among the most important considerations of the period, but warned Congress of his constitutional scruples. Although Henry Clay continually emphasized Federal aid to roads and canals, and embodied it in his American System, which included protective tariff and internal improvements as well as free western lands to build up American enterprise, no amendment appeared. In 1818, at the request of the House, Calhoun, Secretary of War, submitted a report which outlined a system of internal improvements with national defense as the chief objective, but no attempt at legislation followed.

In 1822, the problem of the upkeep of the government-owned Cumberland Road was before Congress. A measure was passed for the collection of tolls to be used in the upkeep of the highway, but Monroe vetoed it on the grounds that the administration of it and the punishment of violators of the law by the Federal government would be an infringement of the rights of states. Two years later, a General Survey Bill was enacted, authorizing the President to have army surveys made of routes for any roads and canals he deemed of national importance. Monroe believed that this measure was within the powers of the government and signed it. In the case of all bills relating to general plans of internal improvements passed by Congress during this period, the opposition came chiefly from the Old South and also from New England which feared that the growing West would depopulate the older region and that it would lose its political, social, and economic power.

During the administration of John Quincy Adams many small subsidies and even land donations were made for internal improvements, chiefly for improved waterways, some of them in the South. Increasing appropriations were made for rivers and harbors and the "pork barrel" laws of later days began to appear in shadowy outline. In the long struggle over internal improvements, the Maysville Road veto was an important episode. In 1830, Congress passed "A Bill Authorizing a subscription of stock in the Maysville, Washington, Paris, and Lexington Turnpike Company." Andrew Jackson, although an ardent nationalist, vetoed the measure, stating that the project lay entirely within one state and that only works of national and general importance should receive Federal aid. The difference between a local and a national road, however, was not made clear. In spite of the veto, appropriations by Congress for canals, roads, rivers, and harbors continued at about the same rate as during the administration of John Quincy Adams. More liberal land donations had been made under Adams, but relatively lavish appropriations were made for improvements during the eight years that Jackson lived in the White House. The controversy that had been waged for a generation prevented the

The Maysville Turnpike, Kentucky

development of a complete governmental system like that suggested by Gallatin and was responsible for the failure of a definite policy as planned by Calhoun.

INLAND WATERWAYS

During the latter part of the colonial period, an interest developed in canal planning, stimulated by a new era of canal building in England about the same time. Suggestions were made in the 1760's by the American Philosophical Society for building canals to connect important waterways, especially in the regions of Pennsylvania, Delaware, and Maryland. Plans were also discussed in different parts of the country for canals around the falls of rivers flowing into the Atlantic, for the falls rendered the Piedmont region less accessible to sea-going commerce than the tidewater area. About the same time, the need of a direct waterway connecting Cape Cod Bay with Buzzards Bay was recognized and a survey was made, although more than a century elapsed before work was actually begun on this project. Between the Revolution and the end of the century many small canals were projected and completed. Among these were the canal around the falls of the Connecticut River near present Holyoke; the canal from Richmond to Westham around the falls of the James River; the Dismal Swamp Canal, and many others. Most of these projects were local in character.

As the canal era got under way, the great Erie Canal was projected. In the last two decades of the eighteenth century Elkanah Watson had stressed the possibilities of a canal from the Hudson River through the Mohawk Valley to the Great Lakes. Others shared his vision of such a great waterway. Among these was De Witt Clinton who pointed out that the project would benefit the state of New York and also the expanding country as a whole. In 1810 a State Canal Commission composed of leading citizens said that "by tests of efficiency, economy, and financial capacity private enterprise was incapable of building the Erie and Champlain Canals." [1] Delayed by the war it was not until 1817 that the New York legislature finally authorized raising about $7,000,000 on the credit of the state for the Erie and Hudson-to-Lake Champlain canals. The funds for the indebtedness and interest charges were obtained from legislative appropriations, private donations, lotteries, and taxes on auction sales, salt, and certain Hudson River steamboat fares. After the canal was completed, tolls were collected

[1] Quoted from Nathan Miller, *The Enterprise of a Free People* (Ithaca: Cornell University Press, 1962), p. 32.

and applied to the indebtedness. Ten years of tolls paid its cost and for a long period of time the state of New York enjoyed a large income from the profits of the canal.

Digging the Erie Canal was accomplished in a period when there were no giant steam or electric shovels to assist in the task. The work, done largely by hand labor, was a remarkable feat. Engineers like Benjamin Wright, James Geddes, and Canvass White overcame tremendous obstacles and completed a canal 363 miles long, over a land rise of 500 feet, accomplished through eighty-three locks. Across the route of the canal lay the Montezuma Swamp. The canal was dug through by doing the work in winter when the bog was frozen solid. In many places, the canal had to be cut through dense forests. The resourceful engineers designed a special plow with a sharp edge to cut through the spreading and tangled roots of the forest trees. They devised special machines of drums and cables to pull down trees and uproot stumps. But only human and horse power were used to remove the soil and only black powder was used for blasting rock which had to be drilled with hand drills. The quick-lime mortar for the masonry of the locks gave way to a new "hydraulic cement," and for this purpose suitable "cement rocks" were discovered by White at Fayetteville, New York. After many experiments, he obtained a patent for making cement and has been called the father of the cement industry in America.

While the first section of the canal between Rome and Utica was finished and used in 1819 and more sections followed, the entire canal was opened with appropriate ceremonies in 1825. Governor Clinton, the canal commissioners, and other officials, after much speechmaking in Buffalo, left on the *Seneca Chief* and a number of other gaily bedecked and garlanded canal boats for the Hudson River. Two kegs of Lake Erie water were taken along to be poured into the Atlantic at New York. Symbols of the West, including two Indian boys, two eagles, two fauns, and a bear were also on the boats. As the parade of boats started, cannon, which had been placed along the route, were fired in rapid succession until the sounds reached New York City. The boats were drawn slowly between the banks, thronged at many places with spectators. A few days later they arrived in the Hudson and were towed by steamboat to Sandy Hook where the kegs containing the water from Lake Erie were emptied into the Atlantic together with small quantities of water from the Mississippi, Columbia, Thames, Seine, Rhine, Danube, Amazon, La Plata, Orinoco, Ganges, Indus, Gambia, and Nile. Dinners, parties, and balls followed and souvenir

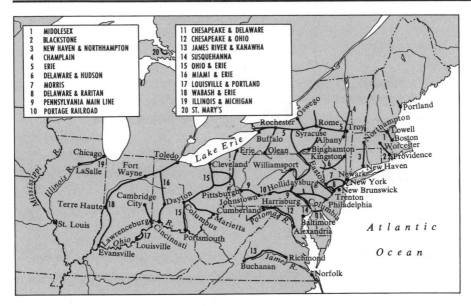

CANAL ROUTES IN THE LATE NINETEENTH CENTURY

medals were made for the gala occasions. The building of the canal had stirred the imagination of Americans, and the ceremonies and celebrations were worthy of the great achievement of "Clinton's Ditch."

The economic effects of the canal in the years that followed were far-reaching. The route lay chiefly through an uninhabited wilderness and the canal therefore speeded up the settlement of an immense territory. While many new settlements were established, the canal also contributed largely to the growth of New York, Buffalo, and intermediate places, as well as to the future great centers of Cleveland, Detroit, and Chicago. New York which had already outstripped Philadelphia, Boston, and Baltimore in population and wealth, was unrivalled as the leading metropolis of the United States. The canal became the great artery of passenger and freight traffic between the northeastern section of the United States and the newly-settled states and territories of the West. The time required for freight shipments from Buffalo to New York was cut down from twenty to six days and the costs from $100 to $10 a ton. The lower rates of transportation likewise reduced the cost of eastern manufactures to westerners. But many a New England farmer, adversely affected by competition with western farmers, left his unfertile and stony farm for the new mill town of his own region, or joined the ever-increasing tide of pioneers moving westward. Europe also felt the effects of the Erie Canal, for American

Upper village of Lockport, Niagara County, New York — 1836

grain from the West could be obtained more cheaply and easily. In England, the Anti-Corn Law League, a well-financed association which revolutionized England's fiscal system, argued that a British market for American wheat would encourage agriculture in the United States and prevent the growth of manufactures there, thus decreasing competition with British industry.

Even before the Erie Canal was completed, many regions became apprehensive over its effects on their western trade. In 1825, the Massachusetts legislature created a commission to consider the question of a canal from Boston to the Connecticut River and then to the Hudson near its junction with the Erie Canal. However, the topography of the region made the project impossible. Most seriously affected by the Erie Canal were Pennsylvania and Maryland. Pennsylvania's reply to the Erie Canal was the "Pennsylvania Public Works" system, a state-supported project, chartered in 1826, on which the first freight reached Pittsburgh from Philadelphia in 1834. The system consisted of a railroad from Philadelphia to Columbia, canals along the Susquehanna and Juniata Rivers to Hollidaysburg, then the Portage Railroad carried the line over the mountains to Johnstown, and from there a canal continued to Pittsburgh. Several subsidiary canals were also built. There were forty aqueducts, 111 locks, and two tunnels in the system, which by 1840 included 606 miles of canal and 118 miles of railroad. The system by this time had cost the state

$32,000,000, although the original estimate had been $5,000,000. The tolls did not pay the expenses and interest, but the system enabled this region to retain a large share of the western trade, which otherwise would have gone to New York. In 1846 the Pennsylvania Railroad was chartered to build a line paralleling the main canals from Philadelphia to Pittsburgh, the state imposing a tonnage tax on the railroad to protect its own transportation system. Owing to continued losses, the state sold its main system to the Pennsylvania Railroad, which shut down the Portage Railroad and, during the Civil War, abandoned the canal from Johnstown to Pittsburgh. The eastern section was turned over to a subsidiary corporation, the Pennsylvania Canal Company.

Maryland and Virginia's answer to the Erie Canal was an all-water route from the Chesapeake Bay to the Ohio—the Chesapeake and Ohio Canal. The project was the legal successor of Washington's Potomac Company and was begun jointly by the United States, Maryland, and Virginia. It was planned to construct locks and canals around the rapids and falls of the Potomac from Georgetown to Cumberland, and then across the mountains to the Youghiogheny River, a tributary of the Monongahela. Work was begun in 1828, but the canal did not reach Cumberland until 1850. The plan failed because of the great cost and the engineering problems of such a task, and especially because of competition from the Baltimore and Ohio Railroad, which reached Wheeling in 1852. The section of the canal that was completed has continued down to the present as a local enterprise along the Potomac River.

The decades of the 1820's and 1830's saw a tremendous amount of canal building all over the country, but most of it in the North and West. Some states like Illinois and Pennsylvania engaged in elaborate systems of internal improvements. By 1861, $188,000,000 had been invested in canals and improved waterways, a tremendous debt for a country that was relatively sparsely settled. Seventy-three per cent of the money came from local and state governments, but they, in turn, sold securities to domestic and foreign investors and local bankers. Baring Brothers of England and Hope Company of Amsterdam led European financial houses in selling state bonds abroad. But excessive loans were made for waterways which could never be financially successful for as the population grew so did the railroad net. Speculation and overexpansion in internal improvements led to disaster and were factors that helped to produce the Panic of 1837. A number of states, including Indiana, Maryland, Pennsylvania, and Illinois, defaulted on their canal debts during the years of depression.

After the panic, canal building increased again, but more care was taken in projecting the plans, and states adopted a more conservative policy regarding their systems of internal improvement. Many important canals were opened, the one that became the most famous being the St. Marys Falls Ship Canal. This artificial waterway on the St. Marys River was built in 1855 by the state of Michigan to connect Lake Superior with Lake Huron. It was improved by the United States in 1870–1871 and was entirely taken over by the Federal government in 1880.

THE STEAMBOATS

While turnpikes and canals required large amounts of capital from the states, steamboats needing capital only in small units for each boat could rely on private financing. Only river and harbor improvements were asked of the states. In the beginning, however, with the steamboat an unproved innovation, the pioneer inventors had the usual trouble raising money.

Experiments in using steam power to propel boats began during the latter part of the Revolution. In the years that followed, many inventors applied their ingenuity to the problem. Among these were John Fitch, James Rumsey, Oliver Evans, Henry Voight, Arthur Donaldson, and William Thornton. While many of them contributed to early steam navigation, it was John Fitch who made the most important advances.

In 1786, Fitch organized a joint-stock company in Philadelphia and had an engine built and installed on a small boat to drive twelve oar-like paddles, six on each side. The next year Fitch demonstrated his queer-looking "water beetle" to a group of skeptical members of the Constitutional Convention. A few of them were persuaded to take a ride in it on the Delaware, but the trip was not very successful, for the boat traveled at a speed of only two and a half miles an hour

John Fitch's second steamboat

against the current and finally was grounded in the mud. However, during the summer of 1790, Fitch's new steamboat made daily trips between Philadelphia and Trenton, took excursion parties to Chester on Sundays, and made occasional evening trips up the Schuylkill. Engineering difficulties and failure to make any profits led to the withdrawal of Fitch's financial backers.

Most of the difficulties came from lack of a boat big enough to hold a more efficient engine, that is, from lack of capital. But propulsion by vertical paddles was also unsatisfactory. Fitch tried to overcome this last problem by experiments with a screw propeller, which, half a century later, proved to be the best solution. Unable to raise money to continue his experiments, Fitch committed suicide, a disappointed man.

More than a score of steamboats had been built and tried with ultimate failure before Robert Fulton successfully demonstrated his boat on the Hudson in 1807. Six years earlier he was in Paris trying to interest Napoleon in his invention of a submarine. In the French capital, he met Robert R. Livingston, the United States minister to France. The diplomat himself had earlier experimented with steamboats, and the two men decided that they would work together. Livingston financed the building of the *Clermont*, a 160-ton sidewheeler, 150 feet long, big enough to use profitably the heavy, low pressure steam engine. The English government had now relaxed its restrictions and permitted Boulton and Watt to ship the engine to America. The boat made the 150-mile run from New York to Albany in thirty-two hours. As a result of the first successful trip of the *Clermont,* or "Fulton's Folly," as some mocking skeptics referred to it, a regular passenger service was inaugurated, other steamboats were built, and a new era in river transportation was begun.

In 1811, a year of comet and earthquake, the first steamboat on what used to be called the "western waters" descended the Ohio and Mississippi Rivers. Built at Pittsburgh by Nicholas Roosevelt under Fulton-Livingston patents, the *New Orleans,* a side-wheeler of 116 feet left Pittsburgh on October 20, 1811, and after safely navigating the falls of the Ohio and surviving the New Madrid earthquake, reached New Orleans on January 10, 1812. The vessel was put into service between New Orleans and Natchez. The steamboat was added to the many different kinds of river craft, including bull-boats, bateaux, canoes, dugouts, Mackinaw boats, flatboats, keelboats, rafts, and barges. In time, the river steamboat became a most important means of moving the migrant to new lands and his produce to market. It transported his manufactured goods and supplies, the lumber that built his home, and the equipment used in the expanding railroads. It played a part in the building of the West and left its influence on the rising nation, for it affected even the manners and language of the people. The metaphors, "letting off steam" and "loaded to the guards," are reminiscent of the steamboat age.

During the earliest years of steamboat development, however, progress was slow. Engineering problems had to be overcome, especially the building of engines powerful enough to gain more speed in moving the boat upstream against strong currents. There were many tragic accidents as boilers exploded. Rivers had to be cleared of submerged rocks, shoals, snags, and fallen trees. But the monopolies granted by states to small groups were the chief obstacle to immediate steamboat expansion. As early as 1803, Fulton and Livingston, with Nicholas Roosevelt, received the exclusive right to navigate the waters of the state of New York. In 1811, the partners received a monopoly from Louisiana to navigate in the lower Mississippi. Other states also granted steamboat navigation rights to a limited few. From the very beginning, new operators attempted to infringe on the monopolies and litigation followed.

Fulton and Livingston had granted a license to Aaron Ogden to run a steam ferry between New York City and Elizabethtown, New Jersey. Thomas Gibbons operated boats over the same route, without any such franchise, although his boats were duly registered and licensed under the laws of the United States governing the coastal trade. Gibbons was enjoined by the state courts from continuing operations and carried his case to the Supreme Court. In Gibbons vs. Ogden, handed down by Chief Justice Marshall in 1824, the court smashed state-chartered monopolies of steamboat traffic and held that only Congress had power to regulate interstate commerce. The threatened return of strife among the states similar to that of Confederation days was ended, and the way was open for any man or group of men to engage in steamboat traffic.

Removal of monopolies, decreased cost of transportation, reduced time of travel, advances in engineering, and the three million dollars spent by the Federal government between 1822 and 1860 for improving traffic conditions on the Mississippi, Ohio, Missouri, and Arkansas Rivers, were factors that aided steamboat development. By 1846, about 1,200 steamboats were plying western waters and more than 10,000,000 tons of freight valued at over $400,000,000 were transported annually, about double the volume of American foreign commerce for the same year. By the time of the Civil War, steamboats were navigating more than forty tributaries of the Mississippi system; Pittsburgh, Cincinnati, and Louisville were the important Ohio ports, while New Orleans and St. Louis dominated the lower Mississippi. The gross tonnage of American steamboats in 1860 was 868,000 tons. By this time, captain-ownership of boats had been largely supplanted by large corporations such as those which owned or controlled the Cincinnati and Louisville Mail Line, the Anchor Line, or the Union Packet Line.

THE RAILROADS

Like canals, railroads needed large capital investments. For the first fifty years, 1830–1880, their development was a mixed private and public enterprise. Cities, counties, states, and the Federal government subscribed to stocks and bonds, remitted taxes and gave lands, but in most cases private interests controlled the voting stock and managed the companies.

The railroad had a long experimental pre-commercial period. During the last two decades of the eighteenth century, many Americans were experimenting with "steam carriages" or "steam wagons," the progenitors of the modern locomotive. Inventors, attempting to use steam to propel boats, also tried to apply it to land transportation. In 1786, Oliver Evans of Philadelphia asked the legislature of Pennsylvania for a monopoly of using "steam wagons" on the highways of that state, but was refused. He received patents in several states which granted him the right to operate his "Columbian," a steam vehicle. In 1804, he produced his strange "Orukter Amphibolos," designed to travel on land and water, and in the years that followed he made many contributions to engineering in the construction of new "Columbian" engines. Among other pioneers in this field was John Stevens of Hoboken, New Jersey, who in 1811, several years before Stephenson tested his first locomotive in England, suggested the practicability of a railway with steam engines and cars having flanged wheels. In 1815, he obtained a charter for a railroad, and five years later, he demonstrated on his Hoboken estate the first narrow gauge steam railway in America. This stimulated many other inventors, who by this time were convinced that rails would be necessary for steam trains.

Primitive wooden rails were used in the United States as early as 1795 at a Boston brick works and in the years that followed many other tramways were built, operated by gravity, horsepower, mulepower, or cable. They were generally used to haul heavy materials in and from quarries and mines. In 1826, the state of Pennsylvania, in the interest of its own system of transportation, sent William Strickland to England to study railroad development there. On his return he published a book, stressing British success with railroads and advocating them. This influenced the chartering of the Baltimore and Ohio Railroad and the South Carolina Canal and Railroad Company (Charleston and Hamburg Railroad) in 1827. Both at first used cars drawn by horses and also experimented with treadmills set in the middle of flat cars with seats for passengers or space for freight on each side, the horses treading the mills to make the car wheels go round. Both companies also tried to drive cars by the use of sails. In the meantime several small railroads attempted to use locomotives, notably the Delaware and Hudson Canal Company, which imported two English engines in 1829, one of them the *Stourbridge Lion*. However, the engines proved to be too heavy for the rails and trestles and were abandoned. It was in this year that George Stephenson and his son Robert demonstrated successfully their *Rocket* in England. In 1830, steam engines made in New York were installed on the Baltimore and Ohio Railroad and the Charleston and Hamburg, although many English-built engines were also used on early American railroads.

In the early 1830's short lines sprang up with surprising rapidity in different places along the eastern seaboard. In spite of opposition from various groups, of prejudice, and of engineering problems, rapid progress was made. By 1840, dozens of railroads had been chartered by the states and the railroad mileage of the country totaled 2,818 miles. By 1850, the railroad mileage had reached 9,021, and, by 1860, a railway web could be traced from the northeastern seaboard to the Mississippi Valley, and even in the South the skeleton of its system had been planned. During the two decades before the Civil War, the railroads competed with canals and emerged victorious, for from 1840 to 1860 railroad mileage grew from 2,818 to 30,600, while canal mileage increased only from 3,300 to 3,700. During this time the superiority of the railroad over the canal became evident. Canals frequently lacked water in periods of drought; at times they broke their banks; often they froze during severe winter weather; and travel on them was always slow. But the railroads had to pass through a painful period before they emerged victorious.

The railroads which spread their parallel rails from town to town, adversely affected turnpike and road companies, stagecoach and stage wagon interests. But as progress was made, the railroads provided a quicker and more flexible form of transportation. Produce and merchandise were sent by railway freight cars, and travelers took the rail-

The "West Point"
The locomotive "West Point" was built in New York City for the South Carolina Railroad and made the first excursion trip, as shown above, on March 5, 1831.

way passenger cars instead of the stagecoach. Toll receipts fell off, and many pikes and roads became public roads. The stagecoach and stage wagon disappeared in the East, but moved westward to regions that were more sparsely settled.

During their early years of development the railroads faced much opposition. Canal, turnpike, steamboat, bridge, and stagecoach companies did everything possible to oppose them, especially in those regions where the railroads were threatening competition. It should be noted that the rivalry was concerned not only with business itself but also with raising capital. Towns along the Erie Canal held mass meetings to oppose the grant of charters to railroads, and in a few parts of the country tonnage taxes were imposed on railroads. Highway tavern keepers added their voices to the chorus of opposition, and many farmers, whose barns or fields were set afire by the trail of sparks from early wood-burning locomotives, condemned them in no uncertain terms. Some farmers, also, believed that the new means of transportation might interfere with the market for horses, hay, and grain.

The rising railroads had to contend also with much ignorance and prejudice. Early trains were ridiculed by some who maintained that they could never be as dependable as stagecoaches, and in the beginning of railroad development a number of races took place between trains and stagecoaches. A distinguished group of Boston doctors gave ominous warning that the jars occasioned by traveling at such excessive speeds as fifteen or twenty miles an hour would lead to many cases of "concussion of the brain." In several parts of the country, school authorities refused the use of school buildings for meetings in the interest of railroads. For example, a school board in the progressive state of Ohio, replying to a request for the use of a schoolhouse for a debate on the value of railroads, wrote: "You are welcome to use the schoolhouse to debate all proper questions; but such things as railroads . . . are impossibilities and rank infidelity." Religious fanatics assured the public that an age of moral decay had set in, and even many sincere and sane citizens believed that the railroad was a device of the devil "to lead immortal souls down to hell." As the railroad net expanded, opposition and prejudice gradually disappeared.

Many engineering difficulties with engines, equipment, roadbeds, and tracks had to be overcome by the early railroads. Engineering had not progressed to a point where the strength of material could be

RAILROADS BEFORE THE CIVIL WAR

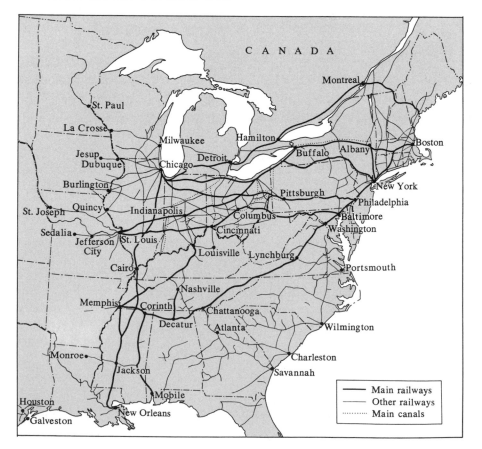

tested scientifically and, therefore, during these years when it was an empiric art, rather than an applied science, locomotives exploded when boiler plates refused to stand the strain of increased steam pressure and cylinder heads blew out with amazing regularity. Brakes, which first were only wooden blocks operated by a foot pedal, were gradually improved, but the air brake did not appear until after the Civil War. Cabs to protect the engineer were not used until the 1840's; chain couplings gave way to bars and finally to couplers and pins which allowed some play between cars. Cow catchers first were iron bars placed at the front of the locomotive to protect it by impaling large animals that crossed its path, but this device gave way to bumpers and later to the V-shaped protection. Patents were granted for flanged wheels, for devices to multiply tractive power, and for mechanical legs designed to assist trains uphill. The records of the patent office show that Americans were becoming skilled inventors in their own right. The first railroad passenger cars were built from ideas taken from contemporary stagecoaches, market carts, and Conestoga wagons. In Europe they remained short, but in America they grew rapidly in size and gradually assumed a box-like structure. During the early age of experimentation, open coaches were tried on a few railroads. But by 1850 the ultimate type of closed passenger coach with a center aisle and doors and platforms at the ends had emerged.

Among early railroad engineering problems, those relating to roadbeds and tracks were exceedingly difficult to solve. Limited finances resulted in quickly constructed roadbeds with dangerously sharp curves on many lines. But the hazards of such roadbeds soon proved that it was less expensive of money and life to construct them to withstand the strain of heavy rolling stock. To hold the rails in place wooden, iron, and even granite piles were tried, before the wooden cross tie was adopted. The earliest tracks were wooden rails with flat strips of strap iron secured to their upper surface to protect the wood from wear. The iron strips often became loose as a train passed over and curled up at the end, forming what was called a "snakehead," sometimes derailing the train and causing serious accidents. Because of these mishaps and the heavier and speedier trains which were soon rolling over the rails, heavy iron rails were imported from England. Until 1844, except for strap rails and a small amount of cast iron rails, all the rails used in the United States were imported. In that year the rolling of heavy iron rails in the United States was begun at the Mount Savage Rolling Mill in Maryland. Rails of the inverted U, or Evans type, and of the T type, designed by R. L. Stevens, son of John Stevens, the American inventor, were manufactured. Other rolling mills began producing heavy rails, but much railroad iron continued to come from abroad. Steel rails were not used until after the Civil War when the Bessemer process came into use. Another problem of the early railroads arose from the use of different gauges. The width between tracks varied from three feet, four inches, to six feet. The disregard for uniformity made it necessary for passengers and freight to change from one railroad to another, with inconvenience to passengers and increased cost of freightage. When Congress had to decide the gauge of the proposed Union Pacific Railroad during the Civil War, it decided on a width of four feet, eight and one-half inches, the English standard gauge. Later, American railroads rebuilt their tracks to conform to this gauge. The consolidation of the small lines into larger system, beginning in the 1850's, hastened this standardization.

About $1,250,000,000 was invested in railroads between 1830 and 1860. It was not easy to gain financial support for new enterprises because there was much competition for capital with the shipping, canal, and turnpike interests, and with growing manufacturing and industry. But businessmen, bankers, and manufacturers took the lead, and the money was usually forthcoming for new lines. Mass meetings were held to encourage the sale of railway stocks and bonds; enterprising chambers of commerce and boards of trade in many cities and towns did everything possible to publicize the advantages of railroads; and communities bought stock, granted subsidies, and remitted taxes. Europeans invested large sums in American railway securities. Even after the losses to European holders of American securities during the Panic of 1837, which included repudiation and default by several states, British, French, and German investors showed their faith in the future of America by investing heavily in American railroad securities.

In addition to financial encouragement from communities, towns, and cities, many states aided railroads and some even established their own. Georgia built a railroad across the mountains to Tennessee; Pennsylvania introduced some railroads in its state-owned system; Indiana and Illinois planned state railroads, and the former began building one; Michigan took over two private lines whose construction had stopped during the Panic of 1837, and, after operating them, sold them at a large loss to eastern capitalists. A number of states granted subsidies; most granted loans. Massachusetts and Ohio in the North, and Virginia, South Carolina, and other states in the South, subscribed for stock; and a few states guaranteed a part or all of a railroad's securities. State aid was also given by authorizing railroad corporations to issue paper money, redeemable at a future time, to pay for equipment and labor; states paid for surveys; and, grants of land were made. Many corporations looked to the Federal government for aid, but the constitutional argument, supported especially by the southerners in Congress, prevented direct assistance until the Civil War. However, a new policy was begun in 1850 when Federal land grants were made to states which in turn could give them to railroads. Largely through the efforts of Stephen A. Douglas, the Illinois Central Railroad received 2,595,000 acres of land in this manner. Then followed a veritable deluge of grants of public lands to railroads until the practice stopped in 1871.

THE TELEGRAPH

Experiments with the magnetic telegraph go back to eighteenth-century Europe, although attempts were made in America almost at the same time to send messages with the aid of the mysterious power, electricity, which absorbed the attention of many scientists and inventors, including the ingenious Franklin. While many Europeans and Americans made contributions to the development of the electromagnetic telegraph, it was Samuel F. B. Morse, a professor and portrait painter, who made practicable the sending of spaced impulses—dots and dashes— over highways of copper thread. In 1837, he gave a private exhibition of the telegraph. Lacking money, he and his friends appealed to Congress for financial aid. Several years passed before that body finally voted $30,000 for the construction of a forty-four mile line from Washington to Baltimore. On May 1, 1844, when the line had reached Annapolis Junction, the Whig nomination of Henry Clay was telegraphed from that point to Washington, reaching that city an hour before the train arrived with the news. This incident brought the possibilities of the telegraph to the attention of many congressmen.

Alfred Vail, the assistant of Morse, did much by his skill and knowledge to aid Morse in perfecting his instrument. Some people were of the opinion at the time that Vail and not Morse was the real inventor of the telegraph. But in a controversy between the two men over some of the patents, Morse's claims were sustained. Vail, however, did help improve the mechanical construction of the instrument. It was unfortunate that, as improvements appeared, much litigation arose, and the first decade of the telegraph was marked by unending lawsuits.

For months after the first message was sent, the line between Washington and Baltimore remained almost idle while the government debated whether to make the telegraph a governmental agency. Soon, however, private companies were organized; lines were extended to Philadelphia, New York, Pittsburgh, and elsewhere; and telegraph poles began to dot the American landscape. Ezra Cornell became the financial backer of a line built to Cleveland, Chicago, and Milwaukee. Henry O'Rielly, an Irish-born firebrand and a dynamic promoter, built 8,000 miles of line in the Middle West and South. Within a few years there were fifty companies in the United States. Consolidation began with the organization of the Western Union in 1856, which had grown out of earlier companies. By 1860, its lines reached from the Atlantic Ocean to the Mississippi River and wires were being strung across the prairies into the far West. Within a year the Western Union extended its system to San Francisco. By the eve of the Civil War, about 50,000 miles of telegraph had been strung over the country.

It is difficult today to realize the importance of the telegraph to those who lived during the mid-nineteenth century. The vision of such quick communication enchanted men, but its practical uses soon became apparent and were put to good service. Financiers, businessmen, and manufacturers could now communicate instantly with their representatives, agents, or customers, and the telegraph became an important factor in the rise of "big business." It was also invaluable to railroad development as the location of every train could now be known and traffic intelligently directed without confusion over a developing network of lines. Some railroads, like the Pennsylvania, constructed and operated their own telegraph lines.

The telegraph stimulated men to ponder other means of quick communication. Many bizarre patents were filed and plans were even made by an Atmospheric Telegraph Company to lay a tube two feet in diameter between New York and Boston to provide parcels with winged speed. But more important and in the end more practicable was the suggestion for the extension of the telegraph across the seas. In 1850, John Roebling wrote a series of newspaper articles on the practicability of a transatlantic cable. This finally became a reality through the work and perseverance of Cyrus W. Field of New York. In 1854, through his efforts the Atlantic Telegraph Company was organized and the cooperation of English capitalists was obtained. Both the British and American governments loaned ships for the undertaking. The first cable of 1857 broke, but the next year President

Buchanan and Queen Victoria exchanged greetings over the Atlantic cable. Within a few months, however, the cable again ceased to function and was not successfully laid until the end of the Civil War.

THE EARLIEST EXPRESS COMPANIES

Not long after the beginning of railroad development, the first express companies were established. It had been customary to send money and valuables from one place to another in the care of stagecoach drivers, ship or steamboat captains, and railway conductors. In 1839, William F. Harnden, a former conductor on the Boston and Worcester Railroad, became a special messenger between New York and Boston, carrying valuables and papers for businessmen and merchants of those cities. He found the business profitable; he soon employed others and opened offices in Philadelphia as well as in Boston and New York. Within a few years his business extended overseas. In the same year that Harnden began his special service, Alvin Adams, a produce merchant ruined by the Panic of 1837, worked out the same plan between Boston and Worcester. He became prosperous and organized Adams and Company, whose activities soon covered the East and penetrated the South. Reorganized later as the Adams Express Company with a capital of $1,200,000, it absorbed many competitors.

In 1850, after many express companies had sprung up, two of them operating in the Northeast—Wells, Butterfield and Company, and Livingston, Fargo and Company—united to form the American Express Company, capitalized at $150,000. Two years later, its chief incorporators, Henry Wells, William G. Fargo and associates organized Wells, Fargo and Company to function in the far West, which before the Civil War eliminated nearly all competitors in that area. It handled mails, goods of all sorts, gold, and silver in the region between the Mississippi Valley and the Pacific. By 1860, five large companies controlled most of the express business of the country: the Adams Express Company, the American, the United States, the National, and Wells, Fargo and Company.

THE TRANSPORTATION REVOLUTION

The period from 1815 to 1860 in American economic history has been called "the transportation revolution." Certainly the effects of the railroad and telegraph were profound. The innovating force of the railroad went far beyond the new management practices, engineering knowledge, and speed of transportation that it inevitably brought about. The new forms of communication penetrated deeply into the life of towns and cities; time became important in hours and minutes instead of weeks and days; merchants and financiers began to think in terms of the section and the nation rather than the town and county; the promoters of new developments enlarged the scope of their plans and dreamed of great commercial centers that were to arise at railroad junctions; and on a more immediate and humdrum level, mines, forges, and shop industries arose to supply the needs of the railroad. The principal railroads were necessarily big corporations with widely-held stock. As such they led to questions of division of interest between insiders and other stockholders, speculation in securities on a far greater scale than before, and, in short, the manifold problems of the modern corporation.

CHAPTER 9

Finance and Credit

Transportation systems, farms, factories, and other buildings were the real capital stock of the nation. As seen in the previous chapter the states, using the device of the corporation, aided private entrepreneurs in this investment. The present chapter will concentrate on the mechanisms such as government fiscal policy, banking, and stock and money markets that helped to allocate both public and private financial resources for economic use. Since the formation of capital could also be speeded up by foreign investment, a good financial reputation for the United States as a whole was an important asset.

ESTABLISHING THE CREDIT OF
THE NEW GOVERNMENT

The development of the government's fiscal policy fell largely into the hands of the able financier Alexander Hamilton, the first Secretary of the Treasury. Hamilton was well-equipped for his task, especially in his knowledge of the financial affairs of Britain and other foreign countries. He made recommendations to Congress which became the basis for the laws passed to restore the public credit and to stimulate general prosperity. Through his inspiration, the financial powers of Congress under the Constitution were shaped, the treasury became solvent, and the young Republic soon acquired a credit that few European nations enjoyed.

After taking office, the first concern of Hamilton was the indebtedness of the nation. In 1789, the United States owed $11,710,378 to foreign countires and $42,414,085 at home, including principal and interest. In a report to Congress, Hamilton proposed the payment of these debts at par by creating new certificates to be exchanged for the depreciated old ones. In addition, the new Secretary of the Treasury suggested that such Revolutionary war debts of the states as were still unpaid should be assumed by the Federal government. He believed that this action would bind the states into a unified loyalty to the central government. He recommended the creation of a sinking fund to stabilize the price of government securities and to provide for repayment of the principal. Most daring of any part of his report was the suggestion for a Bank of the United States, incorporated by Congress, which would provide much needed banking facilities for the government and the country as a whole. He favored an institution patterned after the Bank of England, but having branches in different parts of the country.

In Congress, all agreed that the foreign debts should be refunded in full, and a law was passed to this end, but here complete agreement ended. Opposition appeared when a measure for funding the domestic debt was considered. Bonds and certificates, representing the nation's debt from the time of the Revolution, had been selling below 25 per cent. Speculators had bought up many of the securities from the original holders at depressed prices. Payment at par would mean large profits for the speculators. In spite of opposition, and of benefiting the money-changers, the measure passed.

The proposal to have the Federal government assume the state debts brought tremendous opposition within the halls of Congress. Some of the states, like New York and Virginia, had reduced their debts considerably. The debt of Massachusetts was large, as was that of South Carolina. It was natural that the states with large debts and also those who held state securities should be impressed with the wisdom of Hamilton's proposal for assumption. The remonstrance of Virginia to the plan, drafted by Patrick Henry, caused Hamilton to say: "This is the first symptom of a spirit which must either be killed or will kill the Constitution of the United States." The failure of the measure in the House did not cause Hamilton to despair. Instead he skillfully worked out a plan to insure success. Jefferson had returned from Europe to take up his duties as Secretary of State. With Jefferson's assistance, Hamilton procured an agreement by which southern votes in Congress were to secure the assumption of state debts when the bill came up again, in return for northern votes to locate the national capital on the banks of the Potomac. This issue was a serious one at this time, for many different locations were being advocated including New York, Philadelphia, Trenton, Princeton, Baltimore, and the banks of the Susquehanna. The agreement between Hamilton and Jefferson went through as planned. Measures were passed for the assumption of the state debts and for location of the capital at Washington. Many years later, Jefferson lamented the fact that he had used his influence for assumption, stating somewhat unkindly that "the more debt Hamilton could rake up, the more debt for his mercenaries." The question of assumption had arisen in the Constitutional Convention, and it was therefore not an entirely new one. The real danger to men like Hamilton was the disintegration of the union.

The proposal for a central bank was made by Hamilton in a separate report in December, 1790. In it, he pointed out the need for such an institution together with its advantages. The proposal brought the defenders of states' rights to their feet. Even Madison, a member of the House, opposed it on constitutional grounds and called attention to the fact that the Constitutional Convention had rejected a proposal granting Congress specific powers to incorporate.

Hamilton defended this part of his program on the ground that a central bank could serve as a fiscal agent of the government, provide a depository for public money, regulate the currency, and assist in increasing active capital so necessary if commerce and manufacturing were to expand. For the first time in American history, he suggested that such an act of Congress would be constitutional on the basis of the implied powers of the Constitution, but each implied power must rest, he asserted, on expressed powers and in the "necessary and proper" clause. He also pointed out that Congress representing a sovereign state possessed "resultant" powers—those that any sovereign state could assume, and the right to incorporate was one of these. When Congress voted on the measure, it passed, and Washington signed it after much consideration and consultation with his cabinet.

The bank was chartered for twenty years and was capitalized at $10,000,000. The government could hold one-fifth of the stock and on that basis could appoint one-fifth of the directors. It was authorized to receive deposits, to make loans to individuals and to the Federal and state governments, to handle deposits and disbursements for the Treasury, to issue notes up to the amount of its capital and deposits, and to establish branches.

The establishment of a system of coinage and a mint was based on another Hamiltonian report. The Mint Act of 1792 created a mint in Philadelphia and established a bimetallic standard. The silver dollar was to contain 371 grams of silver, the content of the Spanish dollar. The ratio between gold and silver was set at fifteen to one. Owing to a scarcity of the precious metals, it was not until 1807 that the annual output of coins exceeded $1,000,000.

When the early customs duties failed to produce sufficient revenue, on the advice of Hamilton, Congress passed the Excise Act (1791), imposing taxes on distilled spirits and on stills. This resulted in hardships for the people of western Pennsylvania and the Virginia back country, who turned much of their corn into whiskey, the chief transportable western product, and the Federal government had to quell an insurrection by military force.

THE RISE OF BANKING

The excellent profits of the state-chartered banks opened in 1784 in New York and Boston, and the congressionally chartered Bank of North America in Philadelphia soon attracted scores of entrepreneurs to the business of banking. The new corporations with widely-held stock brought members of the leading merchant families together on their boards and strengthened the American financial community. By 1811 there were 88 banks receiving deposits and lending money in the form of engraved notes of various denominations. Since there were no generally agreed upon principles governing such lending, some banks loaned less than their capital and deposits and required good security, while others loaned two or three times the money they had received in stock subscriptions and deposits. In general, big city banks were able to observe reasonably safe, conservative practices, because their borrowers were chiefly financing operations in salable goods. But the banks located in smaller towns, which were the great majority, had to make loans secured by land and buildings which could not quickly be sold. Hence most of the banks were not in a position to redeem their notes in specie if uncertain times should lead people to prefer gold to paper. But, against this weakness, which caused many bank failures from 1807 to 1815, must be balanced the service the banks rendered by providing the currency and credit needed for rapid economic growth.

The First Bank of the United States, with its main office in Philadelphia and eight branches scattered throughout the country, was an important economic factor in the new banking community. During the twenty years of its existence (1791–1811), it stimulated business, manufactures, and commerce by providing additional financial facilities; it served the government in a most satisfactory way by acting as its fiscal agent; and it exercised a wholesome, though not always welcomed, influence on the rising state banks, especially in regulating their note issues by refusing to accept bank notes not redeemable in specie. In fact, its power was a basic reason for hostility toward it. In spite of its good work and manifest advantages, its charter was not renewed. Personal hostility to Secretary of the Treasury Gallatin who recommended that its life be extended, political jealousies and dissensions, the question of constitutionality, and opposition to the large number of foreign stockholders, resulted in the defeat by a single vote in both House and Senate of a bill for a new charter. The bank wound up its affairs and eventually paid shareholders $434 for each share of stock held.

The central bank was greatly missed in the war with England from 1812 to 1815. As the war began and the government found itself financially unprepared, it became more and more evident that a serious mistake had been made. In 1811, when the bank went out of existence, there were eighty-eight state banks; this number rose to 246 in 1816. Most states exercised little regulation over their banks, which enjoyed the right to issue bank notes with almost no restriction. By 1814, the expansion of bank note circulation, the disorders and depreciation of a large part of this currency, and the drain of specie to Europe, including the export of $7,000,000 which had been invested by Europeans in the First Bank of the United States, compelled banking institutions to suspend specie payments except in New England, where methods were more conservative.

With much difficulty the government financed the War of 1812, which cost altogether about $113,000,000. The tariff was doubled to secure much needed revenue. Bonds and treasury notes of various varieties were issued. Direct taxes—apportioned among the states— were assessed for the first time in the history of the Republic, and, in spite of much opposition, internal revenue taxes were imposed in 1813 and were repealed late in 1817. The disorders of the currency made government financing very difficult. John Jacob Astor of New York, Stephen Girard of Philadelphia, and other wealthy men formed syndicates to purchase war bonds which could only be sold well below par, and lacked a good public market.

THE SECOND BANK OF THE UNITED STATES

Before the war was over, proposals were made for a Second Bank of the United States and many who had opposed the First Bank now changed their views.

In 1814, on the recommendation of Secretary of the Treasury Alexander J. Dallas for a new central bank, Congress debated several proposed measures. Dallas pointed out the need for such an institution and stressed the necessity for it in rendering aid to the embarrassed treasury as well as in restoring a sane monetary system to the country. In 1815, a bank bill passed both Houses, but was vetoed by President Madison not on the grounds of its constitutionality but because he did not agree with all its provisions. The next year a bank bill sponsored by Astor and Girard and steered through the Senate by John C. Calhoun was passed. It followed the ideas suggested earlier by Secretary Dallas. Although Henry Clay, representing middle-western interests, had opposed a new charter for the First Bank of the United States, he now supported the measure. Leaving the Speaker's chair, he stated that he had been instructed by his state to vote against the recharter of the earlier bank, but that now the "force of circumstances and the light of experience" had changed his views and he was sure that the bank was needed. He agreed that Congress possessed the "constructive power" to charter it. Strangely enough, the Federalists in Congress, led by Daniel Webster of Massachusetts, were opposed, but the measure became law in April, 1816.

While the Second Bank of the United States had been able to force state banks to resume specie payments and, to a certain extent, to adopt more conservative methods, it did not prevent the financial crisis of 1819. Many factors were responsible for that disaster. Years of overexpansion of bank credit had encouraged speculation in land and commodities. A depression began in England in 1819, cutting down cotton orders as well as those for other American raw materials. In the United States the contraction of state bank currency and of credit initiated by the Second Bank of the United States pricked the bubble of inflation and brought about the collapse of business as prices of commodities tumbled. Cotton, for example, fell 50 per cent. Contributory to the causes of the panic had been the flood of foreign goods since 1816 with which American manufacturers had not been able to cope. The Federal government also experienced financial difficulties, as war taxes had been repealed before the depression began.

As financial distress increased and swept across the country, many banks suspended specie payments. The Second Bank of the United States was investigated by Congress and went through a process of financial rehabilitation. There was much distress everywhere as workers were thrown out of employment, banks became insolvent, business men were bankrupt, sheriffs' sales grew larger in number, and imprisonments for debt increased. Manufacturers held conventions and ascribed their distress to the need for adequate protection for home industry against the "cheap production, fraudulent invoices, long credit and unlimited sales at auction, whereby the country has been deluged with foreign merchandise." Petitions were sent to Congress asking for the abolition of credit on import duties and for increased protection on certain types of manufactures. But the bill of 1820, drafted while economic problems were still serious, failed. Debtors clamored for relief legislation, but without much success. The government did little except to revise the system for sale of public lands (p. 156). The depression was not quite so severe in New England as in other parts of the country because of a better banking and currency system, greatly diversified industry, and seafaring activities. By 1821, the effects of the depression were wearing off as prosperity returned.

The Second Bank of the United States was chartered for a period of twenty years. Its authorized capital stock was $35,000,000, one-fifth of which was subscribed by the Federal government. Its management was vested in a board of twenty-five directors, one-fifth of whom were appointed by the President of the United States. Its powers were in many ways similar to those granted to the First United States Bank. It could issue bank notes up to the amount of its capital stock and was required to pay specie on demand for both notes and deposits with a penalty of 12 per cent for failure to do so. It became the fiscal agent for the government, looking after its deposits without paying interest and transferring public funds without charging commission. In return for its charter it was required to pay the government a bonus of $1,500,000.

The main office, as with the earlier bank, was in Philadelphia. Branches were established at Baltimore, New York, Boston, New Orleans, and other cities in various parts of the country. Hostility to the bank appeared, especially during the financial crisis of 1819, when an unsuccessful attempt was made in Congress to revoke its charter. In several states, heavy taxes were imposed on the branches in the expectation of getting rid of them. The action of Maryland in this respect led to a famous case, McCulloch *vs.* Maryland (1819). In the Supreme Court decision, handed down by Chief Justice Marshall, the right of Congress to charter the bank was upheld and the law of Maryland, taxing the bank, was declared unconstitutional, for, Marshall pointed out, the power of a state to tax a creation of the Federal government was equivalent to the power to destroy it. The western states, especially, opposed the decision. The *Kentucky Herald* commented:

"This monster of iniquity is to be saddled upon us. We are to be taxed by a corporation unknown to the Constitution and known to us only by its oppressive and vindictive acts. . . . If the bank may tax us without our consent, . . . and if these branches are to be free from State taxation, we had better give up our Constitution and return to the condition of a Territory."[1]

While the first president William Jones had not tried to check the credit inflation of 1818 and early 1819, under Langdon Cheves who became president in 1819 and Nicholas Biddle who succeeded him in 1823 the bank was well managed. It stabilized the currency system and exerted a conservative influence on the entire banking structure of the country. But it did not possess the power of a modern central bank to control credit.

When Andrew Jackson became President in 1829 he assailed the bank and, in spite of the Supreme Court decision, raised the question of its constitutionality. In reply to a letter from Biddle asking his views, Jackson stated that he was no economist or financier, but that he was afraid of all banks since he had read the history of the South Sea Bubble; he also questioned the right of Congress to charter a bank outside the District of Columbia. Greatly miscalculating public opinion regarding the bank, Jackson's enemies made recharter an issue in the campaign of 1832. Urged by Clay, Webster, and even some Calhoun adherents, Biddle formally applied to Congress for a recharter although the old one would not expire for four years. The measure providing the bank with an extension of life for ten years passed both houses of Congress by small majorities. Those who opposed Jackson were sure that he would veto the measure, thus providing an issue which they expected would defeat him in the election of 1832.

As was anticipated, Jackson vetoed the bank bill and returned it to Congress with a vigorous veto message, intended to be a campaign document. He struck a popular chord when he emphasized that the bank was a monopoly, enjoying the special favor of government at the expense of the public. He stressed his belief that some of its powers and privileges were "unauthorized by the Constitution, subversive to the rights of the States, and dangerous to the liberties of the people." He rejected the finality of the opinion of the Supreme Court as to the constitutionality of the bank. He attempted to arouse national spirit against the bank by pointing out that foreigners held much of its stock, which in time of war would make it "an internal enemy." Finally, he

[1] Quoted by J. B. McMaster, *History of the People of the United States* (New York, 1903), IV, 505.

Plain sewing done here
(symptoms of a locked jaw)

appealed to the masses—for whom the document was really intended—
by calling attention to the age-old conflict between despotic wealth
and honest poverty and stressing the idea that: "Many of our rich
men have not been content with equal protection and equal benefits,
but have besought us to make them richer by act of Congress."

The re-election of Jackson and a majority of his followers to Congress sealed the doom of the Second Bank of the United States. Despite
all that the opposition to Jackson, including Biddle, could do, the hero
of New Orleans was still the idol of the masses, and the ending of the
bank was in harmony with the philosophy of the West. Biddle and his
friends, however, refused to accept the verdict of the election as final,
for to close up the business of the bank and its branches by 1836 would
mean the calling in of a mass of loans and the withdrawal from circulation of much bank currency, as well as the removal of government
deposits, which it was believed could not be done at once without
causing disaster. Biddle, therefore, was still hopeful and believed that
in order to avert this calamity, Congress would pass a bill extending

the bank's charter even over the President's veto. But Jackson, fully aware of the situation, resolved to withdraw the government deposits gradually so that they could be finally suspended altogether without an economic shock, and he believed that three years were sufficient for the bank to wind up its affairs without hurting the financial system of the country.

Since Secretary of the Treasury W. J. Duane, appointed for the purpose, refused to order the removal, he was dismissed by Jackson and replaced by Roger B. Taney, who carried out the President's wishes. The "removal of the deposits" consisted in ordering the fiscal agencies of the government not to deposit any more funds in the United States Bank. Government funds on deposit in the bank (about $6,000,000) were to be checked out gradually until no more remained. All new funds were to be deposited in the designated state banks, called "pet" banks. When Congress met in December, 1833, it received a large number of petitions from businessmen and others asking that the order be rescinded.

Jackson and Taney also reported their action to Congress, declaring that they believed the bank unsound. A bitter partisan fight followed between the friends of the bank and its enemies. All that resulted, however, was the adoption of resolutions of censure against Jackson and Taney in the Senate, and a few years later these were expunged from the record. Thus Jackson in his fight with the bank was completely victorious. Biddle obtained a state charter for the United States Bank of Pennsylvania, which continued the private business of the bank until 1841, when it became insolvent chiefly because of the depression.

DEPRESSION, 1837–1843

The Panic of 1837 was the most severe financial and industrial disturbance experienced up to that time. It was followed by a series of depressions and partial recoveries which continued until 1843. Its causes were complex. Rapid investment in social overhead capital and overexpansion of credit were largely responsible. Land speculation in the West was an upsetting factor. Much of the money used in such speculation was borrowed, especially from "wild-cat banks," which were increasing rapidly in number. Canal and railroad building by states and private companies, and the expansion of industry rapidly increased total indebtedness to a point where it was difficult to raise more capital. The increasing use of luxuries by an ever-growing portion of the population increased the payments owing to England for imports. High protectionists found an important reason for the panic in the declining tariff—a debatable question, of course.

Several events precipitated the crisis. In 1834 an attempt was made by the government to change from a paper to a gold currency. The coinage acts of 1792 and 1793 made the ratio of gold and silver one to fifteen, but the market ratio of the two metals until 1833 had been about one to 15.6. This kept gold at a premium, with the result that it could not be kept in circulation. In 1834, therefore, the change in the ratio of coinage to one to sixteen encouraged the minting of gold. A new mint, with its machines operated by horsepower, was set up and every encouragement given to develop a coinage system. For example, an attempt was made to abolish small notes and to increase the silver circulation; collectors of customs and receivers of public money were required to accept only designated forms of currency. To aid the movement toward a coin currency, the President, in 1836, issued his famous Specie Circular which provided that only gold and silver should be accepted in payment for public land. This had the effect of abruptly deflating western land speculation. By 1834 the national debt had been paid off and high tariff returns were creating an overly large Federal surplus. Congress passed a law (1836) distributing the surplus in installments among the states, which caused the depositary banks from which the money was taken to contract their credit. Another factor that aided in precipitating the panic was the financial crisis in England, including the failure of Wilkes, Wilde, and Wiggin, three English companies interested in American cotton and credit. British and other European creditors began to call their loans and to seek specie for their American securities. Still another adverse factor was the record-breaking cotton crop of 1837 at a time when the market was already saturated.

Evidences of the coming storm were experienced early in 1837. As the back country banks drew on their balances kept in New York, specie payments were suspended by the metropolitan banks and they were followed by the other banks of the country. Many banks failed, all metallic currency disappeared and "notes and tickets" took the place of subsidiary coins. Many business and manufacturing firms issued their own currency, promises to pay at some future date.

The full force of the depression, however, was not felt during the first two years after the panic. Nicholas Biddle mobilized a group of banks to issue jointly guaranteed notes ("post notes") to state governments in return for bonds. The bonds were then marketed in London and the proceeds used to buy cotton to support its price.

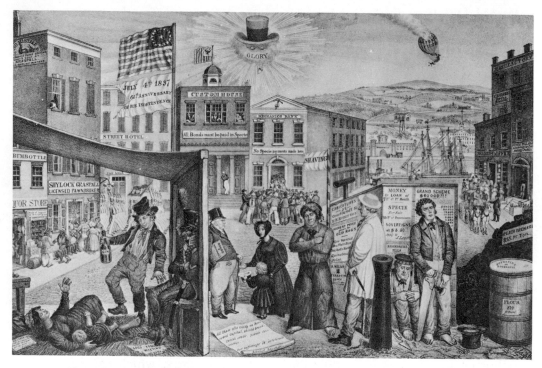

The effects of the Panic of 1837

In this way the burden of the mammoth crop of 1837 was eased, and the capital continued to flow from Britain to the United States. If recovery had occurred in England by 1839 the system might have worked, but unfortunately the English depression became deeper, post notes unacceptable, and state bonds nearly unsalable. The collapse from 1839 to 1842 was the major impact of the depression.

During these four years industrial activities of all sorts slowed down as thousands of individuals and companies became bankrupt. Large numbers of factory workers, artisans, and laborers were thrown out of work, and misery and poverty increased in the new industrial urban centers as well as in the older ones. Before the close of 1837 nine-tenths of the factories of the eastern states were closed at a time when flour and other food prices were rising because of poor crops. In New York, handbills were circulated and posted on buildings demanding: "Bread, Meat, Rent, Fuel—the prices must come down!" Riots occurred. Many people starved to death in different parts of the country, for the government did not intervene to help feed the distressed, and charitable organizations were unable to cope entirely with the situation. The South and West as well as the East felt the stark hand of industrial depression as it gripped the entire country.

The Federal government, too, soon found itself in serious difficulties. The surplus which was being distributed to the states now melted away like snow under a bright sun and the fourth installment was never paid. President Van Buren, fearful that the "pet banks" holding government funds would fail, asked Congress to provide an independent treasury system whereby government funds would be kept in vaults in the important cities of the country. In 1840, this was accomplished and government finances were divorced completely from the banking system for the time being. Congress was also forced to pass a Bankruptcy Act in 1841, providing for voluntary bankruptcy. Under its provisions approximately 40,000 people were relieved of debts amounting to about $450,000,000. By the time that the act was passed the bank note circulation of the country was declining rapidly. In 1837, it stood at $149,000,000; in 1842, it had sunk to $59,000,000. State governments were in serious difficulties. Efforts were made to have Congress assume all state debts, but without success. Eight states including Pennsylvania and one territory defaulted interest payments on their bonds. Arkansas, Florida, Michigan, and Mississippi repudiated bond issues in whole or in part. Foreign investors and American holders of the securities suffered. The panic affected individuals and groups all over the country, and recovery came slowly and painfully.

THE INDEPENDENT TREASURY SYSTEM

The plan proposed by President Van Buren in 1837 for an independent government treasury was not entirely new, for years before, Jefferson had proposed a plan whereby government officials would look after government moneys, and, in 1834, Representative William F. Gordon of Virginia proposed an independent treasury system as an amendment to a bill. In his message to Congress, Van Buren argued that since the government was well established financially there was no further need as there had been in the early years of the Republic to rely on banks. He avowed that state banks were unsafe depositories of public funds and that a national bank was also unsatisfactory. He pointed out that government funds in the hands of banks led to serious results through the overexpansion of credit and rash speculation. He recommended the separation of the "fiscal concerns of the government from those individuals and corporations." Stiff opposition arose from Whig leaders, including Clay and Webster, as well as from a large section of the Democratic party which objected to the restrictions upon state banks that such a system would bring. Not until 1840 did a measure pass, establishing a new system for looking after government funds.

The Independent Treasury or Sub-Treasury Act provided that government vaults be built at Washington and other leading cities where all public moneys should be kept and handled only through the United States Treasury Department and its fiscal agents. Government funds in the "pet" banks were withdrawn, and the new system began operation—but not for long. As soon as the Whigs gained power for a brief period, the law establishing the independent treasury was repealed (1841), government funds were placed again in "pet" banks, and steps were taken to establish a third United States Bank. Had President Harrison lived, it is probable that this part of the Whig program would have been carried out. But "Old Tippecanoe" died a month after his inauguration and John Tyler of Virginia, who was really a states' rights Democrat, became President. As a result, the ambitious Whig program collapsed when he vetoed the bank measures.

The Whigs had drawn up a plan for creating a "Fiscal Bank of the United States," free from the old constitutional objections, for its home was to be the District of Columbia and branches could be established only with the consent of the states. Tyler vetoed the measure as unconstitutional. Congress drew up a new bill providing for a "Fiscal Corporation of the United States" and designed to overcome the objections of the President. Tyler, however, decided to assent to no bank bill whatsoever and returned it with his veto. With anger and contempt, the cabinet resigned, except for Webster, Secretary of State, who remained long enough to complete separation from England regarding the northeast boundary and other problems. The Whigs issued a manifesto declaring their complete separation from the President as their brief period of control came to an end.

In 1846, with the Democrats again in control, the Independent Treasury was re-established. The new treasury building at Washington as well as the mint at Philadelphia and the branch mint at New Orleans were made places of deposit. Sub-treasuries were opened at New York, Boston, Charleston, New Orleans, and St. Louis. As time went on additional depositaries were established. Since some sub-treasuries, such as New York, were large collectors of funds while Washington, and other points on occasion, were payers, a great deal of transfer was necessary. For this purpose the Treasury commissioned agents such as the private banking firm of Corcoran and Riggs, that agreed to receive money where it came in and pay it out where needed at a suitable fee. Thus the government funds were often in the commercial money market for considerable periods of time.

STATE BANKING SYSTEMS

During the boom years of the 1830's, state banks grew like weeds. In 1829, there were 329 banks in the country; in 1837, there were 788. They issued countless notes of varying worth. The weakest types were nicknamed "sick Indian," "red dog," or "blue monkey." Many notes became practically worthless because of bank failures. Such currency was widely used in speculation and was a factor in causing the Panic of 1837. During the financial breathing spell provided by Biddle and his associates from 1837 to 1839 (p. 217), bank chartering continued at a rapid rate. By 1840, there were 901 chartered banks, but by 1842, only 692. The collapse of many banks and the depreciation of bank shares prolonged the depression into 1843.

The excessively large number of small independent banks and the problems of agricultural credit led to loose banking practices in most areas. In a number of states, banks were well regulated, but in most the absence of restrictions resulted in reckless banking. In many western and southern states a bank could be established without stated capital and sometimes even without a place of business. All that was necessary in such cases was to deposit with a state treasurer authorized stocks and bonds as security for bank notes. Since many of the authorized state securities had very low market values, often the bank notes issued were in no way secure. Other banks were established with specie borrowed only long enough to show the banking commissioners or other officials that there were actual reserves. These serious banking abuses were encouraged by inadequate or ineffective supervision, the borrowing of capital to start a bank, the excessive note issues that were permitted, the lack of rigorous requirements for redeeming notes, the lack of uniformity of the notes which made counterfeiting easy and their real value dubious, and the unsoundness of loans due to the desire of banks to get their notes into circulation while little attention was paid to the security given. While the system helped to make credit available for local purposes, it could also impede business, for merchants had to become familiar with counterfeit detectors and had to keep informed on the values of notes offered in payment of goods and debts.

Sound banking systems, however, were developed in those sections of the country where there were good business risks or state-controlled

NUMBER OF BANKS AND THEIR PRINCIPAL ASSETS, 1834 – 1865

(Money figures in millions of dollars)

Year	Number of Banks	Total Assets or Liabilities	Total Loans	Total Investments	Total Cash	Year	Number of Banks	Total Assets or Liabilities	Total Loans	Total Investments	Total Cash
1834	506	419	324	6	76	1850	824	532	364	21	115
1835	704	498	365	9	108	1851	879	597	414	22	132
1836	713	622	458	12	129	1852*	913	620	430	23	137
1837	788	707	525	12	140	1853†	750	577	409	22	127
1838	829	682	486	34	119	1854	1,208	795	557	44	163
1839	840	702	492	36	129	1855	1,307	817	576	53	155
1840	901	658	463	42	99	1856	1,398	880	634	49	167
1841	784	608	387	65	112	1857	1,416	953	684	59	177
1842	692	472	324	25	82	1858	1,422	849	583	60	170
1843	691	393	255	28	74	1859	1,476	983	657	64	229
1844	696	427	265	23	104	1860	1,562	1,000	692	70	196
1845	707	434	289	20	93	1861	1,601	1,016	697	74	198
1846	707	456	312	22	95	1862	1,492	1,012	647	99	221
1847	715	458	310	20	94	1863	1,532	1,209	654	186	307
1848	751	512	345	27	112	1864‡	1,556	973	555	150	236
1849	782	749	332	24	97	1865‡	1,643	1,357	518	412	392

* Estimates based on previous 5 years for number of banks and on 10 years (1854–1863) for assets and liabilities.
† Incomplete.
‡ For non-national banks, all figures except number of banks and capital accounts are estimated.

Source: U.S. Bureau of the Census, Historical Statistics of the United States, Colonial Times to 1957, Washington, D.C., 1960, p. 624.

banks. When the Suffolk Bank was chartered in Massachusetts in 1818, it agreed to redeem the notes of any New England bank at par if the issuing bank maintained a reserve of $2,000 or more according to its capital and also deposited sufficient funds to redeem its notes that might reach Boston. At first many country banks refused to keep a permanent reserve with the Suffolk Bank, but they were forced into line when that bank began to collect and demand redemption of country notes. By 1824, the Boston banks joined with the Suffolk Bank in making the plan effective throughout New England and thus a form of clearing system for that section of the country was established. The plan was strengthened by several Massachusetts laws, one passed in 1858, requiring a reserve of 15 per cent in specie against both notes and deposits.

The state of New York also established a fairly stable banking system. In order to abate some of the banking abuses prevalent at that time, a plan was formulated in 1829 whereby each bank incorporated in the state was required to contribute each year to a safety fund an amount equal to .5 per cent of its capital stock until it reached 3 per cent. When a bank failed and was liquidated, the fund could be drawn on to settle the remaining debts. This was actually a mutual insurance plan. The law also provided for the inspection of all banks at least three times a year. The system gave way to free banking when in 1838 the legislature of New York passed a law permitting any person or group of persons to engage in banking and to circulate notes secured by stocks, bonds, mortgages, and other collateral approved by and deposited with the state comptroller. An amendment to the law required that the securities should be limited to state and national bonds. This plan was followed by some western states.

Even before the Panic of 1837 the territory of Wisconsin had steadily refused to charter a bank, but the great wave of anti-bank sentiment in the West followed the banking collapse from 1839 to 1842. As late as 1852 there were no incorporated banks in Arkansas, California, Florida, Illinois, Iowa, Texas, or Wisconsin. Illinois and Wisconsin quickly deserted the ranks and chartered many banks in the 1850's under general incorporation acts called "free" banking laws, but some of the state prohibitions remained for many years. This did not eliminate the banking function in these states, but simply put it in the hands of unincorporated private bankers or money lenders.

Other western states tried different systems of regulation. Many of these met disaster through politics, corruption, and inefficiency, but there were exceptions. The State Bank of Indiana—one-half of its capital owned by the state—was established in 1834 after the model of the Second Bank of the United States. While it suspended specie payments during the Panic of 1837, it recovered and provided a stable system until its charter expired in 1859. The State Bank of Ohio (1845–1866) with branches throughout the state, also provided a good plan of banking, combining the safety fund and bond deposit aspects. After the Panic of 1837, an excellent system took shape in Louisiana putting an end to loose banking there. An act of 1842 set up a board of currency with broad powers of supervision. Deposits were protected; a one-third specie reserve was required; banks were prohibited from speculating; and bank notes had to be exchanged daily while specie settlements had to be made weekly. The value of the system became evident during the Panic of 1857, for New Orleans suffered less than any other commercial city in the nation during that depression. The Louisiana plan, like the New York system, influenced the organization of the National Banking System.

By mid-century New York was the undisputed financial center of the nation. Bankers all over the country kept deposits in New York banks to pay for imports and other purchases in the great metropolitan market. With no central bank, what financial leadership there was came from the heads of the big New York financial houses, usually in conjunction with their counterparts in Boston and Philadelphia. But, since each bank had first to think of its own interests, and had no obligation to help others, the 1,550 banks of 1860 scarcely constituted a banking system.

RISE OF STOCK EXCHANGES

Stocks and bonds were at first bought or sold by merchants meeting at selected taverns or coffee houses. Frequently they were auctioned. Public securities, including the obligations of the United States as well as the bonds of the states, were handled in the same way. Early in March, 1792, an office was opened at 22 Wall Street in New York by a number of brokers for the purpose of holding "public sales daily at noon, selling in rotation." Later in the same month several of these together with a number of other brokers and merchants—twenty-four altogether—met around a table under a buttonwood tree in Wall Street and signed an agreement which resulted in a securities market, the forerunner of the New York Stock Exchange. The refunding of the federal debt, the assumption of the state debts, the establishment of the First Bank of the United States, and the increase of banks, insurance companies, turnpike companies, and canal companies gave an impetus to the sale and exchange of stocks and bonds.

A stock exchange was organized in Philadelphia in 1800, a year before one was established in London. The expansion of business during the War of 1812 was partly responsible for the formal organization of the New York Stock and Exchange Board in 1817 and this name remained until 1868 when it was changed to its present one. Securities markets arose in other cities, but the New York Stock Exchange became the leading stock market of the country.

During the early years of stock exchanges, members could trade in any sort of security and there were few restrictions. Thus bad stocks as well as good had equal chances of gaining the attention of the purchaser, for no distinction was made between them. Ultimately this defect was recognized and eradicated. Regulations were put into effect; only the best stocks and bonds could be traded; and an approved list was made of all securities that could be bought and sold at the exchanges.

The volume of trade in the exchange of securities increased rapidly after the establishment of the New York Stock Exchange. In the period before the Civil War railroad stocks, mining stocks, and, from 1859 on, petroleum stocks were heavily traded in. State and municipal bonds were issued in large amounts. Manufacturing securities appeared more slowly. Large amounts of capital came from abroad, but foreign investors generally preferred public bonds and railroad issues rather than manufacturing, banking, or commercial stocks.

THE PANIC OF 1857

While ups and downs of the business cycle were generally only one or two years in length, from 1843 on there was no major panic or depression until 1857. The decade after the Mexican War was a "boom" period as investment of both foreign and domestic capital proceeded with unprecedented rapidity in industrial development, railroad construction, and land. There was also a considerable expansion of state banking. Bank note circulation increased from $58,000,000 in 1843 to $214,000,000 in 1857, while loans rose from the depression low of $254,000,000 to a moderate $684,000,000. The discovery of gold in California, the completion of railroads from the East to Chicago, and a great upsurge in manufacturing made 1849 to 1854 one of the major periods of economic advance in the nineteenth century. Such sharp periods of expansion appear inevitably to bring recessions. The boom broke in the United States in 1854, but the demand for American shipping because of the Crimean War, the land graduation act, (p. 158), and other stimulants to activity prevented a major break occurring until England suffered its post-Crimean depression in 1857.

A panic began with the failure of the New York branch of the Ohio Life Insurance and Trust Company of Cincinnati, which had financial connections in different parts of the country, with large liabilities to eastern financial houses. All banks in the city of New York except one suspended specie payments and nearly all the banks elsewhere followed. Stocks and bonds fell and commodity prices declined sharply. The depression was most serious in the industrial regions of the East and the wheat belt of the Middle West, which were hit by bank failures. In the larger manufacturing centers, workers and laborers held protest meetings in which they denounced speculators, the New York Stock Exchange, the banks, and the wealthy as being responsible for the depression.

The Cotton Belt and the South in general were not so seriously affected as other sections of the country. In the South crops had been large, and the section was relatively prosperous. But the panic affected southern regions as prices fluctuated, some cotton brokers failed, and loans were more difficult to negotiate. Foreign markets were not suf-

A cartoon which appeared during the Panic of 1857

NEW YORK to PHILADELPHIA BANK. "Going to suspend yourself, eh? Is that your Brotherly Love?"

ficiently depressed to interfere severely with the exportation of cotton and tobacco. As a result, many southerners came to feel that their section of the country was economically sounder and more secure than the North, and during the sad years that followed, secessionists emphasized their belief that the South would be better off if it built up a financial system of its own, entirely independent of the North. Agitation for a higher tariff by northern protectionists, who believed that the low tariff policy was one of the chief causes of the panic, also aroused southern fears and built up a desire to become free from the economic domination of the North.

CHAPTER 10

Industrialism

Ably borrowing and improving upon the British advances in technology that are collectively referred to as the "industrial revolution," the United States was by 1860 a great manufacturing nation. While England was still the world leader, in many lines America had gone further in machine technology. The rise of factory processes using power machinery in the United States began around 1800, but the big upswing, sometimes called the "take-off" was from 1843 to 1857.

In contrast to the social overhead capital in transportation and other public utilities that came in large blocks from governments and foreign investors, most initial capital in manufacturing was small-scale and domestic. In the early decades of the nineteenth century, the states encouraged manufacturing by small loans and tax exemptions. By 1817, New York, for example, had loaned $1,500,000 to manufacturing enterprises. The state had also passed a general incorporation act for manufacturing. But as time went on, encouragement in new areas was generally limited to tax exemption, and occasionally community subscriptions to stock.

Over the whole period from 1800 to 1860, the great bulk of manufacturing capital came from private savings. Entrepreneurs started on a small scale with their own money plus some from friends, relatives, and venturesome local banks and expanded operations by reinvestment of earnings. Although the corporate form was often used, stocks or bonds were generally unsalable to the public. And investors were wise to be wary, for initial failure and reorganization were probably as much the rule as the exception.

If one looks at the entire national economy in this period it can be said that staple exports, principally cotton and tobacco, brought in the surpluses necessary for building transportation and public utilities. The North received much of this money from handling the trade in staples and from direct southern investment in northern enterprise. With the need for social overhead capital largely met from the proceeds of export agriculture, domestic capital was released for developing manufacturing.

THE ENGLISH INDUSTRIAL REVOLUTION

While importation of capital for manufacturing was small, the importation of technological knowledge and skill was large, continuous, and probably essential. Technological advances which resulted in the rise of the factory system and later evolved into mass production first took place in England. The term "industrial revolution" was coined by the French economist Jerome Blanqui to cover this English breakthrough in technology, but in fact, the change was gradual. Iron smelting, coal mining, building construction, shipbuilding, cloth finishing, and the making of bricks, leather, paper, glass, and gunpowder had reached relatively large scales of production long before the eighteenth century. For some time, there had been continual changes in technology in many fields—new procedures in smelting and refining metals, and advances in the use of motive power of wind, water, and animals. By the mid-eighteenth century expanding commerce and increasing demand brought rapid changes in a number of manufacturing processes which gave rise to the factory system. The changes were ushered in by a series of inventions that were related to the demand for increased production. Mechanization made important advances in the textile industries partly because they lagged behind most of the other industries.

In 1733, John Kay made the first of the important textile inventions. His drop box and flying shuttle made it possible for one person instead of two to weave wide cloth. His shuttle was equipped with wheels and was shot back and forth over a traverse raceway by the alternative impact of suspended hammers. The increased speed of weaving, as a result of the new technique, brought about a greater demand for woolen yarn and cotton thread. But a generation passed after Kay's remarkable improvement of the loom before important changes came in spinning. Then suddenly a flood of mechanical inventions descended on the country. The many-spindled spinning jenny of James Hargreaves (1764), the roller water-frame of Richard Arkwright (1769), and the combination of the two improvements into the hybrid "spinning mule" of Samuel Crompton (1779), resulted in the acceleration of spinning. Improvements in the loom came slowly, although Edmund Cartwright patented a power loom as early as 1785. The Jacquard loom, invented in France in 1801 by Joseph Jacquard, was an important advance in the technology of textile manufacture. Improvements also took place in carding and other processes as numerous changes were made in English factories. The new machinery gave an impetus especially to cotton manufacture and opened the way for the production of raw cotton in the United States.

The first textile factories used machines constructed largely of wood, driven by horsepower or waterpower. Soon, metal machinery came into use when steam power began to compete with that of water. As a result of the demand for iron, the production of that metal underwent many changes. Since Europe lacked the wood necessary for an iron age based on charcoal smelting, the Darbys' successful substitution of coke in blast furnaces in the latter half of the century was the next important advance. The blowing cylinders of John Smeaton, introduced in 1768, which slowly displaced the old wood and leather giant bellows, and the application of steam as motive power resulted in a greatly increased output as furnaces were made larger and new ones built. Changes occurred also at the forges where bar iron was produced. Experiments begun by several men earlier in the century were carried to completion by Peter Onions in 1783 and by Henry Cort in 1784. Cort's "puddling" process made it possible to produce a better grade of malleable iron and also substituted grooved rolls to squeeze or roll the iron into bars instead of the slow, cumbersome process of beating out the metal under ponderous hammers. In the manufacture of machines, many advances were made as greater accuracy and precision in lathes and other machine tools became necessary, especially in the production of steam engines. The changes affected other industries as well as textiles and iron, but to a lesser extent, although in the potteries the changes should not be minimized as the Wedgwoods, Spodes, and others contributed to the production of improved pottery, stoneware, earthenware, and china. In time, the factory system was applied to other manufactures and the system of mass production took form.

A most important aspect of industrial changes was the application of steam to drive the new machinery. By the late seventeenth and early eighteenth centuries, the experiments of Thomas Savery, a gentleman trained as a military engineer, and Thomas Newcomen, a blacksmith and ironmonger, resulted in two different steam pumps which represented the progress that had been made in the use of steam power up to that time. Such contrivances, however, could be used only for such work as removing water from mines and pumping water "for fountains and the supply of gentlemen's houses." They could not be used for driving machinery.

More than half a century after the patents granted to Savery and Newcomen, James Watt, a maker of scientific apparatus at the University of Glasgow, began experiments with models of Newcomen's engine. Watt transformed Newcomen's atmospheric engine into a steam engine by introducing a separate condenser chamber and closing the cylinder at both ends so that the piston could be driven up and down by steam. Watt received the first of many patents in 1769 and formed a partnership with Matthew Boulton, a Birmingham manufacturer. The contributions of James Watt in bridging the gap between pure science and empirical discovery were substantial and his systematic investigations led to many improvements. Most important was the perfection of the device for converting the power generated by steam into rotary motion (1781). Industrial capitalism soon realized the importance of the improved steam engine. It came to be used to furnish power for producing the blast at the iron furnaces, for the hammers at the forges, and for the machinery at the new rolling mills. It was introduced into flour mills, sugar cane mills, and stone-crushing mills. In 1785, steam power was first applied in a spinning factory. Before the end of the century it was replacing water power in mills and factories in many parts of England. The location of industry was no longer required to be on rapid flowing streams. It came to be determined by the availability of raw material, nearness to markets or shipping points, and the source of labor supply.

As England built up her manufacturing technology in the eighteenth century, a policy was developed to safeguard it from being copied by other countries. As early as the reign of George I a law was passed imposing penalties on anyone convicted of enticing from England any "artificer or manufacturer" (1718). This was renewed by an act in 1750 which also prohibited the exportation of "tools and utensils" used in the woolen and silk industries. In 1774, a similar prohibition was laid on the exportation of machinery used in the cotton

and linen industries, although this law had a special provision except-
ing wool cards shipped to North America. Seven years later (1781)
Parliament imposed drastic penalties for the attempt to export any
"machine, engine, tool, press, paper, utensil, or implement used for
preparing, working, completing, or finishing woolen, cotton, linen, or
silk manufacture." The next year the earlier acts relating to enticing workmen from Great Britain were elaborated, and in 1785, a
law was passed prohibiting the exportation to any foreign country of
tools, machinery, engines, models, or plans of machines used in the
iron industry. Heavy penalties were also laid for enticing English
workmen employed in iron and steel manufacture. Many English
statesmen maintained that this law was not directed against the
United States, but at Europe, especially Germany. However, it was
quite evident that it was aimed at the new nation, which only a short
time before had secured independence from the mother country, as
well as at European countries. This policy of protecting British manufactures was enforced as far as possible until the 1820's, when the growing industrialization of other countries proved its futility. The restrictive act was formally repealed in 1843.

PROMOTING MANUFACTURING IN AMERICA

Although detailed knowledge of British advances could not
readily be secured, the rise of local industry during the late colonial
and Revolutionary period made Americans anxious to push ahead.
Promotion of manufacture became a popular cause at the national,
state, and community levels. Organizations for this purpose were soon
formed, the most important of which was the Pennsylvania Society
for the Encouragement of Manufactures and the Useful Arts, in
Philadelphia, an outgrowth of an earlier one with similar aims—the
United Company of Philadelphia for Promoting American Manufactures, founded in 1775. Other similar societies were organized in
Boston, New York, Baltimore, Wilmington, and elsewhere. They held
meetings to promote manufacturing; they published articles; members
agreed to use only American products; prizes and premiums were
offered inventors of machinery; and financial aid was sometimes given
to encourage certain industries. A few of these societies went so far
as to undertake their own manufacturing operations. For example,
the Pennsylvania Society for the Encouragement of Manufactures and
the Useful Arts established textile shops and attempted to emulate
the rising factories of Great Britain.

In 1791, Alexander Hamilton made his famous "Report on the Subject of Manufactures." He listed seventeen distinct lines of manufacture which he stated were flourishing. These included leather and leather goods, iron manufactures, shipbuilding and woodmaking, flax and hemp manufactures, bricks and tiles, spirits and liquors, paper of different sorts, hats, refined sugars, oil and its products, copper and brass wares, tinware, carriages, snuff and tobacco, starch and hairpowder, lampblack and other painters' colors, and gunpowder. A detailed statement was made in regard to manufactures under each heading. Hamilton also pointed out that great quantities of cloth and clothes of all sorts were made in the "household way," not only for supplying families but also for exportation. He wrote that textile factories were beginning to appear in New England and were producing goods equal in quality to those of old England. He recommended protective duties, bounties, premiums, and every other possible aid to stimulate manufactures. Rejecting the Jeffersonian exaltation of agriculture, he insisted that manufacturing should be developed to increase the national income and to provide a dependable home market for agricultural commodities. All that he got from Congress, however, was a small increase of duties in some of the schedules of the tariff. The report was resurrected and its arguments utilized by the manufacturing interests in the period after the War of 1812.

Hamilton's actions suited his words. He organized the Philadelphia Society for the Promotion of National Industry and the Society for Establishing Useful Manufactures, which became known as the S. U. M. A perpetual charter granted by the New Jersey legislature in 1791 authorized the latter society to carry on manufacturing of different kinds, to sell commodities, to acquire real estate, to improve rivers and project canals, and to incorporate the municipality of Paterson. It was authorized to issue capital stock up to $1,000,000. A large tract of land was bought and a small cotton factory was established at the Great Falls of the Passaic River. Lack of experienced management brought operations to an end in 1796, but long after Hamilton had died the region became a great textile center.

Neither Hamilton nor his associates fully visualized the problems involved in establishing factory industry. British competition and scarcity of capital were obvious; less obvious were lack of managerial know-how, marketing facilities, reliable machinery, maintenance men, and skilled and disciplined workers. Early managers tried to do everything—superintend shops, fix machinery, keep books, buy materials, and deal with customers—and consequently did none of them well. People were used to English goods and distrusted the quality, often rightly, of things made in America. Labor was relatively high-priced, unaccustomed to factory routines, and lacking in skill.

This shortage of skilled labor, which persisted throughout the nineteenth century, contributed a valuable characteristic to American industrialism—the continued quest for labor-saving machinery. A member of an English Commission of 1854 said: "The whole energy of the people is devoted to improving and inventing labor-saving machinery." [1] From the 1820's on American factories began to be more mechanized than those of England or the Continent. The added fact that raw materials for both machinery and products were generally cheaper than in Europe meant that extra-heavy machinery and wasteful processes caused little concern if they saved in labor costs.

The character of American operations also lent itself to crude processes. The chief demand was for cheap, relatively durable products. Fine finish and artistic design were not worth their cost to most American consumers. Manufacturers paid little attention to the possibilities inherent in theoretical study and the applications of science. Mechanical devices, if relatively simple, would be adopted, but intricate processes were distrusted. As a result, early American industry presents the paradox of being scientifically crude, but mechanically ingenious; wasteful of materials, but highly productive per worker.

THE TEXTILE INDUSTRY

Prior to 1790, progress had been made in developing American spinning machinery for textile mills or shops and such machines were used in Philadelphia, Beverly, Hartford, Worcester, New York City, and elsewhere, a few of them being operated by waterpower. Advances were made in the production of woolen and cotton cloth. But the factory system really got under way in the United States when the Englishman, Samuel Slater, introduced the more efficient Arkwright machinery in Rhode Island.

Slater, an employee in an English cotton mill, carefully read the advertisements in American newspapers that found their way to England. Attracted by the prizes offered by the Pennsylvania Society for the Encouragement of Manufactures and the Useful Arts for improvements in cotton machinery, he decided to leave England and come to the United States to seek his fortune. To evade the British laws

---

[1] Quoted in H. J. Habakkuk, *American and British Technology in the Nineteenth Century* (Cambridge: Cambridge University Press, 1962), p. 100.

designed to prevent the migration of artisans, he disguised himself as a farmer boy, slipped away to London, and embarked for New York. Here he found employment for two months in the woolen establishment of the New York Manufacturing Society and then met Moses Brown, a Quaker merchant of Pawtucket, Rhode Island, who persuaded him to make an agreement with his firm, William Almy and Smith Brown. This company had made some progress in the manufacture of textiles but was having difficulties with their machines. In Pawtucket, Slater reproduced from memory plans of water frames, carding machinery, and spinning machines. Men, sworn to secrecy, were employed to make the wooden and iron parts of the machines. Late in 1790, the first cotton factory in the United States containing machinery modeled after Arkwright's began operations. The cotton spun into yarn in the mill was "put out" to poor families to be cleaned and whipped. The goods produced by Almy, Brown, and Slater were marketed by the mercantile firm of Almy and Brown.

In spite of Slater's attempts to keep the machinery secret, other cotton mills appeared in the years that followed. They were operated by horse or water power. Many other English workmen came to America and made contributions to the rising factory system. Not all who came, however, were endowed with the skill and genius of Slater. Many were merely pretenders and quite often American manufacturers were deceived and imposed upon by such unqualified men. The English methods took hold relatively slowly. Difficulties in perfecting machinery and competition with English cotton goods were partly the reason. But more important, there was little knowledge of factory management and inadequate capital for the necessary equipment. As in other "underdeveloped countries" most of the capital found its way into a rapidly developing commerce and trade, or into land and buildings. As the factory system slowly arose, shops containing simpler jennies and looms, but often driven by water power, appeared in increasing numbers in the North and South and even in the new West. Home manufactures of cotton goods also grew and competed with the factory product. The Embargo of 1808, the Non-intercourse Act, and the War of 1812, however, stimulated the factory system. In 1814 a mill was started at Waltham, Massachusetts, that took in raw cotton and turned out finished cloth. The dozen or so cotton mills of 1800 increased to eighty-seven in 1810, and by 1815 many millions of dollars had been invested in the factories of New England alone. Progress was also being made in the middle states and to a small extent in the South.

Partly protected by the tariff, mills continued to increase. In 1830, there were 795 cotton mills in the country, representing an investment of $45,000,000. By 1860, the capital invested reached $98,585,000. The number of mills decreased from 1,240 in 1840 to 1,094 in 1860 due to consolidation and the establishment of large works, a process which was going on in most important industries. By 1860, about 122,000 people were employed in cotton manufacture. The total value of cotton goods produced in 1860 was about $115,500,000. Of this, New England produced $79,000,000; the middle states, $26,500,000; the South, $8,500,000; and, the West, $1,300,000. At this time, almost seven-eighths of the cotton goods used in the country were made in the United States. It should be noted that in addition to factory-produced cotton goods, some cotton was still being spun and woven into cloth in many homes, although household manufactures were rapidly declining.

Many inventions and the resulting growing efficiency of machinery in cotton manufactures characterized the industry during this period. Among the inventions and changes in technology were improvements in carding and spinning machinery, better looms, the introduction of cylinder machines for printing calico, especially the engraved cylinders which permitted the production of finer qualities and attractive colored patterns, and the application of water and steam power to drive the machinery. By 1860, as a result of technological advances, Americans were producing the best qualities of cloth in competition with importations from Europe and were beginning to export

The textile mills of Lowell, Massachusetts

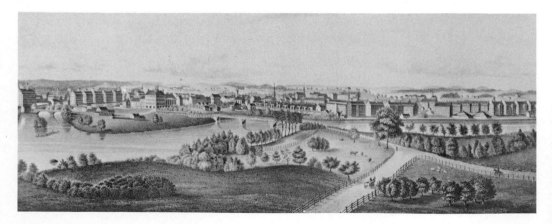

cotton yarns, sheetings, and coarse calicoes to Spanish America, China, India, and the Levant.

The home production of woolen cloth and mixtures of wool and other material, especially linsey-woolsey, continued longer than in the case of cotton, well into the nineteenth century. Woolen mills appeared along with those for cotton but were generally smaller. In the period that followed the Revolution, spinning jennies, carding machines, and looms were used and improved. A "woolen manufactory" organized in Hartford, Connecticut, in 1788 marked an important advance in the manufacture of wool, for it produced 5,000 yards of cloth a year. At his inauguration in 1789, Washington wore a dark brown suit made from cloth manufactured by this company. Woolen factories emerged from the shops where woolen cloth was produced when the different processes were brought under one roof, machinery was improved, and power—water or steam—was used to drive the machinery. Technological progress was aided by English workmen like Arthur and John Scholfield of Yorkshire who migrated to Massachusetts in 1792. Improvements were also copied from the cotton machinery. By the beginning of the nineteenth century, increasing numbers of woolen mills were established and a better grade of cloth was produced as a demand arose for the fine-grained wool of merino sheep which were imported in large numbers. As was the case with cotton, the maritime problems from 1808 to 1815 resulted in the increased investment of capital in additional mills. According to the census of 1810, there were twenty-four woolen factories in the country. At the same time there were 1,682 fulling mills to which the domestic or home producers took their cloth to be fulled. The War of 1812 itself gave an impetus to the manufacture of woolen cloth as the demand for military equipment increased. Although many mills were ruined by competition with British goods after the war, there were more than 100 factories in 1820, possessing a total of 700 looms.

Overproduction abroad which resulted in an overflow of woolen goods to the United States made the decade from 1820–1830 a serious one for woolen manufacturers. Although the tariff of 1824 encouraged new mills, the rate of failure in the industry was high. The "Tariff of Abominations" of 1828 hurt the manufacturers of coarse wool because of the heavy duty on raw materials, but the industry revived in the boom of the early 1830's. The census of 1840 reported 1,420 woolen mills in the country, though the cotton industry, which employed more than three times as much capital and labor, was confined to 1,240 plants. This was because woolen mills were much smaller

than the cotton establishments. The woolen industry recovered slowly
from the depression of 1837–1843 and increased about two-thirds
during the decade before the war. In spite of the setback of 1857
which ruined a few large companies, by 1860 there were nearly 1,700
woolen mills in the country employing about 60,000, and possessing
640,000 spindles and 16,000 looms. A few small mills could be found
in Texas and even in California and Oregon, but Massachusetts was
the leading woolen state and Pennsylvania ranked second. Among the
types of woolen cloth woven in mills in New England and the middle
states were broadcloth, worsted, flannel, cassimere, and even alpaca.
Mousseline-de-laine for women's dresses, composed of cotton and wool,
became an article of large production in Massachusetts after 1840 and
reached high perfection. Home manufactures of linseys and other cheap
cloth for Negro slaves persisted in many places, especially around
Philadelphia and Baltimore. Including carpets, blankets, hosiery, and
mixed cloths, in addition to the usual types of woolen cloth, the value
of goods produced in the woolen industry amounted to $80,000,000 by
1860.

Closely related to the manufacture of textiles was the clothing industry, which rose during this period. While home and shop-made
woolen jackets, clothes of homespun, stockings, caps, and mittens had
been articles of trade during colonial days, machine-produced, "ready-
made" clothes appeared in New York stores by 1836 and were first
bought chiefly by the poorer people, such as youths starting work in
the city. Such clothes soon came to compete with those made by tailors
and in the homes, and were offered for sale in all the leading business
centers. The manufacture of men's ready-made clothing was much
more important than women's at this time, for in 1860, only about
$7,000,000 worth of women's clothing, including cloaks, corsets, hoop-
skirts, and millinery, were machine-produced—about one-tenth of the
value of men's clothes. The invention and improvement of the sewing
machine gave an impetus to the manufacture of clothing and also
marked the beginning of the sweat-shop system.

PROGRESS IN OTHER INDUSTRIES

As early as 1798, standardization in industrial production began
when Eli Whitney devised a plan for producing interchangeable parts
in making muskets. Identical parts were produced by means of the jig,
a device for guiding a tool. In its simplest form, the jig is a metal plate
in which a pattern is cut out and which can be followed in drilling

Samuel Slater   Eli Whitney   Charles Goodyear

or cutting out large numbers of the part. The idea was not entirely new, for it had been applied to making complicated instruments long before. Jig-guided and power-operated machine tools as applied to fire-arms were improved and perfected by Simeon North, Samuel Colt, and others. The principle was applied to the sewing machine, to clock and watch making, and to farm and other machines. The plan became known throughout the world as the "American system" and became the basis for more advanced mass production.

Many changes and much progress took place in the iron industry, the foundations of which were laid in the colonial period. From the beginning of the nineteenth century to the Civil War, northern river valleys from the Hudson-Champlain region southward were the im-portant areas of iron production, and the valleys of the Lehigh, Dela-ware, Schuylkill, and Susquehanna in Pennsylvania became the chief centers of iron production. Beyond the mountains, the industry de-veloped rapidly in western Pennsylvania and eastern Ohio. In parts of Kentucky and Tennessee, quantities of iron were also produced.

Much of the pig iron during this period was made on iron planta-tions as in the colonial period. But changes were beginning to take place. These were largely due to the adoption of new fuels. As long as charcoal was used, vast areas of woodland were necessary and iron-works were located in rural areas. The first serious experiments in using anthracite coal in blast furnaces dates from the time of the patent received by Frederick W. Geissenhainer in 1833 which provided for smelting iron with anthracite and a hot blast secured through the utilization of the hot gases escaping from the furnace. By 1840, a number of larger blast furnaces had been built and it was amply demonstrated that anthracite could be profitably used in smelting iron. As entire dependence on charcoal came to an end and with the use of steam to drive the cylinders that provided the blast, many of the new furnaces were built in urban regions. By 1855, the use of anthracite in the production of pig iron had surpassed that of charcoal. During the same period, raw bituminous coal was tried in a number of blast furnaces, which were altered for the purpose, and new ones were also built, especially in western Pennsylvania and eastern Ohio. Some American furnaces used a mixture of anthracite and bituminous coal. Many experiments in the use of coke (produced from bituminous coal) were made in the decade of the thirties. Slowly, coke gained in favor as a blast-furnace fuel, but it was not until the latter part of the century that it surpassed its rivals.

Technological changes also took place in the production of bar iron. The English invention by Henry Cort of the puddling furnace and rolling mill (1784) was first adopted at the Plumsock ironworks in western Pennsylvania in 1817. Other works of a similar type were built, although much bar iron produced during this period was hammered out at forges and bloomeries. Until 1844, all the rails used in this country, except the strap rails fastened to the top of wooden rails, were imported from England. In that year the rolling of heavy rails was begun and by 1850 there were sixteen mills where rails were rolled, with an annual output of 100,000 tons. By 1860, the number of such mills had doubled and one-half the rails, axles, and other forms of manufactured iron required by American railroads were rolled in this country.

During the several decades prior to the Civil War many changes took place in the production of secondary and finished iron products, from heavy machine castings down to the smallest household gadgets. The metal industries received an impetus from the contemporary industrial and agricultural revolutions. Castings, hammered iron, and rolled iron were required for engines, machines, agricultural machinery, and ironmongery. In 1860, almost every state produced machinery of some sort. Pennsylvania, Massachusetts, Ohio, and New Jersey led the others.

In 1810, the production of pig iron in the United States amounted to 53,908 gross tons and the blast furnaces numbered 153. In 1860, 563,755 tons of pig iron were produced by 377 furnaces. At the same time 256 works made 513,213 tons of bar iron and ninety-seven produced 51,290 tons of blooms. The amount of steel made in the United States prior to the Civil War was small indeed, for there were only thirteen works that produced 11,838 tons of steel in 1860.

The foundations of the shipbuilding industry had been laid in colonial days, and prosperity continued after a brief interruption during the transition from colonial to national status. The advantages of large supplies of excellent lumber at low prices together with a supply of skilled labor resulted in low construction costs, and vessels were built not only for the American merchant marine, which was second only to that of England by 1793, but were sold throughout the world. As in the earlier period, shipbuilding yards were located largely along the North Atlantic coast, although many vessels were built for internal commerce on western rivers, and a few ocean-going vessels were constructed as early as 1793 on the upper waters of the Ohio.

After the War of 1812, the reputation of Yankee shipbuilders became known everywhere and American-built vessels could be found in any important port of the world. Between 1815 and 1840, about 540,000 tons of shipping were sold to foreigners. From 1854 to 1859, Europeans bought 50,000 tons of shipping annually but, unfortunately, as American shipbuilding reached its height, technological, political, and economic factors were at work which brought about its downfall and with it the decline of the American merchant marine (p. 271).

The outstanding industries of this period in the order of their importance were: flour and meal, cotton goods, lumber, iron and iron manufactures, boots and shoes, clothing, leather and skins, woolen goods, sugar refining, provisions, printing and publishing, and carriages. The distribution of miscellaneous manufactures was general throughout the country although not quite so advanced in the newer sections of the country. New York, Pennsylvania, Massachusetts, and Ohio led in the value of output of the various miscellaneous manufactures. A trend toward localization was evident in a number of industries. This can be best seen in the textile industries and the production of boots and shoes in New England, the coal and iron industries in Pennsylvania, the manufacture of lard in Ohio, and the production of lead in Wisconsin.

THE INFLUENCE OF INVENTIONS

While important English inventions influenced the beginnings of the factory system in the United States, American ingenuity soon made itself evident and in the period that followed, both countries learned much from each other in regard to technological developments.

In addition to the advances made in the textile and iron industries, the development of agricultural machinery, improved flour-milling technology, the improvement in steam engines and railroads, the perfection of the telegraph, the introduction of the sewing machine with its factory applications, and rotary printing presses (especially Hoe's), there were thousands of other inventions and applications of simple machinery to hand processes such as nail manufacture.

The "curing" of rubber, now called vulcanization after Vulcan, Roman god of fire, is illustrative of American improvement of European devices. Although a fairly satisfactory waterproof cloth had been developed by Thomas Hancock and Charles Mackintosh in England beginning about 1820, the effect of changes in temperature on rubber confined its uses to narrow limits. Charles Goodyear of New York, bringing a mixture of rubber and sulphur accidentally in contact with a hot stove in 1839, discovered the secret of vulcanizing rubber, received a patent in 1844, and made possible the beginnings of innumerable industries in that field. The search for labor-saving machinery never ceased. An Englishman writing at the time of the Civil War declared: "Mechanical contrivances of every sort are produced to supply the want of human hands. Thus we find America producing a machine even to peel apples; another to beat eggs; a third to clean knives; a fourth to wring clothes; in fact there is scarcely a purpose for which human hands have been ordinarily employed, for which some ingenious attempt is not made to find a substitute in a cheap and efficient labor-saving machine."[1]

A system of patent law gradually developed. During the colonial period a few patents were issued by special acts of the legislatures of the different colonies. The first American patent was given in 1641 by Massachusetts Bay Colony to Samuel Winslow for a new process of making salt. Five years later, Joseph Jenkes received the first American patent on machinery in the same colony for a mill for manufacturing scythes. In the brief period of Confederation the states issued patents through special legislation. The first Congress under the Constitution passed a general patent law in 1790, authorized by the clause: "Congress shall have the power . . . to promote the progress of science and useful arts by securing for limited times to authors and inventors the exclusive right to their respective writings and inventions." The law placed the responsibility for granting patents in the hands of a board consisting of the Secretary of State, the Secretary of War, and the

[1] Sir Morton Peto, *Resources and Prospects of America* (London, 1866), p. 100.

Attorney General; obviously, such a board could not spend much time on patents. Three years later the board was abolished and the duty of authorizing patents placed upon the Secretary of State. In 1802, Secretary of State James Madison gave the Patent Office the status of a unit within the Department of State when he appointed Dr. William Thornton at a salary of $1,400 "to have charge of issuing patents." But patents were granted without proper investigation of their novelty and there were many infringements. In 1836, the Patent Office was established by law under a Commissioner of Patents as a distinct and separate bureau in the Department of State, and for the first time workable and accurate procedures were established for granting patents. In 1849, the Patent Office was transferred to the newly created Department of the Interior, and in 1925 to the Department of Commerce. From 1791 to 1860 the number of patents increased from three in the former year to 4,819 in the latter.

THE CONTROVERSY OVER
A PROTECTIVE TARIFF

The first United States tariff, which went into effect on July 4, 1789, was a revenue measure. Its preamble stated that it was intended "to support the government," to "discharge the debts of the United States," and for the "encouragement and protection of manufactures." But its average rates were about 8 per cent and its highest only 15 per cent, which hardly made it protective in any sense. In design, however, it was partly intended to aid industry as individual members of Congress voiced a demand for protection and local interests played a part in adjusting its rates through "log-rolling" and compromise. It levied specific duties on more than thirty types of commodities, *ad valorem* rates from 7.5 per cent to 15 per cent on a few specified articles, and a straight 5 per cent on all articles not enumerated. While Hamilton was Secretary of the Treasury, slight increases were made several times and, later, the tariff laws of 1804, 1807, and 1808 raised the rates slightly on many products, but no basic change occurred in the tariff until the eve of the War of 1812 when the urgent need for revenue resulted in doubling all its rates for the period of the war and for one year thereafter.

The end of the war brought apprehension about the rising manufacturing industries which had been encouraged by the war and the maritime difficulties which had preceded it. Cotton, woolen, and iron manufactures, especially, had expanded as commercial capital found new uses in industrial enterprises and the European wars forced Americans to manufacture for themselves. With the close of the long period of strife and bloodshed in Europe, many Americans foresaw keen competition between European and American manufactures. Thus, President Madison in his message to Congress in February, 1815, submitting copies of the Treaty of Ghent, said: "No subject can enter with greater force and merit into the deliberations of Congress than a consideration of the means to preserve and promote the manufactures which have sprung into existence and attained an unparalleled maturity throughout the United States during the period of the European wars." Even Jefferson, who earlier had been quite hostile to manufacturing, declared: "To be independent for the comforts of life, we must fabricate them for ourselves. We must now place the manufacturer by the side of the agriculturalist." The speech of Lord Brougham in the English Parliament in which he declared that it was necessary for British manufacturers and mercantile interests "to incur a loss upon the first exportation, in order by a glut to stifle in the cradle those rising manufactures in the United States which the war had forced into existence, contrary to the natural course of things" also aroused much sentiment in favor of protection in the United States.

As in the period following the Revolution, British goods were "dumped" on the American market and were sold for whatever they would bring. In 1816, imports reached a peak not exceeded until 1850 and distress was general among manufacturers. In his message of December, 1815, Madison recommended to Congress a measure designed to protect American manufacturing industries. With a few exceptions, the political leaders of the country favored tariff protection, some to protect the investments and prosperity of the owners of the new plants, others because it was necessary that the country become entirely self-sufficient economically. A bill was introduced, not by a representative of northern industry but by William Lowndes of South Carolina. The southern leader, John C. Calhoun, led the debates in favor of it, supporting protection on the ground that it was a wise national policy necessary to bind the different sections together. "Neither agriculture, manufactures, nor commerce, taken separately," he insisted, "is the cause of wealth. It flows from the three combined and cannot exist without each." Henry Clay from Kentucky joined Calhoun in advocating the protective policy. Among those who opposed, the brilliant but erratic John Randolph of Roanoke emphasized his belief that the principle of protection amounted to "the levying of an immense tax on one portion of the community to put money into the pockets of another." Daniel Webster, representing the commercial interests—not the industrial group—of New England also opposed the measure, but was in favor of a moderately protective tariff which should be permanent. With the aid of southern and western votes, the industrialists of the North succeeded in passing a bill which Senator Benton pointed out inaugurated a new policy of protection.

The tariff of 1816 provided duties which ranged from 7.5 per cent to 30 per cent. The duties imposed on cotton and woolen goods were 25 per cent. For the first time the minimum principle was applied —no cotton cloth was to be valued at less than twenty-five cents a yard— the object being to exclude cheap Indian cotton goods. The law, however, did not completely suit the most ardent friends of protection. Further demands resulted in increases in 1818 on pig iron and also on hammered iron, which was now suffering from competition with English rolled iron.

The financial crisis of 1819 brought renewed clamor for protection. Manufacturers ascribed their distress to the want of adequate protection to home industry against the cheap production of foreign goods, fraudulent invoices, unlimited auction sales (p. 273) and long-time credit. Conventions of manufacturers were held and petitions sent to Congress asking for an increase of duties. The bill of 1820, drafted while the emergency still continued, increased duties considerably. It

VALUE OF MERCHANDISE EXPORTS AND IMPORTS, 1790 – 1860
(In millions of dollars)

Year	Exports	Imports	Year	Exports	Imports
1790	—	23	1830	59	63
1795	40	70	1835	100	137
1800	32	91	1840	112	98
1805	42	121	1845	98	113
1810	42	85	1850	135	174
1815	46	113	1855	193	258
1820	52	74	1860	316	354
1825	67	90			

Source: U.S. Bureau of the Census, *Historical Statistics of the United States, Colonial Times to 1957*, Washington, D.C., 1960, p. 538.

passed the House by a comfortable majority vote, but failed in the Senate by a single vote. It was becoming evident that as the movement for protection gained in the North, the southerners increasingly opposed it.

After the defeat of the tariff bill of 1820, members of Congress in favor of high protection tried each year to have the duties on imports raised but without success until 1824. At that time, it was no eastern representative of industry who led the debates for increased protection, but Henry Clay of Kentucky, who stressed protection as a part of his American System. Speaking for some constituents who wanted protection against imported hemp, he held that his object was to establish a home market and "to lay the foundations of a genuine American policy," thus eliminating dependence upon foreign goods and markets. He advocated protection, not to favor local interests and special industries but as a general system which would make the United States independent of foreign nations. He argued for improved roads and canals so that the farmers might more easily transport their products to industrial centers and over which manufacturers could send their goods to the farmers. He expected the industrialists to support transportation projects in return for western agricultural support of the tariff. Clay's plan explains his leadership in sponsoring the tariff bill of 1824, but the Old South objected to the two major premises of the American System. That South, largely agrarian, was beginning to look with misgivings on a protective tariff, which it believed raised prices, and also opposed systems of internal improvements at government expense. The votes on the measure showed that the middle states, Kentucky, and the Northwest were entirely in favor of it, the South and the Southwest (except Kentucky) were solidly against it, and New England was divided. Outside the latter area it was evident that the tariff had become a sectional issue.

The tariff of 1824 granted increased protection to the manufacturers of woolen goods, iron, hemp, lead, and glass. Duties were raised on silks, linens, cutlery, and spices, although it was recognized that the commodities did not interfere with any home production or manufacture. A specific duty was levied on raw wool and the principle of minimum value was extended from cotton to woolen goods. The principle of the law was definitely protective. For a time it satisfied most of the manufacturing interests.

Not long after the passage of the tariff of 1824, Great Britain reduced the duty on foreign wool from sixpence to a half-penny per pound with the result that the British woolen manufacturer could still undersell his American rival. At the same time new mills were built in the United States in the expectation of protection against foreign competition. It became evident, also, that defects in the tariff law were responsible for the frauds practiced by many English shippers who, by falsely evaluating their goods, escaped the high duties. As a result of competition with English goods, the woolen manufacturers of the country were in serious difficulties and made pleas to Congress for increased protection in which they were joined by the producers of wool, whose interests were also depressed. Congress took heed and in 1827 a Woolens Bill was drafted. It aimed to apply the full establishment of the minimum principle to wool and woolens, thus granting additional protection. Although the measure passed the House, it failed in the Senate by the casting vote of the Vice-President, John C. Calhoun.

The failure of the Woolens Bill was followed by attempts to secure combined and systematic action for protection. A Tariff Convention was held in Harrisburg, Pennsylvania, in the summer of 1827, and a campaign was inaugurated for increased protection to raw and manufactured wool, hammered bar iron, hemp, flax, and other commodities. In these activities the Pennsylvanians had the aid of the German economist, Friedrich List, who was editor of a Reading, Pennsylvania newspaper from 1825 to 1830, and of Matthew Carey of Philadelphia, the most widely-read American economist in favor of protection. A plan for a complete protective policy was set forth in a memorial to Congress and in an address to the people of the country.

After a number of Machiavellian political maneuvers connected with the presidential candidacy of Andrew Jackson, a tariff bill was passed that did not truly represent majority opinion. The tariff of 1828 reached the apex of protective legislation prior to the Civil War. Increases on iron products went further than the recommendations of the Harrisburg Convention. The law granted high protection especially on woolen manufactures and raw wool received added protection. Rates were increased on many types of manufactured goods. The duty on hemp, as on many raw materials, was high and added to the expense of rope-makers, shipbuilders, and shipowners.

The new measure was derisively termed the "Tariff of Abominations" or the "Black Tariff." The South now became not only impatient but hostile. As the news of its passage reached that section, flags were placed at half-mast while parades and meetings expressed opposition to it. Leaders threatened resistance, the press condemned the law, and legislatures adopted resolutions voicing popular feeling. It was South

Carolina, however, and not Virginia, mother of the South, that led the active resistance.

Jackson, elected President in 1828, was lukewarm toward the tariff issue, although in his messages he pointed out that the abuses of the law should be remedied. Nullification sentiment increased in South Carolina but the Unionists there prevented a call for a convention. Attempts were made in Congress to revise the tariff downward and to remove the inconsistencies. The law of 1832 which followed did obliterate the "abominations," but the protective policy remained. Events now moved swiftly in South Carolina. A convention in that state adopted an Ordinance of Nullification declaring the acts of 1828 and 1832 null and void, after February 1, 1833. The legislature passed laws providing machinery for enforcing the ordinance even to the point of using military force. Threats of secession were made if the Federal government should try to enforce the law. In December, 1832, during the excitement of threatened revolution by the planters, Jackson urged Congress to reduce the tariff to the lowest possible point consistent with protecting those products that might suffer from foreign competition. He issued a Proclamation to the People of South Carolina in which he appealed to them, but also condemned nullification and threatened to enforce the federal laws at all costs.

South Carolina called for a convention of southern states, but without success, for the rest of the South opposed nullification. Henry Clay prevented the Nullification Ordinance from going into effect by engineering the compromise of 1833. It provided for a gradual reduction of all duties exceeding 20 per cent so that by 1842 no duties would be above that rate. It enlarged the free list somewhat, provided for home valuation of goods after 1842, and abolished the credit system in payment of duties, also after that date. Clay was motivated by the seriousness of the situation and by the fear that the protective system might be overthrown entirely.

As the compromise tariff reached its minimum rates in 1842, vigorous protective sentiment revived. The time was auspicious, for the Whigs who were more favorable to the tariff had a majority in Congress. The loss of government revenue brought about by the Panic of 1837 also provided an opportunity for the protectionists, who argued that the tariff was so low that it could not protect certain vital industries nor even produce a sufficient revenue for the government. The law of 1842 restored protection as duties were raised, but not uniformly, to the level of the tariff of 1832. The average rate on dutiable commodities under the measure was about 35 per cent.

The Whig policy lasted no longer than their period in power. The Democratic Walker tariff of 1846 inaugurated a low tariff policy which continued to the eve of the Civil War. Aside from this, the measure, which largely followed the recommendations of Secretary of the Treasury Robert J. Walker, was remarkable for its brevity, condensation, and comprehensiveness. It introduced well-organized, classified, and graded schedules beginning with A, which included chiefly luxuries at 100 per cent duties, down to I, which was the free list schedule on such commodities as coffee, tea, and copper ore. The law also defined methods of appraisement more clearly than ever before and established a system of government warehouses where goods could be kept for a specified length of time without the payment of duties. The act of 1857 reduced the tariff still lower chiefly because the income of the government exceeded its requirements. It reached an average of 18 per cent. Soon after it was passed a commercial panic broke, and the country as well as the government suffered from its effects.

BEGINNINGS OF ORGANIZED LABOR[2]

The germ of American labor unions may be found in the temporary associations of journeymen that were formed in a few crafts during the colonial period. While some of these organizations occasionally carried out strikes against the masters or employers and in other ways protested against certain conditions of labor, they were primarily beneficial societies. All were local and ephemeral. As the cleavage between the employer and employee classes began to broaden in the latter part of the eighteenth century and the early nineteenth century, they increased in number and while they still stressed mutual aid and friendly benefits for sickness, accident, and death, many of them took collective action in the defense of standards of apprenticeship, resisted competition with inferior workmanship, defended themselves against charges of combination and conspiracy, and sought better working conditions. Among these craft organizations, a few of the most important were the Philadelphia carpenters (1791), the Philadelphia shoemakers (1792), the Philadelphia Society of Journeymen Cordwainers (1794), the Baltimore printers (1791), the Baltimore tailors (1795), and the New York Society of Journeymen Shipwrights (1803). A number of these craft and beneficial societies were in-

[2] Unfortunately, statistics are lacking for a proper discussion of comparative wage rates and living standards in the period before 1850.

corporated by state legislatures, twenty-four being chartered in New York between 1800 and 1810, such as the New York Masons Society and the Albany Mechanical Society. The textile factories which arose at this time, employing women and children as well as men, were not touched by this early movement.

Although the number of labor organizations increased during the first quarter of the nineteenth century, progress was slow and labor gains were small. This was due partly to the fact that public opinion generally opposed such organizations on the grounds that they were unpatriotic, dangerous, illegal, and were responsible for increasing the prices of commodities. Labor did have the sympathy of a minority who insisted that workmen be given the right to organize to improve their condition. But the courts were opposed. In England the Combination Acts (1799 and 1800) made it illegal for workmen to form unions in order to get higher wages or a decrease of hours. These influences had the effect of discrediting labor organizations in the United States. Employers were vigorously opposed and formed associations. The Society of Master Cordwainers (or shoemakers) of the City of Philadelphia (1789) and the Boston shipowners are examples of early employers' associations, which, while promoting social and educational activities and attempting to secure legislation to aid their particular trades, also opposed the rising unions of workmen within the various crafts.

By the latter part of the eighteenth century, craft societies carried out a number of strikes or "turn-outs" as they were called which revealed the growing separation between employers and workers. In 1776 and 1786, the Philadelphia printers struck against a reduction of wages; in 1795 and 1805 the tailors of Baltimore walked out of their shops, making certain demands; and the journeymen shoemakers of Philadelphia called strikes in 1796, 1798, and 1799. In 1805, the Philadelphia Cordwainers went on strike demanding the wage scale prevailing in New York and Baltimore and a discontinuance of the rebate of wages for export work. Eight union leaders were arrested on a charge of criminal conspiracy. The case was tried in the Mayor's Court. The prosecution quoted British authorities to the effect that a "conspiracy" of workmen to raise their wages was criminal at common law. The employers complained of their inability to carry out contracts, the refusal of the union members to work with nonmembers, violence, and the application of a boycott. The men were found guilty of conspiracy and each fined $8.00. The strike came to an end and an important precedent was established for the prosecution of labor union activities in the years that immediately followed.

Five other criminal conspiracy cases were brought against union shoemakers during the period, three of which were decided against the workmen. By 1809, such terms as "scab," "general turnout," and "strike" were commonly used. In the celebrated trial of the journeymen cordwainers of New York City in 1810, as well as in the labor disputes among such groups as shipbuilders, carpenters, printers, and hat workers, it became evident that the strike was beginning to rise to some importance as a weapon of labor. But the number of strikes to 1835 was not large—records of twenty-four exist—nor were they of serious consequence.

Beginning in 1827, the labor movement entered a new phase, characterized by the combination of local societies or unions into trade associations. As a result of the failure of a strike of the Philadelphia journeymen carpenters, who sought a ten-hour day, labor leaders of that city, in 1827, were successful in uniting a number of craft societies into one unit, known as the Philadelphia Mechanics' Union of Trade Associations. Six years later, this organization became the Trades-Union of the City and County of Philadelphia, and by 1836 included fifty-three societies with more than 10,000 members. The movement took hold elsewhere. The General Trades-Union of New York City included fifty-two societies. Similar movements could be found in other cities, including Baltimore, Boston, Albany, and Newark. A regional union, the New England Association of Farmers, Mechanics, and Other Workingmen, also appeared. After these general trade unions were formed, an attempt was made to organize them nationally. Conventions were held in New York in 1834 and 1835, and in Philadelphia in 1836 and 1837. The latter was poorly attended and the entire movement was obliterated by the Panic of 1837.

The establishment of the Philadelphia Mechanics' Union of Trade Associations in 1827 produced a workingmen's party in that city. Such labor parties were formed in other localities from Maine to Georgia. Labor candidates met with success especially in New England, New Jersey, and Delaware. This political aspect of the labor movement was short-lived, but was not bare of results. It supported a number of reforms, including free, tax-supported schools, the abolition of imprisonment for debt, mechanics' lien laws protecting worker's tools from attachment for debt, and changes in the compulsory militia system. These reforms were achieved in many states during the period. Among other demands, not as successful at this particular time, were the restriction of child labor in the factories, the abolition of chartered monopolies, and election and judicial reforms.

Between 1834 and 1837 a large number of new craft unions appeared, including a few women's organizations among factory workers, seamstresses and bookbinders. Some of the new local unions joined the trade associations in their respective communities; others remained independent. At this time, the first attempts were made to form national organizations of a single craft. The cordwainers from different cities sent forty-five delegates to a cordwainers' convention held in New York in 1836. The combmakers, carpenters, weavers, and printers also held separate national conventions in the same year. But this movement did not get far. The Panic of 1837 put an end to most labor organizations when large numbers were thrown out of work. The progress made by local unions, associations of local unions, the national organization of trade unions, and national organizations of single trades, came to an end. Only a few local unions lived through the disastrous years, 1837–1843.

During this period of labor activity, the first labor papers appeared. The earliest wage-earners' newspaper published anywhere was the *Mechanics Free Press* of the Philadelphia Mechanics' Union of Trade Associations. Its initial number was published in January, 1828, antedating the first similar journal in England by two years. Other labor journals appeared in America. George H. and Frederick W. Evans began publishing the *Daily Sentinel* and *Young America* in 1830. A little later, George H. Evans became editor of the important *Working Man's Advocate*. These labor papers supported many of the reforms demanded by labor during this early period.

Following the crushing blow given to labor organizations by the panic years, labor was affected by the humanitarian and socialistic ideals of the decade of the forties. Labor congresses were held and workingmen's associations formed, but most often by philanthropists who had an interest in labor rather than by the workers themselves. The New England Workingmen's Association (1845) is a good example of the type of labor organization of the period. Many groups of workingmen developed cooperative buying. At the meetings and congresses of the various workingmen's associations a number of reformers, such as Robert Dale Owen, Albert Brisbane, George Ripley, and Wendell Phillips, took part. Among the reforms discussed and demanded by workmen in the cities were land reforms—free lands for homesteads and a limitation on the amount of land one person could own, the ten-hour day, and improved working conditions. Under the leadership of utopian reformers a few experiments were tried in communal living, but these all failed (p. 256).

At the time when workers' organizations were at a low ebb, there were a number of legal gains for labor. In 1842, the Supreme Court of Massachusetts in the case of the Commonwealth *vs.* Hunt declared that a trade union was a lawful organization, that a strike for a closed shop was legal, and that the members of a union were not collectively responsible for illegal acts committed by individuals. While some aspects of the decision were not upheld by other courts in later times, the decision was a turning point in the legal history of American trade unionism. Another example of a gain for labor was in the executive order issued by President Van Buren in 1840, establishing the ten-hour day for laborers and mechanics in the employ of the Federal government. In 1843, Massachusetts forbade the employment of children under twelve years of age for more than ten hours a day. Although little was accomplished, the Massachusetts legislature in 1845 led the way in appointing a committee to investigate labor conditions. In 1847, New Hampshire enacted a ten-hour factory law. The next year Pennsylvania provided for a ten-hour work day and forbade the employment of children under twelve in cotton, woolen, silk, and linen mills.

During the decade of the fifties, labor organizations revived and the number of local craft unions increased rapidly. The origin of several labor unions of the present can be traced to that decade. Many were now organized on a national scale. A Convention of Journeymen Printers met in 1850 and two years later became the National Typographical Union of North America. National unions were also formed among the stonecutters, hat finishers, ironmolders, machinists, and blacksmiths. On the eve of the Civil War, twenty-six American trade unions had national organizations. The Panic of 1857 caused much unemployment and affected the labor movement adversely to some extent, but, because of the shortage of workers during the war, labor emerged after that conflict in a greatly strengthened condition.

All of this union activity was confined to the skilled crafts, whose members generally worked not in factories, but in small shops. Skilled labor was to remain scarce and, by English standards, well paid. As the factory system arose, industrial or mill towns made their appearance. The movement of unskilled workers from country districts toward urban centers became rapid after 1820 as the textile industries expanded. The population of the mill towns of New England, New York, and Pennsylvania grew rapidly. Other types of manufacturing industries also aided the rapid growth of population in the new industrial centers.

Closing time at the
Washington Textile Mills,
Lawrence, Massachusetts

As increasing hordes of workers left the farms for the towns, they
had to adjust themselves to a new way of living. Their former freedom of action was now changed to regimentation; the broad spaces
they once commanded disappeared as they crowded into barrack-
like homes; and the evils ever present in city life made their appearance. Drunkenness, pauperism, juvenile crime, and other ills grew.
In the older commercial cities, the old-time craftsmen, the organized
groups, were decreasing in relation to the new skilled and unskilled
industrial workers.

While most of the towns were similar in many ways to English industrial centers of the same period, with their attendant misery and
poverty, there were some exceptions. The traveler, Harriet Martineau,
wrote in glowing terms of the factory operatives at Waltham with
their lyceum, library, and lectures. She took note of the "well-nourished
and intelligent dandy mechanic" in places that she visited in the North.
For several decades, Lowell factory girls with their white dresses and
excellent deportment, housed in strictly chaperoned boarding houses,
lived relatively happily and correctly even though hours were long and
wages not high. Fair conditions and programs of entertainment were
provided to attract operatives from the farms. Charles Dickens
visited the Lowell mills and was enthusiastic about the life of the
workers there. But such conditions were not representative of most
of the towns, where squalor and evil were widespread. And even at
Waltham and Lowell conditions deteriorated in the 1840's as immigrants displaced natives. For the factory workers hours of work were
long; wages were low; and, there was a constant speeding up of pro-

duction. In an age when the demand for capital exceeded the supply, low wages seemed a social gain. But wages in the United States were higher than elsewhere.

EXPERIMENTS IN REORGANIZING INDUSTRIAL SOCIETY

The misery that rising industrial urban centers brought, as workers were crowded together in factories and tenements, and as poverty increased because of depression or misfortune, led many thoughtful persons to wonder whether society could not be better organized. The utopian dream goes far back into the past, long before industrialization and no doubt is as old as the imagination of man itself. At first, most of these plans were religious in scope and the celibate ideals which were common to many of them brought a natural end to those experiments. But during the decades prior to the Civil War, experimental Utopias appeared which were practical attempts to apply cooperative principles to small communities in order to reshape the rising capitalistic form of society. Many were definitely filled with the religious spirit as people tried to escape the first hideous impact of the industrial revolution on an older agrarian civilization. But others were systematic attempts to create a happier form of industrial order. The first, and one of the most important attempts to accomplish this was made by Robert Owen, the British philanthropist and industrialist.

Robert Owen, the owner of a textile factory in New Lanarch, Scotland, devoted himself to improving the living conditions of his employees. He stressed the principles that the environment shaped character, that the profit system was wrong and that wealth belonged chiefly to the labor which created it. As a beginning, he reduced working hours; he ruled that no children under ten years of age should work in his factories; he built decent homes; he provided free schools and free medical service for his employees; and he opened stores where provisions could be obtained almost at cost. Although his community was greatly improved, he could not put his socialistic principles completely into effect because his partners and other industrialists opposed, ridiculed, and prevented him. After publishing his *Social System* in 1821, in which he condemned the existing social order in its stress on individualism, competition and gain, and declared that the happiness of the many should be placed above the enrichment of the few, he turned to America as the best place to begin the establishment of his self-sufficient communities.

In 1825, Owen founded the New Harmony settlement on the Wabash river in Indiana. "The New Harmony Community of Equality" provided for the equality of property, labor, and opportunity as well as complete freedom of speech and action. All were to cooperate and each member of the group was to contribute to the general effort and receive its benefits according to his needs. Religious and political fanatics as well as a number of conscientious and well-meaning individuals, in all about 1,000 men, women, and children, joined the new colony. Some farming was begun, and a hat factory, sawmill, candle factory, and shops of different sorts were built at the expense of the founder, who left his son Robert Dale Owen in charge of the community as he toured the United States and Mexico giving lectures on his socialistic concepts and plans. There was no dearth of inquisitive travelers to the community, who stopped at its tavern and made it pay. But the experiment itself failed. The constant clashes between differing personalities, the dislike of work on the part of many, and the lack of any real authority in the community, which resulted in virtual anarchy, brought about its end. In 1827, Owen admitted failure.

In other plans to establish ideal communities, the ideas of Charles Fourier, a pioneer French socialist, were followed. Unlike Robert Owen, who was sure that the environment shaped character, Fourier insisted that human nature was unchangeable and that society, therefore, must be adapted to the individual. He believed that groups should be organized into ideal communities, each consisting of about 1,600 persons living in a state of self-sufficiency on several thousand acres of land. In each of the cooperative communities, surpluses should be produced and equitably distributed among the three classes: labor, capital, and talent. Albert Brisbane, an American disciple of Fourier, returned to the United States from France in 1834 and began lecturing and writing about Fourierism. Inspired by the Fourier idea some forty communities sprang up of which Brook Farm, 1841–1847, was the most famous. All were unsuccessful.

Among the more radical communal experiments in social and religious thinking, the Oneida Colony in New York state was outstanding. It was the most prosperous and the best organized from the industrial point of view. The Perfectionists, as they were called, worked out new forms of social relationships, especially in regard to economic communism and a plan of "complex marriage." John Humphrey Noyes, leader of the group, and his fellow members believed in industrial progress but rejected the "evils of competition."

From its beginning in 1848, the community grew. Machine shops, canning and silk factories, and other types of works were built. A branch colony was established in Wallingford, Connecticut. The Oneidans survived when other similar experiments were only memories. In 1879, chiefly because of objections from the surrounding communities to their communistic method of living, especially to the plan of "complex marriage" and also on account of dissatisfaction from the younger element within the group, communism was abandoned, but the industries were continued under joint-stock ownership at Niagara Falls, Ontario, and in the State of New York.

THE EXTENT OF INDUSTRIALIZATION

These Utopian efforts to capture and preserve a simpler organization of society and production emphasize the continuing agricultural character of American life in the 1840's and 1850's. Yet the basic change that was taking place was the great upsurge of factory production. In 1839, agriculture accounted for roughly three-quarters of American commodity production and manufacturing for about one-sixth—the remaining shares being a negligible fraction for mining, and about one-tenth for construction. By 1859, the agricultural product was only a little more than half the total and manufacturing had risen to one-third.

The nation of 1860 could still be called agricultural. Farming, for example, was the pursuit of more than four times as many workers as manufacturing. But the rate of growth of industry, with its product and employment nearly doubling each decade, left no doubt that the industrial process had a momentum that would not be checked. The known resources of the United States and its rate of population growth assured all thoughtful forecasters that it was only a matter of time before the nation would surpass the production of the industrial leaders of Europe.

CHAPTER II

Commerce and Trade

The history of United States foreign trade from 1790 to 1860 was one of a very gradual movement toward self-sufficiency. Products, once imported, came to be made or grown within the nation, and the great American exports of agricultural staples ultimately suffered from the competition of other areas. Aided by European wars, imports and exports reached a peak in 1807 that was presumably never again approached as a percentage of the gross national product, although the latter has not been calculated for this early period.[1] During the first half of the nineteenth century, however, growing exports of cotton and imports of finished and semi-finished manufactures increased foreign trade almost as rapidly as the probable growth of the national product.

Until the mid-nineteenth century the United States carried a large percentage of its trade in its own ships. The consequent payments by foreigners for freight charges plus foreign investment in the United States allowed the nation to import more than it exported. Only in occasional years of depression in which foreign investment lagged and trade decreased did the United States have to part with more goods than it received.

---

[1] "In broad terms, national product . . . is a comprehensive measure of the nation's total annual production of commodities and services. Only the end products of a year's economic activity are included." *Historical Statistics,* p. 131.

Meanwhile, a great rise in trade was taking place within the country. Cotton from the South fed the mills of New England and the Middle States; food products from the West freed eastern agricultural workers for factory labor. The east coast cities stood in relation to the back country as Liverpool and London stood to the United States. The domestic metropolitan centers not only sent manufactured products to the interior to pay for food and raw materials, but Eastern capitalists financed additional shipments that represented investment in the West.

THE RISE OF AMERICAN FOREIGN COMMERCE

Independence brought the problem of finding new markets, for the protection and advantages that the British navigation system had furnished were ended. The British colonies were in general officially closed to American vessels; the encouragement that American shipbuilding had enjoyed within the Empire no longer existed; and the protection that the British navy afforded against pirates and enemies had come to an end. But within a decade after independence, American commerce was thriving again and was beginning to expand. Wars in Europe reopened British Empire and other European trades to neutral shipping. The efforts made by Americans to find new markets and ports for commerce and trade succeeded as Yankee sea captains and sailors scoured the Seven Seas; made contacts with Asia, the East Indies, and Africa; carried American products around the world; and, returned home with new and exotic products from these distant lands.

When the new government went into effect in 1789, Congress promptly began exercising its authority to give advantages to American shipping. The tariff law, passed at the very beginning of the life of Congress, was intended to raise revenue, and even to encourage and protect manufactures, but it also aided American shipping by granting a discount of 10 per cent of the duties on imports brought to the United States in vessels built and owned by Americans. To encourage direct trade with the Far East, American vessels carrying tea were required to pay much less duty than foreign vessels, and relatively high duties were imposed on tea brought from Europe in the vessels of any country, a blow directed principally at the British East India Company. Another act of Congress passed at this time gave American-built and American-owned vessels a decided advantage in low tonnage duties, whereas foreign vessels were required to pay high tonnage rates on entering American ports. To permit a monopoly of coastal trade, American vessels engaged in home commerce paid tonnage duties only once a year, while foreign ships in the American coastal trade had to pay at each entry. In 1790, an act regulating the employment and activities of seamen provided the basis for a policy satisfactory enough to remain in force until the changes made by the La Follette Act of 1915.

Many factors contributed to the rise of American foreign commerce during the early years of the Republic. But most important was the demand from Europe for American products, consisting chiefly of agricultural commodities and raw materials, as well as for American vessels to carry European goods. This demand came as a result of the European wars that followed the bloody French Revolution. The execution of Louis XVI early in 1793 was the signal for England to enter the war already begun by other European powers against France. The withdrawal of millions of Europeans from their farms or industrial pursuits in the years that followed brought shortages of commodities in Europe and resultant prosperity to America. The carrying trade of France and her allies was in large part taken over by American merchantmen and from time to time, royal governors of the British West Indies under special proclamations permitted a broad American trade with those islands. Not only were American vessels engaged in the carrying trade of England and France, but by 1800, about 92 per cent of all imports and exports to and from the United States were carried in American vessels—a contrast from the period, 1783–1789, when British vessels carried most American commerce, as England furnished the large bulk of manufactured goods. The tonnage registered for foreign trade increased from 123,893 tons in 1789 to 981,017 tons in 1810.

Although the period to 1808 was one of increasing maritime prosperity, a number of difficulties had to be faced and solved. The young nation, at the beginning of its career under the Constitution, was almost drawn into the war over the question whether the United States should aid France on the basis of the treaties of 1778, under which France assisted the Americans in their struggle for independence. Hamilton maintained that the French treaties were no longer in effect since the governments that had made them—both American and French—no longer existed. Jefferson believed that the treaties were made between the peoples of the two countries and were therefore in effect, but he had no desire to get into the war. President Washington issued a Proclamation of Neutrality (1793) which stated that the United States would "adopt and pursue a conduct friendly and impartial toward the belligerent powers," and warned Americans against aiding any of the belligerent powers. The word neutrality was avoided out of deference to Jefferson and in the hope that Great Britain would note its absence and grant maritime concessions to the United States to keep it neutral. The proclamation was enacted into law by Congress in 1794, setting an American precedent for neutrality.

As prosperity came, difficulties also arose with England. In addition to the border problems remaining from the treaty of 1783, new problems had arisen as American vessels engaged in the carrying trade for France were captured, and Americans were seized on the high seas and impressed into the British navy. On the other hand, prewar debts had not been paid to British merchants and no steps had been taken to reimburse Loyalists for their confiscated estates. John Jay was sent to negotiate a treaty which averted the danger of war between the two nations but which contained features very unsatisfactory to most Americans. Under the terms of the Jay Treaty the English promised to evacuate the northwestern posts, which they did in 1796. A mixed commission was created to adjudicate American shipping losses in return for certain maritime measures for the duration of the war. By 1802, more than $10,000,000 had been paid, but England did not end the capture of vessels, which continued throughout the period. The Jay Treaty also provided that the United States would guarantee the payment of the pre-Revolutionary debts owed by Americans to British merchants, the amount to be worked out by a commission. Settlement was made in 1802 when the United States government agreed to pay £600,000, which was really only a part of the claims. Two commissions were set up to consider the boundary questions. In regard to West Indian trade, a clause provided that American ships of a burden less than seventy tons could trade with the British West Indies, but on condition that the vessels would not carry molasses, sugar, coffee, cocoa, or cotton to any ports other than American. The Senate struck out this clause as insulting and ignominious. No provision was made in the treaty regarding the impressment of American seamen or payment for the slaves carried to England during the Revolution. The treaty was ratified by the Senate with difficulty and attempts were made in the House to block the necessary appropriations to carry it into effect. Many considered it a shameful treaty and Jay was severely and bitterly condemned. But Great Britain had granted some concessions in order to keep her best foreign customer and to insure American neutrality.

France objected to the Jay Treaty and refused to receive American diplomats or representatives. France went further and began to capture an increasing number of American ships engaged in the British carrying trade. Hostilities broke out on the high seas between the two nations, and vessels were attacked and captured by both sides. An undeclared war was waged with France for two years (1798–1800). Military preparations were made; the tiny navy was enlarged; privateers were commissioned; and, seventy captured and condemned prizes yielded $700,000. Damages suffered by Americans ran into the millions. In 1800, Napoleon, planning a revival of a French colonial empire in the region of Louisiana, agreed to a "Convention of Peace, Commerce and Navigation." Its terms put an end to the treaties of 1778 in return for our relinquishing claims against France for the loss of American ships and cargoes, which then became claims of the shipowners against the government of the United States. The maritime principles of the treaties of 1778, including the principle "free ships make free goods" and a most-favored-nation clause, were continued. With this settlement, commercial prosperity continued with few interruptions as American vessels continued to engage in carrying trade for England and France.

INTERNATIONAL COMPLICATIONS

Many American shipowners, in order to evade the Rule of 1756, a dictum of British prize courts enforced during the Seven Years' War that neutrals could not engage in a commerce during war time from which they were excluded in time of peace, worked out a policy whereby French colonial goods were taken to ports of the United States and re-exported as American goods. In the case of the *Polly* in 1802, during a brief interval of peace in the European wars, a British court decided that this practice—known as the "broken voyage" —was not a violation of the Rule of 1756. But in 1805, in the case of the *Essex,* the decision was reversed. The British court this time decided that such goods were subject to confiscation. Thus the doctrine of the broken voyage was discredited by England and an increasing number of American vessels were captured.

Higher American maritime wages led many sailors to desert the British navy and take service, with false citizenship papers, as United States seamen. To try to recover some of these men the British navy stopped American vessels, examined the crews, and impressed those suspected of being runaway subjects. In these inquests the naval officers adhered to the rule "once an Englishman, always an Englishman." Regardless of protests, British men-of-war patrolled the American coast, even within the three-mile international limit. In addition came the British Orders in Council declaring most of the coast of western Europe in a state of blockade, and Napoleon's decrees, by which he tried to ruin England economically by closing the continent to her trade. Thus neutral shipping was liable to seizure by either England or France. It meant that if the measures were even partially enforced, they would be destructive of American and other neutral commerce.

Failing to solve the maritime problems that confronted the country through diplomatic channels, President Jefferson suggested to Congress that an Embargo Act be passed, intended to bring the belligerent powers to terms through economic pressure. By means of a policy of "peaceable coercion," Jefferson believed that the economic boycott would bring England and France to terms within a short period of time, because of their war needs. The law, passed late in 1807, closed American ports to all foreign commerce and prohibited the departure of American vessels to any foreign country. It permitted American coastal commerce, but, as vessels took advantage of this liberty and sailed to foreign ports, a supplementary act required such vessels to give heavy bond that they would not violate the law.

The embargo failed in its objectives. After fourteen months, it was evident that the warring nations of Europe could continue their struggle without American help. In the United States, the results of the embargo soon became evident. While the law was grossly violated, it put an end to most American foreign commerce. Vessels were tied up in the great seaports of the country and thousands of seamen were thrown out of work. New England commerce suffered most, but some compensation was obtained in the stimulus given to manufactures as imports of foreign manufactured goods were cut off and commercial and merchant capital found its way into industry in the middle states as well as in New England. Coastal trading kept up a semblance of commercial activity. The South suffered severely as its staples could not be exported abroad and depression spread over that region. Many of the vessels that illegally left port for France were seized by Napoleon on the ground that they could not lawfully leave the United States. Within a year vessels and cargoes valued at $10,000,000 were confiscated.

New Englanders strenuously opposed the passage of the Embargo Act and the unprofitable boycott, for in spite of the diplomatic tangles over maritime questions and the loss of ships, profits were high. In Congress, the Federalists maintained that such a policy was unconstitutional, for they stressed that it was not the regulation of commerce, but its annihilation. In New England a few talked about secession which was even advocated at meetings and in pulpits. Timothy Dwight of Connecticut suggested secession in a series of sermons that he preached on the Biblical text: "Come out therefore from among them and be ye separate saith the Lord." An enforcement law, passed to prevent the evasions of the embargo, especially stirred many New England Federalists who objected to turning the United States navy "into a police squadron to assist in destroying American commerce." It is interesting to note that, by the time of the embargo, the Federalists and Republicans had reversed their stand on the question of the constructive powers of Congress under the Constitution.

In coercing foreign states, the embargo was ineffective. It affected English industries adversely but increased the British carrying trade and shipping. Toward the close of his administration Jefferson admitted the failure of the embargo to influence England and France to adopt more reasonable policies toward neutrals and asked Congress to repeal the measure. In its place a non-intercourse act was adopted opening commerce again with all the nations of the world except France and Great Britain, and prohibiting all commercial intercourse with those two nations. Madison, who followed Jefferson, first attempted to solve the foreign problems that confronted him through diplomacy but he also failed. Then, like his predecessor, he turned to legislation. The Macon Act (1810) attempted to play England and France against each other for the benefit of the United States by permitting trade with all the countries of the world but providing that if either England or France should revoke its edicts, the United States would prohibit trade with the other. Napoleon accepted the terms immediately and commerce was cut off with Great Britain in spite of the objections of an infuriated minority in Congress, while England warned that France would not in fact remove restrictions on American commerce or stop the capture of American vessels.

THE WAR OF 1812

The trend of events indicated that America's peace program had failed and the country appeared to be headed toward war. National feeling was also aroused because of the belief that the British were actively inciting the Indians to hostilities against American settlers in the Northwest. That region held Great Britain responsible for the Indian battle at Tippecanoe in Indiana territory. The West demanded the expulsion of the British from Canada as the remedy for such troubles. Recent research has shown that there was little truth in the assertion that British officials had anything to do with the Indian uprisings. But events such as these created the psychological situation necessary for war.

President Madison called Congress together in November, 1811, and recommended that the country prepare for hostilities. The twelfth Congress which received the message included many younger men to whom the name "War Hawks" was given. They were chiefly from the South and West and resented the insults to national honor inflicted on the high seas and supposedly in the West. They were also ardent expansionists in a period when nationalism was broadening. They demanded the annexation of Canada and Spanish East and West Florida. After months of debate in Congress few steps were taken for adequate financial, military, or naval preparations. Yet President Madison sent Congress his war message on June 1, 1812. He stated that a declaration of war had been forced upon the United States and he reviewed the story of British aggressions upon neutral rights including the "continued practice of violating the American flag on the great highway of nations and of seizing and carrying off persons sailing under it," the hovering over and harassing of the American coast, and the inauguration of sweeping blockades that could not be enforced. He insinuated that the British were responsible for "the warfare just renewed by the savages on one of our extensive frontiers." The declaration of war adopted by the House of Representatives was largely sectional—New York, New Jersey, and New England casting seventeen votes for it and thirty-five against it, while the rest of the country cast sixty-two votes in favor of war and only fourteen for peace. Murmurs of secession were again heard in New England as opposition was expressed in various ways. The lack of preparation of every kind for such a war might have quickly resulted in a national calamity if it had not been for the fact that British power was concentrated in Europe in a final struggle with Napoleon.

The war affected commerce immediately. Imports and exports dropped drastically. During hostilities, 515 letters of marque and reprisal were granted to Americans as all the seaboard states from Maine to Louisiana sent privateers to sea against England. They brought home 1,345 British prizes valued at almost $40,000,000— to the consternation of British shipping interests and to the alarm of marine insurance companies forced to increase their rates. Aroused by these American successes on the high seas and by spectacular sea duels in which Americans were usually victorious, the British government tightened the blockade of American ports. Early in 1814 the entire eastern seaboard was blockaded, including New England, which had been exempt until this time because of pro-British sentiment in that area. So effective was the blockade that by the late summer of 1814 only rarely did a swift American vessel steal through it. Commerce came almost to a standstill. The carrying trade was ruined and exports for the entire year were only a fifth of the pre- and post-war average. Coastal commerce also felt the effect of the blockade. Ship-owners, mercantile interests, and shippers were in distress; the destruction of exports was ruinous to planters and farmers; imports practically ceased except through a few favored New England ports; and government revenue from duties declined to a low level. The China trade and the whaling industry both suffered seriously. It is true that the cutting off of commerce, as during the embargo, encouraged the transfer of capital to manufacturing enterprises and woolen, cotton, and iron production expanded. However, this did not offset the damages of war and the disasters to commerce. A serious economic crisis was averted only at the end of the hostilities in 1814.

On the military front the war was equally discouraging. Inept leadership and untrained troops led to defeats on the Canadian border, and inadequate defense resulted in the burning of Washington, D. C. by a naval expedition. Early in 1815, two weeks after the peace treaty had been signed, Andrew Jackson won the only important military victory of the entire war at New Orleans.

Both nations were war-weary—England especially, after twenty years of continental warfare—and agreed to a peace on the basis of a return to the *status quo ante bellum* as to territory. Older problems regarding the Indians, disputed boundaries, the fisheries, and others, were to be decided later by commissions. The Treaty of Ghent secured none of the ends for which the United States went to war. The problems relating to impressments and interference with neutral trade and commerce were dropped because of the termination of the European struggle. The campaigns of Andrew Jackson against the Creeks in the South, however, broke the Indian power there and opened the lower Mississippi Valley to settlement.

RECOVERY AND EXPANSION

Because of a flood of British manufactured goods and an accumulated and rapidly rising demand for American cotton, commercial recovery was rapid after the War of 1812. In spite of high exports, the surplus of imports, many of them carried on British credit, was much larger in both 1815 and 1816 than in any other year prior to the Civil War. But late in 1818 foreign trade declined and remained at lower levels as the country suffered an economic depression. A substantial part of the English credit was lost in business failures, making British investors wary of American risks for nearly a decade.

At the cessation of hostilities, it was clear that England and other countries would try to regain their lost carrying trade. In 1817, as part of the movement toward national self-sufficiency which followed the war, a Navigation Act, similar in spirit to earlier British legislation, was adopted. It provided that all goods and commodities must be carried between American ports in vessels owned entirely by American citizens. This policy has remained unchanged. The law also prohibited the importation of goods from any foreign country except in American vessels or in the vessels of the country from which the goods came. Provision was made for the repeal of these restrictions if a foreign nation removed similar restraints on American vessels.

Until 1820, the number of treaties made by the United States was small. During the next forty years, the field and scope of treaty-making were greatly extended. Among the varied commercial subjects involved were neutral rights, release of shipping tolls, and consuls. Conventional relations of commerce and navigation came to be established with the nations of Europe, the rising republics of Latin America, and with other regions of the world. In time these agreements and treaties bore commercial fruit.

The decade 1820–1830 was a flourishing one for American ship-owners as the percentage of American goods carried in American vessels reached the peak of 92.5 (1826). But the amounts of foreign commerce, both imports and exports, did not increase proportionately with the growing population, dispersion of peoples westward, expansion of industry, and the increase of national wealth. During this period packet or liner service as distinguished from the "regular trader" and the "tramp" came into use. Packets or liners were vessels sailing on a printed schedule of fixed dates between specified ports. The first packet service was the Black Ball Line out of New York which began monthly service with Liverpool in 1818. After a year or two, its packets sailed on weekly schedules. Among other lines that followed were the Red Star Line, and the Blue Swallowtail Line. By 1824, New York had also inaugurated packet service with London and Le Havre. About the same time packet lines of full-rigged ships, brigs, and schooners were established in coastal commerce.

During the boom of the 1830's foreign trade again increased, particularly with Great Britain, France, and the countries of northern Europe. In 1830, the British West Indies were at last opened to American shipping, but relatively the trade with that area was not as important as it had been during the colonial period.

Following the recovery in 1843 from the long depression many factors aided the expansion of commerce. The victory of Great Britain over China in the Opium War of 1842 was shared by the United States. In 1844 Caleb Cushing made a treaty with the Chinese, permitting trade with several ports—not only Canton as heretofore—and granting other privileges. Trade expanded with the Hawaiian Islands especially after California was acquired and the Oregon question settled. Ports were also opened in Japan after Commodore Perry sailed into the Bay of Yedo on his memorable voyages in 1853 and 1854 to demand from Japan humane treatment for American sailors abandoned on Japanese shores. For twenty years the United States had attempted to prevent the maltreatment, and often death, of its sailors shipwrecked in Japanese waters while scouring the north Pacific in quest of whale. For more than two centuries the Japanese had continued a national policy of seclusion and exclusion which prevented any contacts with them except through the Dutch trading station on the little island of Deshima in the harbor of Nagasaki. Examples of the "benefits" of western civilization, presented to the Japanese when Perry forced his way into Japan, included sewing machines, clocks, a telegraph instrument, a telescope, a model steam locomotive, and many other products of an industrialized culture, but it was the fear of the guns on Perry's battleships that helped to bring the first treaty between the two nations.

In addition to these factors that increased American commerce, the repeal of the corn laws, the ending of tariffs, and the removal of the entire navigation system by England aided the American carrying trade. The failure of crops in both England and Ireland between 1845 and 1850 increased American grain exports and Irish immigration. The Crimean War and the Sepoy Mutiny also benefited American shipping, when England for a time depended upon other maritime nations to transport much of her commerce. The gold rushes to California and Australia not only expanded shipping through the carrying of passengers and supplies to those regions but increased specie and enlarged the purchasing power of the United States and other countries, which in turn also stimulated economic development.

The decade of the 1850's was one of intense activity in all aspects of American economic life and this was reflected in a reversal of the

American ships in Mocha Harbor, Arabia

long-run trend of imports and exports. In 1850 the total volume of trade was $239,000,000, a decrease from the best years of the 1830's. By 1860 the total, in constant dollars, had risen to nearly $700,000,-000. Again, cotton accounted for a large part of the increase in exports. Imports had always been greater in variety than exports and these relations did not change greatly over the entire period between 1790 and 1861. Finished manufactures always constituted more than 50 per cent of the total, although importations of raw materials and semi-finished products increased from 15 per cent in 1820 to 25 per cent in 1860, paralleling the growth of American manufactures. Sugar, coffee, tea, cigars, tobaccos, and molasses constituted about 20 per cent of all imports. Luxuries made up the balance. Among imported manufactures, the textiles—wool, silk, cotton, and linen—held chief place and made up almost one-third of all imports in 1860. Iron and steel manufactures ranked next in importance. By 1860, trade with Europe accounted for three-fourths of the exports and three-fifths of the imports, although commercial relations were growing with Canada, South America, and Asia. Trade with Africa was small, in fact almost negligible.

THE CONTEST FOR THE ATLANTIC TRADE

The total tonnage of the American merchant marine, foreign and coastal, expanded from 202,000 gross tons [1] in 1789 to 5,354,000

---

[1] Gross tonnage refers to the space measurement of vessels, 100 cubic feet being called one ton.

in 1860. After the Civil War American tonnage in foreign trade declined and did not recover until the twentieth century, although
coastal tonnage continued to grow. In 1845, tonnage engaged in foreign
trade first exceeded the pre-1812 level. From then on it expanded
rapidly to reach 2,379,000 in 1860. The remarkable rise of the merchant marine during the middle years of the century was due partly
to advantages American shipbuilders possessed over foreign competitors
in building wooden sailing vessels, and the subsequent decline, to
a disadvantage in building iron steamers.

In the transatlantic trade the high revenue freight and passenger
business went to the companies whose ships were fast and reliable. By
1840 subsidized British lines of steamers like Cunard were getting the
best traffic away from the sailing ships. The initial American answer
was not to subsidize steam but to improve the sailing ship.

The remarkably long and narrow, wooden sailing vessels with
broad and lofty expanse of sail that from the middle 1840's on came
to be known all over the world as American clipper ships were developed to compete with the speed of the steamer. With good winds
they were faster than the early side-wheelers, much steadier riding,
and more economical to run. The discovery of gold in California
gave an added impetus to clipper construction. Many vessels took
cargoes and passengers to California and then crossed the Pacific
to the Orient, returning with tea, silk, and spices. These Valkyries
of the sea, with their long narrow bows and tapering hulls, could
travel faster than any other type of sailing vessel afloat. The names
of many clipper ships—the *Flying Cloud,* the *Comet,* the *Andrew
Jackson,* the *Flying Fish,* the *Lightning,* and the *Donald McKay,*
named after one of the greatest of shipbuilders—were well known to
Americans of the mid-nineteenth century, for races between clippers
to the Orient and elsewhere, and the breaking of speed records, were
given broad publicity and were the subjects of excited discussion.

Meanwhile, England, lacking wood but possessing quantities of
iron and coal, experimented with steam-driven iron vessels. It had
been an American vessel that had made the first ocean trip using
some steam power. The *Savannah,* under Moses Rogers, without
passengers or freight—for few were willing to risk life, possessions,
or freight on what seemed to be a fantastic voyage—left Savannah,
Georgia, for Liverpool in 1819. During the trip, the engines with
which the vessel was equipped furnished power only six times for
a total of eighty hours; the vessel's sails were used for the rest of the
voyage. The tremendous amount of wood necessary and the imper-

fections of the engines at that early date marked the experiment as a failure. English initiative and inventive genius, spurred by the disadvantages that Great Britain was under in building wooden sailing vessels, produced the first oceangoing steamships. In 1838, the 700-ton, 250-horsepower *Sirius* and the 1,340-ton 450-horsepower *Great Western,* wooden side-wheelers, traveling entirely under steam power produced by coal, reached New York from Queenstown and Bristol respectively, the former in seventeen days and the latter in fifteen. Two years later, a Canadian, Samuel Cunard, with the aid of a British government mail subsidy, organized a steamship line of his own between Liverpool and Boston. Other companies followed. Britishers continued their experiments with steamships until they proved their superiority in speed over sailing vessels. Experiments with large iron vessels also proved successful when the *Great Britain* driven by a screw propeller was launched in 1843. The first propeller boats were slow, but by the 1850's they were demonstrating their superiority, particularly in rough weather, and the clipper ship was doomed.

Another influence that contributed to the decline of the American merchant marine was the fact that Congress was tardy and ungenerous in aiding American companies, while Great Britain heavily subsidized such companies as the Peninsular and Oriental Company (1837) and the Pacific Steam Navigation Company (1840) as well as the Cunard Line. In 1845, Congress passed a subsidy act authorizing the Postmaster General to make mail contracts with the owners of American vessels, preferably steam. Because of southern opposition on constitutional grounds to a policy granting financial aid to shipping, Congress was not as liberal in this respect as the British Parliament. The Ocean Steamship Company operating between New York and Le Havre and Bremen did receive $200,000 a year for a time. The temporarily successful but ill-fated Collins Line, the American competitor of the Cunard Line, also received subsidies but failed, largely as a result of disasters at sea, in 1857. The policy of granting subventions was discontinued by Congress in 1860, although the decline of the American fleet after 1862 induced Congress to turn again to ocean mail payments as a means of keeping some American vessels in the transoceanic trade.

In addition to these factors, American yards with high labor costs and distant sources of metal could not build iron steamships as cheaply as the shipbuilders of England or certain other European nations. From colonial times on, cheap wood had been the basis for the American shipbuilding industry. In 1860, wood was only economically useful for slow freighters, and coastal and river boats. By this time, only 66 per cent of American foreign trade was being carried in American ships compared to over 90 per cent before the coming of steam.

THE COASTAL TRADE

The coastal trade had been extremely important during the colonial period not only in the exchange of local products between colonial ports but also in distributing imports. With the increasing diversity of sectional production, the tonnage of coastal vessels grew from 68,607 in 1789 to 2,644,867 in 1860. Manufactured goods, iron products, fish, ice, rum, boats, shoes, and other commodities were distributed among the northern ports and were exchanged for the cotton, rice, tobacco, and naval stores of the South, while surplus agricultural products, sugar, hemp, and foodstuffs, as well as cotton from the Mississippi Valley, reached the Atlantic coast by way of New Orleans. Coastal commerce grew to a greater volume than foreign trade. At the time the Federal Union was formed in 1789 a prohibitive tax was placed on foreign-built and owned ships operating between American ports and this was followed by their complete exclusion from the coastal trade under the Navigation Act of 1817.

After 1848, when California became a part of the United States, trade and commerce between the eastern and western coasts expanded tremendously. The discovery of gold in California greatly stimulated this trade and in 1849 about 700 vessels cleared for the west coast from various Atlantic ports. This trade at first was around Cape Horn, but within a few years some of it crossed the Isthmus of Panama where a railroad built by Americans was opened in 1855. Part of it also went overland across the Isthmus of Nicaragua. Vessels plied the waters from the Atlantic ports to Colon or Greytown and between Panama or Brito to Sacramento and other Pacific coast ports. Of course, the vessels used in the Pacific coastal trade were oceangoing craft including the queenly clippers.

While the schooner was the typical American coastal vessel in the period prior to the Civil War, American steamboats made short coastal voyages as early as 1809. The first regular lines, however, were not put into operation until about 1825 in the sheltered waters of Long Island Sound and between Boston and points along the coast of Maine. A line was established in the Gulf of Mexico by Charles Morgan in 1835, and in 1848 the United States Mail Steamship Company began operating its steamboats from New York to Charleston, South Carolina, New Orleans, Havana, and the Isthmus of Panama. Beginning at the time of the gold rush, the Pacific Mail Steamship Company opened a pioneer line from Panama to San Francisco and Oregon.

INTERNAL TRADE

During the first three decades of the nineteenth century a great deal of the goods brought into east coast ports by ships from abroad was sold at auction. New York merchants, particularly, found that large cargoes could be disposed of quickly in this way, and the lower prices brought at the auction were compensated for by not having to hold and handle the goods. The buyers at the auctions were wholesalers and jobbers who would, in turn, distribute the goods to storekeepers and smaller wholesalers from the interior. New York City became the chief center for auction selling which reached its height between 1815 and 1830. New York State aided the system by strict regulation of commissions and sales. As wholesale merchants grew larger, more numerous and more specialized, and ocean freight service more regular, the auction system gradually reverted to direct relations between sellers and large buyers. In 1846, New York City had nearly sixty specialized fields of importation. In dry goods and allied articles, one of the fields, there were over one hundred importers.

With better transportation and growing cities domestic trade grew faster than foreign. More and more farmers were able to send a surplus of some kind to market and buy in return the goods distributed by wholesalers and retailers. Looked at broadly, increasing agricultural efficiency from fuller utilization of farm resources supported a higher standard of consumption of non-farm products and more distributors. By 1840 distribution was on its way toward becoming the chief form of business. It is estimated that there were 1,400 firms in foreign trade, nearly 3,000 in domestic trade, and 58,000 stores, not counting eating-houses or taverns. The total is probably slightly less than for all mill, factory, and household manufacturing enterprises, but by 1860 distribution was undoubtedly in the lead.

The system built up for the distribution of imports was also useful for marketing local factory and mill products. A host of middlemen appeared in the big east coast cities, the gathering points from which goods were distributed to the back country. Jobbers, without any storage facilities of their own, made a living by bringing manufacturers' agents together with wholesalers who supplied the country shopkeepers. Brokers executed orders from remote places like Cincinnati on commission. Wholesalers with warehouses bought goods outright for future sale to stores or smaller wholesalers.

Goods reached the consumer whether in the city or on the farm in several ways. Outside the cities with their stores and shops of all kinds, the village general store which kept, sold, and bartered an endless variety of provisions, goods, and commodities was the most important. Throughout the period the general store continued to be the typical retail distributor. In rural areas, the store was a social center. It also supplied newspapers, magazines, and perhaps books. The proprietor probably went to a big city once or twice a year to buy, and brought back ideas about the world. Business methods were primitive, simple, and almost changeless, for systematic methods of bookkeeping and taking inventory were almost unknown.

As local markets grew, specialized stores appeared. Dry goods, for example, meaning textiles, clothes, sewing equipment, and other "notions," were separated in the larger towns from foods, drugs, or hardware. By 1860 big city dry goods shops were beginning to offer the variety of wares that would soon make them into department stores.

As in the late colonial period, the peddler was also an important agent of trade in all regions. As the population moved westward, shrewd Yankee traders, transporting their commodities by foot, by carriage, by horse, or by boat, traveled the highways, turnpikes, trails, and rivers from the East to beyond the Mississippi and from Maine to the Gulf of Mexico. Clocks, cheap watches, tinware, articles of brass and copper, pins, scissors, combs, buttons, and a host of other Yankee notions made up the stock. Many of these peddlers grew wealthy and became city merchants or wholesalers. The peddler helped to ease the early marketing problems of factory industry. The consumers in rural areas were usually acquainted with particular peddlers and looked forward to their periodical visits. With improvement in transportation and communication, and the building up of communities, the old-time peddler declined in importance, although there were still 16,594 in the United States in 1860.

A more efficient device for retail distribution to back-country areas near rivers was the trading boat. West of the Allegheny Mountains, each year from about 1800 to the Civil War, flatboats or "arks" descended the Ohio, Tennessee, Mississippi, and other western rivers, fitted out as store boats or trading boats. With an array of shelves and counters, they carried stocks of groceries, hardware, notions, and liquors and peddled their goods from wharf to wharf at plantations, villages, and hamlets. Blasts from a tin horn announced the arrival of the water merchant. After the boat was tied up, goods were sold or exchanged for farm products which in turn were disposed of in the

A nineteenth century
general store

larger cities or towns. The rise of the railroads was an important factor in bringing to an end the career of the floating stores, for, as the West became more densely populated, that region grew into one great market.

The wholesale centers of trade were at first confined to the cities along the coast, especially Boston, New York, Philadelphia, and Baltimore. During the first half of the nineteenth century, additional wholesale centers grew up in the Ohio and Mississippi Valleys, in such cities as Pittsburgh, Cincinnati, Louisville, St. Louis, and New Orleans. Wholesalers from the older East often opened branches in the rising western cities. Agents of great merchants traveled to the newer regions in search of trade and played a part in developing new methods of marketing. These agents were important in distributing credit information among the wholesale merchants. Such knowledge was important as terms often were for six months or more, which really meant until the storekeeper had sold most of the goods. Not until 1841, following the large number of business failures in the Panic of 1837, was the first mercantile agency established in New York by Lewis Tappan who had accumulated a large amount of credit information for the wholesale firm of A. Tappan and Company. In 1859, it became R. G. Dun and Company. About ten years earlier, the Bradstreet Company was established by John M. Bradstreet, a Cincinnati lawyer. Other mercantile or credit information agencies were started but few survived. In 1933, the firm of Dun and Bradstreet was formed.

American internal trade was characterized by the successive opening of new areas—the Old Northwest, the Old Southwest, the Great Lakes region, and the newer sections of the Mississippi Valley. With the aid of steamboats and later railroad trains, all of these mid-continental markets became tied to the domestic system of wholesalers, jobbers, and brokers operating in the major metropolitan centers. But overland trade with the Far West was more like the earlier trade with Europe. The covered wagon took the place of the boat, and merchants, usually located at St. Louis or Kansas City, arranged for shipment in trains of wagons with suitable protection from robbers.

On the plains of the Southwest, a colorful trade developed between Missouri and the old Spanish—later Mexican—city of Santa Fe. Beginning with the expedition of William Becknell over the Santa Fe trail in 1821, caravans carried to that city cotton and woolen goods, cutlery, and notions. They returned with gold and silver coins and bullion, coarse Mexican blankets, beaver furs, and mules. Despite occasional military protection, Indian attacks, robbery, and death on the prairies accompanied the rise of this trade. In the face of occasional confiscations, high duties, and mistreatment by Mexican officials, profits were usually high, and with a few interruptions trade continued until after the Civil War. The completion of the last section of the railroad from Topeka to Santa Fe in 1880, however, ended the importance of the wagon road. In 1846, the value of merchandise transported to Santa Fe was estimated at $1,752,250. In twelve months of 1848–1849, 3,000 wagons, 12,000 persons, and 50,000 animals traveled over the road, many journeying to California in the search for gold. After Santa Fe became American in 1848, large commercial houses were established there and the city became a center to supply merchandise to northern Mexico as well as to the rising regions of Arizona and New Mexico. Another center of trade in the Far West was the Mormon settlement near Great Salt Lake (p. 176). In many sections of the Pacific area, the new mining settlements were opening up markets which were to play an important part in the economic development of the country in the years that followed.

CHAPTER 12

Agriculture

Basic to the rapid rate of American economic growth was good agricultural land in what seemed limitless quantity. Even with poor methods of cultivation, farmers could produce large surpluses above the needs of subsistence. The economic problem was transportation to markets where the surplus could be sold. Thus behind every turnpike, canal, and railway venture from the east coast to the Mississippi Valley lay great potential agricultural productivity.

Farming differed from that of Europe in that American farmers were on the move. Land was bought and improved with an eye to resale. Only in certain areas of the east coast was there much permanency of ownership. Since land values generally rose, a farmer could profit greatly from buying more land than he needed and selling all or parts of it later. In many areas farmers may have made more money from buying and selling land than from raising crops. As a result, American farmers took a more businesslike and less sentimental view of the land. They saw in acreage potential gains that could not be hoped for by the European cultivator.

AMERICAN AGRICULTURE IN 1790

When the republic was established, nine out of every ten adults devoted themselves to farming. Only one in ten was engaged in commerce, manufacturing, or other industries. Northern farming, westward to the frontier, was largely self-sufficient, for the ideal was to produce almost everything that each family needed, including food, clothes, furniture, and tools. Near the seaports, a number of farmers grew surpluses of wheat and other agricultural products for the coastal urban centers and also for export. In the South, the farms which outnumbered the larger tobacco plantations were chiefly of the self-sufficient type, although the plantation owners dominated the area economically, socially, and politically.

The methods of agriculture practiced at the end of the eighteenth century had not changed much from those of the late colonial period. There were some exceptions among a few gentlemen planters in the South, some ironmasters in the North, and a number of progressive farmers in all parts of the country, who tried to apply the agricultural knowledge obtained from Europe or were interested in experimenting. Implements and tools were primitive: wooden plows and harrows were in general use; oxen or horses were used to plow and break up the ground; seed was scattered by hand; the cultivation of the soil was accomplished with ironshod wooden spades; reaping was done with scythes and sickles; and the grain to be threshed was beaten out with flails or stamped by oxen or horses. Both widespread subsistence farming and the commercial farming of the plantation type exploited the soil, robbing it of its fertility and causing waste through erosion. This "land butchery" continued almost everywhere. The abundance of virgin soil permitted the opening up of new fields and areas; therefore, little attention was paid to the care of land or to the intensive farming practiced in many parts of Europe. The process of wearing out land by continual use, without fertilization or crop rotation, was repeated over and over again, resulting in ruined areas.

Travelers from Europe, curious to observe American activities in the morning of the new republic, wrote much about the general backwardness of American farming and ascribed the lack of progress to an ignorance of scientific farming as practiced in their home countries; to the conservativeness and lack of initiative of most American farmers, who were content to achieve nothing more than self-sufficiency for themselves and their families; to the vast extent of land in the New World, which encouraged wastefulness; to the problem of securing help, with the resulting expense of labor; to the difficulties of transportation all over the country; and to a lack of money, banking, and credit facilities, which might have enabled agrarians to expand their enterprises. Most of these contemporary writers neglected one of the most important reasons: the general lack of markets for farm products.

With the exception of plantation crops, which were largely exported, and of the surpluses absorbed by nearby commercial towns, there were few markets for farm products at this time.

SOUTHERN CROPS

One of the most striking features of the agricultural history of the first half century of the republic was the rise of cotton culture in the deep South. During the colonial period relatively little cotton was grown in the South for commercial purposes, although cotton plants decorated many a prim southern garden. Some cotton was used in making fustian, a blend of cotton and flax, but wool and flax were the ordinary raw materials for homespun. The interruption of trade with Great Britain during the Revolution turned the attention of southerners to the production of cotton to promote the making of textiles; the legislatures of Virginia, South Carolina, and Maryland encouraged its culture at this time. In the years that followed, because of the general decline in the cultivation of tobacco and the rising demand for raw cotton from the new English cotton mills and later from the factories of the North, a remarkable change took place in southern agriculture in the type of the chief crop and the expansion of the plantation areas. Eli Whitney's cotton gin of 1793 solved the mechanical problem of separating the seeds from the cotton, and the way was open for large-scale production. By 1800, about 35,000 bales were produced in the South, chiefly in South Carolina and Georgia. Soon the culture spread rapidly in central North Carolina and southeastern Virginia as far as soil and climatic conditions permitted, and into the fertile gulf regions. Exhaustion of the soil from continuous cotton cultivation resulted in a westward movement in search of new and better lands until cotton and slavery had moved westward from the Atlantic to Texas. By 1860, Mississippi, Alabama, and Louisiana produced more than one-half the total cotton crop in the United States, while Texas produced more than South Carolina.

By 1835, more than a million bales were produced annually, and by that time cotton had become the principal southern crop and the largest single item of export from the country, a position it held until 1861. Returns from the export of cotton to England aided greatly in expanding transportation and industry and gave foreign investors confidence in America's ability to pay.

In 1790, tobacco, the South's chief staple during the colonial period, still ranked first on the list of American exports. This recovery after the setback of the Revolution, however, was only temporary. International trade difficulties during the European wars; the developing rivalry with cotton; the overseas demand for wheat; the attempts of England after the War of 1812 to stimulate West Indian importation; and competition with Cuba, Sumatra, Colombia, and other regions affected the position of United States tobacco in world markets. Not until after 1820 were old levels regained, and not until the middle of the century was there a real spurt in tobacco production. By this time its culture had expanded into the Mississsippi Valley. In 1850, Kentucky, Tennessee, Ohio, and Missouri were raising more tobacco than the states east of the Alleghenies, although Virginia maintained leadership until 1860. The western product, grown on virgin soil, was successfully competing in foreign markets with the tobacco of the older sections. Louisville, St. Louis, and New Orleans became important trade and manufacturing centers for tobacco in the West.

During the decade 1850–1860, the total production of tobacco more than doubled. This was due to general business expansion and prosperity; to the discovery and production of the bright yellow-leaf variety—lighter than the old varieties—which stimulated consumption considerably; and to the new methods of flue-curing which supplanted the charcoal fire method. The cigar market also broadened as standards of living were raised, for in earlier times, the smoking of cigars was a mark of social distinction. In the Old South, Richmond, Lynchburg, and Petersburg were important tobacco manufacturing centers and Durham, North Carolina, was just beginning its phenomenal career. Among the northern centers of tobacco manufacture, New York and Philadelphia became outstanding, especially in the production of cigars.

The production of rice, begun during the colonial period, expanded considerably. The rice plantations of the South Carolina and Georgia coasts were centers of wealth and culture, although in many cases they were operated by overseers because the absentee owners feared the malaria of the lowlands. The plantations with their irrigation systems of ditches, sluices, and water gates for flooding and draining the areas represented an achievement in agricultural engineering. Drills and harrows were used generally and threshing machines were also adopted. After 1820, steam was introduced as motive power in threshing mills which consequently were moved from the plantations to the towns. Unlike the expansion in cotton and tobacco in the decade before the Civil War, the production of rice declined from 215,000,000 pounds in 1850 to 187,000,000 in 1860. The Civil War dealt a blow to rice culture in the older regions of the South, although there were partial recoveries for a generation. But the failure of free black labor to accomplish the work done earlier by slaves in the unhealthful swamps, together with destructive storms and competition with the increasing production of rice in the Southwest, put an end to the rice plantations of the Carolina and Georgia coasts. By the twentieth century they were swamplands or shooting preserves of the wealthy. Prior to the Civil War, there was a slight development of rice culture in Louisiana, Mississippi, and Alabama. In the latter part of the century, however, Louisiana became the leading rice-producing state in the country and in later years Texas and Arkansas made important gains.

The production of sugar also became important. As early as 1751 Jesuits introduced sugar cane from Santo Domingo into Louisiana. In the half century that followed, it was used for making syrup and "tafia." In 1795, Étienne Boré discovered a satisfactory method of granulating the syrup, which stimulated the growing of sugar cane in that region. When Louisiana became part of the United States in 1803, sugar cane was an established crop and in the years that followed, it was cultivated along the Gulf coast and in parts of the Old South, chiefly for syrup. In 1818, the total production of sugar in the United States was only 25,000 hogsheads, but a few years later the introduction of steam power for crushing the cane gave the industry an impetus.

The production of sugar cane fluctuated in a most erratic manner because of the varying prices of sugar and cotton, caused chiefly by changes in the tariff. For instance, in 1835, sugar fell to six cents a pound, below the cost of production, and the next year most planters changed to cotton culture. In 1842, the price of cotton fell at the time that the new tariff imposed a duty of $2\frac{1}{2}$ cents a pound on brown sugar. Many planters shifted from cotton to sugar production. By the middle of the century and during the years that followed, cotton culture was prosperous and prices were high enough to check the further expansion of sugar production in the South. In considering these fluctuations, the effects of floods and damaging early frosts should also be noted. In spite of these variations, production increased from about 20,000 short tons in 1823 to 270,000 in 1861. By this latter date, the sugar plantations were using 180,000 slaves and the drain of labor from the Atlantic seaboard westward increased the price of slaves. The industry was in general limited to Louisiana, although it extended over to the Brazos River area of Texas and some cane was raised in the region eastward to Georgia.

Slave markets and auctions could be found in all the important towns of the Old South and the Southwest, but the large markets were located in Richmond, Alexandria, Charleston, Savannah, Mobile, Natchez, New Orleans, Memphis, Louisville, and Lexington. Many slaves, bred in the older states, were transported to markets in the Southwest in ships by way of the Gulf; others were sent down the Ohio and Mississippi Rivers. Some were taken part of the way overland from Alexandria. During the decade of 1850–1860 it was estimated that the annual turnover of slaves was about 80,000, valued at $59,000,000. This was an important source of revenue to slave owners in the older areas such as Virginia where a steady surplus of slaves was produced. While the foreign slave trade legally came to an end in 1808, slave traders continued to smuggle their captives into America until the Civil War in spite of the law of 1819 which made slave trading piracy and a capital crime. The attempts of patrols to extinguish the trade were only partly successful.

NORTHERN CROPS

North of the Potomac and the Ohio Rivers wheat was the great cash crop. It would grow almost anywhere in the nonarid parts of the United States, required little weight in seed for planting, and had a ready sale if the farmer could reach a local market. In the period before the Civil War, grist mills to grind wheat into flour were the principal type of mill or factory. The following table of wheat production in the United States from 1839 to 1859 shows the use of wheat as an initial crop in the new areas, and also the fact that it was grown in large quantities in Virginia.

A good corn crop was worth more to the farmer per acre than wheat, but it needed a slightly warmer growing season, required much more weight in seed—important to farmers who moved every few years—and more cultivation. Corn was excellent feed for hogs and poultry which were easier to take to market than the grain itself. But men busy with cutting trees, removing stumps, breaking virgin sod, and the numerous other tasks of developing a new farm generally preferred wheat if they could market it.

Hay, letting the land lie fallow and the grass grow, was a universal crop. As the greater productivity of the middle west made grain farming unprofitable on the poor lands of northern New England, the fields were used for pasturage and hay that fed cows for dairy products.

WHEAT PRODUCTION IN LEADING STATES, 1839 – 1859

	1839		1849		1859	
	Thousands of Bushels	Percentage of Total Crop	Thousands of Bushels	Percentage of Total Crop	Thousands of Bushels	Percentage of Total Crop
Ohio	16,571	20	14,787	14	15,119	9
Pennsylvania	13,213	16	15,367	15	13,042	8
New York	12,286	14	13,121	13	8,681	5
Virginia	10,109	12	11,216	11	13,130	8
Illinois	3,335	4	9,414	9	23,837	14
Indiana	4,049	5	6,214	6	16,848	10
Wisconsin			4,286	4	15,657	9
United States	84,823		100,485		173,104	

Source: Louis Bernard Schmidt, "The Westward Movement of the Wheat Growing Industry in the United States," *Iowa Journal of History and Politics*, July, 1920, pp. 399 – 410.

CORN PRODUCTION IN LEADING STATES, 1839 – 1859

(In thousands of bushels)

	1839	1849	1859
Illinois	22,634	57,646	115,174
Ohio	33,668	59,078	73,543
Missouri	17,332	36,214	72,892
Indiana	28,155	52,964	71,588
Kentucky	39,847	58,672	64,043
Tennessee	44,986	52,276	52,089
Iowa	1,406	8,656	42,772
United States	317,531	592,071	838,772

Source: Compiled from *Eighth Census of the United States, 1860, Agriculture*, p. cxl.

Since land around the big cities was too valuable to use for crops yielding low return per acre, hay farmers could market their surplus as feed for animals in the more urban areas.

Land that could not grow competitively profitable grain or grass crops could still be used profitably. Thus northern New England continued as an area producing potatoes and apples, and these products spread westward through the colder areas. Garden vegetables, requiring large amounts of labor, could be grown on small plots and were planted by New England and other farmers near cities.

The growth of industrial urban centers during the early nineteenth century led to a demand for food products from wider and wider areas. Factory towns removed from the farms many workers who then became dependent upon others for their food, clothes, and general needs. As a result, gradually-enlarging markets were provided for meat, grain, vegetables, dairy products, firewood, and other commodities. Around the growing urban centers, farmers specialized in market gardening, fruit growing, and dairy farming. Many regions in time became highly specialized. Wool growing expanded on New England hills; the raising of cattle increased in the Connecticut Valley and in central Massachusetts; and regions in New York became noted for butter and cheese. Each big city drew on cattle driven in from the back country, and sometimes fattened on idle suburban land that was being held for an increase in value. The southern states that found it most profitable to specialize in cotton or sugar bought most of their meat from the Middle West.

Improvements in transportation aided and stimulated the movement toward specialization as crops and products could be more easily moved. With the improvement of roads and waterways, the building of turnpikes and canals, the development of the steamboat, and the railroad, specialization spread to the West. Western wheat, corn, pork, beef, and wool competed with the same eastern products. The Erie Canal inaugurated direct western competition with eastern production, and a little later the trunk line railroads connecting the East and the West increased the competition. This expanded transportation meant that grain and cattle farming for distant markets like New York City was no longer profitable in northern New England. Many western regions became highly specialized. Cincinnati, the "Porkopolis" of the West, became the country's great packing center long before the Civil War, although western regions in Missouri and Illinois were also building up livestock and other farm industries, made possible by demands from the industrial and commercial centers of the East.

IMPROVED TOOLS AND
LABOR-SAVING MACHINERY

As specialization increased, better tools and labor-saving machinery improved the methods of farming. By the end of the eighteenth century, a number of gentlemen farmers and planters were busy with the problem of improving the plow. Thomas Jefferson, through mathematical calculations, attempted to change its shape for greater efficiency without increasing its weight and designed a mouldboard based on scientific principles. It was Charles Newbold, of New Jersey, however, who patented a cast iron plow in 1797. Although he spent a small fortune in attempting to market his invention, he was unsuccessful. Many farmers were prejudiced and maintained that solid iron plows would poison the soil and encourage weeds to grow, that the cost was too high, or that the plow, cast in one piece, was worthless if any part of it was broken. By the time that Jethro Wood of Scipio, New York, had patented his inventions, between 1814 and 1819, most of the prejudice against iron plows had disappeared, and while the cost of his plow was relatively high, the mouldboard, share, and landslide were cast separately and the various parts were joined by lugs and interlocking pieces, making the replacement of any broken part simple and cheap. Within a decade or so, many designs of iron plows appeared, some imported from England and Scotland. But so successful was Wood that he was obliged to fight patent infringements until his death in 1834. By that time, improved iron plows were in general use in the East. As early as 1830, two works built at Pittsburgh produced thousands of the implements a year, and plow factories were established in New England, the middle states, and the West.

Among the many improvements of this period were those leading to plows made of steel. Steel-faced plows of English make appeared in the early 1830's, but it was John Deere, blacksmith of Grand Detour, Illinois, who in 1837 invented a steel plow suitable for the heavy sun-baked soils of the western prairies. Ten years later he set up a factory in Moline, Illinois, and, in 1858, organized the family-controlled firm of Deere and Company, which became the largest producer of plows in the world and also manufactured other types of farm implements.

During the period before the Civil War, many improvements were made in farm tools and implements of all sorts, including spades, hoes, hand rakes, mattocks, scythes, and hay forks. Harvesting machinery first became practicable through the inventions of Cyrus Hall McCormick, in Virginia, and of Obed Hussey, a New Englander, who constructed a successful reaper in Cincinnati and obtained a patent in 1833, a year before McCormick received his, although it is probable that the latter's actual invention preceded Hussey's. But before this time, there had been forty-seven reaper patents, twenty-three of them American. The rivalry between McCormick and Hussey over patents and markets was long and bitter and led to much controversy and many court scenes. Hussey at first sold more machines than his competitor, especially in western New York, but they were heavy and subject to breakdowns, and in the long run he was defeated by his rival. Despite much advertising, McCormick did not sell his first reaper until 1840. His machine then proved to be superior, for it utilized all seven principles which have since been found essential to successful mechanical harvesting: the side draft, the knife, the divider, the fingers, the reel, the platform, and the wheel. As sales expanded, the horse-drawn reaper proved to be revolutionary, for with two men the McCormick machine could do ten times the work of two scythe or cradle harvesters. One of the factors that made for McCormick's success was his removal to Chicago in 1846, where he found a partner who paid $2,500 for a half interest. The reaper invaded the Middle West, made extensive wheat growing possible, and encouraged frontier migration. By 1856, more than 4,000 McCormick reapers a year were being sold, largely on the installment plan. In 1860, there were 80,000 to 90,-000 reapers in use, chiefly on middle western farms. By this time, the reaper had been improved by devices such as the self-raker.

As late as 1840, almost all the hay produced in the United States was harvested with a scythe. The early reapers of McCormick and Hussey could be used as mowing machines by removing the platform at the rear of the cutter bar, but the hay had to be raked up after the machine had passed. The use of the reaper as a mower was not satisfactory for it could operate only on comparatively level fields and not on uneven pastures and uplands where hay was often grown. In 1856, Cyrus Wheeler patented a two-wheeled mower with a flexible cutter bar, permitting operation on rough and uneven ground. By 1860, a number of different types of mowing machines similar to modern mowers were on the market.

Early hand-driven threshing machines were imported from Scotland in the last part of the eighteenth century. In 1788, Andrew Meikle of Scotland patented a thresher and, before 1800, had added to it a separator and a fanning mill. Sometimes water power was used to operate his threshers and sometimes horse treadmills. Such machines were too expensive and difficult to operate for the ordinary American farmer, but early in the nineteenth century, the cheap hand-driven fanning mill came into use on many farms. Beginning in the 1820's Jacob Pope marketed with much success a cheap hand-operated thresher. Then threshers driven by horse power appeared. In the decade prior to the mid-century, Wheeler and Meikle as well as H. L. Emery and Company were the most popular distributors of small thresher-separators in the East, while Jerome I. Case turned out similar machines in Racine, Wisconsin. The first American machine to combine the three operations of threshing, separating, and cleaning was built by John and Hiram Pitt of Winthrop, Maine. John Pitt established a factory at Albany, New York, in 1849, which was moved later to Buffalo. Hiram Pitt began the manufacture of threshers in Alton, Illinois, in 1847, and four years later moved to Chicago. The manufacture of threshers tended to follow the extension of the wheat belt in the West. Since a thresher was expensive, farmers often cooperated in purchasing and operating it, moving it from one farm to another. In some places, enterprising entrepreneurs traveled from farm to farm at harvest time with their threshers and crews, doing the work for a fixed charge. Horse power was used for threshing long after the Civil War; steam tractors came into general use before the end of the century; and finally cheap portable gas engines took the place in many cases of horse and steam power.

Among other improvements was the seed drill. Although Jefferson had experimented with grain drills in the 1790's, mechanical seeding did not really develop until the Pennock brothers began their work in 1842. Corn planters, which required a different technique, were not highly successful until after the Civil War. Disk harrows appeared about this time. The horse-drawn rake was improved and hay tedders, mechanical hay forks, and hay balers were beginning to lighten the work of many farmers.

American machines were well known in Europe by the Civil War because they were relatively light, simple, and cheap. In European fairs, they were awarded many prizes. When the McCormick reaper was demonstrated at the London World's Fair of 1851, it was ridiculed at first. The London *Times* called it "a cross between Astley's chariot and a flying machine." But sentiment toward it changed in the field trial. So successful was the demonstration that the reaper was awarded the Council Medal; the *Times* apologized for its remarks; and the reaper had more visitors than the Koh-i-noor diamond at the fair. At the International Exposition at Paris in 1855, the American threshing machine entered by John and Hiram Pitt won first prize, and an American reaper cut an acre of oats in twenty-one minutes, which was one-third of the time of foreign entries. Europeans were beginning to recognize Yankee ingenuity and ability.

The introduction of labor-saving agricultural machinery marked the threshold of a new epoch in the history of man. It meant the beginning of an era of plenty if intelligence could be applied to its proper use and distribution. Earlier periods of history had experienced periodic famines and want partly because of crop failure and partly because of the inability of labor to provide surpluses that could be drawn upon in days of stress. The new machinery meant that there was no limit to production through inability to plant or harvest, and as further progress was made, it became evident that an economy of plenty was about to displace an economy of scarcity.

THE BEGINNINGS OF SCIENTIFIC FARMING

Eighteenth-century England saw a real movement in the direction of scientific farming. By the middle of that century, many important Englishmen became interested in improving agriculture. Jethro Tull, an Oxford graduate, toured Europe studying agricultural practices and returned to England to experiment. In his work and achievements, he stressed the importance of double-plowing, the seed drill, improved planting, frequent hoeing and cultivating, and the value of clover and turnips as a substitute for fallow. Others carried on his experiments, including Lord Townshend, nicknamed "Turnip Townshend," who showed through experimentation on his estate that root crops like turnips would restore the fertility of a field by replacing the lost nitrogen and obviating the necessity of leaving it fallow. He urged the spreading of barnyard dungs on fields and advocated the use of lime and marl. Coke of Holkam and George III, called at times "Farmer George," also made contributions to agriculture.

Robert Bakewell led the innovations in stock-breeding, and his ideas and labor did much to transform English sheep and cattle. To meet the growing demand for food, he produced, by constant cross-breeding and inbreeding, larger and fatter types that yielded more mutton and beef. As a result, the average weight of English sheep and cattle more than doubled during his lifetime. The many improvements and changes in English farming during this period have been called by some writers the agricultural revolution.

The transformation in English agriculture was noted by some

American planters and large farmers, who kept in touch with England by travel or through correspondence with relatives and friends. But even by the end of the century only a few attempts had been made to apply agrarian principles that had been proved and accepted in England. Washington, Jefferson, Webster, and others discussed the new methods and applied them to some extent. But in spite of articles in farm journals, the mass of American farmers paid little attention.

With the expansion of intensive commercial farming, increasing markets, development of machinery, improvement in transportation, and rise of agricultural societies, some attention was paid to scientific farming. During the eighteenth century, in many places along the seacoast, fish and seaweed had been applied by a few farmers directly to the land. Ground gypsum, marl, and limestone, crushed or burned, had been used as correctors of soil acidity. There were limekilns on the farmsteads of many Germans, especially in Pennsylvania, but improved agricultural practices were not general. In the early nineteenth century, partly as a result of the increasing price of land in older sections of the country and partly because of the rising scientific spirit which was affecting some farmers, such fertilizers as barnyard manures, rockweed, fish, and guano came into increasing use. An early form of commercial fertilizer to be widely used was Peruvian guano. The production and application of such commercial fertilizers in America dates from about 1840 with the work of Liebig, Lawes, and Gilbert, whose findings aroused much popular interest, but their discoveries were often exploited by quacks and imposters, many of whom styled themselves as "professors." Chemists in early agricultural schools and colleges gave attention and publicity to fertilizer analysis and experiments, although their contributions, especially in the new state colleges, became more important after the Civil War. The use of gypsum, lime, and marl also increased. Gypsum or "land plaster" first came from Nova Scotia, but during the War of 1812 large deposits were opened up in the state of New York, reducing the price and giving this material publicity as a corrector of soil acidity. Marl, composed of clay mixed with calcium carbonate, valuable for soils deficient in lime, was extensively used in the East, especially in New Jersey where large deposits were found. Edmund Ruffin of Virginia, an outstanding agricultural leader, was an enthusiast for marling and, in 1821, published his *Essay on Calcareous Manures,* which went through many editions.

Closely related to the use of fertilizers, gypsum, lime, and marl in improvement of the soil was crop rotation. Washington had adopted a system of rotation of crops at Mount Vernon, growing wheat, corn, clover, and oats, as well as tobacco, which had proved destructive to the land. German and a few other farmers in the North had also given some attention to the rotation of crops long before 1800. In the nineteenth century, with the broadening of markets, the rise of agricultural societies, and the beginning of an agricultural press, farmers were continuously reminded of the value of rotation, with such crops as corn, barley or oats, wheat, and clover in various modifications, but the great majority still preferred to plant their usual crops.

More attention, also, came to be devoted to the improvement of cattle, especially after 1820. The best English breeds were imported, such as Herefords, Jerseys, Guernseys, and Durhams. Interest increased in producing superior breeds by crossing the new importations with the more common cattle of the United States, although many wealthy owners built up herds of pure-blooded stock. The results of crossbreeding in time became evident as cattle increased in size, the quality of beef improved, and the yield of milk grew larger. There developed a differentiation between beef cattle and dairy cows, which met with great success in the East, but little progress was made at this time in the West. Better management, improved stabling, and more scientific feeding, as well as better breeding and selection, brought desirable results by 1860.

The first decades of the nineteenth century witnessed improvements in sheep-breeding, for American sheep were small and not very productive of wool compared with European flocks. The introduction of the fine-wooled white Merino sheep with the exclusion of English breeds from the American market during the period of the embargo, the Non-intercourse Act, and the War of 1812 brought about important changes. About 1800, the first real attempts were made to improve the native stock by importing Merino rams and ewes from France and Spain. As woolen factories were built in increasing numbers in the United States, the demand for the fine wool grew larger and a Merino craze followed. Between 1809 and 1811, more than 24,000 Merino sheep entered the United States and the demand did not die down until after the War of 1812. It was followed in the early 1820's by large importations of Saxony sheep. New Leicester rams were also imported for crossing with American breeds in order to develop better mutton types. In the next decade, wool growing in the East reached its height, for 60 per cent of American sheep were in New England and the middle states. After 1840, greater demands for meat, westward migration, improved transportation, and an increase in the price of foodstuffs caused the center of sheep raising to move westward to the Ohio Valley.

Striking improvements took place also in the breeding of swine. In 1800, farms all over the country raised at least a few hogs. By 1860, common varieties known as the "razorback," "alligator," "hazelnut splitter," and "prairie rooter" had been crossed with better breeds, with resulting improvements. Breeds such as Poland China, Berkshire, Suffolk, Essex, Chester County White, and Byfield could be found on the best farms. After the Erie Canal was opened, western corn-fed pork displaced to a great extent the eastern product, fed on swill, mash, and skim milk. Hog raising followed the corn belt in its westward extension as farmers found that it was very profitable to send their corn to market in the form of hogs. Pork packing increased in importance in the West. Cincinnati was the chief center of the pork packing industry before the Civil War; then Chicago became the leading city of the industry.

By the middle of the nineteenth century, the sturdy ox was being largely displaced as a draft animal by the horse and mule, especially in the East. Fine race, show, and farm horses had been bred during the colonial period by the Narragansett planters and on many other northern farms and southern plantations. But for draft work and as long as implements were crude and heavy, oxen were generally preferred since they were strong and docile, and although tough and stringy, could be used for food when working days were over. The requirement of the new machinery and the needs of increased production doomed the ox as far as farm work was concerned. Among the best draft horses in 1850 were those of the Conestoga breed, descendants of large Flemish horses. By this time the Percheron was being imported from Europe and for a time was a popular type. After the Civil War, Belgian, Clydesdale, and Shire breeds appeared on the American market.

The mule, like the horse, was introduced to the American continent by the early Spaniards. After the American Revolution, Washington produced mules from stock he received from the king of Spain and from Lafayette. These found favor with his fellow planters. Henry Clay and other leading stockmen in Kentucky imported asses and bred mules. The mule was especially adapted to plantation economy and quickly came into general use in the South. Prior to 1860, the main source of supply was the Ohio Valley, but later the southern and Mississippi states, especially Missouri, became important in mule breeding. During the Civil War, mules were used extensively for supply trains and from that time the "army mule" became proverbial. General classification of mules included plantation, heavy draft, mine, and farm animals.

THE RISE OF AGRICULTURAL SOCIETIES

Agricultural societies through meetings, prizes, and publications sought to stimulate better farming. The establishment, in 1785, of the Philadelphia Society for Promoting Agriculture, whose members included Washington and Franklin, and the Agricultural Society of South Carolina was followed by the organization of many similar societies in Maine (1787), New York (1791), Massachusetts (1792), and Connecticut (1792). These pioneer agricultural organizations were composed largely of "gentlemen farmers," professional men, and business men. They were "literary" or "learned" societies, which published accounts of the best practices abroad and the results of agrarian experiments at home, and offered premiums and prizes for improvements in agriculture. Unfortunately, they did not reach the ordinary "dirt farmer," who rejected "book learning" as useless. In 1807, Elkanah Watson, called "the father of the agricultural fair in America," exhibited two Merino sheep in the public square at Pittsfield, Massachusetts, and three years later twenty-six neighbors joined him in an exhibition on the village green. This led to the organization, in 1811, of the Berkshire Agricultural Society, consisting largely of Pittsfield farmers. Massachusetts and other states granted money to such societies for prizes for the best products in many categories. Activities gradually increased at each annual fair or exhibition to include a parade, plowing matches, a public meeting opened by prayer and characterized by addresses and songs, and an agricultural ball at the close. The new type of society in contrast to the older "literary" agricultural organizations spread rapidly. By 1819, Watson estimated that 100 existed in the United States and for a few years continued to increase due to the allotments of state funds to county organizations. Between 1825 and 1840, when state funds were withdrawn, many societies disappeared. After 1840 a revival took place and hundreds of new local, county, and state societies were formed. In 1858, the Commissioner of Patents listed 912 county and state societies, five-sixths of which were organized after 1849. Many of the state societies began to exercise an influence on legislation. A national organization appeared when the United States Agricultural Society was formed in 1852. This society influenced the creation of a federal Department of Agriculture in 1862.

The agricultural societies played an important part in improving farm conditions and also in bettering relationships among farmers. The fairs sponsored by them were different from the eighteenth century borough fairs, which had been held for the purpose of buying and selling and were carried on somewhat after the pattern of medieval fairs. The prizes offered at the county fairs of the nineteenth century stimulated the improvement of livestock, farm products, and even tools and machinery. Methods of scientific farming generally were encouraged by exhibitions, demonstrations, addresses, and pamphlets. The annual gatherings also did much to make the farmer a more social individual by bringing him into contact with others in his community.

THE BEGINNING OF THE AGRICULTURAL PRESS

American farmers at the beginning of the nineteenth century were not especially given to reading, except the sacred Bible and the venerated farm almanac. The latter recorded astronomical data, rules for planting and regulating farm activity according to the various phases of the moon, occasional verse, anecdotes, riddles, "cures," recipes, and interesting bits of general information. In 1831, the editor of *The American Farmer* said that the farmers "will neither take an agricultural paper, read it when given to them, nor believe in its contents if by chance they can hear it read." He estimated that not one farmer in fifty subscribed regularly to a farm paper. Yet between 1820 and 1860 the American agricultural press experienced a mushroom growth. More than 400 different periodicals devoted primarily to agriculture and its related interests appeared. But on the eve of the Civil War the number stood at less than 100, distributed to about 250,000 subscribers. If all the subscribers were in different farm families, journals were reaching 12½ per cent of the 2 million farms. *The American Farmer, The New England Farmer, The Prairie Farmer,* and *The Southern Planter* were representative of various sections of the country. The farm periodicals mirrored in some detail the life of rural America at a time when the nation was awakening to the glories of democracy and when the country was young and vigorous as economic life expanded apparently without limit. The best papers contained accounts of the agricultural fairs; technical articles, including discussions of drainage, plowing, fertilizers, crop rotation, improvement of livestock, and new machinery; advertising, not only of farm supplies, but also of patent medicines, hair restorers, and instruments for discovering gold, silver, platinum, coal, iron, copper, and other valuable metals and minerals; special features such as articles for children and young men, and educational articles on chemistry, physics, electricity, travel, nature, and history; ladies' departments which stressed cooking recipes, the care of children, advice about choosing a husband, and propaganda for reform; puzzles, conundrums, and stunts; and rural poetry such as "The Milk-Maid's Song," "The Hen Fever," "Sabbath in the Country," and other poetic "effusions" to nourish those who craved the "delight of melancholia." The journals remain a rich depository of the economic and social history of the period.

Books on agriculture also appeared in increasing numbers: Edmund Ruffin's long *Essay on Calcareous Manures,* 1821, eventually ran through five editions, and by 1852 totaled 493 pages; Jesse Buel's *The Farmer's Companion* (1839), composed largely of material from English works and extracts from the *Cultivator,* of which Buel was editor; John J. Thomas' *The Fruit Culturalist* (1846), which was enlarged into *The American Fruit Culturist* (1849); and,

Farm magazines of the early nineteenth century

Henry Colman's *European Agriculture and Rural Economy from Personal Observation* (1844) and other works, based on his investigations in Europe. Books on chemistry also appeared, especially after the American edition of Justus von Liebig's *Chemistry in Its Application to Agriculture and Physiology* (1841), which stressed the idea that constituents lacking in the soil could be furnished through the application of mineral manures.

In spite of the advances made in agriculture, especially the beginnings of a scientific approach and the development of a farm literature, most American farmers remained superstitious, preparing the soil and doing their planting "according to the moon." Editors and scientists attacked the age-old superstition, yet farmers continued to adhere to it. Not only were planting and harvesting done when the moon was auspicious, but dependence upon the phases of the moon was a factor in the killing of hogs, the roofing of houses, and the weaning of children. The idea of the transmutation of wheat to chess (a noxious grass) was another fallacy which was debated in periodicals at intervals over a period of forty years. The superstition, caution, and skepticism of farmers toward innovations and scientific farming retarded progress, although the changes which took place between 1800 and 1860 laid the basis for a new type of agriculture.

GOVERNMENT AID TO AGRICULTURE

A plan for a board of agriculture was made as early as 1776 when resolutions designed to aid agriculture were introduced into the Second Continental Congress. One contained a clause creating a standing committee to "correspond with and assist" the agricultural societies proposed for each of the colonies. The clause, however, was struck out and the plan abandoned. Twenty years later, President Washington recommended to Congress the establishment of a Federal board of agriculture to encourage agrarian improvement and to collect and diffuse information. No action was taken and although the question came up from time to time, many decades passed before any plans were worked out by the Federal government in the interests of the farmers of the country.

In 1836, the Commissioner of Patents, Henry L. Ellsworth, assumed the responsibility for distributing among farmers seeds obtained from abroad, and three years later his work received official recognition when Congress appropriated $1,000 for "collecting and distributing seeds, prosecuting agricultural investigations, and procuring agricultural statistics." The appropriations were granted irregularly until

1847, and they were made annually thereafter. The amount appropriated by Congress in 1856 reached $105,000. In 1854, the work received a scientific emphasis when a chemist, a botanist, and an entomologist were added to the agricultural division of the Patent Office.

States also assisted agriculture. Such aid was not new, for bounties and premiums had been paid by colonial assemblies to encourage the production of certain farm commodities. In 1792 and during the years that followed, the Society for Promoting Agriculture in Massachusetts received grants from the legislature. When the new type of agricultural societies appeared in the nineteenth century, financial aid was given by many states. Beginning with New Hampshire in 1817 and Massachusetts and New York in 1819, small sums were given to local and state societies. Between 1819 and 1845, Massachusetts paid $115,800 to such groups. State boards were also set up in many states, made up at first of the presidents of agricultural societies or their representatives. A few states encouraged the production of certain crops. Massachusetts, for instance, tried to stimulate the growing of wheat by paying bounties, but the results were not very successful.

The demands of agricultural societies and the farm press for state aid came to fruition after 1835 as appropriations increased and plans were made for agricultural and geological surveys. A demand arose also for financial aid to agricultural education. From 1823 when Jesse Buel introduced the first bill to establish an agricultural college in the state of New York, such agitation continued in increasing crescendo. Private schools, such as the Gardiner Lyceum at Gardiner, Maine, the first exclusively agricultural school in the United States (1822), were beginning to appear, but private institutions received no government aid. At last, when in 1837 a state university was authorized in Michigan, instruction in agriculture was specified in the act, but because of lack of funds, such instruction was not furnished for many years. In 1855, an agricultural college was established in Michigan separate from the university, and it began to function two years later. In the meantime, after years of struggle, the New York State Agricultural College was established by law (1853). Maryland endowed an agricultural college in 1856, and the next year Pennsylvania appropriated $24,000 to match an equal sum raised by private subscription for an agricultural college which in time blossomed into Pennsylvania State University. The inadequacy of state support for agricultural education, however, led to the plan of federal aid through the Morrill Act of 1862 (p. 348).

CHAPTER 13

Sectionalism and War

Economic development has contributed to many wars and revolutions. New types of economic interest grow and impinge upon the favored position of older economic interest groups. If the old group is strongly enough entrenched it may require physical force to end its special privileges. Almost inevitably such struggles involve noneconomic factors as well. The powerful older group may be mainly of a different religion, as in the Puritan Revolution in England, or represent a different social status, as in the French Revolution. In America, as the North grew increasingly more powerful in relation to the South, the latter feared that it might be deprived of the legal protection necessary to keep its slave labor from escaping to the North. Furthermore, the economic policies best suited to export agriculture were not acceptable to the rising industrial interests of the North. But as in the English and French examples, other noneconomic factors such as humanitarian reform and sectional loyalties became involved in the conflict of economic interests.

THE BACKGROUND

Both the economic realities and the spirit of sectionalism, ever-present in American development, produced many regional conflicts, struggles, and disagreements which hindered the rising spirit of nationalism. Differing ideas and ideals naturally emerged from divergences of occupation, climate, soil, natural resources, and ethnic and cultural backgrounds. By the time of the Civil War, there were at least five distinct regions: the East, including New England and the Middle States; the Old South; the Northwest; the Southwest; and the Pacific Coast. On the eve of the conflict a much larger and broader division revealed two general areas: the North with its rising industrial life and the South with its agrarian economy.

By 1860, the progress of manufacturing industries in New England and in the middle states was striking. Commerce and finance, largely in the hands of easterners, were also flourishing. While the interests of different groups in the East—industrial, commercial, and agrarian —often seriously conflicted, the dominant groups favored protective tariff, privileges and subsidies for business enterprise, and a better integrated banking system. During most of this period, the agrarian interests of the South and the West were strong enough to obstruct these policies, as can be seen in the failure to levy high tariffs in the years preceding the war, in the few Federal subsidies granted to business, and in the defeat of a centralized banking system after 1836.

Among the demands made by the West during the period, governmental aid for internal improvements was foremost. With the exception of the Cumberland Road, the amount of Federal funds invested in western transportation was not large. Localities and states had to develop and finance plans of their own. The West also demanded disposal of Federal land to settlers, which was continually opposed by the South and the East. Not until the middle of the century did politicians seriously advocate "free land for the landless." A homestead bill passed in the House in 1852, but was defeated in the Senate; in 1860, a similar bill passed both houses and was vetoed by a Democratic president. Cooperation between East and West in the war finally brought the Homestead Act of 1862. The agricultural states in general opposed a strict centralized system of banking and were successful in this policy after the demise of the Second Bank of the United States. The same states opposed high protective tariffs, but as industry developed in the West defenders of protection increased in number.

By 1860, the Old South opposed a protective tariff, a centralized banking system, internal improvements at national expense, and privileges and subsidies for business. The interests of the Southwest were in many ways similar to those of the Old South, as westward expansion there meant the extension of southern culture and economic life, particularly in the production of cotton. But the Southwest desired internal improvements and free lands, demands that were opposed by the Old South.

THE SOUTH AS A SECTION

Characteristics of crop production for export and the slave-plantation system differentiated the South from other sections. Less than 8 per cent of the population lived in towns of 4,000 or more, and these were largely dependent upon the surrounding agricultural communities. The South, however, was not without industry. Iron furnaces and forges flourished in many parts of Virginia, Tennessee, and Kentucky. The Tredegar Iron Works of Richmond, Virginia, established in 1836, came to rival some of the Pittsburgh mills, for in 1860 they included rolling mills, foundries, machine shops, and metal works. Locomotives and railroad equipment of all kinds were turned out as well as other types of iron products. Much coal was mined in certain areas. Cotton mills were also built in the South, but the industry was relatively small. Likewise the number of factories and shops did not grow very rapidly. The South produced a little less than 10 per cent of all the manufactures of the country in 1860.

Southern leaders recognized the fact that the South was increasingly falling behind the North in population, manufacturing, transportation, commerce, and in other lines of economic development. Many southerners preached the importance of manufactures. Conventions were held from time to time to discuss economic development. The Southern Commercial Convention met successively at Baltimore, Memphis, Charleston, New Orleans, Richmond, Savannah, Knoxville, Montgomery, and Vicksburg between 1852 and 1859. Representatives from different parts of the South attended its meetings and plans of all sorts were suggested. Many felt that the financial, manufacturing, and commercial dependence of the South upon the North resulted in a drain of southern wealth and in the economic debilitation of the region. Among the proposals made to promote economic activities were the building of a southern transcontinental railroad, the establishment of southern steamship lines for oceanic trade, the improvement of harbors and shipping facilities, the promotion of trade with Europe and Latin America, the encouragement of southern manufactures through bounties and premiums, the imposition of discriminatory taxation on northern-made goods, and the promotion of industrial and commercial education. In spite of these proposals to broaden the economic life of the South, little was accomplished.

In the years prior to the Civil War the plantation system reached its peak. Every phase of life in the South was under the domination of this system, although in 1860 only 383,000 persons out of a population of more than 8,000,000 in the plantation states owned slaves. While less than 2,500 planters owned 100 or more slaves each, it was this latter group that largely controlled the South. About 1,000 families received nearly half of the cash income from the export of cotton. The wealth and power of the entire section were in the hands of a few.

Between the small number of the important planter class at the top of the social scale and the Negro slaves at the bottom were several other groups. The lesser planters and middle-class farmers, who possessed from five to twenty-five slaves, together with the professional men and merchants of the towns and cities, who usually held one or more slaves as servants, were in sympathy with the ideals of the plantation system and provided the most vigorous defenders of southern civilization. The skilled workmen, yeomen farmers, and small tradesmen usually gave support to the ruling order. Another class of southern society, separate from the rest and with little or no contact with slavery, were the white inhabitants of the mountain areas of Virginia, the Carolinas, Georgia, Tennessee, and Kentucky, who for the most part were small farmers. Still another group were the poor whites, low in the social scale. They were often squatters on the poorest lands, but usually inhabited the pine barrens of the low country, the sand hills farther inland, or remote mountain districts. Known by such names as "hill billies," "crackers," "sand hillers," and "red necks," their existence was aggravated by poverty, hookworm, malaria, corn whiskey, and a poor diet. They were descendants of frontiersmen who had not been able to prosper in the rugged environment. They hated the ruling class as well as the Negro with whom they were forced to compete. The free Negroes, about 250,000 altogether, who lived chiefly in the upper southern states, constituted a problem, for they found it difficult to fit into the southern scheme of things, although many were good carpenters, blacksmiths, coopers, and shoemakers. At the bottom of the social scale were the 4,000,000 Negro slaves, who worked both on the plantations and in the cities and towns.

THE ANTISLAVERY MOVEMENT

Few protests on moral grounds were made against slavery during the colonial period. At its close, much concern was being shown in South Carolina and Virginia over the large and increasing slave population which was threatening to become a burden. Attempts to restrict the slave trade were prevented by England on the ground that it would interfere with the trade of the empire. In 1774, the Association of the Continental Congress forbade importations from England and, in the original draft of the Declaration of Independence, Jefferson severely condemned the traffic in slaves. The philosophy of the Revolution included a stress on the rights of man, which benefited to a certain degree the Negro of the South, for a number of plantation owners freed their slaves or made provision in their wills for their emancipation. The movement was influenced by the egalitarianism then dominant in England and by the essays of Quakers like John Woolman and humanitarians like Thomas Jefferson. It was also stimulated by the decline of tobacco culture, and it can be seen in the legislation ending the foreign slave trade by all the southern (as well as northern) states before 1803, prior to the Federal law of 1808. Between 1776 and 1800, all the northern states passed laws providing for the abolition of slavery, but early in the nineteenth century the increasing demand for cotton once again made Negro slaves a valuable labor force. The philosophy of the rights of man as it touched the slaves was forgotten, and while Negroes could not be legally imported from foreign shores, the breeding of slaves in the Old South increased in importance.

Under the impetus of the philosophy of the Revolution, antislavery societies had been established. As early as 1775, the "Pennsylvania Society for Promoting the Abolition of Slavery, the Relief of Free Negroes Unlawfully held in Bondage, and Improving the Condition of the African Race" was organized. Others followed in different parts of the country, and they were strongest in the border states between North and South. Members of these societies advocated gradual emancipation and hoped that through education and enlightenment, slavery at some future time would come to an end. During the first part of the nineteenth century the crusade against slavery was not militant or bitter. Leaders like the pious Quaker Benjamin Lundy, a native of New Jersey, who in 1821 began the publication of the *Genius of Universal Emancipation* in Ohio, traveled over the country lecturing and organizing societies.

The question of colonizing Negroes who had been given their freedom was discussed at this time. As early as 1802 the legislature of Virginia adopted resolutions favoring the colonization of the Negroes in Africa or South America by the Federal government, but without result. In 1816, a private organization, the American Colonization

Society, was established by such men as Bushrod Washington and Henry Clay. Local branches were established in every state; many legislatures and churches contributed funds. Money was raised to buy slaves, transport them, and settle them in Liberia, Africa. Between 1821 and 1867 about 6,000 free Negroes were sent to the new colony which in 1847 became an independent republic. While the work done by the society was worthwhile, the number of Negroes aided was relatively small because of a lack of funds.

About 1830, an abolition movement began. It was a part of the general awakening of the humanitarian spirit as seen in the growth of the temperance movement, the beginning of the agitation for women's rights, and reforms of many kinds. By some, slavery now came to be identified with tyranny and opposed to a growing democracy. The leader of the new movement was William Lloyd Garrison who founded the weekly antislavery *The Liberator* in Boston in 1831. Though it never had a large circulation, it was the leader among journals which advocated and demanded immediate, uncompensated emancipation. Garrison denounced the Constitution of the United States as "a covenant with death and an agreement with hell" because some of its clauses pertained to the institution of slavery. The movement grew as can be evidenced in the development of new societies led by the New England Antislavery Society and the American Antislavery Society.

While the new radical movement expanded in the North, it met with hostility, especially on the part of businessmen who feared the loss of southern trade. Opposition was occasionally expressed in violence as abolitionist meetings were broken up and printing presses destroyed. The murder of the Reverend Elijah Lovejoy, an abolitionist editor of Alton, Illinois, and the burning of Pennsylvania Hall in Philadelphia where abolitionist meetings were held were two spectacular instances of the attempts to suppress the movement. While the radical movement grew slowly, the moderate abolitionists increased in number and another plan to oppose slavery also took form—the Underground Railroad.

The informal, secret system of aiding fugitive slaves to escape to free states or Canada became known as the Underground Railroad. Quakers, Methodists, northern Negroes, and others aided fugitives to escape northward, assisting them from one place to another at night and hiding them during the day. The system of secret routes developed until it extended through fourteen northern states from Maine to Kansas. Thousands of slaves were lost to their masters each year and, prior to 1850, the southerners demanded a stricter fugitive slave law.

The several antislavery movements put the southern slave holders on the defensive. In Congress, a gag rule to prevent the consideration of antislavery petitions was pushed through the House of Representatives in 1836 and remained in effect for eight years. At the same time, there was much excitement over the freedom of the mails as abolition literature was refused in parts of the South. The growing opposition to slavery led to many arguments justifying it. Led by John C. Calhoun, slavery was defended and religion, history, and economics were marshalled to prove its soundness. The change in the southern attitude toward slavery since the Missouri Compromise was evident. In 1819, it was argued that more territory should be opened to slavery in order to dilute it. By 1850, slavery was depicted as a "positive good" which should be protected even in the territories.

Among the arguments in favor of slavery, the scriptural one was important. It was pointed out that many passages in the Bible relating to slavery were a justification for the institution and therefore it was as old as civilization itself, receiving divine sanction. It was shown that great cultures had been based more or less on slavery and therefore history had placed its seal of approval on it. Stress was laid on the work of the founding fathers in recognizing it in the Constitution and, although the words "slaves" or "slavery" did not find a place in the basic law of the country, certain agreements regarding slavery were written into the Constitution. Justifying slavery from the economic point of view, it was stated that about $2 billion had been directly invested in slaves and other billions indirectly through investments in lands, cotton, and tobacco. It was shown that the Negro as a respectable Christian slave was superior to his previous status of savagery in Africa and was also better off in many respects than the factory workers of the North who, it was declared, were slaves to machines and worked for pitiful wages in foul factories, uncared for in times of unemployment and cast aside in old age. Still another argument emphasized that cheap slave labor meant low-priced cotton which resulted in cheap cotton goods, benefiting people everywhere who wore such material. A final argument which ran through the whole period was based on fear. It was stated that the southerners had inherited the institution and that the safety of the whites was involved when the question of emancipation was raised. The massacres in Haiti, the Nat Turner insurrection in Virginia, and other slave conspiracies and uprisings, actual and imaginary, placed the South on its guard. The argument that evolved from the question of emancipation set forth the idea that the two races could not live in the same region on terms of equality, for it was believed that the Negro race was inferior and would therefore destroy white culture and civilization.

EVENTS LEADING TO WAR

The first serious sectional alignment that threatened the Union came in 1819–1820 over the admission of Missouri (p. 173). That controversy regarding the extension of slavery startled the nation. To Jefferson it was "like a fire bell in the night," even more serious than the crisis that had arisen during the Revolution. In the years that followed, other alarming sectional issues had to be met, especially the revolt of the planters in South Carolina in opposition to the policy of protection to northern manufactures. While the controversy over slavery increased after 1830, it became dangerous at the time of the Mexican War over the question of territory to be acquired from Mexico.

In Congress, at the beginning of the Mexican War, the Wilmot Proviso, an amendment to an appropriation bill, proposed: "That as an express and fundamental condition to the acquisition of any territory from the Republic of Mexico by the United States, by virtue of any treaty which may be negotiated between them, and to the use by the Executive of the moneys herein appropriated, neither slavery nor involuntary servitude shall ever exist in any part of said territory." The Proviso precipitated a bitter and serious debate over the question of slavery in the territories. Although it failed to pass both Houses, it was brought up in one form or another more than a score of times during the Mexican War.

After the Treaty of Guadalupe Hidalgo which ended the war and rounded out the possessions of the United States to the Pacific, the issue of slavery became critical. Many northerners, convinced that slavery was an evil, determined that it should be limited to the states where it already existed and that it should be kept out of the territories. Southerners resented the moral issue that had been forced to the front and decried the attempt to exclude slaveholders from territories acquired by common effort. The question as to whether the Constitution followed the flag was ably debated by Webster, representing northern business interests, and Calhoun, representing the South. The former insisted that the basic law of the country did not automatically go into effect in newly acquired territories and that only those provisions that Congress saw fit should be extended there. Calhoun, on the other hand, championing the extreme southern view maintained that the Constitution, protecting the property of all citizens, was in effect in all American possessions and therefore it was the duty of Congress to uphold slavery in the territories. The critical aspects of the controversy brought many suggested compromise proposals, among them extending the Missouri Compromise line to the Pacific; permitting the people who settled in a territory to decide the question (popular sovereignty); or throwing the responsibility for deciding the issue upon the courts. The seriousness of the issue can be seen in the call for a southern convention at Nashville as threats of secession increased.

Congress in its session of 1849–1850 effected a compromise and averted the possibility of war. The aged Clay had been returned to the Senate by his constituents for the purpose of bringing peace. Since several issues had to be adjusted, he suggested solutions by means of a series of resolutions and pleaded for compromise. Calhoun's last message was one of despair, for he could see no solution to the attacks of northern abolitionists on the institution of slavery. In a few days he was dead, but his spirit and ideas led the party of secession in a much stronger manner than he was ever able to do during his lifetime. Webster, like Clay, pleaded for compromise and stressed his belief that slavery could never be profitable in the new territories because of the character of the terrain and climate. He was assailed and condemned by radical abolitionists for his stand. In Congress, William H. Seward and Salmon P. Chase were the spokesmen of the radicals. After bitter debates extending over nine months, five laws were passed, each formerly included as sections of a proposed omnibus bill which could not secure sufficient votes to be passed as a whole. One by one a majority was obtained for each measure and the Compromise of 1850 was effected.

Under the terms of the Compromise, Utah and New Mexico were made territories to be admitted with or without slavery when they applied for statehood as their constitutions should provide. Thus, popular sovereignty was written into law. California, now teeming with gold hunters who had no interest in slavery, was admitted as a free state without the requirement of going through a formal territorial period. A boundary dispute between Texas and New Mexico was settled in favor of the latter, but Texas received $10,000,000 which was intended to liquidate the war debt of that state. A strict fugitive slave law, demanded by the South to replace the ineffective law of 1793, vitiated by such Supreme Court decisions as Prigg *vs.* Pennsylvania (1842),[1] was included. The new law was stringent for it did not permit a jury trial; the master or his agent could bring the charge against an alleged runaway; the judge or commissioner received a double fee if he decided in favor of the slave owner; the testimony of the fugitive was not admitted; anyone hindering an arrest or attempting to rescue a supposed runaway slave was liable on conviction to a fine and to imprisonment; and Federal marshals could deputize bystanders to help them in making arrests, with heavy penalties for refusal. Another law at last abolished the slave trade, but not slavery, in the District of Columbia. No longer could slave markets be held in the shadow of the Capitol.

Attempts were made to make the Compromise final. This can be seen in the speeches of northern and southern leaders, pledges made by congressmen, the "finality resolutions" introduced into Congress, the messages of President Fillmore, the weakness demonstrated in the Nashville Conventions and the attitude of the moderates in both sections. Many southern states held conventions to consider and pass judgment on the Compromise. Several endorsed the sentiment of the Georgia Conventon as set forth in the Georgia Platform which stated that while the Compromise could not be wholly approved, it was accepted in order to preserve unity, but only upon the "faithful execution of the Fugitive Slave law by the proper authorities depends the preservation of our much loved Union."

On the passage of the fugitive slave law, thousands of former fugitive slaves who had been living in northern cities for years fled to Canada. Radical abolitionists denounced the law and frequently aided the Negroes. They even attempted to seize runaways from marshals who had placed them under arrest. Riots occurred in several places. Northern states passed a new series of personal liberty laws, requiring rigorous proof of ownership, severely penalizing illegal seizures, denying the use of jails for the detention of runaway slaves, and guaranteeing to fugitives the right of jury trial. It seemed that this section of the Compromise would be the first to result in failure. Its operation, however, was overshadowed by other events which widened the breach between the North and South, and led inevitably to the Civil War.

The passage of the Kansas-Nebraska Act of 1854, which repealed

---

[1] While this decision stressed the right of the slave owner to recover a fugitive slave without obstruction from any state law, it pointed out that the Federal statute did not require the state authorities to assist in capturing fugitives.

the Missouri Compromise by allowing both territories to decide on whether or not they would permit slavery, intensified the controversy over slavery in the territories. Bloody warfare was waged on the plains of Kansas when northerners and southerners sought to control the government of the territory. Then followed the Dred Scott decision of the Supreme Court (1857). Seven justices, led by Chief Justice Taney, agreed in deciding that a Negro was not a citizen and therefore could not sue in a Federal court, although the minority of two justices hotly contested the arguments and opposed them. But the part of the decision that stirred the North was the statement that Congress had no power to exclude slavery from any of the territories because the Constitution protected the institution everywhere in the country. This idea had been the extreme contention of Calhoun and other southern leaders. It struck a blow at the arguments of the antislavery forces. By this interpretation, the Missouri Compromise had always been unconstitutional and the newer doctrine of popular sovereignty was of little meaning. The decision created a sensation. It was condemned in the North as purely political and not the reasoned judgment of the jurists; if enforced, it meant that Congress could not abolish slavery in the territories but was bound to guarantee to all slave owners the protection of their slaves; it increased the hostility between North and South, and the inflamed discussions that followed did much to precipitate the war.

An event that further led to the crisis of war was John Brown's raid at Harpers Ferry, at the junction of the Potomac and the Shenandoah. Fresh from "bleeding Kansas" and from participation in raids against slavery there, John Brown planned to liberate the slaves of the South through a series of revolutions, beginning in the Allegheny Mountains in Virginia. Aided by a small band of relatives, friends, and a few Negroes, he tried to seize the government arsenal at Harpers Ferry in order to use the weapons in freeing the slaves, and to establish a Negro republic. The raid failed. Brown was convicted of treason and hanged. Southern newspapers were especially incensed at the sympathetic comment on Brown in some of the northern papers. While the event in itself was not of outstanding importance, a thrill of horror ran through the South as it suspected that other mass attacks on the South financed by wealthy abolitionists would follow. Actually, Brown's supporters in the northern states were few in number and none possessed complete knowledge of his plans. Most northerners repudiated the plot, for they saw in it not only an assault against the South but an attack upon organized society and democracy. Yet a few, like Emerson, called Brown a new saint who was to "make the gallows glorious like the cross."

A final step that led to war was the election of Lincoln and the "Black Republicans." The South had threatened secession if the election went against that region. Lincoln won the Presidency but by a minority vote as four presidential candidates participated in the election. In the South, he did not receive a single electoral vote. The party that supported him was wholly in the North. In December, South Carolina seceded from the Union and in time was followed by ten southern states. Upon taking office, Lincoln swore to preserve the Union and his efforts to do this brought on the tragic war that for four bitter years drenched a divided country in blood.

Opinion varies somewhat as to the relative importance of the fundamental reasons for the Civil War. Some writers insist that the quarrel over the question of slavery and its extension was the most important cause for disunity; others emphasize that the war was the result of a struggle for power between the planter aristocracy of the South and the industrial magnates of the North, involving such issues as the tariff, banks, and subsidies; still others suggest that southern political leaders, fearing the growing power of the North, were largely responsible. Taking a broader view, however, almost all agree that the struggle was a product of the widening breach between two civilizations with basic differences in climate, soil, social structure, economic life, labor systems, and general culture.

The events of the 1850's stimulated the increasing controversy which led to the conflict. Northern pulpits, forums, and the press spread propaganda and created misunderstandings about slavery and the plantation system. Books like Harriet Beecher Stowe's *Uncle Tom's Cabin; or Life Among the Lowly,* a sincere but inaccurate, emotionalized attempt by a northerner to depict plantation life, which went through many editions before the war and was also dramatized and produced on the stage, added fuel to the fire that was to sear and almost consume the nation. Retaliating against the attacks of the North, southern agencies of public opinion vigorously defended their institutions. Tracts and pamphlets were published. Editors, writers, and orators became more and more antagonistic to the North. James D. B. DeBow, editor of the important *DeBow's Review,* argued in 1860 that the prosperity of the independent farmer of the South rested largely upon slavery and pointed out that: "The non-slaveholder knows that as soon as his savings will admit, he can become a slaveholder, and thus relieve his wife from the necessities of the kitchen and the laundry, and his children from the labors of the field." His journal emphasized continually that the wealth of the South was permanent and stable, whereas that of the North was "fugitive and fictitious."

Another eventful book in the slavery controversy was H. R. Helper's *Impending Crisis of the South and How to Meet It* (1857). It was an economic appeal to the non-slaveholders of the South written by one from the small-farmer class of that region. In spite of the fact that Helper had distorted and misinterpreted his figures, the book convinced many northerners who had not been influenced by the moral argument that slavery was an economic fallacy. The book had serious repercussions in Congress and deepened the cleavage between the sections. Thus, in innumerable ways, the psychological basis for war was laid. The serious controversies and countless irritations made the conflict inevitable in spite of the fact that the apparent important issue in 1860 was opposition to the extension of slavery into a region which most people realized could not foster or support the plantation system.

MATERIAL STRENGTH OF NORTH AND SOUTH

In material strength and power, the North was far ahead of the South. Altogether twenty-three states with a population of 22,000,000 were aligned against eleven southern states having 9,000,000 people, of whom 3,500,000 were slaves. The border states of Delaware, Maryland, Kentucky, and Missouri, together with the area that became West Virginia (1863), and the southern portions of Ohio, Indiana, and Illinois were largely southern in sentiment, though their economic ties were with the North. All of these states remained loyal to the Union. Of the border states, only Delaware and Kentucky kept slavery until the end of the war.

The North was far superior economically. Its banking capital of $330 million was more than seven times that of the South. Most important was its great superiority in transportation, industry, and commerce. How then did the South expect to win? It had the advantage of superior military leadership, trained horsemen, martial spirit, and of waging a defensive war on interior lines. The South counted on a short struggle and looked abroad, especially to England, for an alliance or at least for aid. It expected that the West would join forces with it, but the West since 1850 had developed increasingly closer economic ties with the East. On the promise of free homesteads, transcontinental railroads, and agricultural aid, it cast its lot against the South and did its part to create a solid North. As the war dragged on, the superior resources of the North played a most important part in the accomplishment of final victory.

AGRICULTURE DURING THE WAR

The North was in complete control of the chief granaries of the country during the war, as the constantly enlarging wheat and corn areas of the Middle West remained loyal to the Union. Increasing prices and the demand for foodstuffs of all kinds brought prosperity to the northern farmers. In spite of enlistments, the drafting of large numbers of men into the army, and the continual stream of migrants westward, especially to the newly opened mining regions of the Rocky Mountains, northern agricultural production remained adequate. The problem of the shortage of farm labor was solved by the increased use of labor-saving machinery and more work by farm families. No invading armies caused destruction to harvests in the North, which not only fed itself but exported surpluses of wheat. In the year just preceding the war, the United States exported about 20,000,000 bushels of wheat annually. Loss of the southern market allowed increased exports, which reached 60,000,000 bushels in 1862. During the first three years of war, the harvests of Great Britain were poor and the fact that England depended partly on the North for wheat contributed in some degree to prevent British recognition of Confederate independence. With domestic and foreign markets for their products, together with remarkably successful crops, farmers were active, prosperous, and optimistic.

In contrast to the North, southern planting declined, but every available effort was made to produce foodstuffs. In the years before the war, the staple crops of cotton and tobacco had been exceptionally good. While there had always been much general farming in all southern areas, the South as a whole depended upon the North for a large part of its food. As war approached, many believed that cotton would save the South. In 1859, Senator Hammond said: "Without the firing of a gun, without drawing a sword, should they make war upon us, we could bring the whole world to our feet. What would happen if no cotton was furnished for three years? I will not stop to depict what every one can imagine, but this is certain, England would topple headlong and carry the whole civilized world with her. No, you do not dare to make war on cotton. No power dares to make war on it; cotton is king."

While large quantities of cotton were exported from the South at the beginning of the war despite the menace of northern warships, the shipment of cotton dwindled pathetically as the blockade tightened

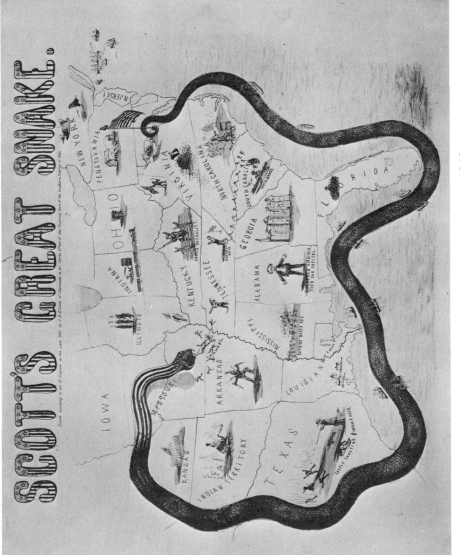

Satirical map of the Union blockade, 1861

and it became evident that England was not going to war to save "King Cotton." During the early years of the war, Great Britain's 2,650 cotton factories were not adversely affected by a lack of raw materials because a trade depression overstocked England with raw cotton. In fact some of the surplus raw cotton was reshipped to the North at handsome profits. By the close of 1862, however, as the war continued, England, France, and other European countries were beginning to feel a shortage. English and French cotton factories were forced to shut down and thousands of workers were turned out of work. Most of the English aristocracy and most of the manufacturing and commercial classes sided with the South, but a minority of the leaders and the several million unenfranchised workers sympathized with the North, and supported new antislavery societies. Because of excessive profits and the need for ammunition, shoes, blankets, medicines, and many other things from Europe, southern companies continued to operate blockade runners, but the amount of cotton and tobacco exported and the quantities of badly needed supplies imported grew less as the blockade became more and more effective by the spring of 1865.

Many Negro slaves were put to work raising grain and food crops instead of cotton and tobacco. As the war continued, the Confederacy found that it was almost impossible to feed itself. In some sections, food was relatively plentiful, for there were no crop failures during the entire war. But in many, there was a great scarcity of food because of problems of distribution as railroad lines were destroyed by northern troops and as roads and waterways were taken over or closed by them. Sherman's sixty-mile path of ruin in Georgia and the havoc wrought in the fertile Shenandoah Valley stripped these regions of provisions. Inflation also increased the problems of distributing farm products. Early in 1864, in Richmond, flour sold at $300 a barrel in Confederate currency at the time that a gold dollar was worth $22 in Confederate money. At different times, owing to the scarcity of food and to soaring prices, riots occurred in Atlanta, Mobile, and elsewhere. The Confederate troops were often fed on northern food obtained in exchange for cotton, although a Confederate law prohibited the exportation of cotton except by way of southern seaports. But northern laws permitted and closely regulated a restricted trade in southern cotton. By 1864, this trade, legal and illegal, provided the North with sufficient cotton to supply its factories. About $500,000 worth of goods and provisions each week were sent to the Confederacy from the North, chiefly through Memphis. General Grant and other army officers insisted that this trade prolonged the war at least a year.

INDUSTRIAL LIFE DURING THE WAR

As the war began, depression settled over the North and West. It was brought on by many factors, such as the failure of business to recover satisfactorily following the Panic of 1857, the breaking of economic ties with the South, the question of $300,000,000 worth of debts owed by southern merchants to northerners, the fact that the currency of many western banks was secured by the bonds of seceded states, and the uncertainties wrought by the war itself. Depression was particularly severe in the West where bank closings and the cutting off of the river trade threw business into confusion. But by 1862, new demands for war supplies and prosperity in the East were aiding recovery.

The demand for woolen cloth for army uniforms, undergarments, blankets, and overcoats stimulated woolen manufacture at once. Many cotton factories were converted into woolen mills and new plants established. The war department found it necessary to purchase army cloth in England and France during the emergency, but not without general criticism and demands to patronize home industry. After the first year of war, American mills were able to produce all the cloth that was needed, but most worked day and night, including Sundays. Profits were tremendous as government contracts were made at high prices and many woolen companies declared unbelievable dividends. It was, perhaps, inevitable that there should be some fraud and corruption caused by the necessity for speed in supplying the demands of war. The production of shoddy, a cloth made of compressed rags, not pure wool, made fortunes for a few unscrupulous manufacturers and brought indignant protests. Most of the cloth made for the troops, however, measured up to high standards. The woolen interests held conventions, influenced the woolen schedules of the rising tariff, and organized the National Association of Wool Manufacturers.

During the beginning of the war, the cotton manufacturing industry, largely centering in New England and employing 200,000 workers, declined. By 1862, the production of American cotton mills had dropped more than 50 per cent as the war cut off the supply of raw cotton. Substitutes were sought for cotton thread as the price of cotton goods soared. In time, under regulations of the government, shipments of cotton from the confiscated and abandoned plantations were slowly moving northward, and treasury agents, charged with this trade, were exchanging northern produce for southern cotton. Importations from abroad also continued. By 1864, there was no serious shortage of raw cotton. Many mills, like the woolen mills, now enjoyed unprecedented prosperity and declared high rates of dividends. With the aid of the increasing war tariffs, cotton products enjoyed protection as never before. Evidence of new interest of the industry in the tariff can be seen in the organization of the New England Cotton Manufacturers Association, later merged into the National Association of Cotton Manufacturers.

Other textile industries were less important. The cotton shortage stimulated efforts to revive the linen industry, but the high cost of dressing domestic flax and the high duties on imported fiber prevented much success. A large amount of Irish linen was imported, and as a result linen manufacture in Ireland was greatly stimulated. Silk thread, trimmings, and ribbons were manufactured chiefly in Connecticut and in the Paterson-Philadelphia area, both accessible to imported raw materials and to metropolitan markets for the finished material. However, silk materials were made only on a small scale and broad silk goods were not produced extensively until after the war.

The war coincided with the spread of labor-saving sewing machinery in clothing and shoes. From 1849, when Elias Howe put his machine on the market, many inventions were patented, the perfection of ideas current in America and Europe. In 1856, by the "Albany Agreement," the principal patents of the leading makers of sewing machines were pooled. Factories for the manufacture of such machines soon ranked among the country's largest establishments. The manufacture of clothing was thus stimulated, and before the war machines were used not only in the homes, but were adapted for use in factories where clothing, footwear, saddlery, and harness were produced in large quantities. In the manufacture of shoes, the McKay machine for sewing soles to uppers marked a revolution in that industry, especially as steam power was applied. The leather industry as a whole was prosperous, providing materials needed in shoe factories and also in saddlery and harness shops which furnished the equipment for the mounted troops, the artillery, and the long army trains.

The manufacture of firearms, of course, received a tremendous impetus. The usual equipment of the Union Army was the muzzle-loading Springfield or Enfield rifle, the loading being accomplished through the muzzle with a greased patch and hickory ramrod. Although there were in use in 1861 many types of breech-loading rifles, including the famous Colt revolver-rifles, and pistols, the improved weapons were not widely adopted by the army in spite of their increased rapidity of firing and greater ease of manipulation. Early in the war, many regiments provided their own arms of nondescript types, from up-to-date arms to those of a musty vintage. In some instances, contractors provided at high prices antiquated and discarded weapons which they bought from European governments. A large part of these were useless for military service. Almost a year was required for private contractors to provide facilities for manufacturing rifles on a large scale. The Gatling gun was patented in 1862. Mounted on a light carriage, its six barrels were placed in a circular frame which was revolved by means of a crank, each barrel in turn being automatically loaded and fired. It was described as "a regiment of men put into half a dozen gun barrels" and fired up to 250 balls a minute, according to the speed with which the crank was turned. Except for those used by General B. F. Butler in Virginia during the latter part of the war, the Gatling gun was generally neglected by the army. The older type cannon and heavy ordnance were retained. Less than 8,000 cannon were issued to the Union armies as against more than 4,000,000 rifles.

After initial depression iron manufacture reached normal levels by 1864. Most of the pig iron of the country was produced in Pennsylvania, New Jersey, and New York. Pittsburgh was the iron center, although there were others that were important. Iron products included cannon, guns, shot, engines, machinery, rails, tools, and implements. The production of steel was small, although experiments were carried on in making Bessemer steel. With the possibility of receiving high tariff protection, the iron producers strengthened their American Iron and Steel Association which dated back to 1855.

Prospecting and mining continued in the West in spite of the war. Mineral deposits of iron, copper, and salt were opened up in Michigan. New sources of metals and minerals were discovered and exploited in the regions of the Rocky Mountains. The output of the older gold mines of California, which had reached its height in the fifties with an annual production of $65,000,000, was declining, but increasing quantities of gold, silver, and other metals were mined in Nevada, Colorado, Idaho, and Montana. Large numbers of people crossed the plains on their way to the newly opened mining areas. A motley group of older men, draft evaders, workers from agricultural areas, and some seeking escape from the disorders of the border states and even from the South, provided the labor necessary for the mines.

In the North, railroad building was retarded first by depression and then by inflation. Wise managers hesitated to lay track at 50 to 100 per cent above what they assumed to be the normal cost. New mileage which had been growing by 2,000 miles a year in the late

1850's fell to about half that level from 1861 to 1865. On the other hand, inflation and war had raised railroad revenues in relation to their bonded indebtedness. In 1862, Congress gave the Union government power to seize and operate the railroads, and General Daniel C. McCallum was placed in charge of operations. He never found it necessary to take over a major road, but United States Military Railroads laid or seized for strategic purposes over 2,000 miles of track. These and other roads greatly facilitated Union operations in the Confederacy.

In the South the railroad net was inadequate for military purposes, and a shortage of material prevented substantial new construction. The speed of the inflation upset private operation for profit,

RAILROAD MILEAGE, 1830 – 1880

Year	Miles of Road Operated	Year	Miles of Road Operated	Year	Miles of Road Operated
1830	23	1844	4,377	1858	26,968
1831	95	1845	4,633	1859	28,789
1832	229	1846	4,930	1860	30,626
1833	380	1847	5,598	1861	31,286
1834	633	1848	5,996	1862	32,120
1835	1,098	1849	7,365	1863	33,170
1836	1,273	1850	9,021	1864	33,908
1837	1,497	1851	10,982	1865	35,085
1838	1,913	1852	12,908	1866	36,801
1839	2,302	1853	15,360	1867	39,050
1840	2,818	1854	16,720	1868	42,229
1841	3,535	1855	18,374	1869	46,844
1842	4,026	1856	22,076	1870	52,922
1843	4,185	1857	24,503	1880	93,262

Source: U.S. Bureau of the Census, *Historical Statistics of the United States, Colonial Times to 1957*, Washington, D.C., 1960, p. 427.

but the Confederacy was slow in seizing roads and controlling traffic and maintenance. By the end of the war the southern roads were in very poor condition. With relatively little industrial development up to this time, all the resources of the South had to be directed toward equipping and maintaining the fighting forces. Buildings were taken over or erected for the purpose of producing uniforms, clothes, supplies, and equipment. Iron furnaces, forges, and manufacturing plants within the Confederacy were turned to war production and new ones built. The Tredegar Iron Works of Richmond, operated by Joseph Reid Anderson, carried on experiments in military and naval armaments, and provided the southern forces with a large part of their munitions. The Shelby Iron Company of Alabama was also important for war supplies. At the outset of the war, arms and munitions from European countries, together with heavy ordnance and supplies from captured Federal seacoast fortifications and arsenals, as well as the requisitioning of privately owned arms, aided the Confederacy. Arsenals appeared at Richmond, Fayetteville, Augusta, Charleston, Savannah, Nashville, and Mount Vernon, Alabama (later Selna, Alabama). Munitions depots were also established in various places and a government ordnance laboratory at Macon, Georgia. Saltpeter and sulphur were plentiful, but labor and equipment for their conversion into gunpowder were difficult to secure. As the war progressed, lead-smelting works, foundries, rifle and pistol shops, and other plants for making military equipment were built. On the plantations and in the shops, the Negroes played an important part in the war effort. One serious handicap in the South was the lack of sufficient transportation facilities to carry the materials and supplies to the war zone.

FINANCING THE WAR

The condition of Federal government finance was not good on the eve of the war because in the years following the tariff reduction and Panic of 1857 deficits had to be financed through issues of bonds. The unbalanced budget shook the confidence of many investors. When Salmon P. Chase reluctantly accepted appointment as Secretary of the Treasury in Lincoln's cabinet, he realized the enormous task which would be placed on his department by war. At this time the public debt was $75,000,000 and available funds in the Treasury were inadequate for immediate expenses. He decided on a program of taxation to cover the ordinary expenditures of government and on a plan of loans to carry on the war. As the struggle continued, many different ways had to be found to finance it. Not until 1866, the year after the war, did most of the receipts of the government come from taxation.

During the war, the larger part of its cost was obtained through loans. This was the result of many circumstances including the inexperience early in the war of those in charge of raising funds, the belief that it was going to be a short conflict, the hesitation of the government to impose heavy internal taxes which were almost unknown to that generation, the fact that the Republican party was new and lacked solidarity, and the belief that the Morrill tariff would provide more money than it actually did. In the first year of the war, the banking system broke down under the strain of badly arranged government borrowing, and specie payments were suspended on December 30, 1861. By this time the government had a deficit of $143,000,000 and a debt of $267,000,000 in obligations of different kinds. Throughout the war, the government issued a great number of bonds and short term notes, varying in interest up to 7.30 per cent (bearing two cents a day interest on each $100 bond) and expiring at different dates, mostly within a period of five years. These had to be refunded in the period after the war. Between 1861 and 1865 inclusive, loans, including treasury notes, amounted to a total of $2 billion. As a result of the difficulties involved in selling bonds, Jay Cooke and Company of Philadelphia were appointed agents to sell several issues. By means of a comprehensive organization and effective publicity, the firm was quite successful.

The first Federal income tax in August, 1861, authorized a rate of 3 per cent on the excess of all incomes above $800 a year. It was so increased in 1862 and 1865 that incomes between $600 and $5,000 were taxed at 5 per cent and above that figure at 10 per cent. After the war, the limit of exemption was raised and in 1867 placed at $2,000. The tax law was in force until 1872 and, although its constitutionality was questioned, no cases were decided by the Supreme Court while it was in effect. Internal revenue taxes were not new, but they had not been levied by the Federal government since 1817. At first, Secretary Chase did not emphasize the need for such taxes, but as the necessity for increased revenue became evident in 1862, Congress enacted a system of excises and set up the machinery for their collection. It imposed moderate duties upon a large number of items rather than heavy ones on a few. Levies were imposed on beer, liquor, and tobacco; manufactures and products; railroads and steamboats, banking institutions, and insurance companies; advertisements and legacies; and legal documents of all kinds. The law also provided for license fees for certain occupations. Between 1862 and 1865, internal revenue and income taxes amounted to $356,000,000.

At the same time that Congress passed the internal revenue act in 1862, changes were made in the tariff. The Morrill tariff had been planned in 1860 and passed on March 2, 1861. Representative Morrill of Vermont was a protectionist by conviction, but the measure was moderate because its purpose was to bring revenue to a depleted treasury and because a highly protective tariff had no chance of passing in the waning Democratic Congress. In 1862, the internal revenue taxes furnished a unique reason for protecting certain domestic industries. It was pointed out that if manufactures of certain products were to survive they should be protected, "otherwise we shall have destroyed the goose that lays the golden egg." Except for the protective schedules, there were few other changes in the act of 1862, but it is important to note the beginning of a new protective policy. In 1864, because increased excise duties were levied on manufactures, many schedules were made highly protective and the general level of the tariff was raised. The average rate on dutiable commodities was raised from about 37 per cent to 47 per cent and the new measure remained the basis of tariff legislation in the years that followed.

The need in 1862 for immediate war funds led to an act providing for the issue of $150,000,000 in paper currency. Although its constitutionality was questioned, Secretary Chase reluctantly gave his approval to the proposal. Some who opposed were sure that it would bring economic disaster through inflation. In spite of this view, during the war Congress authorized a total of $450,000,000 of United States notes. These greenbacks, as they were popularly known, were made legal tender for all debts, public and private, and for all taxes and debts due the United States except tariff duties and interest on the public debt. No specific gold or silver reserve was set aside nor was any date announced for their redemption, although on their face they bore the promise of the government to pay gold on demand. On being issued, they drove out of circulation the last vestiges of gold and silver coins, including subsidiary coins. Gold and silver now ceased being part of the circulating money supply and became representative of world prices in relation to those of the United States. Put another way, bond and currency issues in excess of real savings brought domestic inflation which was roughly measurable by comparison with gold values. In terms of gold, the greenback dollar was worth eighty-seven cents in July, 1862; seventy-seven cents in July, 1863; thirty-nine cents in July, 1864; and seventy cents in July, 1865. Not for many years did it come to equal the gold dollar in value. Because there was need for subsidiary currency, Congress authorized the use of postage and other stamps in 1862 and in 1863, but this awkward medium of exchange was replaced by notes of fractional currency or "shinplasters" in denominations as low as three cents. Altogether $50,000,000 of this unique money was authorized and it added to the income of the government in the war emergency. As a result of the shortage of currency, shopkeepers and tradesmen issued quantities of tokens and store cards.

In his annual report of December, 1861, Secretary Chase proposed a national banking system in order that the government could exercise its authority over the credit distribution of the country. He believed that a uniform bank note circulation was necessary instead of a multitude of currencies provided by banking systems dependent on the laws of thirty-four states. He also felt that it would give security to the Union because a common interest would be secured by requiring national securities as a basis for circulation. Little stress was placed on the requirement for government bonds as security in his report, but this was an important reason for the recommendation. These reasons were elaborated in later reports of Chase, but not until 1863 was "An Act to Provide a National Currency" passed. It authorized the establishment of banks which would have the right to issue notes up to 90 per cent of the current market price of government bonds, which were required to be deposited with the treasurer of the United States. The system developed slowly. As defects in the law became evident, it was recast in the measure of 1864 and was called the National Bank Act. By October of that year there were 584 national banks having a circulation of $65,000,000. Thus a market had been provided for the sale of a small amount of Federal securities and at the same time a uniform system of banking and currency had been established. Since state banks hesitated to join the system, an act of March, 1865, imposed a tax of 10 per cent on the circulation of state bank notes beginning in July, 1866, to achieve the ideal of a uniform currency. This put an end to local bank notes. By October, 1866, the number of national banks had increased to 1,644, but contrary to Chase's hopes, the new banking system had been only a minor factor in war finance.

The financing of the war in the South was much more serious and difficult because that section had been financially dependent upon the North. The fiscal machinery organized by the Confederate government was similar to that of the Federal government, with its

Treasury Department and several divisions. Under the Confederate constitution, the government was authorized to coin money and to regulate its value, to authorize paper money as legal tender, and to borrow upon the public credit. The new government started without funds and the first step taken was to seize about $1,000,000 in the custom houses and mints of the South. At the same time, in order to conserve specie and strike at the North, a law of 1861 forbade the payment of private debts to northern creditors and required that such debts be paid into the Confederate treasury.

Believing that the war would not be a long one, the southern Secretary of the Treasury, C. G. Memminger, at first emphasized loans. On February 28, 1861, the Confederate Congress authorized an issue of $15,000,000 ten-year bonds at 8 per cent. An export duty of one-eighth of one per cent on raw cotton was pledged for the payment of the interest. This loan drained the southern banks of specie. Other issues followed and, as it was impossible to secure specie, a number of them were made payable in produce including cotton, tobacco, sugar, and other commodities. By the end of 1862, gold had been drained out of the country, the result of the South's unfavorable balance of trade with Europe. The outflow was accentuated by a brief embargo on the export of cotton when it was hoped that England would intervene on behalf of the Confederacy before allowing her cotton industry to perish. By this time the northern blockade was also beginning to be felt. Early in 1863, however, a loan was arranged with the French banking firm, Emile Erlanger et Compagnie, for a secret issue of twenty-year bonds bearing interest at 7 per cent and secured by raw cotton. Although the loan was authorized at $15,000,000, it netted the Confederacy only about $6,500,000. In the last years of the war, treasury notes had to be issued in increasing quantities with the result that inflation undermined the entire fiscal system.

At first the Confederate Treasury justified paper as the establishing of a national currency. In May, 1861, the southern Congress authorized an issue of $20,000,000. By the end of the year, $105,000,000 of such notes were outstanding. Issues of treasury notes followed one another in rapid succession. Attempts were made to bolster some of the issues and to prevent them from declining in value by making them exchangeable for interest bearing bonds at a future date, but without much success. As a result of the continued policy of issuing fiat money, more than $1 billion, including fractional currency, had been authorized before the war came to an end. In addition to the paper currency of the Confederate government, states added to the flood and notes were also issued by municipalities, banks, factories, and business concerns. As a result of the disappearance of specie and the increase of paper money, inflation more serious than in the North set in, and before the end of the war Confederate paper money became worthless.

Although at the beginning of the war it did not wish to impose high taxes, in August, 1861, the Confederate Congress apportioned among the states a direct tax on real estate, slaves, merchandise, bank stocks, railroad and corporation stock, cattle, horses, mules, and many other types of property. It was not very successful, as some states raised their quotas by issues of bonds or paper money and others took no action at all. Two years later an internal revenue tax of 8 per cent was levied on naval stores, salt, wine, liquors, tobacco, cotton, wool, sugar, molasses, syrup, and similar commodities. Among other taxes, in addition to the small customs duties, were those on incomes, license taxes on certain occupations, and a 10 per cent tax on agricultural products payable in kind. In spite of the variety of taxes, only about $125,000,000 were raised in this manner out of total receipts from all other sources of $2.3 billion.

During the last part of the war, economic demoralization spread over the South. Financial problems became acute. The confusion and depreciation of the currency together with the large borrowings made a major change in policy inevitable. Repudiation of the currency was forced by the loss of the war but without doubt would have occurred in any event. More upsetting to the economic life of the South after the war was the emancipation of all slaves without compensation to owners and the outlawing of the entire southern debt. The former was written into the Constitution by means of the Thirteenth Amendment; the latter by the Fourteenth.

CHAPTER 14

The Transportation System

While the United States had vast resources in farm land, timber, and minerals that promised industrial greatness, full realization of the promise required railroads. In the period between 1850 and 1900, a closely meshed railway net was spread over the eastern and central parts of the nation, and more than half a dozen single track lines reached the Pacific Coast. By 1887, the railroad had become so basic to the economic life of the nation that it was the first major industry to be placed under Federal government regulation. The 250,000 miles of railroad track in the United States in 1914 exceeded the mileage of all of Europe and equalled one-third of the world's total.

THE TRANSCONTINENTAL RAILROADS

The idea of connecting the Atlantic and Pacific by means of railroads was conceived early in the history of railroad transportation. In 1845, Asa Whitney, a merchant engaged in the China trade, petitioned Congress for a charter for a railroad from Lake Michigan to the north of the Columbia River. He believed that goods from the Orient could be transported from the Pacific coast to the Great Lakes and thence by the rapidly developing transportation system of the East to the cities of the Atlantic seaboard. He estimated the cost of the proposed road at about $65,000,000 and asked that a strip of

323

land sixty miles wide along the route be granted for the purpose. He believed that cheap labor then migrating from Ireland and Germany could be used to build the road and proposed to pay the workers as far as possible in land. It was therefore planned to have them settle along the route, aiding in building up that part of the country. Whitney lobbied in Congress; meetings were held in eastern cities in favor of the project; boards of trade and chambers of commerce became interested; and many state legislatures petitioned Congress in support of the plan. Whitney's dream received much publicity, but Congress took no action.

The acquisition and rapid growth of California after 1848 brought the need for a Pacific railroad again to the attention of the country. In Congress there was general agreement regarding the need for such a road and also that the government should aid in financing it. In 1853, Congress authorized a survey of various routes, which was accomplished under the direction of Secretary of War Jefferson Davis. The work was performed in an excellent manner by army engineers and the report set forth all possible routes. But the project of a transcontinental railroad was delayed because of sectional differences. The South wanted a southern route with a terminus on the Mississippi, while the North demanded a northern route with a terminus in Chicago or some other northern city. Stephen A. Douglas tried to harmonize the conflicting interests by suggesting a northern, central, and southern road, constructed with Federal aid, but his proposed bill failed. Most people believed that one railroad would be sufficient.

The secession of the southern states made possible a northern or a central route. The latter was decided on. In 1862, the Pacific Rail-

MILEAGE OF FIRST MAIN RAILROAD TRACK, 1890 – 1930

Year	First Main Track	Year	First Main Track
1890	156,404	1910	240,831
1895	177,746	1915	257,569
1900	192,556	1920	259,941
1905	216,974	1930*	260,440

*From 1930 on, first main track declined slowly.
Source: U.S. Bureau of the Census, *Historical Statistics of the United States, Colonial Times to 1957*, Washington, D.C., 1960, p. 429.

Construction of the first transcontinental railroad
in the Nevada desert, 1868

way Act authorized the Union Pacific Railroad to build a line west
from the Missouri River to the western boundary of Nevada. It permitted the Central Pacific Railroad to build a road from Sacramento
to the eastern boundary of California. Both companies were granted
five alternate sections on each side of a right of way, 200 feet wide.
Loans were also made at the rate of $16,000 per mile in flat country,
$32,000 per mile in hilly country, and $48,000 per mile in mountainous country, all secured by first mortgage bonds. In spite of such
aid, it was difficult to attract private capital for an undertaking whose
future earning power seemed remote and uncertain. An act of 1864
doubled the land grants and Congress took second mortgage bonds
for its loans to the railroads. The Central Pacific was authorized to
build 150 miles east of the California-Nevada line, and two years later
it was permitted to advance eastward until it met the westward-
moving Union Pacific. Although work was begun on both lines in
1863, it was not taken up in earnest until after the Civil War when it
was pushed to completion.

The Central Pacific Railroad was largely built by Chinese coolies in pigtails, wearing basket hats, colored blouses, and flapping pantaloons. The Union Pacific Railroad was constructed by Irish laborers and ex-soldiers of the Civil War. The hostility of the Indians of the plains made necessary trains equipped to resist attack, and much of the work was done under the protection of armed men. Engineering problems also had to be solved. These were most difficult in the far West, for a larger number of tunnels, deep rock cuttings, and high trestles which spanned ravines and gorges were required in that region because of the topography of the country. All work was accomplished without the aid of steam shovels, giant derricks, and other modern appliances and machinery. Under the leadership of Grenville M. Dodge, engineer of the Union Pacific, and Theodore D. Judah of the Central Pacific, the lines were completed. The last two years were marked by a spectacular race between the two companies bidding for government subsidies, land grants, and public favor. The race culminated in the dramatic union of the two lines at Promontory Point, near Ogden, Utah in 1869. Amid appropriate and impressive ceremonies, the "wedding of the rails" was celebrated. The Union Pacific had laid 1,086 miles of track; the Central Pacific, 689. It now became possible to travel from ocean to ocean entirely by rail and the time for such travel was cut down considerably.

The problem of railroad construction in unsettled areas presented financial as well as physical difficulties. There was a vicious circle: it was hard to sell stock in an unfinished railroad with little traffic, and hard to raise money to finish the road without selling stock. The usual solution was to establish a separate company for construction, which could attract additional private capital by promising quick profits. The construction company could be paid in the stock of the railroad, at a large discount from par. In addition to selling its own stock, the construction company could borrow from banks with the railroad stock as security. In this way quite large additional funds could be drawn into construction of the road, but the price reckoned in par value of railroad stock (which, of course, could not be sold for as much as par) was generally so high that the construction company came to control a majority of the voting shares of the railroad. Since the big stockholders in both railroad and construction company were mainly the same people, this did not bother them, but it meant that in financial dealings these "insiders" would tend to favor their smaller wholly owned construction company rather than the larger widely owned railroad in which their proportionate interest was much less.

The building of the first transcontinental railroad was unfortunately associated with speculative construction company operations. A group of leaders of the Union Pacific organized a construction company, called the Credit Mobilier, to which contracts were awarded to build much of the road. Proceeds from the sale of the railroad's first mortgage bonds and from government bonds which had been loaned the road on a second mortgage together with the sale of stock, income bonds, and land grant bonds, a total of some $75,000,000, was turned over to the Credit Mobilier to pay for construction that cost less than $60,000,000. In order to prevent Congressional interference with the activities of the Credit Mobilier, Oakes Ames, a member of the construction company and of Congress, as early as 1867 distributed a number of shares of the company to senators and representatives, permitting some to pay for their stock out of future dividends. The scandal did not become known generally until the presidential campaign of 1872, when charges were made by the *New York Sun*. Congressional committees investigated and the House formally censured Oakes Ames and James Brooks, the government's directors of the road. Vice-President Schuyler Colfax, who had received some of the stock, had to retire from public life and many others in high positions, including James A. Garfield, had their reputations besmirched. But other railroad men at the time and some later economists doubt that private enterprise could have been expected to build the road more cheaply. The profit was not great in proportion to the risks, and it was hard to raise the initial capital. The Central Pacific Railroad also organized an inside construction company to build its line. Under the leadership of Leland Stanford, Collis P. Huntington, Charles Crocker, and Mark Hopkins, officials of the Central Pacific, the firm of Charles Crocker and Company was organized. Larger profits were probably made than on the eastern end of the line. An attempt by Congress to investigate the company failed, as all records had been burned.

Before the first transcontinental railroad was built, Congress chartered several others. In 1864, the Northern Pacific Railroad Company received the right to build a railroad from Lake Superior to Puget Sound. It received large land grants but no government loans. In 1869, Jay Cooke and Company became its financial agents. Construction was begun in 1870 and had reached Bismarck, North Dakota, in 1873, when Jay Cooke and Company failed because of heavy advances to the railroads. In 1876, the Northern Pacific became insolvent but work was later resumed under the leadership of Henry Villard. It was completed to Portland, Oregon, in 1883 and three years later reached

Seattle, Washington. Congress chartered the Atlantic and Pacific Railroad in 1866 to run from Springfield, Missouri, down to the 35th parallel and across the Colorado River to Needles. It also received land grants, but encountered difficulties in financing its work during the Panic of 1873. It was reorganized, but a few years later was merged with the Atchison, Topeka and Santa Fe. The last of the continental Federal land grant railroads was the Texas and Pacific, chartered by Congress in 1871.

The total land area of continental United States is about 1.9 billion acres. Of these some 1.2 billion acres belonged to the Federal government in 1856. Direct Federal land transfers to railroads from that time on came to about 130,000,000 acres and to railroads from land first transferred to the states nearly 50,000,000 acres more, or a total of about 15 per cent of the mid-century public domain. In making these grants, the Federal government made a better bargain than it anticipated. In return for the land the railroads had to carry mail, troops, and government property at rates fixed by Congress, which could be reduced to 50 per cent below normal. Competing non-land grant roads had to meet these rates to secure Federal business. Up to the Second World War these Federal rebates were a small problem, but in that war the railroads lost so heavily on government business that they were forced to seek an adjustment.

THE IMPROVEMENT AND CONSOLIDATION OF THE RAILROADS

During this period when the railroad system was being completed, many improvements were made and greater efficiency was attained. A standard railway gauge was adopted which replaced the multiplicity of gauges of the earlier period. Steel rails, first Bessemer, then open-hearth, superseded iron rails, providing tracks of greater uniformity, strength, and hardness. Steel bridges and equipment also aided in railroad development. Tank cars, cattle cars, and other types of cars were developed for freight and express traffic. Out of the crude signaling system emerged the highly efficient automatic electric block system. The Westinghouse air brake and automatic car couplers were important advances and the Federal Safety Appliance Act of 1893 required standard safety equipment. Better passenger cars and more comforts were provided for the traveling public, as many improvements such as better lighting—from oil to electric, and heating—from stoves to steam, gradually made travel safer and more comfortable. The consolidation of small units into large systems and the building of longer lines made progress possible and provided for a more efficient and smooth-running operation of the railroads in an age of industrial expansion.

The consolidation of the railroads began about the middle of the nineteenth century. The disadvantages of transferring merchandise, freight, and passengers from one short line to another when distances had to be covered made consolidation inevitable. In most cases, varying gauges of railroads made impossible uninterrupted travel over several lines. Changes from one road to another were inconvenient and expensive. The first important long-distance consolidation was that of the New York Central Railroad in 1853, when eleven short roads were combined into one system. At the same time longer lines were planned, to be consolidated later. As early as 1833 a company was organized to connect New York City with Lake Erie by a railroad. Small sections of the line were built from time to time, but not until 1851 did the track reach Dunkirk, the original objective on Lake Erie. The next year connection was made with Buffalo. This was the origin of the Erie Railroad, which after the Civil War annexed many short lines and gained the attention of the country as it became the center of scandals. The Pennsylvania began with a line from Philadelphia to the Susquehanna River and then absorbed many smaller railroads, reaching out to Cincinnati, Chicago, and St. Louis. By 1871 it controlled more than 3,000 miles of track. The Michigan Southern was formed by the unification of a number of small roads. The rate wars in New England began the consolidation of the Boston and Maine system. These are but some of the examples of the consolidations of the period.

Late nineteenth and early twentieth century consolidations were aimed not so much at avoiding transshipment as at establishing regional controls over railroad transportation. The Interstate Commerce Act of 1887 which prohibited pooling led investment banking houses interested in railroad bonds to seek new ways of avoiding cutthroat competition. One such means was to establish common ownership of competing roads, or as J. Pierpont Morgan said, "a community of interest." The depression of the middle nineties, by making many roads dependent on the bankers for survival, speeded the formation of ownership systems. Two investment banking houses, J. P. Morgan and Co., and Kuhn, Loeb and Company took the lead in railroad finance. The roads financed, and hence strongly influenced by the House of Morgan, included: The Vanderbilt, or New York Central system; the James J. Hill group in the Northwest; the Southern system; and a New England system—some 70,000 miles in all. The Kuhn, Loeb interests, in which the firm operated through Edward H. Harriman, included lines from Chicago south and west to the Gulf and the Pacific Coast, such as Illinois Central, and Union and Southern Pacific, totalling 25,000 miles of track.

RAILROAD MISMANAGEMENT

As consolidation increased after the Civil War, many came to look upon the growing railroad systems as monopolies operating against the public interest. The farmers of the more settled regions of the West, hard pressed as prices of their products declined while rates remained high, grew exceedingly antagonistic. Businessmen, also, condemned the roads, for it became increasingly difficult for them to compete with large enterprises which were favored in various ways by the carriers. The flames of such opposition were fanned by disclosures of mismanagement, corruption, and the domination of a few influential financiers.

The dishonest manipulation of the issues and sales of railroad stocks was an unsavory practice that was fairly common during the generation after the Civil War. This was often done by insiders throwing new stock on the market to force down prices and then buying the shares back at a lower figure. As we have noted in connection with the transcontinentals, many roads were highly overcapitalized in the beginning and unable to pay reasonable dividends. Not only was the investing public defrauded by railroad financiers, but executives cheated and fought each other. The most flagrant example of the latter was the terrific battle for the control of the Erie Railroad, which was waged by Jay Gould, James Fisk, Cornelius Vanderbilt, and Daniel Drew. Gould was finally forced to give up control, but he left the road so impoverished that no dividend was declared until 1942.

Private car companies were also organized to insure fast or special handling of goods. These companies were generally owned by small groups of directors or inside stockholders. Thus express and special freight was not always in the hands of the railroads, and the stockholders in general did not participate in the profits brought by the "cream of the traffic." The Star Union Line and Empire Line of the Pennsylvania Railroad, and the Merchant's Dispatch Transportation Company of the New York Central were examples of such companies. Cattle cars, poultry cars, coal cars, and others were owned and controlled by outside companies, often organized by railroad officials.

Discrimination in rates provoked more antirailroad feeling than any other practice, yet there seemed no way out of the dilemma if free competition was to be the rule. To begin with, since loading, unloading, and other terminal costs were a very large part of the total, the cost per ton mile of hauling freight diminished with the distance. In addition, long-haul rates were usually set in competition with other roads, whereas short hauls were likely to be in monopolized territory. Since competitive rates were often driven so low that they did not cover overhead costs, the inevitable tendency was to make up the deficiency by charging higher short-haul rates where the shipper had no alternative but to pay. Similarly, big shippers located at competitive points could command special discounts, called rebates, by threatening to shift their business to another road, whereas the little businessman had no such leverage. In addition, there were many other rate differences based on the unequal demand for space in different directions and the value of the goods being shipped. The railroads' solution to these dilemmas of competition was legalized pooling: allowing the roads involved in a competitive area to divide the traffic among them and to fix reasonable rates. But public authorities did not trust such semimonopolistic private rate making. While the roads pooled certain traffic, the agreements had no legal force as the courts generally regarded pooling as a restraint of trade.

As a result of these difficulties, the general principle adopted by the railroads was to "charge what the traffic would bear." For example, domestic groceries from Chicago to New York were transported at seventy-five cents per 100 pounds, while imported sugar and coffee were charged only thirty-five cents per 100 pounds. An illustration of discrimination between competitive and non-competitive points can be seen in the fact that it cost about as much to ship coal from the mines on the Reading Railroad to Philadelphia, a distance of ninety miles, as from the same mines to Boston, 350 miles away. An investigation showed that between January and June, 1880, the New York Central Railroad granted more than 6,000 special rates. This was typical of many railroads.

Another indictment against the railroads resulted from their participation in politics. Judges and legislators were often bribed to protect or favor the interests of certain railroads. An investigating committee discovered that the Erie Railroad in one year expended $700,000 for bribery and corruption, carried on the books as an "India rubber account." The manipulation of the New York courts by the New York Central Railroad was scandalous. It was common practice to grant free passage to men such as politicians or editors who could influence legislation, and once the system was established no individual road dared to stop it. As disclosures of mismanagement and corruption were made in the seventies and eighties, there is little wonder that the public became hostile toward the carriers. Of course, many railroads such as the Chicago, Burlington & Quincy or the Pennsylvania railroads were honestly and well managed, but they received little or no publicity compared to the unscrupulous ones.

RAILROAD REGULATION

By the late sixties, business interests in Massachusetts and New York, middle-western farmers, and many other small shippers were demanding state regulation of railroads. As a result, a number of states, particularly in the Upper Mississippi Valley, passed laws placing restrictions on railroad rate making. An Illinois law of 1871, for example, established maximum freight and passenger rates and a board of railway and warehouse commissioners to enforce the law. Other state legislatures passed laws similar to those of Illinois for the purpose of regulating railroads, warehouses and elevators. The Grange, a farmers' organization, at meetings, picnics, and socials, exhorted its members to elect to office only those who favored strict regulation. Thus railroad regulatory acts by the states became known as Granger laws.

At first railroads refused to obey the regulatory laws, pending appeal to the courts. The carriers argued that the assumption of such powers by states violated the due process clause of the Fourteenth Amendment, which sets forth that no state shall "deprive any person of life, liberty and property without due process of law." Another line of argument stressed that within the meaning of Article I, Section 10 of the Constitution, the charters granted to railroads were contracts which were being impaired by the Granger laws. Still another argument insisted that only Congress had the right and power to regulate interstate commerce. The courts, however, decided against the railroads—until 1886.

One of the first important decisions of the Supreme Court regarding state regulation of storage and railroad rates was Munn vs. Illinois (1876) involving the validity of the Illinois law of 1871 which fixed maximum rates for storing grain in warehouses. A Chicago warehouse company, Munn and Scott, was found guilty in 1872 of charging higher rates than the law stipulated. The case was taken on appeal through the courts and finally reached the Supreme Court. In answer to the contention that the fixing of maximum rates amounted to the taking of property without due process of law, the Court stated that the government could regulate prices in businesses "affected with a public interest" as had been done in England and other countries for centuries. Replying to the argument that only Congress could regulate warehouses which "may become connected with interstate commerce," the Court decided that such regulation was of domestic concern and "until Congress acts in reference to their interstate relations, the State may exercise all the powers of government over them, even though in so doing it may indirectly operate upon commerce outside its immediate jurisdiction." The decision was of great significance and was followed by another which applied directly to the question of railroad rates. In the case of Peik *vs.* Chicago and Northwestern Railway Company (1876), the railroad contended that the legislature of Wisconsin could not lawfully regulate rates because the railroad crossed the boundaries of the state. The Court decided that the state had the right to do so within its boundaries, even if the carriers traversed them, because of the absence of Federal legislation in this respect. Once again it was emphasized that "until Congress acts," the states possessed the power of regulation, otherwise there would be no control over such corporations.

Though regulatory legislation affecting the railroads was held constitutional, it became impossible to make such laws really workable and efficient because a uniform policy could not be achieved. Nor could state boards or commissions effectively regulate railroads operating in several states. In addition, the remarkable expansion of railroad building in the decade of the eighties, declining rates, and perhaps some personal pressures made regulatory commissions more friendly to the railroad point of view.

In 1886, the Supreme Court handed down a decision in the Wabash case [1] which seriously modified the decision in the Granger cases and made necessary Federal legislation if the railroads were to be regulated at all. The case involved the "long-and-short haul" evil, for the railroad charged certain shippers more for carrying the same amount and type of goods from Gilman, Illinois, to New York City than from Peoria to New York City, although Peoria was eighty-six miles farther away. The Court decided that the state had no jurisdiction in the matter, as such regulation was in the field of interstate commerce and therefore strictly reserved to Congress. It was maintained

[1] Wabash, St. Louis and Pacific Railway Company *vs.* Illinois.

that the authority of the state was limited to control over intrastate commerce.

The problem of regulation had long been debated in Congress. In 1872, President Grant, influenced by the discontent of the farmers and by the early railroad legislation in the states, called the attention of Congress to the prevailing high rates and asked for an investigation. The Windom Committee was appointed and made a report in 1874. It recommended that the government improve the waterways of the country and build lines to compete with the railroads for the purpose of forcing a reduction of their rates. It also advocated a bureau of commerce for collecting information relating to internal trade and commerce in order that steps could be taken to remedy such abuses as stock watering, rebates, and discrimination. The McCrary bill was drawn up in the House and passed (1874) but the Senate refused to consider it. While it did not follow many of the suggestions of the Windom Committee, it provided for a Federal railroad commission and for regulation of the carriers. In 1878, a more conservative measure—the Reagan bill—passed the House, but no action was taken on it in the Senate. It forbade pools, discriminatory rates, and drawbacks; it required the publicity of rates; and it prohibited charging more for a shorter distance than for a longer one over the same route. In the years that followed, many similar bills were passed by the House but were pigeonholed in the Senate.

The business depression of 1884–1885 increased public pressure for Federal regulation. Bills were passed in the Senate which provided for an interstate commerce commission, but they were not so highly regulatory as the Reagan bills which had been passed by the House and no compromise was reached. Finally the nullification of state regulation by the decision in the Wabash case made action by Congress imperative. As a result the Interstate Commerce Act was passed in 1887.

The Interstate Commerce Act laid down the general principle that all rates must be just and reasonable. It forbade discriminations between shippers, localities, and classes of freight. It prohibited charging more for a short than for a long haul over the same line, in the same direction, and under similar conditions, except with the consent of the proper authorities. It declared the pooling of railroad traffic or earnings illegal. And it required that all rates and fares be printed and publicly posted. The law also provided for the Interstate Commerce Commission (originally five members) to administer the act. It was given certain regulatory powers over the carriers including those of investigating the railroads, prescribing systems of accounting, making reports, and providing publicity. Its important function was the administration of the rate policy, for it was authorized to hear complaints and examine the evidence of shippers and the railroads regarding unfair rates and to make decisions. But it had to depend upon the Federal courts to enforce its rulings and it discovered that the courts were not friendly.

From the time that the act went into effect until 1906, the Interstate Commerce Commission enjoyed neither high repute nor authority, nor did it succeed in enforcing its rulings. The chief weakness of the Commission lay in the fact that its decisions were not compulsory and it had to take action in the courts to force acceptance by the railroads. The willingness of the Federal courts to receive new evidence in cases of appeal from the decisions of the Commission as well as to pass stern judgment on such decisions undermined its authority. Until 1896, the courts refused to force witnesses to give evidence of an incriminating nature, and the next year the Supreme Court held that while the Commission could declare a specific rate unreasonable and unjust, it did not have the power to decide on the proper rate. In 1897, the Supreme Court declared that certain conditions might warrant a railroad charging more for a short haul than for a long one, thus vitiating the "long and short haul clause." Of forty-two appeals taken by the Commission to the Circuit Courts between 1887 and 1905, twenty-four were reversed and only seven were fully sustained. During the same period the Supreme Court reversed the Commission's ruling in fifteen out of sixteen cases. Abuses continued and the Commission became little more than a bureau of statistics. But it had made several thousand decisions informally, which were accepted by the carriers and shippers, and it had achieved much in securing rate publicity as well as in reducing the number of freight rate classifications. Its work during these early years was of educational value and as new laws gave it increased power, it became obvious that the period of railroad laissez faire was over.

Partly on the initiative of some of the carriers, Congress passed the Elkins Anti-rebate Act in 1903, which strengthened that section of the Interstate Commerce Act relating to rebates and to rate-cutting. It struck at trusts and corporations which had gained power and influence as a result of secret and unfair rebates on the transportation of their freight over smaller competitors. The law provided for the prosecution and punishment of railroad corporations as well as their agents and officers for deviating in any way from the published schedules of rates. The receiver of a rebate as well as the giver was to be regarded as guilty of violating the law. About the same time (1903) the Expediting Act was passed, largely for the purpose of securing the more effective regulation of the carriers. It provided that any suit brought by the United States to the Circuit Courts under the Interstate Commerce Act, the Sherman Antitrust Act (see p. 483), or laws having a like purpose, should have preference over all other cases and in every way be "expedited and be assigned for leaving at the earliest practicable day." But it was the Hepburn Act that raised the prestige of the Interstate Commerce Commission and provided for a stricter regulation of the railroads.

The Hepburn Act of 1906 was largely the result of a crusade led by "progressive" leaders in Congress and was passed only after a battle. It empowered the Interstate Commerce Commission in cases brought before it to fix reasonable rates that should be observed until set aside by the courts. Thus, its decisions were binding, requiring the carriers to assume the burden of initiating litigation to test the validity of the Commission's orders. The law authorized the Commission to determine, prescribe, and enforce uniform systems of bookkeeping; it strengthened the Elkins Act of 1903 regarding discriminations; it forbade railroads from transporting commodities they had produced or mined except those necessary for their own use; it placed under the jurisdiction of the Commission, in addition to the railroads, agencies directly connected with railroad transportation, such as industrial railroads, private car lines, and pipeline companies; it forbade railroads to issue free passes to certain groups of individuals; and it increased the number of commissioners from five to seven.

Another step was taken to tighten government control over the carriers when the Mann-Elkins Act was passed in 1910. This law placed telegraph and telephone companies under the jurisdiction of the Interstate Commerce Commission. It gave the Commission the power to suspend proposed changes in railroad rates until the courts had the opportunity to investigate such increases. It provided for the establishment of a special commerce court to hear railroad cases which arose from the orders of the Commission. It also made vital the "long and short haul clause" of the Interstate Commerce Act. Several amendments were made to the parent law between 1910 and 1914. One of the most important was the Physical Valuation Act of 1913 which authorized the Commission to undertake the valuation of railroad properties as a basis for regulation. By 1914, most of the defects of the act of 1887 had been corrected, and the railroads were being strictly regulated, perhaps to a degree that sapped the energy and initiative of management.

THE AGE OF THE ELECTRIC TROLLEY

Ultimately the automobile was to be the most important force in changing the ways of urban living and transferring people and their work to the fringes of metropolitan areas, but before 1914 the electric trolley was the major factor. The first commercially successful traction systems using overhead trolley wires were established in Binghamton, New York, in 1886 by Leo Daft, and in Richmond, Virginia, in 1887 by Frank J. Sprague. By 1902, there were 22,500 miles of electric urban and interurban railways in the United States; by 1912 the mileage had increased to 41,000. After the First World War, buses, using pneumatic tires for the first time, rapidly made this vast trolley system obsolete.

Meanwhile, cheaply constructed trolley tracks branched out in all directions from the center of cities and connected nearby cities with more frequent service than could be afforded by trains. Along the thickly populated east coast one could go hundreds of miles by connecting trolley lines. Suburbs which had previously clung close to the relatively few railroad lines, leaving great areas of open country in between, could now be developed in a more uniform ring around the central city. People ten or fifteen miles out in the country could commute to work for less than the cost of railroad fares, and the thousands of employees that filled central city skyscrapers could be brought to their work by subways and elevateds. The capital investment in surface lines all over the country and in subways and elevateds in the largest cities gave an additional buoyant push to the economy from 1897 to 1912. This period of generally prosperous years can be thought of as the electrical utilities boom.

THE INLAND WATERWAYS

Until the 1850's, the inland waterways were the most important agencies of transportation in the country. By 1860, commerce on the Mississippi had reached a peak. The war then interrupted river traffic between the North and the South. Steamboats continued to run on the upper Mississippi and Ohio Rivers, but southward traffic on the great artery of commerce ceased almost entirely. In the North, the war worked greatly to the advantage of traffic on the canals and rivers as well as to the railroads, and transportation thrived in that region. Every means was used to transport war supplies. The South, far behind the North in water transportation facilities as well as rail, found its war efforts greatly hampered by the lack of canals, improved waterways, steamboats, and railroads.

After the war, most of the passenger traffic of the country came to be carried by the railroads, and the trend to ship express and lighter freight by rail, which had really begun with railroad expansion about the middle of the century, developed in a most remarkable way. By 1870, the railroads were carrying more than four-fifths of such bulky products as grain. Cotton from the southwest, also, was no longer sent exclusively by water routes, but reached Atlantic or Gulf ports, such as Charleston, Savannah, and Galveston, by rail. The high water mark of river commerce for the lower Mississippi was reached in 1880. More than 1,000,000 tons were received and shipped from St. Louis in that year. It fell to 141,000 tons in 1905.

Changes in transportation affected the river towns, although the railroads brought prosperity to most of them. New Orleans declined as a great river port, but it made material progress. St. Louis, whose commerce in 1850 had been almost entirely by water, within a generation had become a railroad center and its trade was largely carried by the railroads. By the time of the Louisiana Purchase Exposition in 1904, the largest world's fair held up to that time, the commerce of St. Louis was a hundred times greater by rail than by river.

With the exception of the Monongahela and the Ohio, whose banks were dotted with mills and mines, river trade diminished in spite of large sums of money spent by the Federal government for the improvement of channels. Navigation on such rivers as the Hudson and Potomac came to be limited to ferry service, excursion trade, and transporting products locally. After the building of the transcontinental railroads and the settlement of the far West, transportation on the Upper Mississippi, Missouri, and Columbia also declined in relative importance.

Canal operation also suffered after the Civil War as a result of rail competition. By 1900, almost 1,700 miles of these artificial waterways had been abandoned and by 1914, one-half of the canals of the country had ceased to be used. But many important canals continued to serve many areas and a few new ones were built.

The Erie continued to be one of the important canals. In spite of the railroads that paralleled it, annual tonnage reached a peak of more than 4,500,000 tons in 1889. This declined to 2,000,000 tons in 1905 and to 891,000 in 1920, although all tolls were ended in 1882. In 1903, as traffic was waning, the state of New York projected the New York

State Barge Canal, a system of four canals, of which the Erie was the most important. It required an expenditure of about $150,000,000 to complete the system, which was opened to traffic in 1918. Another important canal was the Illinois and Michigan Canal, completed in 1848. It competed successfully with parallel railroads and reached its peak in 1882 when it carried more than a million tons of traffic, maintaining its position by cutting tolls to the lowest possible level. By the beginning of the twentieth century it had lost its importance. After many proposals and failures, the eight-mile long Cape Cod Canal, connecting Buzzards Bay and Cape Cod Bay, was built in 1909–1914 by a private company. The Federal government bought it in 1928.

The greatest of all canals within the United States was the Sault Sainte Marie Canal around the rapids in the Saint Mary's River at the outlet of Lake Superior. It was first built by the state of Michigan in 1855 and was taken over by the United States in 1881 and reconstructed. Tolls were abolished. By 1918, the United States government had built four locks (or canals) and the Canadian government one. Measured in terms of traffic it became the most important canal in the world before the end of the nineteenth century and has maintained its position as the world's greatest waterway. In the best year on record, 92,622,000 tons of freight were borne through the canal. The traffic passes from Lake Superior to the lower lakes and has carried not only iron ore, but also coal, lumber, and grain.

During the first decade or so of the twentieth century a movement developed in the interest of improving and using the waterways more widely. It arose largely because of the congestion of the railroads as the United States became a great manufacturing nation and was also given impetus through the conservation movement as evidenced by the Inland Waterways Commission, appointed by Theodore Roosevelt. Not until the period of the First World War, however, did the movement bring tangible results in the greater use of the country's waterways.

Railroad competition was responsible for the decline of inland waterway transportation. The building of lines parallel to canals and unfair methods of competition were often important factors. But the railroads were also faster and more reliable; they had no navigation problems such as the shifting sandbars and hidden snags of the rivers and they were not impeded during the freezing weather of winter as were most of the northern canals. Further, they usually possessed better loading and terminal facilities than the waterways. Then, too, the courses of rivers were fixed, while railroads could be built in any direction to meet the changing demands of trade. The great rivers flow southward, whereas most of the trade of the country during this period tended to move east and west. Thus, transportation on the inland waters came to be confined largely to bulky and nonperishable goods, such as coal, iron, lumber, gravel, and sand which did not demand rapid transportation.

THE GREAT LAKES

After the Civil War, as river and canal transportation declined, traffic on the Great Lakes grew in a most remarkable manner. The freight of those regions, being bulky, was well suited to lake transportation. Coal was transported north and west, while iron ore, grain, flour, copper, and lumber were moved eastward. Duluth, Minnesota, and Superior, Wisconsin, became the great ore shipping ports. Other lake ports such as Milwaukee, Chicago, Detroit, Toledo, Cleveland, and Buffalo shared the growing prosperity of the lake trade. Shipments on the Great Lakes increased from 25,000,000 short tons in 1889 to 125,000,000 in 1916.

The size of vessels on the Great Lakes increased with the volume of traffic. In 1860, there were 400-ton vessels on the lakes. By 1900, lake steamers averaged 6,000 tons each and later these grew to 14,000 tons. Steel vessels increased in number from six in 1886 to about 300 in 1900. The whaleback boat, cigar-shaped with a small pilot house at its stern, was perfected for lake traffic. Improved steel barges carried the ores to the East and ingenious and speedy loading devices were developed for the ores and other commodities. By 1914, the tonnage of vessels on the lakes amounted to one-fifth of the entire merchant marine of the country.

The early vessels on the lakes were independently owned by individuals or small companies. By 1914, six steamship lines owned by the New York Central, Pennsylvania, Erie, and Lehigh Railroads were the most important in carrying passengers and light freight. Various companies controlled the traffic in coal and iron. For example, the Pittsburgh Steamship Company, a subsidiary of the United States Steel Corporation, by 1914 owned about one-sixth of the American tonnage relating to the transportation of bulky commodities and exclusive of passenger traffic and light freight. Thus, most of the traffic, largely through consolidation, had fallen into the hands of a number of large corporations which for the most part worked together through interlocking directorates and other plans of cooperation.

The lake system was made possible through a number of canals.

The Sault Sainte Marie, as noted (p. 339), became of outstanding importance. Among others were the Welland, connecting Lake Erie with Lake Ontario, around the falls in the Niagara River, and the system of canals around the rapids in the St. Lawrence. By means of the Erie Canal, and later the New York State Barge Canal, and the St. Lawrence Seaway, the Lake routes extended to the Atlantic Ocean.

THE PANAMA CANAL

The greatest single feat in the field of American transportation during the period under discussion was achieved outside the continental boundaries of the United States when the Panama Canal was built. The work was begun under the vigorous leadership of Theodore Roosevelt. It was completed and opened to commerce in 1914.

The story of the Panama Canal goes back in time to the earliest Spanish occupation of the continent. Balboa, the first white man to see the Pacific Ocean in 1513, suggested that the two oceans could be connected at the isthmus. But it was the French who first attempted to make the dream of centuries come true. A Panama canal project was discussed at the Congress of Geographical Sciences at Paris in 1875. A company was formed and three years later Colombia, the nation controlling the isthmus, granted the French company the right to build a canal within twelve years, but without impairing the rights of free passage granted to the United States under the treaty of 1846. In 1881, the French company, under the guidance of Ferdinand de Lesseps, the chief engineer of the Suez Canal, purchased The American Panama Railroad, built in 1855, and began construction. The popularity of de Lesseps led thousands of Frenchmen to invest in the company, but many things militated against the success of the great project. The lack of foresight to prepare accommodations for workers; the ravages of yellow fever among the employees and the inability to cope with disease; unexpected engineering difficulties; and financial mismanagement in Paris brought failure. Between 1881 and 1888, about $262,-000,000 were spent by the company, but only one-third of this amount had actually been expended on work at the canal. Extravagance, bribery, and corruption doomed the project to failure. In 1888, work was suspended and the company became insolvent. Only one-fourth of the canal had been completed. A new company was organized and received permission from Colombia to complete the canal by 1904, but it, too, made little progress.

The activity of the French company at Panama led President Hayes to state in 1880 that an isthmian canal should be under American control. Garfield and Cleveland also protested. In 1887 and 1888, concessions were obtained by Americans to build a canal across Nicaragua, and in 1889 Congress chartered the Maritime Canal Company for this purpose. Operations were begun at Greytown the next year but the Panic of 1893 put an end to the work. Congress now became active and appointed several canal commissions between 1895 and 1906 for the purpose of investigating a proposed route. All commissions endorsed the Nicaraguan route, although the rights of the French company at Panama were now for sale at $109,000,000. At the beginning of the new century, President McKinley and Secretary of State Hay began negotiating with Great Britain for the abrogation of the Clayton-Bulwer Treaty of 1850 which forbade the United States to build a fortified canal. After McKinley's death negotiations were continued by Theodore Roosevelt. As a result, the Hay-Pauncefote Treaty of 1901 was ratified. It put an end to the pledge of 1850 and provided that the United States could build, control, and defend a canal between the two oceans, subject to the principle of equal privileges to all nations.

Although American canal commissions had recommended the Nicaraguan route, Roosevelt was pursuaded by William Nelson Cromwell, American attorney for the French company, and by Philippe Bunau-Varilla, chief engineer for the company, to express preference for the Panama route. Congress, undecided as to the better route, passed the Hepburn bill in 1902, which authorized the President to pay $40,000,000 to the French company if a clear title could be obtained. If not, work was to be undertaken at Nicaragua. The next step was to secure the consent of Colombia. Secretary of State Hay negotiated with Herran, the Colombian minister in Washington. In the proposed Hay-Herran Treaty of 1903 the United States agreed to pay Colombia $10,000,000 and $250,000 each year for the lease of a strip of land six miles wide across the isthmus. The treaty, however, was not approved by the Colombian Congress. Since the rights of the French company were to expire the next year, it looked as though the Panama plan had come to an end.

The failure of the Hay-Herran Treaty was a great disappointment to the inhabitants of the Panama isthmus, who looked forward to becoming prosperous after the completion of the canal. Prominent citizens including Dr. Amador and Bunau-Varilla conferred with Americans as to the advisability of breaking away from Colombia. Roosevelt took immediate action by sending American war vessels to within easy reach of the isthmus and ordered the commanders to keep the transit open and to prevent any armed force with hostile intent from landing on the isthmus. One vessel, the *Nashville,* arrived off Colon on November 2. The next day the local garrison at Panama seized control of the city and proclaimed the Republic of Panama. The movement was motivated and financed by Bunau-Varilla, working in the interests of the French company. Colombian forces, sent to the opposite side of the isthmus, were prevented from crossing to Panama by the commander of the *Nashville.* American interference was based on the authority of the treaty of 1846.

Three days after the bloodless Panama revolution, the United States recognized the new republic and a week later Bunau-Varilla was received by Roosevelt as its minister. A treaty between the United States and Panama followed. It was ratified by the Senate early in 1904. The United States guaranteed the independence of the Republic of Panama and agreed to pay it $10,000,000 on exchange of ratifications and $250,000 annually, beginning in nine years. Panama granted the United States in perpetuity a strip of land ten miles wide with "all the rights, power, and authority within the zone," which it would possess "if it were sovereign of the territory." The French company was paid its $40,000,000 and plans were immediately projected for building the canal. President Roosevelt was severely criticized in Colombia and in other Latin American countries, as well as by many in the United States for his part in the revolution. In a special message to the Senate, he held that Colombia had no right to prevent the transit of the world's traffic across the isthmus and that intervention by the United States was justified by treaty rights, international interests, and the well-being of "collective civilization."

Work at the canal was begun in 1904 when President Roosevelt appointed a canal commission, but little construction was done until 1906 when Congress finally adopted the report of the engineers for a lock canal. Bids from contractors were opened the next year, but none was satisfactory. Roosevelt then placed the work under the control of the corps of engineers of the United States army. Colonel George W. Goethals became chief engineer and chairman of the Isthmian Canal Commission. Many engineering problems had to be met and the difficulties of securing labor overcome. Under William C. Gorgas, the sanitary department installed drainage systems and waged war on yellow fever and other tropical diseases, which made it possible for white men to live and work efficiently in that region. The canal was opened in August, 1914. For various intervals in 1915 and 1916, traffic was interrupted because of landslides at the Gaillard Cut (formerly called the Culebra Cut), but since 1917, shipping in the canal has been un-impeded. The total cost of construction was over $370,000,000—more than two and one-half times the original estimate, but tolls collected equally from both United States and foreign vessels passing through the canal have more than paid for its cost.

In accord with his Latin American policy, Woodrow Wilson de-cided to appease Colombia, which had been hostile to and suspicious of the United States since the establishment of the Republic of Panama. He proposed a treaty including an apology for the action of the Roose-velt administration and an agreement to pay Columbia $30,000,000. Roosevelt denounced it as a "blackmail treaty" and his friend Senator Lodge led the fight against its ratification. As a result it failed. In 1921, partly because American interests found it difficult to do business in Colombia and partly because of the desire for oil concessions in that country by American capital, the treaty was revived. In the meantime, Roosevelt had died and the way was open for its passage. The apology was omitted from the treaty, which provided for the payment of $25,000,000 to Colombia. Senator Lodge reversed his position and under his leadership the treaty was ratified by the Senate.

COMMUNICATION

After the Civil War, marked advances were made in telegraphic communication. By 1867, the Western Union Telegraph Company, with a capital of $41,000,000, had absorbed many smaller companies and its lines stretched from the Atlantic to the Mississippi Valley and from the Ohio River to the Great Lakes. In the years that followed it was threatened by several rival companies, the chief being the Atlantic and Pacific. Jay Gould obtained control of this company in 1874 and seven years later sold it to the Western Union. The capital stock of the company was now $80,000,000. In the years that followed, the Western Union maintained its position as the chief telegraphic company on the continent. In 1940, there were 2,401,000 miles of telegraph wire strung over the country, of which Western Union owned 1,915,000 miles and Postal Telegraph Incorporated, 398,000 miles.

Many improvements and new inventions were made in the field of telegraphy. The stock ticker, a printing telegraph system, was first introduced by the New York Stock Exchange in 1867. In 1872, Thomas Edison invented a device for sending two messages in opposite direc-tions over the same wire at the same time. In the years that followed, the multiplex telegraph was improved to send many messages at once over the same line. In 1919, improvements in the multiplex system were perfected so that the wire could be used for both telephone and telegraph messages simultaneously. Other devices for rapid telegraphy, made necessary by the great amount of business in the cities, appeared and were projected. After 1900, printing telegraphs began to displace clicking keys and in more recent years the Teletype has improved efficiency.

Experiments with the wireless or radio telegraph were also begun, although these were first tried by Europeans. Long ether waves were discovered by Heinrich Hertz, a German scientist, in 1887. In 1895, Marconi in Italy began experimenting with wireless waves and produced the first practical transmitter. Two years later, he sent a message a distance of fifteen miles, and in 1901 the first wireless message was flashed across the Atlantic. In 1906, DeForest projected the three-element vacuum tube. Its introduction as a detector opened a new era in radio telegraphy. More recently this invention has made possible the development of the radio telephone.

The telephone was also perfected during this period. For generations men had attempted to transmit the human voice over distances. Between 1872 and 1875, Alexander Graham Bell of Boston, a teacher of diction and of the deaf, and Elisha Gray, an electrical inventor of Highland Park, Illinois, worked independently along lines of producing a "harmonic telegraph." Both men on the same day in 1876 filed applications for patent rights at the Patent Office, but Bell received the patent in spite of the attempts of Gray to prove his own priority. Few in the United States realized the value of the invention and the Western Union Telegraph Company refused to buy it for $100,000, although a short time later the company attempted to manufacture and install telephones under the rights of another patent. In England the London *Times* called the invention the "latest American humbug." Bell and the two men who financed him, Thomas Sanders and Gardiner G. Hubbard, organized the Bell Telephone Company. No sooner had Bell received his patent in 1876 than many other inventors who had been working on the idea made themselves known. For many years the holders of Bell's patent had to defend themselves against innumerable law suits, but they were able to fight off all claimants. Stock in Bell's company jumped from $50 to $800 within a year.

In 1880, the American Bell Telephone Company was established; five years later a subsidiary company, the American Telephone and Telegraph Company, was built to own and operate long distance lines. In 1900, the American Telephone and Telegraph Company became a great holding company. Five years later an attempt was made to take over the Western Union Telegraph Company, but the government brought suit under the Sherman Antitrust law and forced the separation of the two companies (1913). Following the expiration of the original Bell patent in 1893, a number of small companies sprang up, reaching their greatest strength in the early years of the twentieth century.

The first public exhibition of the telephone took place in 1876 at the Centennial Exposition in Philadelphia. Within a year, 800 telephones were in use and by 1900 more than 1,000,000 had been installed in the United States alone. The expansion of the system was phenomenal. In 1926, there were 57,000,000 miles of telephone wires in the country and $3,350,000,000 invested in telephone plants and equipment. Of the 26,000,000 telephones in the world at that time, 17,000,000 were owned by the American Bell Telephone Company. Many improvements were also made during this period of development, including the multiple switchboard, the Pupin coil which made transmission over smaller wires possible, and, more recently, the automatic telephone.

NUMBER OF TELEPHONES, 1900 – 1960
(In thousands)

Year	Number	Year	Number
1900	1,356	1935	17,424
1905	4,127	1940	21,928
1910	7,635	1945	27,867
1915	10,524	1950	43,004
1920	13,329	1955	56,243
1925	16,936	1960	64,980
1930	20,202		

Sources: U.S. Bureau of the Census, *Historical Statistics of the United States, Colonial Times to 1957*, Washington, D.C., 1960, p. 480; and *Statistical Abstract of the United States 1962*, Washington, D.C., 1962, p. 516.

CHAPTER 15

The Settlement of the Far West

By the time of the Civil War, the frontier was pushing westward beyond a line, roughly speaking, drawn north and south through sections of Kansas and Nebraska and central Texas, although the Mormons had made a settlement in the cheerless region of Great Salt Valley. A new frontier, begun by the gold-seeking "forty-niners," was also pushing eastward to the regions of the Sierra Nevadas and the Rocky Mountains, where the precious metals constituted a magnet drawing people into new areas in the search for wealth. Before the end of the century, these two movements—eastward and westward—finally culminated in the so-called "last frontier." This, however, did not mean that the West was even sparsely settled, for even in 1960 there were still vast areas of unoccupied land.

Many factors contributed to the rapid settlement of the West. The various land laws enacted by Congress, the promotional activities of states and companies with land to sell, the transcontinental railroads and the railway web that followed in the vast region west of the Mississippi Valley, the attraction of the precious metals and other mineral wealth, the development of ranching, and a new policy regarding the Indians were some of the most important factors. Beyond the fertile regions of the Mississippi Valley lay the vast expanse of plain, plateau, and mountain extending to the Pacific coast.

347

THE HOMESTEAD ACT AND OTHER LAND LAWS

The Homestead Act was passed in 1862. The Republican party had thus fulfilled this part of its bargain made in 1860 to insure western support. Under the law, 160 acres of government land could be obtained by any person over twenty-one who was an American citizen or who had filed his intention of becoming one. After five years of residence or cultivation, the settler received his title by paying a nominal registration fee. Provision, however, was made for the purchase of the land by the homesteader after six months of residence at the prevailing minimum price, usually $1.25 an acre. The residence requirement was raised to fourteen months in 1891. In spite of the liberal terms of the act, the problem of credit was a serious one for the western settler. Capital needed for breaking the prairie, seeding and stocking the land, obtaining tools and machines, building a house, and fencing pastures had to be borrowed in the pioneer period at excessive rates of interest.

The Homestead Act has been described as "the greatest democratic measure of all history." Actually it was not. The frontier had leaped across the Mississippi before this time and the law applied largely to areas which were not suitable for homesteading at all, but were chiefly mineral, timber, grazing, and semiarid lands. In general it applied to the region west of the 100th meridian, from the Great Plains to the Pacific, for the area east of this region, well suited for small farms, was already largely settled or was held by speculators, although some good unoccupied lands were obtainable and were taken up in the years immediately following the passage of the act. The government also continued the cash sale of land under the terms of other laws. A total of 130,000,000 acres were given to the railroads from laws passed between 1862 and 1871, when Congress ceased its policy of railroad grants. Homesteaders were required to move at least twenty to forty miles away from projected routes, with the result that many preferred to pay the required $400 or more to the government or railroads in order to be close to transportation facilities. Among other laws which helped to dispose of the national domain were the Dawes Act of 1887, modified by the Burke Act of 1906 and others, which threw on the market some 100,000,000 acres of Indian lands. The Federal government also turned over to the states many millions of acres of land to be sold for the purpose of financing agricultural and technical colleges under the terms of the Morrill Land Grant Act of 1862.

To encourage tree planting in regions where timber was sparse or absent, rainfall insufficient, and hot winds and dust storms prevalent, Congress passed the Timber Culture Act in 1873. It provided that settlers could obtain 160 acres of land on condition that forty acres were set out in trees. At the time that the law went into effect, land could be obtained in Iowa, in Minnesota, and immediately west of the Missouri River. But in a few years, it actually applied only to the plains and the semiarid regions where it was largely impossible and even undesirable to fulfill the requirements of the government regarding the production of timber. About 10,000,000 acres were disposed of by this act, but much fraud was involved in its administration, land companies benefited, and little permanent tree growth resulted. It was repealed in 1891. Under the Desert Land Act of 1877, semiarid lands were offered in 640-acre tracts to settlers who would irrigate them. The provision for irrigation was vague and it became evident that effective ditch construction would require more capital than most settlers could obtain. As a result, the law chiefly benefited grazing interests and irrigation companies. Most harmful to the public interest was the Timber and Stone Act of 1878, which provided for the sale of quarter sections of land unsuited for agriculture but valuable for timber. The law operated to transfer public timberlands to large corporations and speculators. Over 13,000,000 acres of the national domain were thus alienated.

With vast areas of land obtainable, speculation increased and great tracts in the most desirable regions were obtained by domestic and even foreign syndicates. Under these conditions, homesteaders had to take up their free lands in less fertile or advantageous regions, while settlers who were willing to pay for better lands had to compete with speculators or pay the prices set by the states or the railroads. Under the various land laws, it was indeed possible for a person to acquire a total of 1,120 acres of public lands: 160 acres each under the Homestead, Pre-emption, and Timber Culture Acts, and 640 acres under the Desert Land Act. But the laws did not benefit large numbers of bona fide settlers as they should have done. Instead, large operators and companies got control of much of the land. Fraudulent entries were common; "floaters" were employed by predatory interests to pre-empt lands; claims were turned over to land, timber, and mining companies; perjury and bribery of land officials were common; and the Federal Land Office did not have the organization, personnel, or backing to insure careful and honest administration. By 1900, 25,000,000 acres of land were in the possession of fifty-four companies and individuals. Almost half the farmlands in the Rocky Mountain and Pacific states were in units of about 1,000 acres or more, tilled by laborers or tenants, some of them Japanese. Beginning in 1891, when the Pre-emption and the Timber Culture Acts were repealed, a movement was inaugurated to reform the land policy of the country, which in time bore fruit, although much of the best government lands by the early twentieth century had been distributed in a manner contrary to the spirit of the Federal laws.

THE PRAIRIE FARM

The majority of farmers who went West in the last half of the nineteenth century bought their land from railroads, land companies, or other previous holders. Usually credit was extended, allowing for several annual payments. Railroads, in particular, were extremely anxious to settle farmers along their tracks, and offered attractive terms to get them there. But acquiring land was but a small part of the problems of the farmer in the practically treeless plains that stretched from Illinois west and northwest. Lumber commanded very high prices, and thousands of farmers in the drier regions first lived in houses built of chunks of tough prairie sod, piled up like bricks. This same sod defied breaking. Six- or eight-horse teams and two men holding the plow were necessary for initial cultivation—which meant either hiring the equipment or getting community cooperation. Most prairie farms lacked water. Deep wells had to be dug. For efficient farm operation it was best to have a windmill and a water storage tank—a costly installation that required either capital or recourse to a money lender.

The first year the farmer would probably be too busy building, getting water, fencing with barbed wire, and raising food to live on to do much about a cash crop. His first market crop was usually wheat, but success was by no means certain. Kansas, Nebraska, the Dakotas, Minnesota, and even parts of Iowa had uncertain rainfall and climate. Late winter freezing and heavy spring rains could flood the prairies, produce crops of mosquitoes, and make an unhealthy environment. Then summer droughts might dry up the crop, grasshoppers might eat it, or hail storms beat the grain to pieces. But two or three good harvests could pay off the farmer's debts. In this perpetual gamble with nature many succeeded and many failed. The failures either moved back to work in cities or towns, or sold out to later comers and tried again farther west.

THE MINING INDUSTRY

During the last half of the nineteenth century, the mining industry of the far West developed. Wandering prospectors, disappointed in not achieving their dreams of wealth in California during the gold

Sutter's Mill, California
Gold was first discovered in the
mid-nineteenth century on this site.

rush, turned eastward toward the Rocky Mountains and followed
streams, creeks, and rivers to the real supply of the precious metals
in the hills and mountains. They found gold on the bottom of streams
which they recovered by "panning" off the muddy gravel from the
heavy gold. The metal was also extracted from exposed quartz veins
with a pickax.

From time to time there were exciting stampedes here and there
as new discoveries were made and new gold rushes developed. In
the frantic attempt to find metals men rushed to Colville, a Hudson's
Bay Company post in the region of Washington, to places along the
Fraser River in Canada, to the Snake River region, as well as to the
Southwest, frequently reopening old Spanish mines. The precious
metals became a powerful incentive to rapid settlement as prospective
miners from the East as well as from the west coast opened up new
communities. The Comstock Lode at Virginia City, discovered in
1859, attracted many settlers to that region and held the attention of
the world for some time as fabulous wealth was secured. During the
first twenty years, more than $500,000,000 in silver and gold were
taken from these mines. But it was evident that the miner working

only with hand tools could do little in regions where hoisting machines, giant pumps, heavy drills, stamp mills, and cables, among other things were necessary to extract ores from their rocky gangue, requiring large amounts of capital and a corporative form of enterprise. The wandering miner had to give up his free and easy life and become the employee of large companies, working fixed hours at regular rates of pay. The regions of Montana, Idaho, New Mexico, Wyoming, and Arizona, as well as Nevada and Colorado were settled in much the same way, the metal attracting the first settlers. The last one of the important gold rushes within the United States was to the Black Hills in 1874, which called the warlike Sioux to action as their reservations were overrun, and led to the massacre of Custer and his men at the Little Big Horn River. This gold rush marked the opening up of the South Dakota region.

While gold and silver were chiefly sought in the West during this period, lead, copper, and other metals were ultimately to be more important. For a time Colorado became the largest lead-producing region in the world. After 1885, lead production steadily increased in Idaho and Utah. Since 1900, these two regions and the Mississippi Valley have been the most important lead-mining areas in the country. Copper was another metal that rose to importance. For some time after the Civil War, the Michigan mines led all others in supplying this metal. In 1864, copper mines were opened in Montana and then in Arizona. In 1881, the Anaconda copper mine near Helena, Montana, began its famous career. The growing demand arising from the rapidly developing electrical industries and the increasing use of copper in alloys resulted in a remarkable development of this industry.

THE CATTLE COUNTRY

During the two decades or so after the Civil War, the Great Plains became the scene of an important range cattle industry, which contributed much to the color, romance, and folklore of the West. The driving of cattle to distant markets was not entirely new in America when Texas cattle men began to use the Chisholm Trail and other routes as they established "long drives." The Spaniards in Mexico in the sixteenth century drove great herds from place to place. In the eighteenth century and later, Spanish settlements in Texas, built around missions or forts, derived a meager revenue from horses and cattle sent occasionally to Louisiana, though such trade was often contraband. Then, again, as the American frontier moved beyond the

Appalachians, and especially after improved roads were built to connect the new West with the older East, cattle and swine were driven from Ohio, Kentucky, and Tennessee to Philadelphia, Baltimore, and other urban centers of the East. But the cattle industry of the plains, emanating first from Texas, possessed some aspects not found in these earlier examples of the long drive to distant markets.

Before the Americans living in Texas had rebelled against Mexico in 1836, a "Beef Trail" had been established to New Orleans. Years before the Civil War, markets had been found in Sedalia, Springfield, and St. Louis in Missouri, and longhorn steers even reached Chicago. During the Civil War, cattle were driven from Texas to different places along the southern line of battle for the Confederate forces, and at its close Texas had about 5,000,000 cattle and few markets in which to sell them. Then began the period of the long drive as attempts were made to find outlets in the north country. At first these efforts were not very successful because of the hostility of the settlers of Missouri and eastern Kansas who feared the introduction of Texas fever. The establishment by Joseph G. McCoy in 1867, of Abilene, Kansas, on the route of the Kansas Pacific Railway as a depot to which Texas cattle could be driven for shipment by rail to Kansas City, marked the beginning of a large number of similar cow towns. Wichita, Ellsworth, Dodge City, Kansas; Ogallala, Nebraska, Cheyenne, Wyoming; Medora in the Dakotas; Prescott, Arizona, and Las Vegas, New Mexico, were some of the most important cattle centers that arose during this period. Dodge City came to boast it was the "cowboy capital of the world." Trails were thus established to towns on the railroads all over the Great Plains.

Two types of cow towns appeared. In one, the cattle were slaughtered for the town's own needs and for the constantly growing community of which it was the center; the other marked the terminus of the long trail and the railroad shipping point to great packing centers. Stockyards and packing plants were built in such cities as Chicago, St. Louis, Kansas City, and Fort Worth as the railroads extended their lines. The Chicago packers came to dominate the field and set prices. In the period after the Civil War, men like Cudahy, Armour, Swift, and Libby became leaders in the packing industry. Brokerage companies and banks specializing in cattle loans sprang up to finance the industry and the railroads provided special cars for the shipment of cattle and meat products. The increase of population and the settlement of new regions provided expanding markets both in the East and the West.

During the period of the open range cattle industry, cattle associations—local, district, sectional, and national—functioned. The Colorado Cattle Growers' Association was organized as early as 1867. Others quickly followed. The Wyoming Stock Growers' Association, formed in 1873, expanded into most of the regions of the West. In 1884, the National Cattle and Horse Growers' Association was established at St. Louis. The cattle associations supervised the sale of cattle, laid out roundup districts, promulgated rules for mavericks or stray cattle, and recorded the brands, made up of letters, figures, geometric designs, symbols, or representations of objects that denoted ownership. They attempted to eliminate through agreements the overcrowding of the range which resulted in flooding the market; they cooperated with officials in enforcing laws relating to cattle; and they urged legislation favorable to their interests.

The Texas Longhorns were a hybrid of Spanish, Mexican, and mixed American blood. Narrow-hipped, high-shouldered, and flat-ribbed, they possessed a spread of horn that varied from three to six feet, occasionally more, from tip to tip. Texas steers were tough and hardy in all respects. They could travel over the roughest ground, climb high mountains, fight wolves, panthers, or bears, survive during arid months on liquid nourishment obtained from the leaves of the prickly pear and yucca stalks, and fortified by range grasses and browse, could survive the blizzards of the Northwest. The Longhorns were in no way pampered and received little attention except when they were branded and again when they were herded north to be sold. But even in the seventies, purebred Shorthorns, Herefords, and other breeds were imported into parts of the West, as well as the East, from England and Scotland.

The story of the long drive over the plains and prairies is the epic of the adventurous cowboy. He became master of the plains for a brief period after the first transcontinental railroads sounded the death-knell of the vast herds of buffalo and as the Indians of the plains were subjugated and confined to restricted areas. The cowboy tended the stock, did the branding, and drove the cattle to market. His costume and equipment, selected for utility, not for color, were patterned after those of the earlier Spanish cowboys in Texas and California. Chaparejos (leather "chaps") over loose, heavy trousers protected his legs from thorns and goring cattle; high-heeled boots made walking awkward but prevented entanglement in the stirrup; the neckerchief across the mouth and nose kept out stifling dust and was also protection against the raw wind; the partly-buttoned vest, worn over a woolen shirt, provided pockets for watch, tobacco, and matches; and, the broad gray or brown leather-thonged hat served as protection against sun, rain, snow, and sleet. On horses largely of Spanish stock, the cowboys—adventurous youths from Texas, eastern and western farms, and the British Isles—herded and handled the longhorns with skill in horsemanship and in the use of the lariat. They possessed courage, resourcefulness and stamina.

When the cowboys took to the trail, it was usually with herds of about 2,500 to 3,500 and rarely more. A herd requiring enough cowboys to keep one cook and one manager busy was the optimum size. For example, there were 33,000 steers and 2,000 wild horses in the big stampede at the Red River in 1882, but they were made up of eleven herds that had been waiting for the water to go down. Stampedes were hazardous and occurred occasionally during roundups and the long drive. Sudden noises and sights could start a stampede. Thunder, lightning, the jump of a jack rabbit, the sudden scream of a panther, the whir of a rattlesnake, or a horse shaking an empty saddle were causes of stampedes. Such disasters rarely cost human life, but many cattle were trampled to death, and horns and legs were broken. To prevent disturbing noises and to avoid stampedes, the cowboys crooned to the cattle under the stars on the lonely plains. They sang old ballads, popular sentimental songs, made up new ones, and adopted old ones.

Cattle thieving was common throughout the period. Although cattlemen's associations registered the various types of brands adopted by the cattle raisers, thieves became expert in changing original designs by making additions to them. As protection against such marauders, vigilance committees were formed and hanged the guilty. In addition, the horse rustler was always a menace. And the professional bad men of the West sometimes seized the cattle on the open plains, sometimes waylaid the cowboy as he came to town with his pay for an occasional spree.

While there were many individual owners of ranches and also partners who engaged in breeding cattle for the long drive, often companies were formed. Businessmen, bankers, politicians, and others formed companies to engage in the cattle trade and much eastern capital was invested in it. British capital also was applied. By 1884, it was estimated that more than $30,000,000 of British funds had been invested in the industry. Among large Scottish and English enterprises were the Prairie Land and Cattle Company, the Matador Company, and many others. At this time more than 100,000,000 pounds of beef were being shipped annually from the plains to Great

Britain. As a result, a commission of Parliament was sent to the United States to visit the West and to report on conditions.

The range industry of the plains reached its height about 1884, but factors were working against the continuance of the long drive. The railroads which had made possible the range industry also put an end to it as they penetrated all parts of the West, bringing permanent settlers. But by that time the farmers or nesters (so called contemptuously by the cattlemen) were settling on the range, homesteads were being taken up, and towns and communities were developing. The use of barbed wire (patented first by J. F. Glidden, a farmer of Illinois, in 1873) was becoming universal. Prairie farmers were enclosing their lands with wire fences, and ranchers were fencing their sources of water. Thus the settlement of the West doomed the longhorn, the cattle trails, and the cowboys of the plains. In addition, severe blizzards and prolonged droughts in the late eighties and nineties decimated the herds and bankrupted many of the cattle companies. The character of the industry changed in the twentieth century. From the great ranches of Texas, Wyoming, and other western states, many ranch owners came to live in the towns; hands were no longer limited to the restricted work of cowboys but performed all types of ranch work; and through improved practices cattle of very high quality were bred.

THE SHEEP DRIVES

Sheep raising was first introduced into the West by early Spanish colonists when they occupied New Mexico, Arizona, Texas, and California. It was not until after the Civil War, however, as large populations moved into the vast areas of the West that sheep production, both for wool and meat, increased in a remarkable way in that section of the country. From 1840 to 1860 the raising of sheep for wool in the East had declined drastically. But during the same period, the annexation of territory that was formerly Mexican brought under the American flag vast grazing areas already possessing Spanish flocks. In the East, as the Civil War came on and cotton grew scarce, wool production was speeded up. But the westward trend in sheep raising continued and crossed the prairies to the far West as many eastern sheep farmers turned to cereals and other more profitable products. Descendants of Spanish flocks were also moved north from New Mexico to California and to Oregon.

After large flocks had been bred in Pacific coastal areas in the seventies and eighties, they were driven into Montana, Nevada, Wyoming, and Colorado, and from New Mexico they were driven especially to Wyoming, Colorado, and Texas. From Colorado and Wyoming the drives trailed into Kansas and Nebraska. By 1885, Texas had become the principal southern market for California sheep. By the end of the century, the sheep trails had ended as lands were taken up and occupied. Shipment by railroad took the place of the long sheep drives. The states of the Rocky Mountains and Pacific areas became important in producing wool, mutton, and lamb while the East, under the stimulus of urban food markets, stressed mutton breeds.

The story of the sheep drives across the great areas from the Pacific, over the mountains and across the plains as the trails changed from westward to eastward during the last quarter of the nineteenth century is full of interest. The shepherds or *pastores* were perhaps not quite as picturesque as the cowboys of the same period, but their lives were filled with similar dangers and adventures—perils from floods, Indians, outlaws, wolves, coyotes, eagles, and poisonous plants. They had to contend also with the problems of gathering the flocks from small owners, of preparing for the drive, of shearing, of controlling disease, of passing inspection in territories and states, and of finding running water, especially in the sun-baked desert country. Flocks were driven in bands of from 2,500 to 7,000 or even more. The cowboys loathed the sheepmen and when their paths crossed on the prairies and plains, there were frequent clashes and fights. Intense rivalry developed between the cattlemen and sheepmen over the use of the best grazing lands. After sheep had nibbled short grasses on the range for months, the land would often become barren. The hoofs of browsing sheep destroyed the grass of the plains and foothills, and cattle would not drink from watering places used by sheep. *Pastores* were often driven from fertile ranges and at times besought the nearest court for a redress of their grievances, while a few controversies ended in bloodshed. As was the case with the cow country, the story of the sheep drives ended before the close of the century, but by this time great sheep ranches had been established in the mountain and Pacific areas of the Far West.

PROBLEMS OF THE INDIANS

As the frontier swept into the western prairies and plains, the plight of the Indians became tragic. As early as 1825 a plan was evolved to move all Indians living east of the Mississippi to the region west of the river. The law of 1830 was intended to carry this out. Then followed the attempt to establish a "permanent" Indian frontier by a line of military posts from Fort Snelling southward. Every effort was made by treaty and otherwise to move the red man to his home in the "Indian country" where he might live on reservations. At the same time a project was discussed for building a series of strong stone forts to guard the boundary. But before it could be carried out, Americans were pushing through Indian country over the Oregon Trail, the Santa Fe Trail, and other routes to Oregon and California. The opening up of the territories acquired from Mexico in 1848 and of Kansas in 1854 put an end to the plan of dividing the continent between the white man in the East and the red man in the West.

After the Civil War, because of widespread Indian uprisings, it was decided not to permit the tribes to rove over the West. In 1871, Congress abolished the system of making treaties with the Indians and assumed jurisdiction over the administration of their affairs. By this time the building of railroads, the establishment of army garrisons, the development of cattle and sheep ranges, the unending caravans over westward routes, the building of communities, and the killing off of the buffalo or American bison seriously interfered with Indian life on the plains.

During the building of the Union Pacific and Kansas Pacific Railroads, vast herds of bison crossing the tracks frequently stopped trains. Yet within a few years the bison were almost totally destroyed by hunters from all parts of the country and from Europe, as well as by those who systematically exploited the hunting grounds for the purpose of selling the meat in the East and the robes in many parts of the world. By 1875, there were two groups of the animals—the northern herd extending into Canada and the southern herd. The latter was practically extinct by 1878, although a few survivors were not killed until 1889. The northern herd was exterminated by 1884 except for a few scattered animals. A census made in 1889 showed a total of only 1,091 American bison existing throughout the entire world. Since that time individuals and organizations have been aroused and as a result the number of buffaloes has increased. The American Bison Society was organized in 1905, and largely through its efforts the danger of the complete extinction of the great animal was ended.

The extermination of the buffalo seriously affected the life of the Indians of the plains, for their civilization, including their religion, was bound up in the shaggy creature in the same manner that maize was vital in the culture of the tribes farther east. The Indians used the bow and arrow as well as the rifle to capture and kill the animals which

THE EASTERN BOUNDARY
OF THE INDIAN LANDS

were stalked, stampeded over cliffs, driven into cul de sacs, or pursued on horseback. The Indians utilized all parts of the buffalo—the hide for shelter, clothing, and bags, the flesh for food, the bones for knives, hoes, and other implements, the teeth for ornaments, and the tendons for thread and bowstrings. As a result of the disappearance of their means of livelihood, the Indians of the plains were helpless at a time when they were caught viselike between the moving frontiers of the east and the west. At the same time the lack of cooperation between Indian agents, the army, and Congress in administering Indian affairs became more and more apparent and many tribes took to the warpath again.

The predicament of the Indians brought a renewed interest in their plight, although agitation for reform in their treatment had been going on for more than two decades. Helen Hunt Jackson was inspired to write *A Century of Dishonor* (1881), which was widely read. Eastern humanitarians organized the Indian Rights Association and the Lake Mohonk Conference of Friends of the Indians. Because of the interest in the red man and because of the need for a new way of treating with him, Congress passed the Dawes or General Allotment Act of 1887. The new policy was designed to break up Indian tribal relationships and to put an end to the idea of the Indians as "domestic nations." It provided that the President through special agents could allot lands to the members of any tribe—160 acres to the head of a family and lesser amounts to each of the others, including children. The lands were to be held in trust by the government for twenty-five years and full title was then to be granted the individual. In the meantime citizenship was conferred upon those holding allotments. The surplus tribal lands were to be open to white settlement by the United States and the proceeds from their sales were to be used in the interests of the Indians. Thus millions of acres of tribal lands became available for white settlement.

The Dawes Act proved to be unwise in many respects. Some Indians strenuously objected to the twenty-five year waiting period for a clear land title; others who received allotments showed that they were not ready to assume the responsibilities of citizenship as drunkenness increased. Frauds were also perpetrated on the government and on the red men regarding Indian lands. As a result of the defects of the law, the Burke Act of 1906 provided that citizenship should not be granted until full title had been obtained to the land, that complete ownership was to be granted at the discretion of the President, and that liquor should not be given or sold to Indians who were not citizens. This enabled the government to continue paternalistic control over the Indian in order to safeguard him against debauchery and exploitation. But the legal and political status of most Indians was anomalous. As a result, an act of 1924 conferred citizenship upon all those who were not already citizens. Ten years later, the Wheeler-Howard Indian Reorganization Act of 1934 reversed the policy of land allotments and provided for the conservation and enlargement of remaining Indian lands held by the United States in trust for the Indians. On reservations, by a majority vote, Indian tribes could adopt a constitution for social self-government. Provision for educating promising Indian youths in trade schools, high schools, and colleges, adopted in earlier acts, was continued. In order to encourage economic development on the part of tribes and individuals, a revolving fund provided loans to be made to Indian-chartered corporations.

The Dawes Act of 1887 did not apply to the so-called Five Civilized Tribes: the Cherokee, Creek, Choctaw, Chickasaw, and Seminole. These tribes had been moved in 1820–1845 to what was called Indian Territory, originally what is now most of Oklahoma. They held Negro slaves and joined the Confederacy during the Civil War. After the war they were forced to cede the western part of their lands to the government as a home for other tribes. One area near the center of Indian Territory was not included in any reservations and was known as "Unassigned Lands." Boomers attempted to settle here from time to time, but were ejected by United States troops. Demands from squatters and cattlemen resulted in opening up to settlement in 1889 the Unassigned Lands and the Panhandle (the proposed territory of Cimarron), which was also outside any state or territory. The next year the Territory of Oklahoma was created. In the years that followed "runs" occurred as parts of the western lands were opened up. In the meantime, because the Dawes Act did not apply to the Five Civilized Tribes, the Dawes Commission was appointed in 1893 to induce them to abolish their tribal governments and to take up their lands in individual allotments. By 1906, this was accomplished. The next year the Territory of Oklahoma and Indian Territory were united and admitted to the Union as the forty-sixth state. By this time, oil production, which had begun about 1900, was rapidly increasing and in time it brought great prosperity and wealth to the region, in which many Indians shared.

THE INFLUENCE OF THE WEST

As early as 1844, Ralph Waldo Emerson suggested the influence of the West on American thought and culture. Others expressed similar ideas in the years that followed. It was Frederick J. Turner, a young professor in the University of Wisconsin, who, in 1893, in a brief paper "The Significance of the Frontier in American History," which was followed by other writings, led the way for a school of American historians who held that the frontier as a moving area was a powerful and unique factor in the development of America.

Turner stressed the idea that the experiences of westward-moving peoples on the successive frontiers had a great influence on American culture. The existence of cheap and free lands; the advance of western settlement; the development of self-reliance, especially the restless optimism, the coarseness, the acuteness, and the physical toughness of the frontiersmen; the tolerance of diverse religious and national backgrounds; and the feeling of equality together with the spread of democracy explain American development and civilization. Turner assumed that the age of the frontier, with its opportunities as well as its problems, had passed and become a part of history, but that its influence underlay all American culture.

Students of population (demographers) while agreeing with many of his conclusions have pointed out that the characteristics associated by Turner with the American frontier are those common to all areas of rapid in-migration. Migrants have been predominantly young people seeking to make their own way in new communities without benefit of inherited position, family, or friends, and hence they had to be self-reliant, tolerant, and democratic whether they moved to a frontier or to a city. Furthermore, since traders, lawyers, land speculators, and other business types often preceded the actual settlers in frontier areas and controlled the developing communities, the frontier areas were not by their nature more democratic than other areas. Consequently, mobility of population, a factor still powerful in 1960, rather than the influence of a transitory region such as the frontier, appears to have been a more important physical agency in differentiating Americans from their European ancestors.

CHAPTER 16

The Conservation of Natural Resources

EXPLOITATION, WASTE, AND MONOPOLY

By the latter part of the nineteenth century Americans in increasing numbers were becoming alarmed at the rate at which the nation's natural resources were being exploited and especially at the destruction and waste involved. Throughout the growth and development of the country there had been much waste. Pioneers attacked the forests with ax and fire without thought of the future; hunters wantonly destroyed wild life, often for the sport of it; farmers broke up rich soils and exhausted the fertility of the land without attempting to provide for its restoration; and miners adopted the easiest and most wasteful methods of securing the earth's treasures without concern for posterity. Investment groups, both domestic and foreign, acquired large holdings and exploited the rich natural resources of the country. Moreover, little attention was paid to losses due to the ravages of nature or the carelessness of man. For example, fire swept vast woodlands and forests, damaging the soil and destroying timber, forage, and wild life. At the end of the nineteenth century economists and conservationists were pointing out that the forests would last only about a generation or so at the existing rate of wasteful exploitation, that coal would disappear in about a century, and that the usefulness of most other forms of natural resources would come to an end largely through greed and waste.

Before 1900, most of the lands containing known deposits of gold, silver, copper, lead, nickel, and other metals and minerals had passed to private control. During the last half of the nineteenth century vast areas were secured in various ways by private interests. The Mineral Lands Act of 1872 provided for the sale of mineral lands, except coal properties, after a certain amount of development, at prices ranging from $2.50 to $5.00 an acre; a series of laws permitted the sale of coal lands at prices varying from $10 to $15 an acre; the Timber and Stone Act of 1878 resulted in the sale, at a minimum of $2.50 an acre, of land valuable for timber and stone but unfit for cultivation; the railroads received rich deposits of minerals in the government lands freely granted to them; areas of lands containing valuable natural resources were alienated under the Homestead and Pre-emption Acts in spite of the fact that these laws were designed for pioneer farmers; and the rich ore lands of Minnesota, Michigan, and Wisconsin were exempted from the Mineral Lands Act and sold at even lower prices than that law provided. Confusion of national policy, corruption, greed, and inefficiency had brought about the loss to private interests of the nation's most valuable birthright—its minerals and metals.

Because of the abundance of drier and better lands, little attention had been paid in the early nineteenth century to swamp and overflowed lands. Until 1850 all the great swamp tracts, except some in the thirteen original states, such as Dismal and Okefinokee swamps, Jersey marshes, and tidal lands in New England, remained in the possession of the Federal government. In 1850 and 1860 about six-sevenths of these regions were turned over to the states, a total of about 64,000,000 acres. Florida and Louisiana alone received 20,000,000 and 9,000,000 acres respectively. Many frauds were perpetrated in selecting lands by the states and in disposing of them. During this period few states made efforts to drain the swamp lands. Illinois and Iowa granted them to counties, which sold them for the benefit of schools, and to companies for bridge construction, or they offered them as military bounties during the Civil War. In Michigan, Minnesota, and Florida, railroad companies were given areas of swamp lands. The grants to capitalists and syndicates of large tracts of land in most of the sixteen states containing vast marshes and swamps furthered the trend toward the monopoly of land.

THE BEGINNING OF CONSERVATION

The Washburn-Langford-Doane expedition into the Upper Yellowstone country in 1870 publicized the natural beauties of that region.

News of the wonderland, its travertine terraces, hot springs, spouting geysers, brilliantly colored canyons, plunging waterfalls, blue lake, game herds, and ghostly fossil forests, spread over the country. The suggestions of a group of Montana citizens who, around a wilderness campfire in 1870, conceived the idea of establishing the region as "a pleasuring ground for the benefit and enjoyment of the people," led to an act of Congress in 1872 to hold the area in government ownership as a national park.

In the decades that followed, a few other national parks were established for public use. But the movement was accelerated in the period when Theodore Roosevelt was preaching the doctrine of conservation. Several parks were set aside as a part of his program and the way was opened for others to follow. They were reserved because of the great scenic beauty that made them of interest to the general public, and also in order to reserve splendid forests and protect wild life in danger of extinction. From time to time, other national parks were opened in various parts of the country.

The first steps in conservation can also be seen in the establishment of the office of the United States Commissioner of Fish and Fisheries in 1871, because of the growing concern over the decline of the fisheries; in the communication to Congress of the American Association for the Advancement of Science in 1874, regarding conservation policies; in the authorization given to the Department of Agriculture in 1876 to investigate the country's forest resources; in the earliest attempts made to irrigate semiarid lands in the West; and in the laws passed toward the end of the century relating to forest lands. Irrigation had been adopted to a small extent from the earliest days of settlement and could be found in the areas inhabited by the early Spanish settlers, the Pennsylvania Germans during the colonial period, some tribes of Indians, the Mormons in Utah, the early immigrants to California during the gold rush, and along the trails to the Far West. It was not until after the Civil War that the Federal government undertook to encourage the reclamation of barren lands. A demand for the amendment of the land laws relating to these lands appeared. Obviously the usual tract of 160 acres in semiarid regions was not large enough for farming such areas, and if these waste areas were to be utilized they would have to be developed under careful plans of irrigation. President Grant after visiting the Far West in 1875 suggested to Congress the appointment of a commission to inspect the dry regions and to make recommendations. Two years later the Desert Land Act was passed. It provided for the sale of 640 acres at $1.25

an acre to any who would irrigate the land within three years. Although only a small part of the land had to be cultivated under the law, the requirement for irrigation was vague, and it became evident that the average settler could not afford to build an adequate system of water works. Little progress was made until the cattle industry of the plains was disrupted by cold and drought after 1886. Then land and irrigation companies were formed, and a boom resulted. By 1890, more than 3,600,000 acres had been granted to 54,000 irrigators. In that year Congress reduced the amount that an individual could purchase to 320 acres, but the law operated in the interests of grazing groups and irrigation companies and not the settler.

Westerners pointed out that title to land under the Desert Land Act was not given until after the land was irrigated and that settlers therefore could not give their land as security for the cost of reclamation. As a result of the demand for a change in the desert legislation, Congress passed the Carey Act in 1894. It provided for the transfer of up to a million acres of Federal lands to each state having semiarid lands within its borders on the condition that the state would irrigate not less than twenty of each 160 acres cultivated by actual settlers within a period of ten years. Colorado, Idaho, Montana, Nevada, Wyoming, and other western states immediately accepted the proposal. The states contracted with private companies to build irrigation works, and in turn these companies sold or leased "water rights" to settlers. By 1914, more than 7,000,000 acres had been applied for under the Carey Act, but only 460,000 acres had actually been reclaimed. Of this figure, 62 per cent was in Wyoming.

A CONSERVATION MOVEMENT

In the nineties German-educated scholars and American-trained engineers, such as Frederick W. Taylor, began thinking in terms of efficiency. Applied to government, the "gospel of efficiency" meant control by experts who were above politics. The leaders of the movement for government control and conservation of natural resources were often men close to the engineering societies and the movement for scientific industrial management. As President, Theodore Roosevelt took a leading part in this movement and with his vigorous personality and dramatic flair urged the necessity for a well-rounded program of conservation. Beginning with his annual message of 1901, he did everything possible to bring the matter to the attention of the entire country until the masses came to understand the meaning of conservation and national welfare.

As early as 1891, a law of Congress gave the President the right to withdraw government forest lands from sale and to establish national forests. Under Presidents Harrison, Cleveland, and McKinley, about 46,000,000 acres of forest reserves were set aside. When Theodore Roosevelt became President, he recognized a major problem of conservation—that of adjusting the conflict between the interests of the present and those of the future. In his first annual message he stated:

Wise forest production does not mean the withdrawal of forest resources, whether of wood, water or grass, from contributing their full share to the welfare of the people, but, on the contrary, gives the assurance of larger and more certain supplies. The fundamental idea of forestry is the perpetuation of forests by use. Forest protection is not an end in itself; it is a means to increase and sustain the resources of our country and the industries which depend upon them.

By the close of Roosevelt's presidency the larger part of the Federal forest lands, more than 148,000,000 acres, had been set aside to be used perpetually in the interests of the whole nation.

In 1901, the Division of Forestry, which had been established twenty years before in the Department of Agriculture, became the Bureau of Forestry. Gifford Pinchot, a man of wide experience who knew what other countries were doing to preserve their forests, was made Chief Forester. In 1905, the Bureau became the United States Forest Service and control of the national forests was transferred to it from a Division of the Land Office in the Department of Interior. Thus the foresters and forests, which had been under two different Departments, were brought together. Under the direction of Pinchot, plans were made and carried out to prevent the destruction of the forests that remained, especially from fire, and a beginning was made to retimber denuded areas. Through programs and publications much was accomplished in the scientific care and control of government forests. But it was not until after the Capper Report of 1920, the Report of President Hoover's Timber Conservation Board, and the Copeland Report of 1933, that national forestry was placed on a solid foundation.

Other parts of the Department of Agriculture were given new life under President Theodore Roosevelt. Many of its undertakings were in effect conservation enterprises. It helped the American farmer to understand more efficient and scientific methods of farming; it made discoveries and circulated information to combat animal and plant

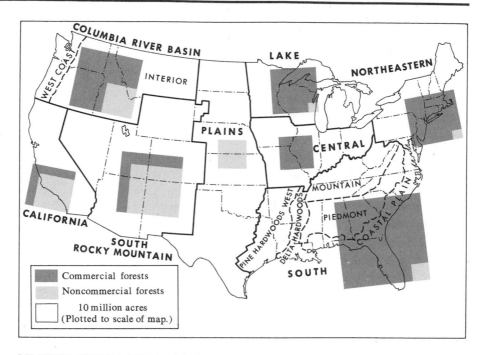

RELATIVE FOREST AREAS, 1940

diseases as well as destructive insects; and it gathered statistics, distributed seeds, and studied soils. Although only a little progress was made at this time in regard to soil conservation, the department played an increasingly vital part in the conservation of natural resources.

By 1900, the most important mineral lands remaining in the hands of the government were coal, phosphate, and oil lands. Legislation was adopted during President Roosevelt's administration which authorized the President to withdraw from sale the mineral lands of the national domain. In order to protect the mineral resources that remained, Roosevelt reserved from sale and settlement a total of 75,000,000 acres of land that contained coal, oil, and other subsurface wealth. Laws were also passed providing for the separation of the surface of coal lands fit for agriculture from the mineral wealth beneath, thus permitting the separate disposal of each or their separate retention by the government.

THE MANAGEMENT OF WATER

As the conservation movement got under way, a demand was made for the construction of irrigation projects by the Federal government. In 1902, the Newlands Reclamation Act provided for federal construction of irrigation works for the first time, outside of Indian reservations. The law required that the receipts from the sales of Federal lands in Oklahoma, Kansas, Nebraska, North Dakota, South Dakota, and all states to the west and southwest (except Texas) be set aside as a reclamation fund to be used to survey, construct, and maintain irrigation works in the semiarid states. The users of water in each region were to repay the government for the cost of construction over a period of ten years without interest on the deferred payment. It was discovered, however, that settlers who took up lands could not pay for these projects within the stated period and Congress was forced in 1914 to extend it to twenty years. Later the government was required to lease water rights in many different localities rather than to sell the entire irrigation works because of the financial inability of the settlers to buy them.

Under the Newlands Act, much was accomplished in the reclamation of semiarid lands. By 1914, more than $96,000,000 had been spent in the building, operation, and maintenance of irrigation projects. Only $7,000,000 was received from settlers by the Federal government in return. But such huge dams were built as the Shoshone Dam in Wyoming, the Roosevelt Dam in Arizona, and the Arrowrock Dam in Idaho, as well as many smaller irrigation works. Millions of acres of lands were reclaimed and such crops as sugar beets, alfalfa, rice, cereals, and fruits were grown on them. Although the projects were largely financial failures to the government, they inaugurated the movement to open for settlement the great dry areas of the West and began policies which in more recent years have been elaborated, contributing to the improvement and well-being of large groups of people. Although the impetus to the irrigation movement was given during the administration of Theodore Roosevelt, it was not until the decades of the twenties and thirties that a beginning was made in analyzing such projects in terms of cost and economic evaluation.

Along with opening land by irrigation went restoring land by drainage. Federal funds were increasingly appropriated for the purpose. In addition, private initiative, and to some extent state enterprise, did much to reclaim certain areas. The interstate character of many large drainage projects was urged as sufficient reason for increased national aid. In 1914 and 1915 Congress appropriated large sums of money for investigating the problems of wet lands in general and of flood control in particular. In time it became evident that there were many sides to the question of the reclamation of swamp lands other than the recovery for agricultural tracts or for industrial or other uses. Thousands of square miles of drained bottoms proved useless for growing purposes. Slowly it was recognized that swamps, like forests, were often valuable for maintaining the flow of streams, which were impeded by draining.

Throughout most of the nineteenth century, the policy of the Federal government had been to sell or grant outright to industrial and other companies lands which contained valuable water power sites. Thus private enterprise came to control the valuable sources of power. States likewise had given water power rights to private interests. By the end of the nineteenth century, the most valuable watersheds and power sites were in private hands. In 1889, a systematic study of the water resources of the country was begun by the United States Geological Survey at the request of Congress. The acts of 1895 and 1902, passed in the interests of water supply rather than that of power, reserved certain watersheds from settlement. In 1906, a new policy was established when Congress leased to the Edison Electric Power Company in southern California certain water power sites for a period of forty years in return for an annual rental paid to the government. Other companies received similar contracts. The policy was not accomplished without a vigorous fight by the water power interests. The Attorney General, however, sustained the right of the government to charge for water power.

In 1910, Congress enacted legislation authorizing the President to set aside public lands for water power or irrigation purposes and Taft made good use of this authority. Ten years later the Federal Water Power Act provided that no lease or grant of Federal water power

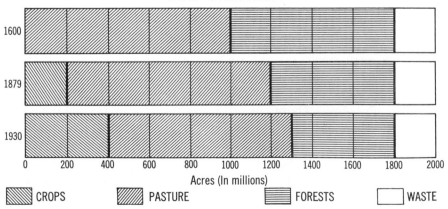

Source: National Education Association.

should be made for more than fifty years. It also permitted the "re-capture" of power plants by the Federal government, state, or municipality, if deemed necessary, at the expiration of the lease, provided a fair payment be made for the plant. A Federal Power Commission, consisting of the Secretaries of War, Agriculture, and Interior, was established to administer the law. It laid the basis for future developments in regard to the control and conservation of valuable water power sites. The public interest in power sites was protected; programs were worked out cooperatively with the power commissions of several states; and the way was paved for rate-making, which was later to become a vital issue. In 1930, the Commission was reorganized with five full-time commissioners.

INLAND WATERWAYS AND THE GOVERNORS' CONFERENCE

In 1907, President Roosevelt appointed the Inland Waterways Commission to study the relations of the forests and streams to the other natural resources and to prepare "a comprehensive plan for the improvement and control of the river systems of the country." The interest in waterways, long dormant, grew out of the desire to conserve natural resources, to control floods that periodically devastated sections of the country, to relieve the congestion of the railroads, to provide a more adequate transportation system, and to establish competition with the railroads in order to reduce transportation rates. In 1908 the Inland Waterways Commission submitted a bulky *Preliminary Report* on rivers, lakes, canals, and railroad competition. It recommended that all future plans for improving navigation should consider power development, flood control, water purification, and reclamation of land. The Commission recommended a conference for a discussion of the conservation problem as a whole. This was called by President Roosevelt, and a group of state governors and others met at the White House in 1908.

Governors of the states, cabinet members, justices of the Supreme Court, educators, and scientists took part in the discussions. This national conference gave widespread publicity to the need for conservation and for the first time brought together the governors of the states. Its recommendations set forth a general and complete scheme of reform. A plan was drawn up which provided for cooperation between Congress and the states in developing a program. As a result, the states entered enthusiastically into plans for the conservation of state forests, for reforestation, and for the reservation of mineral lands. Little, however, was actually accomplished by the states at this time. Some state programs, begun years before, were now revitalized. Inspired by the work of the Federal government, forty-one states appointed commissions within eighteen months after the conference had adjourned. In order to develop even further interest and coordination in the work, President Roosevelt appointed the National Conservation Commission, headed by Gifford Pinchot. In 1909, it made its exhaustive inventory of the natural resources of the country and emphasized the great waste of minerals still taking place. As a result, more efficient practices in mining came into use, and more government lands containing coal and phosphate were withdrawn from private entry. In the same year, the North American Conservation Conference met in Washington for the purpose of extending the program as far as possible into international affairs.

Partly as a result of the conference and partly on the recommendation of the Inland Waterways Commission, Congress established the National Waterways Commission in 1909. It was charged with the duty of investigating the water transportation system of the country. The Commission, consisting of twelve congressmen, reported to Congress in 1910. It suggested the continuance of investigations by army engineers and the completion of projects that had been started, but advocated a careful study of projects that were not vital and essential to navigation. In 1911, however, Congress passed the Weeks Law allowing Federal purchase of forest lands wherever necessary to improve the navigability of rivers. Under this law lands in the White Mountains and Southern Appalachians were purchased. The following year a report of the Commission recommended the Lake Erie-Ohio River Canal, suggested further study on the question of the Lake Erie-Lake Michigan Canal, opposed certain other suggested projects, and urged, unsuccessfully, that all water carriers be brought under the regulating jurisdiction of the Interstate Commerce Commission. As a result of the inland waterways movement, traffic on the rivers, canals, and streams increased. In 1920 more than 125,000,000 tons of freight were transported on the inland waterways of the country, other than the Great Lakes.

OPPOSITION TO THE CONSERVATION MOVEMENT

The interest in conservation did not develop without opposition, particularly from the West. One writer stated that: "In the East, Pinchot conservation means resistance to private greed and corporate fraud that have sought to despoil and waste the public domain at the expense of the public," while "in the Far West, Pinchot conservation is held to mean obstruction of settlement and public progress that comes from opening of new lands."[1] Westerners argued that the settlement of new lands should not be restricted in any way because this policy would hold back national development; that government grazing lands had cost the nation little and therefore should be open to all; that the timber of the country had not been wasted but had been used for industrial purposes and the building of towns; and that conservation policies should be confined to the states as not being within the province of the Federal government.

Much stress was placed on the constitutional argument that conservation was a sovereign right of the states. It was emphasized that the powers of the states were sufficient to handle all conservation problems; that Federal control was unjust because it involved bureaucratic methods and taxed the few for the benefit of the many; and that the new states should have the same right to their resources as the older states had to theirs. But up to this time the states had done little or nothing to promote the policies of conservation.

Those in favor of Federal control insisted that conservation was properly a function of the Federal government because the resources belonged to the people of the country and therefore the Federal government had the right to regulate and control them. They stated that the Federal government could enforce a uniform policy and supervise it more economically than the states. Then again, conservation projects on rivers and streams as well as reclamation of lands were often interstate in scope.

Attempts to create a nonpolitical conservation authority with real decision-making power, however, were always defeated by the combination of local interests and states' rights. Whenever some Federal agency was able to practice conservation, its office quickly came to be a ring for bouts between many interest groups. Hence, while forest acreage was withdrawn from harmful exploitation and a number of dams were built, no planned system of soil conservation, flood control, and utilization of hydroelectric power was established. In carrying out Roosevelt's policies, President Taft was harassed by a major conflict similar to the many lesser ones that went on in all bureaus trying to administer conservation. Chief Forester Gifford Pinchot publicly accused Secretary of the Interior Ballinger of granting to powerful private interests cer-

[1] Leslie M. Scott, "Why East and West Differ on the Conservation Problem," *Independent*, March 31, 1910, LXVIII, 697.

tain public lands containing water power sites in Montana and Wyoming. These lands had been withdrawn from public sale by President Roosevelt. Pinchot also defended L. R. Glavis, an investigator for the Federal Land Office, who had lost his position because he accused Ballinger of favoring the powerful Cunningham syndicate in its claim to coal lands in Alaska. Pinchot was dismissed, but public opinion demanded an investigation. A joint congressional committee exonerated Ballinger. Failing to secure public confidence, his position became intolerable, and he resigned. Later, the courts ruled that the Cunningham claims were fraudulent. The affair served to widen the breach that was developing within the ranks of the Republican party. The dispute was an intensely bitter one and led many to think that Taft was not doing all he could about conservation and that he was a poor judge of men. The results of the controversy from one point of view were encouraging, showing that public opinion could be highly aroused over the question of policies regarding the public wealth.

As will be seen in Chapter 26, conservation continued to be a national problem involving political interests. But the details of the problem changed from decade to decade as technology developed and employed new resources. Conservation of natural gas did not seem an important issue in 1900—by 1940 it was. Timber was one of the earliest interests of conservationists, but the development of plastics may make it a less important resource in the future. Natural resources, in other words, only seem important when they are needed, and it is impossible to predict accurately the needs of future generations.

CHAPTER 17

The Southern Region

PROBLEMS OF RECONSTRUCTION

For more than a decade and a half after 1861, the South suffered from the ravages of war and its aftermath. It was tragic for the morale and spirit of that section as well as for its recovery that political reconstruction was carried out at the point of the bayonet as northern troops took charge of the region under the acts of reconstruction. It was also unfortunate that a large part of the former ruling classes had little voice in solving the problems that followed the war, as many of them were disfranchised and in disrepute. Hordes of demagogues and unscrupulous politicians descended on the South, largely as office holders or financial adventurers. These carpetbaggers took part in shaping the new state constitutions, in bringing the Negroes and former white unionists together into the ranks of the Republican party, and in controlling the machinery of the state governments. Through reckless expenditures they helped to increase the state debts and were partly responsible for preventing a more rapid economic recovery. It should be noted, however, that in addition to the carpetbaggers, many northern missionaries and teachers, who had a sincere interest in the newly emancipated Negroes and in the problems of reconstruction, also went to the South during this period. Their numbers and influence, however, were not great enough to combat the evils of reconstruction,

backed by the authority of the Federal government. Some Federal soldiers saw opportunities for a better living in the South and returned
after the war to become substantial citizens.

Economic problems were manifold. In addition to the devastation
in the war areas, almost one-fourth of the white male population was
killed or incapacitated; capital resources were dissipated; banks and
commercial houses were bankrupt; the credit system was disorganized;
economic ties with foreign countries were broken; the production of
the staple crops was greatly retarded; livestock was reduced by almost
two-thirds; and land values had greatly depreciated. In addition, emancipation suddenly redistributed ownership of the factors of production
by wiping out about $2 billion worth of slave property. Thus sweep-
ing changes were made in the economy of that section and in time
a new South arose on the ashes of the older one.

POPULATION AND LAND CHANGES

The war affected the South economically in many different ways.
There was a shifting and redistribution of population. A number of
southern citizens, including businessmen, artisans, and small farmers,
whose source of livelihood had been destroyed by the war, moved westward; many disfranchised southerners who had been valiant soldiers
in the Confederacy sought new homes in the Northwest; increasing
numbers moved from the country to the towns; and a few sought
foreign lands, as for example, the colony of southern émigrés which
existed for a time in Brazil, while some distinguished soldiers sought
service in foreign armies. Foreigners flocking to the United States from
Europe continued to avoid the South. In 1900, only 2.4 per cent of
the population were foreign-born.

Another change brought by the war was a redistribution of land.
The old plantation system with its characteristic economic and social
life was ended. During the years of reconstruction, the sale of plantations for taxes was a common occurrence. In such sales, plantations
were broken up and the fragments passed to new owners, especially
to small farmers and Negroes. Those plantation owners who were able
to keep their ancestral homes and estates found that the lack of cash
and the problem of labor supply made it impossible to continue the
old type of life. The sale and rental of parts of many plantations accelerated the movement of the redistribution of land. The average farm
in Georgia in 1860 was about 430 acres; in 1880, only 187 acres. In
Alabama in 1860, there were 55,128 plantations and farms; twenty
years later the number had increased to 135,864.

The breakdown of the plantation system resulted in a new social pattern in the South. The former rigid strata of southern society—from the great plantation owners to the lowliest slaves—had ended. The fall of the old aristocracy was complete. Power passed into the hands of a new composite group drawn from all the earlier groups but represented largely by those who had had little power of any sort before the war. Many outside interests helped the Negro. Most conspicuous were the George Peabody Educational Foundation, established by a Boston philanthropist, and similar foundations created by other northerners such as John F. Slater and Julius Rosenwald. Negro industrial schools such as Hampton and Tuskegee, and institutions of higher education including Howard, Fisk, and Atlanta Universities came into existence.

Before the war the South had been at a serious disadvantage in relation to the North owing to the lack of development of its industrial potential. During the emergency of war everything possible was done to place that region on a self-sufficient basis as blast furnaces, forges, and foundries produced cannon and other arms; powder mills were established, and textile factories and tanneries increased. The first step in reconstruction was the conversion of war industries to peace-time activities. Many plants made the change without difficulty as there were broad markets for all types of merchandise, if the seller would extend credit. Some that had been destroyed during the war were rebuilt. Northern investors helped southern industry from the beginning of reconstruction to the early 1870's when panic and depression checked investment.

As the war came to an end in the spring of 1865, an attempt was made by many to plant as much cotton and tobacco as possible. But because of the lateness of planting, the difficulty of securing cash or credit, the scarcity of seed, the lack of horses and mules, the handicap of worn-out farming implements, and the problems of labor resulting from emancipation, the crop of 1865 was relatively small. In the years that followed, plantation owners, small farmers, tenants, and share-croppers gradually increased the staple crops. But the cotton crop of 1860 (2,275,372,000 pounds) was not surpassed until 1879 (2,404,410,-000 pounds). During these years, the southern states passed lien laws to enable landowners and tenants to secure loans on land, crops, livestock, and other property in order to obtain supplies from commission merchants.

The new system of financing, however, worked to the disadvantage of whites and Negroes alike. Farmers went into debt for tools, machinery, seed, and even food, giving the merchant who supplied their needs a lien or mortgage—even on the next year's crop. The result was that it became impossible for a farmer to trade with anyone else because no other merchant would grant credit to one whose property or future crop was already mortgaged. The merchant was therefore in a position to dictate prices and also to name the crops that the farmer should raise. Naturally these were chiefly cotton and tobacco, which promised a quick money return, while the raising of grain from the merchant's point of view tended to make the farmer independent of him for provisions. The lack of capital, the dependence upon merchants, the restriction of the types of crops, and unscientific methods of cultivation were real problems that had to be faced. Consequently economic progress was slow, especially in the diversification of crops, during the entire period of reconstruction. But some changes in this direction took place even during this period.

The problem of developing a new labor system had to be solved during the reconstruction years. The abolition of slavery put an end to an agricultural system which had been in existence in the South since the seventeenth century, although even before the war this system was beginning to change in certain sections as many ante-bellum planters hired slaves by the year. After the war they engaged Negroes under written agreements, the terms of which bound the freedman to the white in much the same way as the hired slave. But the immediate effects of abolition were disastrous. It meant the loss of the slaves to their owners, as well as the loss of taxable property to the communities, and it also caused the general breaking up of the labor organization of the plantation system. While a number of Negroes remained faithful to their old masters and continued to labor for them, usually for low wages, many hoped for better wages and opportunities in newer regions, either the North or the Southwest. In the months after the war, the roads were full of Negroes on their way to offices of the Freedmen's Bureau or to the nearest fort or garrison now in the hands of Federal troops. Rumors were rife that food and clothes could be obtained free, and that each Negro was to receive forty acres of land and a mule from confiscated plantations. This latter hope, prevalent especially before Christmas, 1865, probably arose from the distribution among freedmen of lands on the southeast coast by General Sherman's order in January, 1865. Thousand of idle men and women lived in camps or wandered seeking imaginary opportunities, in many cases stealing and pilfering in order to live. Lawlessness, immorality, and sickness resulted, while at the same time much of the land was uncultivated for lack of laborers. The Freedman's Bureau cared for many Negroes and sent numbers back to work for wages. The problem, however, was too large for the Bureau to handle and as a result southern state legislatures and municipalities took action. Many laws and ordinances were passed to control and regulate the lives and the activities of the Negroes. These became known as black codes.

The black codes varied in the different southern states. They dealt with such matters as vagrancy, apprenticeship, property rights, penalties for crime, and marital relations. Some southern legislatures provided that idle Negroes could be arrested. Vagrancy was variously defined but the definitions were more or less obviously applicable to Negroes moving about without sanction or employment, and penalties included fines or imprisonment, labor on public works, or labor for private employers, who might be required to pay the fine. Some states provided that a Negro would have to produce a license if he wished to engage in trade or preach; in others, he was required to carry a license, showing where he lived and for whom he worked. The laws varied greatly among the states, but were most repressive in South Carolina and Mississippi where the colored population outnumbered the white. Such regulations seemed necessary to the South, but in the North, they aroused indignation, some asserting that they were an attempt to restore slavery in another guise. Far from this, however, the laws were partly an attempt on the part of the southern states to restore order to the disorganized labor system.

As Congress put into operation its radical reconstruction plan of 1867, the black codes fell. During the years that followed, through a division of land, working for wages, and sharecropping, a new labor system emerged. In the Black Belt—the crescent shaped area of black alluvial soil extending from the Alabama River in Alabama and up the Tombigbee in northern Mississippi—cotton was practically the only crop and this area became the leading cotton-producing region of the South until 1880, when it began to turn some attention to food crops. The expense of the maintenance of labor was less than under slavery, but the yield under free labor was relatively low. In other regions during the latter part of the period of reconstruction, diversified farming and the raising of food crops on small tracts of land leased, shared, or independently owned showed that changes were beginning to occur in the South.

Sharecropping offered the tenant more of a feeling of independence than he could enjoy as a wage laborer, but, more important, it allowed the owner who lacked the capital to advance money for wages a chance to have his land cultivated. The tenant planted an agreed-upon crop, usually cotton, under specified conditions and divided the proceeds of the harvest with the landlord. The terms meant that except for small vegetable patches the tenant had to be a single-crop farmer with no power to improve the land or to try new products. The terms usually left the tenant with no alternative to living on store credit until the crop was sold. Such tenants seldom made a surplus above meagre subsistence. In the states along the coast of the Gulf of Mexico, except for Florida, this form of tenure came by 1880 to be the rule on nearly a third of all farms, while tenants of all types ran between 40 and 50 per cent of the cultivators.

During reconstruction years, as the South was slowly recovering, the entire country was severely shaken by the Panic of 1873 in the leading industrial nations. The North was most seriously affected, but it also had grave effects on the South as the foreign cotton markets collapsed. Cotton dropped from twenty cents a pound in 1872 to seven cents a pound in 1873. This price brought ruin to many planters and farmers as well as to their creditors. Other crops were affected in similar manner. In the early and middle seventies, state governments were won back by the Democrats from northern Republican-Negro coalitions, the large postwar debts were in many cases repudiated or scaled down. For several years the South again suffered from hard times. Slowly progress was made and there emerged out of the political and economic wreckage of the past a new and better South. Based on a realization of its natural resources and with a will to throw off the shackles of the earlier period, a new economic era began.

DIVERSIFIED AGRICULTURE

From the close of the period of reconstruction more interest was displayed in diversified agriculture. The changes that took place helped to relieve the South from its almost complete dependence on cotton and other staple crops. Prior to the Civil War, Savannah, Charleston, and Norfolk steamship lines carried early vegetables and fruits to northern ports but the quantities were quite small. Fruit, vegetables, and nut growing for commercial purposes received little attention. Problems of transportation, lack of large city markets, emphasis on staple crops, and difficulties of labor supply prevented development in these fields. After the war, consignment by boat increased, but not until shipments were made by rail in the 1880's did they grow rapidly in volume. Demands from rapidly expanding northern cities, including vegetables out of season, the development of the transportation system, together with reduction of rates, the introduction of fast freight and express service, and the use of ventilator and refrigerator cars together with the changed economic conditions of the South were responsible for this expansion of southern agriculture.

All parts of the Old South contributed to the new trade in truck crops and sent their products first to such cities as Baltimore, Philadelphia, New York, and Boston. The movement expanded into the Southwest and markets were found all over the country. Florida assumed a new importance as a source for early vegetables and fruits, including oranges, for northern markets. In 1900, the states of Virginia, North Carolina, South Carolina, Florida, Kentucky, Tennessee, Alabama, Mississippi, Arkansas, and Louisiana produced for sale potatoes and other vegetables, fruits, and peanuts to the amount of almost $100,-000,000. Thus a new type of industry, which was almost nonexistent before the war, was prospering.

Broadening markets, an increase in the demand for green vegetables the year round in the American diet, motor trucks, and good roads all aided to increase commercial fruit and vegetable growing to large proportions in the twentieth century.

THE STAPLE CROPS

After reconstruction the production of cotton increased rapidly. The crop of 1880 was 6,605,750 bales; by 1890, the crop had increased to 8,652,590 bales; and in 1900, to 10,425,000. By 1914, it had reached 16,134,000 bales, which was four times as large as the bumper crop of 1860. But most of the cotton during the period after reconstruction was cultivated by tenant farmers and not by those who owned the land. Even the landowners were heavily in debt, for farms in the leading cotton-growing states in 1900 were mortgaged to at least half their value.

During the decade of the 1880's the condition of cotton culture was relatively prosperous as there was a broadening demand for the commodity in Europe and in the United States, especially in the South itself where cotton mills were increasing. But in the last decade of the nineteenth century a severe depression hung over cotton production and the lot of cotton growers was similar to that of agrarians in the West and in other parts of the country. As a result, attempts were made to combine southern and western farm organizations, particularly through the alliances (p. 398), but without success. The price of upland cotton fell during the years 1889 to 1894 from 11.5 cents to 7.5 a pound. As the depression continued, its price fell to 6 cents and in 1898 to 4.9 cents. Such a price was ruinous and in many cases did not pay or cover the cost of production. Foreclosure resulted; much of the land fell into the hands of merchants, manufacturers and corporations; and farm tenancy increased.

Between 1899 and 1914, the price trend of agricultural products was sharply upward. The average annual price of cotton in New York during the period rose from nine cents to fourteen cents a pound. The total acreage in cotton increased 35 per cent. The gain was notable in the new regions of Texas and Oklahoma. At the outbreak of the war in Europe in 1914, the price fell from 12.5 to seven cents a pound, but during the war prices recovered, and cotton producers shared a measure of prosperity never known before as prices climbed to reach thirty-eights cents a pound in 1919. Postwar deflation hurt the cotton growers, but alarming distress and deep suffering did not come until the country was caught in the grip of the depression of the 1930's.

It took some time after the Civil War for the production of southern tobacco to recover. In 1880, the total crop in the United States was 472,661,000 pounds; in 1910, it exceeded 1,140,000,000 pounds. By this time it had become largely a product of the small farm, grown in connection with diversified farming, the acreage being limited by the amount the farmer could properly store and cure during the brief

PRODUCTION AREAS OF COTTON, TOBACCO, AND SUGAR, 1900

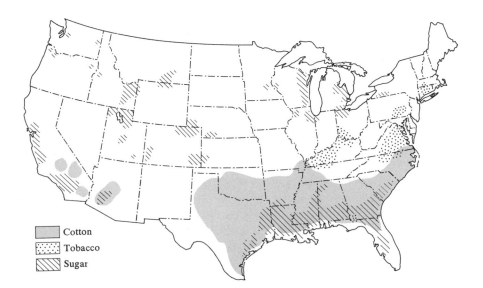

Cotton
Tobacco
Sugar

period that curing must be done to insure a high quality of tobacco. After the Civil War, Virginia no longer was the leading tobacco state. Production shifted to the newer regions of Kentucky, Tennessee, and North Carolina. Kentucky assumed leadership until 1927 when North Carolina became the chief tobacco-growing state, cultivating largely the bright or flue-cured tobacco used in making cigarettes. The production of tobacco also increased in states outside the South. The cultivation of cigar leaf became localized in the Connecticut Valley, Pennsylvania, Ohio, and Wisconsin, especially after 1875 when Havana seedleaf was adopted. About 1900, a shade-grown cigar wrapper was introduced in Florida and the Connecticut Valley. As in earlier days, tobacco continued to be auctioned in different centers in the South. Ordinarily the United States exported two-fifths of its tobacco crop in raw form.

Growing sugar cane for commercial purposes was largely confined to Louisiana. After reconstruction, the quantity of sugar produced annually fluctuated widely, reaching a maximum of 355,000 short tons in 1908. The story of sugar cultivation in the United States is closely interwoven with the periodic changes in tariff protection on the commodity. The First World War brought prosperity to sugar growers and stimulated production. The culture of beet sugar was attempted in different parts of the country quite early, but not until 1880 was it placed on a commercial basis when California expanded its production. It took hold in the western states rather than in the South, Colorado coming to lead the nation's output. By 1910 more beet than cane sugar was produced in the United States. In 1920, the output of beet sugar exceeded 1,000,000 tons.

After 1880, the southern crops of corn, wheat, oats, barley, hay, and forage increased. Between 1865 and 1914, the greatest expansion took place in the newer states west of the Mississippi. Wheat production decreased almost to a vanishing point in Georgia, Florida, Alabama, Mississippi, and also in Louisiana. The raising of beef and dairy cattle made slow progress. Not until after 1914 did the latter became a strong commercial factor in the southern states.

The advances made in scientific farming greatly aided the South's progress in agriculture. Not long after the Civil War, the United States Department of Agriculture and state colleges of agriculture began to experiment on worn-out lands in the Old South and also in many barren regions. Great tracts were made fertile by putting into the soil certain elements in which it was deficient. Long before the Civil War, plans had been carried out to improve farming, but now progress

PERCENTAGE OF FARMS CULTIVATED BY TENANTS,
1880 – 1930

1880 – 25%	1910 – 38%
1890 – 28%	1920 – 39%
1900 – 35%	1930*– 41%

* 1930 is the decennial peak of tenancy. After that date, tenancy rapidly declined. See Chapter 30.

Source: U.S. Bureau of the Census, *Historical Statistics of the United States, Colonial Times to 1957*, Washington, D.C., 1960, pp. 278–279.

was rapid and more expansive. The knowledge of a proper rotation of crops was spread to many regions, and increasing numbers of southern farmers learned to use cotton seed for fertilizer, feed, and for cottonseed oil.

Sharecropping became one of the serious problems of the South. Tenant farmers, whether white or Negro, owning neither tools nor working stock and receiving a share of the cotton, tobacco, or other crops, continued to increase. The low income obtained by such families and their reduction to serfdom by the credit system which continually obligated them to the landowners held back progress in many parts of the South.

DEVELOPMENT OF INDUSTRIES

Gradual progress was made in manufacturing in the South. The tendency for cotton manufacture to migrate to the source of the raw materials and at the same time seek the advantage of low taxes, cheap labor, and abundant power led to an increase in the production of coarse fabrics. In 1880, the South had about 500,000 active cotton spindles whereas New England had almost 9,000,000. In 1915, the South possessed 13,265,000 spindles; New England, 17,526,000; and the rest of the country, 2,050,000. By 1920, the South had almost one-half the spindles in the country. Massachusetts, South Carolina, and North Carolina were the leading textile states. Ten years later Massachusetts still led and was followed by North Carolina, South Carolina, and Georgia.

Cities such as Albemarle, Durham, and Winston-Salem in North Carolina were typical of the rising textile towns in the South. The economic and social development of these regions was similar in many ways to the changes that took place in New England and the middle states as the factory system arose during the first part of the nineteenth century. Low wages, long hours, and child labor characterized the southern factory system for many years.

Tobacco manufacture increased with the growth of the tobacco crops. Leaf was shipped from the warehouses in the various regions of the South to such manufacturing centers as Durham, Winston-Salem, St. Louis, and Louisville. Much was also sent to New York, Philadelphia, and other manufacturing cities of the North. The annual product of all the tobacco factories of the country in 1860 was valued at close to $31,000,000; in 1919, at over $1 billion. The increasing consumption of cigarettes was an important reason for the expansion, for by 1914, more than 10 billion cigarettes were manufactured annually. Chiefly around the production of machine-made cigarettes, James B. Duke organized the American Tobacco Company in 1890. By 1911, the "Tobacco Trust," as it was known, largely controlled all branches of the tobacco manufacturing industry except the production of cigars. In that year, the Supreme Court found the company guilty of attempting to restrain commerce and monopolize the tobacco industry in violation of the Sherman Anti-Trust Act, and ordered it dissolved into competing units.

Among the growing manufacturing industries of the South, the production of furniture was important. North Carolina became second in furniture manufacturing only to Grand Rapids, Michigan. The production of coarse paper made headway in the pine regions. An increase occurred in the manufacture of boots and shoes. Milling and packing industries expanded. Cotton seed became the basis for many manufactures. Prior to the Civil War relatively small amounts of cottonseed oil were made in New Orleans, Natchez, Mobile, and Petersburg, but the great bulk of cotton seed was discarded. After the war its commercial value as a fertilizer was recognized. The seven cottonseed oil mills of 1860 increased to 119 in 1890, crushing annually 1,000,000 tons of seeds, with products valued at $19,700,000. From that time on, industrial chemistry found many new uses for the seed in producing fertilizers, cattle feed, cooking oil, and salad oil.

One of the most important factors in southern industrial development was the establishment of a new iron and steel industry. In 1850, the entire South produced about 12 per cent of the total iron output of the country. The war almost destroyed the industry and recovery was slow. As late as 1890, the output of southern iron amounted only to 6 per cent of the nation's total, but by 1896 it had reached a maximum of 19 per cent. However, production by this time had increased enormously in the North, and the progress of southern industry proportionately must be gauged in the light of northern advancement.

In 1871, when Alabama was declared politically reconstructed, a group of railway and business leaders decided to establish a city devoted to iron manufacture in a region where iron ore, coal, and limestone were known to be in abundance and in close proximity. At the junction of several railroads, Birmingham arose with amazing rapidity, growing from a village of 3,000 to a city of 178,000 in 1920. It became the center of iron, coal, and coke production of that area. At first, pig iron became the most important iron product and by 1900, the Birmingham district exported more pig iron than all other regions. Experiments with the Bessemer steel process were not very successful at first, but as the open-hearth process was introduced in the closing years of the nineteenth century by the Tennessee Coal, Iron and Railroad Company and by other companies, much progress was made in producing steel. The Tennessee Coal, Iron and Railroad Company, though originally incorporated in Tennessee in the 1850's, was operating almost entirely in Alabama by 1890.

Between 1880 and 1890 about fifty blast furnaces were erected in Alabama, Virginia, and Tennessee. Until the Panic of 1893, a speculative fever ran through many regions of the South as land sales boomed, towns were laid out, railroads extended, and plans made for developing the coal and iron industries. From the end of the nineteenth century, as the country recovered from the effects of the panic, much progress was made in the iron and steel industry of the South. During the Panic of 1907, the United States Steel Corporation took over the Tennessee Coal, Iron and Railroad Corporation in Alabama and began its activities in that region. All forms of rolled iron and steel were manufactured in the South. Meanwhile, the foundry industry, long established in the southern states, expanded. The manufacture of stoves, car wheels, locomotives, general railway supplies, and cast iron pipes flourished in such cities as Richmond, Birmingham, Atlanta, Roanoke, Chattanooga, and Anniston.

Much progress was also made in the production of petroleum and natural gas. In 1876, oil wells were opened in West Virginia. Kentucky, Tennessee, and Missouri followed. In Texas, the commercial production of petroleum began in 1896; Oklahoma followed in 1901; and Louisiana became an active producer in 1902. Arkansas did not begin its career in oil until 1921. Among other southern industries that should be noted was sulphur, which became an important export. By 1906, the South had a monopoly of the world's sulphur production.

Louisiana was the first center, but later Texas became the chief source of supply of the mineral.

The southern lumber industry reached great proportions. By the end of the nineteenth century, lumbering had become a large-scale industrial enterprise. Northern capital increasingly was invested in southern forest lands and sawmills. The South came to rival the Northwest in the output of lumber and timber. Lumbering became the leading industry of Mississippi and among the chief industries of Alabama, Georgia, Louisiana, North Carolina, and Texas. In 1900, the South produced 41 per cent of the nation's lumber, and in 1910, 53 per cent. Another of America's oldest industries—the production of naval stores, also flourished in the South. The United States produced in this period about 65 per cent of the world's supply of naval stores and almost all of this was obtained from the pine forests of the coastal plains region from North Carolina to Texas.

Many factors have contributed to the rise of a new South. The destruction of the plantation system, with the division of land and the development of a new labor system that followed, has been one. The South's natural resources including minerals, water power sites, and new fertile lands have been another. The extension of the transportation system, the development of public utilities companies also contributed to the economic development of the South. Northern capital, too, aided in laying the foundations for a diversified form of economic life, which slowly came to displace the earlier agrarian civilization.

THE NEW SOUTH

The term "the New South" has been generally applied to denote the economic and social changes and developments which have taken place in that part of the country since reconstruction. After a dark period of suffering and corruption, the South slowly developed economic and cultural patterns based on rising industries. With the increase of manufactures, the growth of urban population, the expansion of railroads, and the building of improved roads, the characteristics of the older agrarian South receded and in many regions its appearance became more like that of the industrial North.

In the period after the war southern leaders of a new generation arose to encourage and guide the expanding industrial life of the South. Such men as J. D. B. DeBow and William Gregg, who had championed manufacturers and urged agricultural diversification in the Old South, had a legion of followers in the New. Men like Henry W. Grady, editor of the *Atlanta Constitution,* Richmond H. Edmonds, founder of the *Manufacturer's Record,* and D. A. Tompkins, owner of the

Charlotte Observer, were leaders of a group that preached the gospel of business and industrial enterprise and engaged actively in stimulating the movement. Although many planters of the older generation looked back to a "golden past" and held tenaciously to the beliefs of ante-bellum days, a new spirit and energy was arising which found expression in the industrial transformation of certain areas.

From the close of the Civil War, southern editors, promoters, real estate men, merchants, state commissioners of immigration, and others appealed through newspapers, periodicals, and pamphlets for capital and settlers to aid in establishing a new economy in the South. As early as 1865, men like W. S. McElwain obtained capital from the North to rebuild furnaces and factories that had been destroyed during the war. Truman H. Aldrich of New York, who went to Alabama in 1872, was representative of northerners who took capital to the South and engaged in many economic enterprises there.

The scaling down and repudiation of state debts in the decade of the seventies following the weird financing of the carpet-bag governments met with a storm of denunciation in the North and left many northerners hesitant regarding southern securities of all kinds. But as businessmen, investors, and financiers realized the economic possibilities of the South they again invested increasing amounts in southern public and industrial securities.

The growing economic ties between the North and South can be seen in several expositions. Northern manufacturers sent machinery and fabrics to the International Cotton Exposition, held in Atlanta in 1881, and General Sherman contributed $2,000 to it in order to begin a general subscription fund in the North. Congress appropriated $1,000,000 for the Cotton Centennial Exposition, held in New Orleans in 1885, and spent an additional $300,000 for a national exhibit. In these and other expositions, growing cooperation was manifested between the two sections. This was true also in the Louisiana Purchase Exposition, held in St. Louis in 1904. The exposition covered 1,240 acres and was the result of the preparation of several years. It cost more than $31,500,000 and was attended by almost 20,000,000 people. Foreign governments participated and erected buildings. The exposition also called attention to a new type of transportation. Many automobiles were on display, one of which had made the trip all the way from New York under its own power, which was advertised as a marvel of a new age.

As a result of the growing economic activities and relations between the two sections, the deep wounds of war slowly began to heal.

CHAPTER 18

Farm Organizations

BASIC PROBLEMS OF THE FARMERS

From the time of the Civil War to the early twentieth century the western migratory movement resulted in the establishment of more than a million farms in areas that had never before been settled. Prior to the Civil War agriculture had been predominant as evidenced by the control of the agrarians over the economic, political, and social life of the country in spite of the influence of industrialists, merchants, bankers, shippers, lawyers, and speculators. After the war, industrialism continued to develop in the East in a remarkable way and a dynamic urban society came to dominate the national scene instead of a relatively static, individualistic rural society. The farmer felt his loss of political prestige and tried through organization to retain his former power.

The rapid movement of farmers into remote areas of the West, the need for machinery in order to produce grain profitably, and a steady tendency toward oversupply in the world market caused trouble for farmers in less advantageous areas. In a period of generally falling prices those of farm products fell faster than the rest. Hundreds of thousands of independent farmers could not easily combine to raise prices or to control output as large numbers of new farms appeared each year. Farm associations that sprang up from time to time could

389

not adequately cope with such problems. Production increased so rapidly that stabilization was impossible. Then, too, the single crop system and the intensive farming of the Middle West requiring machinery and labor-saving devices forced the farmers to become businessmen. The production of wheat, for example, expanded commercial farming where the risks were greater and crop failures more hazardous than in subsistence farming. Farmers frequently had to mortgage their lands in order to purchase equipment or to tide them over an emergency. Eastern mortgage companies loaned money at rates from 8 to 15 per cent or more. During the period from 1870 to 1897, such fixed charges plus increasing taxes were constant burdens to the farmers who were powerless to prevent the prices of their products from sliding downward. Several crop failures or a sharp decline in farm prices often meant foreclosure. Following the drought in the upper Mississippi Valley from 1887 to 1889, more and more American homesteads were mortgaged. By the latter years of the century more than half the farms in the Middle West were mortgaged and large numbers of mortgages had been foreclosed. As a result, many owners were forced to become tenants. Yet farmers in favored sections were saved from disaster by the increase in land values as settlement grew more dense. Hence there was a pressure to sell high-priced land and buy cheaper land further west, and to move every few years so as to live from capital gains.

Farmers sought many other remedies—lower railroad rates and charges, increased currency and inflation, and other panaceas. But neither farm organizations, third political parties, nor legislation could solve the basic problems. A bitter and unhappy struggle was waged until the end of the century. Then new conditions brought prosperity for about two decades as prices rose, crops on the whole were good, and domestic and foreign markets absorbed surpluses. However, farm mortgages remained a problem, and farm tenancy increased.

THE GRANGER MOVEMENT

Out of the problems faced by the growers of staple crops came the first important farmers' organization in American history. The Patrons of Husbandry, from which blossomed the Granger movement, had its beginnings in the work of Oliver H. Kelley, a clerk in the federal Bureau of Agriculture. After the Civil War, Kelley was sent on a tour of investigation through the impoverished South. He was impressed by the traditional and outworn methods of southern agriculture and by the lack of cooperation among southern farmers. He gave up his position and with a number of associates organized the first Grange in Washington in 1867. Attempts to interest farmers in the East in his organization failed and in 1868, he went to his early home in Minnesota. His plan met with almost immediate and phenomenal success in the Middle West. By the close of 1869 there were thirty-seven active Granges in Minnesota and by the next year the organization had expanded into nine widely-separated states. The Panic of 1873 stimulated the movement and Granges were established throughout the country. In 1876, the order reached its peak with a membership of more than 850,000 and then drastically declined until more recent years, which have witnessed a slow but steady growth of the National Grange. The center of early Grange activities was the grain-growing regions of the upper Mississippi Valley.

When Kelley organized the Patrons of Husbandry, he was simply applying to the farmers ideas that were current in the post-Civil War period as numerous organizations—patriotic, fraternal, labor, and others—were being formed. The Grange was a secret ritualistic order, open to both men and women. Its local units were knit together by a state and a national organization. One of its objectives was to encourage sociability among farmers through picnics, socials, and meetings, thus developing a bond of unity and an understanding of mutual problems, which could result in joint action. Another aim was educational, as fairs and exhibitions of livestock and machinery were promoted and provision made for lectures and educational meetings, especially during the winter season when farmers could attend. Still another aim was that of cooperative buying and selling.

While the National Grange in the beginning failed to work out a comprehensive program of cooperative enterprise, local and state Granges undertook various plans and methods. The most general procedure was to employ agents who would market farm crops most profitably and force manufacturers of farm machinery and other products to sell more cheaply. Grange cooperative stores, where goods were sold at cost, were also common. In 1875, the National Grange recommended the British Rochdale plan, whereby stock was widely distributed in small shares and savings were effected, not by selling at cost, but by charging regular prices, the profits being divided among the members according to their purchases. Stores modeled on this plan prospered for a time in parts of the South and West, particularly in Texas. Cooperative creameries, cheese factories, pork-packing establishments, farm implement works, and linseed oil factories were established. In a few places cooperative banks to provide credit at low rates of interest to farmers were projected and in a dozen states mutual fire and life insurance companies were set up. All the cooperative enterprises, however, were short-lived because of lack of capital, unfamiliarity with business methods, and the hostility of businessmen and bankers. Serious competition also came from mail-order houses which were formed at this time, among them Montgomery Ward and Company of Chicago. Another objective of the Grange was to force down railroad rates and to secure regulation of the carriers in the interests of the farmers. In this objective (see p. 332), they were successful.

THE GREENBACK MOVEMENT

While the Grange was attacking the railroads a new movement arose which was based largely on the quantity theory of money. It was similar in many respects to the movement of the agrarians in the years of distress following the Revolution. Again there was a demand for an inflated currency to benefit the debtor classes. As the condition of farmers of the Middle West became more and more serious, many Grangers joined with others in supporting a third party which emerged from the agitation. In tracing the origin of the Greenback movement it is necessary to go back to the years immediately following the Civil War.

After the war, conservative eastern interests demanded the reestablishment of specie payments in place of the paper basis of exchange which had prevailed since the first issues of greenbacks in 1862. On the other hand, Democratic politicians anxious for a popular issue thought that currency expansion might be the answer. The central point of the "Ohio Idea," sponsored by Democratic George H. Pendleton, was the payment in greenbacks of the large issue of war bonds known as the "five-twenties," for no specific provision had been made for their payment in gold. The idea was endorsed by the Democratic convention in 1868. In addition to wiping out the government's large interest payments and ending such tax-exempt securities, the increase of greenbacks would result in the desired inflation of the currency. The plank in the Democratic platform read: "One currency for the government and the people, the laborer and the officeholder, the pensioners and the soldier, the producer and the bondholder. . . ." The movement included opposition to national bank currency and also to national banks which could not lend money on the security of real estate, the only collateral that most farmers had. These ideas had some support in both major parties in rural regions,

Purposes of the Grange, 1873

Brother Jonathan greets with
joy the return of the specie

BROTHER JONATHAN (*loq.*) "Ah, Specie! Glad to see you, Specie! Been looking for you
for some time.   Your substitute, Greenback, was very well in his day; but, fact is, I wanted
some *Change!*"

but they were chiefly part of the agitation carried on by minor parties
in the years that followed. In 1872, only the new Labor Reform party
officially supported Greenback policies.

The Panic of 1873 brought an increase in local Greenback clubs
which provided the background for a new third party. Few state
Granges were avowedly inflationist. But two of them, the Indiana and
Illinois Granges, furnished the leadership for a Greenback party. A
group of agrarians from several states together with representatives
from the Labor Reform party met in Indianapolis in 1874. A permanent organization was effected and a national nominating convention
met in the same city in 1876. Although the party is usually referred
to as the Greenback party, it was known at different times as the
Independent National, National, and Greenback Labor party. It presented tickets in three presidential campaigns, calling for a number of
reforms, radical for that day, and also for the non-resumption of specie
payments. Its greatest strength was exhibited in the congressional election of 1878 when it polled a million votes. It died in the campaign
of 1884. By this time, Congress had already made greenbacks redeemable in gold.

Meanwhile, a political struggle had been taking place in Congress
between the inflationists, who represented agrarian and business
debtors, and the conservatives or "sound money" men, who demanded

the resumption of specie payments in order to bring the greenbacks to par, stabilize the currency, and enhance the credit of the government. At the close of 1874, about $382,000,000 in greenbacks was in circulation. Partly because of the Panic of 1873 the Republicans lost their majority in the House the next year. While they still had the necessary votes, they passed the Resumption Act in January, 1875. It provided for the retirement of greenbacks to $300,000,000; it recalled fractional paper currency which was to be replaced by silver coins; it withdrew the charge for coining gold; and it directed the Secretary of the Treasury to sell bonds in order to obtain the gold to be used in redeeming legal tender notes presented for redemption on and after January 1, 1879. The inflationists, however, were able to modify the law in 1878 before it went into effect, by securing the enactment of a measure providing that the amount of greenbacks then outstanding, a total of $346,681,000, should remain in circulation. Resumption was accomplished without difficulty. There had been rumors of a conspiracy to make a run on the Sub-treasury in New York, but on the first day that greenbacks could be redeemed for gold, only $135,000 worth of notes were presented there for coin and $400,000 worth of gold exchanged for notes. By this time, greenbacks had risen to par, and it was quite evident that, except in the silver-mining states, people preferred paper to metallic money.

BEGINNING OF THE FREE SILVER MOVEMENT

Under an act of 1837 silver could be taken to the United States mint to be made into silver dollars, but actually none had been presented for years because the ratio was 16 to 1. With gold less than sixteen times more valuable than silver, the owner of silver could get more in the open market than in having the silver minted. Thus the silver dollar was omitted from the mint reform act of 1873, although provision was made for a special Oriental trade dollar weighing 420 grains instead of the older standard of 412½ grains. After 1876, this Oriental trade dollar was no longer legal tender within the United States.

Owing to the mining of vast quantities of silver in Nevada and other far western states the price of silver in the world markets began to decline after 1873. As the price declined, the producers in the West decided to send their bullion to the mint to be coined into dollars. But they discovered that the law of 1873 had omitted the standard silver dollar from the coinage. Persistently, westerners tried to show that eastern bankers and legislators had conspired to demonetize silver. Excited partisans denounced the whole affair as the "Crime of '73." The result was a political movement, promoted by the silver-mining interests and backed by agrarian and other inflationary elements, for a return to bimetallism or the free coinage of silver.

The increasing labors of the new pressure group almost achieved bimetallism. The chief opposition came from conservative business interests which believed that the free coinage of silver would drive gold into hiding and upset foreign and domestic trade. In Congress, representatives of the western silver interests and the farmers made speeches stressing that silver was the people's currency whereas gold belonged to the aristocracy. Senators from the West and South, especially, indulged in flowery oratory during the years 1875–1878 as silver was personified and almost deified. Senator Morgan's remarks were typical:

Silver enjoys this natural supremacy among the largest number of people because the laboring people prefer it. They use it freely and confidingly. It is their familiar friend, their boon companion, while gold is a guest to be treated with severest consideration; to be hid in a place of security, not to be expended in the markets and fairs. It is a treasure and not a tool of trade with the laboring people. A twenty-dollar gold piece is the nucleus of a fortune, to remain hid until some freak of fortune shall add other prisoners to its cell. But $20 in silver dimes is the joy of the household, the substance of things hoped for, the evidence of things not seen. . . . Silver is [to] the great arteries of commerce—what the mountain springs are to the rivers. It is the stimulant of industry and production in the thousands of little fields of enterprise which in the aggregate make up the wealth of the nation.

During these years a crop of silver bills were started on their way through the legislative hopper. In 1877, a bill sponsored by Representative Richard P. Bland of Missouri providing for the free coinage of silver passed the House by a large majority vote. In the Senate it was stressed that the measure would jeopardize Secretary of the Treasury Sherman's plans for resuming specie payments. The Secretary suggested limited purchases instead of free coinage and an amendment to the bill sponsored by Senator William B. Allison of Iowa was made and accepted by both Houses. President Hayes vetoed the measure on the ground that the market value of the bullion in the silver dollar would not be equal in value to that of the gold dollar and therefore harm would result from making it legal tender. But Congress promptly passed the bill over his veto by the necessary two-third majority vote.

The Bland-Allison Act of 1878 provided for the coinage of silver dollars of 412½ grains of standard silver, which were to be legal tender for all debts, public and private except when otherwise expressly stated in the contract. The Secretary of the Treasury was authorized to purchase at market value each month not less than $2,000,000 or more than $4,000,000 worth of silver to be coined into silver dollars. Any seigniorage—the difference between the cost of the bullion and the money coined from it—was to be paid into the Treasury. Holders of the silver dollars could deposit them with the Treasury in sums of $10 or multiples and receive silver certificates. The President was authorized to invite the countries composing the Latin Monetary Union and other European nations to join the United States in a conference to fix the ratio between gold and silver.

In complying with the Act conservative Secretaries of the Treasury purchased the minimum of $2,000,000 of silver bullion each month. Between 1878 and 1890 while the law was in effect, a total of $308,279,000 of silver was obtained and from this 378,166,000 silver dollars were coined, the difference of about $70,000,000 in seigniorage accruing to the government. Thus the currency of the country was greatly expanded, for under earlier laws from 1794 to 1873 only 8,000,000 silver dollars had been coined. The law also introduced a new kind of paper money—silver certificates, at first in denominations of $10 or higher but by a measure of 1886 silver certificates of $1, $2, and $5 were authorized. Not more than 60,000,000 silver dollars were in circulation at any one time; the rest of the coins were stored in specially-constructed vaults. From causes affecting world currency conditions, prices resumed their decline after 1882 in spite of the coinage of silver.

THE FARMERS' ALLIANCES

As the Grange declined in the decade of the eighties, agricultural organizations known as alliances rose to prominence. Two great national alliances were formed. The National Farmer's Alliance (Northern or Northwestern Alliance) was established in 1880 by Milton George, editor of the *Western Rural*, a Chicago farm periodical. It developed into a loose confederation of strong state alliances having a large number of local societies in the Middle West, especially in Kansas, Nebraska, Iowa, the Dakotas, and Minnesota. By the late 1880's farmers in the newly-settled areas of these states were in dire trouble. When they bought their farms, land values were booming, rainfall adequate, and mortgage credit available at high-interest rates. From 1886 on, nearly a decade of drought left these farmers with no way of meeting their debts. The farmers of the "middle border" joined the Northern Alliance by the thousands in the hope that they could find some relief from their financial difficulties. By 1890, when no relief came from the major political parties, the Alliance had organized third-party tickets for local and state offices throughout the Middle West.

The origin of the Southern Alliance or the National Farmers' Alliance and Industrial Union goes back to 1874. It declined soon after its origin but took on new life in 1879. After 1886, under an aggressive president, C. W. Macune, it absorbed the Louisiana Farmers' Union, the Arkansas Agricultural Wheel, and other local associations. Under varying names it became a strongly centralized organization. With the downward trend of cotton prices, many new members were obtained, cooperative buying and selling became more general, and a number of business exchanges were formed. The Southern Alliance, like the Northern, went into politics to secure relief, but avoided third parties for fear that a split in white solidarity might lead to Negro participation in politics. During the period a subordinate Colored Farmers' Alliance and Cooperative Union was founded to look after the welfare of Negroes.

An attempt was made to bring the Northern and Southern Farmers' Alliances together at a meeting of a number of farmer and labor organizations in St. Louis in 1889. Unity of purpose was achieved to a certain degree, but union of organization failed. The declining Knights of Labor joined the farm groups wholeheartedly in a program designed to bring rural and urban workers closer together. The two alliances in their programs called for the free coinage of silver and increased paper money. They agreed on the need for reducing and equalizing taxation and for reclaiming from the railroads all lands held in excess of actual needs. Both favored government ownership and operation of the means of communication and transportation. But from this point on, the divergent economic interests of the western and southern farmers forced them farther apart, especially as the Northern Alliance undertook to form a new third party which became known as the People's or Populist Party.

The distress of the farmers in the late eighties, the meetings at St. Louis and elsewhere, together with the declining price of silver—to a ratio of 20 to 1—and the discontent in mining regions brought the smouldering issue of the free coinage of silver once again prominently before Congress. Promoted by the representatives of the silver interests together with the agrarians and inflationary elements, the demand for complete bimetallism was renewed with vigor as the expansion of the currency continued to be one of the strongest tenets in the economic creed of westerners. In 1889 and 1890 the admission of six northwestern states—North and South Dakota, Montana, Washington, Idaho, and Wyoming—gave the West increased power and strength in Congress. It was obvious that the silver issue was again important.

In 1890, with the drive for tariff increases by eastern representatives, the inflationists tried to get the free, unlimited coinage of silver. As a result of the two issues, the westerners supported the high McKinley tariff bill although opposed to its protective schedules, while the representatives of the East stifled their conservative consciences and voted in return for the Sherman Silver Purchase Act. This law did not provide completely for free silver because of eastern opposition and because it was feared that President Harrison might veto such a bill. It did provide for an increase in the purchase of silver to 4,500,000 ounces a month, practically all the metal that was produced in the country at that time. The act also authorized payment for the silver bullion and for the issuance of notes which were made full legal tender except where other provisions were made in a contract. It also made the notes redeemable on demand in either gold or silver at the discretion of the Secretary of the Treasury. Between 1890 and 1893 the government bought $155,931,000 worth of silver. Because of eastern financial pressure the Treasury kept the notes redeemable in gold, which put the government in serious financial straits after the Panic of 1893. To save the dwindling gold reserves of the Treasury the Silver Purchase Act was repealed, in the face of bitter western opposition, and in the deepening depression no provision remained for the coinage of silver.

THE POPULISTS

The success of local parties in the West, sponsored by members of the Northern Alliance, led to a new national political party. Under the leadership of the Alliance together with representatives of the Knights of Labor, a convention was held at Cincinnati in 1891 to form a third party. About 1,400 delegates were present, most of whom represented five western states. Plans were laid to meet the following year. In February, 800 delegates met at St. Louis and a nominating convention was held at Omaha on July 4, 1892. At the

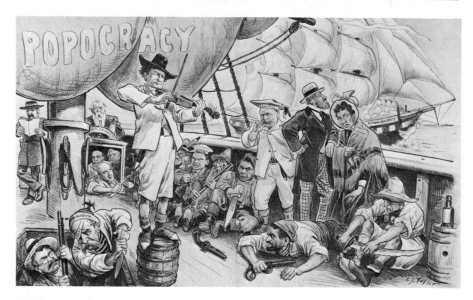

Political Pirates

Trying to lure a rich prize, in good old buccaneer fashion.

St. Louis meeting a platform was drawn up which revealed the emotions, impulses, and principles of the new party. In part the preamble stated:

> The national power to create money is appropriated to enrich bond-holders; a vast public debt payable in legal-tender currency has been funded into gold-bearing bonds, thereby adding millions to the burdens of the people.
>
> Silver, which has been accepted as coin since the dawn of history, has been demonetized to add to the purchasing power of gold by decreasing the value of all forms of property as well as human labor, and the supply of currency is purposely abridged to fatten usurers, bankrupt enterprise, and enslave industry. A vast conspiracy against mankind has been organized on two continents, and it is rapidly taking possession of the world. If not met and overthrown at once it forebodes terrible social convulsions, the destruction of civilization, or the establishment of an absolute despotism.

With a declaration "that the union of the labor forces of the United States this day consummated shall be permanent and perpetual," the platform demanded "a national currency, safe, sound, and flexible, issued by the general government only," the free and unlimited coinage of silver and gold at a ratio of 16 to 1, a plan for government purchase and storage of surplus staple crops, a graduated income tax, government ownership and operation of railroads and telegraph lines, and the abolition of land monopolies. In order to attract the labor vote, resolutions were adopted endorsing restrictions on immigration, the eight-hour day, and the abolition "of a large standing army of mercenaries, known as the Pinkerton system" (see p. 458). The new party showed remarkable strength in the election. With General Weaver of Greenback fame as its presidential candidate, the party secured a million popular votes and won twenty-two places in the electoral college. Six senators and seven representatives were elected.

By the time these men assembled in Congress the economy was deeply depressed. Succeeding years were marked by severe unemployment, the lowest prices ever recorded for farm commodities up to that time (1896), and the failure of the conservative Cleveland administration to act in the situation. The Populists looked forward to the next election and carried on a vigorous and spectacular campaign emphasizing the free coinage of silver. All over the country meetings were held in which monetary panaceas as well as economic theories were discussed. Songs were sung and the cause of silver became a holy crusade in which gold was the diabolical symbol of capital, wealth, and plutocracy, always opposed to the interests of the masses. Mrs. Mary Elizabeth Lease, an able orator and organizer, expressed the spirit of the western movement when she said: "We want money, land, and transportation" and insisted that "Kansas suffers from two great robbers, the Santa Fe Railroad and the loan companies." Her most famous statement was "Kansas had better stop raising corn and begin raising hell."

Many Populists thought they could win in 1896 if neither major party endorsed free coinage of silver. But when William Jennings Bryan persuaded the Democrats to advocate silver, the Populists decided to join them in backing Bryan for the Presidency. He presented the free coinage question as a "cause as holy as the cause of humanity." He called for another Jackson to lead the Democratic hosts "against the encroachments of organized wealth" and brought his listeners to their feet with his closing defiance to those who advocated a gold standard alone: "You shall not press down upon the brow of labor this crown of thorns. You shall not crucify mankind upon a cross of gold." The party committed itself to the "free and unlimited coinage of both silver and gold at a ratio of 16 to 1 and that the standard silver dollar be of full legal tender for all debts public and private." Bryan through the magic of his speech also made himself the candidate of the party. The Populists with their chief issue taken over by a major party were in a quandary but maintained a separate identity, with Bryan also as their presidential nominee. The Republicans stood for a gold standard and thus the issue on this point between the two major parties was clearly drawn.

The campaign preceding the election was one of education as people everywhere tried to understand basic monetary questions. Politicians and others tried to simplify such ideas as Gresham's law, the quantity theory of money, and monetary standards. A flood of pamphlets and other publications descended on the country. *Coin's Financial School,* by W. H. Harvey, published in 1894, was the first of a large number of similar pamphlets issued in the interests of silver. Coin, depicted as a "smooth little financier," set forth the principles of money against a background of silver and replied to the questions of economists, bankers, merchants, and others. He discussed the iniquity of the Crime of '73, problems of bimetallism and the repeal of the Silver Purchase Act. Through the use of graphic illustrations, homely allusions, glib arguments and the use of real names of prominent people, the book was clever propoganda for the cause of bimetallism. Other pamphlets appeared by those who believed in the gold standard. Newspapers and periodicals took up the fight. Professor J. L. Laughlin of the University of Chicago replied with *A Freak in Finance.* The Sound Currency Committee of the Reform Clubs in its semimonthly publication *Sound Currency,* for May 1, 1895, included Horace White's article "Coin's Financial Fool," which attacked the arguments and conclusions of Coin. As the election drew nearer, publications about the controversy increased and the battle of the standards was on.

While the popular vote of the two major presidential candidates was relatively close, the Republicans under William McKinley were completely victorious. The election settled the question of the gold standard although Congress did not enact the issue into law until 1900, for immediately on regaining power the Republicans directed their attention to the tariff.

FARM PROSPERITY

By 1897, prosperity had returned. As prices rose in the years that followed, the Populist movement died. Between the end of the nineteenth century and the outbreak of the First World War prices rose quite steadily and continued an upward trend. From 1897 to 1913 the wholesale prices of commodities increased 50 per cent, or an

average of over 3 per cent annually, while the prices of farm commodities rose about 20 per cent faster. During the same period farm
property doubled in value.

While many farmers did not succeed in liquidating all their debts,
and others paid off old debts and contracted new ones as they expanded
their holdings or strove for a higher standard of living, rapidly rising
agricultural prices had a psychological effect in quieting agitation. A
new degree of self-confidence and hope appeared, inspired by widening
opportunities. The growing prosperity could be seen in better farm
homes, especially in certain regions of the Middle West where sod
houses and other types of temporary homes of the newer areas disappeared. In the most progressive parts of the country after 1900, gas
and electricity came into use in many farmhouses and barns. The
introduction of septic tanks, of heating and lighting systems, and of
new household gadgets was another indication of the rising status of
the farmer. More frequent train services and regular free mail delivery
added to the conveniences of country life. By 1914 the more prosperous farmers were using trucks to take their produce to markets
and some could boast of owning an automobile.

Between 1900 and 1910 more than 3,000,000 people left farms
for urban areas, but a large number of immigrants and others found
farm homes in the West. New England and the eastern-north-central
states, however, were experiencing a loss of farm population and income, a trend that was spreading to the Middle Atlantic states. It was
also true that during the first decade of the twentieth century while
population increased 21 per cent, improved farm acreage rose only
15 per cent, and during the next four years the number of cattle in
the country fell amost 13 per cent, thus creating a balance between
supply and demand more favorable to the farmer.

Improved economic conditions stifled any serious outbursts, but
the agrarian movement did not entirely die out. No new farmers'
parties appeared, but various organizations were established, which
for the most part emphasized economic cooperation. In 1902, two new
farmers' associations were started—the American Society of Equity,
and the Farmer Cooperative and Educational Union (the Farmers'
Union). The former based its program on the principle of controlling
production and withholding surpluses; the Farmers' Union stressed
cooperative marketing. A Southern Cotton Growers Protective Association, in 1900, began a campaign for a reduction of cotton production through programs of diversification but without much success.
In 1910, representatives of the American Society of Equity and of

another farm society known as the Gleaners joined with several state farmers' organizations to form a Farmers' National Headquarters in Washington to serve as a lobbying agency. Seven years later a rival group created the National Board of Farm Organizations, which also lobbied in the interests of farmers. The National Grange continued its activities during the period although it was not as powerful as it had been earlier. While aggressive tactics and political third parties disappeared, farm organizations remained to serve a useful purpose in holding groups of farmers together to promote their own interests.

The period 1898–1914 was one of the most satisfactory for the farmers in American history as prices and land values increased, as the agricultural standard of living rose and as agriculturalists obtained more recognition in national affairs. But farm debts remained large and there was an increase in tenancy. Soil erosion and declining fertility were serious in many sections. Older sections in the Northeast were especially affected, and many farmers were forced to abandon their century-old farms in the hill country of New England and New York. The chief problems were largely of production and not of the disposal of unmarketable surpluses. The United States was selling to foreign customers annually from about 150,000,000 to 200,000,000 bushels of wheat, about 8,000,000 bales of cotton, 1 billion pounds of pork, and also large quantities of tobacco and fruit. Agricultural commodities were the chief medium used to meet foreign obligations, for the United States was still a debtor nation. The government fostered research and education to make production more efficient and to solve farm problems.

GOVERNMENT AID TO AGRICULTURE

The Department of Agriculture, established in 1862 under a commissioner, continued the gathering and distribution of seeds as well as the scientific work which had been started by the Commissioner of Patents (p. 296). The work of the divisions of Chemistry, Entomology, and Botany of the Department made much progress and new divisions were created from time to time. The success and achievements of the Bureau of Animal Husbandry in the field of animal diseases hastened the Department's elevation to cabinet status in 1889, when its head was made the Secretary of Agriculture. The Department then passed into a most expansive period when its work came to cover almost all phases of agriculture.

Much was done during the period in the field of agricultural education. The Morrill Act of 1862 provided that a state might receive

30,000 acres of public lands within its borders for each Senator and Representative it had in Congress, the proceeds from the sale of such lands to be invested and the income used to establish colleges to teach especially "agriculture and the mechanical arts." The land-grant colleges established under this law potentially provided a comprehensive system of agricultural research and experimentation. But, since the curricula and activities of these institutions were prescribed by state legislatures and were under separate state administrations, the materials of instruction and methods of teaching were not unified or systematized. By 1890, many influences aided to make the work in the land-grant colleges more effective and efficient. Among these, experimentation was most important.

Agricultural experiment stations were first established to provide instructional materials for the colleges and to investigate occupational problems. They proved to be a vital link between the Department of Agriculture and the colleges. The first state agricultural experiment station was set up at Wesleyan University, Middletown, Connecticut, in 1875. By 1887, fourteen states had such stations and colleges in thirteen others carried on equivalent work. In that year, the Association of American Agricultural Colleges and Experiment Stations was organized under the leadership of the Commissioner of Agriculture to coordinate the work of the individual stations. The Association of American Agricultural Colleges together with the National Grange and the Alliances brought about nation-wide sentiment in favor of legislation. Congress passed the Hatch Act (1887), which provided for annual grants for the stations in all the states and territories. The subsidies were increased from time to time by subsequent legislation.

The Second Morrill Act of 1890 appropriated to the states funds for current educational purposes and encouraged the states to provide regular agricultural instruction. In the years that followed, Federal aid was asked to carry on extension and institute work. From about 1870 state farm organizations, including the Grange, had made provisions for lecturers at farmers' meetings. By the end of the century the farmers' institute movement to spread agricultural knowledge was strong and it continued to grow in the twentieth century. Demands arose for government aid for such activities. In 1914, the Smith-Lever Act provided Federal appropriations for agricultural extension work by county agents in farm communities. Through this act students not attending colleges could secure instruction in agriculture and home economics, thus indirectly enjoying some of the benefits of the work of agricultural colleges and experimental stations. The promotion of extension work on a national scale, aided by state and Federal appropriations, brought an end to the farmers' institutes of the older type as their functions were absorbed by the newer movements. Agricultural education entered the secondary schools with the passage of the Smith-Hughes Act of 1917, which created a Federal Board for Vocational Education for the purpose of promoting training in agriculture, trades, industries, commerce, home economics, and the teaching of vocational subjects. It furnished funds for vocational education on condition that the states contribute an equal amount. Supplementary laws have extended the original activities in many ways, especially to vocational rehabilitation.

CHAPTER 19

Banking and Finance

In theory the commercial banking system was regarded chiefly as a supplier of short-term credit to facilitate business transactions rather than capital for long-term investment. But prior to the First World War a great deal of bank credit, perhaps as much as half, was used by business firms for working capital or plant expansion. In addition to mortgage lending on business property ninety-day paper or demand loans were continuously renewed, and thus bank credit became a source of capital for economic growth.

In addition to bank resources the reserves of life insurance companies were important pools of capital that could be drawn upon for mortgages or high-grade corporate bonds. By 1890 the reserves of insurance companies were one-sixth as large as the resources of all banks, and by 1914 they were about one-fifth as large. Additional pools of savings existed in the funds of building and loan corporations and fire and casualty insurance companies.

Aided by the easy incorporation policies of many states, the spread of credit institutions was rapid in the United States. By the 1850's the real problem was in quality not quantity of credit. State banks made many of their loans in bank notes secured by state bonds (p. 210) which were of varying worth. So many different types of notes circulated that only an expert using one of the illustrated volumes pub-

407

lished to detect counterfeits could set the value of the currency of an out-of-town bank. The cost of such services and the problem of making payments in distant cities were a burden to business.

THE NATIONAL BANKING SYSTEM

The need for a uniform currency and a wider market for government bonds led to the creation of a new banking system during the Civil War. The National Currency Act of 1863 and its complete revision by the National Bank Act of 1864 established the new system. It was based largely on a number of reforms that had taken place in some of the states shortly before, such as note-issues secured by bonds and strict supervision and inspection. Under the national banking law, banks could be organized by five or more persons. They were authorized to issue notes for circulation by purchasing government bonds with their capital stock. Bonds amounting to at least one-third of their capital were required to be deposited with the government. At first the issue of notes was limited to 90 per cent of the face value of these bonds, but a change was made in 1900 to permit circulation up to the full value of the bonds, as long as they stood at par or above par. Meanwhile, state bank notes were put out of circulation by a prohibitive 10 per cent tax. The capital stock required for organizing a national bank varied with the size of the city or community in which it was located. The minimum capital required by the act of 1864 was $50,000 for banks in towns of 6,000 or less; the minimum for the largest cities was $200,000. Under the act of 1900 national banks could be organized with a capital of $25,000 in towns not exceeding 3,000 in population.

Reserve requirements also varied with the size of the community. Seventeen places were designated as "redemption" cities. National banks in these cities had to maintain reserves equal to 25 per cent of their notes and deposits, while banks in other cities were only required to keep reserves of 15 per cent. The Act continued the prevailing state practice of allowing banks to keep part of their reserves in the form of deposits in other banks in the redemption cities. The banks in redemption cities had to keep half their reserves in cash in their own vaults, the banks in other cities only 40 per cent. New York City national banks had to keep all their reserves in cash. An Act in 1874 relieved the national banks of keeping reserves against their notes, which were already secured by government bonds. The varied reserve requirements mirrored the greater need for bank liquidity (ability to pay cash) in major financial centers, since some of the deposits in these centers represented the reserves of other banks. Strict supervision of the banks was provided by a system of examiners, directed by the comptroller of the currency, under the jurisdiction of the Treasury Department.

Until 1913, when the Federal Reserve Act was passed, the Treasury Department had entire administrative control over national banks. It chartered them, printed and issued circulating notes, examined and supervised them, and assumed complete charge when a bank became insolvent. Most of these duties are still carried on by a special bureau under the direction of the comptroller of the currency, although changes have occurred, as for example, the elimination of national bank notes. The Treasurer of the United States has custody of the bonds deposited and performs other duties.

Soon after the national banking system was established, popular opposition to it appeared. Criticism continued throughout the period. In the West, especially, antagonism became pronounced. The banks were not permitted to issue loans on real estate and since this was the only form of property that most farmers possessed, they naturally opposed institutions that were so restricted. Since the practice of using checks spread slowly in the country areas, prohibition of state bank notes made money scarce. In the depressed seventies western farmers demanded "bloodstained" greenbacks in almost limitless quantities in order to secure higher prices for their commodities (p. 392).

Opposition also came from different groups all over the country who believed that the banks received a double profit through the interest on the bonds deposited with the government and the interest on their currency issued on the security of the government bonds. The old cry of monopoly was also heard throughout the land from time to time as critics of the system proclaimed that bank officials and financial interests controlled elections and sent stockholders to Congress. Opposition to the banking system, however, centered in the rural sections of the growing West where population was scattered, the supply of capital small, and distrust of the richer East more deeply rooted.

The national banking system was an improvement over the older heterogeneous state systems that prevailed before the war, and it played a useful role in providing a strong uniform currency for the country during a period of tremendous industrial and agricultural growth. But by the end of the nineteenth century the proportion of state banks not in the national system had increased to such an extent that they greatly exceeded the number of national banks. With checks now the common way of making payments, inability to issue currency was not a serious handicap. Beginning about 1887 changes and improvements were made in state banking laws. As time went on two major faults in the national banking system became more evident. These were the inability of the currency to expand and contract according to the changing needs of business; and the scattered deposit reserves, kept in the banks of the larger cities, which in times of distress resulted in the ruin of good as well as weak banks when the lesser banks demanded a part of their reserves and runs occurred.

THE DEPRESSION OF THE 1870's

As compared to Western Europe the American business cycle continued to have steep ups and downs. Periods of prosperity tended to generate great expectations, dreams that might be fulfilled eventually, but not until another generation. Excessive optimism led to massive investment in producer goods such as railroads, plants, and office buildings. Toward the peak of each major boom, investment exceeded business and private savings and was carried on by inflationary bank credit. This inevitably raised interest rates, prices, and wages. At some point wise entrepreneurs would decide to delay further expansion until costs were less, and the boom would collapse in bankruptcies and stock exchange panics.

The first serious depression after the Civil War began in 1873 and extended over a period of almost five years. While it was largely the result of domestic over-investment and inflated credit, it had many causes and was closely related to world-wide conditions. In 1872 and 1873, booms collapsed in England and France, and foreign investors proceeded to call in their American loans and sell American bonds. These foreign holdings had become excessive from the time of the Civil War, for between 1861 and 1870 the United States had borrowed abroad on national, state, railway, and other securities more than $1,500,000,000, which meant large annual interest charges. French indemnity payments for defeat in the Franco-Prussian War, the failure of railroad speculation in Russia and middle Europe, and commercial dislocations caused by the opening of the Suez Canal, all contributed to Europe's problems, which reacted on the United States.

Within the United States the North after 1865, had gone through a period of rapid expansion, which had resulted in investment in railroads, manufacturing, and building at a rate that exceeded domestic saving. The result was rising interest rates and prices, and increasingly tight credit. At the same time that prices of manufactured goods were advancing, increasing agricultural exports tended to reduce the premium on gold, which meant a smaller return to the farmer in domestic currency. Thus, overspeculation, fluctuating prices, and a large indebtedness brought the country to the brink of disaster. With its great confidence in progress, the United States had again mortgaged itself to the future and a day of reckoning was near.

The element of fear also did its part to extend the depression which affected every operation of finance, industry, transportation, and commerce. The faith of investors—both foreign and domestic—was shaken by the exposures of political, economic, and social corruption during the first administration of President Grant. The disclosures regarding the waste and extravagance of the carpetbag governments in the South which resulted in increasing the debts of the southern states, the Crédit Mobilier scandals in connection with the building of the Union Pacific, the activities of the Whiskey Ring—which included men near the President—in defrauding the government of large amounts of internal revenue taxes, the bribery of the New York judiciary by the Erie Railroad, and the strangle hold of corrupt politicians on the cities, such as the Tweed Ring in New York and the Philadelphia Gasworks ring brought apprehension and undermined the confidence of many in the country's securities and in the economic structure of the nation. The losses in the fires in Chicago, Boston, and Portland also added to the worries of businessmen generally as nerves were stretched taut to the breaking point.

While there had been earlier warnings in the bankruptcy of some financial houses, the panic was precipitated in September, 1873, by the failure of Jay Cooke and Company, which was desperately trying to raise money to continue the construction of the Northern Pacific Railway. The business of the entire nation soon revealed its own instability. Business firms, banks, and industrial corporations failed; manufacturing plants shut down. President Grant hurried to New York to consult with Vanderbilt and other prominent businessmen. The New York Stock Exchange closed its doors for ten days. Bankruptcy overtook a host of companies and individuals. Business failures increased from about 6,000 in 1874, to almost 8,000 in 1875, and to more than 9,000 in 1876. Many railroads went into receivership, and railroad construction practically ceased. In 1875, more than 500,000 men were out of work. Long bread lines and soup kitchens appeared in the cities, and tramps swarmed the countryside. In the absence of organized public relief, private charities did the best they could to aid and keep alive the destitute. During the long depression, wage reductions in the industries that were able to keep going resulted in strikes —especially among the Pennsylvania coal miners, the New England textile operatives, and the nation's railroad workers.

The difficulties in securing currency led to the issuance in many cities of clearinghouse certificates. These were notes secured by the combined credit of the banks that used the clearing house. Owing to the clamor for money, the Secretary of the Treasury, under the stress of the emergency issued additional greenbacks. Congress passed a bill in 1874 for the permanent increase of the paper currency to $400,000,000. President Grant vetoed the measure. The next year an act to resume specie payments was passed, thus adding a further deflationary pressure to falling prices. Its enactment, however, was not part of any far-seeing program. It was essentially a compromise between the inflationists and those who demanded a currency based on gold alone. The amount of greenbacks to remain in circulation was limited to $300,000,000 although this figure was changed in 1878 to that outstanding—a total of $346,681,000.

In 1878 the business curve turned upward. Readjustment had taken place as the depression spent itself. The bumper crops of 1878 and 1879 together with increasing demands from Europe for farm products aided recovery. Manufacturers found new markets in distant lands; machinery, especially, was exported in increasing quantities. The balance of trade improved; gold began to flow in the direction of the United States; foreigners invested in American securities. As railroad and other construction was resumed, employment increased, immigration figures grew larger, and confidence was restored. Good times followed, but were interrupted in 1881, 1884, 1890, and especially after 1893. During the last half of the nineteenth century, periods of prosperity were short and were usually followed by long downward swings. Yet it should be remembered that these business difficulties did not prevent a very high rate of capital formation and economic growth.

THE DEPRESSION OF THE 1890's

The year 1893 marked the beginning of another severe business depression which lasted until 1897. The failure of the English financial house of Baring Brothers in 1890, as a result of the collapse of gold-mining enterprises in South Africa and speculation in Argentine securities, seriously affected the United States. The financial problems that followed forced English investors to sell their American securities, which caused a brief panic at the New York Stock Exchange. The warning that economic conditions were not sound, however, was not heeded. Speculation in stocks and merchandise continued. In 1892, national bank loans rose about $165,000,000. The Sherman Silver Purchase Act of 1890 (p. 399) resulted in increasing a depreciating silver currency. The election of 1892 which brought the Democrats completely into power caused uncertainty and fear among many businessmen regarding the free coinage of silver and a possible reduction in the tariff. The stage was thus set for a depression which left misery, suffering, and distress in its trail.

The failure of the Philadelphia and Reading Railroad in February and the National Cordage Company in May ushered in the panic of 1893. Many banks all over the country suspended business; an increasing number of commercial and industrial failures followed; a stock market panic occurred; the gold reserve of the government fell below the accepted minimum of $100,000,000; business was demoralized. The Erie, Northern Pacific, the Union Pacific, and other railroads followed the Philadelphia and Reading into bankruptcy until one-fourth of the railroad capital was in receivership. In the first year of the panic there were more than 15,000 business failures with liabilities amounting to $437,000,000. During the same year, 158 national banks, and several hundred state and private banks closed their doors. Securities fell in value; the dividends of companies that survived were cut or omitted; factories were shut down; committees were organized in the cities to provide food and relief for large numbers of unemployed; the West suffered through the failure of the corn crop in 1894 as well as the continued decrease of farm prices. One of the chief difficulties of the period was hoarding of currency which made circulation inadequate, and as in the depression of 1873, clearinghouse certificates had to be used in many cities.

The distress of the unemployed led to marches on Washington. The most publicized march was that led by Jacob S. Coxey, a self-made businessman of Massillon, Ohio, who advocated the building of good roads financed by Federal issues of fiat paper money as a means of solving the unemployment problem. Together with Carl Browne, a spectacular and picturesque western associate, Coxey organized "The Commonweal of Christ" and made preparations at Massillon for the journey to Washington to begin on Easter Sunday, 1894. The "petition in boots" or the "living petition" of the unemployed to the capital left on schedule, but instead of the expected 100,000 men only a few hundred reached their destination in spite of extensive advertising, newspaper publicity, and picturesque leaders. On May Day a parade was held in Washington, but when Coxey, Browne, and others advanced toward the steps of the Capitol, they were arrested, tried, convicted, and sent to jail for carrying banners and walking on the grass of the Capitol grounds. Congressmen did not wish to hear their pleas. Other industrial armies were formed as far west as the Pacific coast and ambitiously planned to travel to Washington. The most important were Fry's army from Los Angeles and Kelley's from San Francisco. They took free rides on freight trains that traveled across the plains. Many communities furnished them with provisions and in some cases paid their transportation a part of the way eastward in order to get rid of them. Although thousands joined them along the line of march, not more than 1,000 reached Washington. As in the case of Coxey's army, they found that government officials were not interested in their petitions or in their condition.

Early in the depression the government found itself in difficulties, for expenses proved to be larger than income and it became more and more difficult to maintain the legally required gold reserve of $100,000,000 to cover in part the circulation of greenbacks. Under such conditions, the Treasury was faced with two choices: (1) the borrowing of gold by means of issues of bonds; (2) the redemption of the government's paper currency in silver. The Sherman Silver Purchase Act provided that silver certificates might be redeemed in gold or silver and that it was the policy of the United States to maintain the two metals at a parity with each other. Since silver was selling for much less than the legal ratio between the two metals, everyone demanded redemption in gold. The ebbing gold reserve presented a serious problem since President Cleveland refused to consider redeeming the paper currency only with silver. The depreciated silver dollars would have driven gold out of circulation and put the currency system of the country on a silver basis. This, in turn, would have increased the sums needed for redemption of American gold bonds held abroad, but would probably have stimulated exports. As the first step in the solution of the problem, the President in June, 1893, summoned Congress to meet in special session to repeal the Sherman Silver Purchase Act. After much heated debate and many lengthy speeches, the act was repealed, and the purchase of silver by the government came to an end.

As early as April, 1893, the government's gold reserve fell below the generally accepted safety level of $100,000,000. By January, 1894, in spite of the repeal of the Sherman Act, it had declined to $70,000,000, which was considered by many to endanger continued

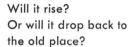

Will it rise?
Or will it drop back to
the old place?

redemption of currency in gold. Under the authority of the Resumption Act of 1875, the Secretary of the Treasury in January, 1894, issued a $50,000,000 ten year series of bonds, at 5 per cent interest, to be sold for gold. A syndicate of New York bankers took the issue which cost them $58,660,000, but as part of the payment, they obtained $24,000,000 in gold from the Treasury in exchange for greenbacks and silver certificates. In November, 1894, another $50,000,000 government bond issue was made, but one-half the gold used to purchase it was likewise secured from the Treasury. Since a large part of the eventual subscribers also withdrew gold from the Treasury to buy the bonds, an "endless chain" was created, and the drain on the gold reserve became serious. In February, 1895, it declined to $41,000,000. It was useless to try to secure gold under ordinary conditions of borrowing and therefore the government made an agreement with J. P. Morgan and a group of bankers for the purchase of 3,500,000 ounces of gold to be paid for with United States 3¾ per cent thirty-year bonds. The bankers agreed to import one-half of the gold, not to withdraw any money from the Treasury, and to use all possible efforts to prevent others from securing Treasury gold. Since the bonds quickly reached 120 on the market, the President was severely criticized by the free silverites and was unjustly accused of being in league with Wall Street interests. A fourth issue in January, 1896, was offered to the public through bids. In spite of this $100,000,000 issue, bearing 4 per cent interest, which was sold at premium of $11,000,000, the reserve did not rise much above the traditional danger line and by July, 1896, fell to $90,000,000. This was due to the speculative hoarding of gold by the public in anticipation of the victory of the bimetallists in the November elections of that year. The victory of the Republicans, who were pledged to a gold standard, brought much of the precious metal from its hiding places in the months that followed. As a result, large amounts found their way to the Treasury. As business conditions improved and revenue income increased, the problem of the endless chain was solved and the reserve could be maintained.

The year 1894 marked the depth of the depression. Bankruptcies, marches the unemployed, strikes, soup kitchens, the condemnation of the new Wilson-Gorman Tariff, the failure of the corn crop, and the widespread belief that trusts were largely responsible for the tragic condition of the country made the year one of the darkest in American history. Many adherents were added to the cause of free silver and the movement, led by the West, gained momentum. While conditions improved in 1895, they deteriorated again in 1896, and it was not until late in the year that the turning point in the economic condition of the country occurred. The result of the election of 1896, which restored confidence to the financial and business interests, the gradual depletion of stocks of manufactured goods, the poor European crops of 1897, which stimulated American exports and gold imports, and the increase in the world's supply of gold through new discoveries, such as those at Klondike, together with improved processes in gold mining—all aided in restoring prosperity.

THE GOLD STANDARD

From December, 1861, to January 1, 1879, the country was on a paper money standard, although government currency bore on its face the promise to pay gold on demand. The currency law of 1873 authorized the free and unlimited coinage of gold and made it full legal tender at a time when the silver dollar was dropped from the list of coins to be minted. But the country remained on a paper basis for almost six more years. Greenbacks and national bank notes comprised the principal money of the period. The nation returned to specie payments at the beginning of 1879 in accordance with the terms of the Resumption Act of 1875. Paper currency then reached a parity with gold.

The struggle for a bimetallic currency, sponsored largely by the

Westerners, which resulted in the silver legislation of 1878 and 1890 (pp. 396, 414), was decided finally by the election of 1896. The victory of the Republicans put an end to the general demand for the free coinage of silver. But it was not until 1900, on the eve of another political campaign, that the pledge for a gold standard was enacted into law. The Gold Standard (or Currency) Act of 1900 remained the basis for the monetary system of the United States until 1933. It provided that the unit of value should be the gold dollar consisting of 25.8 grains of gold, nine-tenths fine; that all other money of the United States should be maintained at a parity with gold, and that a reserve of $150,000,000 in gold should be maintained at all times by the Sceretary of the Treasury. Under this system the mints were opened for the unlimited coinage of gold, and imports and exports of gold were unrestricted.

By adopting a gold standard, the United States, like other nations in a similar position, hoped to give stability to the purchasing power of its money unit and provide a uniform medium for international payments. The value of the legal money unit was tied to the value of a fixed weight of gold. The gold standard, however, was not successful in accomplishing the first objective—stabilizing the domestic price level, for from 1879 to 1933 when it was actually in effect, prices changed considerably. Taking the wholesale prices of 1913 as 100, wide variations may be noted throughout the period. In 1882, the index figure was 98, in 1897, 67, and in 1920, 226. Thus prices declined while the country was on a partial bimetallic base and severe inflation occurred during the period of the gold standard. The lack of price stability was due to many factors other than the monetary base, including the demand for commodities, the activities of producers, the velocity of circulation of checks and cash, and banking practices.

A second reason for the adoption of the gold standard was the expectation of each country to establish the value of its own money unit in a fixed relation to the value of gold units adopted by the other countries. Thus foreign trade and investment could be encouraged and facilitated. This was largely attained. But at the same time, the relations between powerful central banks and governments became closer. The banks, as they learned to control the flow of gold to some degree, came to occupy a position whereby they were able to serve the purposes of their governments, which were not primarily in the interests of international trade. Thus, by the time of the First World War certain practices were being developed within many nations in the direction of the control of gold for the individual benefit of those nations.

BANKING PROBLEMS

A large part of the ultimate reserves of American banks consisted not of cash or specie but of deposits in New York City. The New York banks that held these deposits often had large amounts invested in loans to stockbrokers, and, as a result, withdrawals of these deposits could cause a panic. Both state banks and trust companies had grown in number more rapidly than national banks. In New York City in 1870 there had been 84 national banks in the city and only 24 state banks. By 1910 there were 39 each of national and state banks and 35 trust companies.

The latter were in some cases old institutions, that, as their name implies, had developed for the management of estates. Gradually they found commercial banking a profitable addition to their business. Whereas national banks had to keep a reserve of 25 per cent against deposits and state banks 15 per cent, New York State required only a 5 per cent reserve of trust companies. In 1906 the reserve was raised

NUMBER AND TOTAL ASSETS OF NATIONAL AND STATE BANKS, 1897 – 1914

(Money figures in millions of dollars)

	National Banks		State Banks			National Banks		State Banks	
Year	Number	Total Assets	Number	Total Assets	Year	Number	Total Assets	Number	Total Assets
1897	3,610	3,563	7,828	2,912	1906	6,047	7,781	13,739	7,820
1898	3,581	3,978	7,949	3,193	1907	6,422	8,472	14,939	8,390
1899	3,582	4,709	8,253	3,780	1908	6,817	8,710	15,714	7,954
1900	3,731	4,944	8,696	4,115	1909	6,886	9,365	16,212	8,780
1901	4,163	5,674	9,261	4,897	1910	7,138	9,892	17,376	9,432
1902	4,532	6,007	9,956	5,420	1911	7,270	10,378	17,913	9,941
1903	4,935	6,285	10,879	5,905	1912	7,366	10,857	18,478	10,638
1904	5,330	6,653	11,707	6,382	1913	7,467	11,032	19,197	11,024
1905	5,664	7,325	12,488	7,217	1914	7,518	11,477	19,718	11,679

Source: U.S. Bureau of the Census, *Historical Statistics of the United States, Colonial Times to 1957*, Washington, D.C., 1960, p. 633.

to 15 per cent, but only 5 per cent had to be held in cash. Since the New York Clearing House required higher reserves if trust companies wished to belong, very few did. In addition, trust companies could invest in common stocks.

The dangers in the banking situation had been recognized for many years, but it took the Panic of 1907 to bring them forcefully to the attention of state and Federal governments. From 1897 on the generally prosperous condition of business had fostered a great increase in the number of banks. Some of the new trust companies were deeply involved in stock market manipulations. The panic started with a stock market break and the consequent failure of one of the most vulnerable trust companies. Other failures followed in rapid succession.

The situation was prevented from developing into a serious depression by support given to banks and trust companies by the New York Clearing House, through issuing certificates to its members that they could use in lieu of cash, through the help of strong private interests and the United States Treasury, and perhaps most of all through the assistance of J. P. Morgan and a group of bank and trust company presidents. While the latter type of aid, in the form of large loans, was effective, both the public and many bankers thought it represented a discriminatory type of control of the New York money market by a powerful inner group.

Following the panic, New York State passed a law requiring trust companies to keep a 15 per cent reserve in cash. In 1911, the Clearing House took the larger trust companies into its membership. But, nationally the situation was not improving as state banks steadily grew in number, and the problem of unstable reserves deposited in New York City continued.

MARKETING SECURITIES

The United States grew rapidly because of the high productivity of capital which, in turn, allowed and induced a high rate of capital investment. In the nineteenth century most of the production, saving, and investment was by farmers and other small proprietors for the purpose of improving and expanding family enterprises. Even relatively large companies with a million dollars or more in capital grew chiefly from reinvestment of earnings. Until late in the century the selling of stocks and bonds to the public was largely confined to banks, public utilities, railroads, and governments. In 1900, of the total assets of the United States, estimated at $159 billion, stocks made up only $13.9 billion and corporate bonds, $5.2 billion. Vital as security marketing had been for the expansion of state activities and railroads, it was still a minor mechanism of capital growth.

The public marketing of stocks and bonds was done through investment bankers, and as big companies became more numerous in the eighties and nineties the leading investment firms also became bigger and more important. Occupying the bridgehead between the company needing capital and the investing public, the security sellers were able to dictate financial policy to many public utilities, railroads, and large industrial firms.

Investment banking involved wholesaling of stocks and bonds to big buyers such as banks and insurance companies, and retailing to individual investors or other small buyers. The partners of the investment bank would calculate the price at which the securities could be sold and underwrite the issue at a certain figure for the company needing funds. Since the United States market was limited and relatively unstable, strong connections with investment houses in London, Paris, Amsterdam, or Berlin were essential to safe conduct of this business on a large scale. The half-dozen houses that had such connections dominated security selling in the United States. Outstanding for English and French connections was Drexel, Morgan, formerly J. P. Morgan and Company; chief among the houses with central European ties was Kuhn, Loeb and Company.

Because of the risks involved in marketing a fifty or hundred million dollar security issue the large houses and the scores of banks and brokers who served as retailers generally cooperated in syndicates. The house that had initiated the deal served as the syndicate leader and each of the others agreed to handle a certain number of the securities. Obviously, it was an advantage to the syndicate leader to control a group of outlets such as banks, trust, and insurance companies so that their share in operations could be relied upon. For this reason J. Pierpont Morgan, for example, built up two big trust companies, influenced the financial policy of three of the biggest life insurance companies, and formed a close alliance with the two leading commercial banks. With such outlets Morgan could estimate his market with considerable accuracy.

As the money was received from security sales a deposit was created to the credit of the company being financed. In this way investment bankers came to do commercial banking business, while, as just noted, commercial banks also sold securities. Thus the dividing line between security selling and commercial banking became indistinct by 1900 and remained so until 1933 when the two types of activity were separated by law (p. 571). Since investment houses also held seats on the stock exchange and traded in securities for themselves and their clients, they were stockbrokers as well as bankers.

The reputation of the investment banker rested on the performance of the securities associated with his name. Therefore, it was important for him to try to guide the financial policies of the companies whose stocks and bonds he marketed. To facilitate this continuing relationship the investment banking firm asked for representation on the boards of directors of the companies financed. By 1910, representatives of the leading investment houses sat on the boards of all but a few of the two hundred largest companies in the United States.

The group of financial firms closely associated with J. P. Morgan and Company became so powerful in both finance and the control of railroads, utilities, and big industrial companies that they were investigated by a congressional committee in 1911 and 1912, and condemned as a "Money Trust."

While this concentration of financial power, which also occurred to a considerable extent in England, France, and Germany, was the result of the marketing of securities of big corporations in uncertain, private security markets, in the United States it fulfilled a special need. In the absence of any central banking authority someone had to take the lead in trying to achieve stability in the financial markets. The combination of J. P. Morgan and Company, the National City Bank of New York and their close associates assumed this function. Pierpont Morgan generally assumed the role of leader, and James Stillman, President of the National City Bank, supported him with the largest commercial banking resources in the nation.

To a degree the system achieved its purpose of increasing stability and order in United States money and security markets, but this concentration of private power, noted in connection with the Panic of 1907 was open to criticism from many angles. Criteria of soundness in financing were imposed from above with no possibility of discussion, and often based on an inadequate knowledge of the situation. Banks and financiers approved by Morgan and his friends were favored whereas others were excluded from profitable business or aid in times of trouble. Monopoly, or community of interest as the bankers expressed it, was openly favored, and technological change was often regarded as a menace to financial stability.

In estimating the general economic effects of the "Money Trust," however, it should be remembered that its direct influence reached only to the larger banks and the public marketing of big security issues.

The major areas of trade, service, and light industry, lay beyond the immediate influence of Wall Street. Of 265,000 manufacturing firms in 1910, for example, less than 200 were big enough to be of much concern to investment bankers. The vast majority of American firms were still financed by family capital, that of friends and local business associates, and local bank loans. The public marketing of small issues was a prohibitively expensive process for the ordinary corporation. Some of the power concentrated in Wall Street was ended by the Federal Reserve Act in 1913, and the government financing of the First World War, while no financier assumed J. Pierpont Morgan's leadership after his death in 1913.

THE FEDERAL RESERVE SYSTEM

The Panic of 1907 led to demands in Congress for legislation that would strengthen the banking and currency system of the country and remedy their defects. Many suggestions were considered but finally the Aldrich-Vreeland Bill of 1908 was passed. It aimed to give elasticity to the currency by permitting national banks to issue emergency notes on the security of the bonds of states, counties, cities, and towns or through national currency associations on the pledge of commercial paper. A tax up to 10 per cent a month was intended to discourage abundant issues. The banks did not take advantage of this provision to issue emergency currency until the dark days in the fall of 1914 when the war in Europe upset financial balances all over the world.

The Aldrich-Vreeland Act also authorized the appointment of a National Monetary Commission composed of eighteen members of Congress. The Commission, with Senator Aldrich as chairman, was charged with the duty of investigating the currency and banking systems of the United States and other countries and of suggesting improvements in the existing laws. Experts were appointed to aid in the work, and members of the Commission visited Europe to get first-hand information about the systems of foreign countries.

Early in 1912, the Commission submitted its report to Congress and also the text of a proposed law designed to remedy defects pointed out in the report. Recommendations were made for the establishment of a National Reserve Association, chartered by the Federal government to act as its fiscal agent and also to deal with other banks. To avoid objections to the establishment of a central institution which might dominate local banks it was suggested that district associations of banks be formed, each with a certain degree of independence. It was also proposed ultimately to give the National Reserve Association the sole power of note issue. The Commission published its report in thirty-eight volumes, a most comprehensive banking library. No definite action was taken by Congress in the direction of improving the banking and monetary systems of the country until Woodrow Wilson became President.

President Wilson appeared personally before Congress in 1913 and asked for a measure which would embody the following principles: (1) an elastic currency based on the commercial assets of the country rather than on the bonded indebtedness; (2) a reduction in the number of cities holding bank reserves; (3) strict public control of the banking system; (4) a system that provided for decentralization rather than one headed by a central bank. A bill was drafted by Senator Robert Owen and Carter Glass, chairmen of the Senate and House Committees on Banking and Currency, together with Secretary of the Treasury William G. McAdoo and the President. It represented, however, the ideas of many persons who had been concerned about the financial system of the country for many years. The measure was introduced when the progressive movement was at its height and must be evaluated on the background of enlightened public opinion. In Congress there was general agreement regarding the first two points made by the President, but much opposition to strict government control and to a decentralized system. For six months Congress wrangled over the measure, while important bankers and western farmers severely criticized it. The bill

FEDERAL RESERVE DISTRICTS

was passed toward the close of 1913 and went into operation late the next year.

The Federal Reserve Act provided for a new decentralized system, based on regional lines. Federal Reserve banks were to be created in certain districts, the number eventually being fixed at twelve. Banks were established in Boston, New York, Philadelphia, Cleveland, Richmond, Atlanta, Chicago, St. Louis, Minneapolis, Kansas City, Dallas, and San Francisco. The law provided that each national bank in the country should invest 6 per cent of its capital and surplus in the stock of the Federal Reserve bank of its district, on which dividends of 6 per cent were to be paid; state banks and trust companies were invited, but not required, to join the system. Each reserve bank was to be a depository only for funds of its member banks and at the discretion of the Secretary of the Treasury, for government funds. The member banks were given the right to elect six of the nine directors of the Federal Reserve bank in their district. The Federal Reserve Board, which consisted of the Secretary of the Treasury, and the Comptroller of the Currency, *ex officio,* together with five others appointed by the President, supervised the system and was given power to control the general credit situation and to insure the sound operation of the Federal Reserve banks.

The law provided a means of securing greater currency elasticity through Federal Reserve notes. A member bank could secure Federal Reserve notes in any amount by rediscounting with its Federal Reserve bank the eligible commercial paper of businessmen and others to whom it had made loans. Since the reserve bank would charge for these discounts, banks would only use them when the demand for money was high. In times when large amounts of currency were needed a member bank, therefore, could expand its issues to the amount of its paper eligible for rediscount. The Federal Reserve notes were planned to replace the inelastic national bank notes, which were dependent on government bonds.

The new system was established on the basis of the four points set forth by President Wilson: elasticity of the currency, mobilization of reserves, public control of the banking system, and decentralization. While there was bitter resistance at first from bankers who opposed regimentation of their operations and although the system through amendments and administrative policy moved away somewhat from the democratic ideals of its sponsors, it provided for a superior banking and currency system. It proved its worth in a convincing manner during the First World War and in the years that followed.

CHAPTER 20

The Continuing Growth of Industry

In the late nineteenth century industrial greatness depended physically on iron ore within economic reach of coking coal, and psychologically on able and energetic entrepreneurs who would exploit the physical opportunities. The United States had both these requirements. Its high-grade ore deposits were greater, its bituminous coal more limitless, and its businessmen more committed to using machines than in the other industrial nations. And with the coming of oil as a source of industrial power in the 1890's United States superiority grew even greater.

With these cheap raw materials, including lumber and stone, and other favorable factors, American industrialism progressed mightily. Because of the diversity in bulk and utility between such products as lace and sheet steel it is very hard to decide how to measure the growth of industrial production. The table on page 426 gives a widely accepted index of the growth of manufacturing based on quantity of goods and value added to them by the factory process. Except for the 1890's the rate of growth in the United States increased every decade ultimately leaving other nations far behind.

SOME BASIC TRENDS

Industrialization was the chief force in greatly increasing man-made wealth and annual production of goods and services, or gross

INDUSTRIAL PRODUCTION, 1860 – 1910
(1900 = 100)

Year	Index	Year	Index
1860	16	1890	71
1870	25	1900	100
1880	42	1910	172

Source: Edwin Frickey, *Production in the United States, 1860–1914*, Cambridge, Mass., 1947, p. 54.

national product. Total man-made goods per capita, called reproducible wealth, measured in dollars of constant value rose from $441 in 1850 to $1910 in 1912.

This growth, amazing to the rest of the world, did not occur steadily. Three upward spurts, one in the early fifties, one in the late seventies and early eighties, and one from the late nineties to the early nineteen-hundreds stand out clearly, while the Civil War retarded growth in the sixties. The major increases all coincide with upswings in the business cycle and heavy investment in social overhead capital: primarily railroads in the first two periods, and electrical utilities including street railways in the third period.

In all of this great advance it must be remembered that the industrial sector of the economy was only the generator. Prior to 1914 manufacturing workers did not reach 25 per cent of total workers or manufacturing 25 per cent of the total gross national product. The major activities of the nation were still farm production, services, and trade.

While the United States industrial plant was becoming colossal in size, American scholars were not keeping up with England and Western Europe in basic scientific knowledge, and the understanding of complicated chemical processes. In this stage of American development the factory overshadowed the laboratory, and experience was more highly regarded than learning. Fortunately there were no restrictions on the transfer of knowledge, and Americans dipped into the growing fund of European scientific understanding for practical ideas in metallurgy, electricity, and transportation, often adding ingenious improvements, such as Edison's incandescent light, that had great value.

From the 1880's electricity, metallurgy, and oil presaged a new economic era. By 1914 experimental airplanes, reliable automobiles and trucks, electrically-driven trains and ships, fine tool steels and light alloys, telephones, power stations and the wireless were all in use, but the great impact of this new technology was only beginning.

In contrast, bigness in business organization had reached maturity by the First World War. The size of the American market opened by the railroads, and the savings that could be made through large-scale production and marketing encouraged the growth of the best located and most efficient companies at the expense of their competitors. Hence by 1890 companies like Standard Oil and American Sugar Refining were doing over 90 per cent of the business in their respective fields. The fear that all production might be monopolized by giant firms fostered a strong antitrust movement (see Chapter 22), that checked monopoly but often left two or more companies so strong that they could control price and production policies. Because it was the chief financial market, the biggest companies moved their head offices to New York City, but everywhere the movement in industrial business was from the smaller towns to the major industrial centers.

ENLARGING MARKETS

A most important factor in the expansion of industry and business was the continually increasing demand for products of all sorts. Population increased tremendously through the growing birth rate and immigration. In 1850, the population of the country was 23,261,000; by 1900, it had reached 75,995,000; in 1910 it was 91,972,000; and in 1920, 105,711,000. The continual stream of immigration supplied the demand for laborers necessary for industrial expansion and at the same time built up markets which would take the increased production. Many immigrants passed by the industrial regions and joined the native-born in taking up homesteads in the West, thus creating new markets for manufactured goods in the agricultural regions of the country. Improvement in living conditions also helped the domestic market. Prosperous farmers and well-paid skilled workers probably created a larger middle-income group than elsewhere in the world.[1]

The fact that interstate commerce could be carried on unhampered by custom duties or racial prejudices was important in the development of industrial life in America. Goods were transferred from section to section without much regulatory hindrance. The economic growth of the nation gave rise to a movement for uniform state legislation which was partly achieved in the field of commerce during this period.

[1] H. J. Habakkuk, *American & British Technology in the Nineteenth Century* (Cambridge, Mass., 1962), p. 124.

Foreign markets also expanded. Between 1860 and 1914, American foreign trade increased approximately eight times in value. Exports of crude materials grew in volume but not in proportion to the increase in export of other commodities. Exports of manufactured or semi-finished goods in 1871–1875 were 20 per cent of total exports; in 1911–1915, they were 46 per cent. The increasing exportation of manufactured goods, together with the high protective tariff policy, resulted in a relative decline in exports to Europe. In 1881–1885, almost 81 per cent of American exports went to Europe; in 1911–1915, only 61 per cent. New markets opened in Asia, Canada, and Latin America. In addition to wheat, cotton, grain, petroleum, animal products, tobacco, lumber, naval stores, and metals, manufactures of all sorts were exported.

THE EXPLOITATION OF NATURAL RESOURCES

In the period following the Civil War, natural resources were exploited as never before, contributing to the industrial expansion (see Chapter 16). Coal, necessary for the production of steam, in the new age of industrialization and railroad transportation, was mined in ever-increasing quantities. Because of abundant wood, however, it had come to use very slowly. In the seventeenth century, French explorers, including Jolliet, Marquette, and Hennepin, were the first to note its presence in this country; they pointed out that there was much of it in the region that is now Illinois. The commercial mining of bituminous coal first began in the Richmond basin of Virginia about 1750 and for many years this was the only important source of coal in America. But there was no demand for coal except from a few blacksmiths. Partly, also, because of the difficulties of transportation, markets for bituminous coal did not broaden until after 1820. Mines were opened up in Illinois, Maryland, Kentucky, Ohio, and Pennsylvania. In 1850, 4,000,000 tons[2] were produced annually, and through 1890 the amount more than doubled each decade.

Anthracite, or hard coal, was first used by blacksmiths in the Wilkes-Barre region of Pennsylvania in the last years of the colonial period. During the Revolution, anthracite was shipped to the gun-lock factory at the Carlisle Armory. But it was not until the nineteenth century that it came into general use. In 1808, Jesse Fall of Wilkes-Barre, who twenty years earlier had demonstrated its possibilities as a fuel in nail manufacturing, now related it to domestic life by burning it in an open grate with a natural draft. But from 1808 to 1820, the

---

[2] All statistics relating to coal and coke are given in short tons (2,000 pounds).

total output was but 12,000 tons. By 1840, nearly 1,000,000 tons of anthracite were mined annually and ten times this amount in 1860.

During the period from 1860 to 1914, both anthracite and bituminous coal were mined extensively, unfortunately by the most wasteful methods. Coal was employed to produce steam for factory purposes; it was used by the thousands of locomotives that carried passengers and freight all over the country; it was the chief fuel for heating and cooking in homes. As coke displaced charcoal as a blast furnace fuel, large quantities of bituminous coal were used in the form of coke in the iron industry. More than 6,000,000 tons of coke were shipped from the Connellsville region in 1890, and coke ovens were springing up in other sections. By 1914, about 40,000,000 tons of coke were produced in the country annually. In 1890 nearly 160,000,000 tons of coal were mined in the United States—45,000,000 tons of anthracite and 111,000,000 tons of bituminous. The total was more than 25 per cent of the production of the entire world. The annual average reached by 1914 amounted to 510,000,000, of which 90,000,000 tons were anthracite and 420,000,000 tons bituminous.

The petroleum industry also developed at a remarkable rate. Long before "Colonel" Edwin L. Drake drilled the first well in Titusville in 1859, the Indians first and later the white settlers of northwestern Pennsylvania used petroleum as a medicine and at times for lighting, although it burned with a smoky flame and an offensive odor. Oil was obtained from seepages along Oil Creek and the Allegheny River, and occasionally when salt wells were drilled. But it was chiefly sold as a cure for rheumatism, headaches, coughs, colds, sprains, toothaches, and other human ailments. By 1850, Samuel M. Kier, a Pittsburgh druggist, had succeeded in "double-distilling" it and was selling it also as an "illuminant." The first scientific report on the chemical and physical properties of Pennsylvania "rock oil" was made in 1855 by Benjamin Silliman, Jr. at the request of Jonathan G. Eveleth and George H. Bissell. Silliman pointed out the commercial possibilities of the oil. Experiments were also made in refining it. Eveleth and Bissell organized the Pennsylvania Rock Oil Company of New York, which was followed by the Pennsylvania Rock Oil Company of Connecticut. A group of the Connecticut stockholders, under the leadership of James M. Townsend, formed the Seneca Oil Company, leased a plot of land on Oil Creek near Titusville, engaged Drake to supervise the work, and hired two brine-well drillers to sink the well. Work was completed when a depth of sixty-nine and one-half feet was reached; initial production was about twenty-five barrels a day. This marked the beginning of the petroleum industry.

The success of Drake led to an oil boom. Thousands flocked to the region of Oil City. Farmers granted rights to individuals and companies to drill on their lands in return for a royalty of one-eighth to one-fourth of the oil produced, lands were leased by groups of speculators, and those who sought to purchase land found that prices quickly soared. By 1862, production exceeded 100 million gallons per year. Many of the early wells were drilled by the spring-pole method, although in time steam was applied to cable tool-drilling rigs. On the tops of derricks, flags and signs with strange mottoes were placed, including such slogans as "Hell or China," symbolizing the determination of the drillers to strike oil regardless of where it might be found. At first crude oil was transported by teams and barges, but soon railroads were built and pipelines came into use. Mushroom towns sprang up, like Pithole, whose population increased from less than 100 to 14,000 between January and September, 1865, but whose population quickly dispersed to other areas when production declined, leaving it a ghost town. Hundreds of companies were organized, some of which returned rich profits to their stockholders, while a larger number failed completely. During the first few years of the oil boom, buyers and sellers of petroleum gathered in hotels and on streets in Titusville, Oil City, and other centers to carry out their transactions. An Oil Dealers' Exchange was established at Petroleum Center in 1867, and four years later several exchanges were opened in the oil regions. Pennsylvania remained the chief source of oil for many years, but small quantities were also produced in New York, Ohio, West Virginia, Kentucky, Tennessee, and California. After 1884, the production of petroleum in Ohio and West Virginia expanded. Ten years later Wyoming began producing oil, and, at the turn of the century, the development of oil lands had been begun in Texas, Indian Territory (Oklahoma), Kansas, Louisiana, and Illinois. Early in the twentieth century, increasing quantities were obtained in Colorado, Indiana, Kansas, and Texas.

A new era in iron mining began with the opening up of the Lake Superior regions. As early as the eighteenth century, there were rumors of mineral wealth in this section, for Indians had used the reddish oxide from exposed iron and copper ores as pigment for their war paints. Even after the discovery of deposits of ore in 1844 by United States government surveyors near what is now Marquette, few realized the economic importance of this region. Although some small shipments were made to the East prior to 1856, the vast deposits were not widely developed until the period after the Civil War. In the decades that followed the war, many other ranges were opened up in Michigan and Minnesota, including the Menominee, Gogebic, Vermilion, Mesabi, and Cuyuna. The iron deposits of the Lake Superior region vary considerably both in quality and in accessibility. Some are soft and loose; others are hard and fairly difficult to mine. Some are found close to the surface and the soft ones are scooped up from great pits by steam and electric shovels, particularly in the Mesabi region; others occur at greater depths and are mined by shaft and underground methods. The story of the exploitation of these vast deposits include the rapid rise of mining towns, the problems incident to creating a civilization in the wilderness, the mingling of different races, advances in the technology of mining, tragic mine disasters, the superstitions of the workers, serious labor disputes and strikes, unsuccessful attempts to smelt the ores in mining areas, and the development of transporting ores to the East by way of the Great Lakes.

Further west, in the area of the Rocky Mountains, gold and silver mines were opened up and copper, lead, nickel, and other metals were obtained (p. 351). From the 1850's on, the exploitation of mineral wealth expanded tremendously. Without the vast quantities of metals and minerals industrial life in the East could not have made such rapid progress. Thus a most remarkable economic development took place at the same time in both the East and the West.

INVENTIONS AND TECHNOLOGICAL IMPROVEMENTS

As industrialism spread it speeded technological advance. The increasing number of patents illustrates the interest in technology. In the decade 1860–1869, the Patent Office granted 77,355 patents; during the years 1890–1899, this number had increased to 234,749. Among the many inventions of the period that influenced social and economic change were the air brake (1869) of George Westinghouse and a number of patents leading to automatic braking of trains; barbed wire (1874), invented by Joseph F. Glidden, which made possible the cheap and efficient fencing of vast areas of western lands; the telephone (1876) by Alexander Graham Bell and Elisha Gray, resulting in a new type of rapid communication that brought remarkable changes to social and business life; the phonograph (1877) and the incandescent lamp (1879) by Thomas A. Edison; and the dynamo and arc light developed by C. F. Brush and Elihu Thomson. In the 1880's and 1890's the trolley car, the automobile, the cash register, transparent film, electrical welding, the steam turbine, and the electric furnace were invented or introduced.

Even by 1876, remarkable progress had been made. In that year, the wonders of the industrial development of the preceding century were shown to the public at the Centennial Exposition held in Philadelphia, marking the one hundredth anniversary of the Declaration of Independence. This was the first great international exposition held in America. Altogether thirty-seven foreign nations constructed buildings and the exposition housed more than 30,000 exhibitors from fifty nations. The seven principal divisions of exhibits were mining and metallurgy, manufactured products, science and education, fine arts, machinery, agriculture, and horticulture. The Woman's Building, something new in expositions, pointed significantly toward the emancipation of women. Three-fourths of the space in Machinery Hall was taken up by American machinery and mechanical contrivances of all sorts. Visitors were thrilled by the exhibits which varied from small household appliances to the great Corliss steam engine that provided the power for driving the machinery. American ingenuity showed its pre-eminence and demonstrated that the United States was fast becoming a manufacturing nation. Foreign goods and materials also were of much interest and later influenced interior decoration; the superiority of certain types of European goods showed the weaknesses in similar American products. The exposition set a pattern for many others held in large cities to commemorate anniversaries.

Thousands of inventions directly affected manufactures during this period and resulted in improved industrial processes. The most significant of these was in the production of steel, which gradually replaced much of the iron which had formerly been used. Until this period, relatively small amounts of blister and crucible steel were produced and were used chiefly in making cutlery and the finer grades of tools. New methods now resulted in spectacular changes. The Bessemer process was invented in England by Henry Bessemer, who applied for an American patent in 1856. William Kelly of Eddyville, Kentucky, who had been working on the same idea for ten years, objected and proved his claim of priority in an American court. He received a patent for his "pneumatic process" in 1857. Devoid of business ability and unable to develop interest in his invention at a time when sectional antagonism brought the forces of industry and the slave plantation to a bloody civil war, he did little more than continue his experiments. While Bessemer could not obtain a patent for his process in the United States, he was able to secure one for his improved converter in 1865. Abram Hewitt and Alexander Holley received the right to manufacture steel from Bessemer, although the

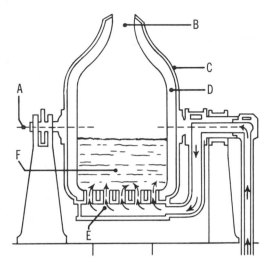

THE BESSEMER CONVERTER

A. Axis upon which the converter turns when it is tilted to pour out the molten metal.   B. Spout. It is from this spout that one sees issuing the burst of flame and the outpouring of sparks when the converted is in operation.   C. Outer steel casing. D. Lining of siliceous rock or other material.   E. Air entering through the holes of the false bottom. F. Molten iron.

former was skeptical of the process. About the same time Ward and Durfee bought the rights to manufacture steel under Kelly's patent and, strangely enough, also acquired the American rights to Mushet's improvement on Bessemer's invention. Both groups began making steel, the former at Troy, New York, and the Kelly Pneumatic Process Company at Wyandotte, Michigan. In 1866, the struggle came to an end when the two groups compromised their conflicting claims and the American method thereafter became known as the Bessemer process.

The new method was relatively simple in principle. By blowing a stream of cold air through molten iron, the carbon was burned out, as an orange-yellow flame tinged with blue burst into a brighter one, accompanied by streams of sparks from the converter. As the flame died down "spiegeleisen," containing carbon, manganese, silicon, iron, lime, zinc and magnesia, was added. During his early experiments Bessemer tried to stop the blast of air when he thought a sufficient amount of carbon and other substances had been eliminated, with the result that too much or too little carbon remained. European inventions led to more reliable quality in steel. Mushet improved the process by adding "spiegeleisen," thus permitting the control of the percentage of carbon needed for different types of steel. The Thomas-Gilchrist process, which substituted a basic limestone lining for the acid lining of the converter, made possible the application of the process to iron containing a high degree of phosphorus. The Bessemer process, plus cheap coke allowed United States steel men to increase volume and offset lower English wages. By 1880 American production of steel was ahead of British.

Another method for making large quantities of steel reached the United States in the late 1860's. This was the Siemens-Martin or open-hearth process. Much slower than the Bessemer method, it proved to be more advantageous, for it could be watched more easily in the relatively shallow bowl of the large furnace. Thus, samples could be taken from time to time; the flame might be shut off whenever the right carbon content appeared and the regulation of the molten metal was much easier than in the Bessemer process. After 1908, most of the steel made in the United States was produced by the open-hearth method. By 1900, the total production of steel of all types in this country exceeded 10,000,000 tons annually. In 1914, the manufacture of steel reached 23,485,900 tons. Of this, 17,175,000 tons were Bessemer, 6,221,000 were open-hearth, and 89,900 crucible steel.[3]

Innumerable inventions increased efficiency in textile factories, and machinery became increasingly automatic. A series of changes led to the Northrop loom in cotton manufacture, which inaugurated fundamental improvements in regard to quick-changing mechanisms and warp-stopping devices. Similar changes occurred in the other textile industries.

From the 1850's on, American machine tools became the world's cheapest and best. Because the United States market was big and tools more widely used, manufacturers were able to specialize. Single-purpose turret lathes or milling machines were cheaper and more efficient than multi-purpose British machines. By 1880, American tools were about half the price of British.

In the food-producing industries, a few illustrations will suggest the revolutionary changes brought about by improved technology. The "roller process" avoided discoloration in grinding wheat into flour by obtaining more separation of kernel and husk. Inventions in the manufacture of tin containers led to completely automatic can-making machinery. European machines for making artificial ice were improved upon, and by 1900 about 4,500 patents had been granted in the United States for various processes of refrigeration, 700 of them relating directly to ice machines. Almost all industries were affected by more automatic machinery.

---

[3] Expressed in terms of long tons of 2,240 pounds.

Improvements also occurred in motive power. During this period steam came into general industrial use. The old-fashioned water wheel became increasingly rare. Among the inventors who improved the steam engine, the name of George H. Corliss ranks high, for his invention of the cut-off mechanism by which valves could be opened and closed instantaneously and automatically was important. Another American inventor, Charles Curtiss, combined the ideas of Gustaf de Laval, a Swedish engineer, and Charles A. Parsons, an English engineer, in producing an improved steam turbine. In the turbine, steam was forced directly against the "buckets" or vanes on a spindle revolving in a cylinder, rather than against a piston; hence no large flywheel was necessary. In the nineties a major change began in sources of energy. The gas engine was used, deriving its power at first from exploding a mixture of coal gas with air. Many different types of coal gas engines appeared, which paved the way for the gasoline engine, making possible the modern automobile. In 1898, Dr. Rudolph Diesel, a German scientist, obtained a United States patent for his engine which could use a heavier and cheaper grade of oil, and in the twentieth century the Diesel engine appeared. The new age was also marked by the rapidly increasing use of both coal-generated and hydro-generated electricity.

Plant procedures were another aspect of technology that made rapid progress after 1890. Frederick W. Taylor, an engineer trained in steel manufacture, observed the inefficiency of human movements and material flows in large plants. Setting himself up as a consultant he gradually developed a system involving specialized foremen, time-motion analyses of worker efficiency, and wage payments based on productivity which he called "scientific management." By 1910, many plants were adopting parts of his system, and his book, *Scientific Management,* published in 1911 was read throughout the western world. Meanwhile, his ideas were taken up by others and a new profession of management advice began to flourish leading to highly important ideas regarding quality control and the measurement of productivity (p. 548).

A POLICY OF TARIFF PROTECTION

At the developmental stage of the United States in the late nineteenth century tariff protection was probably an aid to industrial growth. The years prior to the Civil War were marked by low tariffs in spite of the struggle by industrialists for protection. This was due principally to the fact that the agricultural sections, especially the

South, dominated. With the Civil War, however, the balance shifted. The rising industrial East now wielded power, and a policy of protection was inaugurated and maintained.

The Morrill Tariff, passed in 1861 on the eve of conflict, increased rates for the purpose of obtaining more revenue for the struggle. From time to time during the war, custom duties were raised, so that at its close many schedules were highly protective. While at first the necessity for more revenue was the motive for tariff increases, the argument was later advanced that domestic industries, which had to pay heavy war taxes, should be protected from competition with foreign goods by increasing custom duties.

After the war, the question of the tariff policy again became controversial. In the agricultural parts of the West, sentiment was strongly against the high levels that had been reached. When the proposal to reduce the tariff was made in Congress, an outcry arose from the manufacturing interests and every effort was put forth not only to maintain the high wartime duties, but to increase them on behalf of special industries. Swarms of lobbyists descended on Washington, led by such men as John L. Hayes, secretary of the National Association of Wool Manufacturers. In Congress, William D. Kelley of Pennsylvania championed extreme protection and his persistent support of duties on iron won him the sobriquet, "Pig Iron Kelley." On the other hand, in order to oppose a high tariff policy, the American Free Trade League was formed and included a number of influential writers and editors. Many congressmen took the middle course and approved the sentiments uttered by John Sherman that Congress should "dismiss to future generations extreme ideas of free trade and protection, which are inconsistent with a revenue system." The conflict of opinion within both parties resulted in failure to make any drastic modifications of any kind in the trend that had developed during the war. The high level remained.

The changes of 1869 and 1870 in no way affected the high tariff policy. Some duties were slightly reduced, but increases were made on copper, marble, flax, and a few other commodities, while a small reduction on pig iron was offset by an increase on steel rails. The discontent among western farmers and the growth of the Liberal Republican movement in 1872 with its advocacy of a reduced tariff frightened the protectionist leaders in Congress to such an extent that on the eve of the political campaign of that year a horizontal cut of 10 per cent was made. In addition, duties on tea and coffee were abolished and the free list of raw materials was slightly extended. This hasty and ill-advised law resulted in difficulties. The loss of duties on tea and coffee in the years of industrial depression that followed cut off an annual income of $20,000,000 and customs receipts as a whole fell from $216,000,000 in 1872 to $163,000,000 in 1874. In 1875, duties were restored to their former level where they remained for almost a decade.

Many factors contributed to the failure of tariff reform: the pre-occupation of Congress in the struggle with President Johnson in the reconstruction of the southern states; the repeal of internal revenue taxes and the fear that a simultaneous reduction of import taxes would seriously affect the government's revenue; the fact that party lines were not clearly differentiated in regard to the tariff; the political weakness of the South, which was not at first fully represented in Congress; and the growing belief of many Americans that high tariffs were necessary to prosperity resulted in a protective policy, which became a permanent political issue.

In 1882, the government was in an unusual financial position, for there was a large surplus in the treasury. Alignment in Republican and Democratic ranks over the tariff was not yet clear-cut, for a group of eastern Democrats, chiefly from Pennsylvania and New Jersey, did not favor reduction, while a number of Republicans in the West did so. Congress authorized a tariff commission to recommend changes. This was a new method of approaching the tariff. The commission appointed by President Arthur, however, was made up of protectionists with John L. Hayes, of the National Association of Wool Manufacturers, as its chairman. It seemed obvious that the high tariff was to be reformed by its friends. The commission junketed around the country, holding hearings at more than a score of cities and examining several hundred witnesses. Its report was a surprise as it reached the conclusion: "No rates of defensive duties except for the establishment of new industries which more than equalize the conditions of labor and capital with those of foreign competitors can be justified." It recommended reductions up to 50 per cent, but the average was from 20 to 25 per cent. However, the recommendations on the whole applied to necessities rather than to luxuries, and to raw materials chiefly instead of manufactured goods. As Congress got busy on a bill, lobbyists poured into Washington to guard the interests of pig iron, steel, sugar, wool, and other products. The measure provided for a further reduction of internal revenue taxes. In regard to customs duties, the law of 1883 in general reduced rates only about 4 per cent. Duties were increased on some commodities and reduced on others. *The Nation* condemned the law and characterized its schedules as "taking a shaving off the duty on iron wire and adding it to the duty on glue."

In 1885, President Cleveland, the first Democratic Party President since Buchanan, recommended a reduction of the tariff and two years later devoted his entire annual address to Congress to it. This novel message surprised the country. He stated that information on the various aspects of the state of the nation could be found in the reports of the various departments and then plunged into a discussion of the tariff which he declared was a system of "unnecessary taxation, . . . vicious, inequitable, and illogical." He stressed the fact that the income of the government exceeded its needs and that the surplus was increasing. He maintained that the high tariff policy raised prices of all goods; that it was not needed to keep up wages since only 2,630,000 workers out of 17,392,000 were employed in protected industries; that it injured the farmer as well as the laborer; that it increased prices of raw materials and hindered export trade; and that its complicated schedules were senseless. He did not advocate free trade, but insisted that a drastic reduction of the tariff was necessary.

Following Cleveland's message, the Mills Bill, patterned after his suggestion, was introduced into the House where it passed with only four dissenting votes among the Democrats. The Republican-controlled Senate refused to consider the bill and attempted to work out a measure of its own but without success.

The tariff was a dominant issue in the campaign of 1888. The Republicans won by a narrow margin and began work to redeem their campaign pledges. The McKinley Tariff of 1890 was the result. Throughout the debates the protectionist philosophy was developed to its highest point. With the aid of the rules of "Czar" Thomas B. Reed, the Speaker of the House and of the votes of western Senators who received in exchange eastern votes for the Sherman Silver Purchase Act, the law was passed and an acme of protection reached. While duties on steel rails, steel plates, and iron were slightly reduced, and a number of commodities of little commercial importance were added to the free list, the McKinley Tariff of 1890 increased duties on wool, woolen goods, and dress goods, especially on the finer grades. Higher duties were imposed on linens, silk laces, plush goods, cutlery, and many other types of manufactured goods. A political gesture was made to the farming interests when the protective principle was applied to agricultural products, but the duties levied on wheat, corn, potatoes, flax, and other products were not of great importance to the farmer, since few agricultural staples were imported. To encourage the manufacture of tin plate, duties of about 70 per cent were imposed (p. 443). In order to reduce the government's income, raw sugar was to be admitted free; to placate domestic sugar growers a bounty of two cents a pound was granted on the production of sugar within the United States. A reciprocity clause provided that the President alone could impose duties on sugar, molasses, tea, coffee, and hides if he considered that any country exporting these commodities to the United States imposed unjust duties on the products of the United States. Reciprocity, therefore, became a club to force Central and South American nations to grant concessions and make agreements, although it was adopted largely through Blaine's influence as a part of his plan for a Pan-American commercial union.

The McKinley Tariff measured up to the expectation of its framers; in fact, in several respects it worked in a way undreamed of by them. The loss of revenue on sugar and the prohibitory rates on some schedules, together with the lavish expenditures of Congress, wiped out the surplus in two years; a deficit appeared as the country was plunged into the Panic of 1893. Other clauses worked out to better advantage. A new tin-plate industry was born and made remarkable progress. The reciprocity clause resulted in agreements with Brazil, the Dominican Republic, Cuba, Puerto Rico, Guatemala, Salvador, the German Empire, some of Great Britain's colonies, Nicaragua, Honduras, and Austria-Hungary. But the high rates of the tariff, reflected soon after its passage in higher retail prices, together with objection to many parts of the law, caused widespread dissatisfaction. The election which came a little more than a month after the measure went into effect brought disaster to the Republicans, who lost control of the House; even McKinley himself was one of the defeated candidates. In the presidential election of 1892, the Democrats, led by Cleveland, were victorious.

The change of political party was responsible for the Wilson-Gorman Act of 1894. For the first time since the Civil War, the Democratic Party had majorities in both Houses of Congress and also controlled the Presidency. The majority in the Senate, however, was slight. Since the Democrats had come into power largely on the tariff issue, Cleveland pressed for a downward revision of the tariff. It was an inauspicious time for a drastic change for several reasons, including a government deficit, falling revenue, the industrial depression, uncertainty on the part of businessmen, and continued labor unrest. The measure, as it was brought into the House, provided for considerable reductions on most schedules. Because of the financial situation of the government provision was made for a tax on incomes over $4,000. In the Senate the bill was so amended by those desiring to protect the industries of their constituents that it was completely changed from its original form. The Republicans ridiculed these attempts of the Democrats at tariff making. One Republican Senator stated: "The framers of the Wilson Bill having classified hydraulic hose among articles of wearing apparel will no doubt remodel that extraordinary measure so as to include hydraulic rams and spinning mules in the livestock schedule." In the Senate, 634 changes were made, restoring the protective principle throughout and outweighing any principle of reform. In spite of the attitude and opposition of the President, the House agreed to the changes. Cleveland did not sign the bill, but permitted it to become law without his signature.

With the change of party control in 1897, another tariff was made. Four years of depression had resulted in a Republican victory. Although the chief issue in the campaign had centered on the question of the free coinage of silver versus the gold standard, the victors began work on the tariff. The Dingley law of 1897 advanced rates on dutiable goods about 50 per cent, but through no merits or faults of its own, it marked the beginning of good times. In the years that followed congressional attention was turned to questions of imperialism and other issues. Not until the political campaign of 1908 did the tariff issue again become really important.

From time to time during the administrations of Theodore Roosevent rumblings against the protective tariff were heard in the Middle Border. The "Iowa Idea" was widely accepted in that part of the country. It purported that the tariff was the mother of trusts and that the way to prevent monopolies was to reduce it. The high cost of living and the tariff were discussed in the politcal campaign of 1908; both major parties promised, if elected, to revise the protective tariff. At the very beginning of his administration President Taft called Congress into special session. In accord with his recommendations a bill providing for a much lower tariff passed the House. Under Senator Aldrich's leadership, the Senate pounced upon the measure and finally made 847 amendments to it, most of them for increased duties. In spite of the opposition of the rising "insurgents" under Robert M. La Follette of Wisconsin, the policy of high protection continued. The Payne-Aldrich Tariff of 1909 made a few reductions and abolished the duty on hides and some other commodities. But the average rate on dutiable goods was almost the same as under the Dingley measure it superseded. The law empowered the President to impose a maximum scale of duties on imports from countries which discriminated against American trade; it provided for a tariff board to aid the President in penalizing such imports; and it levied a low tax on the net earnings of corporations. The board disappeared after three years, having made only three reports.

The first important change in the tariff policy since the Civil War was made in 1913, when the Democratic Party redeemed its pledge to reduce the tariff. President Wilson did not ask Congress for a free trade measure. He suggested adherence to the revenue principle and cautioned against sudden and ruinous reductions without giving business time to make adjustments. The Underwood Tariff brought the average rates down to about 30 per cent on dutiable commodities. On 958 articles the duties were reduced; on 307 they were unchanged; and on eighty-six—such as chemicals—they were increased. Reductions were made on some agricultural products and others were placed on the free list in an attempt to decrease the cost of living. The duty on sugar was to be gradually reduced and taken off entirely in 1916. An income tax clause, now made possible by the Sixteenth Amendment, provided for additional revenue. The tariff board, which had been allowed to lapse, was revived in 1916 through the appointment of a bi-partisan commission.

THE RISE OF SOME KEY MANUFACTURING INDUSTRIES

After the Civil War, the age of iron gave way to the age of steel. Prior to this period the small amounts of blister and crucible steel, painfully and expensively produced, were used chiefly in making cutlery, the best grades of tools, and different types of weapons. The Bessemer and open-hearth processes revolutionized the iron industry and provided material that could be used for a variety of purposes and at low cost. Advances were made in the production of steel so that it could be made soft and ductile or hard enough to scratch glass. It could be made tough and resilient for springs or pliable for tin cans; it could be made strong enough to be rolled into great structural beams for skyscrapers or drawn into wire for a fine-mesh wire cloth. It could be rendered magnetic or non-magnetic and also resistant to heat, cold, or rust. Steel came to be woven into the very fabric of America's material civilization as railroad trains, ocean vessels, skyscrapers, factories, bridges, pipe lines, power lines, machinery, and automobiles were made of it.

Iron, of course, was necessary in the production of steel. The principle of making pig or cast iron by smelting it in tall furnaces did not change. The small stone, cold-blast, charcoal furnaces gave way to larger ones using coke as a fuel. The new ones were built of steel and many towered 100 feet or more. They possessed four huge heating stoves, blowing engines that delivered thousands of cubic feet of blast each minute, many tuyeres, an array of dust arresters, gas washers, and automatic ore and coke handling machinery, all essentials of the giants of modern metallurgical devices. At many furnaces, the centuries-old method of casting pig iron in sand continued, but in the larger works, the molten iron from the blast furnace was run into large ladles and moved immediately to the open-hearth furnace or Bessemer converter to be made into steel. After having undergone one of these processes, or a duplex process—a combination of both— the molten steel was poured into molds.

After a strong crust developed on the steel, the molds were pulled on cars to the stripper, where they were removed, leaving white-hot ingots. These were taken to the gas-fired soaking pits where their molten interiors gradually solidified by cooling, while the outer parts were reheated. After equalizing the temperatures of the interiors and exteriors, the hot ingots were ready for rolling directly into rails, plates, slabs, billets, and other shapes before being allowed to cool. Since 1914, the trend toward integrating the processes within one plant has continued. Modern steel works include blast furnaces, Bessemer converters, open-hearth furnaces, rolling mills, coke ovens with by-product plants, as well as foundries and machine shops.

At the coke ovens in large steel plants and elsewhere, the by-products of coal became exceedingly important. Rich coal-gas, used as fuel in the steel furnaces, was the main by-product of coke produced at mills. Coal tar, also, became important, for it was used not only for building purposes, but from it a large variety of beautiful dyes and fragrant perfumes could be manufactured. Among many other derivatives of coal tar, such chemicals as ammonia, naphthaline, benzol, and phenol were manufactured. Research in recent years has also led to medical derivatives of many kinds, such as novocaine, an anesthetic, and sulfanilamide, sulfapyridine and sulfathiazole, used in treating pneumonia, meningitis, and septicemia. An endless variety of products came to be made from the gases and vapors liberated when coal was coked, which formerly were permitted to escape in smoke. In addition to dyes, perfumes, and medicines, products such as T.N.T., nylon, aspirin, billiard balls, smelling salts, and fertilizers were made from coal, which formerly was valued only as a fuel.

In spite of the economics of large-scale production and distribution, there were still hundreds of small steel companies in 1898. During the next few years, however, mergers took place that left only a dozen large general firms, together with many small manufacturers of special types of steel. United States Steel, formed in 1901 from eight companies, dominated production. At the start it made 72 per cent of all Bessemer and 60 per cent of all open-hearth steel. While its share was to drop below 50 per cent in succeeding decades, United States Steel continued to set the general price policies of the industry.

While the head offices of United States Steel and some of the other companies were in New York, the Pittsburgh-Youngstown-Cleveland area came to be the heart of the iron and steel production. Here, and in the Buffalo, Chicago, Detroit, and St. Louis regions, iron and steel were produced from the ores of the Lake Superior region. In the coastal area north of Baltimore, most of the ores used were local or were imported from South America, Cuba, and Sweden. The Birmingham, Alabama, district was unique in that ore and coking coal were adjacent; hence a minimum of transportation was necessary. In the Tennessee region and in scattered far western areas, such as Pueblo, Colorado and Provo, Utah, local ores were largely used.

Many industries developed in connection with the production of steel. One of the most striking was the manufacture of tin plate. Small quantities of tin plate had been made in the late colonial period as small hammered iron sheets were coated with tin obtained from England. The industry made no progress and died in the early nineteenth century. Quantities of tin plate were imported chiefly from Great Britain; these increased greatly from the period beginning with the Civil War. Attempts were then made to establish a tin plate industry in the United States, but the companies could not compete with foreign importations. All the plants stopped operating before 1878. The McKinley Tariff of 1890 placed a duty of 2.2 cents a pound on imported tin plate, not to protect an industry but to create one. The law provided that the duty should cease after 1897 unless domestic production reached specified amounts. The provisions of the McKinley Act relating to tin plate attracted capital, machinery, and workmen from South Wales and within a few years, the American tin plate industry was established. By 1914, large amounts of American capital had been invested in the industry, which surpassed the production of tin plate in Great Britain. By this time, the United States had become the leading consumer and producer of tin plate in the world.

The growth of the canning industry was largely responsible for the development of the tin plate industry, as meats, fish, poultry, soups, vegetables, fruits, milk, jams, and beverages, as well as oil, polish, and tobacco, were sold in tin containers. The use of cans for preserving foods dates back to the beginning of the nineteenth century. The rise of urban centers gave an impetus to this means of preserving and distributing food and other products. Among the improvements in the manufacture of tin cans, the drop press, invented by Allen Taylor in 1847, and the combination press of Henry Evans, a few years later, were important. The lock seamer was invented in 1869 and the automatic soldering of can ends in 1876. The first complete automatic can-making machinery was put into operation in 1885 in Baltimore.

A new industry which experienced a most spectacular rise was the automobile industry. As early as the eighteenth century man had attempted to operate steam-propelled vehicles on the city streets. In the United States, Oliver Evans was one of the most important of the earlier pioneers in this field. As steam railways developed, attempts were made in several European cities to apply steam to stage coaches, but high toll charges and restrictive legislation interfered with the success of such ventures. During the latter part of the nineteenth century much progress was made in Germany in producing self-propelled vehicles. In 1876, A. N. Otto built a four-cycle internal combustion hydrocarbon motor, based partly on the ideas of Beau de Rochas, a Frenchman; in 1886, Gottlieb Daimler exhibited the first motor tricycle; and the next year Carl Benz produced the first automobile driven by a gasoline engine. In the years that followed, many in Europe and America experimented with "horseless carriages," using steam, electricity, illuminating gas, vaporized oil, gasoline, carbonic acid gas, and alcohol as motive power.

As early as 1879, George B. Selden of Rochester, N. Y. applied for his first patent for a gasoline vehicle, which he purposely kept pending for many years; but it was not until 1892 that Charles Duryea and his brother Frank drove the first successful American gasoline car down the streets of Springfield, Massachusetts. During the depression of 1893–1897 advances were made in producing vehicles run by electric batteries, steam power, or gasoline. By this time automobile design had reached a relatively mature stage in France and Germany, but European progress had little influence in America. With one exception the early experimenters with automobiles in the United States were not college graduates. They did not read literature in foreign languages, and, in any case the long heavy European cars did not fit American conditions. Here bad roads put a premium on high light vehicles, and the designers, mainly men with bicycle and wagon building experience, put a small single cylinder motor under the seat of a buggy on bicycle wheels. The resulting vehicle was not only easy to push, but cheap to buy.

Commercial manufacture of these "horseless carriages" started in 1894, and by 1900, the second year of large production, there were some eight thousand motor vehicles in the United States. The amount of capital needed to go into the business of assembling automobiles was quite low. Well-established machine shops, bicycle plants and wagon builders would supply the parts on credit, and the assembler who put his name on the product needed only an empty building, a small amount of equipment, and enough money to pay wages until dealers bought the cars. Henry Ford started on a fairly large scale in 1903 with $28,500. As a result of this low "threshold of entry" from fifty to a hundred car "manufacturers" competed during the first years of the century.

The automobile spread more rapidly in the United States than elsewhere in the world, not only because of cheap simple models, but because of great potential demand. The long distances between farms, towns, and cities made the automobile attractive to farmers, doctors, lawyers, and salesmen, and these middle-class people had the money to buy a thousand-dollar utility. In Europe the automobile remained a luxury item, advanced in design, often because of military subsidies, but beyond the reach of any but buyers with high incomes.

Steam and electricity rivalled internal combustion engines as power for early automobiles. Steam gave the best performance, but waiting for boilers to heat up was a nuisance and several gauges had to be watched to insure safe operation. Electrics were virtually foolproof, but lacked speed and had to have batteries recharged frequently. Although powerful electric traction financiers backed the Electric Motor Vehicle Company, which acquired the Selden patent, they made little effort to invest the money in research needed to improve and service the electric cars or to monopolize the market. Recognizing the patent as a weak one the company licensed all comers at low rates, and all manufacturers except Henry Ford found it cheaper to pay than risk litigation. In 1911 a Federal court decided that the patent did not apply to the gasoline motors then in use.

In the beginning automobile manufacture was scattered wherever there were large machine shops, and wagon firms. New England, the Middle Atlantic states and the Great Lakes area all had numerous companies. But within a decade the industry had begun to concentrate around the western end of Lake Erie. Here there was a good labor supply, competitive transportation rates, established suppliers of parts, and, in Detroit particularly, bank credit not available in the East. In spite of all these favorable locational factors, however, the concentration around Detroit owes something to the accident that William C. Durant and Henry Ford lived in southern Michigan.

These two men brought the stage of big business to this rapidly growing industry, Durant by means of mergers between already large companies, Ford by building one company bigger than the rest. In 1908 Durant, a successful wagon builder, merged Buick, Cadillac, Oldsmobile, and Oakland with several smaller car and supply companies to form General Motors. Had he been able to secure enough financing he could have bought Ford also, but the big investment bankers lacked confidence in him. In this same year Ford finally perfected the plans for a simple, rugged car that could sell at a relatively low price.

The Ford Model T, designed with great care between 1906 and 1908, and marketed in 1909, exactly fitted the needs of the American market. High maintenance cost was the main worry of the man of small means who wanted a car, and the Model T was above all else simple and easy to repair. A short car with high clearance was needed for country roads, one with power to spare (since gasoline was cheap) and not too heavy if it had to be towed. The Model T met these requirements. Finally its initial price of $950 was reasonable for what was offered. Within a year the Model T led all other makes in sales, and as volume rose Ford decreased the price until in 1914, at less than $500 a car, he sold nearly half of the automobiles made in the United States.

Increasing sales put tremendous pressure on the Ford organization for higher productivity. In 1913 two engineers, C. W. Avery and William Klarin, in consultation with Ford, worked out the application of the mechanized assembly line for automobile production. Instead of bringing components to certain stations where parts of the car were assembled and then moving these sub-assemblies to new stations, the developing car was routed on an electrified conveyor belt past parts arranged in appropriate order. In this way more specialization in human operations was possible, and each job had to be done fast enough to keep pace with the line. The results were amazing, the time of assembling a car was cut by nearly 90 per cent. Although relatively few employees worked on mechanized assembly lines, they came in the popular imagination to typify mass production. From the broader standpoint this managerial innovation at Ford was one more example of the increasing use of continuous processes, mechanical, thermal, and chemical, in the twentieth century.

By 1917 the automobile industry had matured both technologically and organizationally. Eight- and twelve-cylinder cars were providing as high performance as roads would permit; half a dozen companies led by Ford and General Motors produced 80 to 90 per cent of the cars; outside capital through investment bankers had entered the industry; and the five million licensed automobiles were being added to at a rate of over a million and a half a year.

Another industry in which amazing development occurred was the electric industry. By 1870, a practical generator appeared, largely the result of the work of Z. T. Gramme of Belgium. Eight years later, Charles F. Brush of Cleveland, Ohio, devised an arc lamp and an ingenious type of generator for furnishing its current. Edward Weston of Newark, New Jersey, and Elihu Thomson of Philadelphia achieved success in the same field. By 1880, several cities had installed arc lights for street lighting and for advertising purposes. The large, sputtering arc lights, however, were not suited for many indoor uses, but when Thomas Edison perfected the smaller incandescent light by sending a current through a carbonized cotton thread in a glass vacuum bulb, he made possible the era of domestic electricity.

In 1882, Edison designed the first commercial generator station at Pearl Street, New York for a corporation financed by Drexel, Morgan & Company. The plant had six dynamos, the largest about 125 horsepower. It first served fifty-nine users, but because of the limitation of its low-voltage current its power could not be sent more than a mile. In the meantime, George Westinghouse had applied electricity to the operation of railroad signals and had built some of the first electric lighting generators. He became interested in the secondary generator system, a product of European experimentation for the long-distance transmission of electricity; from this he developed an American system for alternating current. The first experimental plant was put into operation in Great Barrington, Massachusetts, in 1886; later in the same year the first commercial alternating-current lighting plant was installed in Buffalo. A "battle of the systems"—direct and alternating—followed. The amazing electrical displays produced by alternating current in the Chicago World's Fair of 1893 demonstrated the superiority of that form of current. Electrical engineers began to combine the two systems so that both could be used to advantage. Most of the current produced in the United States in the years that followed was alternating, although as progress was made in generating electricity, a considerable portion of it was transformed into direct current for electric railways, electro-chemical industries, and other uses where direct current was more advantageous. One of the landmarks of the electrical industry was the harnessing of Niagara Falls in 1895 with the first of three 5,000 horsepower alternating-current generators. Not only did it demonstrate the possibilities of electrical development, but it also stimulated the use of water power instead of steam for generating electricity.

At first, electricity was used largely for lighting. Soon it was applied to many other uses. As seen in Chapter 15, electric trolley lines spread rapidly over the large urban areas. Early in the twentieth century, some steam railroads electrified sections of their systems where traffic was heavy. The Baltimore and Ohio at Baltimore, the Pennsylvania in New York, and other railroads operated trains from current obtained from a third rail. In 1907, the New Haven Railroad was electrified by using an alternating current supplied by overhead wires. This plan was generally adopted by other railroads for electrifying parts of their systems. The flexibility and relative simplicity of electric operation and the increased power obtained were the chief reasons for the adoption of the new power by many railroads. Much more slowly was electricity used on the sea. It came into general use for lighting vessels, but marine engineers long regarded it as unsuitable for water motive power. An impetus was given to its use in the marine field when the United States naval collier *Jupiter,* equipped with electrical propelling machinery and steam turbine generators, was commissioned in 1913. Little progress, however, was made in the use of this form of power on merchant vessels, for steam or Diesel oil engines were preferred.

During the period of experimentation, electricity was used for driving such machines as pumps, fans, and printing presses, but not until after 1888, when Nikola Tesla developed polyphase alternating current generation, did electric power find general use in industry. As motors were improved in speed, power, and mechanical characteristics, they came to be used to drive all types of machinery. In addition, when cheap electricity became available through the use of water power, the electro-chemical industry was given an impetus, especially the production of aluminum, graphite, abrasives, chlorine, alloys, and other materials. The use of electric heat for treating and baking processes in industry originated during this period.

From the beginning of the twentieth century electrical devices of many kinds found their place in many homes. As early as 1880, Edison suggested that an electrical motor weighing about eighty pounds could be used for driving a sewing machine, but many years passed before motors were applied to domestic sewing machines. The electric iron and other household appliances were slowly accepted. After 1914, these together with the electric refrigerator, devices for electric heating and cooking, and automatic mechanisms for controlling and feeding coal and oil furnaces were increasingly used.

The story of electrical manufacturing centers in two important companies, the Westinghouse Electric Company (the Westinghouse Electric and Manufacturing Company), which began business in 1886, and the General Electric Company, incorporated in 1892. While many small pioneer companies developed, most were eventually absorbed by one or the other of the two organizations. The two companies shared most of the basic patents for electrical equipment. By 1914 there was a total of 1,030 establishments in the country chiefly engaged in the manufacture of machinery, apparatus, and supplies for use in the generation, transmission, or vitalization of electrical energy. About 150,000 were employed in the industry and net products exclusive of telegraph and telephone equipment were valued at $317,671,000.

THE SINEWS OF ECONOMIC GROWTH

It seems likely that the United States will never again invest such a large share of its national income in capital goods for non-military uses as it did in the period 1850 to 1910. Only in the 1860's was there any large diversion of resources for military purposes, and frequently in this sixty-year period both personal saving and private investment reached levels never again equalled in time of peace. From 1884 to 1893, for example, it has been estimated that over 14 per cent of the national income went into private capital formation as compared with only 11 per cent from 1919 to 1928, and about 10 per cent in decades after the Second World War.

These are the dry statistical results of the American myth of "self-help," or success from saving and hard work. As soon as the successful man's income rose above the needs of subsistence he started saving and investing. Rising businessmen maintained meagre standards of living in order to reinvest their profits in further expansion; literally they lived to work rather than the reverse. It was this period more than any other that gave to the world the image of American free enterprise, of the entrepreneur, materialistic and perhaps coarse, but dedicated to work, progress, and efficiency.

CHAPTER 21

Labor

In 1850, with farming still the occupation of nearly two-thirds of working Americans, there were as many employers as employees. In spite of many large factories, industrial workers were a small minority of the population. By 1910, employees were far more numerous than the self-employed and only a little over one-third of the working population was in agriculture.

The percentage of foreign-born had declined steadily from the late eighteenth century, when most workers were immigrants, to the 1840's when less than 15 per cent had been born abroad. From 1845 on massive immigration from Europe produced an opposite trend, and by 1910 a fifth of the labor force was foreign-born.

Both immigrants, among whom there was a high percentage of men of working age, and increasing employment of women made the labor force grow faster than the population. While gainful workers in the continental United States grew from 7,700,000 in 1850 to 36,700,000 in 1910, almost a five-fold increase, the population increased only four-fold. More jobs for women was the chief contributing factor. In 1850 only one woman in fifteen or twenty worked outside her home; by 1900 the ratio was one in six, and by 1910, had the figures been properly recorded, it would probably have been one in five.

450

The growing number of women in offices, stores, and factories was, in turn, a result of the rise of urban business. If one arbitrarily assumes that a place of 8,000 people or more had the attributes of a city, although many smaller places could be included, urban population grew from 13 per cent of the total in 1850 to 39 per cent in 1910. In addition to making it easier for several members of a family to find employment, cities also facilitated labor organization. The early trade unions stemmed from the largest cities, while the rural areas, even in the twentieth century, were largely non-union.

EARLY ATTEMPTS AT UNION FEDERATION

From 1850 on, local and national organizations of single crafts increased in number and the labor movement as a whole grew stronger. Among the new national organizations were the Brotherhood of the Footboard (the forerunner of the Brotherhood of Locomotive Engineers), the Cigar Makers' International Union, and the Bricklayers' and Masons' International Union. Because wages lagged behind rapidly rising prices in the wartime period of inflation, many strikes and labor disputes occurred, especially during the last two years of the war. In 1864, an attempt was made to organize workers of all types into the International Industrial Assembly of America but with little success. Throughout the period the workers in the various unions sought such practical ends as high wages, a shorter working day, the abolition of the truck system (paying wages through store orders), and the right to organize.

After the war, an attempt was made to bring all labor organizations into one National Labor Union, and Congresses were held each year

POPULATION AND WORKERS, 1850 – 1920
(In thousands)

Year	Population	Gainful Workers	Year	Population	Gainful Workers
1850	23,261	7,700	1890	63,056	23,740
1860	31,513	10,530	1900	76,094	29,070
1870	39,905	12,920	1910	92,407	36,730
1880	50,262	17,390	1920	106,466	41,610

Source: U.S. Bureau of the Census, *Historical Statistics of the United States, Colonial Times to 1957,* Washington, D.C., 1960, pp. 7, 74.

from 1866 to 1872. Made up of local and national unions, trade assemblies, and other organizations, the national craft groups were entitled to three representatives, state organizations to two, and local and other unions to one representative to the National Labor Congresses. In 1868, William H. Sylvis, head of the iron molders' union, was elected president, but died during his term of office. Among a long list of demands, the organization sought an eight-hour day, the creation of a national labor bureau, the restriction of cheap immigrant labor, a reduction of tariff duties on necessities, and the abolition of national banks. The unsuccessful participation of the National Labor Union in the national political campaign of 1872 together with its strong advocacy of social reforms and lack of real power in dealing with employers brought its activities to an end. In its last meeting held in 1872, only seven delegates were present.

THE KNIGHTS OF LABOR

Secret societies of all kinds appeared after the Civil War and labor was not exempt from them. Among these, the order known as the Knights of St. Crispin was organized in 1867 by the shoemakers of the country. It established a journal, endorsed political candidates, started cooperative stores, decried certain evils of the wage system, protested against the abuse of the machine, and demanded social justice. While it was active for a time, it disappeared after the panic of 1873. Secret societies and organizations sprang up among other crafts. Of importance was an order organized in 1869 among the garment cutters of Philadelphia by Uriah S. Stevens, which became known as the Noble Order of the Knights of Labor.

At first this organization was secret, even its name, which was designated by five stars. It possessed an elaborate ritual and was composed solely of garment cutters. Within a short time members of other crafts were admitted and the ideal of craft unionism gave way to the plan of amalgamating all workers into a coherent and disciplined labor army of local and district assemblies. In theory, the government of the Knights of Labor was highly centralized. The chief governing body was the General Assembly, which elected the General Executive Board and the Grand Master Workman, and had much power over the subordinate bodies—local, district, state, trade, and national. The local groups were chiefly single crafts, but some locals were mixed assemblies including men of various trades. The organization admitted to its ranks gainfully employed persons—men and women, whites and Negroes, skilled and unskilled, as well as employers, merchants, and farmers. It excluded those engaged in the manufacturing or sale of intoxicating liquors, bankers, professional gamblers, lawyers, and, prior to 1881, physicians. The Knights of Labor grew slowly at first, but it made much progress after T. V. Powderly followed Stevens as its Grand Master Workman in 1879 and when it abandoned its secrecy two years later. The organization reached its peak in 1886 with a membership of about 700,000, although claims were made of a much larger enrollment.

The Knights of Labor aimed in the direction of broad social reform through political action and through cooperation rather than the use of strikes and other methods of trade unionism. It planned for the betterment of the working class through discussion, arbitration, and careful planning. Among its demands were the gradual introduction of the eight-hour day, land reform, the establishment of a bureau of labor statistics, the prohibition of child labor, graduated income and inheritance taxes, government ownership of railways and telegraph lines, the abolition of national banks, and the introduction of a system of cooperation to take the place of the wage system. Many local groups set up cooperative workshops and stores, but most of these were short-lived as the impossibility of securing credit, inefficient management, competition with private distributors, and unfair practices of the railroads put an end to them.

As the Knights of Labor reached its height of power in 1886 forces were at work which contributed to its rapid decline. The failure of many strikes—including sympathetic strikes—and boycotts, in which the Knights were involved, despite the theoretical opposition of the organization to such a weapon, was partly a reason. Then, too, it did not succeed in enticing to its membership many strong unions, such as the Railroad Brotherhoods. The over-centralization of the organization was partly responsible for many of its difficulties, although the local and district assemblies were often quite independent and at times defied the orders and rulings of the national officers. Because of its welcome to all groups, many radicals, extreme socialists, and other elements entered the order that were opposed to the policies advocated by the skilled crafts. Powderly favored investing the funds of the order in cooperative ventures rather than in supporting strikes. The ideals of his program were too theoretical to relate definitely to the direct interests of various trades and crafts. As a new organization arose, which emphasized a federated organization of skilled craftsmen instead of a mass industrial organization, "job conscious" trade unions turned to it.

By 1890 the Noble Order of the Knights of Labor was overshadowed by the rising American Federation of Labor, which seemed to fit better into the American skilled labor environment. But the brief and spectacular career of the Knights had not been without result. The organization had strengthened many weak local unions and had helped to found many new ones. It did much to secure the Federal Bureau of Labor (1884) and through its lobbies it exerted an influence in obtaining other legislation which benefited labor. It contributed to the forces that brought about the repeal of the Labor Contract Law in 1885, which had limited the importation of foreign laborers under contract. It also laid the foundation for the eight-hour day and other labor reforms, which were accomplished after the activities of the Knights had ended.

THE AMERICAN FEDERATION OF LABOR

A labor convention, which met in Pittsburgh in 1881, formed an association made up of craft and industrial unions with the very cumbersome name of "The Federation of Organized Trades and Labor Unions of the United States of America and Canada." Among the leaders of its most important unions were P. J. McGuire, of the carpenters' union and proposer of Labor Day, together with Adolf Strasser and Samuel Gompers of the cigar makers' union. Gompers had been a socialist, but had concluded that the doctrines of Karl Marx could not solve American labor problems. With his colleagues, he set out to build up a conservative labor federation as opposed to the industrial and centrally controlled unionism of the Knights of Labor. A reorganization took place in 1886 and a new name—the American Federation of Labor—was adopted.

The chief object of the Federation was to promote independent trade unionism based upon craft autonomy. Each craft organization governed itself, worked out its own policies and controlled its own financial affairs. The powers of the Federation were set forth in a written constitution. The organic unit of the Federation was the local union made up of members of a craft who worked together in one community. Each local was a part of a national union in its own particular trade except in a few cases where no national organization existed. In order to achieve greater unity and power, the locals were encouraged to affiliate with the central labor union of the town or city in which they were located and also with the state federation wherever possible. The national union, the city central union or federation and the state federation were all affiliated with the American Federation of Labor. But the individual unionist was not a member of the Federation. At the top were the officers and an Executive Council, both elected by annual Conventions of representatives from the member unions. The Council had certain discretionary powers to administer the affairs of the organization during the period between Conventions, but it could not control either the politics or finances of the national unions. Its revenue was obtained from an assessment on the affiliated unions based on their membership.

From the beginning the American Federation of Labor only pursued policies that would benefit the immediate economic status of its skilled membership. Thus attempts were made to secure the enactment of favorable measures and the repeal of oppressive laws regarding union or skilled labor in state legislatures and in Congress. Stress was laid upon collective bargaining and the working out of trade agreements with employers. The use of the union label—a mark adopted and placed on products made by a labor organization—was promoted, and the buying only of union labor goods advocated. The Federation continually maintained that the strike, the boycott, and the unfair list were necessary weapons of organized labor, but direct action emanated from the unions and not from the parent body. The policy regarding strikes was endorsed; moral support and financial aid, if necessary, might be given. At first an "Unfair List" was published in the *American Federationist,* the official organ of the Federation, but in 1909 a Supreme Court decision required that the list be dropped. Not favoring state regulation of working conditions which could be controlled by union contracts, the Federation did not take an active part in "progressive" politics. It did, however, endorse some political reforms such as the initiative, referendum, and recall; the popular election of Senators; workmen's compensation laws; the restriction of immigration; women's suffrage; a national department of education; old age pensions; and abolition of child labor.

From the beginning, the organization had strong leadership. Samuel Gompers was its president, with the exception of one year, from its origin until his death in 1924. Born in a London tenement, Gompers, of Dutch-Jewish lineage, came to America as a youth and worked his way up from the bottom. A man of forceful personality, great energy, executive ability, conservative idealism, but rather narrow ideas, he was able to stave off the attempts by some groups to commit the Federation to socialism or an American labor party, and by others to assume the burden of organizing the unskilled. While insisting that unions be kept away from partisan politics, during most of the period he was forced into national politics, even to support candidates and to endorse parties. Although he was hated and assailed by many within and without his organization, for his conservative and exclusive policies, the American Federation of Labor grew and prospered during much of his presidency. The total individual membership increased from less than 200,000 in 1886 to 2,000,000 in 1914. In 1920, a peak of 4,000,000 was reached. At the death of Gompers in 1924, the membership was approximately 2,865,000.

INDUSTRIAL WORKERS OF THE WORLD

The very structure of the American Federation of Labor automatically excluded the mass of unskilled workers. It included unions of the skilled crafts, although a few outstanding organizations, notably the Railroad Brotherhoods, preferred to remain unaffiliated. As a protest against craft unionism and the conservative policies of the American Federation of Labor, a left-wing industrial union was formed.

A convention held in Chicago in 1905, supported by the Western Federation of Miners and the socialistically inclined American Railway Union, organized the Industrial Workers of the World. Besides William D. Haywood of the Miners, Daniel De Leon, the veteran Marxist leader, and Eugene Debs, head of the American Socialist Party provided leadership at the meeting. Within the new organization were varying groups, but chiefly the syndicalists who sponsored militant industrial unionism and opposed political action, and socialists who advocated political means in the class struggle. A split

TRADE UNION MEMBERSHIP, 1870 – 1930

Year	Gainful Workers Exclusive of Agriculture (In millions)	Union Membership	Per Cent of Total Non-Agricultural Labor Force
1870	6.2	.3	4.9
1880	8.8	.2	2.3
1890	13.6	.4	2.7
1900	18.1	.9	4.8
1910	25.4	2.1	8.4
1920	30.9	5.0	16.3
1930	38.4	3.4	8.8

Source: Seymour Harris, *American Economic History*, New York, 1961, p. 393.

occurred within the ranks of the organization in 1908 and there emerged the Chicago I. W. W. with most of the original membership including the syndicalist wing, and the Detroit I. W. W., a strict Marxian socialist group. The latter became the Workers Industrial Union in 1915, which was dissolved ten years later.

The Chicago group of the Industrial Workers of the World appealed to all workers. The organization declared that the "universal economic evils affecting the working class can be eradicated only by a universal working class movement" and thus it was planned to be "one industrial union embracing all industries." A manifesto stated: "It must be founded on the class struggle and its general administration must be conducted in harmony with the recognition of the irrepressible conflict between the capitalist class and the working class." Believing in the ultimate revolutionary destruction of capitalism, the members of the I.W.W. advocated direct action as a means to victory. They favored quick strikes, boycotts, and sabotage—violent in the malicious destruction of property or peaceful as "soldiering on the job." The doctrines did not appeal to a large number of Americans, but attracted certain groups of unskilled and migratory workers particularly in the West in lumber camps and harvest fields, as well as some unions of skilled workers. Prior to 1914, the organization was quite aggressive and made itself known through its activities in several spectacular strikes. But it failed to establish stable local and national organizations. At its height in 1912, it had less than 100,000 members. Opposed to World War I, as were most leftist groups, the I.W.W. leaders were arrested under the Sedition Act and given jail sentences up to twenty years. The union never recovered from this virtual liquidation.

LABOR DISPUTES AND STRIKES

As labor became better organized after the Civil War, it was inevitable that disputes with management should increase in number and intensity. The growing complexity of the industrial system and the rise of powerful labor organizations brought strife and even bloodshed. Complete statistics of strikes prior to 1881 are not obtainable, but from that year on a fairly accurate picture of industrial warfare can be obtained as the Bureau of Labor and later the Department of Labor, as well as states and industries kept labor records. From 1865 to 1881, there is evidence to show that industrial disputes and strikes numbered a little less than 500 and, with a few notable exceptions, were not serious.

Soon after the Civil War middle-class opinion hostile to organized labor was strengthened by labor disturbances in the anthracite coal fields of Pennsylvania. For a decade or more, labor trouble between immigrant miners and tough mine bosses was widespread in the hard coal regions. A secret organization, known as the "Molly Maguires," undertook to intimidate, threaten, and punish mine bosses and colliery superintendents who mistreated members of the organization. There were several murders, but local authorities were powerless to apprehend the criminals who kept their activities shrouded in secrecy. Finally, in 1874, Franklin B. Gowen, president of the Philadelphia Coal and Iron Company employed some Pinkerton detectives. One of them, James McParlan, worked as a miner for almost two years. He posed as a counterfeiter and a fugitive from justice, gained the confidence of members of the Molly Maguires, and not only joined the organization but became its secretary. With all necessary evidence in his possession, he secured the arrest and conviction of twenty-four members, ten of whom were executed. The activities of the organization thus came to an end in 1877.

The first serious railroad strikes occurred in the same year. Violent and widespread, they were the first on a national scale and grew out of conditions of the depression years. They began over a third 10 per cent reduction in wages, irregular employment, and the increased tonnage of trains. Serious trouble developed on the Baltimore and Ohio Railroad at Martinsburg, West Virginia. The state militia was called out, but, when it proved sympathetic to the strikers, President Hayes, upon the request of the state governor, sent Federal troops to the scene, ending the strike, but not until it had begun to spread over the country like a wind-fanned fire. The railroad strike touched off disorders by thousands who had been unemployed. Rioting, destruction of property, and loss of life took place in Baltimore and in various places in Pennsylvania. In Cincinnati, Toledo, and St. Louis, mobs often unconnected with the striking railroad workers closed shops, factories, and mills. In Chicago, radical groups staged impressive demonstrations. In these places, and in others in the state of New York, the mobs were dispersed by the militia. The special cause of the great strike on the Pennsylvania at Pittsburgh was the objection of the railroad workers to "double headers," which enabled the company to dispense with the services of half their freight conductors, brakemen, and flagmen on the Pittsburgh division. Rioting and violence broke out in a population many of whose members were antagonistic toward the Pennsylvania and much railroad property was destroyed; the governor of the state called out troops and a battery of artillery; pitched battles in which many were killed resulted. After the strike had ended, the railroad company sued Allegheny County for damages, maintaining that it was liable for losses sustained because it was unable to keep order and to prevent rioting and destruction. The county was required to pay the railroad almost $3,000,000. The workers lost in these railroad strikes. A wave of reaction resulted: the public condemned labor, the courts revived the old doctrines of conspiracy, and the use of Federal troops in labor disputes established a precedent which augured ill for the future.

The decades of the 1880's and 1890's were marked by industrial conflict. From 1881 to 1886 inclusive, 3,902 strikes occurred involving 22,300 establishments and 1,323,000 men. This tempo was kept up for many years. The chief reasons for the strikes included demands for increased wages, opposition to wage reductions, and agitation for reduced hours of work. The whole country was wrought up over the strikes but little could be done. Thoughtful persons raised the question as to how the causes of strikes could be removed.

Among the innumerable labor disputes of the 1880's, railroad strikes again loomed large. During 1884–1885 the Knights of Labor succeeded in winning four of the five major railroad strikes on the Gould lines. Another dispute on the same system began in March, 1886, involving the Texas and Pacific Railroad at Marshall, Texas, on the issue of union recognition, and a daily wage of $1.50 for unskilled laborers. Soon, many railroads were tied up in the central states. Violence provided an excuse for the use of Federal troops, and the strike collapsed. Industrial unionism was unsuccessful and the failure of the Knights in the strike was one factor that led to the decline of their organization.

In 1886, disturbances in Chicago, climaxed by the Haymarket riot early in May of that year, focused the attention of the nation upon the increasing number of anarchists entering the country from Germany. As a protest against the shooting of a number of workmen by the police near the McCormick Reaper Works, August Spies, editor of the *Arbeiter-Zeitung,* issued circulars demanding revenge and calling an indignation meeting at Haymarket Square. Editors of other radical papers also announced the meeting. About 1,400 workmen, among them a number of anarchists, assembled at the appointed time and place. After several speeches had been made, about 180 policemen arrived and began to disperse the group. As one of the speakers was seized, a bomb fell. A deafening explosion followed, killing several policemen and injuring others. A number of men were arrested. Eight alleged anarchists were convicted on conspiracy charges, four were hanged, and the others sentenced for life. In 1893, Governor Altgeld of Illinois pardoned the three surviving prisoners, declaring that the trial had been a farce. The eighth man had committed suicide in prison. The Haymarket riot put an end for the time being to the demand for an eight-hour day, which collapsed under the stigma of radicalism. The turmoil brought fear to many as anarchist "plots" were "discovered" in different parts of the country, in spite of the fact that the number of extreme radicals among the striking workmen was small. Neither the Knights of Labor nor the rising American Federation of Labor had any direct connection with the anarchists, and both organizations opposed and deprecated the violence of the times.

One of the most spectacular strikes of the period occurred at Homestead, Pennsylvania, in 1892. It was a landmark in the development of organized labor as it affected the steel industry. By this time, the Amalgamated Association of Iron, Steel and Tin Workers had become powerful and sought to organize the rank and file in steel mills. The strike arose at the Carnegie Steel Company's work at Homestead chiefly over a reduction of wages and the refusal of the company to recognize the union. The strikers seized the plant and even captured the hired strike-breaking force—300 Pinkerton detectives. Pitched battles were fought along the Ohio River and the strikers used small cannon as well as guns to defend themselves and to attack the detectives. Public opinion at first seemed to be sympathetic to the workers, partly because of the extremely low wages paid them, but their battle tactics and the attempt of Alexander Berkman, an anarchist from New York, to assassinate Henry Clay Frick, the president of the company, turned public sentiment against them. The governor of the state called out the militia. Homestead was placed under martial law, and order was restored. The workmen lost the strike, and most of them were replaced by new employees. The bloodshed—for detectives, workmen, and civilians were slain—led to an investigation by Congress, but nothing was done by that body to prevent the recurrence of such strife in the future. Labor's first great struggle with large-scale capitalism in the steel industry ended in another defeat for industrial organization.

The Pullman strike of 1894 was one of the most important of the times because of its national consequences. The town of Pullman, the home of the Pullman Palace Car Company, adjoining Chicago, was a company town noted for its beauty and cleanliness in contrast to the somber and dirty industrial company towns of the era. It possessed wide streets, distinctive small homes, and green parks. During the Chicago World's Fair of 1893, visitors from all over the world admired the model town, and Englishmen compared it favorably with their own Port Sunlight where Sunlight Soap was made. Although the company owned most of the town, including the homes and many of the stores and also controlled the political life, the employees had been reasonably contented. Because of depressed conditions in 1893 and 1894, however, the Pullman Palace Car Company reduced the wages of its employees several times for a total average reduction of 25 per cent without reducing rents. Early in 1894 several thousand employees sought refuge in the new American Railway Union, organized by Eugene V. Debs. In May a committee of workmen called on George M. Pullman, president of the company, to urge that the wage schedule of June, 1893, be restored. When this was refused, 2,500 employees quit work and forced the closing of the shops. Attempts to arbitrate the differences brought the response from the company that there was nothing to arbitrate.

The local Pullman strike developed into a general railroad strike when members of the American Railway Union refused to handle Pullman cars and equipment. The twenty-four railroads entering Chicago had a Managers Association that took control of the situation, and so handled Pullman equipment that a tie-up of almost all traffic resulted. Meanwhile the sympathetic strike spread to many parts of the country. Because of the interference of the strikers with trains carrying Pullman cars and mail, judges of the United States District Court in Illinois issued a "blanket injunction" prohibiting all interference with trains. The injunction was printed and copies were posted on railroad property. Turbulent scenes followed, and thousands of angry unemployed men and women began looting, destroying, and burning railroad property in Chicago. Much of this, however, was done by migratory workers initially employed at the World's Fair, who had found no other jobs in Chicago as the receding tide carried homeward the visitors to the great exposition. Complaints reached Washington of the seriousness of the situation and President Cleveland ordered Federal troops into Chicago on the ground that the mails were being obstructed and interstate commerce held up. The railroad officials did not ask Governor Altgeld of Illinois to call out the state militia because he held the Managers Association responsible for interruption of the mails, and he was known to have a favorable attitude toward labor. The calling-out of the Federal troops resulted in many lengthy telegrams between Cleveland and Altgeld, the latter vigorously protesting that states' rights were being violated, while the President insisted that he was simply upholding the Federal laws. The troops finally restored order, began running trains under military guard, and soon the strike was ended. At the same time, Debs and other union officials who attempted to direct the activities of the workers were arrested under the authority of the blanket injunction and immediately sentenced to prison. With their leaders gone and the troops against them the strikers gave up in despair. While property losses were largely confined to the area of Chicago, disorders occurred also in cities in other parts of the country.

The Pullman strike was important for several reasons. It reopened the states' rights controversy. In the constitutional question many agreed with the President but others opposed, maintaining that if troops were necessary to put down violence, the state militia should have been called out first. Cleveland demonstrated a vigorous conservatism, for his action showed that he would not let popularity with labor interfere with what he considered to be his duty. Another phase of the strike had to do with the use of the blanket injunction in labor disputes. It had been applied to labor a decade or so earlier, but became prominent for the first time in the Pullman strike. The use of the injunction has played an important part in American labor history since that time.

In an important strike of the early twentieth century, the President of the United States played an important mediatory role. In May of 1902, after vain efforts to secure an agreement, 150,000 miners, members of the United Mine Workers, went on strike under the leadership of John Mitchell. The workers demanded an increase in wages, a working day of eight hours instead of ten, payment by weight and not by car, and the recognition of the union. The operators refused to recognize the union and insisted that the employees of the different companies should deal directly only with their employers. Most of the anthracite mines were owned by corporations which also controlled the coal-carrying railroads, and the dispute affected them.

The strike forced a complete shutdown, but the operators refused to have anything to do with the organized workers. There was little violence and public sympathy arose for the strikers as writers and students of social problems visited the area and presented a picture of sordid living conditions in the coal fields. The public, suspicious of big business and monopolies, was also influenced when a letter of George F. Baer, president of the Philadelphia and Reading Railway Company, chief spokesman for the employers, was given wide and unexpected circulation. In part, Baer wrote: "The rights and interests of the laboring man will be protected and cared for—not by the labor agitators, but by the Christian men to whom God in his infinite wisdom has given control of the property interests of the country and upon the successful management of which so much depends." This gave the cue for a large number of cartoons, which aided in shaping public sentiment.

The strike continued throughout the summer. As the East was threatened with a winter without coal, President Roosevelt, early in October, summoned Mitchell and the employers to the White House. The conference was turbulent, and no agreement could be reached. Later Roosevelt stated: "There was only one man in that conference who behaved like a gentleman and that man was not I." He referred to Mitchell. A secret attempt to intercede had been made through a commission headed by ex-President Cleveland, but without result. Roosevelt now was ready to send United States troops to take over the mines, although his constitutional right to do so was in question. His decision, however, was made known, and the employers yielded on October 13. At a stormy conference they agreed to a commission of arbitration to be appointed by the President. The men returned to work, coal began to flow again from the anthracite fields, and a winter coal famine was averted. The commission under Judge George Gray visited the coal fields in Pennsylvania, heard hundreds of witnesses, and in the spring of 1903 made its report. It concluded that neither side was entirely right, and concessions were made to both. The workers did obtain a 10 per cent increase in wages, and the commission suggested that future disputes be referred to a board of conciliation, chosen by the mine owners and the workers.

The anthracite strike was of significance in regard to the relationship between the government and industry. During the deadlock between the operators and strikers, it was pointed out that such a dispute involved a third party—the public—whose interests were paramount. It is debatable whether the President would have carried out his threat to take over the mines in view of the consequences it would have entailed. In 1909, in reply to a question as to what he would have done if the operators and miners had not compromised, he said: "I would have seized the mines and the roads and would have given the freezing people coal, and Congress could have impeached and be damned."

Strikes by labor and lockouts by employers continued to be the ultimate weapons in bargaining. In the winter of 1909–1910 a strike of 30,000 Jewish, Italian, and American women workers in the shirtwaist trade in New York City established the International Ladies Garment Workers as a major union. These women workers were aided in their fight by wealthy women, college girls, and others.

Many spectacular labor disputes were carried on by the I.W.W. especially in the textile strikes in Lawrence, Massachusetts, in 1912, and in Paterson, New Jersey, the next year. Organizers for the I.W.W. kept up pressure for industrial unionism. The Colorado coal strikes of 1913–1914 resulted in a reign of terror in which men, women, and children were killed. After breaking the strike with the help of Federal troops the Rockefeller-controlled management developed an employee representation plan that was to have important influence on other companies.

NATIONAL EMPLOYERS' ASSOCIATIONS

As labor became more powerful, employers drew together into national organizations. From the time of the Civil War and even earlier, employers had organized against labor, either locally or regionally in certain industries. This was often done through "black-

Samuel Gompers speaking at Cooper Union, New York City

listing"—circulating among themselves the names of union members, labor agitators, strikers, or persons otherwise distasteful. This was practiced in the early thirties. In the sixties, railroads especially maintained blacklists, and the technique was adopted in many industries when unions became more aggressive in their demands. By the end of the century many states had passed laws prohibiting or restricting the practice, but secret methods used by employers made its detection difficult if not impossible. Some employers or groups of employers, resorted to the boycott, used spies, regulated output, and combined to maintain a certain level of wages and prices.

An employers' association is a combination of employers formed chiefly for the purpose of dealing with or fighting labor groups or unions. Among early city organizations of this sort, the Iron Founders' Association of Chicago and vicinity (1864) may be noted as an example. The Associated Employers of Indianapolis was another illustration of an aggressive anti-union local employers' organization. The first important national association of employers was the United States Potters' Association (1875). Other national groups, in marble cutting, ready-made clothing, machine construction, and in various fields followed. In 1886, the Stove Founders' National Defence Association (later the Manufacturers' Protective and Development Association) was formed. It typified a number of organizations which tried to be conciliatory and peaceful in relation to labor and achieved success in making formal wage contracts with employees and in settling grievances. On the other hand the National Association of Manu facturers is an example of an antiunion group. Organized in 1895 to promote domestic and foreign trade, by 1902 it became an employers' association, aggressive in opposing labor demands. It maintained an active labor-relations policy, condemning and opposing the blacklist, boycott, closed shop, and union label. It consistently insisted that employers should be "unmolested and unhampered in the management of their business." Its legislative and political programs were fostered through two affiliated organizations, the League for Industrial Rights (1902) and the National Industrial Council (1907). Among many other organizations of this kind, the National Metal Trades Association is an example of an employers' association in a limited field of industrial enterprise.

LABOR LEGISLATION

Between the Civil War and the First World War, as industrialism and big business became fully established and as industrial relations shifted, many laws were passed relating to labor and many gains were obtained through legislation. The first state labor bureau was established in 1869 in Massachusetts and others followed, bearing witness to the increased interest in labor problems. A Massachusetts law of 1866 prohibited the employment in any factory of children under ten and required an eight-hour work day and six months schooling for those between ten and fourteen. These provisions, however, were not enforced for more than a decade. Then other states passed similar laws. By the end of the century one-half the states set a minimum age of twelve years in manufacturing industries and a maximum of ten hours a day, but only a dozen states regulated child labor in all types of occupations. By 1900, the ten-hour day for women was generally accepted and enforced in a majority of states.

During the last decades of the nineteenth century, state laws were passed to protect the health and safety of workers in factories, workshops, mercantile establishments, sweatshops, laundries, and other places of work. By the end of the century the chief states that produced minerals had mining laws which attempted to regulate hours of labor and to secure safety devices. Railroad labor laws also set forth certain conditions for the protection of workers. In 1892, a Federal law made eight hours the working day for employees engaged in government work, but the courts refused to interpret the law as applying to government work given to private concerns. The courts also threw out laws which attempted to regulate working hours for men. Yet in 1898, the United States Supreme Court in the case of Holden *vs*. Hardy upheld a Utah law which limited underground mining work to eight hours, except in cases of emergency.

CHILD LABOR, 1870 – 1930
(Number of children 10-15 years of age)

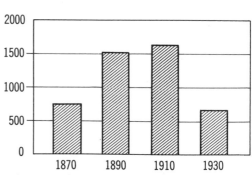

Source: U.S. Bureau of the Census, *Historical Statistics of the United States, Colonial Times to 1957*, Washington, D.C., 1960, p. 72.

Until the troublesome decade of the eighties, Congress had little concern with the problems of labor. However, in 1884, a Bureau of Labor, headed by a Commissioner, was established within the Department of Interior to collect information relating to labor and capital. Two years later, President Cleveland sent a message to Congress in which he recommended legislation and advocated the creation of a Board of Labor Commissioners to act as the official arbiter in labor disputes. In 1888, Congress passed a modest act relating only to the interstate railroads; it provided for a board of arbitration to investigate differences between railroads and their employees. No provision was made for the enforcement of decisions, and the practical results of the law were not important. Ten years later the Erdman Act superseded the law of 1888. It provided that certain officials appointed by the President should act as mediators in railroad disputes, and if they failed, a Board of Arbitration should be appointed whose findings should stand until passed upon by the Federal courts. No cases were brought under the act until 1906. In the years that followed, many controversies were decided under its terms.

From the beginning of the twentieth century, labor made important gains. Under the impetus of the progressive movement, a mass of economic and social as well as political legislation was adopted by the states. Much of the legislation followed the patterns set forth in the latter part of the nineteenth century, but it was now made more effective and was more rigidly enforced. Most important was the change in regard to the responsibility for accidents in industry as mechanization increased employment hazards. Under the common law and under such employers' liability acts as existed in the nineteenth century, the employee was helpless when accidents occurred and was inadequately compensated for injuries. Slowly, the responsibility for accidents was placed upon the employer, unless due to the negligence of the worker. While European countries had passed compensation laws during the last two decades of the nineteenth century, it was not until 1902 that the first compensation law was passed in the United States when Maryland enacted such a law. In that decade other states followed, but all were declared unconstitutional. The compensation movement was given an impetus when a Federal law of 1908, covering certain Federal officials, was upheld by the courts. States amended their constitutions to make possible the enactment of laws for compulsory compensation and framed legislation that would pass the tests of the courts. Between 1910 and 1920, forty-two states and three territories passed similar compensation laws. Prior to

An early labor conference, 1905
Left to right: Andrew Carnegie, William Jennings Bryan, James J. Hill, and John Mitchell.

1914, many states adopted minimum wage laws for women and children. A majority of states set up permanent boards of conciliation and arbitration for the purpose of settling industrial disputes. Many of the laws that benefited workers were contested by employers as unconstitutional, especially under the Fourteenth Amendment. Most of the legislation, however, was upheld by the courts as being within the police power of the states—that inherent right of every sovereign state to make and enforce laws for the protection of the health, safety, morals, public order, convenience, and general welfare of its inhabitants.

During the first part of the twentieth century, the Federal government, also, did much in the interests of labor. In 1903, a Department of Commerce and Labor was established, whose Secretary was given cabinet rank. A separate Department of Labor was set up in 1913. William B. Wilson, a former congressman who had risen from the ranks of labor, was appointed by President Woodrow Wilson as the first Secretary of Labor. According to the act creating it, the duty of the Department of Labor was to "foster, promote, and develop the welfare of the wage earners of the United States; to improve their working conditions, and to advance their opportunities for profitable employment." Within the Department, the important Bureau of Labor Statistics, which had originated in the earlier Bureau of Labor, was continued. The Conciliation Service was continuously vigilant in efforts to promote industrial peace. Many other bureaus and divisions have been established since 1913. Among other Federal laws passed prior to 1914 that benefited labor was one which provided an eight-hour day for workers on government contracts (1912). The Newlands Act of 1913 superseded the Erdman Act of 1898 by creating a formal Board of Mediation and Conciliation for the arbitration of railroad disputes. Many disputes were settled under the terms of this law until the railroads were placed under Federal control in December, 1917, during the First World War.

Although labor made great gains in the first part of the twentieth century, it received many setbacks from the courts relating chiefly to the weapons used by unions to secure their demands. A spectacular case arose in connection with the Danbury hatters' use of the boycott. In 1901–1902, the union known as the United Hatters of North America tried to unionize the employees of the Dietrich E. Loewe Company, a hatmaking establishment in Danbury, Connecticut. As the employers resisted the move, a nation-wide boycott against the company's products was declared by the workers. A suit was brought against 191 members of the newly-formed local union under the Sherman Antitrust Law for combining to interfere with interstate commerce by means of a boycott. A District Court awarded the company $74,000 damages, but the Circuit Court of Appeals overruled the verdict. In 1908, the United States Supreme Court reversed the decision of the Circuit Court and the case was sent back to it for retrial. That court, thus instructed, decided that the damages due the company amounted to $80,000, which was to be trebled under the terms of the Sherman law, the total sum with costs amounting to more than $250,000. Since the union was not incorporated, each of the dependents was liable for a share of the penalty. In 1903 the national union of hatters had agreed to back the local union in their struggle, and later the agreement was taken over by the American Federation of Labor after the United Hatters became affiliated with it. In 1913, the Federation disclaimed further responsibility but took up a collection for the workmen. Later, in order to satisfy the judgment, the savings bank accounts of the individual workers were attached and the homes of 140 of them in Danbury, Bethel, and neighboring communities were ordered sold by the court. The decision was a tragedy for the region of Danbury. In this case as in others, the courts made a distinction between the primary and secondary boycott. The former was declared legal unless accompanied by coercion; the secondary boycott—inducing third parties to stop patronizing or using the products of the boycotted firm—was pronounced illegal.

Another important case in the Federal courts which went against labor was the Buck Stove and Range case, involving the blacklist and the boycott. In 1906, the metal polishers of the Buck Stove and Range Company, St. Louis, struck for a nine-hour day. As a result of the strike, the American Federation of Labor put the company on its "unfair list." The company thereupon brought suit and obtained a sweeping injunction forbidding this boycott. When the Federation tried to circumvent the order which required that it cease printing the name of this firm in the "We Don't Patronize" column of its official journal, Samuel Gompers, John Mitchell, and Frank Morrison were sentenced to prison for contempt. They escaped their sentences on a technicality, but the decision forbidding the boycott was a blow to labor. The case was finally outlawed by the Supreme Court in 1914 under the statute of limitations. Due to the decisions in these cases, labor came to look upon the Federal courts as an enemy.

Federal legislation, passed in 1914, however, was hailed as a great triumph by labor. The Clayton Act, while applying to monopolies and restraints of trade, also referred to labor. Regarding certain union activities which had often been interpreted as restraints of trade, the law stated that nothing in the Federal antitrust statutes was to be construed as to prohibit the existence of labor and agricultural unions. Labor unions were thus declared to be legal. Another clause prohibited the use of restraining orders or injunctions in labor disputes and strikes "unless necessary to prevent irreparable injury to property . . . for which there is no adequate remedy at law." Labor was jubilant, for the use of injunction in labor disputes had been a prominent issue since the Pullman Strike of 1894. But in the years that followed, the courts interpreted this clause narrowly and the victory was not quite as overwhelming as labor first anticipated.

IMMIGRATION

Closely related to labor were problems of immigration. From the earliest days of settlement, immigrants had been welcomed from lands of oppression. From time to time during the national period, fears of alien influence cropped up, but it was not until the decades of the thirties and forties that a nativist movement took form and that hostility toward immigrants, especially Catholics, developed. This opposition was manifested in occasional rioting, in the destruction of property, and in attacks in many publications. Not all Americans were seized by this fever of hate, but nativism continued until the Civil War. During that war, such sentiment died down as the great need for manpower appeared. The government set up an Immigration Bureau to encourage Europeans to come to America and enacted a law which gave legal status to the importation of laborers from Europe and China (1864). Although immigration put more downward pressure on the wages of unskilled than of skilled workers, organized labor in general had consistently opposed large-scale immigration.

Definite records of immigration begin with the year 1820. It has been estimated that between 1776 and 1820, about 250,000 immigrants came to America. From the 1830's, immigration followed the American business cycle, with numbers rising in years of prosperity and plentiful jobs and falling off in years of depression and unemployment. The first important wave of immigrants rose to a high point in the year 1837 when 79,380 reached American shores. Another larger wave starting in 1845 culminated in 1854, when 427,833 were admitted. As immigration increased following the Civil War, peaks of 459,803 in 1873 and 788,992 in 1882 were reached. After 1900, immigration grew tremendously. In 1905, for the first time, the number of immigrants arriving within the year reached the million mark and in 1907, the number amounted to 1,285,349, a high for all time. In 1914, the height of the last great wave of immigration to the United States, the number was 1,218,420. From 1820 to 1914 a total of 30,000,000 Europeans came to this country, more than the population of the United States in 1850. This figure does not take into account those who returned. Accurate statistics of emigrant aliens were not gathered until 1908, and these disclose a relatively large number of emigrants who returned home in that period. For instance, in 1908, alien immigration amounted to 782,870, while 395,073 left the country. The outbreak of the First World War reduced the stream of immigrants to a trickle. After the war a new policy of highly restrictive immigration legislation was begun.

Prior to the eighties the bulk of immigrants came from the countries of northern and western Europe, most being of Teutonic or Nordic stock. By 1890, a shift in the sources of immigration was becoming apparent as ever-increasing numbers came from southern, central, and eastern Europe. The leading countries from which immigrants came during 1890–1900 were Italy, Germany, Austria-Hungary, Russia, and Ireland. From 1900 to 1914 the order was Austria-Hungary, Italy, Russia, England, and Ireland. The influx of immigrants of quite different stock than the older immigration was due to a number of reasons. As the industrial revolution progressed in Germany and the Scandinavian countries new opportunities opened up at home, while good farms in the United States became more expensive. Ireland had depopulated itself by the earlier emigration, and the remaining population was in better balance with the means of living. As in earlier years, religious and political persecution contributed to European emigration. The anti-Semitic persecutions in Russia sent large numbers of Jews to this country. The opening of direct steamship lines between Mediterranean ports and the United States stimulated immigration. "Runners" and agents were paid commissions by steamship companies to travel from village to village, especially in southern Europe, to induce people to emigrate. These agents distributed pamphlets, broadsides, and timetables of steamship lines, railroad companies, land groups, industrialists, and immigration commissions established by many states. They painted America in glowing colors. Contacts between Europeans and their friends and relatives in the United States, who had bettered their condition, also played a part in the vast tide of immigration. The addition of large numbers from the different European countries resulted in complicating the economic, social, and political problems of the nation.

The successive waves of immigration upset the progress of organized labor. Not only were the problems due to cheap, competitive labor and to strike-breaking, but many employers, to oppose unionization, divided wage earners along nationalistic, racial, and religious lines. The minority of alien agitators among the ranks of immigrants, who were classified as anarchists, communists, and syndicalists, also hurt the case of labor with the public, especially after the Haymarket riot of 1886, the Pullman strike of 1894, and the Lawrence strike of 1912. The importation of contract labor from Europe by employers seriously affected labor. Although the law of 1864, legalizing contracts by which immigrants pledged their wages in repayment of their journey across the ocean, was repealed four years later, the importation of contract labor continued. Corporations like the American Emigrant Company, which imported contract labor for employers in return for commissions, flourished. In 1885 and 1888, Congress, under pressure from the Knights of Labor and other labor organizations, made it unlawful to import contract labor except under certain conditions. In spite of these laws, violations occurred. Subsequent legislation designed to tighten the law did not entirely abolish the evil. Italians, Greeks, and Mexicans among others continued to be the victims of such exploitation throughout the period.

In 1882, when the tide of European immigration reached a height not equalled again until the opening of the twentieth century and when the character of the tide was changing, the first important general immigration law was enacted by Congress. Laws had been passed in 1862, 1869, 1873, and 1875 chiefly relating to coolie immigration from the Orient, for the purpose of insuring fair treatment and the safety of immigrants in crossing the ocean. Until 1882, with one exception (the temporary war act of 1864) the Federal government left the control of immigration to the seaboard states. The law of 1882 provided for cooperation between state and Federal authorities. It imposed a tax of fifty cents on each arrival and excluded certain persons, such as those with criminal records or incurable diseases. This mild policy of regulation continued in the years that followed. From time to time new laws increased the amount of the head tax and the undesirable list was expanded. Under the act of 1907 all types of mentally, morally, or physically deficient persons were excluded. Steamship companies were required to be more careful in their solicitation of and advertising for immigrants. Partly through the efforts of labor, literacy tests were advocated—generally to admit only those aliens who could read and write English or some other language. Both major political parties at times included such planks in their platforms. Presidents Cleveland, Taft, and Wilson vetoed bills passed by Congress requiring immigrants

IMMIGRATION TO THE UNITED STATES, 1820 – 1940

	EUROPE	ASIA AND AFRICA	AMERICA
1820-1870	6,717,627	341,575	349,171
1871-1890	7,009,308	191,418	831,011
1891-1930	18,531,411	627,209	3,061,247
1931-1940	348,289	17,094	160,037

Source: U.S. Bureau of the Census, *Historical Statistics of the United States, Colonial Times to 1957*, Washington, D.C., 1960, pp. 56–59.

to pass a literacy test on the ground in each case that such a qualification was a penalty upon the lack of opportunity in the home land and not a test of character, personal fitness, or good citizenship. However, such a test, although a weak one, was included in the measure of 1917, vetoed by President Wilson, but passed by Congress over his veto (p. 535).

After the Civil War a serious immigration problem arose on the Pacific coast. Chinese came to the United States in increasing numbers at the time of the California gold rush. Excluded from staking claims in the "diggings," they did the menial work in the towns and gold camps. The great need for unskilled labor during the Civil War and in the building of the Union Pacific Railroad led to the Burlingame Treaty of 1868, which recognized the right of Chinese and Americans to migrate freely from one country to another without restriction. By 1882 approximately 375,000 Chinese had entered the country.

After the California gold rush had subsided and the transcontinental railroad had been completed, many Chinese were unemployed. Others had small businesses in the cities or were engaged in raising fruits, growing small crops, and in canning. From 1870, unemployment on the west coast increased, and the competition of the Chinese, who were paid low wages, with white labor, whose standards of living were higher, resulted in increasing anti-Chinese feeling. This was expressed through boycotts on Chinese goods, laundry ordinances, anti-alien laws, and the imposition of taxes of different kinds. Riots occurred and a number of Orientals were killed. Men like Denis Kearney traveled up and down the Pacific coast crying "The Chinese must go." In 1877, Kearney organized the short-lived Workingmen's Party of California as a protest against widespread unemployment, land monopoly, railroad domination, Chinese coolie labor competition, and other economic and political ills of the period.

It took some time for the East and for Congress to realize the serious conditions existing on the west coast, but in 1878, Congress passed a measure restricting Chinese immigration (to a maximum of fifteen on each vessel). President Hayes vetoed the measure on the ground that it was contrary to the treaty of 1868, although he favored restriction. He was bitterly denounced in California. However, he appointed a commission to go to China to secure the modification of the Burlingame treaty. The commission was successful and a new agreement reached whereby the United States could "regulate, limit or suspend . . . but . . . not absolutely prohibit" the immigration of Chinese laborers to its shores. As a result, the Chinese Exclusion Act

of 1882 was passed. It suspended the immigration of skilled and unskilled laborers for a period of ten years, but allowed the admittance
of a few classes—teachers, students, merchants, and visitors—on temporary visits. This policy was continued by other laws and was extended
to Hawaii and the Philippines in 1900 and 1902. Largely an economic
one, the Chinese problem was unfortunately handled too often from
the point of view of politics.

During the last decades of the century, small numbers of Japanese, from the newly awakened land of Nippon, landed on the Pacific
coast. As early as 1890, when 2,039 Japanese were enumerated as living
in the United States, citizens of western states began to petition Congress to prohibit Japanese immigration. The lower standards of living
of the Orientals made competition with them difficult. The "yellow
peril" scare, too, which had its genesis in the early contacts between
Americans of European ancestry and the Chinese immigrant laborers,
now increased and racial barriers were emphasized. The number of
Japanese in the country increased from 24,000 in 1900 to 72,000 in
1910, but they were found chiefly in California. An Asiatic Exclusion
League, formed under the auspices of labor in 1905, aided in the movement against the Japanese and led to the segregation of Japanese children in a school in San Francisco. Agitation developed into diplomatic
exchanges. In 1907, President Theodore Roosevelt through a "gentleman's agreement" prevented the passage of legislation in Congress
which would have excluded the Japanese in a way similar to that applied to the Chinese. The immigration law of that year authorized the
President to enter into "such international agreements as may be
proper to prevent the immigration of aliens who, under the laws of the
United States, are or may be excluded. . . ." Secretary of War Root and
Ambassador Takahira made a "gentleman's agreement" whereby Japan
agreed not to issue passports to skilled or unskilled laborers desiring to
emigrate to the United States. In spite of the agreement, the California
legislature passed laws in 1913 and 1920 which made it impossible for
Japanese immigrants to own or lease agricultural or other real property.

THE WELFARE OF WORKERS

Comparisons of the real purchasing power of wages in different
periods is almost impossible. Even if a price index which will reliably
convert the current dollars into real or constant dollars can be found,
the goods and services that the worker may or has to buy change so
in type, quality, and satisfaction that they cannot be equated. The
worker of 1850, for example, did not expect to buy the ready-made

clothes or durable household goods that were commonplace by 1910, and hence their price was unimportant. He probably lived nearer his work and had no bus or trolley fare, and he and his family spent less on commercial amusement. To some extent increases in real wages may be eaten up by changing patterns in consumption that do not represent greater satisfaction.

In addition to all these problems wage statistics are very scarce. Manufacturing and construction workers, always a well-paid minority of the laboring population, are the only group for which there are fairly accurate nineteenth-century wage figures. During the years from 1850 through the Civil War, the real earnings even of these industrial workers probably failed to keep pace with the general upward movement of prices. In the period of generally falling prices from 1865 to 1890, however, real earnings for these favored workers may have doubled. Looked at another way, wage changes lagged behind price movements. In the period of general price increase from 1900 to 1914, real wages rose less rapidly registering an increase of about 20 per cent.[1]

Meanwhile the weekly hours of factory workers had been reduced from about 66, the eleven-hour day, to 55, representing in many cases a ten-hour weekday with a half-day on Saturday. The change was not great. Ten hours plus a half-hour for lunch and the trip to and from home left little leisure time during the week.

The workers' surroundings and living quarters also tended to deteriorate during this stage of urbanism and industrialism. Industry became concentrated in the bigger cities. Slums spread and became more crowded and less sanitary. The overcrowding in some of the largest cities like New York was the worst in the world, and prior to 1910, government took little responsibility for the welfare of the worker or his family. It was during this stage of industrialism that the Marxian prediction of the increasing exploitation of labor still seemed to have a ring of truth.

[1] These figures have been recently re-studied by Albert Rees and other scholars financed by the National Bureau of Economic Research.

CHAPTER 22

Business and the Public

THE DYNAMICS OF GROWTH

In 1850 most American firms were small suppliers of local or regional markets. Only a few companies such as the New England textile mills or hardware producers sold all over the nation, and by twentieth-century standards even the biggest of these firms was small. By 1914, however, big semimonopolistic companies had established the place in manufacturing that they were to maintain thereafter. One to a dozen firms might supply the United States and Canadian markets with sugar, oil, and farm or office machinery.

This evolution appeared to be the direct result of the economic situation. In most manufacturing plants the cost of each unit of product, each gallon of oil, or each reaper decreased as production increased. This was chiefly because many fixed costs such as amortization of buildings and equipment remained the same, and others such as office and selling expenses rose more slowly than returns from increased production. As a result, a firm such as Standard Oil which through extra efficiency and better location could initially reach a level of production above that of its competitors had a snowball-like advantage: as costs declined prices could be cut, and as prices were cut more of the market was captured.

In Europe medium-sized businesses came together in associations or cartels and apportioned the market between them. But in the United States the courts not only refused to enforce such agreements, but frequently held them to be conspiracies in restraint of trade. Efforts to combine on a gentlemen's or voluntary basis repeatedly failed; someone always turned out not to be a gentleman and started selling beyond the agreed quota or below the agreed price. The result, in industries with surplus plant capacity and diminishing unit costs as production increased, was a steady pressure to merge small firms into bigger corporations or trusts.

Opening up a national market, railroads put producers in competition with each other all over the country. By 1890 the United States had the world's largest home market and the firms that captured special parts of it grew very big. Railroads also aided bigness in two other ways. Since rates from cities served by two or more competing roads were lower than from smaller towns served by a single line, many small town manufacturers found it wise either to move to the railroad junction cities or to sell out to better located competitors. This pressure operated strongly on manufacturers of bulky products in which transportation made up much of the final cost, or on processors who needed large amounts of fuel or raw materials. Hence, oil and steel moved to the centers most advantageous for transportation, whereas clocks and shoes stayed where there were skilled workers without much regard to the cost of shipment. The second way in which railroads encouraged bigness was by granting lower rates to producers who could guarantee uniformly large shipments. As a Lake Shore Railroad manager put it, Standard Oil gave them forty carloads of oil a day, and he would be willing to give equally low rates to any shipper who could do likewise. But by this time, thanks largely to the ability of John D. Rockefeller, there was no other shipper, and so in addition to its advantage in lower costs of production Standard enjoyed lower costs of transportation.

But the spectacular rise of the giant corporation in the United States, particularly from 1880 to 1905, should not obscure the fact that such companies did not dominate manufacturing as a whole. Against a score of industries where big firms were dominant, there were hundreds of others where all firms were small. In fact, bigness was fairly well-confined to heavy industry, raw material processing in food and minerals, public utilities, and railroads; or to put it another way to those industries that had to have either large capital investment or large marketing organizations to operate efficiently.

While manufacturing was basic to a high standard of living and a complex national business structure, it was always a small part of the whole. Finance, transportation, trade, and service taken together employed many more workers and many times the number of entrepreneurs. Trade and service alone from 1850 to 1960 always comprised the majority of firms and managers, and there were very few large firms and almost no national monopolies in either of these major activities. Hence throughout this whole period of rapid growth the representative American businessman remained the shopkeeper.

MARKETING

The railroad, the telegraph, and the progress of paper and printing brought revolutionary changes in the means of distributing factory-made goods. Before the spread of the railroad, storekeepers from the back country made tedious and frequently dangerous journeys to the major cities in order to buy goods and make sure that they got them home (p. 273). With the coming of the railroad the larger producers or importers started to send salesmen to visit the wholesalers and retailers. The increasing reliability of the big distributing houses made merchants willing to buy from samples. If necessary, orders could be sent in by telegraph and delivered by express. By the last decades of the century the salesman with his samples and catalogues was everywhere; storekeepers no longer needed to travel. As both business and the market grew, the number of wholesalers and jobbers in small cities as well as large increased greatly.

Selling, both wholesale and retail, became more specialized, and the mechanics of distribution more complex. As in earlier times, the term "wholesaler" was customarily applied to a firm that bought goods, stored them, and resold to either other middlemen or retailers (p. 273). A big wholesaler in dry goods or food located in a major city might supply small city wholesalers all over the country and a few retailers who could order in large quantity. Many standard commodities such as wheat, cotton, or pepper were bought and sold by brokers, or supplied by brokers from foreign agents on commission. In general men called brokers bought on commodity exchanges and did not store the goods, but all of these terms had many exceptions. Whether a man was called a "commission merchant," or "broker," or "jobber," for example, varied with the type of goods handled. In some lines like fresh fruits and vegetables, a "jobber" was a wholesaler who bought in less than carload lots. In other lines he might represent producers or handle transportation. "Factory agents" performed in much the same way as jobbers, but arranged for the sale of the products of only certain firms. An agent for a brewery, for example, tried to get local wholesalers and retailers to buy only the brand of beer that he represented.

Salesmen were employed by all these middlemen as well as by producers. As in the earlier stages of industrialism all over the world, great emphasis was put on personal selling. Trusted salesmen were allowed large expense accounts for entertainment. "Diamond" Jim Brady, a factory representative for railroad equipment, became famous for his parties. But little by little, from 1880 on, national advertising was beginning to substitute for personal sales effort. In general, about half the retail price of goods represented costs of distribution.

Nation-wide competition increased the use of brand names to differentiate products. The use of brand names, in turn, led to distinctive packaging and advertising. Advertising grew from technological advances as well as from business needs. In the late 1840's the rotary printing press made for bigger editions of newspapers, and twenty years later the sulphite process made pulp paper cheap. The way was now opened for the modern type of display advertising in newspapers and mass-circulation magazines.

While agencies to place national advertising appeared before the Civil War, the great growth of advertising activity in the United States came from the eighties on, slightly later than in England and France. As makers of soap, beverages, packaged foods, and consumer durable goods increased their advertising budgets, agencies planned careful national campaigns, hired artists, and consulted psychologists. Billboards and other outdoor displays grew as the use of bicycles and automobiles spread. Car cards in the new trolleys and suburban trains were added to the older media. As the circulation of newspapers and magazines quadrupled during the nineties, cheap slick magazines such as *Ladies Home Journal* and *Saturday Evening Post* carried advertisers' messages to homes all over the nation. The publishers of these magazines were active in soliciting advertising and working with the agencies on campaigns. The many competing automobile companies of the first two decades of the twentieth century spent large sums in various types of media. By 1910 over 4 per cent of the national income was being spent on advertising, a ratio that was only equalled again in the early twenties.

National advertising of brands meant an interest by the producer in the selling practices of the retailer. Factory experts arranged store displays, and the producer assisted in meeting the cost of the retailer's local advertising. Such practices bypassed the old-style wholesalers, brokers, and jobbers in a number of products, particularly automobiles and other expensive durable goods. But in many lines where wide variety and large stocks were necessary, such as in hardware, or where the product was undifferentiated, as in grain, the old, more complicated systems of distribution were still more efficient.

The entire network of wholesalers, jobbers, retailers, and consumers operated on thirty- to sixty-day credit, with even slower payment anticipated in rural areas. This large volume of somewhat uncertain credit had to be reflected in higher prices, and the higher prices, in turn, invited lower-priced competition on a cash basis. Mail order houses such as Sears Roebuck and Montgomery Ward became important in the last decades of the nineteenth century by selling from catalogues for cash in the form of a check or money order. Their illustrated catalogues offered many articles at prices below those of local retailers and also saved isolated farmers the trouble of shopping. Another selling innovation of these last decades was the chain store, Woolworth in five- and ten-cent notions and the Atlantic and Pacific Tea Company in food demonstrated the savings that could be achieved by selling for cash in large volume.

The department store in the larger cities also offered the consumer lower prices based on larger volume with limited credit. The earliest of these big stores, A. T. Stewart's in New York and John Wanamaker's in Philadelphia started before 1850. They were widely copied from the seventies on, with Macy's of New York demonstrating that prices could be cut still more by selling only for cash.

NEW CORPORATE FORMS

By 1870 smart businessmen were using the corporate form for most ventures requiring large capital funds, but incorporation had certain disadvantages. Careful minutes of business decisions had to be prepared, and a lawyer was often required to give advice, whereas a partnership operated in a free and easy fashion. Andrew Carnegie, for example, found it best to keep his firm a partnership for many years, because in this way he was not bothered with directors' meetings and resolutions of the board. Since liability became limited to the assets of the corporation, entrepreneurs such as investment bankers, who wished to inspire confidence that they would back up their commitments, kept the partnership form. Small operators saw no special gain from incorporation that would balance the cost of securing a charter and the trouble of forming a board of directors. Consequently, while the corporate form spread in fields such as manufacturing and transportation, most enterprises remained proprietorships or partnerships. In 1916 there were 341,000 corporations among some 2,000,000 enterprises in the United States.

But relative numbers had little to do with the importance of the corporation in the business system. Not only was it the only device by which tens of millions of dollars in capital could be mobilized from the savings of many people, it was also a flexible device for handling changes in ownership and control. By consent of the stockholders a corporation could be leased for a long period such as 99 years to another corporation at an annual rental. In this way railroad systems were constructed by leasing other lines, which obviated the need for raising additional capital or issuing new shares. Another way of consolidating corporations was the trustee certificate plan put into effect by Standard Oil in 1879 by which stocks and properties in many different companies were finally transferred to a board of nine trustees, with Rockefeller as head. The stockholders received trust certificates for their holdings, entitling them to their share of ownership and profits, but not to any voting privileges. Thus, the administration of the great corporation was centralized in the hands of nine able men. The ingenious system of a trust, whereby the trustees alone had the legal voting right, was copied by other industries. Among these were the American Cotton Oil Trust in 1884, the National Linseed Oil Trust in 1885, and the Distillers and Cattle Feeders' Trust (Whisky Trust) in 1887. While this particular form of industrial centralization did not remain in use very long and was superseded by others such as the holding company (p. 635), journalists came to refer to any big company as a trust.

As large corporations, trusts, and combinations arose, opposition to them developed among the public. Increasing hostility to monopoly grew as knowledge of the methods of the Standard Oil Company and other monopolies became widespread. A demand for regulative and restrictive action by the government appeared. The farmer organizations had opposed monopolies—especially railroad monopolies—and in 1880 a farmer-labor party, the Greenbackers, denounced corporations and called for government action against them. A political anti-monopoly party crystallized in 1884 and took part in the campaign of that year. Both major political parties bowed to public opinion in 1888, pledging Federal action against trusts and monopolies. At the same time an increasing amount of literature appeared that stressed the evils of large-scale industrial enterprise, especially dishonest practices, unfair privileges, the ruthless exploitation of the country's natural resources, the growth of large fortunes, and the concentration of wealth.

The first steps in the control of large-scale enterprise were taken in the states. Before 1890, several of them placed anti-trust clauses in their corporation laws and the number of states adopting such measures increased after that date. Some inserted such provisions in their constitutions. This legislation, however, was largely defeated by the contrary policy of several states. Beginning with New Jersey in 1888, a few states amended their corporation laws to permit "holding companies." Prior to this time, companies were legally competent to own the shares of other concerns only when special charters conferred this privilege, and few such charters had been granted. There are two main types of holding companies: those whose chief business it is to own the stocks of other companies controlling them primarily for investment, and those which acquire all or part of the securities of subsidiaries in order to control or influence their management and to combine such ownership with business operations of their own.

Public agitation over the power and size of giant combinations led to the passage by Congress of the Sherman Antitrust Law in 1890. Only one specific type of combination was named in the act—"trusts," although a blanket phrase covered the others. The law begins: "Every contract, combination, or conspiracy, in the form of trust or otherwise, or conspiracy, in restraint of trade or commerce among the several states, or with foreign nations, is hereby declared to be illegal." The purpose of the law, of course, was to declare illegal all combinations in restraint of trade. The act proved to be weak in several ways. No commission was created to enforce it, as was the case in the Interstate Commerce Act; thus, private individuals or the government would have to bring suits claiming violation of the act. Then, too, it did not define clearly its terms and phrases, leaving to the courts the task of interpretation and developing principles by which industrialists and businessmen could be guided in the development of combinations and great enterprises. At first the law was largely ineffective, for it did little more than put into statutory form the old common law prohibition against conspiracies in restraint of trade.

One of the most important early lawsuits brought under the Sherman Antitrust Law was the case of the United States *vs.* E. C. Knight Company, commonly called the Sugar Trust case (1895). It involved the purchase of four independent concerns in the Philadelphia area by the American Sugar Refining Company, a New Jersey corporation, which gave the company control of 98 per cent of the refining of sugar in the entire country. The Court held that the acquisition of refineries and the business of the manufacturing of sugar within a state was not a matter of interstate commerce and therefore not a violation of the act. Unfortunately, the Attorney General of the United States, who brought the suit, failed to emphasize in the government's brief the monopolistic character of the result of the acquisition of the re-fineries, and as a result the Court held that a combination of manu-facturers was not, in itself, an illegal restraint on interstate commerce. Two years later the Supreme Court further defined its view in the case of the United States *vs.* Trans-Missouri Freight Association (1897). This case involved the attempt of a number of western railroads to fix freight rates by mutual agreement. The Supreme Court decided that the Sherman Act did apply to railroads. In the five to four decision it held that the legislation prohibited all contracts in restraint of interstate or foreign trade whether or not the common action of the companies was to maintain "reasonable rates." The minority of the Court who dissented held that the agreements were reasonable and necessary to prevent destructive competition between the roads. In the Addyston Pipe case (1899), the Court declared illegal a pooling agreement among manufacturers of iron pipe to control prices through the regulation of production and collusive bidding. The pool was ordered dissolved by the Court on the ground that it violated the law of competition and was directly related to interstate commerce. To corporation lawyers these decisions meant that mergers leading to larger individual companies might be legal, but agreements between competitors were not.

A PERIOD OF INDUSTRIAL COMBINATIONS

Between the years 1891 and 1897, the number of great industrial and business combinations that took form was not large. The depres-sion extending over most of this period was chiefly responsible as industrial life suffered from the effects of the panic. But from 1898 to 1903 combinations, especially in the form of holding companies, increased at a most remarkable rate. In 1900, there were 185 in-dustrial combinations with a capitalization of $3 billion engaged in producing 14 per cent of the industrial products of the country. Of these, seventy-three were each capitalized at $10,000,000 or more. In 1904, there were 318 large industrial combinations representing a capitalization of more than $7 billion. These exercised power over the production of petroleum, tobacco products, beef, sugar, iron and steel, and many other industries and manufactures.

The greatest of all the holding companies created during this period was the United States Steel Corporation. Chartered under the laws of New Jersey in 1901, the largest business enterprise in the world, and the first billion dollar corporation, was organized by the combination of a number of large corporations engaged in the manufacture of iron and steel. It was effected largely under the inspiring genius of Elbert H. Gary, president of one of the corporations that was included in the merger, together with Andrew Carnegie, who desired to retire from his vast interests, and the elder J. Pierpont Morgan, whose vast financial power was needed to arrange and finance the deal. The ten large companies involved had an aggregate capital of $867,550,394, owned 149 steel plants, eighty-four blast furnaces, 1,000 miles of railroad, 112 Great Lakes' vessels, and thousands of acres of coal, ore, and limestone lands. The authorized capital of the "Steel Trust," as it became known, was $1,404,000,000, of which the bonds and preferred stocks covered the whole value of the combined companies and the $500,000,000 of common stock was largely, if not entirely, pure "water." In the years that followed, the corporation built up its assets far beyond its capitalization and also gathered under its wing many other companies within the industry.

INCREASED CONTROL OF TRUSTS

When Theodore Roosevelt became President in 1901 as the result of the assassination of William McKinley, one of the most important issues before the country was the control of trusts and monopolies. Public opinion demanded a more effective enforcement of the Sherman Act and additional Federal legislation relating to corporations engaged in interstate business. The increased number of combinations since 1898 was evidence that the Sherman Act had little effect in restraining the growth of trusts or the abuses that accompanied them, and early in the century it became evident that the process of consolidation was making even more progress in the fields of transportation and finance. Combinations were coming under the control of great banking houses. This led John Moody in 1904 to write that ". . . viewed as a whole, we find the dominating influences in the trusts to be made up of an intricate network of large and small capitalists, many allied to one another by ties of more or less importance but all being appendaged to or parts of the greater groups which are themselves dependent on and allied with the two mammoth, or Rockefeller and Mor-

His Flag

He hopes to replace the Stars and Stripes with it before long.

gan groups. These two . . . jointly . . . constitute the heart of the business and commercial life of the nation."[1]

During the era of Roosevelt and under his dynamic personality "trust-busting" became a fixed term in the public imagination. In preaching against monopolies, Roosevelt in his first message to Congress and in speeches to the masses naively divided trusts into two classes—"good and bad trusts"—and declared that "we draw the line against misconduct, not against wealth." Good trusts, he avowed, operated and carried on their activities with a view to public welfare, trading fairly and passing on their economies to consumers. On the other hand, "bad trusts," controlled by malefactors of great wealth, were selfishly seeking their own interests and had little concern for the public. "We do not wish to destroy corporations," Roosevelt asserted, "but we do wish to make them subserve the public good." Translating his stirring phrases into action, he ordered Attorney General Knox to bring suit against the Standard Oil Company, the American Tobacco Company, the DuPont Powder Trust, and others. When Benjamin Harrison was President, only seven suits were instituted

[1] John Moody, *Truth About the Trusts: A Description and Analysis of the American Trust Movement* (New York, 1904), p. 493.

under the Sherman Act; eight were brought by Cleveland; three by McKinley; and forty-eight by Roosevelt. Many of the latter, however, were not decided until Taft's administration.

The most spectacular Supreme Court decision regarding the Sherman Act was not against an industrial combination, but in connection with a plan to combine a number of railroads in the Northwest. The formation of the Northern Securities Company had been the result of a stock market duel for control of the Northern Pacific between Edward H. Harriman, who controlled the Union Pacific System and affiliated financial interests, on the one hand, and J. Pierpont Morgan and James J. Hill of the Great Northern on the other. The two factions finally united in forming a holding company in 1901 which took over all the stock in the Great Northern, Northern Pacific, and Burlington lines in which the Morgan and Hill group held a controlling interest. To the astonishment of Wall Street, President Theodore Roosevelt instructed Attorney General Knox to bring suit under the Sherman Antitrust Act. The potent Republican Senator Marcus A.

THE RAILROAD INFLUENCE OF HARRIMAN AND HILL

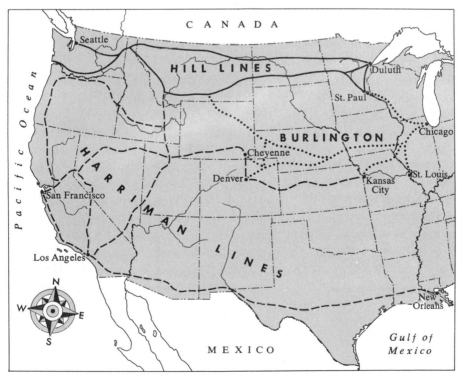

Hanna rushed to Washington to dissuade the President but without result. In a five to four decision the Supreme Court upheld the contention of the government that the holding company had been used as an illegal device for restraining trade. The consequence of the decision, so far as it affected those in control of railroad securities, was of little practical importance, for although the Northern Securities Company was dissolved and the shares were returned to the stockholders in the original companies, actual control of both Northern Pacific and Great Northern Railroads was left in the hands of the Morgan-Hill group by virtue of their large holdings of stock in those companies. But the case was a landmark in the history of "big business." It was a victory for the government; it revitalized the Sherman Act; it increased the popularity of the President; and it gave the public the feeling that at last monopolies were to be controlled.

Another case, more spectacular than important, but one which disclosed that rebating had not ended, was brought to a District Court. The Standard Oil Company of Indiana was accused of receiving "an unlawful secret rate" on petroleum shipped over the Chicago and Alton Railroad. In 1907, Judge Kenesaw M. Landis found the company guilty of violating the Elkins Anti-Rebate Act on 1,462 separate counts and fined it a total of $29,240,000. It is evident that this huge fine was imposed because of prejudice and not in the interests of justice. The next year the decree was reversed by the Circuit Court of Appeals and

"The American Beauty Rose can be produced in all its splendor only by sacrificing the early buds that grow up around it."

This sentence in a speech concerning Standard Oil business tactics inspired this cartoon.

was dismissed, partly on a question of the meaning of the law. The case was not reviewed by the Supreme Court.

Still another example of corruption was disclosed when the case against the American Sugar Refining Company was made public. Late in 1907 it was discovered that the company had defrauded the government of large sums of money which should have been paid as duties on imported sugar. This was done by tampering with the scales on which the sugar was weighed. Suits were brought and more than $4,000,000 was recovered from the company. Criminal prosecutions were brought against officials and employees, and a number of them convicted.

In 1903, when the President recommended the creation of a Department of Commerce and a complete investigation of corporations, Congress created the Department of Commerce and Labor with a Secretary of cabinet rank "to foster, promote, and develop the foreign and domestic commerce, the mining, manufacturing, shipping and fishery industries, the labor interests, and the transportation facilities of the United States." Within the new Department a Bureau of Corporations was set up which was authorized to investigate the activities of interstate corporations. At first its work was undertaken in a weak manner, but finally it thoroughly investigated a number of industries, providing reports and material for the prosecution of some of them under the antitrust laws.

THE "RULE OF REASON" AND TRUSTS

Many judicial cases that had been begun during Roosevelt's period of office were decided during the administration of his successor, William H. Taft. But President Taft was more active than his predecessor in bringing suit against corporations for violations of the Sherman Act. During his four years of office, eighty suits were inaugurated against trusts compared with forty-eight during Roosevelt's seven-year administration.

Perhaps the most important decision brought under the Sherman Act up to that time was in the case of the Standard Oil Company of New Jersey in 1911. The case originated in 1906 when the government filed suit against a number of corporations and individuals alleging that they were conspiring "to restrain the trade and commerce in petroleum . . . in refined oil, and in other products of petroleum." In 1909, the Circuit Court upheld the charge, holding that the combining of the stocks of various companies into the Standard Oil Company of New Jersey in 1899 was a combination in restraint of trade and also an attempt at monopoly. The corporation was forbidden to control its thirty-seven subsidiary companies, which meant a complete dissolution into independent companies and competing units. The case was taken on appeal to the Supreme Court, and in 1911 that body upheld the decision of the Circuit Court. It went further and declared that applications of the antitrust law should "be determined by the light of reason."

The judicial principle, first adopted in the case against the Standard Oil Trust that became known as the "rule of reason," followed the minority opinion of the court in the Trans-Missouri Freight Association case (1897). It was now accepted by the majority of the justices that the Sherman Act prohibited only *unreasonable* restraint of trade. Acts or agreements of a monopolistic nature which affected interstate commerce in an unreasonable manner were to be construed as acts in restraint of trade. The size of the corporation was not to be considered—only its purposes, acts, and the results of its activities. The rule of reason, therefore, was to be derived not from laws or earlier decisions, but from the common sense of the judges. In a vigorous dissenting opinion in the Standard Oil case, Justice Harlan denounced the rule of reason as "judicial legislation" and an attempt to defeat the will of Congress, because the act stated that "all combinations in restraint of trade" were illegal. The principle, however, was accepted and applied to other cases. Subsequent prosecutions under the Sherman Act came to be based not on the size or power of a corporation, but on its unfair, monopolistic, or illegal use of its power.

In the process of dissolution, the Standard Oil Company of New Jersey gave its stockholders pro rata shares in the companies that it had controlled. The immediate effect of the decision was simply to break up the trust into a number of smaller companies, all still controlled by the Rockefeller interests. The increasing market value of the various stocks in the now "competing companies" show clearly that the stockholders had not suffered in any way, nor did it seem that the public had benefited by the decision.

In the six years following the decision, the value of shares of the original holding company, a number of which were not exchanged for some time, rose almost fourfold. But one of the results of the case was to increase the demand by the public for more specific legislation. The interpretation by the court of the language of the law was not sufficient, and public opinion in a progressive age was demanding legislation that was clear and which would provide remedies for many abuses that were becoming more and more evident.

THE PROGRESSIVE ERA

The first fourteen years of the twentieth century were marked by intense demands for reforms—political, social, and economic. This movement had its roots in the last decades of the nineteenth century in the clamor against railroads and monopolies, combinations and trusts, privilege and wealth. Agrarian discontent and the growing evils of urban life added greatly to the strength of the reform movements.

The agitation for reform brought results in the early twentieth century. The West led the swelling tide for human betterment, but it was by no means confined to that section of the country. Robert M. La Follette as governor of Wisconsin led a movement which resulted in the adoption of political devices such as the direct primary, the referendum and recall, and also in progressive economic measures for the stricter supervision, control, and taxation of corporations in his state. The cooperation that developed between specialists at the University of Wisconsin and the administration of the state became known as the "Wisconsin Idea." University professors aided the establishment of Tax, Railway, Insurance, Civil Service, Industrial, Conservation, and other commissions, frequently serving as members. Other universities and colleges began to consider vital economic and social issues, alarming big business and small politicians by their daring thought. The masses were made conscious of the changing scene through the Chautauqua movement, the revived lyceums, women's clubs, and other agencies which stressed the need for understanding and participating in democratic life. Corruption was assailed and appeals were made for legislative and judicial action.

In 1902 it was clearly demonstrated that articles attacking corruption sold magazines, and able writers were commissioned to expose political, social, and economic evils. Ida M. Tarbell's series of articles on the "History of the Standard Oil Company" appeared in *McClure's Magazine*. They were based on a study of congressional reports, court records, and other primary sources. Miss Tarbell exposed the ruthless methods and unfair practices used by that corporation toward competitors, the public, and the government. In the same magazine Lincoln Steffens' "The Shame of the Cities" was published. These articles and others like them marked the beginning of a crusade which continued for over half a dozen years. Ray Stannard Baker's "The Railroads on Trial," stressing the unfair manipulation of rates, appeared in *McClure's* (1905–1906). Thomas W. Lawson, a well-known stock market operator, revealed what he called the strangle hold of Wall Street on the financial system of the country in a series of articles, "Frenzied Finance," published in *Everybody's*. *Munsey's Magazine, Collier's,* and other periodicals entered heartily into the crusade. The political activities of railroads and industries, child labor, the exploitation of women, conditions in factories, the unethical practices of big business, the adulteration of food or drugs, and a thousand other ills became the theme of many magazine articles. Some were published later in book form.

Many novels and books also attacked current abuses. Examples of these are Frank Norris' *The Octopus* (1901) which exposed the strangulation of the California farmers by the Southern Pacific Railroad, and *The Pit,* which set forth the activities and evils of speculation in wheat. Elliott Flower wrote a story of the practices of the Chicago utilities in *The Spoilsman* in 1903. Upton Sinclair's *The Jungle* (1906), which told of the grip of the beef trust on the meat supply of the nation and stressed the unsanitary conditions of Chicago's packing plants, was directly influential in the passage of the pure food and drug acts by Congress.

Much concerned by the exposé of the control of the Senate by big business as set forth in such articles as David Graham Phillips' "The Treason of the Senate," published in *Cosmopolitan* (1906–1907), Roosevelt referred to the authors of such literature as muckrakers, likening them to the man with the rake in *The Pilgrim's Progress* who was more interested in raking the filth at his feet than in obtaining a celestial crown. A short time later in his characteristic fashion he attacked both big business and the "lunatic fringe of muckrakers."

Backed by public opinion the reformers were quite successful. They were partly responsible for a mass of political, social, and economic legislation which was adopted in the states. Included were laws regarding compensation for accidents at work, child labor, factory inspection, and safety (p. 466). Stricter control was also effected within the states over corporations. Among the laws passed by Congress were those pertaining to railroads, the establishment of the Department of Commerce and Labor with its Bureau of Corporations, the Pure Food and Drugs Act (1906), which applied to goods shipped in interstate or foreign commerce and was designed to prevent the adulteration or misbranding of foods or drugs, and the Meat Inspection Act (1906), which gave the Secretary of Agriculture under the interstate commerce clause the power to inspect all meats shipped across state boundaries and to condemn products that were "unsound, unhealthful, unwholesome, or otherwise unfit for human food."

THE CLAYTON ACT

As noted on p. 490 there was a growing demand for progressive legislation to make clearer the clauses of the Sherman Act and to prohibit many evils which had grown with the development of trusts. Clarification of the Sherman Act was achieved by the Clayton Act of 1914. In its passage, it encountered much bitter opposition. Although the Clayton Act reflected the ideas of President Wilson and other administration leaders regarding the regulation of business and industry, only the strength of the bipartisan progressive movement made possible such a law. The new law set forth a number of definitions which eliminated much of the ambiguity of the Sherman Act so that henceforth the courts could be guided by the meaning of certain terms. It prohibited discriminations in prices in favor of certain purchasers or suppliers where discrimination lessened competition or tended to create a monopoly; it forbade exclusive selling or leasing contracts (tying contracts) which would prevent purchasers from handling the products of competitors; it made it illegal for a company to acquire the stock of a competitor, although this clause did not apply to corporations purchasing such stock solely for investment and not for the purpose of lessening competition; it imposed complicated limitations on interlocking directorates of industrial combinations and banks; it placed restrictions on the relation of common carriers to construction and supply companies; it made the directors of corporations personally liable for violations of the law by their companies; and it provided that individuals, not only government officials, could secure injunctions to restrain continued violations of the act. Clauses referring to labor were also important. The law proclaimed that "the labor of a human being is not a commodity or article of commerce"; it exempted labor and agricultural organizations from the antitrust laws, and prohibited the use of injunctions in labor disputes unless necessary to prevent irreparable injury and damages.

In the same year, Congress established a Federal Trade Commission of five members for the purpose of administering the antitrust laws. It was authorized to investigate any "corporation engaged in commerce, except banks and common carriers, and to require from them annual and special reports and other information." It was empowered to prevent business enterprises from using unfair methods of competition in interstate commerce by issuing "cease and desist" orders. These orders could be enforced, however, only by the Federal courts, on the application of the Commission. The Bureau of Corporations, established in the Department of Commerce and Labor (p. 468), was taken over and its work was enlarged. During President Wilson's administration the Commission heard about 2,000 complaints and issued 379 "cease and desist" orders in connection with unfair competition, bribery, false advertising, adulteration, and misrepresentation. Through its efforts, it was largely responsible for bringing about the break-up of the International Harvester Company and the Corn Products Refining Company.

The antitrust legislation of 1914 represented a new concept in regard to the trust problem. While monopoly was still forbidden, the chief stress was placed on the maintenance of fair competition. It was evident that the lawmakers did not want to interfere with the growth of big business enterprises. The evils arising from combinations were attacked and not the combinations themselves. By this time the advantages and benefits of large-scale production were being recognized. The change in government policy reflected the changes in political and judicial opinion; while monopoly was condemned, limited or "monopolistic competition" was tolerated.

CHAPTER 23

Foreign Trade and Expansion

Except for the Crimean and American Civil Wars, the period from 1850 to 1914 was unusually free from major international interference with trade. People, capital, and money moved freely from nation to nation, and the movement of goods was restricted only by tariffs. The United States from 1862 on was the most highly protected of the major industrial nations. Looked at broadly, the most important element in our trade with foreign nations was the movement of people. As noted in Chapter 21, during this period immigrants added a quarter or a third to the American population. These people, more than foreign capital or goods, speeded the economic growth of the United States.

The general pattern of American foreign trade continued unchanged. Wheat, corn, meat, and their products were added increasingly to cotton as major exports. Refrigeration on railroads and steamers from the 1870's on allowed the United States to invade the European market with fresh beef. Exports of American canned and salted food also increased. As a consequence, although exports of American manufactures and semimanufactures rose, the bulk of exports remained agricultural, and cotton remained the most valuable single type. Trade as a whole grew more slowly than the gross national

495

AMERICAN FOREIGN TRADE CLASSIFIED BY COMMODITY TYPES, 1860 – 1920

United States Exports as a Per Cent of Total

Fiscal Year	Crude Materials	Crude Foodstuffs	Manufactured Foodstuffs	Semi-manufactures	Finished Manufactures
1860	68.6	3.8	12.2	4.1	11.3
1880	29.4	32.3	23.5	3.5	11.3
1900	24.8	16.5	23.3	11.2	24.2
1920	23.3	11.4	13.8	11.9	39.6

United States Imports as a Per Cent of Total

Fiscal Year	Crude Materials	Crude Foodstuffs	Manufactured Foodstuffs	Semi-manufactures	Finished Manufactures
1860	11.4	12.9	16.9	9.9	48.9
1880	21.3	15.0	17.7	16.6	29.4
1900	33.1	11.5	15.7	15.8	23.9
1920	33.8	10.9	23.5	15.2	16.6

Source: Adapted from U.S. Bureau of the Census, *Historical Statistics of the United States, Colonial Times to 1957* Washington, D.C., 1960, pp. 544–545.

product. Whereas the latter, in current dollars, increased nearly five-fold between 1870 and 1910, the total of merchandise imports and exports rose less than four-fold.

Changes in the invisible items in the trade balance forced the United States from 1875 on to produce a surplus of exports. Ocean freight charges were now largely collected by foreigners. American tourists spent more abroad than visitors spent here. Money sent or carried home by immigrants exceeded the amounts they brought to the United States. But most important of all the nation became a mature debtor country, one owing more in dividends and interest on previous investments than the annual amount of new capital invested by foreigners. Thus, while the tariff undoubtedly held down imports, and in this way total trade, a surplus of exports would have been necessary regardless of tariff policy.

The international distribution of United States exports did not change greatly (p. 498). Exports to the Far East steadily increased, but were still less than 10 per cent of the total in 1910. After declining in the early nineteenth century exports to North America rose in the early twentieth. Europe continued to dominate the trade of South America.

Imports showed more variation than exports from decade to decade, but the same gain by the Far East and North America at the expense of Europe was noticeable after 1895. South America steadily contributed a surplus of imports to the United States.

AMERICAN INVESTMENTS ABROAD

From 1850 to 1890 the United States was one of the most desirable areas for the investment of European capital. The greatest decades were the 1860's, because of the bargains offered in United States government bonds, and the 1880's because of the appeal of American railroad and cattle companies. By the 1890's both depression and the relative maturity of American western expansion made domestic capital more plentiful in relation to good investments. In 1870 the yield on United States railroad bonds, for example, had averaged nearly 8 per cent, in 1890 the average was 4.6 per cent, and in 1900 under 4 per cent. As a result, European capitalists turned to areas of higher yield such as Latin America and Africa, and capitalists in the United States became interested in investment opportunities outside the country.

American capital went abroad in a number of ways. So-called "direct" investments were by American companies setting up foreign subsidiaries, buying physical property or the stock of foreign companies. "Indirect" investment was the buying of foreign government securities. The total amount of American investments abroad in 1897 amounted to $684,500,000. By 1914 this had increased to $3.5 billion, compared with $7.2 billion of foreign investments in the United States.

During the period, American firms established many foreign sales offices, agencies, and warehouses. The Standard Oil Corporation, for

NET FOREIGN INVESTMENT IN THE UNITED STATES BY DECADES, 1820 – 1899

(In millions of dollars)

1820 – 1829	−5	1860 – 1869	765
1830 – 1839	215	1870 – 1879	485
1840 – 1849	−105	1880 – 1889	1,135
1850 – 1859	195	1890 – 1899	60

Sources: Douglass C. North, "The United States Balance of Payments, 1790–1860," conference paper, National Bureau of Economic Research, Inc.; and Matthew Simon, "Statistical Estimates of the Balance of Payments and the International Capital Movements of the United States, 1861–1900," conference paper, National Bureau of Economic Research, Inc.

example, came to have sixteen subsidiaries in different parts of the world and the United States Steel Corporation 268 agencies in sixty countries. By 1914, the largest American corporations had almost $500 million invested in foreign factories, chiefly in Canada, Europe, and Latin America. Investments in foreign railroads, largely in the Caribbean area, rose from $143,300,000 in 1897 to $255,100,000 in 1914. American capital also went into agricultural enterprises abroad— sugar plantations and mills in Cuba, Puerto Rico, Hawaii, and the Philippines; the production of tropical fruit, coconuts, cacao, coffee, tea, spices, sisal, jute, hemp, rubber in various areas, as well as ranches and farms in Canada and Mexico. Direct investments in American-controlled foreign ventures were also large. These included

VALUE OF UNITED STATES EXPORTS BY CONTINENTS, 1821 – 1920
(In millions of dollars)

	1821	1830	1840	1850	1860	1870	1880	1890	1900	1910	1920
EUROPE	36	48	92	109	249	381	719	684	1040	1136	4466
ASIA	2	1	1	3	8	4	12	20	68	78	872
AMERICA	15	23	30	30	69	79	93	133	227	479	2553
AFRICA						2	5	5	19	19	166
AUSTRALIA AND OCEANIA						5	7	16	41	34	172

VALUE OF UNITED STATES IMPORTS BY CONTINENTS, 1821 – 1920
(In millions of dollars)

	1821	1830	1840	1850	1860	1870	1880	1890	1900	1910	1920
EUROPE	35	40	62	124	217	241	371	450	441	806	1228
ASIA	5	5	10	11	29	37	74	81	146	210	1397
AMERICA	15	17	25	38	104	153	212	238	224	503	2424
AFRICA						3	4	3	11	17	150
AUSTRALIA AND OCEANIA		1	1	1	4	2	7	17	29	20	80

Source: U.S. Bureau of the Census, *Historical Statistics of the United States, Colonial Times to 1957*, Washington, D.C. 1960, pp. 550–553.

investments in oil, copper, aluminum, lead, nickel, tin, zinc, iron, nitrates, and coal.

Americans held more than $1,000,000,000 in the securities of foreign governments and foreign-controlled corporations in 1914. Branch banking in foreign countries was carried on by the International Banking Corporation of New York, so that exporters and importers in many areas no longer had to depend upon British, French, German, and Dutch banks and their branches. The Federal Reserve Act of 1913 and subsequent banking legislation provided for the establishment of foreign branches by national and state banks, which led to the purchase of the International Banking Corporation by the National City Bank and to the creation of foreign branches by other companies such as Chase National Bank.

THE NEW IMPERIALISM

By about 1870 the fusion of nationalism and industrialism created a renewed European imperialism which resulted in the division of the backward countries of Africa and Asia among the leading nations. England, France, Germany, and Italy sought control in different parts of the world through military conquest, agreements and treaties with native governments, establishment of "spheres of influence" in various ways, setting up protectorates, annexation, and economic penetration, especially through investments. The ultimate purpose of the new imperialism, like that of the old, was political and economic power, but the struggle for markets and investments among the Western powers came to be viewed in a new light as countries became highly industrialized and sources of raw materials and food became increasingly valuable.

In the new imperialism, as in the old, could be found motives other than political and economic. From the beginning of European expansion, missionaries had blazed the trails for soldiers and merchants and there had been a sincere desire on the part of Europeans to convert the peoples of the world to Christianity. The argument that sparsely settled lands should absorb the surplus populations and products of Europe was also interwoven with the theory of imperialism. More closely connected with the new imperialism was the excuse of the "white man's burden"—the term used by Rudyard Kipling to denote the supposed duty of the white race to manage the affairs of backward peoples and to impose on them a new type of civilization. Regardless of purpose, during the last three decades of the nineteenth century, Great Britain added to her possessions 5,000,000 square miles of territory containing a population of 90,000,000; France added 3,500,000 square miles and 37,000,000 people; while Germany took 1,000,000 square miles with a population of 14,000,000. Other European nations, likewise, extended their control into distant regions.

The expansion of the territory of the United States in the nineteenth century might be viewed as containing elements of the earlier type of imperialism. To many, however, it was the process of taking possession of their natural heritage. But it was destructive of Indian culture and institutions, although the continent was very sparsely settled. By the middle of the nineteenth century, control of the continent had extended into the possessions of Spanish Americans as the Pacific was reached. In addition to the mid-century manifest destiny fever to extend the benefits of American institutions to other parts of the continent, elements of the old imperialism can be discerned in the forced expansion of trade and commerce as ports in China and Japan were opened up, as unsuccessful attempts were made to annex the Hawaiian Islands, and in the proposal made by Secretary of State Marcy and Senator Gwin of California to buy Alaska from Russia in 1856. The Civil War interfered with such expansionist motives. After the war, Alaska was bought for $7,200,000 because of the decline of the Russian American Company, Russia's disinclination to administer the region, and the inability to defend it. Attempts to expand into the West Indies through the purchase of St. Thomas and St. John in the Danish West Indies were defeated in Congress, and President Grant's attempts to annex Santo Domingo met with no success. Thus until the latter part of the century, the United States was not an imperialistic nation in the modern sense of the term, and a policy of relative isolation was generally accepted. Active American expansion into world affairs came with the Spanish-American War, which to some critics was a pretext for imperialistic expansion, especially the economic penetration of other regions of the world.

THE SPANISH-AMERICAN WAR

At the beginning of the nineteenth century, during the Napoleonic Wars and in the years that immediately followed, the Spanish colonies in Central and South America revolted under the leadership of Miranda, San Martín, Bolívar, and others and set up independent republics. Spain lost her great empire in the New World and only Cuba, the "ever-faithful," and Puerto Rico, in the West Indies, remained as sad memories of the departed glories of Castile. The firm loyalty of Cuba to Spain was due to the fact that many Spanish officials and refugees from Central and South America had fled there during the days of bloody revolution. This loyal and conservative element, for a time at least, controlled Cuba and kept the miserable lower classes aligned with Spain.

The strategic position of Cuba in relation to the United States was recognized by statesmen from Jefferson on, especially before the railroads were built to the West, for western commerce at first developed largely by way of the Mississippi and the Gulf of Mexico. Therefore, many Americans advocated the purchase of Cuba. Suggestions for its purchase, however, continued after the railroads were in operation. President Polk's attempt to buy the island in 1848 for $100,000,000 brought a retort from the Spanish government that it would sooner see it sunk in the Atlantic Ocean than sold to the United States. A few unimportant filibustering expeditions followed. While the slavery interests in the South during the decade prior to the Civil War were anxious to secure Cuba in order to extend slave territory, the abolition of slavery removed one of the sources of the annexationist movement, but the desire for Cuba was not entirely ended.

By this time, the Cuban masses became restless. A revolution flared up in 1868 and a war continued for ten years. It resulted from the failure of the Spanish government to carry out fiscal and political reforms in Cuba and Puerto Rico. Failure to heed the demands for the abolition of slavery together with increased taxation marked a turning point in the relations between Cuba and Spain. The fighting dragged out until 1878, when an agreement was reached which provided pardon for the revolutionists, freedom for the slaves, forgetfulness of past animosities, and partial autonomy. But bribery and corruption were continued by the Spanish officials on the island until by 1895 the public debt of Cuba amounted to $283 per capita, larger proportionately than the debt of any European state; the promised autonomy was not forthcoming; and relatively few rich Spanish and Cuban merchants controlled the business and political life of the island. It was not strange, therefore, that another revolution should break out in 1895.

American attention was focused on Cuba because of the disorders, the destruction of property, and the loss of life there. The ruthless attempts of the Spanish authorities to stamp out the rebellion, especially the policy of herding non-combatants into concentration camps where large numbers died from lack of food and disease, brought severe condemnation from Americans. The United States government was confronted with the task of putting down many filibustering expeditions and millions of dollars were spent for that purpose. The Cuban Junta with headquarters in New York for almost a generation had done its work well in favor of Cuban independence and had raised much money for the struggle. The revolution also affected American investments in Cuba (estimated at about $50,000,000 at this time), for sugar and tobacco plantations were destroyed and trade between the United States and Cuba, which had received a severe blow by the United States tariff act of 1894, was reduced still more. While a number of commercial and shipping firms along the Atlantic and Gulf coasts desired intervention to end their problems, and appeals were made to Congress, the business interests of the country in general were opposed to any interference in Cuba. President Cleveland resisted all pressure for intervention, although in his addresses to Congress he warned the Spanish government that order would have to be restored on the island.

Newspapers, led by the competing *New York Journal* of Hearst and Pulitzer's *New York World*, kept Cuban events before the American public in a most sensational manner, and a part of the religious press preached the sacred duty of American intervention to end Spanish misrule. Humanitarian interest, sentimental sympathy with the Cubans in their struggle for independence, and general indignation at Spanish methods of warfare were inflamed by the sensational picture presented by the jingo press.

Not long after President McKinley took office, a liberal ministry assumed control in Spain. Plans were made by it to change objectionable military methods and the way was opened to grant the Cubans limited autonomy. But early in 1898, the De Lôme letter from the Spanish minister in Washington to a friend in Havana, which was intercepted by insurgents, given to American reporters, and published in the newspapers, stirred up American opinion to white heat, for the minister had written that the President was "weak and a bidder for the admiration of the crowd, besides being a would-be politician who tries to leave a door open behind himself while keeping on good terms with the jingoes of his party." It was the sinking of the *Maine* in Havana harbor, with its tragic loss of life, however, that brought a new outburst of anti-Spanish feeling and led directly to war. Investigations made by Spain and the United States brought no agreement regarding the real cause for the explosions which resulted in the destruction of the battleship. Many congressmen now insisted on war, and early in April, President McKinley delivered his war message, although the day before, Woodford, the American minister at

Madrid, had cabled him asking patience on the ground that the Spanish ministry was doing everything possible to satisfy the demands of the United States. But American patience was at an end with Spain's persistent policy of vacillation, and Congress declared war.

The Spanish-American War was short. In spite of the unpreparedness of the army, inefficiency in sending supplies to Cuba—the chief scene of land warfare—and bungling by army and navy officials, the Americans were completely victorious. The destruction of the Spanish fleet at the Philippines by Dewey, the total loss of a second fleet in Santiago Bay, and the land victories in southern Cuba in which Theodore Roosevelt and his Rough Riders took a prominent part forced the Spanish government to sue for peace. About four months after the declaration of war a peace protocol was signed. Exactly one year after McKinley's war message, ratifications of the permanent peace treaty were exchanged in Washington. The provisions included the relinquishment by Spain of Cuba, Puerto Rico, and Guam. Spain also ceded the Philippines to the United States. In the same article, the United States agreed to pay Spain $20,000,000, although this was not stated as a purchase price for the islands. Spanish ships and merchandise for ten years after the ratification of the treaty were to be admitted to the Philippines on the same terms as ships and merchandise from the United States.

THE UNITED STATES AND CUBA

In the resolutions that declared war against Spain, in the protocol which brought hostilities to an end, and in the final treaty of peace, the United States set forth its purpose regarding Cuba. It was to pacify the island and secure freedom and independence for its people. But before withdrawing the American troops from the island it was necessary for the United States to see that a permanent government was set up which would preserve peace and order.

At the close of the war, American control of the island began under the most depressing economic conditions. In many places farm houses, sugar mills, plantations, crops, domestic animals, buildings, bridges, and roads had been destroyed. Agriculture had suffered severely. Havana, although not ravaged by the war, had suffered a decline of business because of the disorders and the demoralization of agriculture. Many who had left the concentration camps remained in the cities to live by public or private charity. Disease was widespread and bandits roamed the countryside. Political confusion was added to economic and social disturbances when the Spanish officials left their positions and neglected their duties as the power of Spain ended. It required a high degree of statesmanship and philanthropy on the part of the United States to restore the normal activities of the island.

Under American military occupation, Major General John R. Brooke, who was succeeded by Major General Leonard Wood, had complete charge. Starving people were fed, medical supplies were provided for the sick, and every attempt was made to put men back to work. In order to disarm Cuban soldiers and to aid them to return to peaceful vocations, each was given $75 upon the surrender of his firearms, the $3,000,000 for the purpose being obtained from the unexpended balance of the war appropriation. Laborers were employed on public works and $6,000,000 was spent for this purpose during the first year following the war. Although the powers of the military were absolute, every attempt was made to put municipal laws and ordinances into effect, thus giving local control to the people. Elections were arranged, plans were carried out to make local governments financially independent, laws were codified, the police system was reorganized, a school system was established, and much work was done to improve sanitation in order to combat disease.

In the summer of 1900, President McKinley, Secretary of War Root, and Governor-General Wood met and decided that the island had been pacified and that it was time to withdraw. The next year a duly elected Cuban convention met in Havana to draw up a constitution for a new Cuba. Its delegates were instructed to consider several suggested provisions relating to the future relations between Cuba and the United States. The constitution, modeled upon that of the United States, was completed, but only one of the proposed clauses was included. It related to commercial reciprocity between the two countries. The others were ignored. As a result, the administration in Washington refused to approve the constitution and military occupation continued. In the Platt Amendment, which was added to an army appropriation bill, Congress set forth these provisions and added several new ones.

The Cubans were required to include all of them in the new constitution and also to embody them in a treaty between the two countries. The Platt Amendment of 1901 provided that: (1) Cuba should never make a treaty with any foreign power that might impair its independence, nor grant to any foreign nation lands for colonization or naval purposes; (2) Cuba should not contract any public debts which could not be repaid from its ordinary revenues; (3) the Cuban government should grant to the United States the right to intervene at any time to preserve Cuban independence and to protect life, property, and liberty; (4) all acts of the military authorities during occupation were to be ratified, validated, and maintained; (5) Cuba should sell or lease to the United States lands for coaling or naval stations in order to protect the independence of Cuba, its people, and to defend American coasts from foreign attack. In spite of much protest and opposition the terms were finally accepted. Military occupation ended and control of the island was given to the Cubans in 1902.

The disorders which attended the Cuban election of 1906 led to a second military occupation which lasted three years. President Theodore Roosevelt made it clear that the United States had no designs on Cuba, but that the island could not continue independent if revolutions became a habit. Riots and disorders in 1917 led to sending marines to Cuba to help the regularly constituted government maintain order. The policy of the United States in this respect saved Cuba from a career of turbulence. The Platt Amendment, however, caused continued resentment among the Cuban people who strongly objected to foreign interference. By the treaty of 1934 the Platt Amendment was abrogated. The Roosevelt-Hull "good neighbor" policy and the violent strife in Cuba in 1933 and 1934 largely account for abdicating responsibility for Cuban affairs.

As an American protectorate, Cuba prospered. Economic ties grew closer. By a treaty of 1903, a reduction of 20 per cent was made on all imports into the United States from Cuba in consideration for a reduction made by Cuba in its duties on American machinery, iron and steel manufactures, textile goods, foodstuffs, cattle, rice, and other products. Soon after Cuba was released from the terms of the Platt Amendment in 1934, a reciprocal agreement was made between the two countries under the terms of the Trade Agreements Act of that year, which authorized the President to make such pacts. The greatest part of Cuban imports and exports were with the United States. The latter included chiefly sugar, tobacco, cigars, hides, iron, copper, asphalt, and valuable woods.

American investments in Cuba were large. In 1898 they amounted to $50 million. In a generation they increased to $1.5 billion. Ninetenths of all foreign capital invested in Cuba belonged to citizens of the United States. These holdings included real estate, sugar mills, public utilities, railroads, tobacco manufacturers, mining, commercial establishments, and banking. While American penetration brought a measure of prosperity and stability to the island, it made the country economically dependent upon the United States, and it made agricultural laborers out of a number of small farmers who worked for large sugar interests.

PUERTO RICO

Problems regarding the organization of Puerto Rico and the Hawaiian Islands were somewhat different from those of Cuba, for these islands were to be American territory. The 950,000 Puerto Ricans, strongly Spanish in culture, had a rather advanced agricultural-trading economy based on sugar, coffee, and tobacco cultivation. Leaders of the Puerto Rican aristocracy had hoped that they would be given independence to the same degree as Cuba and resented the decision of the United States to retain strict control, although this offered important economic benefits.

Civil government was established by the Foraker Act of 1900, which declared the island to be "unorganized territory" and set up a form of government similar in many respects to the non-democratic phase of territorial government in the United States. The inhabitants, however, were not granted American citizenship by this law.

In certain "insular cases," the Supreme Court determined the relationship of outlying possessions and dependencies with the United States and thus helped to shape colonial policy. Congress had made provision in the Foraker Act for levying 15 per cent of the Dingley tariff on goods from Puerto Rico. In the case of Downes vs. Bidwell (1901), the validity of the legislation was tested on the basis that the Constitution requires that "all duties, imports, and excises shall be uniform throughout the United States." The Court decided that Puerto Rico had not become a part of the United States within the meaning of this provision. In 1902, Congress provided for complete free trade with Puerto Rico. In several of the insular cases the Court held that outlying territories and possessions were of two kinds: incorporated, such as Hawaii and Alaska, and unincorporated, such as Puerto Rico and the Philippines. In legislating for incorporated territories, Congress is bound by all provisions of the Constitution, but in legislating for unincorporated territories Congress is bound only by certain fundamental provisions such as the guarantee against deprivation of life, liberty, and property without due process of law.

Inclusion within the United States customs system greatly benefited Puerto Rican sugar growers, led to American investment in plantations, and generally increased prosperity. But political discontent remained in spite of the Jones Act in 1917, which granted full American citizenship, together with representation in a legislative assembly. The majority party, the Unionists, desired independence. While advances were made in sanitation, education, and public improvements, the United States did little to develop the island through capital investment and, by mainland standards, economic conditions remained poor, even in the nineteen-twenties.

THE PHILIPPINE ISLANDS

The Philippine Islands, discovered by Magellan in 1521 and occupied by Spain after 1565, became a possession of the United States in 1898 as a result of the Spanish-American War. At that time the population of the islands was about 7,000,000 consisting of many different ethnic groups speaking almost a hundred different languages or dialects. Indians, Malayans, Chinese, Japanese, and Arabs had settled there long before the coming of the Spanish. In 1898, the people varied from highly-educated Spanish Catholics to the wildest of primitive races, some of them head hunters and cannibals. Spanish control had been largely in the hands of the Catholic friars for centuries and centered in Manila on the Island of Luzon, the largest of the 7,083 islands that make up the Philippine archipelago. Many of the islands, being nothing more than small rocky islets, have never been inhabited.

Spanish occupation resulted in the establishment of Christianity among the principal Filipino tribes on a few of the most important islands. The rising tide of Mohammedanism, which had begun centuries before Spain established authority there, was now restricted to Mindanao, the Sulu Archipelago, and adjacent regions. In the nineteenth century, under the direction of the Friars on Luzon, well-to-do Filipinos began to send their children to European countries to complete their education. Some imbibed the liberal ideals of Europe and a few were touched by the revolutionary ideas that were burning brightly about the middle of that century. In the decades that followed, as education broadened, Filipino secret societies built the framework for the beginning of a national movement which matured in the last part of the century. Anti-Spanish feeling increased. Dr. José Rizal bore a conspicuous part in the new movement and for it he was executed by the Spanish authorities in 1896. An insurrection at this time was put down by the Spanish authorities.

After the Spanish-American War, American occupation resulted in the Philippine Insurrection, as natives, disappointed in not securing immediate independence, proclaimed a republic and elected Emilio Aguinaldo its president. American blood and money were spent in suppressing the uprising, which came to an end after the spectacular

capture of Aguinaldo who took the oath of allegiance to the United
States and encouraged his followers to do the same. By 1902, other
recalcitrant leaders followed Aguinaldo's example, and peace was restored. In the meantime, a Philippine Commission under William H.
Taft was appointed in 1900 to assist the military governor, especially
in the capacity of a legislative body. The next year civil government
was established and Taft became governor-general. In 1902, he arranged for the purchase by the United States, at a cost of about
$7,000,000, of the lands formerly owned by the Catholic friars, who
had been forced to flee from the islands. In 1907, the Commission
became the upper house of legislature as the first Philippine Assembly
was opened. In 1916, Congress passed the Jones Act which encouraged
the Filipinos to look for early independence. It provided for an extension of powers to the natives, giving them a large measure of control
in the government, but subject to the President of the United States
and Congress. In the years that followed, agitation for independence
increased, commissions were appointed to investigate, and reports were
made, but no action was taken.

During American occupation of the Philippines, progress was made
along commercial, agricultural, sanitary, and material lines generally, as well as in education and the rise of free democratic institutions. Large sums of money were spent by the United States for the
betterment of the people. Agriculture was the most important industry.
The chief crops were rice, hemp, manguey, sugar cane, tobacco, and
coconut. Coffee-raising became unprofitable on account of destructive
insects. Land laws restricted the development of large estates and
the Filipinos owned almost all the land under cultivation. The most
important manufacturing industry was that of cigars and cigarettes.
Large modern coconut oil factories and central sugar mills of modern
type were built in the chief sugar producing sections. The islands
possess large mineral resources, but these have not been greatly
exploited.

The United States supplied about three-fifths of the imports of
the island including machinery, tools, automobiles, flour, oil, coal, and
cotton goods. On the other hand it took about three-fourths of the exports, including practically all the sugar exported and most of the
coconut oil, desiccated coconut, copra, lumber, and cigars. By the
act of 1902, Philippine products entered the United States at a reduction of 25 per cent of the rate of the Dingley tariff. The tariff of 1909
provided free trade except that a limit was placed on the amount of
sugar and tobacco that could enter the United States duty free; the

tariff of 1913 provided for complete free trade. Imports from foreign countries were subject to a tariff of 20 per cent. This benefited both the United States and the Philippines, the balance of trade, however, favoring the latter.

By the early 1930's American businessmen were disappointed in their expectation of the economic exploitation of the Philippines, for American investments there, except for government securities, were relatively small, and increased trade between the Philippines and China, which many expected to flourish, had not materialized. In the Senate, leading proponents of Philippine independence were the senators from Louisiana and Utah, leading cane and beet sugar states, which for years had faced competition with duty-free Philippine, as well as Puerto Rican, sugar. At the same time, many naval experts pointed out that the islands would be a liability rather than an asset in case of a war with Japan. Largely as a result of these factors a measure was passed in 1933 which provided for independence ten years after the inauguration of a government. On account of a provision restricting immigration to the United States, the abrogation of free trade enjoyed since 1909, and other clauses, the Philippine legislature rejected the offer. The Tydings-McDuffie Act of 1934 eliminated certain objections of this law and was accepted by the Philippine legislature on the thirty-sixth anniversary of Dewey's victory at Manila Bay. It provided for the recognition of Philippine independence after a ten-year transitional period. Restrictions on Filipino immigration to the United States, however, were included and also the gradual application of an American tariff. Army bases were to be ceded to the Philippines but the question of naval bases was to be negotiated at a later date. Manuel Quezon was elected first president of the Philippine Commonwealth in 1935 and the people looked forward to independence in 1946. In 1942, the Japanese seized control of the islands and although the government had fled, the United States proclaimed the Philippines an independent nation on Flag Day, 1942.

THE HAWAIIAN ISLANDS

Although the Hawaiian Islands, the "Paradise of the Pacific," were not annexed to the United States until 1898, relations between the two countries go much further back. The islands had been visited by early Spaniards, but they were really discovered by the ill-fated English explorer, Captain James Cook, at the time of the American Revolution and were named the Sandwich Islands after an English noble. Before the end of that century, Yankees who traded in furs with the

Pacific Northwest and China called at Honolulu and added another aspect to their Pacific activities in a developing trade in sandalwood. Early observers pointed out that the Hawaiian natives, who were of Polynesian origin, lived in a land of volcanic peaks, rugged valleys, lava plains, desert tracts, fertile lands, semitropical vegetation, and luxuriant plant life, the varied background presenting a wealth of scenery. The Hawaiians lived very simply by agriculture and fishing, and possessed neither metals, pottery, nor beasts of burden. Their implements were of stone, wood, or bone, and they had no looms or cloth; they used a fibrous bark instead of textiles.

Before 1820, American whalers began to make Honolulu a port for repairing their vessels, and the number of ships stopping there soon increased. In 1820, Boston missionaries reached the islands, and during the years that followed American influence was promoted by them. They found that their chief difficulties came not from the natives, but from resident Europeans and Americans who exploited the islands and their people. Increased American economic interest followed in the wake of the missionaries. By the middle of the century, Honolulu with its American missionaries, Yankee whalemen, and growing trade with the United States was seemingly an American outpost, although by this time European influence—including English and French—was also increasing.

The settlement of Oregon and the acquisition of California increased American interest in the Pacific, especially in the Hawaiian Islands. From 1848 to 1855, urged by American sugar interests, the native government appealed to the United States for a reciprocal treaty, but the Senate, responding to the sugar interests of Louisiana, rejected the idea. About the same time the question of annexation was raised. Several times prior to 1850 Hawaiian rulers had offered—either voluntarily or under pressure—their sovereignty to Great Britain, but without result. In 1850, the French intervened in Hawaiian affairs. The United States government objected and Daniel Webster, Secretary of State, asserted that he would not see the islands taken over by any of the great European commercial powers. The Hawaiian ruler sought unsuccessfully to place his kingdom under American protection. A treaty of annexation was also negotiated between the two countries but was not submitted to the Senate. By 1875, Americans owned 75 per cent of the Hawaiian sugar plantations, the investments amounting to $25,000,000. In this year the Hawaiian king visited the United States and his commissioners signed a reciprocal treaty which the Senate accepted. By its terms unrefined sugar and other Hawaiian products were admitted to the United States free of duty and American manufactured articles could enter Hawaii on the same terms. It provided further that no lands, harbors, or ports should be granted other nations, nor should other countries be permitted free trade. From this time on the sugar industry under the impetus of a ready American market expanded considerably. In 1887, the Hawaiian government granted the United States the exclusive use of Pearl Harbor. This step was taken because of the importance of the harbor for the defense of the islands, its value to the United States in wartime, and American fears that Hawaii might turn to Asia since Chinese immigration to the islands was increasing.

The year 1887 also marked a new liberal government in Hawaii, the king Kalakaua, under American influence, giving suffrage to the whites and recognizing cabinet responsibility. After his death, his successor, Queen Liliuokalani, attempted to restore autocratic rule and to eliminate white control. As a result, early in 1893, influential Americans, with the help of the United States Minister John L. Stevens and the support of 160 Marines, brought about a revolution. The queen was deposed; a provisional government was organized with an American, Sanford B. Dole, as its head; and steps were taken for annexation to the United States. While President Benjamin Harrison signed the treaty in the last days of his administration and submitted it to the Senate, it was not ratified when his term ended. President Grover Cleveland, who followed Harrison, withdrew the document from the Senate and ordered an investigation which revealed a conspiracy between the American planters and United States Minister Stevens. He ordered the restoration of the queen, but the provisional government refused and set up the Republic of Hawaii, which was soon recognized by foreign governments, including the United States.

As a new administration under President William McKinley came into power in 1897, interest in annexing Hawaii again burst forth. However, a majority could not be obtained for a new treaty of annexation in the Senate. With the outbreak of the Spanish-American War and Dewey's victory in Manila Bay, the strategic importance of the Hawaiian Islands was realized. President Dole of the Republic of Hawaii offered the use of the harbors to the United States and proposed a treaty of alliance if annexation could not be achieved. The value of Hawaiian harbors during the war together with the fear of Japanese designs upon the islands strengthened sentiment for annexation in Washington. Instead of waiting to annex the islands by treaty, which would have required a two-thirds majority vote in the Senate, a joint resolution of a simple majority by both houses resulted in an-nexation. Sovereignty was soon transferred to the United States (1898). Japan protested vigorously while the resolution was before the Senate, which probably helped to bring about annexation, but the American government assured that country that the rights of Japanese living there would in no way be affected by the change.

By the Organic Act of 1900 Congress made Hawaii a formal terri-tory of the United States and conferred American citizenship upon its people. As in other outlying possessions economic and social prog-ress followed. Trade continued to be largely with the United States, the principal crop being cane sugar and second in importance the production of pineapples. Other semi-tropical crops and foodstuffs of all kinds are grown. Coffee is produced especially on Hawaii Island; rice is cultivated on the lowest flats mostly by Chinese; and livestock flourish on upland pastures. An added income has been obtained from tourists, travelers, and visitors. The islands furnish valuable bases for strong American military and naval outposts, which proved highly important in the Second World War. The census of 1900 showed the total population to be 154,001. The Hawaiians and part-Hawaiians comprised 24 per cent of this total; Caucasians, chiefly Portuguese, 17 per cent; Chinese and Japanese, 56 per cent; and others 3 per cent. In 1942, the Japanese comprised one-third of the total and the Oriental element altogether made up two-thirds of the total. Even in 1960 the state's population of 600,000 was ethnically a mosaic with people of Asiatic ancestry dominating the pattern.

OTHER PACIFIC ISLANDS

By the end of the nineteenth century, possessions had been secured in other parts of the Pacific. During President Grant's administration, Commander Richard W. Meade was sent to secure the excellent harbor of Pago Pago in the Samoan Islands as a naval base and coaling station for the United States Navy. A treaty, ratified by the Senate in 1878, ceded Pago Pago to the United States and granted certain commercial and extraterritorial privileges. In 1889, it became evident that Germany was planning to seize the islands. An international conference followed and a tripartite agreement, including England, was made—the Berlin Act of 1889—which guaranteed the neutrality and independence of Samoa through what virtually amounted to a three-power protectorate. Problems in administration and continued difficulties led to a proposal by Germany for a division of the islands. American interest in the Pacific at the end of the century also made a new arrangement inevitable. A convention was agreed upon by the three nations in 1899. England renounced its Samoan claims in return for recognition of its occupation of other south Pacific islands. The United States received the island of Tutuila with its harbor of Pago Pago. Germany obtained the islands of Upolu and Savaii. As a result of the First World War, German interests in Samoa were transferred under a mandate to New Zealand. American Samoa has remained the outpost of the United States in the southwest Pacific.

Many small islands were occupied by the United States during the last part of the nineteenth century. Under the Guano Islands Act of 1856, Americans were authorized to take peaceable possession of islands or rocks that did not belong to other nations on which guano deposits —used for fertilization—were found. Many small islands came under American control, but most were abandoned after the deposits were removed. Guano was obtained from Baker and Howland Islands by Americans and Britishers. They were leased under British protection to the Pacific Islands Company, but were later abandoned. In 1935, the United States revived its claim and extended sovereignty over them. An executive order placed them under the Division of Territories and Island Possessions. In 1867, the Midway Islands were occupied and the Aleutian Islands purchased in connection with Alaska. By the end of the nineteenth century many other small islands came under the jurisdiction of the United States, which aided in expanding American influence and which were to be of value as cable, radio, and coaling stations.

THE UNITED STATES AS A WORLD POWER

The expansion of United States trade and investment, and a new sensitivity to naval defense growing out of the Spanish-American War and subsequent building of the Panama Canal led to a more active participation in international affairs. The Far East, partly because of the Philippines, and the Caribbean, because of the Canal, were regarded as particularly sensitive areas.

In the 1890's almost all the major ports of China were "leased" by various European powers, and Japan took over the Korean peninsula. Alarmed by the potential threat to United States trade, Secretary of State John Hay attempted to establish the Open Door policy in China. In 1899, encouraged by Great Britain, he sent identical notes to the other powers asking them not to set up any tariffs but to abide by Chinese tariffs and not to levy higher railroad or harbor rates than those imposed on their own nationals. England, Italy, and Japan partially accepted the new policy. Germany, France, and Russia were evasive. But Hay announced that he considered their assent final and definitive.

The Open Door policy was soon tested in 1900 when the Boxers, a Chinese religious and patriotic society, rose up against the foreigners living there, some of whom, including missionaries, were murdered. The Chinese government did not try to quell the uprising. A joint expedition of European, American, and Japanese troops assembled at Tientsin and started for Pekin, where they put down the uprising. Fearing that the presence of foreign armies on Chinese soil would lead to the dismemberment of China, Hay notified the powers on July 3, 1900, that the United States was opposed to any disturbance of existing Chinese territorial and administrative rights, and stated further that American policy was to "safeguard for the world the principle of equal and impartial trade with all parts of the Chinese Empire." It required skill for him to carry through the American program and to protect China. Aided by the distrustful attitude of the powers to each other, he was successful in having the troops withdrawn and the Open Door policy continued but on certain conditions. These conditions included punishment for the leaders, the adoption of measures by the government to prevent future outbreaks, and indemnities. In spite of Hay's efforts, the total indemnities of $333,000,000 were twice as much as the United States deemed proper. The latter received $24,-000,000 although actual losses of Americans were estimated at $11,-000,000. Congress returned the excess which China set aside as a fund for supporting Chinese students at American universities. The Open Door policy, however, was never maintained with any great success.

In 1904, the bankrupt Dominican Republic was in financial difficulties because of its debts owed to foreigners. As a result of the situation, Roosevelt proclaimed what became known as the Roosevelt corollary to the Monroe Doctrine. In his annual messages of 1904 and 1905, he set forth the principle that, since the United States would not permit European countries to intervene in the affairs of Latin America, this country would have to assume responsibility for preserving order and for protecting life and property there. He based his assumption on the ground that where international obligations had been flagrantly disregarded and there had been chronic wrongdoing, the United States had the right to assume a measure of control in Latin America under the authority of "international police power." In order to prevent European action against the Dominican Republic, an agreement was made with that country and the United States, which granted American control of its customs. Revenues were collected by American officials who set aside 55 per cent of the proceeds for the benefit of the creditors. A treaty, signed in 1905 providing for American assistance in adjusting the debt, was not ratified.

Luis M. Drago, Argentina's minister of foreign relations, sent a protest to Washington. He held that in making loans to foreign countries, capitalists knew the conditions and risks they took. He declared a sovereign state could not have proceedings instituted against it, and he denounced armed intervention as a means of collecting debts incurred by an American nation. The Drago doctrine, as it became known, was given a place on the program of the third Pan-American Conference at Rio de Janeiro in 1906; as a result of its recommendations, resolutions were adopted at the Second Hague Conference, which made the doctrine, in modified form, international law.

General acceptance of this doctrine made it desirable for the United States to act under the sanction of treaty arrangements rather than police power. In 1907, a treaty with the Dominican Republic provided for an American customs receivership to secure a funding loan floated by American bankers. In the meantime, plans had been worked out and accepted by the creditors of the Dominican Republic. Although the financial affairs of that country became satisfactory, intervention was not ended until 1924, and the American customs receivership continued until 1941.

Similar difficulties occurred in Nicaragua in 1913 and in Haiti in 1915. Treaties were negotiated, at gun point in the case of Haiti, giving the United States the right to land troops for police purposes and to administer the customs and other taxes. Both occupations continued into the 1930's, and both provoked determined local resistance.

These efforts to bring financial order to the Caribbean, plus the United States activity in wresting Panama from Colombia, led to a great wave of anti-Yankee sentiment in Latin America. Although the intervention policies were abandoned in favor of the good neighbor policy in the 1930's, the damage to Western Hemisphere foreign relations was not easily undone.

While naval defense was the chief motive in the interventions and the investments involved were very small, they have often been called examples of "dollar diplomacy." President Taft expressed its meaning in 1912: "The diplomacy of the present administration has sought to respond to modern ideas of commercial intercourse. This policy has been characterized as substituting dollars for bullets. It is one that appeals alike to idealistic humanitarian sentiments, to the dictates of sound policy and strategy, and to legal commercial aims. It is an effort frankly directed to the increase of American trade upon the axiomatic principle that the government of the United States shall extend all proper support to every legitimate and beneficial American enterprise abroad."

Dollar diplomacy was also applied to China where the United States participated in loans to the imperial government. In 1913 President Wilson repudiated dollar diplomacy in the Far East as American bankers were about to cooperate with those of other nations in floating a large Chinese loan. Without diplomatic support, the major American banking interests were not inclined at that time to lend money in any areas of unstable government, or to become involved in competition with the nationally supported bankers of the European powers.

"THE AMERICAN PERIL"

The remarkable economic expansion which the United States had attained by the end of the nineteenth century brought expressions of fear of the new imperial power from many Europeans. Territorially, industrially, and commercially, the United States had reached a position that made it one of the great nations of the world. Just before and during the Spanish-American War, European writers, especially British, French, and German, approved and disapproved of America's stand against Spain. One of the most sarcastic critics of American policy during that period stated:

Among the caricatures published by the satirical journals . . . there is a particularly characteristic drawing: it is the map of the universe where Brother Jonathan occupies the surface of the two America's and assigns to himself fantastic limits: to the north, the Aurora Borealis; to the South, Tierra del Fuego; to the west, the Valley of the Last Judgment; . . . as far as the east, it does not appear on the map because the east is Europe and Europe, decayed territory, no longer counts.[1]

An increasing number of Europeans denounced American political, commercial, and territorial ambitions. The term "American peril", however, was more used on the Continent than in the British Isles, but apprehension was discernible in the writings of English journalists and economists.

By the beginning of the twentieth century, American influence was spreading all over the world. As early as 1902, the English writer, W. T. Stead, in his *Americanization of the World*, referred to expan-

---

[1] Henri Alexis Moulin, *L'Expansion des États-Unis et la Doctrine de Monroe*, p. 3.

sion of the United States as the greatest phenomenon of the time. Similar books were written in the same period. England was caught between two competitors—Germany and the United States—and was battling against the activities and influence of both. Since 1870, Germany had made tremendous economic gains. By 1914, it had risen from a collection of loosely-knit states to become the second greatest power in the world and in many ways surpassed both Britain and America. Its industries were great and were growing; its commerce was expanding; and its army was the greatest and its navy the second greatest on the globe. But American influence through commerce, invention, machinery, and investment as well as through dentistry, medicine, education, and literature was rapidly penetrating Europe and the rest of the world.

CHAPTER 24

War and Reaction

In the long view the first half of the twentieth century will probably be seen as the period in which the era of the self-regulating economy came to an end and was replaced by an age of government planning for the general welfare. While governments here and abroad had never completely divorced themselves from aiding private enterprises or undertaking economically useful work, the theory of the nineteenth century, in the English-speaking world particularly, had been that the economy if left alone would automatically rectify errors and move toward a condition of full employment. In the language of automation, the economic system had "feedbacks" that corrected man-made errors.

An English philosopher, Herbert Spencer, had merged the idea of the self-regulating economy with Darwin's theory of evolution through competitive struggle and the survival of the fittest. The resulting doctrine, later called Social Darwinism, held that any government interference with the competitive struggle would retard the evolution of society. Thus as the problems of industrial society multiplied, the resistance to government interference gained in strength among the upper income groups.

While men of above average income continued to control government, circumstances worked strongly against a strict adherence to Social Darwinism. Spreading slums, industrial accidents, child labor,

518

and mass unemployment during depressions menaced the stability of society and forced action upon state politicians. Wars demanded national organization and sacrifice that had no place in the theory of the self-regulating economy and could only be brought about by the Federal government. So between wars and depressions the power of government steadily increased, while political and business leaders deplored the situation but found no substitute for government action. The next chapters are a record of the growing role of all branches of government in economic affairs.

ECONOMIC EFFECTS OF THE FIRST WORLD WAR

The outbreak of the conflict in Europe in 1914 resulted in a collapse of the financial markets of the world, which were unprepared for the coming of war. The London Stock Exchange, in an unprecedented move, closed on July 31. European investors had already begun to convert their American securities into cash, and as wholesale liquidation of American stocks and bonds was threatened, the New York Stock Exchange also suspended on the same day. The stock exchanges all over the country, likewise, closed their doors. Not until December 12 was the New York Stock Exchange opened for limited trading. In April, 1915, unrestricted trading was permitted.

Banking suffered during the early months of the European war. Money was withdrawn from banks and hoarded. The shortage of currency made necessary almost $68,000,000 of emergency currency which was issued for the first time under the provisions of the Aldrich-Vreeland Act of 1908, while the New York banks also used clearing-house certificates. In November, the Federal Reserve Banks opened for business and exerted a wholesome influence on the banking structure of the nation. The ability of American bankers to pay all maturing obligations in gold increased the financial prestige of the country. The gold, however, did not find its way to Europe but was used in the United States by the Allies to secure needed supplies. In order to finance their purchases the Allies also obtained loans largely through Wall Street, although at first the State Department opposed them. By the time the United States had entered the war Americans had loaned the Allied governments about $1.5 billion against only $27,000,000 to the Central Powers. The Federal Treasury also benefited by the war, for its gold amounting to $1.25 billion in July, 1914, had doubled by April, 1917. As a result of these developments, the United States changed from a debtor to a strong creditor nation.

At the beginning of the war, American manufactures were somewhat depressed. The steel industry, often used as a barometer of trade, was slowing up. The first effects of the war were to depress still further many industries. The export of steel manufactures, copper, cotton, grain, meat, and other commodities to Europe received a serious setback. This was due not only to the loss of European markets but to the fact that many foreign vessels which carried most of America's export trade were no longer available. The chemical industries also suffered severely, especially the manufacturers of dyestuffs and fertilizers, as the war cut off the materials necessary for these industries, which came largely from Germany. The opening months of the war were marked by a commercial depression that extended all over the country.

By the late spring of 1915, foreign trade was on the upswing and was developing impressively. Trade with the Central Powers was largely prevented by British sea power, but commerce with England and France mounted rapidly. Cotton, wheat, and beef, together with manufactures, found a profitable and an ever-enlarging market. Cargoes seized by the Allies on the ground that they were destined directly or indirectly to Germany were paid for. Trade in munitions became most prosperous and increased from $40,000,000 in 1914 to $1.29 billion in 1916. The amount of foreign commerce was limited only by the dearth of ocean-going vessels. All types of ships were pressed into service. A law of Congress passed in 1914 admitted foreign vessels to American registry under most liberal terms. This gave an impetus to shipping as 175 vessels sought the protection of the neutral American flag. The Shipping Act of 1916 created the United States Shipping Board, which was empowered to construct or buy vessels for use in commerce and to sell or charter them to Americans. Important regulatory powers over shipping were also given the board. By 1916, shipping tonnage under American registration reached 2,191,715. Exports to the five leading Allied nations increased from $927,000,000 in 1914 to $3.013 billion for the fiscal year 1916.

As commerce began to increase in the spring of 1915, American industries also started to recover. In addition to agricultural products and provisions, certain manufactures relating to war were in demand. Prosperity marked the manufacture of munitions of all sorts, iron and steel products, together with brass, bronze, and zinc commodities, and automobile parts. Metal industries expanded chiefly to supply the machinery and weapons of death. New plants were built and old ones remodeled. The chemical industries grew in a most remarkable way in the absence of German competition. Exports of chemicals, drugs, and dyes increased from $21,924,337 in 1914 to $181,028,432 in 1917. Textile manufactures, especially the production of cotton linters, used in guncotton, also shared the increasing prosperity, but many other industries not related to war production suffered severely. Building operations slowed down almost to a standstill and many factories devoted to manufactures not essential to war purposes were shut down. Unemployment figures revealed that the entire country was not sharing in the prosperity, and rising prices adversely affected large numbers of salaried workers and those employed in the nonessential war industries.

The fabric of American economic life became interwoven with the economy of the Allied powers. Finance and trade bound the United States closer and closer to Great Britain and the other Entente nations, but evidence is lacking to support the charge that President Wilson was influenced by America's financial interests in the Allied nations when he asked Congress to declare war on the Central Powers. Nor did Wall Street bankers and financiers desire war. They were satisfied with good profits without the immediate sacrifices and high taxation that war would bring. In 1936–1937 Senator Nye's Committee on Munitions and Loans revealed sensational data regarding profits and high finance, pointing out the relations between American interests and the Allies during the First World War. But the committee found no evidence to show that bankers and manufacturers had led the country into the war. A more important cause for our entry in the war was the unrestricted submarine policy of Germany.

MOBILIZING INDUSTRIAL RESOURCES

The first attempts to adjust and coordinate American industry to war production were made before the United States entered the war. In August, 1916, the Council of National Defense, consisting of six cabinet officers and seven experts in designated fields, was established for the purpose of utilizing the resources of the nation for war in case of need. However, it was limited in its activities, for its powers were only advisory and it lacked authority to enforce its decisions. In July, 1917, the War Industries Board was created, but it, too, at first did not possess the authority to do effective work, although it was able to modify the soaring prices of some commodities.

As the need for a stricter control of industry became imperative, and as prices rose in an alarming manner when the great increase in governmental purchases interfered with the normal relationships between supply and demand, President Wilson, early in March, 1918, appointed Bernard Baruch as chairman of the War Industries Board and gave the board greatly augmented powers. It was given authority to adapt industries to new uses wherever necessary, to determine priorities on productions and deliveries, to fix prices, to promote industrial efficiency and eliminate waste, and to increase the volume of munitions. It was given control of the manufacturing facilities and resources of the entire country and was authorized to make purchases for the United States and the Allies.

Under the dictatorship of Bernard Baruch, the War Industries Board carried out an industrial mobilization unprecedented in American history up to that time. The rights of free enterprise were annulled and manufacturing was regimented. Through the use of subcommittees a great amount of excellent work was done. The production of about 30,000 articles came under the supervision of the board. Yet it was able to regulate manufacturing in a most remarkable and minute manner. Nonessential industries were turned over to war production, as piano factories made airplane wings, automobile plants produced Liberty motors for airplanes and airplane parts, and radiator works manufactured large guns. In order to save materials, tin was eliminated from children's toys, the use of steel in corsets restricted, and the styles of clothing changed to save fabrics. As a result of the work of the War Industries Board a partial mobilization of the industries and resources of the country was achieved.

Leaders of industry cooperated with the board in a generally efficient manner. They submitted to the arbitrary fixing of contracts, to priorities, and to distribution, but many agreements were on a "cost plus" basis. A number of industrialists and businessmen volunteered as "dollar-a-year men" and went to Washington. While there were many who sacrificed their personal interests in the war effort, some profited greatly during the period of regimentation. Competitive bidding by agents of the Allied powers sent prices of certain non-regulated supplies sky-high until the government and the Inter-Allied War Council set up joint purchasing agencies which reduced this type of abuse. The scarcity of goods and lack of mandatory price controls made profiteering in many fields inevitable and increased the number of millionaires in the country.

Organized labor cooperated and also profited in the war effort. Membership in the American Federation of Labor increased from 2,000,000 in 1914 to 3,260,000 in 1919. Gompers and other labor leaders, conciliated and recognized by the government, enthusiastically supported the war. They adopted the official stand "Work or Fight" and took advantage of the labor shortage caused by the diversion of millions of men to the armed forces and a great decline in immigration. Women were employed in increasing numbers in factories and shops, and unskilled labor was trained to make up in part the scarcity of skilled labor. At the beginning of the war, industries under government control accepted trade-union standards. In March, 1918, a National War Labor Conference Board, made up of representatives of employers and employees, drew up certain principles and policies. Labor agreed to give up the right to strike for the duration of the war in return for the abolition of all restriction on output, the unlimited organization of labor, the right to collective bargaining, recognition of the right of all workers to a living wage, and the agreement that the basic eight-hour day be observed where the law required it. The board reported that it was favorable to the creation of a permanent War Labor Board. In April, 1918, when many labor disputes were threatening to hurt the war effort, President Wilson established by proclamation the War Labor Board. Its function was to secure voluntary, peaceful arbitration of labor disputes, and its authority was based largely on the patriotic cooperation of employers and employees and on public opinion. It followed the principles adopted earlier by the National War Labor Conference Board. By April, 1919, a total of 1,244 cases had reached the board and all had been disposed of except thirty-three. In order to aid and supplement the work of the board, the War Labor Policies Board was created. It furthered the standardization of working conditions in accord with the principles adopted by the War Labor Board and developed policies to improve the relations between capital and labor.

GOVERNMENT OPERATION OF RAILROADS

As early as August, 1916, when danger of hostilities threatened, the President was authorized by an act of Congress to take over the railway system of the country in time of war and use it to the exclusion of other traffic if necessary. Upon the entrance of the United States into the war, it became evident that the railroads acting independently could not meet the demands of the emergency. In April, 1917 the Railroads' War Board, consisting of railroad presidents, was established. Much was done to improve conditions, but heavy use of the port of New York for shipment, an unusually cold and snowy winter, and the threat of the antitrust laws against railroads' merging equipment produced a traffic crisis in the New York yards. In December, 1917 under the authorization of the act of the previous year, the government took over the railroads and proceeded to operate them as a unified system, guaranteeing to the railroads an annual income equal to the average net income of their respective lines for the three years preceding June, 1917. Secretary of the Treasury W. G. McAdoo was made Director General of the Railroad Administration, and later W. D. Hines took his place. The action in "leasing" the railroads to the government was an emergency military measure and was in no way intended to be a socialistic experiment.

Under government management, many wasteful practices, some the result of competition, were eliminated. Greater efficiency and economy resulted. Equipment was standardized; unified terminals were organized; freight reached its destination by the shortest routes; unnecessary passenger trains on parallel lines were cancelled; ticket offices in large cities were consolidated; advertising was eliminated; freight and passenger rates were increased. The administration raised the wages of railroad employees and recognized the basic eight-hour day, established under the Adamson Act of 1916, for 2,000,000 railroad employees. After a short time, the freight congestion was removed and the government was able to speed up the transit of men and war materials to France.

At the end of the first year of government operation of the railroads, the Director General recommended that Congress extend such control for five years. The war was now over and while railroad men generally favored the proposal, public opinion in general opposed it. In 1920, therefore, under the terms of the Transportation Act (Esch-Cummins Act), the railroads were returned to private ownership. But because rates were kept uneconomically low in an effort to check inflation, Federal operation of the roads cost the government more than $860,000,000, not counting the money spent in replacement of equipment.

SHIPPING AND AIRPLANE CONSTRUCTION

As a part of the preparedness program, Congress passed an act in September, 1916, which created the United States Shipping Board first under General George W. Goethals and later under Edward Hurley. The new agency began its work of securing vessels for the American service. With the participation of the United States in the war, its activities expanded. It seized ninety-one German-owned vessels in American ports, adding 660,000 tons to American shipping; it assumed control of all shipyards; it requisitioned ships; it trained officers; it enlarged port facilities; and it organized the Emergency

Fleet Corporation. The Shipping Board took complete control of the overseas shipping aspects of the war.

Until the beginning of 1917, the Allied nations had lost more than 7,000,000 (deadweight) tons of shipping. Vessels built in American shipyards could not replace the losses, for in 1916 American yards completed only 300,000 (deadweight) tons of ships. As the United States entered the war, the urgency of a shipbuilding program of unprecedented size became obvious if troops and supplies were to be sent to Europe to win the war. The slogan "Ships will win the war," reiterated by Prime Minister Lloyd George before an American audience in London, gave emphasis to the idea of a "bridge of ships" across the Atlantic. In April, 1917, Congress chartered the Emergency Fleet Corporation to build, own, and operate a merchant fleet for the United States government. The members of the Shipping Board became the directors and officers of the corporation. In 1918, Charles M. Schwab, a steel executive, was made Director General of the corporation.

The Emergency Fleet Corporation began work immediately. Within six months it had a capital of almost $2 billion and a program for building 1,200 vessels with a total (deadweight) tonnage of 7,500,000. It took over the 431 steel vessels that were under construction in American yards for foreign owners. It built several great shipyards, the largest being the Hog Island Shipyard on the Delaware River, which cost about $65,000,000. Here more than 41,000 men were employed at one time. Investments were also made in many private shipyards for the purpose of enlarging them. The available tonnage was greatly increased but at staggering costs for engines and other equipment. Vessels were built of steel, wood, fabricated material, and even concrete. By the time of the armistice in November, 1918, although the program called for the construction of more than 3,000 vessels, less than 400 steel ships and about 300 wooden vessels had been completed. At the close of the war, contracts totaling 25 per cent of the original program were cancelled. The balance of construction was continued and not until 1922 was the last vessel delivered to the Fleet Corporation. By this time its chief problem was the disposition of the government-owned vessels.

The airplane did not play a very outstanding part in the First World War. In spite of the fact that the United States had pioneered in this field, several other countries led in airplane construction. After entering the war, this country planned to mass-produce planes and parts. The automobile industry joined the five principal United States airplane manufacturers in turning out planes and motors. Fourteen thousand planes and 42,000 airplane engines were produced before the armistice, but less than two hundred planes built in the United States saw service at the front. The experience illustrated the time required to organize mass production. Hundreds of American aviators sent to battle fronts were provided with machines of British and French manufacture. At the close of the war twenty-four large factories found themselves with millions of dollars of cancelled orders.

FOOD AND FUEL CONTROL

The Food and Fuel Administrations were created by executive orders to administer the provisions of the Lever Act of August, 1917, which authorized fixing of the price of certain commodities; licensing of producers and distributors; and prohibited unfair trade practices. The United States Food Administration was organized and Herbert Hoover, who had been appointed by President Wilson in May as voluntary food controller, was named Food Administrator. Through his work as chairman of the Commission for Relief in Belgium, Hoover was well known and had gained valuable administrative experience and much prestige.

The hoarding and unequal distribution of sugar, flour, potatoes and other goods together with extortionate prices that were being charged were among the chief reasons for the creation of the Food Administration. The need to conserve and equitably distribute all foodstuffs and to prevent hoarding and speculation was necessary not only because of the demands of the American armed forces, but also to increase the surplus for export to the Allies, who were in dire need of supplies of all kinds. The Food Administration was authorized to fix prices, license food distributors, prohibit hoarding and profiteering, regulate exports, and stimulate production. It exercised its power partly through voluntary agreements and a licensing system, but regulations were also made and enforced. Campaigns were waged to cut down waste and to reduce food consumption. Wheatless and meatless days were proclaimed, and substitutes were sought and tried for wheat flour, meat, and even candy. It became a patriotic duty to have a war garden.

Wartime expansion brought into cultivation 20,000,000 additional acres of wheat and 5,000,000 more acres of rye. The total acreage of grain (corn, oats, wheat, barley, rye, buckwheat, and rice) increased from 203,000,000 in 1914 to 227,000,000 in 1919, a total of 12 per cent, although poor crop years in 1917 and 1918 held back production.

Cattle and hogs increased more than 2 per cent. Gains were made in all basic foodstuffs. By 1918, exports of farm commodities including cotton were 45 per cent above the prewar level. In 1919 farm exports were almost 20 per cent of the total farm production of the country.

In order to purchase and sell grain and other products, a Grain Corporation was incorporated in Delaware with officers from the Food Administration and with a capital stock of $50,000,000, owned by the government. It bought and distributed wheat and administered the established price of $2.20 a bushel. Another agency of the Food Administration was the Sugar Equalization Board, which was also incorporated to stabilize the price of sugar and to secure better distribution. It bought and distributed the cane sugar crops, while a Sugar Distribution Committee controlled beet sugar. In 1919, a Wheat Director was named to license the storage, distribution, export, and

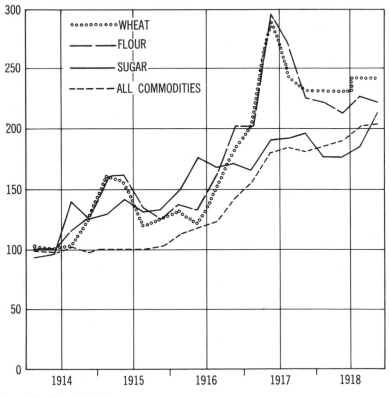

PRICE INDEX OF CERTAIN FOODSTUFFS, 1914 – 1918

Source: Brookings Institution.

import of wheat and flour. In the same year the authority of the Food Administration ended and its remaining functions and powers were transferred to the Attorney General, except those relating to wheat and its products which were administered by the Wheat Director.

In August, 1917, under authority of the Lever Act, the Fuel Administration was established to exercise control over the production, distribution, and price of coal and oil. It stimulated an increase in fuel production, encouraged economy in the consumption of fuel, restricted its use in industries that were considered nonessential to winning the war, regulated the distribution of coal through a zoning system, and fixed maximum prices. Under the direction of Fuel Administrator Harry A. Garfield, the administration introduced daylight saving and induced some motorists living east of the Mississippi to observe "gasless Sundays," while electric displays were banned to save fuel. The expansion of coal mining into submarginal deposits was encouraged and every effort put forth to stimulate the production of anthracite and bituminous coal. The life of the administration ended in 1919.

FINANCING THE WAR

When the United States entered the war, it was faced not only with financing its own war activities but those of the Allies as well. In July, 1917, the British Chancellor of the Exchequer, Lord Northcliffe, informed Colonel House that Allied financial resources were almost exhausted. "Unless the United States government," he stated, "can meet in full our expenses in America . . . the whole financial fabric of the alliance will collapse." During and immediately following the war, Congress authorized loans to the Allies to the amount of $10 billion, of which about $9.5 billion were actually advanced. Almost all of this amount was spent in the United States for supplies.

The war revolutionized national finances. In 1916, the cost of running the government was but $734,000,000. Congress enacted special revenue laws in October, 1917 and February, 1919. Income, inheritance, and corporation taxes were increased. Old excise taxes were raised and new ones levied on luxuries, amusements, gasoline, and many other commodities. An excess-profits tax, a war-profits tax, a transportation tax, a tax on insurance companies, and others were imposed. The new taxes brought greatly increased revenues, although they were somewhat offset by the loss of revenue that followed the prohibition of the sale of intoxicating liquor in 1918. Tariff increases were not made, for such violated the traditions of the Democratic

Party. The drop in imports, also, had an adverse effect on the Federal revenues. Yet from April, 1917 to June, 1919, a total of $9.4 billion was received from taxes. After the war the special war taxes were dropped and reductions made in the income tax rates.

In 1916 the national debt was only $1.2 billion. In 1919, government expenditures reached almost $19 billion, while the national debt had jumped to $26.5 billion (August 31, 1919). The total cost of the war to the United States from 1917 to 1919 has been estimated at more than $42 billion, of which $9.5 billion were loaned to the Allied na-

COST OF FIRST WORLD WAR TO THE LEADING NATIONS AS OF SPRING, 1919

Dollars spent (In billions)

This chart shows government expenditures only to the spring of 1919. If we add nearly $10 billion loaned to foreign governments by the United States and other items to the $22 billion it cost us up to 1919, we have the ultimate amount of over $36 billion as the direct cost to the people of the United States. This means the war cost us $2,000,000 an hour for twenty-five months following our entrance into the war.

Source: War Department.

tions, $26.5 billion were spent at home, and $6 billion were dispensed in indirect outlays. About 20 per cent of the total was raised by taxation, 50 per cent by loans, and 30 per cent by creating government deposits, the equivalent of issuing paper money. Thus the methods of finance were more inflationary than those of the North in the Civil War.

Three methods of borrowing were used. The Treasury Department issued short-term certificates of indebtedness, borrowing from the Federal Reserve banks. These were retired as income was received. A more permanent form of borrowing was by means of a series of bond issues. The first four issues were known as Liberty Loans, while the fifth and last was called the Victory Loan. The former were long term bonds bearing from 3½ to 4¼ per cent interest. The Victory Loan consisted of two series of 3–4 year notes bearing interest at 3¾ and 4¾ per cent. A total of $21 billion was realized from the sale of the five issues and at the same time they were effective agencies for sustaining morale. As far as possible, the bonds were sold directly to the people. Liberty Loan Committees were organized in all sections of the country and canvassed almost the entire population; rallies and mass meetings were held; four minute speakers delivered sales talks in theatres, moving picture houses, and hotels, and ministers from the pulpits made pleas for the purchase of bonds. Since member banks could use bonds for rediscount with the Federal Reserve, and individual purchasers could borrow over 90 per cent of the value of the bonds, each issue was over-subscribed, but since only a part of the money came from real savings the effect was strongly inflationary. Still another means of borrowing was through the sale of war saving certificates and thrift stamps. This plan netted $1.1 billion. In the years that followed the Liberty bond issues were paid or refunded as Treasury bonds at a considerable saving of interest.

A RETURN TO NORMALCY

After the First World War, a return to "normalcy" was desired by a large number of people. To most, who anticipated some form of economic reconstruction, the term at first was vague and devoid of meaning. In an address early in 1920, Warren G. Harding stated: "America's present need is not heroics but healing, not nostrums but normalcy." During the period that followed, the word came to mean a desire for change from the liberalism of the preceding decade.

To many powerful American economic interests, "normalcy" soon symbolized the abandonment of the important domestic and foreign policies of Woodrow Wilson's administrations. It signified a return to the high protective tariffs of earlier years, a drastic reduction of taxes, a laissez-faire policy of government in regard to business and industry, favors to corporate groups, the subservience of labor, and a vigorous nationalistic foreign policy. The "back to normal" slogan was used very effectively by the Republican Party in the political campaign of 1920. The philosophy, as it unfolded, dominated the country in the following decade when the pursuit of prosperity became the chief American goal.

At the same time, in demobilizing the great American war machine which had been built up through regimentation, partly along the lines of state socialism, there was a general feeling that much of what had been done during the emergency of war was foreign to the American principle of freedom. In their reaction to the restrictions and regulations of wartime, they elected to office an administration that brought a return of the philosophy of the pre-Progressive years of the late nineteenth century. Yet, during the period of Harding's "return to normalcy," Coolidge's "prosperity," and Hoover's "rugged individualism," businessmen were ready to retain some of the advantages of nation-wide organization and integration of business and industry. This can be best seen in the business codes directed by the Department of Commerce and in the attempts to help the farmers of the country. Thus, some lessons had been learned; but in national government the reform movement of the previous decade had collapsed.

The year 1919 marked the beginning of demobilization, but it took the country some time to put an end to the activities of the war machine. When the armistice was signed in November, 1918, military production was getting under way and it continued for a time on its own momentum as the war abruptly ended. The first serious problem was to demobilize about 4,000,000 soldiers and sailors together with the 11,500,000 civilian workers engaged in war work and to adjust their activities to peacetime industry. About 2,000,000 troops had to be brought back from France and fitted into the new economic pattern. The adjustment from wartime production to peacetime industry was accomplished without serious difficulties in spite of only a small amount of government aid in the task and the abolition of most of the emergency boards without much regard to their possible use in solving postwar problems.

Every effort was made to put returned veterans into their old jobs or to find new ones for them. Many returned to find that women had taken their positions. In spite of many difficulties, men found work as industrial adjustment took place. The demand for products of all kinds from devastated Europe immediately after the war kept factories and farms prosperous for a time. These purchases, however, were financed for the most part by American loans.

Another problem that had to be solved concerned the railroads, which were being operated by the government. The Railroad Administration proposed the extension of control for five years in order to give unified operation a fair test. Labor, through Glenn E. Plumb, counsel for the organized railroad employees, proposed the so-called Plumb plan of public ownership to replace the Railroad Administration. A bill was introduced into Congress which provided that the government purchase the railroads and that they be operated by a quasi-public corporation representing the government, operators, and classified employees. Improvements were to be financed by Federal and local funds; profits were to be used to retire the bond issues and other indebtedness, reduce railroad rates, and increase wages. Such proposals, however, had no chance of public acceptance in view of America's postwar mood.

The Transportation Act (Esch-Cummins Act) of 1920 provided for the return of the railroads to private ownership and control. It guaranteed the roads for a period of six months a net return equal to one-half the rental paid during government operations. The Interstate Commerce Commission, which was reorganized and its membership increased to eleven, was given authority to fix minimum and maximum rates and was granted exclusive jurisdiction over the issue of new railroad securities. The Commission was to decide rates that would enable the roads as a whole or in groups to earn a "fair return." Railroads earning more than 6 per cent were to set aside one-half the excess in their reserve funds and were to pay the other half to the government to be placed in a fund from which loans could be made to weak railroads. This was called the "recapture" clause of the act.

Reversing the earlier trend, the Transportation Act authorized the consolidation of railroads, thus relaxing the policy of enforced competition. Wartime control had demonstrated the public advantages of combination. The Commission was given power to approve pooling arrangements and traffic agreements when in the public interest. Not only could it approve mergers and voluntary consolidations, but it was required to "prepare and adopt a plan for the consolidation of the railway properties of the United States into a limited number of systems," preserving as far as possible competition and the existing channels of trade. The law also provided for voluntary adjustment boards for the settlement of labor disputes, these provisions to be enforced by a Railway Labor Board, consisting of nine members, having national jurisdiction.

Much controversy arose over the measure both in and out of Congress. It was maintained that the favorable terms of the act were necessary if the carriers were to survive the competition of interstate omnibus and motor truck lines operating on roads maintained at public expense, as well as the extension of pipe lines and the increasing use of the country's waterways. On the other hand, those who opposed insisted that the railroads and financial interests had really dictated terms that were far more to their advantage than to the public interest. The bill, however, was passed and the railroads returned to private control.

The Interstate Commerce Commission granted increases in rates varying from 25 to 50 per cent, while wages were raised about 20 per cent. The "recapture clause" would not work and, although its constitutionality was upheld by the Supreme Court, it was finally repealed. Under the terms of the law, the Commission and the courts encouraged and urged the consolidations of lines and systems so that by 1928, 6,000 railroad lines had been reduced to about 800. By 1930, the railroads themselves proposed the consolidation of the northeastern lines into four systems: the Pennsylvania, Baltimore and Ohio, New York Central, and Chesapeake and Ohio. The depression, however, prevented the plan from being carried out. The Railway Labor Board failed to prevent a shopmen's strike in 1922 and proved so ineffective that it was abolished in 1926 to be replaced by a new agency known as the United States Board of Mediation.

During the period from 1920 to 1930, in spite of keen competition from buses, trucks and water-traffic, as well as the beginning of airplane commerce, the railroads, except for a few weaker lines, were able to hold their own. In fact, from 1925 to 1930, they were remarkably prosperous, the returns for 1929 marking the highest point in railroad history. This was due to the work of the Commission, economies and improvements in transportation made by the carriers and to the general prosperity of the period. But the depression after 1929 seriously affected the carriers as it did all industries. In 1938, one-third of the mileage of the country's greatest railroads was in the hands of the courts.

Another step in taking down the wartime structure was the disbanding of the government-owned merchant marine. The Jones Merchant Marine Act of 1920 rearranged the duties of the Shipping Board and authorized it to dispose of the wartime merchant fleet to private corporations controlled by Americans citizens as well as to operate unsold ships. A fund was established to lend money to shipowners in order to encourage shipping. The Shipping Board found it difficult to sell the government fleet. Vessels were sold for what they would bring, which was but a fraction of their worth. Henry Ford secured 200 in

1926 as "junk" for $800 each, although almost $1,000,000 had been originally invested in each. Robert S. Dollar of the Dollar Line in 1928 obtained the last government-owned merchant vessel on the Pacific. By this time the Shipping Board's fleet numbered about 800 vessels of 6,000,000 (deadweight) tons and seventy auxiliary craft. Some were being operated; others were deteriorating chiefly in the Delaware and Hudson Rivers. American citizens had bought 1,100 vessels totaling 5,000,000 tons for about $84,000,000. But the total of American shipping had declined from 18,000,000 tons in 1923 to 16,000,000 tons in 1928. Great Britain had regained her leadership and Germany, Japan, France, and Italy were building much more shipping annually than the United States.

The La Follette Act of 1915, upheld by the Supreme Court in 1921, prescribed standards of wages, food, and accommodations for sailors which made it difficult for Americans to compete with foreign shipping. In view of these conditions, Congress passed the Jones-White Act of 1928. Increased subsidies were offered to encourage private shipping. Larger loans bearing lower rates of interest could now be granted private concerns for the purpose of displacing outmoded vessels with modern ones; and large sums were to be paid under long-term contracts for carrying the mail. One-half of the crew of a vessel could be foreigners, who need not be paid at La Follette Act levels. The Act also changed the name of the Emergency Fleet Corporation to the Merchant Fleet Corporation. But because of the surplus tonnage overhanging the market, old vessels could still be sold only at ridiculously low prices. As a result of a congressional investigation in 1932, dissatisfaction became widespread regarding the ocean mail contract system as a means of providing operating subsidies, and at the same time it was evident that the construction loan features of the acts of 1920 and 1928 had not materially encouraged new shipbuilding. The Merchant Marine Act of 1936 continued low-interest construction loans and inaugurated a new policy of operating subsidies for new ships based on the necessity for an American flag merchant marine for purposes of national defense as well as of commerce. The Shipping Board was superseded in 1933 by the Shipping Board Bureau of the Department of Commerce which, in 1936, gave way to the Maritime Commission.

IMMIGRATION RESTRICTION

In the year 1914, more than 1,200,000 immigrants passed through American ports of entry. The First World War stayed the tide of immigration, but it also clearly revealed that aliens had been coming to the United States faster than they could be assimilated and that it was impossible to fuse foreign elements within a short period of time. Labor leaders had long demanded restrictive laws. After the war, civic and political leaders joined labor in protesting against the expected influx from Europe. Many advocated a policy of selective restriction, which would reduce the number of immigrants from those parts of Europe where illiteracy was high and where political tradition, cultural environment and governmental philosophy were opposed to those of the United States. Others urged a highly restrictive policy to keep out the hordes of Europeans who were looking forward to beginning life anew in this country now that the great conflict had ended. Commissioner of Immigration Wallis warned of the prospect of a tidal wave of immigration: "The world is preparing to move to America."

During the war, the Immigration Act of 1917 was passed. It marked a turning point between the older "welcome" policy and the highly restrictive plans that followed. The act provided for a literacy test. President Wilson, like Cleveland and Taft before him, vetoed the measure, but it became law over his veto. It increased the head tax to $8 and provided the usual exclusions to guard the health, morals, and institutions of the United States. A noteworthy clause provided that all aliens over sixteen years of age, physically capable of reading, should be able to read English or some other language. Some exceptions were made, for example, such as applied to close relatives of those in the United States who were fleeing religious or political persecution. A new era in the regulation of immigration was beginning.

The immigration law of 1921 limited the quota which any country could send to the United States to 3 per cent of its people here according to the census of 1910. The act was a temporary one but was extended to 1924. It did not apply to natives of the Western Hemisphere nor to those of Asiatic countries already restricted. Exceptions were also made in the case of government employees, businessmen, students, and travelers from a number of specified countries.

The law of 1924 provided for an even more drastic limitation of immigration by reducing the quotas to 2 per cent on the basis of the census of 1890. This achieved the purpose of automatically increasing the proportion of immigrants from northern and western Europe. One provision, aimed at the Japanese, which barred all aliens ineligible to citizenship, was vehemently protested by that nation but without avail. The law also set forth that after July 1, 1927, there should be applied the "national origin" principle, whereby each country was to be accorded "that proportion of 150,000 which the number of persons of a given national origin residing in the United States in 1920 bears to the country's total population." Although such calculations were complex and attempts were made to simplify the plan, the new quotas totaling 153,700 were proclaimed by President Hoover in March, 1929. In general the nations that had supplied the early immigrants had larger quotas than would be used, whereas the eastern European nations had relatively small quotas. But, in any case, depression cut the flow of immigrants to a low level.

GOVERNMENT FAVORS BUSINESS

The tariff policy was reversed after the war. The Republican-dominated House in 1920 was able to secure the passage of a higher tariff measure on the grounds that European manufactures would compete more than ever with American goods, making protection necessary. President Wilson vetoed the bill. When Harding became President, he called a special session of Congress in 1921 to aid the farmers, who were experiencing widespread suffering. An emergency tariff was passed and relatively high duties were imposed on wheat, corn, meat, wool, sugar, and other agricultural commodities. Duties were increased on textiles, and a special retaliatory "dumping duty" was authorized against countries attempting to unload their surplus products in the United States. Chemicals and dyes were also granted protection from European competition, especially German.

In 1922, a permanent law, the Fordney-McCumber tariff, was enacted. It protected American manufactures even more than did the Payne-Aldrich Act of 1909. Agriculture products were highly protected. Duties were reimposed on iron, steel, textiles, and silk. The law authorized the President to alter by proclamation prevailing rates of duties, not to exceed 50 per cent, upon the recommendation of the Tariff Commission which had been created in 1916. The law remained in effect until the Hawley-Smoot tariff of 1930 superseded it and raised the general tariff level still higher. The new tariff policy prevented Europe from paying a part of its debts in goods, and it resulted in trade reprisals from foreign countries.

A trend that became more and more evident during the twenties was the relaxation of the regulation and control of industry by the government and the courts. The trend to restrict monopolies, which had reached a height just before the war, was now reversed. Heralding a new era was the Supreme Court decision in the United States Steel

Corporation case in 1920. Suit had been brought against the "Steel Trust" during Taft's administration, but the war had interfered with its disposition. Despite the fact that the corporation controlled more than half the steel output of the country, the Court refused to dissolve it on the grounds that mere size was not illegal, that it had abandoned many monopolistic practices, that there was competition within the entire industry, and that a potential power to restrain trade was not necessarily a violation of the law. The decision went even further, declaring that the dissolution of the corporation would injure the public interest and disturb foreign trade. Apparently the principle of the "rule of reason" had ended. A new trust movement now got under way. The merger became the chief method of combination, but public utility empires were built up through the instrumentality of the holding company. In the twenties, more than 4,000 public utilities companies disappeared through mergers. The new combinations were most evident in the telephone and telegraph systems and in the automobile industry. By 1929, about 200 out of a total of 456,000 nonfinancial corporations owned 49.2 per cent of all corporate wealth and 22 per cent of the national wealth. Yet great individual monopolies had declined somewhat. For example, the control by the Standard Oil companies of the oil business which had been 80 per cent in 1911 declined to 42 per cent in 1929, while control of the United States Steel Corporation over steel production dropped during the same period from 70 to 40 per cent. But the trend toward laissez faire continued throughout the period. As late as 1933, the Supreme Court in the Appalachian Coal case declared that the joint sales agency, which included producers of 75 per cent of the output of coal, was not contrary to the Sherman Act.

The antitrust laws were weakened by the courts in other ways. Trade association efforts to avoid price competition were declared to be legal in the cases of the Cement Manufacturers' Protective Association and the Maple Flooring Manufacturers' Association (1925). Regarding labor, the Supreme Court decided that a clause in the Clayton Act could not be interpreted to legalize the secondary boycott or prevent the use of the injunction in protecting property right (Duplex Printing Press Company *vs.* Deering *et al.*, 1921). In the years that followed, the courts increasingly granted injunctions against labor unions. The Fourteenth Amendment was also used to protect business enterprise against the encroachments of state legislatures. Thus the courts pursued policies generally designed to aid business development.

The Department of Justice, also, was more friendly to "big business" and was in general accord with the new trends. Suits were brought for unfair practices and activites, but there was very little interference with the development of large-scale enterprise. The Federal Trade Commission, likewise, although attempting to prohibit such practices as fraudulent advertising and the misbranding of commodities, did not attack interlocking directorates which thrived during the period in spite of the Clayton Act. Nor did the commission interfere with the development of holding companies, which reached an unbelievable extent through pyramiding, as could be seen in the giant system of Samuel Insull in public utilities and the Van Sweringen brothers who controlled railroads valued at $2 billion on an investment of less than $20,000,000. Congress, the courts, and agencies of government all felt that the antitrust laws hindered business prosperity and they acted accordingly.

The Federal government attempted to aid business in other ways. A high tariff and lower taxes provided additional capital for expansion. The Department of Commerce under Herbert Hoover promoted industrial efficiency through standardization, uniform policies, the elimination of unfair practices, the dissemination of information, and research. Trade organizations were fostered and during Hoover's eight years as Secretary of Commerce over 400 "trade associations" were formed. They pooled information and reached profitable agreements. More than 200 "codes of fair practice" were drawn up and accepted—some of them to be copied later by the NRA. The Federal Trade Commission condemned the Department as an agency for price-fixing, but the Supreme Court at this time upheld the codes. The Department also acquired jurisdiction over the Patent Office (1925) and expanded the work of many of its agencies.

THE EXPANDING ROLE OF GOVERNMENT

Guided by the laissez-faire concepts of the administrations from 1921 to 1929 the Federal government avoided any marked increase in civilian employees, although the prevailing level was 50 per cent higher than before the war. Similarly the Federal budget stayed around four billion dollars a year from 1922 to 1930. Coupled with the prosperity of the period, this thrifty Federal policy made it possible to lower the initial income tax rate from 4 per cent in 1921 to ⅜ per cent in 1929, with exemptions of $1,000 for single and $3,500 for married taxpayers.

But while the Federal government was construing its regulatory functions narrowly and aiding business chiefly in ways that did not

VALUE OF STATE AND LOCAL EXPENDITURES, 1902 – 1957

(In millions of dollars)

Year	Current Operation	Construction	Education	Public Welfare	Total
1902	796	164	255	37	1,095
1913	1,505	442	577	52	2,257
1922	3,477	1,236	1,705	119	5,652
1927	4,590	1,921	2,235	151	7,810
1932	5,179	1,558	2,311	444	8,403
1940	6,176	1,828	2,638	1,156	11,240
1950	15,948	5,169	7,177	2,940	27,905
1957	27,983	10,386	14,134	3,404	47,553

Source: U.S. Bureau of the Census, *Historical Statistics of the United States, Colonial Times to 1957*, Washington, D.C., 1960, p. 726.

add to the budget, state and local governments were growing mightily. Faced with the physical and educational problems of expanding industrialism, the states could not retreat from progressive legislation. Streets had to be paved and bridges and tunnels built—these were government aids to the increasing amount of business done by truck and automobile. Industrial technology and management needed more high school and college graduates, and local communities had to raise school levies. The prewar compensation laws had to be revised to match the inflation, and a better educated and more affluent society demanded more in the way of state care for the poor and the sick. In 1913 the total of state and local expenditure was $2,257,000,000, of which $577,000,000 was for education. In 1927, when the Bureau of Labor Statistics Cost of Living Index was less than 60 per cent higher than in 1913, state and local expenditures stood at $7,810,-000,000 up $2,150,000,000 from 1922. Of the 240 per cent increase from 1913 to 1927, education ran only a little ahead of the average. The biggest increase in a major item was for construction and other capital outlays. Looking at the total picture the 1920's were a period of continuing increase in government expenditure.

CHAPTER 25

The Impact of Technological Change

Electricity and the gasoline engine, two major technological forces for economic change, were relatively mature by 1914, but their effect on the economy was only beginning. Supplementing each other in many ways, these two new forms of energy relocated people and industry in the twentieth century just as the railroad had in the second half of the nineteenth century.

SPREAD OF THE AUTOMOBILE

The automobile industry reached relative maturity in the 1920's and effected major policy decisions that were to hold for many decades. Presented with a choice between a cheap and simple automobile and more elaborate models at higher prices, American consumers chose the latter. By 1927 Ford had to abandon his famous Model T and bring out a more luxurious and expensive Model A. No doubt the development of easy installment credit for purchasing automobiles enabled people with low incomes to pay higher prices, and more reliable used cars also competed with the Model T. Once embarked upon the policy of bigger and better cars at increasing retail prices, the industry pursued this course until 1959, by which time the average price of a Ford in real dollars was about four times that of the middle 1920's.

540

With revolutionary rapidity in 1925 and 1926 closed cars replaced open ones, marking the shift from the automobile as a recreational device to a year-round family utility. This change in automobile design produced a major rise in the glass, paint, and upholstery fabric industries. By 1930 there was one passenger car for every five and a half people in the nation, nearly three times as many cars as a decade earlier.

Even in the prosperous twenties three big companies, Chrysler, Ford, and General Motors, had been doing an increasing percentage of the business. The ability of the very big company to afford large advertising budgets and support a large dealer organization was a great advantage. In the great depression all but the strongest independents dropped out and the three big companies came to make over 85 per cent of the sales. Following World War II the uptrend in automobile ownership resumed, but even in years of prosperity the major companies continued to increase their share of sales, until the

MOTOR VEHICLES AND ROADS, 1915 – 1960

Year	Passenger Cars	Buses and Trucks	Miles of Surfaced Rural Road (In thousands)
1915	2,332,426	158,506*	276
1920	8,131,522	1,107,639*	369
1925	17,481,001	2,587,542	521
1930	23,034,753	3,715,100	694
1935	22,567,827	3,978,299	1,080
1940	27,465,826	4,987,407	1,367
1945	25,793,493	5,241,927	1,721
1950	40,333,591	8,828,100	1,939
1955	52,135,583	10,558,236	2,273
1960	61,724,000	12,217,000	2,165

* Trucks only.

Sources: U.S. Bureau of the Census, *Historical Statistics of the United States, Colonial Times to 1957*, Washington, D.C., 1960, pp. 458, 462; and *Statistical Abstract of the United States 1962*, Washington, D.C., 1962, pp. 552, 562.

percentage held by the dwindling independents was around 5 per cent. By 1960 there was an automobile for every three Americans.

After World War II the American producers lost the dominant position in world markets which they had enjoyed in the 1920's. In the earlier period United States prices had been below those of most European auto manufacturers, but in seeking to serve the affluent American buyers with ever larger, more complex cars, American companies not only priced themselves out of foreign markets, but invited a flood of lower-priced imports. The American companies, in turn, established plants abroad and competed in the home markets of foreign producers with small inexpensive cars.

RELOCATION OF PLANTS AND PEOPLE

Automobiles, buses, and trucks made possible both ex-urban living and production, as well as new ways of traveling and shipping goods. The automobile also accounted for much of the new capital investment, some of it going directly into automotive factories and those of suppliers of glass, rubber, paint, fabrics, and parts, but more still aiding automobile production in indirect ways. Public construction of streets and highways became, next to home and business building, the largest single category of investment, surpassing by 1940 the value of the railroad network. After World War II, particularly, a large part of the building construction resulted from possibilities opened up by the use of motor vehicles.

In the twenties the development of pneumatic tires strong enough for trucks and buses started a change in industrial location. By 1950 trailer trucks with oil-burning Diesel engines were capable of carrying heavy commodities such as steel for long distances at rates little higher than those of the railroad, and in much less time. The truck cost more per ton mile to operate, but the expenses of loading and delivery were much less. While one truck could move about with maximum efficiency, railroads had to operate on the basis of making up trains with all the switching and other terminal costs involved. Trucks could be selected to fit the size of the shipments whereas shipping less than carload lots—and freight cars are very large—was quite expensive. Furthermore, and this was often important, the truck could start whenever the shipment was ready whereas the railroad ran on schedule and trains were adjusted to what could be hauled by the available engines.

Essential to the use of trucks were hard-surfaced, durable highways. The superiority of concrete for this purpose was demonstrated just before World War I. In 1916, the Federal government started the practice of aiding the states in the construction of arterial highways. By 1925, local, state, and Federal expenditures for new roads and bridges involved a government investment in the economy of nearly a billion dollars a year. While this figure was enormous by the standards of the day, it was to increase rapidly in both good and bad times. In 1933, the annual capital investment by all forms of government in roads and bridges was slightly higher than in 1925; by 1937 it was a billion and a third; and in 1956 over five billion dollars.

Taking advantage of this vast public investment, truck and bus service grew rapidly. By 1950, there were ten interstate trucking companies operating common carrier service with revenues from ten to nearly thirty million dollars a year. Although some operated routes across the continent, none of these companies were really big business by United States standards. All interstate common carriers were regulated by the Interstate Commerce Commission, but the greater majority of trucks were owned or rented by private companies and their movements were not subject to Federal regulation or statistical measurements. Bus transportation reached an all-time peak in 1948, when for the first time total passengers carried surpassed the figure for the railroads. From then on the number of railroad passengers declined rapidly and the number of bus passengers declined slowly, both losing business to private automobiles and airplanes. In comparing the 6.8 billion bus passengers of 1957, for example, with the 2.5 billion railroad passengers of that year, it should be remembered, however, that the average rail passenger undoubtedly traveled farther than the bus passengers for which passenger mile figures were lacking.

The other new form of transportation, the airplane, also involved large government investment, and had its early commercial development in the twenties. Although for centuries a few men had experimented with flight, particularly with balloons, the work of the Wright brothers early in the twentieth century marked the beginning of practical aviation. Until the First World War gave it an impetus, flying was largely experimental. Commercial flying in the United States began in May, 1918, when the government established an experimental route between Washington and New York. Slowly other routes were projected and private companies began passenger service. The Kelly Act of 1925 provided that companies could carry mail at rates that amounted to a substantial subsidy. In addition, the Federal government supplied beacons marking routes and weather information, while local governments built airports. Supported by mail subsidies, companies for air transport service carried passengers on regular schedules, by night as well as by day. The series of sensational flights by Americans such as Richard E. Byrd and Floyd Bennett over the North Pole in 1926 and Charles A. Lindbergh's nonstop flight across the Atlantic in 1927 created interest and enthusiasm in aviation.

The Second World War with its millions of passenger miles of operation between accidents greatly reduced the fear of flight which had been holding back commercial air service. By that time statistics indicated that a passenger was safer in a plane than in an automobile. As more planes became available for civilian use in the closing years of the war, air passenger service started a period of growth that by 1957 put domestic air passenger mileage ahead of that of the railroads, excluding commuters, and by 1960 ahead of all forms of rail passenger traffic. Plane fares remained higher than rail coach, but considerably lower than first-class rail plus Pullman. This meant that long-haul passenger traffic passed largely to the airlines. Cities as big and as near each other as Philadelphia and Detroit ceased having direct passenger train connections.

While planes became important carriers of equipment needed in emergencies and of perishable luxuries such as flowers and exotic foods, the total of air express and freight service was negligible compared to that of trucks or railroads. The rising figure for ton miles of railroad cargo indicated the continuing economy of tracks for hauling bulky slow-moving freight. Meanwhile, prosperity and inflation had reduced both the dollar total and the relative burden of railroad debt, and Diesel engines had cut fuel costs and speeded service. Buying

DOMESTIC AIR AND RAILROAD OPERATIONS, 1940 – 1957

Year	Number of Companies		Miles of Route		Passenger Miles (In thousands)		Ton Miles of Freight	
	Air	Rail	Air	Rail (First main track)	Air	Rail*	Air	Rail
1940	19	574	42,757	245,740	1,052,156	19,773,000	3,476,224	375,369,000
1950	38	471	77,440	236,857	8,002,825	26,781,000	151,351,080	591,550,000
1957	30	415	88,325	232,177	25,339,560	21,060,000	266,483,000	621,907,000

* Excludes commuters.

Source: U.S. Bureau of the Census, *Historical Statistics of the United States, Colonial Times to 1957*, Washington, D.C., 1960, pp. 429–431, 467.

into truck and bus companies and merging their competing lines, the railroads showed an ability to survive in the new competitive situation.

Coastwise and intercoastal shipping did not fare as well. Mainly using ships constructed before or those built by the government during the First World War, ships that were sold afterward at ten dollars a ton or less, freight and passenger services along the coast and through the Panama Canal had been able to survive and make moderate profits. But, aside from oil tanker service, these trades could not support the cost of new ships. Hence when the old ships were sunk in the Second World War, and in addition stevedoring rates rose to high levels, there was no incentive to resume these trades. Some special services such as bringing ore from Labrador or oil from California and the Gulf Coast did continue, but basically the coastwise truck had eliminated the ship.

THE EFFECT OF ELECTRICITY

Unlike steam power plants, whose efficiency increased with size, electric motors were efficient in all sizes. With a separate motor on each tool, a factory no longer had to depend on drive shafts, belts, and gears operated from a central engine room. With electricity a single operation in a small shop might be just as inexpensive as though it were part of a large factory process. By 1930, electric power was available in all the major industrial areas at reasonable rates. This, coupled with shipment by truck, meant that many small businesses could operate with as low cost per unit of output as in the case of big factories, and they had the additional advantage of flexibility in filling small orders, modifying products to suit the customer, or taking on new products.

This technological flexibility was reflected in the business structure. Instead of the number of firms in manufacturing declining and production falling into the hands of a few big companies, the number of enterprises increased. In 1920 there were 270,000 firms in manufacturing, and in 1957 there were 332,000. Many of the smaller firms were subcontractors for final assemblers. The big automobile producers worked with one thousand or more small companies.

While the essential technology for dispersed manufacturing and country living was available by 1925, changes in location were delayed by a slow rate of economic growth prior to the Second World War. The big change came with the location of new war plants and the expansion of the postwar economy. The movement was chiefly from central cities to the urban fringe areas, with a tendency to locate new plants in rapidly developing regions. The truly rural areas, those without any large cities, tended to lose population, while all large metropolitan areas, which from 1950 on included much of the surrounding country, grew faster than the average.

With electric rapid transit and the automobile, employees could come from a wide area to work either in central city plants or factories built on cheap land in the surrounding countryside. Acres of factory parking lots demonstrated how many employees could afford to come in private automobiles. Unfortunately workers using public transportation suffered a loss in prestige, and therefore bus and trolley lines often went out of operation even in rapidly growing areas. Higher wages and government-guaranteed mortgages allowed factory workers to buy homes in the suburbs or nearby countryside. A great building boom developed from 1945 on, basically dependent on gasoline transportation and electrical power and communication.

The new types of transportation and the continuing geographical mobility of Americans brought some changes in the relative importance of manufacturing areas. The large, old, metropolitan areas continued to advance more rapidly than the country as a whole, but the growth of Los Angeles was phenomenal in both population and light industry. From 1947 to 1954 manufacturing in the area grew 150 per cent, making it the third largest center in the country, and the rate of growth indicated that it would eventually surpass Chicago and become second to New York. Other changes in rank were more moderate. Detroit outstripped Philadelphia and St. Louis grew bigger than Boston. Similar data for metropolitan areas is not available for 1920, but the first ten areas of 1960 were presumably nearly the same as for the earlier date except for the inclusion of Los Angeles.

INCREASING EFFICIENCY

Productive efficiency increased greatly from 1920 to 1960 partly as a result of better machines, but also because of better management practices. Schemes for better management were as old as big companies. From 1850 to 1880 the railroads took a leading role in introducing new arrangements. Then the Society of Mechanical Engineers became interested in analyzing shop problems. The famous Frederick W. Taylor, sometimes called the father of modern management, soon assumed the leading role in the deliberations of the engineers. From 1900 on he devoted all his time to spreading his system of "task management" and incentive pay. The system included careful job definitions, study

of workers' motions, incentives for higher production, careful accounting methods, and specialized foremen. Soon Taylor's chief disciples
such as Henry T. Gantt, Carl G. Barth and later Frank B. Gilbreth
set up consulting management services. By the time Taylor published
Shop Management (1911) and *The Principles of Scientific Method*
(1912), his ideas were well known in Europe and America.

While the pioneer work of Taylor and his associates became a
world-wide symbol of the coming of scientific management, these early
studies in job requirements and proper working arrangements were
only a prelude to later managerial improvements. In the nineteen
twenties and thirties better understanding of employee morale, standardization of products, and quality control achieved still more important results from the standpoint of productivity and profit.

A heritage of the Taylor era and the army intelligence tests of
the First World War was a belief that the man with the highest ability
would perform the best. Psychologists left the academic world to set
up aptitude testing services, and personnel managers, themselves a
product of the war, started relying on intelligence tests. But a decade
of experience showed little connection between high test scores and
good performance on the job. Obviously something was missing.

In 1930, Professor Elton Mayo of the Harvard Business School,
working with data accumulated at the Hawthorne plant of Western
Electric, found an answer. Workers responded favorably to stimulating
human relations, including recognition of their importance as individuals. For these reasons a small group working as a team would produce
more than the same number of workers merged anonymously with
hundreds of others. To put it another way, most jobs did not need an
unusually high level of ability as much as they needed the worker's
interest in doing the job. Based on Mayo's findings a new science of
industrial relations developed in which psychologists might manipulate
the worker in the interest of management, but reconcile him to it
at the same time. The repercussions of this new recognition of morale
reached all the way to the top executive offices and led to increasing
use of committees and group consultation, rather than arbitrary one-
man decisions.

The net effect of some of these psychological theories on production was still open to question in 1960, but there could be no doubt
about the gains made from standardization of products. Reducing
the number of different sizes and shapes was an obvious need of mass
production with interchangeable parts, but its accomplishment was
a problem in business persuasion. The biggest manufacturers gained

an advantage by having parts for their machines more readily available than the different-sized parts of their small competitors. By the Second World War Sears, Roebuck, for example, carried parts for Ford automobiles, but not for those of a score of Ford's nearest competitors.

When Herbert Hoover became Secretary of Commerce in 1921, he joined with progressive trade association executives and some of the engineering societies in a campaign for standardization. By 1925 the battle was being won. The big automobile, electrical, and tire companies were cooperating, and the movement was spreading to all types of production. For example, twenty standard bottles replaced 210 different sizes; seven shapes of bricks did the work of 66; and screws, nuts, bolts, and gear wheels were similarly reduced to numbers that a dealer could keep in stock.

Quality control was another advance originated in the area of management supervision, but carrying with it great impetus for technological change. Prior to the First World War automobile makers could not get the producers to give them steel with a strictly controlled chemical content. As a result, all steel parts had to be extra heavy to allow for brittle steel. This was just one example of waste through variable quality that ran through all industries. Another problem, uneven sizes, was solved by better boring and cutting machinery and careful measurement with Johansen blocks which reached American factories in the 1920's. But more important generally was careful scrutiny of the components of cost in each operation with a view to eliminating elements that were needlessly expensive and adding to quality where there were weaknesses. Careful inspection of products and laboratory testing of samples taken at random accompanied more careful planning. New devices such as X rays and photo electric cells could be used to detect flaws or wrong sizes and colors.

Another element in increasing technological efficiency was the substitution of continuous for broken processes. The Ford assembly line for automobiles was an example of this principle. The substitution of continuously flowing chemical processes for separate stages of operations, carried to a high point in the petrochemical industry, was another example. One of the most spectacular early instances, the continuous hot strip mill for steel plates, depended on the saving that came from avoiding cooling and reheating as well as the necessity of handling between rolls. Such mills were built in the middle 1920's, largely to supply the vast demands of the automobile industry for very thin steel plates.

Photoelectric controls, chemical flows, and other aids to continuous processes were all types of what came by the 1950's to be called automation. Each eliminated the unskilled manual labor needed for carrying material around the plant, and each required a smaller number of semiskilled workers competent to respond to the warnings of meters and gauges or to adjust electrical devices. Maintenance of the machines also required many more special technicians or engineers. By 1955, automation had at least two generally used definitions: (1) self-regulation through feedback and (2) the integration of machines with one another. Feedback refers to any self-correcting control device such as a governor on a motor that holds it at constant speed, or an automatic pilot mechanism that adjusts for wind or wave movements. Such mechanisms had been used commercially in the nineteenth century, but the principle had not had wide application. In fact, by almost any definition, automation was advancing steadily from the early days of industrialism and was only emphasized by the rapid commercial development after 1940 of electronic devices for the control of processes.

Electronic control devices tended to lessen the difference between shop and office work. By the late 1950's, for example, a control apparatus for automatic automobile engine machinery was a hundred yards long, and the operatives had to watch dials and push buttons. Meanwhile computers, the basic electronic control devices, were moving office processes in the same direction.

Computers were of two types: the analogue in which a simple model of procedure was laid out and the computer saw to it that the model was followed; and the digital which was a far more complicated device, having a storage capacity or memory for many patterns that had been fed to it, as well as the ability to make mathematical calculations. Vannevar Bush developed the first practical analogue computer at Massachusetts Institute of Technology in the 1930's, and John Mauchley and J. P. Eckert, Jr. developed an electronic, as distinct from partly mechanical, digital computer at the University of Pennsylvania in 1946.

But electronic computers were merely the most recent step in a long history of mechanizing office work. Without going into a background of ingenious but little-used calculating machines going back to the early seventeenth century, it may be noted that by 1810 French weaving looms were being controlled by Joseph Marie Jacquard's punch cards, and in 1870 Jean Baudot introduced punched tape in the French Ministry of Posts and Telegraph. As punched tape was

. perfected and office equipment such as typewriters, mechanical cal-
culators, and punch card machines were developed in the early twentieth century, a common language in the form of punched holes on
cards or tapes came into use between these machines.

All these devices made it easy to coordinate the work of many
plants and offices. Punch cards or tapes could do bookkeeping, keep
track of inventory, make out payrolls, or in general do any job that
did not require varying judgment, and do it faster, more accurately,
and on any large scale, more cheaply than human beings. Added to
these controls executives had teletype transmission of letters, closed
circuit television, inexpensive telephone service, and transportation by
plane as various means of coordinating far-flung operations.

THE RISE OF CONSUMER DURABLE GOODS

The continued development of new types of more or less durable
machines for personal and family use was a striking feature of technological development from 1914 to 1929. Before the First World
War automobiles had only just matured and less than two million
were in operation. Electric refrigerators, washing machines, and other
electrical household appliances were even less developed, record
players were mechanical, and home radio receivers nonexistent.

While the commercial development of new consumer goods was
delayed by the First World War, the twenties was a period of rapid
perfection and large sales. Economically, household machines diverted
income from payments to servants to payments for the machine, often
on an installment basis. Since machines were bought by families too
poor to have servants, they also absorbed some of the increase in real
wages that occurred from 1918 to 1929. In the period 1907 to 1911 only
8 per cent of the money spent by consumers went into durable goods.
By 1929 the figure was above 12 per cent, and in the forties and fifties
the fraction leveled off at 14 to 15 per cent, but it should be remembered that this was 14 to 15 per cent of a much larger real income.

Still other economic changes were associated with the rise of the
automotive-electrical complex. The final stages of production were
largely in the hands of big companies and profits tended to be high.
As a result these companies could invest in expansion and seek security
through diversifying products. Automobile companies moved into the
electrical field, rubber companies made clothing and even motion
pictures, and each of the big electrical companies developed complete
lines of appliances. To stimulate new sales, styles were changed fre-

quently, generally every year in automobiles, and prestige came to be attached to having a new model. To facilitate purchase of these expensive items by people with low incomes installment payment plans became the rule. Time payments had been used for pianos and some other expensive household goods before the First World War, but the general adoption of such plans came right after the war. In 1919, General Motors Acceptance Corporation was created to handle such business, and soon the purchase of secondhand as well as new cars and appliances could be done in installments.

THE RISE OF SYNTHETICS

Another aspect of technology that affected personal and family buying habits after 1914 was the rise of synthetic products. The term applies to any chemical imitation of a material derived from nature. Thus drugs, rubber goods, foods, and countless other products made from laboratory formulas were called synthetics, and many such compounds, particularly among drugs, dated back to the mid-nineteenth century. The rise of a large-scale United States chemical industry, aided by the protection from European competition given by the First World War, greatly accelerated the domestic development of non-medicinal synthetics.

Synthetic fibres of major importance owed much of their rapid advance to the DuPont company. Building upon original English and French processes, rayon was perfected sufficiently by 1935 to displace 80 per cent of natural silk. In the next two decades nylon, orlon, and dacron took over most of the remaining market for silk, an import from Japan, and cut deeply into the market for wool.

From the chemical standpoint plastics were closely allied to synthetic fibres, but their uses were quite different. Celluloid, the first cheap plastic, had been developed from high-cost foreign processes by John Hyatt in 1869. It was widely used before 1900 for billiard balls, toilet articles, and men's collars. Another early plastic, Bakelite, was used for electrical insulation. With new formulas and processes developed in the 1930's, plastics became less brittle and could be substituted for wood or metal wherever the stress was small and a hard durable finish was desired.

Processes by which natural products were recombined to form new products fell under the general heading, synthetic. One of the most important areas of the chemical alteration of natural products was the petroleum industry. A large part of the chemical industry drew its raw material from fractions given off in the cracking of crude petroleum. The Second World War forced European nations to substitute synthetics for gasoline and rubber. The United States did not have to resort to high-priced synthetic gasoline, but it had to make synthetic rubber.

For many years, attempts had been made to use farm products for new purposes. It was discovered that wheat and other grains, as well as potatoes and sugar cane, could be converted into industrial alcohol; corn was used in making glycerines, dry ice, paper, and wallboard; flax furnished a straw which was converted into cigarette paper by a process developed almost overnight when the war cut off the supply of linen cloth paper from France, Belgium, and other European countries; cotton was used in the manufacture of automobile tires, and also in road building; skim milk was converted into casein, a valuable plastic material for coating paper and finishing leather as well as for making glue, buttons, artificial leather, and paint; and soybeans, grown in increasing quantities, came to be used not only for feed but for plastics—for automobile steering wheels, table tops, radio cabinets, flooring tiles, buttons, and many other things. Thus, through chemistry, new uses were discovered for utilizing constituents of agricultural products such as cellulose, starch, legnin, proteins, and resins. But the field was in its infancy, for synthetic products were made chiefly from nonagricultural raw materials like coal, petroleum, limestone, sulphur, and salt. However, experimentation began to open new vistas for farm products and led the way in bringing together in closer harmony America's two greatest productive forces—the farm and the factory.

MILITARY TECHNOLOGY

The needs of the Army and Navy had always had an accelerating effect upon United States technological development. Eli Whitney's interchangeable parts, for example, were developed for an Army contract and the Springfield arsenal was one of the most important sources of new machine processes in the early nineteenth century. The need for synthetic dyes, and the seizure of these and other German chemical patents during the First World War, gave a great impetus to the chemical industry, while plans for military planes did much to advance civil aviation after the war. But from 1939 on the effect of military demand became far stronger than ever before. In 1940 an Office of Scientific Research and Development was set up with Vannevar Bush, then of the Carnegie Institution of Washington, at its head to put research scientists to work on military problems. Many of the improvements needed for war were also useful for peacetime purposes. The development of heavy, long-range bombers was reflected in bigger, more profitable passenger planes after the war. Radar, first developed by the British, was useful in commercial transportation for detecting the approach of ships or planes. Many synthetic fabrics designed for special military purposes were useful for peacetime operations. The enormous demand for airplane fuel built refining knowledge and capacity that led to higher octane gasoline for automobiles; DDT, the all purpose insecticide, not only allowed occupation forces to live in the tropics with less danger of malaria or yellow fever, but was a powerful weapon in the endless war against mosquitoes, ants, and roaches at home.

In the long run the most important government contribution to technology in the Second World War was the development of atomic energy. The United States government, knowing that the Germans were well advanced in techniques for splitting the atom, made an investment of two billion dollars in research in this one field. The investment paid returns in a process for atomic fission in 1944, when intelligence agents could still report that the Germans were stalled. Had the reverse development taken place, Germany might well have won the war. The wartime use of atomic energy came in the bombs on Hiroshima and Nagasaki, in August of 1945; the peacetime importance, save for the upsetting effect on international relations, was slow to emerge.

After the war, scientists and others brought pressure to place the use of atomic energy under civilian control. The Atomic Energy Act of 1946 set up an Atomic Energy Commission concerned with the production of atomic weapons together with the development of atomic-powered engines for planes and submarines and the use of radioactive isotopes in medicine. Public concern over the new bomb grew, especially when it became known that Soviet scientists were making similar experiments at top speed and that Communist spies were getting secret information from the United States, Britain, and elsewhere for Moscow. Russia, aided by ex-German scientists, did well in the atomic race with the United States.

When it became known that Russia had exploded the atom bomb, President Truman ordered the development of the hydrogen super-bomb in 1950. Two years later the Atomic Energy Commission announced that the terrible instrument of destruction had been completed. Eyewitnesses told of experimental blasts in the Pacific. In 1953 Premier Malenkov reported to the Supreme Soviet in Moscow that the United States no longer had a monopoly on the hydrogen bomb, but said that Soviet policy called for peaceful settlement of international differences.

Meanwhile, attempts had been made in the United Nations for the international control of atomic energy. The Soviet government opposed the American plan to set up an International Atomic Authority which would control uranium and all raw material involved and would control, license, and inspect all atomic activities, as well as foster the beneficial use of atomic energy. Russia proposed instead the outlawing of the atomic bomb by treaty and the immediate destruction of all existing bombs. It opposed the inspection plan and demanded that the veto privilege be retained on questions of atomic energy. Thus international control was blocked.

In 1954, after a heated fight, Congress passed a bill which opened the door for the development of a private atomic power industry within the United States. It was declared that the law would speed the time when atomic energy would be "wholly devoted to peaceful purposes." The measure permitted the Atomic Energy Commission (AEC) to grant forty-year renewable licenses for private industry to operate atomic facilities and handle fissionable materials. With the approval of Congress, the AEC could build electric power plants for experimental purposes. Cooperatives and public-owned utilities were to receive preference in buying such power. The law authorized the President to give friendly nations secret details regarding atomic weapons. Subject to review by Congress the President could also negotiate to carry out his plan for a global A-pool to help backward nations and to grant friendly powers information on producing civilian atomic power.

Private development, however, was slow. Well aware of the numerous unforeseen problems that would have to be solved, corporations hesitated to invest in atomic power plants unless aided by government subsidy, just as capitalists had refused in the 1860's to invest in a transcontinental railroad. By 1957 two power plants, subsidized from funds at the disposal of the Atomic Energy Commission, had been completed. Because of the massive capital investment required, much larger than a conventional steam plant, atomic-generated electricity was still expensive. By 1963, eleven private plants had been completed and fourteen more were projected. AEC estimated that the atom would account for 5 per cent of new power installations in the decade of the Sixties. Atomic costs were competitive with those of coal or gas on the East and West Coasts, where the fossil fuels were high-priced.

Except for submarines, atomic energy was not being used to power transportation in 1960, but atomic surface ships were being constructed.

The radioactive waste from atomic fission and the scarcity of fissionable material were major drawbacks to the commercial use of atomic energy. Once power could be generated from fusion, which could use elements abundant in air and water, and diminish radioactive waste, the true age of atomic power would begin. Estimates in 1963 placed this date five to ten years in the future.

Meanwhile, the development of rockets for military purposes had turned scientists and technicians to a new set of problems. In October and November of 1957 the Russians put two satellites known as Sputniks I and II into orbit. On January 31, 1958 the United States successfully launched Explorer I. But whereas Sputnik II weighed 1,120 pounds, Explorer I weighed only 18. Spurred by this demonstration that the Russians had fuels that gave rocket engines greater thrust, experiments with both solid and liquid fuels went on continuously both by government agencies such as the National Bureau of Standards and by private contractors. While Russian fuels were still more powerful in 1961 a safe liquefied hydrogen that could be used for many purposes had been developed in the United States. Since rockets could provide propulsion without atmosphere, outer space was now open for travel. The known limiting factor was the amount of "payload" a rocket engine could propel for a given time. Unknown factors were various rays, particles, and magnetic fields that might be deadly to human beings.

In 1961 and 1962 the Soviet Union and the United States, respectively, made modest beginnings in the exploration of outer space. Yuri Gagarin, a Russian major, made one orbit of the earth in an externally-controlled ship on April 12, 1961 in 108 minutes. In August another Russian major, Gherman S. Titov, completed eighteen consecutive orbits around the earth. Less than a year later John Glenn, an American colonel, piloted a space craft three times around the earth and landed in a designated area of the ocean. By 1963, both Americans and Russians had completed voyages of over 20 orbits.

Rocket manufacture introduced a new emphasis in big business processes and management. From the beginning large-scale United States industry had aimed at mass production of standard products of medium quality. Rockets were few in number but demanded absolute precision and perfect parts. A director of a large firm working on missiles and satellites said it "is like building a television set that will operate four hours a day for 500 years without an adjustment." In the early 1960's management was still trying to reorient plant practices to this ideal of precision. Although jet airplanes used the same principle of propulsion, by 1963 the only immediate economic use of rocket engines appeared to be sending up small orbiting satellites from which radio, television, and telephone waves could be reflected to spots beyond the reach of direct projection.

The idea of space travel was so exciting that it tended to obscure other lines of government-aided scientific progress of greater potential economic importance, such as the "farming" of the ocean, including removal of its salt content. Ocean water was full of nutrition and could theoretically solve the food problems of the world for many years. But of still greater importance was the problem of supplying additional fresh water to heavily populated, rapidly growing industrial areas such as those on the west coast. Continuous research was carried on to develop processes for lowering the salt content of sea water, and by 1960 systems had been developed that could convert sea to fresh water at high, but not economically prohibitive prices. For massive uses such as in steel manufacture, however, cheaper supplies would be necessary.

THE RISE OF RESEARCH

Spectacular achievements such as radar and the atom bomb from large-scale directed effort gave new prestige to scientific research for both military and commercial purposes. Industrial research in a crude and lowly form may be traced back to an early period of American history, but not until the twenties did it attain an important position. In the nineteenth and early twentieth centuries, industrial research was stimulated by observing such progress in Germany and other countries. In 1910, Robert Kennedy Duncan began his industrial fellowship system, which lead to the establishment of the Mellon Institute of Industrial Research at Pittsburgh in 1913. Chemical, physical, and engineering societies grew more interested and expanded their research activities. World War I gave an impetus to research as the need for quick and cheap manufacture of new and substitute products emphasized the necessity for scientific methods. In 1916, the National Research Council was organized by the National Academy of Sciences at the request of President Wilson for aid during the war and afterwards for the encouragement of research in the natural sciences, especially through cooperation. Its members, representing scientific societies and research institutions, were divided into a number of groups including the physical sciences, engineering, industrial research, and chemistry. Manufacturing companies in some fields, also realizing the importance of research, established laboratories. Through all these means in addition to the work carried on by educational institutions, government bureaus, and consulting laboratories, expenditures for research gradually increased. In 1938, about $180,000,000 was spent by American companies for industrial research, but three-quarters of it was by companies in the electrical, chemical, rubber, petroleum, and power machinery industries. Other industries such as steel, nonferrous metals, textiles, paper, and food supported well below a quarter of the trained specialists in industrial research.

The same pattern persisted after the Second World War, with the aircraft and scientific instruments groups added to the five earlier industries with heavy spending. The research of these newcomers and also of the electrical industry was largely supported by government funds, whereas government played a much smaller role in chemicals, rubber, petroleum, and power machinery.

Increase in expenditure for all forms of research showed a rather steadily mounting curve from one-tenth of one per cent of the gross national product in 1920 to one per cent in the year 1955. Then the curve began to mount rapidly as research salaries rose and new government funds were poured into the missile program. In 1950, for example, Congress had set up the National Science Foundation, but only in 1959, after Russia had launched its first satellite, was the Foundation given a significant budget. By 1960 expenditures were over three times the 1955 figure and still rising rapidly. While university and corporate laboratories carried on most of this research, the new work was largely directed to military rather than commercial or social progress. The total of between two and one-half and three per cent of gross national product, however, was still considerably less than the total national expenditure for advertising.

Both government and corporate-sponsored research was generally directed toward perfecting some theoretically known process, or what is called "developmental" research. Relatively little money from these sources was used to support "pure" research, or experimental inquiry into the unknown for purposes of testing imaginatively conceived propositions. In fact, the very pressure for scientific manpower for immediate purposes tended to reduce the number of highly trained scientists left free to pursue their own speculations.

Yet in the long run, the really new trends in human progress had come from such individual theorizing. Falling within this area of new scientific knowledge in the period after the First World War were discoveries regarding cellular growth and reproduction. Biochemists demonstrated that nucleic acids control cell growth, much as punched tape controls the activity of a digital computer. Scientists appeared to be on the edge of controlling certain characteristics in plant, animal, and human reproduction that would permit the development of desired characteristics to degrees far beyond those achieved by selective breeding.

Lest too gloomy a view be taken of the effect of immediate military and commercial demands upon the future of pure science in the United States, it should be emphasized that much developmental work involves the testing of a new theory, and that the vastly greater number of trained scholars engaged in all aspects of science, compared with the very small number of men actively pursuing pioneer research in the United States before 1940, holds great promise for the advance of theory. At least, it seemed likely in the early 1960's that pure science was being advanced as rapidly in the United States as anywhere else in the world, which had not been the case in earlier decades.

NATURAL RESOURCES

The great economic growth of the United States in the nineteenth century had been based on readily available natural resources. As noted in Chapter 15, cheap coal, iron, and oil were basic to industrial supremacy, and in addition the United States had high-grade copper, tin, lead, zinc, silver, and gold. By 1900 the ores for this last group of metals were no longer high-grade, and by 1920 there were not many known deposits worth processing. Oil reserves were also thought to be running low. The demands of the Second World War showed the limits of known iron ore deposits, leaving only coal as a mineral still available in proved abundance.

Manufacturers using large quantities of any of these dwindling raw materials now had to think in terms of possible sources of supply outside the United States, or plan for substitutes. While substitutes, such as plastic in place of sheet steel, were slow to develop and usually not as satisfactory as the metal, new sources of mineral supply were opened up in Canada and Latin America. Copper from Chile and tin from Bolivia had been imported before the First World War. Oil wells had been brought in in Venezuela by 1920, and iron ore was subsequently discovered in that country along the Orinoco River. Canadian resources, still only partly explored by mid-century, had great promise. Iron ore was discovered in new areas such as Labrador. Eastern Canadian ores could be brought to the major steel centers of

Oil drilling barge in the Gulf of Mexico

the United States around Chicago, Pittsburgh, Philadelphia, and Baltimore by either the ocean or the St. Lawrence Seaway.

Meanwhile, mid-twentieth century shifts in demand for materials
and fuels and new means of extraction had taught businessmen the
difficulty of predicting where shortages would occur. The United States
was moderately well supplied with materials for atomic fission, but
who could know what materials might prove best for atomic fusion ten
years hence. Offshore drilling for oil and sulphur was bringing in large
new reserves. New methods of mining, refining, and smelting made
low-grade iron ore commercially usable. With the use of atomic energy,
plastics, and lighter metals in the foreseeable future, there appeared
to be less excitement about exhaustion of resources in the 1960's than
there had been in the first three decades of the century. Looked at
another way, business leaders and scientists had been taught to have
greater faith in the flexibility of technology than their predecessors of
earlier decades.

THE UPSWING IN POPULATION

The rapid increase in United States population after 1940 threatened new pressure on national resources. In the early thirties popula-

tion had appeared to be approaching stability in all the industrial nations of the world. The general change to a higher rate of increase came with the Second World War, although during the Hitler regime there was a sharp upswing in German population. When the war was over the United States did not return to its old pattern of a diminishing rate of increase. Whereas from 1926 to 1930 population had risen less than 5 per cent, from 1946 to 1950 it rose over 7 per cent, and increased 18.5 per cent in the decade of the 1950's. The causes of changes in rates of population growth can only be inferred, but undoubtedly a more generally diffused prosperity and less fear of unemployment were important.

The upswing in birth rate meant that a larger part of the population were below working age and in need of education and family care. Combined with the fact that retired people were also living longer, this meant that, other things being equal, productive workers had to support more nonworkers. But the United States was able to draw on the reservoir of women, partly freed from housework by frozen foods, washing machines, and other advances in the technology of the home. In 1920 women had made up 20 per cent of the labor force, by 1947 the percentage was 27, and ten years later it was 31. With at least 90 per cent of families living in urban areas or within

ESTIMATED POPULATION OF THE UNITED STATES, 1940 – 1960
(In thousands)

Year	Total Population Including Armed Forces Overseas	Year	Total Population Including Armed Forces Overseas	Year	Total Population Including Armed Forces Overseas
1940	132,122	1947	144,126	1954	162,417
1941	133,402	1948	146,631	1955	165,270
1942	134,860	1949	149,188	1956	168,174
1943	136,739	1950	151,683	1957	171,229
1944	138,397	1951	154,360	1958	174,054
1945	139,928	1952	157,028	1959	177,103
1946	141,389	1953	159,636	1960	179,323

Sources: U.S. Bureau of the Census, *Historical Statistics of the United States, Colonial Times to 1957*, Washington, D.C., 1960, p. 7; and *The World Almanac, 1962*, p. 252.

BIRTHS, 1940 – 1960
(In thousands)

Year	Live Births	Year	Live Births	Year	Live Births
1940	2,559	1947	3,817	1954	4,078
1941	2,703	1948	3,637	1955	4,104
1942	2,989	1949	3,649	1956	4,218
1943	3,104	1950	3,632	1957	4,255
1944	2,939	1951	3,823	1958	4,204
1945	2,858	1952	3,913	1959	4,245
1946	3,411	1953	3,965	1960	4,247

Sources: U.S. Bureau of the Census, *Historical Statistics of the United States, Colonial Times to 1957*, Washington, D.C., 1960, p. 22; and *The World Almanac, 1962*, pp. 301–302.

reach of industrial jobs, there seemed no immediate limit on the increasing employment of women. The limit to an increasing standard of living that might be imposed by shortage of accessible resources still seemed remote in 1963. Therefore, increasing population with its promise of ever-larger markets gave an optimistic tone to the economy, and helped to prevent a return to the stagnation of the thirties.

Movement of workers and retired people from place to place remained at high levels. People seeking better opportunities continued to go from country to cities or metropolitan areas. Because of migration to eastern and western industrial areas from the central farming states, migration east and west across the Mississippi River became about equal in each direction by 1940. Other continuing major shifts that had been going on since 1900 were from South to North and from sections other than the central farming states to the west coast, particularly California. But these longer treks had never been the chief types. Movements between neighboring cities, counties, and states continued to make up the major volume of migration. A city whose total population changed only slightly from 1940 to 1960 would probably have 30 to 40 per cent of the total population moving in each decade and similar numbers moving out. With these levels of mobility continuing, long residence in any locality was probably the exception rather than the rule.

CHAPTER 26

Emergence of the Welfare State

While increased action by the government accompanied the rise of mass production all over the world, the Federal government of the United States had resisted the trend more successfully than any other nation. Hence, except for wars and their aftermath, government activity has not been the subject of separate chapters. But in 1930 the years of reckoning began, and the Federal government was literally forced to become one of the most important economic forces in American development. Three chapters are necessary to describe the relation of the Federal government to the great depression, World War II and the new postwar economy.

In the initial contraction of the 1930's the economy, unsupported by unemployment insurance, general pensions, high severance pay, or other stabilizing devices, with a banking system geared to the needs of the nineteenth century, and with traditional restrictions on government spending or investment, failed to develop forces that would check the downward force of the great depression. Reluctantly American political leaders, both Democratic and Republican, had to try to use the economic power of the national state to promote the general welfare in ways disapproved of by the preceding administrations.

562

HOOVER AND THE DEPRESSION

The crash of stocks in 1929 (see p. 640) stripped American speculators and investors of about $25 billion, not including their foreign losses. Many individuals lost their life savings. Following the stock market panic, the long depression began. Factories closed down, an increasing number of banks failed, prices of commodities sank, foreign trade languished, railroad loadings declined and railways became insolvent, unemployment increased, and bread lines lengthened. Paralysis struck the nation's buying power. Farmers and factory workers, creditors and debtors, capitalists and brokers all suffered. Every part of America's great economic machine was severely affected as it slowed down to a halt.

The attitude of most leaders, including President Hoover, was that the depression was temporary and would pass away in a few months or at most in a year or two. They felt that fundamental business conditions were sound and on a prosperous basis. Late in 1929, the President held a conference in the White House with leaders of industry and business. He announced plans for the formation of an organization representing industry, trade, and commerce to carry out a policy of stabilization to prevent future financial crashes and business disturbances. "Collective self-help" on a voluntary basis was a part of the President's program. He urged industrialists and business to carry on in spite of lack of markets because he believed that recovery "was just around the corner." What was needed, he asserted, was confidence and a continuance of business, but conditions got worse instead of better.

More than two painful years passed before the realities of the situation were accepted. In 1930–1932, bank failures numbered 5,102, a new record. In 1930, more than 4,000,000 workers were unemployed; in 1932, over 12,000,000 were out of work. About one-fifth of the railroad mileage of the country was in receivership. Falling prices showed overproduction, yet one-half the nation found it difficult to get even the necessities of life. The problem of distribution appeared to be unsolvable. Morale was at its lowest when homes, farms, jobs, businesses, and bank deposits were lost.

As the depression came on, the revenues of the government began to decline and its expenditures to increase. In addition to relief measures and other requirements of the depression, Congress had to face large deficits in revenue. It rejected President Hoover's proposal to save money by reducing the salaries of government officials and it opposed a general sales tax. Instead Congress sought to solve this problem by increasing income tax rates, by raising postage rates, and by taxing amusements, bank checks, gifts, stock sales, automobiles, gasoline, oil, tires, matches, refrigerators, and many other things. But the problem of balancing the budget was not solved at that time nor in the period that followed.

The Hawley-Smoot tariff of 1930 was passed largely as the result of the depression in agriculture. In his message to the special session of Congress the year before, President Hoover stated:

An effective tariff upon agricultural products . . . has a dual purpose. Such a tariff not only protects the farmer in our domestic market, but it also stimulates him to diversify his crops and to grow products that he could not otherwise produce, and thus lessen his dependence upon foreign markets.

After months of debate during which strenuous attempts were made to add further protection to certain manufactures, and after much logrolling, Congress passed the measure. President Hoover found flaws in the bill, but signed it because he believed the defects could be corrected through the President's power to revise rates. He gave it his approval in spite of the fact that more than 1,000 economists urged him to veto it on the grounds that it would raise prices, interfere with the payment of the war debts, reduce exports, and force foreign nations to retaliate in a like manner. The new law provided for increases not only in the agricultural schedules but in many others, such as textiles and clothing. It was a much higher measure than that of 1922. The Tariff Commission was increased to six members and through its work the President hoped to reduce excessive rates and to take the tariff out of politics. But almost immediately after its passage, foreign governments passed retaliatory measures. Within two years, more than twenty had done so and others were threatening similar action in order to force the United States to abandon its prohibitory rates.

As times grew worse, relief appropriations were made by Congress. A program for the construction of roads, public buildings, and airways that seemed large by older standards was begun late in 1930. Many measures were signed by the President for emergency constructon and farm loans. Sums were also appropriated for drought relief, for a heat wave and drought in 1930 had ruined the corn, hay, and other crops and had killed livestock on thousands of farms, especially in the Middle West. Loans were made to states, cities, and other governmental agencies for constructive projects and direct relief. In order to aid and protect sound banks a National Credit Association was established by the government with resources of $500,000,000. The first Glass-Steagall Act of 1932 also permitted member banks of the Federal Reserve System to borrow on collateral not normally eligible for rediscount in order to provide increased credit for businessmen. It also permitted Federal Reserve banks to use United States government obligations as security for Federal Reserve notes. In the same year a system of Home Loan banks was also established to discount home mortgages held by banks, building and loan associations, and insurance companies. The plan was enlarged in 1933.

The most important step was the creation of the Reconstruction Finance Corporation by act of Congress early in 1932. The chief aim of the corporation was to encourage and aid financial institutions to lend money in order to revive business and industry. The decline of prices of commodities, securities, and real estate left banks and credit institutions with loans on their books which could not be paid immediately but which would be good in time. Thus the corporation was established to aid solvent banks that lacked liquid assets which could be readily turned into cash without loss. It was authorized to lend to banks of all kinds, building and loan associations, mortgage companies, insurance companies, agricultural credit corporations, states, and public agencies. It could also aid in temporarily financing railroads which could not secure funds on reasonable terms in other channels, providing the Interstate Commerce Commission approved. This was the first time in history that the Federal government had come directly to the aid of general business. It marked desertion of the idea of the self-regulating economy, and the beginning of the concept of the "welfare state."

The Reconstruction Finance Corporation, under a board of seven directors including the Secretary of the Treasury, and capitalized at $500,000,000, was authorized to sell a maximum of $1.5 billion worth of five-year bonds or notes to the public or to the United States Treasury. The loans that were made aided many banking institutions and industrial concerns to weather the storm. In spite of all that the corporation did to patch the economic structure, it met with little success. Bank failures declined during the months after it was established, but by the end of 1932, the banking situation had become exceedingly grave. In the meantime, the corporation was assailed by many groups. Some congressmen protested against loans to railroads which paid excessive salaries to their officials; certain other policies of RFC were attacked; and public confidence was undermined when it became known that, before retiring as its president in 1932, Charles G. Dawes arranged for a large loan to his own bank in Chicago. Thereafter loans were not made in secret. Before the end of its first year, the Reconstruction Finance Corporation loaned more than $1.5 billion to 6,000 borrowers in all parts of the country and in some of the dependencies and outlying possessions.

Meanwhile the international financial structure built around war debts and reparations had fallen apart. In the German parliamentary elections of 1930, the unpopularity of the Young plan was revealed by the spectacular gains made by the National Socialists and Communists. Foreign creditors, particularly the French, became alarmed at the increasing power of the two groups of extremists and began to withdraw their funds from Central European banks. Collapse threatened Germany as foreign trade dwindled, manufactures decreased, unemployment increased, and business failures became more numerous. Emergency decrees in that country provided for reduced taxes and rigid governmental economies, but all efforts failed to prevent disaster. Early in 1931, Germany and Austria attempted to form a customs union or *Anschluss* to arrest the paralysis that was stifling their economic life. France and other European countries objected and withdrawals from Austrian banks increased. Soon the Credit-Anstalt Bank was in difficulties, and to prevent its collapse, the Austrian government guaranteed the bank's deposits. The Bank of International Settlements extended credit to the amount of $14,000,000 to the Austrian National Bank. In July, 1931, the Danat Bank of Berlin closed its doors and other German banks followed. The withdrawal of foreign credits had a disastrous effect on London, the world's financial center, and England abandoned the gold standard in September, 1931. Other countries suspended specie payments.

The financial collapse of Germany and Austria gravely affected the United States. It injured many American firms and New York banks doing business with those countries; it induced a further decline in the bond market; it caused foreign investors to withdraw their funds from the United States; it shook public confidence as bank failures again increased; and it forced panicky citizens to withdraw their deposits and hoard gold in safe deposit boxes.

In the meantime, on June 20, 1931, President Hoover, following the receipt of an urgent letter from President von Hindenburg of Germany, proposed the "postponement during one year of all payments on intergovernmental debts, reparations, and relief debts, both principal and interest, of course not including obligations of government held by private parties." He hoped that such action would promote a world-wide restoration of confidence and economic stability. Other nations agreed. Congress approved, but refused to accept a suggestion by the President that the World War Foreign Debt Commission be revived to examine the whole question again. Financiers and economists predicted that resumption of payments after the moratorium would encounter insurmountable objections in debtor countries. This prophecy came true as an epidemic of defaults occurred. In December, 1932, only six nations made payments. Then followed "token payments" and finally only Finland met her small annual debt.

In 1932, Germany's creditors reached an agreement at Lausanne, suddenly reducing her indebtedness from billions to millions and fixing it as $714,000,000. This change caused much excitement in the United States where the government was charged with having made a secret agreement with Germany's creditors that the war debts were to be cancelled. The rumor, however, was officially denied by the Secretary of State. On the same day, Prime Minister Ramsay MacDonald in England made a similar denial in the House of Commons.

Various opinions were expressed in the United States about the war debts. Some suggested further postponement until stable conditions returned; others insisted on further reductions; many saw wisdom in cancellation since Allied nations had little gold and since payment in commodities would have interfered with American production. On the one extreme were those agreeing with Calvin Coolidge, who when asked his views on the subject replied: "They hired [borrowed] it, didn't they?" Extremists on the other side favored the view held by Andrew Mellon when he was Secretary of the Treasury that cancellation would be the best course for American economic interests in order to keep the European nations prosperous customers of the United States. The Second World War put an end to the question, at least for the time being.

THE DEPTH OF THE DEPRESSION

The lowest point of the depression was reached late in 1932 and early in 1933. Economic conditions had grown steadily worse in the three years of deflation following 1929. Unemployment had reached a peak conservatively estimated at 13,000,000, although some placed it at 15,000,000. Home building had ceased. Families had doubled up or moved to rural sections. Young people without purpose traveled aimlessly over the country. Several hundred cities faced imminent bankruptcy as their revenues fell. Prices were at their lowest level. More than ever before the paradox of huge surpluses of food and clothing at a time when millions suffered for lack of these essentials became more and more evident. Many groups were demanding increased government action. Thousands of farmers especially in the Middle West, whose farms were being foreclosed, together with large numbers of insolvent businessmen, sought help. Veterans of the World War demanded immediate payment in full of the insurance policy bonus voted them in 1924. Congress had passed over Hoover's veto in 1931 a bill permitting the veterans to borrow up to 50 per cent of the value of the bonus, but this proved insufficient. The next year, after a measure granting them immediate cash failed in Congress, the "Bonus Expeditionary Force" of 20,000 veterans marched on Washington and was expelled by bayonets and tear gas. In the midst of general despondency and suffering, the banking structure of the country threatened to collapse.

Meantime the presidential election took place. Of those who went to the polls almost 23,000,000 cast their vote for a New Deal, although nearly 16,000,000, apparently less affected, voted for Hoover. However, the Democratic party was generally successful everywhere. The House of Representatives, which had a majority of Democrats in the second half of Hoover's administration, was now Democratic by almost three to one. Only eight Republican governors were elected in the states. It was a political revolution. Democratic leadership was given a mandate to solve the economic problems that involved everyone and to free the country from the worst depression that the world had ever experienced.

In the grim winter of 1932–1933, with a lame duck administration in power, the depression reached its lowest depth. Impatient with dilatory political action, various groups offered solutions for economic problems that would not only relieve the current misery, but in time would usher in a utopian society. One of the more prominent of these solutions was the technocracy movement that originated in 1931–1932. Its ideas were not new. In 1923, Thorstein Veblen in *The Engineers and the Price System* stressed the growing breach between the increasing capacity of mechanized industry and the problems of actual production and distribution under the profit system. In this work and in earlier ones Veblen insisted that a distinction be made between industry and business—the former making goods, the latter enabling stock promoters, financiers, and absentee owners to prey on the population. Veblen's solution placed the control of production and distribution solely in the hand of technicians.

During the depression, a group led by Howard Scott, calling

themselves technocrats, called for abolition of the price system and substitution of payments based on energy. No definite program was suggested by them for the problem of distribution, but the public was kept interested and curious by the mystery that the group sought to throw around its "findings." It became evident that there were no new practical proposals in the ideas of technocracy and the movement finally subsided. Other "share the wealth" movements rose and fell. Among these were the Townsend Plan, Senator Huey Long's Share-our-Wealth clubs, Father Coughlin's National Union for Social Justice, William Lemke's Union party, and Upton Sinclair's EPIC (End Poverty in California). None of the radical proposals of these organizations was enacted into law, although many of them were backed by large groups in various parts of the country, but they showed that the masses were seeking remedies in a situation that seemed hopeless.

Before the inauguration of President Franklin D. Roosevelt the banking situation grew even worse. After the election, bank runs increased, failures grew larger, and financial conditions deteriorated. Even the oldest and most conservative banks were no longer immune. Republicans ascribed the condition to the refusal of the partly Democratic Congress to adopt Hoover's proposals for banking reform. In January, 1933, it was revealed that total bank resources had fallen from $74 billion in 1930 to $57 billion in June, 1932, while in 1931–1932, deposits had decreased by $12 billion. Exposures of corruption, dishonest practices, and unscrupulousness by some bankers and financiers as well as by some public utilities companies, brought to light by congressional committees, also served to undermine public confidence still further. Most shattering were the disclosures which followed the collapse of the huge pyramid of utility corporations built up by Samuel Insull. As a result of conditions the public increased the withdrawal of deposits to such an extent that governors in many states were forced to declare bank "holidays" that prevented depositors from withdrawing their money. By March 4, 1933, most of the banks had closed. Never in the history of the country had a President been inaugurated under more difficult and serious economic conditions.

As outlined in his political campaign, President Roosevelt's program revolved around the three R's—Relief, Recovery, and Reform. He had promised the country a New Deal and had explained what he meant by the slogan. It included among other things the need for economic planning, for agricultural improvement, for greater regulation of public utility and holding companies, for changes in the tariff, for the curb of speculation, and for just social relations. The proposals made during the days of the campaign were less drastic than the plans that were actually carried out in the years that followed. This was because of the needs that grew out of the emergency and because of President Roosevelt's developing views, influenced by a succession of advisers. In his inaugural message, the new President stated:

. . . The only thing we have to fear is fear itself. . . . Values have shrunken to fantastic levels; taxes have risen; our ability to pay has fallen; government of all kinds is faced by serious curtailment of income; the means of exchange are frozen in the currents of trade; the withered leaves of industrial enterprise lie on every side; farmers find no markets for their produce; the savings of many years in thousands of families are gone. More important, a host of unemployed citizens face the grim problem of existence. . . . We must act and act quickly.

The President began work immediately. He used liberally his executive authority and asked Congress for further "broad executive power to wage a war against the emergency as great as the power that would be given me if we were in fact invaded by a foreign foe." He received limited emergency powers, which added much to the prestige and strength of the executive branch of government, but the authority granted him was not equivalent to that of wartime. In his work of devising recovery measures and projecting a more planned economy, he was aided by the "brain trust," a group of men of liberal views, with experience especially along professional and business lines. He called Congress in special session, which, from March 9 until it adjourned on June 16, adopted legislation unprecedented in American history, not only from the point of view of its bulk but also its content. These laws formed the basis of the New Deal.

BANKING AND FINANCIAL LEGISLATION

Immediately on taking office, President Roosevelt ordered all banks closed temporarily and placed an embargo on the exportation of gold. The breathing space gave time to formulate a program. Congress provided for the reopening of banks that were able to resume operations. The Emergency Banking Act of March 9, 1933 permitted banks belonging to the Federal Reserve System to reopen if their condition was found to be satisfactory and a license was obtained from the Treasury Department. Banks discovered to be insolvent were placed under conservators for restricted operation or liquidation. Additional Federal Reserve bank notes were to be issued to member banks, and Federal Reserve banks could make private loans on the security of government bonds. The Reconstruction Finance Corporation was authorized to subscribe to the capital stock of banks and trust companies. The law also authorized the Treasury to call in all gold and gold certificates. Under the terms of the Emergency Banking Act, banks were reopened beginning on March 13. By March 15, banks controlling 90 per cent of the banking resources of the country were again in operation and the seriousness of the banking crisis was over, although some banks never reopened and many were restricted in their operations.

A permanent banking law followed. The second Glass-Steagall Act of June, 1933, made provision for a stricter supervision of member banks of the Federal Reserve System; it curbed credit in stock market speculation; it divorced the banks from their security-selling affiliations; it approved branch banking in those states where it was permitted; and it authorized the creation of a Federal Deposit Insurance Corporation (FDIC), for insuring bank deposits from July 1, 1934. In the meantime a Temporary Deposit Insurance Fund was established. Under the Banking Act of 1935, the deposit insurance provisions were amended to insure the deposits of all banks entitled to benefits to a maximum of $5,000 for each depositor in each bank. The FDIC was authorized to purchase, hold, and liquidate the assets of national and state banks that had been closed. The act also reorganized drastically the Federal Reserve Board and changed its name to the Board of Governors of the Federal Reserve System. Changes were also made in the management of the Federal Reserve banks. Power over discount and open-market operations of the banks was increased and centralized in the Board of Governors.

Closely associated with banking legislation were the plans to establish control over the stock exchanges of the country through the regulation of the sale of stocks and other securities. In 1933, Congress passed the Federal Securities Act (FSA) and in 1934 supplemented it with the Securities Exchange Act (SEA). The administration of the first law was entrusted to the Federal Trade Commission. The act of 1934 set up a new organization known as the Securities and Exchange Commission to administer both laws. The Commission was authorized to supervise the activities of all stock exchanges. It was charged with the duty of protecting the public against deceit, trickery, and fraud in the purchase and sale of securities. It was required to see that all proposed issues of stocks and bonds were registered and to insist that true information be furnished investors. In 1938, the authority of the Commission was extended to over-the-counter stock sales. As a result of the work of the Commission, dishonest speculation was curbed to a great extent.

While order was being brought out of the chaos in banking, problems connected with the gold standard were being attacked. The chief objective in the changes that took place was to bring about a controlled inflation in order to force prices upward. The President's several proclamations together with the recall by the Treasury of all gold and gold certificates and the joint resolution of Congress on June 5, 1933, which abrogated the payment of all debts in gold, whether public or private, virtually suspended the gold standard.[1] Until the end of January, 1934, when the Gold Reserve Act was passed, the country was on a paper money basis as the coinage and circulation of gold were discontinued. The Agricultural Adjustment Act of May, 1933, authorized the President to make radical changes in the currency system, including the devaluation of the dollar in terms of gold in order to increase prices. In the fall of 1933, the Warren Gold Purchase plan was put into operation. The Reconstruction Finance Corporation was authorized to buy gold newly-mined in the United States and also, if necessary, in world markets at prices to be determined after consultation with the President and the Secretary of the Treasury. The initial price was fixed at $31.36 an ounce, but it reached $35 an ounce when the plan was ended on January 31, 1934. The theory of the project was to bring an increase in the domestic commodity price level by raising the price of gold. But it failed to achieve this, for after an initial rise in the summer of 1933, brought on by fear of inflation, the price index of commodities remained at 71 (1926 = 100) during October, November, and December, 1933, and rose only one point in January, 1934.

The Gold Reserve Act of January, 1934, passed at the request of the President, nationalized all gold by ordering the Federal Reserve banks to turn over their supply to the United States Treasury. In return they received gold certificates to be used as reserves against deposits and Federal Reserve notes. It also authorized the President to devalue the gold dollar so that it would not possess more than 60 per cent of its existing weight. Roosevelt immediately fixed the value of the gold dollar at 59.06 cents. From the government's profit from the gold impounded, which amounted to $3.5 billion, a stabilization

---

[1] Even the ownership of gold coins, gold certificates, and gold bullion became a criminal offense. In the Gold Clause cases (1935), the Supreme Court upheld in general the action of Congress, although in the case involving the payment of Liberty bonds, it declared the action of the government unconstitutional, but refused the plaintiff damages on the ground that he had not shown any loss of buying power in receiving paper money rather than gold.

fund of $2 billion was created to buy and sell gold, foreign exchange, and government securities in order to protect and regulate the credit and currency of the country by offsetting trade balances, speculation, and foreign influences.

In 1929, silver fell to unheard of levels. Demands for action from the silver bloc in Congress resulted in a flood of proposals to benefit the silver interests. President Roosevelt by proclamation ordered the Treasury to purchase 24,412,410 ounces of silver annually at 64.5 cents an ounce, although the market value was but forty-five cents. In 1934, when general price levels failed to rise as was expected, there were increasing demands for further inflation. In June, 1934, the Silver Purchase Act authorized the President to buy silver until the world price rose to $1.29 an ounce, to increase the monetary value of silver in the Treasury to one-third of the value of gold stocks, and to national-ize silver and regulate movements in trade. The government embarked on a program for the purchase of silver similar to its program for the purchase of gold. The price of silver jumped immediately to eighty-one cents an ounce, which by drawing their specie to the United States weakened the currency systems of Mexico and China. Under the law, the government bought about $1 billion worth of silver from foreign countries at high prices. Most of it was deposited in government vaults, especially at West Point, just as most of the gold that was purchased was stored at Fort Knox, Kentucky. The tremendous in-crease of gold prevented the proportion of silver from reaching the one-third ratio with gold. The unprecedented purchases of gold and silver stimulated American trade in the few remaining world markets, but concentrated $16 billion of gold—over half the world's total supply—and a large proportion of the silver supply in the United States.

RELIEF AND AID TO WORKERS

The great and continuing problem of the thirties was unemploy-ment, with the resulting suffering of workers and their families. An Act of May, 1933, established the Federal Emergency Relief Adminis-tration (FERA). Prior to this, Congress had authorized the Recon-struction Finance Corporation to loan $300,000,000 to aid the states and their subdivisions for relief. Now the FERA took up the work. Under the direction of Harry L. Hopkins, the new agency attempted to alleviate the condition of the millions of unemployed. It functioned through the states, indirectly dictating their policies. Relief offices were set up all over the country and the Federal and state governments worked together to supply food and clothing to the needy and destitute. The attempt was made to avoid the dole for individuals capable of working as labor projects were established. The FERA eventually granted about $3 billion to the states and territories as direct benefits or wages on work projects on public property. It also undertook a separate work program under the Civil Works Administration (CWA). After the FERA was disbanded in 1935, its functions were taken over in part by the Works Progress Administration (WPA), the National Youth Administration (NYA), and the Resettlement Administration (RA).

The Civil Works Administration was created by executive order in the desperate winter of 1933–1934. It planned to provide temporary work for about 4,000,000 persons at regular wages until they could be absorbed by private industry or the more permanent Public Works Administration. Its program included local improvements that would require a maximum of labor with a minimum of materials. It provided such work as laying sidewalks, patching streets, repairing and painting public buildings, improving parks and playgrounds, landscaping highways, erosion control, and pest control. These projects were supervised by public administrators and payrolls were dispersed directly by the Federal government. About $900,000,000 was spent on the undertakings which were ended in the spring of 1934.

Under the provisions of the National Industrial Recovery Act, the Federal Emergency Administration of Public Works (PWA) was established. Secretary of the Interior Harold L. Ickes was appointed as its head to administer a fund of $3.3 billion for a program of constructing public highways, buildings, and parkways, of conservation projects, and of general low-cost housing. Expenditures were made directly by the PWA or other Federal agencies through grants to states and municipalities. The plan was intended to stimulate the private employment of idle machinery and non-relief labor in heavy construction work. Those who looked upon it as a pump-priming measure believed that it would create the necessary spur to business and industry. Others felt that it would reduce the severe fluctuations of the business cycle by increasing public employment in periods when private employment was decreasing. Some hailed it as the beginning of a movement in the direction of a planned economy. Of course, its immediate object was to grant aid and relief through a program of public works, but Secretary Ickes was so conscientious in scrutinizing projects that the rate of spending was slow. In 1937, its slum-clearance and low-rent housing projects were transferred to the United States Housing Authority (USHA) and after July, 1939, emphasis was placed on self-liquidating projects together with loans to private enterprise.

The Works Progress Administration (WPA) was created by executive order under the authority of the Emergency Relief Appropriation Act (ERAA) of 1935 to prevent idle artists, craftsmen, and professionals from losing their skills. In that year and in 1936 appropriations of more than $6 billion were made to finance more than 100,000 projects in different parts of the country. These included the construction of schoolhouses and other public buildings, the laying of streets and roads, and many other useful public works. The Administration carried out many enterprises in the field of adult education and it established a number of white-collar projects. The art projects in painting, sculpture, drama, music, and writing furnished employment to many. Difficulties were encountered in carrying out the WPA work. It was handicapped by the difficulty of finding projects that would not compete with private industry, and problems arose because

NUMBER OF PERSONS EMPLOYED ON WPA PROJECTS, 1935 – 1942

(In thousands)

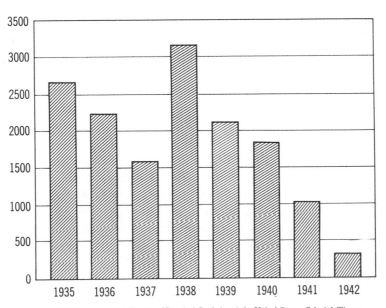

Source: U.S. Bureau of the Census, *Historical Statistics of the United States, Colonial Times to 1957*, Washington, D.C., 1960, p. 200.

the majority of the workers most in need of help were unskilled. Moreover, since the program was primarily one of relief, morale and discipline were often low. In 1939, the name was changed to Work Projects Administration and it became a part of the new Federal Works Agency. In 1942, President Roosevelt ordered the liquidation of the WPA, declaring that employment in war industries had reached a point "where a national work relief program is no longer necessary."

SOCIAL SECURITY

Although social security programs had long been in effect in leading European countries, little progress was made prior to 1935 in promoting such a plan in the United States. In 1934, President Roosevelt appointed a committee and an able group of technical advisers to prepare a program for the consideration of Congress. Following the report of this Committee on Economic Security, Congress drew up a measure embodying its recommendations. After much debate the Social Security Act was passed in August, 1935. To take care of immediate needs, it included provisions for a Federal subsidization of state programs for old age amounting to one-half the total paid each eligible person up to $40 a month. By 1942, about 2,000,000 needy persons were receiving old-age assistance. For the future there was the Federal government annuity system for retired workers sixty-five and over, financed by a payroll tax on employers and employees. The plan originally excluded agricultural laborers, domestic servants, casual employees, public servants, or employees of charitable, scientific, literary, educational, and religious institutions. The amount paid retired workers depended on the wages earned during employment. By 1942, more than 46,000,000 persons had been given social security account numbers. The constitutionality of the plan, which was put into operation in January, 1937, was upheld by the Supreme Court in that year.

Unemployment insurance was also provided through a payroll tax on wages paid by employers of eight or more persons. The states decided what workers were eligible for unemployment insurance and also the amount of the benefit. Certain classes were excluded as in the old-age annuity system. By 1940, about 28,000,000 workers had unemployment insurance. The constitutionality of the state and Federal unemployment insurance plans was upheld by the Supreme Court in 1937.

Among other provisions of the law, Federal funds were made available to aid the states in caring for dependent children, in granting aid to the blind, in promoting the health of mothers and infants, in aiding crippled children, in establishing and maintaining adequate public health services, and in promoting vocational rehabilitation. General supervision of the law was given to a National Social Security Board of three members. In addition, the Secretaries of the Treasury and Labor, the Surgeon General of Public Health, the Bureau of Internal Revenue, and other officials and bureaus were given administrative duties in connection with the law.

Complementing the social security program, a Railroad Employees Retirement Act was passed in 1934. The Supreme Court declared the law unconstitutional (Railroad Retirement Board *vs*. Alton Railroad Company). New legislation was adopted in 1937 and 1938. It provided annuities to railroad employees who retired at sixty-five or after thirty years' service.

AID TO YOUTH

In order to aid the large numbers of unemployed youth, many of whom were roaming the country, a Civilian Conservation Corps (CCC) was formed in 1933. It first absorbed 200,000 unmarried young men in need of employment, and then it was expanded. The enrollees received a cash allowance in addition to food, clothing, shelter, transportation, medical attention, and education. Some acquired technical skills. They lived in camps and worked on reforestation, roads, trails, and drainage; they engaged in pest control, building erosion dams, and in fighting forest fires. Their work was carried on largely in forests, parks, and on agricultural lands. Enrollment was for a period of six months with a maximum service of two years permitted. By 1940, more than 2,000,000 men had served in the CCC in addition to 40,000 Indians and 20,000 living in the territorial possessions.

The work of the CCC well illustrates interdepartmental cooperation that was common among many agencies. The CCC cooperated in regard to conservation with the War, Interior, and Agricultural Departments and Veterans' Administration. In 1942, as the war effort consumed the activities of the nation, the CCC was abolished.

Chiefly in order to aid capable young people with part-time employment to enable them to pursue further academic, vocational, technical, or professional studies, the National Youth Administration was set up by executive order as a division of the Works Progress Administration. Later, it came under the jurisdiction of the Federal Security Administration. The NYA granted aid to thousands of high school, vocational, college, and university students to prepare themselves for a future career and, at the same time, kept them out of the labor market in a period of general unemployment. The NYA also provided apprenticeship training and work projects for young persons not in school. It promoted vocational guidance and placement together with the extension of educational and recreational facilities for young people, especially in neglected areas. In 1942, its work was drastically curtailed, but certain projects necessary to the war effort were continued.

RELIEF TO HOME OWNERS

The Home Owners' Loan Corporation (HOLC) was created by the Federal Home Bank Board as directed by an act of Congress in June, 1933. The corporation was owned and controlled by the government and was planned to refinance home owners who were threatened with the loss of their homes by foreclosure. It was authorized to loan up to 80 per cent of the appraised value of homes worth not over $20,000. Loans were made by exchanging bonds of the corporation for mortgages. By 1936, the corporation held more than 1,000,000 mortgages and had issued $3 billion in bonds, guaranteed by the United States. It ceased its lending operations in June, 1936, and after that date, engaged in the management of its mortgages and the maintenance and sale of properties acquired through foreclosure and liquidation.

In 1934 and 1938 the Federal Housing Administration was established by the National Housing Acts. It was designed to aid economic recovery by stimulating certain industries and trades through small loans to householders for the purpose of financing alterations, repairs, and improvements to real estate. "Renovate" became a familiar word as householders were urged to improve their properties. The FHA was also authorized to make loans to approved financial institutions in order that they might aid individuals to build or buy low cost homes on plans which provided loans of 80 or even 90 per cent of the value of the property and extended over periods up to thirty years. Provision was made for the government to guarantee repayment of such loans through a plan of mortgage insurance.

The first efforts in slum clearance and low-rent housing were made by the Federal government in 1933 by the Public Works Administration, under the National Industrial Recovery Act (p. 579), when an appropriation of $150,000,000 for that purpose was made. But the primary reason for this expenditure was to put people to work. In 1937, the problem was approached directly from the point of view of improved housing when Congress created the United States Housing Authority (USHA) empowering it to make loans up to $500,000,000 to local housing agencies over a period of three years. It could loan up to 90 per cent of the total cost of a project at low interest rates. The USHA took over the work of the PWA in this respect and sponsored a number of projects in different parts of the country. In 1939, for the first time America's slums started to diminish in extent.

THE ATTEMPT TO READJUST
INDUSTRY AND LABOR

In June, 1933, the National Industrial Recovery Act (NIRA), an emergency measure, went into effect. One purpose of the law was to aid in putting to work the 12,000,000 or more unemployed workers through an extensive program of public works and through the stimulation of private industry. A bond issue of $3.3 billion was authorized to finance the construction of Federal, state, and local projects and new taxes were provided to take care of the relatively large appropriation. Other aspects of the law were designed "to eliminate unfair competitive practices," "to remove obstructions to the free flow of interstate and foreign commerce," and "to improve standards of labor." The President referred to the act as "a great spontaneous cooperation to put millions of men back in their regular jobs this summer. The idea is simply for employers to hire more men to do the existing work by reducing the hours of each man each week and at the same time pay a living wage for the shorter week."

To carry out the provisions of the NIRA, President Roosevelt created the National Recovery Administration (NRA), with Hugh S. Johnson as administrator. A blue-colored representation of the American "thunderbird" with outspread wings was proclaimed the symbol of industrial recovery. All who accepted the President's Re-employment Agreement or a special Code of Fair Competition were permitted to display a Blue Eagle poster. The law provided for the self-regulation of business and industry through the formulation of codes of fair competition. Before the depression, the Department of Commerce had sponsored codes and encouraged cooperation in standardizing products and methods of distributing them. Now the plan was broadened to secure agreement in the different industries in order to eliminate variation in prices of similar commodities and to insure all producers a fair return, and agreements were exempted from the anti-trust laws. Altogether, 578 national codes with 200 supplements, affecting about 22,000,000 workers, were put into effect.

The law required the recognition in the codes of the rights of employees to organize and to bargain collectively through representatives of their own choosing. It was also necessary for employers to "comply with the maximum hours of labor, minimum rates of pay, and other conditions of employment, approved or prescribed by the President." Many industrial executives interpreted the plan as meaning the suspension of the antitrust laws in return for the concessions of minimum pay, shorter hours, better working conditions, and the abolition of child labor. As the codes were enforced, it became evident that the interests of small local firms, labor, and consumers were not regarded in spite of the attempts of a Consumers' Advisory Board to offset monopolistic trends. Furthermore, very little of the $3.3 billion appropriated for public works was spent in 1933, and the decline in total spending for public construction by all types of government, local, state and Federal, was barely checked.

In the second year of the experiment, at a time when many codes were being made, it became evident that all was not well with NRA and there was much criticism. Many employers refused to enter into price-fixing agreements with competitors and some who had agreed to the codes refused to give the workers the benefits that they had obtained. The National Labor Board, established in 1933, found it increasingly difficult to protect the rights of workers, especially in regard to collective bargaining. Strikes and labor disputes increased. A part of the public came to believe that the codes were at least partly responsible for the increasing prices of food and other commodities, which, while not high, caused apprehension among those who were suffering from the depression. In the meantime Johnson resigned as administrator and the President reorganized the recovery machinery and at the same time replaced the National Labor Board with the National Labor Relations Board. In the spring of 1935, the Supreme Court in the Schechter case invalidated the code system of NIRA, declaring that it was an unconstitutional delegation of the lawmaking power to the executive and a Federal invasion of intrastate commerce. After a drastic reorganization and continuation for a time of the National Recovery Administration, the President officially ended its life on January 1, 1936.

The Wagner Act of 1935 created a National Labor Relations Board which was destined to become most important in the history of labor relations. The act clearly reasserted the right of collective bargaining, prohibited employer efforts to interfere with organization, and gave a union winning a majority in a plant election the power to speak for all employees. The act also gave the board power to investigate complaints by labor or employers and to hold hearings in regard to unfair practices affecting interstate commerce. The board was authorized to issue "cease and desist" orders and in case of disobedience to petition any circuit court of appeal for enforcement of the order. In a five-to-four decision the Supreme Court upheld the law in the case of the National Labor Relations Board *vs.* Jones and Laughlin Steel Corporation (1937). It granted that the labor relations of manufacturers engaged in interstate commerce were subject to Federal regulation. The decision robbed big business of the victory it thought it had won in the Schechter case and increased the prestige of the board. Violations of the law continued, but court action in each case brought them to a halt.

One of the most important gains for labor was the passage of the Fair Labor Standards Act of 1938, popularly known as the Wages and Hours Act. The measure was considered by Congress, at the urging of President Roosevelt. The proposal resulted in controversy between northern and southern interests, southern employers demanding that southern wages be recognized, while northern employers opposed. The law created a Wage and Hour Division in the Department of Labor and was applied to industries engaged in interstate commerce. It established for the first year after its passage a minimum wage of twenty-five cents an hour, thirty cents for the second year, and forty cents an hour to be sought within the following six years. Geographical differentials were not recognized, but local variances were to be permitted. The law also provided that employers should not require more than a forty-four hour week for the first year, a forty-two hour week for the second, and a forty-hour week thereafter. When these limits were exceeded, time and one-half pay was required. The law exempted certain industries and workers. It also forbade child labor under sixteen and excluded anyone under eighteen from working in hazardous occupations. The law was put into effect late in 1938 with no difficulty. In 1942, however, because of the war, opposition developed to the forty-hour week and unsuccessful attempts were made in Congress to modify the law so that overtime payments would not begin until after forty-eight hours of work.

The gains of labor under the New Deal were remarkable. These can be seen in the unprecedented growth of American unionism under the protection of the administration. They were also evident in the series of Federal laws that were put into effect with startling rapidity, including those on wages and hours, social security, collective bargaining, employment agencies, and other welfare measures. In a series of liberal decisions, especially those connected with the National Labor Relations Board, the Supreme Court changed to some extent

FACTORY AND FARM INCOME, 1925 – 1940

(1925 = 100)

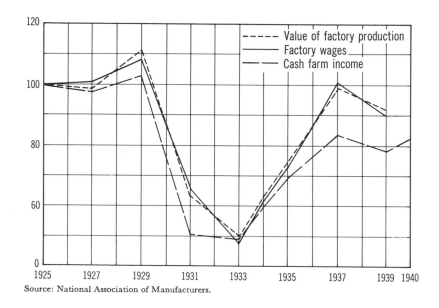

- - - - - Value of factory production
——— Factory wages
— — Cash farm income

Source: National Association of Manufacturers.

the legal background of industrial relations. State legislation and judicial decisions in the East and North also followed the trend that favored labor. Thus, through better wages, shorter hours, safer working conditions, and improved living conditions, large numbers of workers were benefited.

Still another victory for labor came with the passage of the Second Guffey Coal Act. The first one had been declared unconstitutional by the Supreme Court in the case of Carter *vs.* Carter Coal Company (1936). The new law of 1937 established a little NRA in the bituminous coal industry. It imposed a tax of 19½ per cent on the wholesale price of coal, but exempted operators who signed and observed a code under which a commission fixed coal prices.

AID TO AGRICULTURE

In spite of the efforts made during President Hoover's administration on behalf of the farmers, agricultural prices and rural property values continued to drop alarmingly. The debts of farmers increased; thousands were losing their farms; and the impoverishment of those engaged in agriculture meant a lessened ability of a large part of the population of the country to buy, adding to the distress of all. The Democrats had pledged the party in the platform of 1932 to the extension and "development of the farm cooperative movement and effective control of surpluses," as well as "the enactment of every constitutional measure to raise farm prices."

Under the leadership of the President and Secretary of Agriculture Wallace the administration approached the gigantic problem from two angles: (1) direct aid and adequate loans to farmers; and (2) the attempt to adjust farm production to market demands. A Farm Credit Act was passed early in the history of the New Deal (1933). The Farm Credit Administration (FCA) was set up as an agency to supervise the Federal Land Banks, the Federal Intermediate Credit Banks, the Production Credit Corporations, the Regional Banks for Cooperatives in each of the twelve Farm Credit Administration Districts, and in 1934, the Federal Farm Mortgage Corporation. Credit facilities for farmers were thus grouped into four divisions under the Farm Credit Administration: land banks, production credit, intermediate credit, and cooperative credit.

Many laws were passed to carry out this aspect of the new farm policy. The Farm Relief and Inflation Act authorized the Federal Banks to issue $2 billion in 4 per cent bonds to refinance farm mortgages at interest rates not higher than $4\frac{1}{2}$ per cent. The Frazier-Lemke Farm Bankruptcy Act (1934) authorized the courts under certain conditions to grant farmers burdened by mortgages a five-year moratorium. The next year, the law was declared by the Supreme Court to be a violation of the Fifth Amendment, but a new law modifying the terms of the moratorium and limiting it to a three-year period was unanimously approved by the highest tribunal. Under the various agencies of the Farm Credit Administration and the many laws that were adopted to carry out the new policy, farmers were able to get short-term loans to finance current operations and long-term mortgage loans on their farms at relatively low rates of interest. Farm bankruptcies decreased and many farmers were able to get back and refinance property that had been foreclosed. During the first four years of the New Deal a total of more than $3.5 billion had been loaned to farmers.

The Agricultural Adjustment Act was an effort to raise farm prices by both subsidy and restricted production. While it provided for credit extension and mortgage relief, it was designed chiefly to "reestablish prices to farmers at a level that will give agricultural commodities a purchasing power with respect to articles that farmers buy equivalent to the purchasing power of agricultural commodities in the base period." That period was from 1909 to 1914 for wheat, cotton, corn, hogs, rice, and dairy products and from 1919 to 1929 for tobacco. The Secretary of Agriculture was given extensive authority to reduce productive acreage and to foster marketing quotas.

Voluntary agreements were made between the government and growers of enumerated cash crops including cotton, wheat, corn, peanuts, potatoes, rice, rye, sugar beets, sugar cane, tobacco, and hogs. The farmers who assented received cash in return for withdrawing acreage temporarily from cultivation. Within a year 3,000,000 contracts were signed providing for crop control, including 90 per cent of the cotton and tobacco growers, 80 per cent of the wheat producers, and about all the corn farmers and hog raisers. The money to pay the farmers was obtained through processing taxes imposed upon the manufacturers who prepared farm products for public consumption, such as millers, meat packers, and cotton processors. At the same time marketing agreements were made with producers, processors, and distributors of agricultural products in order that "competitive wastes may be eliminated, trade practices improved, surpluses moved into markets for consumption, and producers' prices raised." State and local committees or associations of producers helped to administer the law, which was an extension of Federal aid operating through decentralized agencies.

Aided by the inflationary policies and the agricultural reduction programs of the New Deal, together with severe drought and dust storms in parts of the country, the AAA resulted in rising farm prices in 1934[1] and 1935. But agriculture received such relief at the expense of consumers, who were also suffering from the depression and were complaining about rising prices. Another effect was to reduce labor on farms. By 1935, there was a reduction of about 1,000,000 man hours. In the South, especially, suffering increased. Tenant farmers and sharecroppers, put off plantations by crop restrictions, ignored the color line for the first time and formed a Southern Tenant Farmers' Union, although with few actual results.

A severe blow was given the farm program in January, 1936 when the Supreme Court declared several aspects of the AAA unconstitutional (Hoosac Mills case[2]). It held that the processing taxes were invalid, that the payment of cash benefits to farmers to get them to coop-

---

[1]Total farm income in 1934, including government payments, was some $6.1 billion, about $1 billion more than in 1933.
[2]United States vs. Butler.

erate was coercive, and that the regulation of agriculture did not come within the jurisdiction of Congress but belonged to the states. The decision did not affect such provisions of the law as marketing agreements, loans, the eradication of animal diseases, and sugar quotas.

In order to accomplish what the invalidated clauses of the Agricultural Adjustment Act of 1933 had sought—control of agricultural production to prevent large unmarketable surpluses—Congress enacted the Soil Conservation and Domestic Allotment Act (1936). An earlier law, the Soil Erosion Act (1935), passed after widespread devastation and distress wrought by flood and dust storms, which sought to prevent erosion, control floods, and relieve unemployment, was the basis for the law. By the Soil Conservation and Domestic Allotment Act, indirect production control replaced the system of direct control under the defunct AAA, by making such control incidental to soil conservation. The law authorized appropriations of not more than $500,000,000 annually for payments to farmers for voluntarily planting a part of their lands in clover, soybeans, or other crops to restore its fertility or for directly fertilizing and improving land that otherwise might be put into production and for purposes of preventing erosion and encouraging flood control. While the law was passed chiefly to aid farmers by attempting to re-establish and maintain farm buying power, the government was at last recognizing the need for protecting the nation's most valuable natural resource—the soil.

The Agricultural Adjustment Act of 1938—a series of laws—continued the Soil Conservation Act as a permanent farm policy. The new statute was designed to promote this program through fixing national allotments at a point "to give production sufficient for domestic consumption, for exports, and for reserve supplies." Producers of wheat, corn, cotton, tobacco, and rice could obtain storage loans when prices slumped and for holding surpluses until they were needed. Marketing quotas could be employed to buttress the price-supporting influences of the loans. Quotas could be introduced only after producers of a commodity in a special referendum voted in favor of their use by at least a two-thirds majority vote. Each farmer of that commodity was then given a marketing quota and penalties were prescribed for sales in excess of it. If the loans and quotas stabilized prices that were still too low in the light of parity prices and farm income, the Secretary of Agriculture was authorized to make payments, as far as funds were available, to producers of the five basic crops to raise the income from the sale of crops to parity on their controlled production. Complementing the provisions of the act of 1938, the Agricultural Marketing

Agreements Act of 1937 enabled farmers and distributors to establish rational marketing systems for entire crops. This was done through the orders of the Secretary of Agriculture and not through licenses as attempted earlier. By 1941 the demands of the Second World War were temporarily solving the farm problem.

CONSERVATION

The policies of conservation originating early in the twentieth century had been carefully carried out as a whole, but under the New Deal the program was rapidly extended and expanded and many daring innovations were introduced. The continuance of earlier policies can be seen in the expansion of national control over coal, petroleum, natural gas, and helium deposits and the addition of several millions of acres to the national forests through a greatly expanded program for purchasing poorly administered forest lands. In addition, many projects were undertaken for the conservation of soil, water, forests, fish, game, and other resources carried on by such agencies as the CCC, PWA, and WPA, and the expansion of the work of the Bureau of Biological Survey, as well as in the soil conservation programs provided for the farmers of the country. More spectacular were the projects developed in the Tennessee Valley and similar ones of lesser degree in other parts of the country.

The most elaborate attempt of conservation was carried on in the valley of the Tennessee River involving portions of seven states. During the First World War, the Wilson Dam was built by the Federal government at Muscle Shoals in northern Alabama to provide power for the production of nitrates, important in the manufacture of explosives. After the war the project was abandoned and for many years the issue involved a nation-wide controversy over the question of public or private ownership and operation of power facilities. During these years nothing was done by the government in this region because of the inability of Congress and the several Presidents to agree to an appropriate plan, although the government embarked in the public power business in 1928 when Congress authorized the Hoover (later Boulder) Dam. As late as 1931 President Hoover vetoed a bill to authorize the government to produce electric power in the Tennessee Valley and to sell it to the public, on the ground that it would mean competition with private utility companies. By the time that President Franklin D. Roosevelt took office, general feeling had increased among a large part of the public that rates for electric current were too high. It was believed that most companies were operated solely for profit and

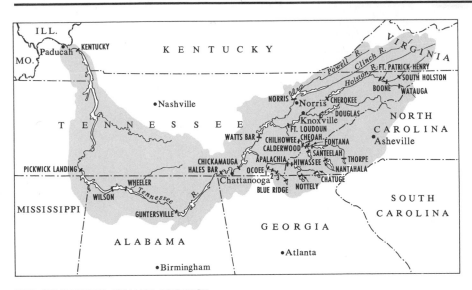

THE TENNESSEE VALLEY PROJECT

not in the interests of the consumers. Many electric companies were controlled by huge holding companies and these especially came under attack.

The Tennessee Valley Authority (TVA) was created by Congress in 1933 to provide for the development of the entire Tennessee watershed of approximately 40,000 square miles. The purpose was to develop the resources of the entire river, in every way possible, for the benefit of all who lived in the region. The experiment went far beyond any previously attempted in the field of conservation. Huge dams were constructed on the Tennessee River and its tributaries. The Norris Dam on the Clinch River, the Wheeler Dam, above the Wilson Dam at Muscle Shoals, and others were completed. The total cost of all the projects when finished has been estimated at about $500,000,000.

Among the several objectives of the project, flood control became one of the most impressive. Through the agency of the Gilbertsville Reservoir it was expected that floods on the lower Ohio and Mississippi Rivers would be reduced by two or three feet. Another purpose of the system was to aid navigation when navigable depths are reached in continuous stretches. Still another aim was the creation of water power for producing electricity to be sold at low rates to municipalities, cooperatives, and industries. In spite of many law suits brought by private power utilities, court decisions favored the Authority. In

FEDERAL IRRIGATION AND POWER PROJECTS IN THE WEST, 1962

addition to extending the use of power by its program of rural electrification, the Authority provided a "yardstick" for rates by private companies. Still another activity was the development of low-priced fertilizers. Much progress was made and a high-grade fertilizer of phosphate concentration was produced in the plant at Muscle Shoals. In addition, other programs for soil conservation, diversification of agriculture, terracing of hillsides, and reforestation of denuded areas have been carried out in the area.

Among other similar projects should be noted Boulder Dam on the Colorado River, authorized before the New Deal, in 1928, for flood control, navigation improvement, irrigation, storage, and power. It was completed in 1936. The huge Grand Coulee Dam on the Columbia River makes possible a portion of the flow of that river into the fifty-mile long Grand Coulee and provides water for a large area of land capable of high productivity when irrigated. The Federal Bureau of Reclamation became interested in the irrigation of this region in 1903, but a dam was not proposed until 1918. In 1933, President Roosevelt authorized the use of PWA funds for its construction as a major part of a plan for the development of the Columbia Valley.

Another broad purpose of the New Deal conservation policies was to provide electric power for farms all over the country. Beginning in 1933 an Electric Farm and Home Authority began work to aid farmers in the extension of power to kitchens, barns, and workshops and to facilitate the purchase of apparatus and appliances. Much was accomplished in this respect. In 1942, President Roosevelt ordered the liquidation of this Authority because of the curtailment of the manufacture of electrical appliances, the purchase of which it financed. In addition to returning to the government its original capital, it also showed a surplus of $650,000.

Closely related to the plans to provide the country with cheap electric power was the increased regulation of public utilities. Under the Public Utility Act (Wheeler-Rayburn Act) of 1935 and the Robinson-Patman Act of 1936, the powers of the FTC, FPC, and SEC were broadened to regulate interstate electric and gas rates and to end the pyramided, holding-company system and its evils. The ICC, FCC, NLRB, and the Maritime Commission also had certain powers of regulation over utilities. Such action together with congressional investigations and newspaper publicity regarding the unsavory activities of many companies put the utilities on the defensive.

The Public Utility Act of 1935 required that all utility holding companies register with the Securities and Exchange Commission and furnish the agency with essential information. Unregistered holding companies were forbidden to engage in interstate commerce; registered companies were subject to rigid control by the commission in regard to issues of securities and the acquisition of subsidiaries. The law also provided for the simplification and reorganization of the holding company systems, for the supervision of accounts, and for the submission of reports by holding companies. The so-called "death sentence" clause limited the operations of each holding company to a single integrated public utility system unless the commission found it more economical for a company to manage and hold more than one system. As the law went into effect, there was much opposition by the companies to registration. Protests were without avail, for in the case of the Electric Bond and Share Company et al. *vs.* the Securities and Exchange Commission in 1939, the Supreme Court upheld the validity of the provision. Following this decision, some of the utility companies were dissolved to escape the requirement, but of course, the dissolved companies were subject to drastic regulation. Obfuscation, speculation, and unhealthy concentration of control were largely ended. The law thus provided for regulation in the interests of the investors, consumers, and the public, and made impossible such pyramiding as that in the gigantic structure known as Insull Utility Investments, Inc.

THE UNANSWERED QUESTION

The New Deal had not produced a satisfactory level of private capital investment. In 1939 there were still 9.5 million unemployed, three-quarters as many as at the lowest point of the depression. But the Federal government had created some of the stabilizing machinery of the modern welfare state: controls that while possibly hindering some enterprise greatly increased security. The Second World War temporarily ended unemployment and made academic the question as to how this could ultimately have been achieved in time of peace. The question remained, however, whether full employment could be achieved without government spending, and if government had to supply jobs in a time of stable peace, where and how it should be done.

CHAPTER 27

The Second World War

BACKGROUND OF THE WAR

The international system for peace and security established after World War I had come to rest both in Europe and the Far East on continued prosperity and American loans. With the coming of depression the liberal Weimar Republic in Germany was unable to meet reparations payments. As left-wing forces gained in strength, the former military leaders agreed to support Adolph Hitler, whose program involved repudiation of Germany's obligations under the Treaty of Versailles. Hitler became chancellor, and soon virtual dictator of Germany just a few days after the inauguration of President Roosevelt. In Japan, also, the military gained the upper hand and began war with the equally militant nationalist Chinese.

By 1935, Germany was rearming, and Italy had joined in disregarding treaty obligations. For a time England and France might have checked the rise of what came to be the German-Italian-Japanese Axis, but fear of the rise of communism in Europe led both England and France to hope for friendly solutions to German and Italian aggression. Thus the situation drifted until by 1939 the newly equipped army of Germany was the strongest machine in the world.

In the middle thirties Congress had passed legislation designed to prevent recurrence of the situation that led the country into the First World War. An Act of 1935 imposed upon the President the duty of placing embargoes on exports of arms and munitions to belligerent nations. After Japan began a relentless invasion of China in August, 1937, President Roosevelt refused to invoke the neutrality laws, theoretically because no war had been declared, but actually because American sympathy was with China, and the provisions of the laws would have worked to the disadvantage of that country, although trade between the United States and China was small. President Roosevelt's suggestion that aggressor nations should be "quarantined" evoked such attacks from isolationists that he did not return to the subject.

Meanwhile, in February, 1936, the Neutrality Act was amended in order to prohibit even the granting of loans and credits to nations at war. In July, civil war began in Spain. The government, composed of a Popular Front coalition of liberals, Socialists, and Communists, was attacked by conservative groups under the leadership of General Francisco Franco, who planned to set up a dictatorship. He was aided by Italy and Germany. England and France adopted a nonintervention program. Early in 1937, at the request of the President, Congress extended its neutrality legislation to include civil as well as international wars. American liberals and interventionists pointed out that the neutrality laws worked to the advantage of the aggressors—Japan in China and the Insurgents in Spain. In May, 1937, a law was adopted which, although a compromise measure, pleased neither interventionists nor isolationists. It prohibited in time of war the exportation from the United States of arms and munitions to belligerents except to American republics engaged in war with a country outside the western hemisphere. It forbade the sale of securities in the United States by a belligerent and even prohibited travel by Americans on belligerent-owned ships. The President at his discretion could enforce "cash and carry" rules by which nations at war purchasing goods other than munitions would be required to pay cash for them and to transport them in their own ships.

International conditions steadily degenerated. Early in 1938, the President asked Congress for a naval appropriation of $1 billion in the interests of national defense and later requested the enlargement of the Air Force to 6,000 planes. The naval program was not approved by Congress for several months. In several speeches, the President stated that the United States must arm against international lawlessness. The reaction to speeches of the President, the Secretary of State, and others who emphasized national defense was quite different from that which greeted similar speeches of Woodrow Wilson in 1916 and 1917. Peace organizations now stressed the futility of war;

a movement among college students condemned international conflicts and stressed arbitration; and the Munitions Committee headed by Senator Nye acquainted the public with the enormous war profits made by munition manufacturers from 1914 to 1918. A resolution providing that a declaration of war be submitted to a popular referendum before the nation could go to war was introduced in Congress, although it did not get far. Public opinion in 1938 was generally opposed to another war. But sentiment was soon to change.

The neutrality acts of 1935, 1936, and 1937 had been passed in the belief that the sale of munitions had been at least partly responsible for America's entrance into the First World War. Impending war in Europe in 1938 and 1939 made President Roosevelt apprehensive lest the neutrality laws would prevent Great Britain and France from purchasing war supplies in the United States. Under international law belligerents had a right to purchase contraband in a neutral country and to take it away, but the American laws prevented this. Although the administration and, to some extent, public opinion desired to aid Great Britain, Congress did not make any changes in neutrality legislation until two months after war had begun in Europe. The Neutrality Act of 1939 omitted any embargo on arms, munitions, implements of war, or on any commodity, but it forbade American vessels from carrying any supplies of war; it prohibited ships from traveling to belligerent ports in Europe or North Africa; it prevented the arming of American merchant ships; it required foreign vessels carrying goods to European belligerent ports to have the title to the cargoes transferred from American ownership on a pass-title, cash-carry basis before leaving United States ports; it gave the President discretionary power in preventing American ships from entering "combat zones" that he might proclaim; and it prohibited Americans from traveling on belligerent vessels. In signing the measure in November, 1939, the President stated:

The revised neutrality law has been signed and has gone into effect today; and I have also, under it, issued a proclamation defining a combat area, described in latitude and longitude.

In plain English, the chief result is this. From now on, no American ships may go to belligerent ports, British, French, and German, in Europe or Africa, as far South as the Canary Islands. This is laid down in the law and there is no discretion in the matter.

The law aided the Allies by removing embargoes, but the purchasers had to take title to goods before their export. The act did nothing to aid the merchant marines and navies of the Allies.

The war began in Europe on September 1, 1939 when Nazi troops marched into Poland without declaring war. On September 3, 1939, two days after the Nazi forces began invading Poland, Great Britain and France, realizing that the policy of appeasement had failed, declared war on Germany, but before aid could be sent to Poland, that country had fallen. Russia joined Germany and moved into Poland from the East. Once again Poland was partitioned. Russia a little later secured the three Baltic states of Estonia, Latvia, and Lithuania, which before the First World War had belonged to it. Russia then attacked Finland. Terrific fighting ensued and in March, 1940, a peace was reached. Finland retained its national independence but at the cost of a number of concessions, including much territory. Then followed in quick succession the German occupation of Denmark, Norway, and the Low Countries as the German blitzkrieg struck territory which had been prepared by fifth columnists. The fall of France in the early summer of 1940 was a tragedy for the Allied cause. At this point Italy entered the war. Then followed the Battle of Britain as London and other English cities were bombed from the air. In 1941, Germany startled the world by turning on her ally and attacking Russia.

NATIONAL DEFENSE

The events in Europe had strong repercussions in the United States and intensified the controversy between isolationists and interventionists. Early in 1940 President Roosevelt asked Congress for immediate appropriations of $1,182,000,000 for defense. These were not granted until after the fall of France. Then, as taxes were increased, there followed a number of defense measures. A total of $4 billion was authorized for a two-ocean navy; and an increase of $500,000,000 was made to the Export-Import Bank for the purpose of expanding its lending power, especially to Latin-American countries.

President Roosevelt appointed a National Defense Advisory Committee. Edward R. Stettinius of the United States Steel Corporation was given charge of the production of raw materials; William S. Knudsen, president of General Motors Corporation, of manufacturing; Sidney Hillman, vice-president of the C.I.O., of labor and employment; Ralph Budd, chairman of the Chicago, Burlington and Quincy Railroad, of transportation; Chester C. Davis, of the Federal Reserve Board, of agricultural export and production; Leon Henderson, of the Securities and Exchange Commission, of price stabilization; and Harriet Elliot, dean of the Woman's College, University of North Carolina, of consumer interests. Changes were made in the President's cabinet, as Republicans Henry L. Stimson and Frank Knox became Secretary of War and Secretary of the Navy respectively. In September, 1940, the President announced that fifty overage destroyers had been traded to Great Britain in return for the use of naval and air bases in Newfoundland, Bermuda, Jamaica, the Bahamas, St. Lucia, Trinidad, Antigua, and British Guiana. Still another step in the interest of defense was the passage of the Selective Service and Training Act (September, 1940), which was America's first peacetime military draft.

Although keeping out of war had been the popular issue of the campaign, the results of the presidential election of 1940, in which President Roosevelt was elected for a third term, were interpreted by the administration as an endorsement of Roosevelt's policy to give all possible aid to the Allies. This policy was broadened after the election and was carried out largely through economic methods. The freezing of funds was one. As early as April, 1940, when Germany invaded Denmark and Norway, funds in the United States belonging to nationals from those countries were frozen by executive order to protect them from being seized by the invaders. The same plan was applied to other seized territories. Assets of the invaders, however, were not touched. Thus Germany, Italy, and Japan were enabled to finance shipments and propaganda, as well as to move their funds at will. Not until June, 1941, were the assets of all European states frozen and not until Japan entered Indo-China in July, 1941, was the plan applied to that country. The freezing orders imposed heavy penalties for trading with the citizens of such states. As a result, in July, Washington announced a blacklist of 1,800 firms in Latin America doing business with Germany, Italy, and Japan. A gray list permitted suspects to engage in transactions under an export license pending investigation but Japanese firms were not blacklisted until after Pearl Harbor had been struck.

Export licensing became another effective method of defense and of aiding the Allies. The Licensing Act of July, 1940 authorized the President to prohibit or curtail the export of materials used in manufacturing munitions. Within a year, the list included almost all metals and retail manufactures, machinery, rubber manufactures, chemicals, wood pulp, oils, and fats. The export-licensing system seriously affected economic relations between the United States and Latin-American countries. Because of increasing American purchases of copper, wool, and other commodities, those countries could buy more from the United States, but the licensing plan interfered. A policy was worked out by the government which granted manufacturers in both hemispheres equal treatment in the distribution of priority materials after the needs of the United States and of other countries under the Lend-Lease Act had been met.

A most decisive step in aiding the Allies was taken when an Act Further to Promote the Defense of the United States, or the Lend-Lease Act, was passed in March, 1941, after long and bitter debate. Proponents of the law hailed it as a defense measure which would keep the war away from America, and they proclaimed the country to be the arsenal of democracy. The law pledged the United States to lend to the limit of its material resources "defense articles to those governments whose defense the President deems vital to the defense of the United States." A supplementary act was passed providing for an initial appropriation of $7 billion to implement the law. By June, 1942, more than $30 billion had been authorized by Congress. Most of this was appropriated to the British Empire and lesser amounts were sent to Russia, China, Latin-American countries, and other powers. By the Lend-Lease Act, the United States underwrote a victory for the democracies at the risk of entering the war herself.

As a part of economic defense, the government attempted to accumulate reserves of strategic supplies. As early as June, 1939, the Strategic Materials Act was passed, which appropriated $100,000,000 for the purchase of important materials over a four-year period. Little was accomplished. In June, 1940, Congress authorized the RFC to organize subsidiary corporations for securing critical materials. The Rubber Reserve Company, the Metals Reserve Company, and the Defense Supplies Corporation were set up. The policy tended to stimulate the importation of raw materials from the countries of Latin America and the Far East, especially the Dutch East Indies but price ceilings robbed the law of much of its effectiveness. In 1941, the policy was broadened by additional legislation, and increased quantities of rubber, tin, tungsten, and platinum were obtained largely in the Far East and copper and other vital commodities chiefly in Latin America. The task was undertaken through the RFC, the State Department, the Office of Production Management (OPM), and the Economic Defense Board (EDB), later the Board of Economic Warfare (BEW). Quarrels between the State Department and the BEW, procrastination and confusion, and a shipping shortage all contributed to render the program ineffective. At the same time valuable materials necessary for defense purposes were being used to manufacture automobiles and appliances of all sorts. Not until the summer of 1941 did the government take steps to control the production of civilian goods.

Early in 1941 the shortage of shipping became alarming, and steps were taken by the government to improve the situation. In April, it was discovered that captains of Italian vessels in United States ports had been given orders to destroy their ships. At the same time Italian and German crews committed acts of sabotage. Under the Espionage Act of 1917, the government took over twenty-eight Italian, thirty-six Danish, and two German vessels. In June, Congress empowered the President to place all idle foreign-owned ships in the American merchant marine. The largest, the French liner *Normandie,* was badly damaged by fire in New York harbor as it was being converted to American use. As a further step toward the control of shipping, a Ship Warrants Act of July, 1941 required all vessels in United States ports to secure priority warrants from the Maritime Commission for using port facilities. In addition to these steps, the shipbuilding program was vastly increased. After the United States entered the war in December, 1941, the program proposed a total of 8,000,000 (deadweight) tons of merchant vessels for 1942 and 15,000,000 for 1943.

Throughout 1941, momentous events occurred in rapid succession. Shortly after the Lend-Lease Law was passed, an agreement was made in Washington with the minister of Greenland permitting the United States to construct naval and air bases in Greenland. Soon afterwards, the American navy began to convoy vessels by the northern route to the British Isles. President Roosevelt also declared that the Red Sea was no longer to be considered a combat zone as specified under the provisions of the Neutrality Act. This made possible a stream of airplanes, tanks, and other sorely-needed supplies from the United States to Britain's armies in the Middle East. American aid to the Allies increased the danger to American shipping from German submarines and in June, the *Robin Moor,* an American freighter carrying automobiles and steel rails to Capetown, Africa, was sunk far outside the war zones. As a result, German consulates in the United States were closed and all Germans connected with the German Railway and Tourist agencies, the German Transocean News Service, and the German Library of Information were ordered to leave the country. All Axis assets in the United States were frozen. Relations between the United States and Great Britain grew closer and in August, 1941, President Roosevelt and Prime Minister Winston Churchill met in the Atlantic off the North American coast where they promulgated the Atlantic Charter. Its eight points, reminiscent of Woodrow Wilson's Fourteen Points, set forth the ideals of the democracies as opposed to the totalitarian program. It disavowed aggrandizement of any kind by both nations; it committed both to oppose boundary changes unless desired by the peoples concerned; it endorsed self-government by all countries; it demanded for all nations access to trade and raw materials on equal terms; it pledged to promote the economic collaboration of all nations for improved labor standards and social betterment; it declared for peace to make all nations free from fear and insecurity; it upheld the freedom of the seas; and it demanded the compulsory disarmament of aggressor nations in the interests of international security. At the same time, President Roosevelt and Prime Minister Churchill pledged aid to Russia, which in June had been invaded by its former ally, Germany. They also notified Japan that aggression in the Far East must cease.

A few days after the declaration of the Atlantic Charter, the sinking by submarine on the Atlantic of a series of American vessels began. President Roosevelt ordered all naval vessels to shoot Axis submarines and surface raiders on sight. In October, the torpedoing of the American destroyer *Kearny* and the sinking of the destroyer *Reuben James,* led the United States close to war. Within a short time, Congress changed many provisions of the Neutrality law, permitting the arming of merchant vessels and allowing American ships to enter the ports of belligerent nations.

DEFENSE OF THE WESTERN HEMISPHERE

Another aspect of defense centered in hemisphere defense. In its relations with Latin America, the New Deal had developed what it called the "good neighbor" policy. Caribbean imperialism was ended by the withdrawal of marines from Haiti, the abrogation. of the Platt Amendment regarding Cuba, the relinquishment of the treaty right to intervene in Panama (1936), and the ending of Dominican customs receivership (1941). Every effort was being made to replace suspicion with friendliness.

The United States sought to combat Axis propaganda in South America. It gave loans and financial support to Brazil and to other Latin-American countries. Reluctant Argentina, incensed at American tariff barriers against its grain and quarantines on its meat, received an advance of $50,000,000 in December, 1940. The next year, the American government announced that it was prepared to lend $70,000,-000 a month to Latin-American countries. The Division of Cultural Relations of the Department of State engaged in a somewhat belated effort to combat Nazi propaganda, especially in Argentina and Brazil.

In 1942, after the United States had entered the war, Nelson A. Rockefeller was appointed Coordinator of Commercial and Cultural Relations with Latin America. As a result of the Good Neighbor policy, some of the nations to the south recognized their growing community of interest with the United States.

A serious problem, however, had to be solved with Mexico. In 1938, the Mexican government expropriated all foreign oil holdings, valued at about $400,000,000. The action was legal if proper compensation was made, but American investors protested and the government made vigorous representations. Although few assurances were given by the Mexican government, the United States did not resort to drastic measures. When war broke out in Europe, there was much bitterness in both countries over the question of the oil lands. In May, 1940, Mexico rejected an American proposal to arbitrate the dispute, but the conquests of Germany in Europe resulted in bringing the two countries closer together. Collaboration in defense matters followed and in November, 1941, the two republics announced the signing of a pact. The United States agreed to purchase Mexican silver, help stabilize the peso, lend money for roads, and negotiate a trade agreement. Mexico promised to make substantial payments on general American claims and agreed to settle the oil dispute. In the spring of 1942, settlement of the oil-expropriation problem was made when a lump sum settlement of about $24,000,000 was arranged. Relations between the two countries became more friendly.

From the military point of view, the Havana Convention of 1940 committed the United States to the defense of the Western Hemisphere. All the American republics were represented at the Convention. The Act of Havana provided for the establishment of a "collective trusteeship" in the Americas. Territory of European powers in danger of falling into unfriendly hands might be taken over and administered jointly by the American republics pending final decisions of the areas. The required two-thirds of the twenty-one republics ratified the measure in about a year. The Act marked an important step in hemisphere defense and broadened the Monroe Doctrine by permitting Latin-American countries to join in applying that historic policy. In January, 1942, the Third Meeting of Foreign Ministers of the American Republics met at Rio de Janeiro. It unanimously adopted a resolution recommending a severance of relations with the Axis, and before the Conference adjourned all but Argentina and Chile had broken with the Axis nations.

During the period preceding the war, relations with Canada were friendly. A most important question between the two countries was the deepening of the St. Lawrence-Great Lakes waterway in order to transform lake ports into seaports and also to develop electric power. The St. Lawrence Waterway Treaty, signed in 1932, after great efforts had been made by President Hoover, failed in the Senate in 1934 because several northern states believed that their economic interests would be adversely affected. There was also a belief on the part of some Senators that American railroads would be injured. A few objected to the government engaging in the power business. The matter continued to be a lively issue in the years that followed, but soon the development of the dictator states in Europe served to draw the United States and Canada into closer unity. In August, 1938, President Roosevelt in a speech made in Kingston, Canada, announced to the people of that country, "I give to you assurance that the people of the United States will not stand idly by if domination of Canadian soil is threatened by any other empire." Exactly two years later President Roosevelt and Prime Minister Mackenzie King, meeting in Ogdensburg, New York, agreed on a plan to establish a Permanent Joint Board of Defense to study problems of defense relating to the two countries. It was an unusual pact for a neutral nation to make with one at war, but it was accepted by the American people as a necessary part of hemisphere defense. As the United States entered the war, much was accomplished in the cooperative war effort of the two countries, especially in breaking down tariff barriers to direct vital supplies to places where they were needed.

THE UNITED STATES IN A GLOBAL WAR

As difficulties with Germany increased, American problems with Japan grew more serious. That country had joined the German-Italian military alliance in September, 1940, and then declared the intention of establishing a new order in eastern Asia. By this time, relations between the United States and Japan were strained, especially because of indignities to Americans in China, violations of the open door policy, and the war in China. In the summer of 1941, when Japan began to widen its conquests and sent troops into French Indo-China, President Roosevelt joined Great Britain in freezing Japanese assets and also issued an order absorbing the Philippine army into that of the United States. Now Japan either had to push further south into the Netherlands East Indies to secure iron and oil or else abandon the dream of Asiatic dominance.

In November the United States restated its basic principles for peace in the Far East. They included the abandonment of Japanese aggression, the withdrawal of troops from China and Indo-China, and adherence to a peaceful economic policy. No compromise with the military government of Japan could be reached on this basis. Japan attacked Pearl Harbor from the air early Sunday, December 7, killing more than 3,000 persons, destroying two battleships, three destroyers, and many aircraft, and damaging a number of vessels. The next day President Roosevelt delivered a war message to Congress and that body immediately declared war on Japan. Three days later Germany and Italy issued declarations of war on the United States. On the same day Congress accepted the challenge. The United States was at war with the Axis and a participant in a global war. In a radio address to the American people, President Roosevelt declared: "We are now in this war. We are in it all the way. Every single man, woman, and child is a partner in the most tremendous undertaking of our American history."

Plans to wage a total war were now necessary. Congress immediately made an army appropriation of some $8 billion and a new Selective Service Act was passed fixing the draft age at twenty to forty-four inclusive and requiring the registration of all men from eighteen to twenty and forty-five to sixty-four for possible civilian work. Before the end of the year the draft age was lowered to eighteen. A Women's Army Auxiliary Corps (WAAC), a Women's Naval Reserve (WAVES), and a Women's Coast Guard Reserve (SPARS), to release men for active combat duty, were authorized and put into service. A Women's Auxiliary Ferrying Squadron, offspring of the Air Transport Command, was established; early in 1943, a Marine Corps Women's Reserve, officially known as Marines, was organized.

Industrial mobilization now made more rapid progress. The first agency established to coordinate the defense effort was the National Defense Advisory Committee in 1940 (p. 594), but it was only an advisory body. In January, 1941, the President established the Office of Production Management (OPM) to provide centralized control over production. William S. Knudsen was made director general in charge of production and Sidney Hillman, director in charge of labor relations. The OPM was given considerable authority, but it relied chiefly on the voluntary cooperation of industry. It decreed priorities on steel, iron, rubber, silk, and automobiles, but was relatively ineffective because it could not control military requisitions. At the same time, Congress authorized the President to requisition defense materials.

COMBATTING INFLATION

In order to supplement the OPM, the President, in April, 1941, created the Office of Price Administration and Civil Supply (OPA), headed by Leon Henderson, to stabilize prices so as to protect the nation from rising living costs and possible inflation resulting from heavy defense expenditures. Price rises in steel, cotton goods, rubber tires, automobiles, and other goods were controlled, but Congress had to grant special price-fixing powers. After the United States entered the war, the dangers from inflation increased as the gap between the supply of commodities and the purchasing powers of the consumers of the country widened. In April, 1942, in order to keep the cost of living from spiraling upward, President Roosevelt suggested to Congress a seven-point anti-inflation program which included heavy taxation, price ceilings, stabilization of wages and salaries, stabilization of prices of agricultural products, the buying of war bonds by earners instead of the purchase of nonessential goods, rationing of all scarce essential articles, and the discouragement of credit and installment buying. Immediately, Price Administrator Henderson issued an order making it illegal for wholesalers and retailers of most commodities to

TOTAL COST OF LIVING COMPARED WITH COST OF RENT, 1940 – 1957
(1947–1949 = 100)

Year	All Items	Rent	Year	All Items	Rent
1940	59.9	86.9	1949	101.8	105.0
1941	62.9	88.4	1950	102.8	108.8
1942	69.7	90.4	1951	111.0	113.1
1943	74.0	90.3	1952	113.5	117.9
1944	75.2	90.6	1953	114.4	124.1
1945	76.9	90.9	1954	114.8	128.5
1946	83.4	91.4	1955	114.5	130.3
1947	95.5	94.4	1956	116.2	132.7
1948	102.8	100.7	1957	120.2	135.2

Source: U.S. Bureau of the Census, *Historical Statistics of the United States, Colonial Times to 1957*, Washington, D.C., 1960, p. 125.

sell their products at a higher price than they charged in March, 1942. Later, rationing was begun in sugar. From time to time other commodities were added to the list and a system of point rationing was finally inaugurated. At its peak, the Office of Price Administration, with its headquarters at Washington, D. C., was organized into nine regional boards, 92 district offices, 305 rent area offices, and more than 3,600 regional boards, which served all the communities of the nation. Its price regulations covered almost everything the American family ate, wore, and used, and applied to several million different commodities at all levels from producer to consumer. It imposed rent regulations and administered thirteen rationing programs covering a wide variety of essential civilian goods, including automobiles, tires, gasoline, meats, and fats.

Congress was slow to enact the necessary legislation asked by the President to prevent inflation, and the President, in turn, was unwilling to delegate adequate administrative authority. In October, 1942, an anti-inflation law was passed. The President was granted broad powers, with some limitations, to hold down wartime living costs. The measure, which had been delayed because of controversy over farm prices, guaranteed the farmer at least 90 per cent of parity prices for his major crops and provided that no ceilings be placed on farm prices at less than parity or below the highest price received for any commodity between January 1, 1942 and September 15, 1942 (adjusted for grade, location, and seasonal differentials).

The President appointed James F. Byrnes, former senator and ex-Justice of the Supreme Court, as Director of Economic Stabilization. A fourteen-man Stabilization Board was set up, consisting of eight heads of departments and agencies of the government and two representatives each of labor, management, and farming. Wide powers were conferred on Director Byrnes by the anti-inflation act and by the President's orders based on it. He was authorized to "formulate and develop a comprehensive national policy relating to the control of civilian purchasing power, prices, rents, wages, salaries, profits, rationing, subsidies, and related matters." He was empowered "to issue directives on policy to the federal departments and agencies concerned."

Prompt action followed the establishment of the Stabilization Board. The Price Administrator, a member of it, clapped price ceilings on exempted food items except a few of seasonal character. Rent control was extended to the whole country and all rents were frozen at the March 1, 1942 level. Wage rates were fixed at the September 15, 1942 level unless decided otherwise by the War Labor Board; increases were granted in the steel industry and in a few others. Finally salaries were frozen and a limit of $25,000 placed on all salaries after taxes, and "with due allowance for the payment of life insurance premiums, fixed obligations," etc. Early in 1943, Congress overruled the President by permitting salaries to rise to the highest point attained up to September 15, 1942. Under the authority of the anti-inflation law, the country had taken a long step toward full-time war economy.

CONTROLLING PRODUCTION

Before the United States was actually at war, the President set up in August, 1941, the Supply Priorities and Allocations Board (SPAB) for the purpose of supervising the entire production program, but at the same time the Office of Production Management remained. In this piling up of agencies it became clear that only the President had real authority. Vice-President Henry A. Wallace was made chairman of the new board and Donald Nelson, of Sears, Roebuck and Company, was appointed executive director. The Vice-President was also head of the Economic Defense Board which controlled exports; the problem of distribution at home and abroad now centered on him. Shortages had already appeared in magnesium, nickel, copper, chromium and even in aluminum, although in regard to the latter it was not entirely due to the lack of bauxite, but to the difficulties encountered in reducing it through tremendous electrical power. To aid in securing copper, the tariff was suspended on government purchases from Chile and bonuses or attractive prices were offered for the product in the United States where the cost of production was high.

Early in 1942, when war had become a grim reality, a Senate investigating committee reported that war production had been impeded by the bungling of government officials, the greed of employers, and the selfishness of labor. The committee severely criticized several government agencies and suggested a reorganization of the Office of Production Management. President Roosevelt immediately created the War Production Board (WPB) with Donald Nelson, who was moved from the SPAB, as its head. At the same time, the National War Labor Board was established, under the chairmanship of William H. Davis, a New York lawyer.

The War Production Board was given full authority to supervise war production, and Congress established criminal penalties for violation of the government's priority orders. It substituted for general priorities a classified system of special allocations of all strategic materials.

INFLATIONARY TRENDS IN TWO WAR PERIODS
(1926 = 100)

FIRST WORLD WAR			SECOND WORLD WAR		
Year	Farm Products	All Commodities other than Farm Products and Foods	Year	Farm Products	All Commodities other than Farm Products and Foods
1914	71.2	66.4	1940	67.7	83.0
1915	71.5	68.0	1941	82.4	89.0
1916	84.4	88.3	1942	105.9	95.5
1917	129.0	114.2	1943	122.6	96.9
1918	148.0	124.6	1944	123.3	98.5
1919	157.6	128.8	1945	128.2	99.7
1920	150.7	161.3	1946	148.9	109.5
			1947	181.2	135.2
			1948	188.3	151.0

Source: U.S. Bureau of the Census, *Historical Statistics of the United States, Colonial Times to 1957*, Washington, D.C., 1960, p. 116.

The production of automobiles, radios, and other manufactures for civilian use was stopped, and production was reduced in some other consumer lines so that the materials could be used for war goods. At last order appeared to be superseding chaos. But Nelson, partly because of the number of conflicting agencies that still surrounded him, was unable to strictly control priorities or to prevent overexpansion in unnecessary directions.

The disorderly production boom was an additional reason for the President's creation of the Office of Economic Stabilization under James F. Byrnes. The President now seemed to have found an administrator to suit him. In May, 1943, Byrnes, as head of the new Office of War Mobilization with his office in the White House, was hailed by Roosevelt as the "Assistant President." While May, 1943, was only eighteen months after Pearl Harbor, war production was approaching its peak, and it is only fair to say that Byrnes and his successor, Fred. M. Vinson, never had to face some of the problems encountered by Knudsen and Nelson.

Because the war was fought on many fronts and United States industry was more dispersed, no traffic tie-ups occurred such as that of December, 1917. Material was shipped from Seattle, Portland, Los Angeles, New Orleans, and Baltimore as well as from New York and Philadelphia. Truck transport was available for short and medium hauls. The government also tried to locate new war plants in uncongested areas of the South and West. As a result the railroads were able to function efficiently and there was no serious talk of government administration. The transcontinental railroads did seek relief, however, from their original charter provisions granting special rates to government freight. Pointing out how much more they had remitted to the government than they had originally received in the value of the land grants, they won cancellation of the reduced tariff clauses in 1947.

When the United States entered the war in December, 1941, William Green, president of the American Federation of Labor, and Philip Murray, president of the Congress of Industrial Organizations, together with other prominent labor leaders promised that labor would cooperate in the war effort to the fullest extent and they made a no-strike pledge. The promise and pledge were carried out, in general, though there were some unauthorized strikes. Exceptions to labor's no-strike pledge were the strikes of the United Mine Workers under its aggressive president, John L. Lewis. Early in 1943 a strike by this union forced the government to take over the bituminous mines, which led Congress to pass the Smith-Connally Act over President Roosevelt's veto, a law legalizing the government seizure of strike-bound war plants. In the fall of 1943 the bituminous miners again went on strike, and in 1945 the anthracite miners walked out. The government seized the mines in both cases, but pay increases ended both strikes. A railroad strike in December, 1943, forced the government to take over the railroads for three weeks while wage disputes were being settled. With few exceptions, however, the record of labor during the war was excellent, for the number of man-hours lost through strikes was relatively small. The War Labor Board (WLB), representing management, labor, and the public, had final jurisdiction over labor disputes and wage adjustments, and in 1942 it inaugurated a policy to limit increases of wages to 15 per cent above the level of January 1, 1941—the so-called "Little Steel formula." Protests against this policy by labor leaders because of the rising cost of living caused the War Labor Board to make modifications through vacation pay, increased wages for overtime, and in other ways.

FINANCING THE WAR

Financing such a global war was a great undertaking. Congress made large appropriations in 1940 for the national defense or rearmament program, but the financing of the war may be considered to have begun when the first Series E Savings Bonds were sold in May, 1941, seven months before the Japanese struck at Pearl Harbor, and continued until January, 1946. Between these two dates the United States Treasury sold $185 billion of war securities; additional borrowing raised the total to $201 billion. Of this amount, seven war loan drives, climaxed by a Victory Loan, brought nearly $157 billion. The Liberty Loans of the First World War, which totaled $21 billion, considered large at that time, now appeared small by comparison.

The war loan drives and the sale of United States Savings Bonds between drives were conducted by the War Finance Division of the Treasury Department. The bonds were sold by volunteer groups all over the nation and its possessions. Headquarters of the War Finance Division in Washington coordinated and directed the activities of the field groups—largely volunteers—and provided pamphlets, posters, and other promotional material to stimulate interest in the drives. In addition to securing public participation in the financing program, the sales of bonds were also intended to draw into savings the increased earnings of the public and therefore to combat inflation. Bonds in denominations as low as $25 and savings stamps at ten cents each were sold. Forced saving by law would have been more effective, but was opposed by workers as well as employers. Although banks and corporations purchased a large part of the war bonds, the public exceeded each of the quotas that were set for it, and many employees bought bonds through payroll deductions. As a result of government borrowing, the national debt, which was less than $49 billion in June, 1941, rose to more than $272 billion in June, 1946, or an amount in excess of $6,000 for each family in the United States.

As usual, neither the President nor Congress was willing immediately to raise the taxes necessary to check inflation. In January, 1942, the President asked only for $7 billion in additional tax revenue although $56 billion was being asked for armament and war supplies. But even this wholly inadequate increase caused long debate. By September nothing had been done, and the President made another urgent appeal. Finally, a bill was passed and signed October 21, almost a year after Pearl Harbor. Inadequate as it was, it was still in Roosevelt's words "the greatest tax bill in American history." The corporation income tax was raised to a maximum of 40 per cent with a 90 per cent tax on profits beyond those earned in a peacetime base period. By dropping the individual exemption to $500 and the exemption for married couples to $1200, the number of taxpayers was increased from 13,000,000 to 50,000,000.

If every worker who earned over $500 a year was to be taxed some means of payment other than an annual lump sum was needed. Beardsley Ruml, the Treasurer of Macy's department store, is credited with suggesting the plan of payroll deduction. This not only made taxation of low incomes workable, but also added another important precedent to the growing practice of paying all large bills on the basis of even installments, one of the major elements of the twentieth-century business system.

For his second annual budget message, January, 1943, the President had a more realistic assessment made of the gap between income and individual savings subscribed to bonds, on the one hand, and proposed spending on the other. He said that $16 billion in new taxes would be necessary to "close the inflationary gap." Again the debate seemed endless and the bill, finally passed in February, 1944, added only an estimated $2.2 billion dollars in new revenue. The President vetoed the bill in the interest of both the fixed income groups who would be hurt by inflation, and what were conceived to be the long-run interests of capitalist stability. But large majorities in the House and Senate, responsive to the immediate needs of enterprise, over-rode the President's veto. A major difficulty was that any system that would prevent inflation would have to tax away much of the overtime pay of labor, or else remove it in the form of forced saving, and it was feared that either solution would diminish the will to work.

Of the total of $370 billion spent by the United States government in the five fiscal years of war from July 1, 1941, to June 30, 1946, approximately $169 billion or 46 per cent came from taxes, while the balance of $201 billion or 54 per cent was obtained by borrowing, relatively a much better showing than that of the First World War, when less than one-third of the cost was defrayed by taxation. Expenditures, however, were so great in the Second World War, that the huge national debt caused grave concern, and economists pointed out that its effect on business, employment, and the cost of living would be felt for a long period of time.

SHORTAGES OF MATERIALS AND MEN

The conquests of Japan in the Pacific cut off the supply of crude rubber from British Malaya and the Netherlands Indies. Other sources of supply were sought in South America where only a small fraction of the country's needs could be obtained (chiefly from trees growing wild). Rubber plantations were developed in South America, but since years must elapse from the time trees are planted until they become productive, the shortage in the United States could not be relieved. Among the new plantations was one established by the Ford Motor Company in the Amazon Valley. Guayule, a shrub from which rubber may be obtained after several years' growth, was planted in California and other parts of the United States. For immediate needs, however, the manufacture of increasing quantities of synthetic rubber was projected. Even in 1941, the Standard Oil Company of New Jersey put into operation the first oil refinery equipment built expressly to produce butadiene, a co-product in the manufacture of ethylene and gasoline and the principal material for the manufacture of buna rubber. In 1942, a controversy was waged in Congress over the question of whether its synthetic rubber program should be carried out by the petroleum interests or the agriculturalists who demanded that alcohol made from grain be used. The oil men received financial backing from Congress to carry out the synthetic program, and President Roosevelt appointed William Jeffers, president of the Union Pacific Railroad, as Rubber Controller, with full power in the conservation of the rubber in use and in the manufacture of that to be produced. To replace the tin formerly obtained from the Pacific areas, funds from the United States were given to Bolivia, the chief tin-producing country in the Western Hemisphere, for the development of smelters. In the past, most of its tin ore was shipped to Europe to be refined and therefore it lacked smelters. The most serious of other shortages of essential materials were in silk, manganese, chromium, and copper.

During 1942, many other actions had been taken in the direction of conserving scarce materials, such as a drive for scrap for the steel industry, the rationing of oil for heating in thirty eastern and north-central states, and the strict rationing of gasoline. In the East where restrictions were first imposed, the chief reason for rationing was the shortage of gasoline because of the difficulty of shipment by sea and the need of the military and naval forces. Nation-wide rationing followed, largely to conserve automobile tires because of the shortage of rubber. Elmer Davis, who was made Director of the Office of War Information (OWI), discontinued or curtailed more than 500 government publications.

To get the best use of scarce labor a War Manpower Commission (WMC) was set up to direct millions of men and women voluntarily into war work in the hope of avoiding compulsory action. The WMC undertook to "freeze" labor in order to put an end to labor pirating by making the United States Employment Service the sole agency for hiring highly-skilled war workers. Late in 1942, Paul V. McNutt, Administrator of the Federal Security Agency, was made chairman of the WMC, with broad powers for controlling manpower for both military and civilian purposes. The United States Employment Service was integrated within the Commission and the Selective Service System was put under its control.

THE END OF THE WAR

By the close of 1943 the allied nations were gaining the initiative in the war as victories were won on the outer rim of the conflict areas and the advances of the enemy were stopped. The struggle for North Africa was begun the preceding year with Anglo-American landings in French Morocco and Algeria from an armada of more than 850 warships and transports; it resulted in the conquest of Tunisia and allied control from Gibraltar to Suez. The Middle East, necessary to crush Germany, was held. The mighty Russian counteroffensive had swept from the Volga River to Poland and was pushing toward Germany; the Anglo-American attack on the "soft underbelly of Europe" brought the capture of Sicily, Sardinia, and all of southern Italy, Naples, and Foggia, although progress into Italy at first was slow. The American drives in the Pacific areas, marked by sea battles, amphibious landings, and jungle fighting, led to the capture of many bases necessary to surround and defeat Japan. The economic might of the United States was turning the tide of the conflict in favor of the Allies as men, airplanes, and supplies were poured into the conflict areas.

The allied strategy of war, a strategy based on the industrial superiority of the United States, was showing results. The decisions to utilize completely the economic power of the United States as the "arsenal of democracy" for all the allied nations and to concentrate first on the defeat of Germany had been fortunate ones. The transoceanic supply lines had been made safe by the defeat of the German submarine campaign, and allied objectives were being achieved. The invasion of France from the west and the south was the logical culmination of all the preceding campaigns.

The invasion of Normandy on June 6, 1944, was followed by continued Russian victories in the East, by the American liberation of the Philippines, and finally by the conquest of Germany. Carrying out plans agreed upon by the United States, the Russian army reached the Oder River and stood poised for the final assault on Berlin, which was captured after bitter fighting. In their drives westward to Berlin, the Russians were aided by the possession of 400,000 American motor vehicles, 6,000 tanks, 13,000 planes, 300,000 tons of explosives, as well as by allied air operations against Germany. A few days before Berlin fell, Benito Mussolini, the Italian dictator, was captured by Italian partisans and executed. Hitler apparently died amid the flames and ruins of Berlin as the Russians entered the city. On May 7, 1945, the Germans surrendered unconditionally, and the following day was proclaimed Victory-in-Europe Day, or V-E Day.

In the midst of the triumphant advances of the Allies and just as victory in Europe seemed assured, people all over the world were shocked to hear of the sudden death of President Franklin D. Roosevelt (April 12, 1945). The previous February the President had conferred at Yalta in the Crimea with Prime Minister Churchill and Joseph Stalin, one of the several conferences held by the allied leaders, and on March 1, 1945, although broken in health, he had appeared before a joint session of Congress to present a report on the Yalta conference. The death of President Roosevelt brought Vice-President Harry S. Truman to the Presidency, and the American people gave him whole-hearted support to complete the task of winning the war.

American successes in the Pacific, although accomplished with many casualties, prepared the way for attack on Japan. An invasion never took place, for early in August, 1945, an American plane dropped on Hiroshima, a city of 300,000 inhabitants, a new and terrible weapon of war—an atomic bomb. The bomb destroyed the city and killed 50,000 of its inhabitants. A similar bomb, dropped on a second Japanese city, Nagasaki, caused great loss of life and much destruction. After President Truman warned the Japanese government that similar bombs would follow if it did not give up, Japan surrendered on August 14, 1945.

CHAPTER 28

Government and the New Order

The combination of the New Deal and the Second World War so increased the strength of organized labor, re-allocated income through higher wages and taxes, increased social security, and tied the economy to government policy that the sum amounted to a revolution. New attitudes toward consumption, saving, and old age arose; old social lines became blurred; and new theories had to be developed to explain the behavior of the economy. The present chapter provides the background of legislation and changes in government policy affecting the economy.

THE COST OF WAR

The Second World War was the costliest and most destructive in history. The total military and civilian dead of all nations reached 22,000,000, while the number of maimed and wounded has been estimated at 34,500,000. The United States shared in these vast losses; her casualties in all branches of the services all over the world exceeded 1,000,000, with almost 400,000 dead. The vast destruction of property during the war is difficult to comprehend. Large armies were engaged in battles in the air, and for the first time the capitals of nations were marked for destruction. London, Berlin, Warsaw, and Tokyo were ravaged by air raids. Many cities, especially in Europe, lay in ruins,

612

FEDERAL EXPENDITURES—WORLD WAR I AND WORLD WAR II
(In billions of dollars)

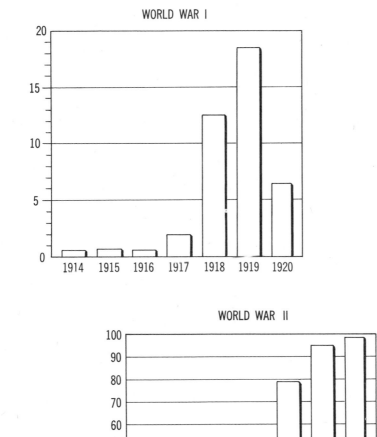

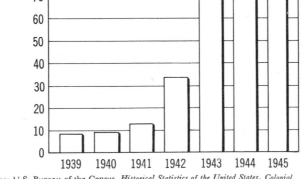

Source: U.S. Bureau of the Census, *Historical Statistics of the United States, Colonial Times to 1957*, Washington, D.C., 1960, p. 718.

and the destruction of private property was appalling. The two Japanese cities, Hiroshima and Nagasaki, were completely leveled by atomic bombs. The United States, except for the Hawaiian Islands and other possessions, suffered no damage from air raids, although precautions were taken against possible attacks. However, hundreds of American merchant ships, as well as the vessels of allied and of neutral nations, were sunk, largely through the attacks of the enemy's U-boats. During the war the United States navy lost 696 vessels, among them two battleships, 11 aircraft carriers, and 10 cruisers. The naval losses of the British Empire totaled almost 800 ships. Germany's navy practically disappeared except for a large fleet of submarines; the Italian fleet had been sunk or captured; at the end of the war, only remnants of the Japanese navy remained afloat. The Second World War cost the Allies and neutral countries a total of 4,770 ships, aggregating 21,140,000 gross tons. Of this, the losses of the United States totaled 3,310,000 tons.

The direct financial cost of the war has been estimated at well over a trillion dollars. Soon after the conflict was over, President Truman stated that the direct war costs for the United States alone amounted to $341 billions, roughly one-third of the total direct cost to all belligerents except China, whose war costs were unknown. America's war expenditure, which forced the national debt to dizzy heights, was used not only to equip the services of the United States in the conflict, but also to aid the Allies in carrying on a global war.

THE ADJUSTMENT TO A PEACETIME ECONOMY

The end of hostilities brought many problems of adjustment as the nation shifted from a wartime to a peacetime economy.

In the Army, men were discharged individually rather than by groups or units, preference being given to those who had served longest, had been overseas, had engaged in active combat, had dependents, and had received certain combat awards. A plan provided for the release of men who had accumulated eighty-five points, a requirement which was progressively lowered, especially as replacements became available. After the fall of Japan, the Marine Corps established a system similar to the Army, while the Navy and Coast Guard introduced a plan, granting one-half point for each year of age, one-half point for each month of active duty during the war, and a number of points for dependents.

Each discharged veteran received information regarding his rights and also advice about agencies which could help him find employment.

Benefits included unemployment payments for a period of time, insurance, priority rights in the purchase of certain supplies and surplus war materials, and financial loans to begin business or to purchase homes. Thousands of veterans returned to secondary schools and colleges under the Servicemen's Readjustment Act of 1944 (the G.I. Bill of Rights), and higher educational institutions experienced an unprecedented expansion. The Veterans Administration was reorganized and General Omar Bradley, well-known infantry officer of the war, was made its head. Although much was done to help the veterans re-establish themselves, many found that in the booming economy transportation facilities were overburdened, hotels crowded, living quarters difficult to secure, certain food products scarce and expensive, and automobiles almost impossible to obtain.

The Selective Service Act of 1940, with its extensions, under which millions had been drafted, expired in 1947. Early the next year President Truman asked for new legislation to bring the armed forces to their authorized strength, and stated that "our badly depleted military strength is one of the nation's greatest dangers." The Selective Service Act of 1948 was the second peacetime draft law in the history of the nation (the first being the act of 1940). The new law provided for building up the armed forces and reserve components; it authorized a total of about 2,000,000 men in the active forces of the United States. In the meantime, in 1947, on the recommendation of the President, Congress enacted a measure unifying the armed forces, making them a single National Military establishment. In place of the Secretary of the Army and Secretary of the Navy, the law provided for a single Secretary of National Defense with Cabinet status. Under him, provision was made for three co-equal departments—Army, Navy, and Air Force—each headed by a Secretary, none of whom, however, is in the Cabinet.

The end of the war required a readjustment of industry from its high-speed production of war materials to peacetime production. After the surrender of Japan, the Federal government cancelled more than $30 billion worth of war contracts on a basis of adjusted compensation, and the government began to work out plans to relax its wartime controls over industry, labor, and prices. Industry re-tooled for peacetime needs and, in spite of shortages of tools, machinery, and equipment, and labor disputes and strikes, the shift was made with surprisingly little difficulty and a minimum of unemployment. By the summer of 1947, employment exceeded 60,000,000, the highest record in American history up to that time. President Truman reported to Congress that the nation enjoyed unprecedented prosperity, with a

VALUE OF GROSS NATIONAL PRODUCT IN 1954 PRICES, 1929 – 1960
(In billions of dollars)

Year	GNP	Year	GNP	Year	GNP	Year	GNP
1929	181.8	1937	183.5	1945	314.0	1953	369.0
1930	164.5	1938	175.1	1946	282.5	1954	363.1
1931	153.0	1939	189.3	1947	282.3	1955	392.7
1932	130.1	1940	205.8	1948	293.1	1956	402.2
1933	126.6	1941	238.1	1949	292.7	1957	407.0
1934	138.5	1942	266.9	1950	318.1	1958	401.3
1935	152.9	1943	296.7	1951	341.8	1959	428.4
1936	173.3	1944	317.9	1952	353.5	1960	440.8

Sources: U.S. Bureau of the Census, *Historical Statistics of the United States, Colonial Times to 1957*, Washington, D.C., 1960, p. 143; and *Statistical Abstract of the United States, 1962*, Washington, D.C., 1962, p. 314.

production for goods and services at about $225 billion a year, a figure that was surpassed in 1948.

Before the war ended, but looking forward to peace and reconversion, Congress established the Office of War Mobilization and Reconversion (1944). Its purposes were: (1) to unify programs and establish policies relating to manpower and industrial needs to carry the war to a successful conclusion; and (2) to coordinate government planning of manpower and all other resources during the reconversion to peace. The agency took over the duties and functions of the Office of War Mobilization, which had been set up in 1943. It established the Surplus Property Administration to dispose of $100 billion worth of surplus war property, including war plants, war materials, and agricultural commodities. Plans to sell or lease the more than 1,500 government-owned plants were begun. The disposal of surplus property abroad was handled by another agency, the Office of Foreign Liquidation, under the supervision of the Department of State. The sale of war surpluses at home and abroad presented many problems and required time, but plans were devised and carried out without great difficulty.

POSTWAR INFLATION

One of the most serious aspects of reconversion was the threat of runaway inflation. The shortages of many commodities, together with the large amount of wartime savings and the expansion of the currency and bank credits, kept prices high and brought apprehension as to whether inflation could be held in check. Shortages of raw materials and finished products were widespread. Manufacturers required new machines and tools as well as materials such as steel, rubber, wood, and copper; the railroads needed equipment of all sorts; and consumers demanded automobiles, refrigerators, and other durable goods, the production of which had been largely cut off during the war. Many food items were in short supply, especially meat, butter, fats, and flour, at a time when the people of Europe and the Orient were facing starvation and Americans were trying to aid them.

As the war ended, many government controls were removed. In the fall of 1945 the War Production Board announced the termination of the Controlled Material Plan, which had immeasurably aided the production of war materials; the priority system of allocating materials was greatly modified. Before the close of 1945, the War Production Board was abolished and the Civilian Production Administration took over its functions. Other war agencies were dissolved and any essential activities remaining were taken over by peacetime bureaus.

Even before victory had been fully achieved, many articles were dropped from the ration list, and after V-J Day consolidation of some of the district offices and local boards of the Office of Price Administration was begun. Special interests and some consumers demanded the elimination of all government controls, though Chester Bowles, head of the OPA, with popular support, opposed the demand, insisting that it was necessary to hold the line against uncontrolled inflation. President Truman insisted upon strict controls, while a divided and turbulent Congress finally gave the President only a weak and unenforceable measure. As a result, the OPA was liquidated and there remained controls only over rents and a few scarce commodities. Meat, which had been difficult to get, was now decontrolled and appeared in larger quantities, but prices of all commodities skyrocketed. Food prices, which had advanced about 50 per cent during the war, spiralled about 60 per cent more during the last half of 1946. The inflationary rise continued, but not as rapidly as in 1946, until the fall of 1948 and the spring of 1949, when it became evident that the postwar boom was slowing down as inventories of goods increased and, in some lines, a seller's market became a buyer's market. Though the downward trend continued, food prices, bolstered by government policies, could not find low levels, and it became evident that there would be no sharp change in economic conditions.

In attempting to solve postwar problems, though congressmen showed honest differences of opinion on many issues, a trend to return to the politics of special interests of the 1920's became evident. In 1946 a Full Employment Bill (p. 644) established an important precedent for government responsibility for the economy. Designed to attack unemployment in periods of depression, the bill was watered down so that when it was finally accepted by the Republican-Democrat coalition, it provided only for a board to advise the President. Bills for a Missouri Valley Authority, the extension of social security to millions not covered, a long-range Federal public housing program, and appropriations for cancer research all failed. Yet congressmen rushed to secure a share in a large pork barrel measure, a River and Harbor Improvements catchall, while the desire for social security moved them to establish a congressional pension system and to increase their salaries to $12,500 with a tax-exempt expense account of $2,500 annually.

INTERNATIONAL ECONOMIC RELATIONS

As a result of the war, most of the countries of Europe were prostrate, and it was obvious that it would take years to repair the damage of six years of ruinous warfare. In the countries that had suffered most severely, it was beyond the ability of private enterprise to rebuild quickly enough, and the people of many European nations turned to their governments for collective action in rebuilding communities and in seeking to restore conditions necessary for full employment and prosperity. A socialistic trend therefore developed in many countries. In Britain, under the leadership of the Labour party, the government developed its program to nationalize mines, banking, transportation, utilities, and the steel industry, as well as to launch government housing projects and to put into effect a comprehensive plan of social security. In France and elsewhere, socialization made rapid gains, but these nations were forced to turn to the United States for financial aid to carry out their plans for rehabilitation.

The United Nations Relief and Rehabilitation Administration (UNRRA), which was set up in November, 1943, to aid the victims of war and invasion, took up the work of relief. Led by the United States, forty-eight nations agreed to aid the peoples of liberated countries with food, clothing, agricultural implements, seed, and other supplies;

the contributions of the nations were levied on the basis of national income. Herbert H. Lehman, former governor of New York, became Director General of UNRRA, and he was succeeded in 1946 by Fiorello H. La Guardia, ex-mayor of New York City. Disbanded in 1947, UNRRA had distributed more than $3.5 billion worth of supplies. In that year the more comprehensive European Recovery Plan was formulated. In the meantime, the United States had granted loans and aid to many governments, including a loan to Britain of $3.75 billion.

Before the war had ended, statesmen realized the momentous problems that peace would bring. Therefore, in July, 1944, representatives of forty-four nations met at Bretton Woods, New Hampshire, to plan international monetary arrangements for the postwar world. The conference agreed to establish a large monetary fund to which each member nation would contribute on the basis of its financial ability for the purpose of stabilizing the money values of their currencies and to assist in international exchange connected with world trade. Under the plan the International Bank for Reconstruction and Development, or World Bank, was established. The Articles of Agreement adopted at Bretton Woods set forth the aims of the plan, which of course centered in reconstruction. Participation by the United States was authorized when Congress enacted the Bretton Woods Agreement law of 1945.

The World Bank began operations in June, 1946, with headquarters at Washington, D.C. Its authorized capital was $10 billion, of which $7.67 billion was subscribed by thirty-eight of the nations represented at the Bretton Woods Conference; by 1949, eight other countries had become members, bringing the total subscriptions to over $8 billion, although each nation paid but 20 per cent of its allotment; 2 per cent in gold or dollars and 18 per cent in its own currency. The unpaid 80 per cent of the subscribed capital was reserved to meet the bank's obligations. The subscription of the United States totaled over $3 billion, of which 20 per cent, or $635,000,000, was paid in.

Loans by the World Bank are financed out of the paid-in portion of the capital stock and from funds borrowed from the capital markets of the world. Beginning in 1947 loans were made to member nations and to private corporations. Loans varied from those granted to the Netherlands, Denmark, and Luxembourg to those in the form of ten-year serial mortgage notes granted to Dutch shipping companies, guaranteed by the Kingdom of the Netherlands.

The hope to maintain international peace after the war resulted in a conference held in 1944 at Dumbarton Oaks, a former private estate just within Washington, D.C. Here representatives of the United

States, Britain, the Union of Soviet Socialist Republics, and China drew up plans for an international peace organization after the war. Proposals were made for an organization similar to the decadent League of Nations, but with power to enforce its decisions in order to control any aggressor nation. As a result of the conference, President Franklin D. Roosevelt issued a call for the United Nations Conference on International Organization to meet at San Francisco on April 25, 1945. The President expected to address the assembled delegates, but died two weeks before the meeting.

The United Nations Conference, held from April 25 to June 26, 1945, at San Francisco was a most impressive gathering of delegates from all over the world, made colorful by different races, languages, and costumes. Presiding over the conference was Edward R. Stettinius, American Secretary of State, successor to Cordell Hull, who had planned the conference but had been forced to resign because of illness. After two months of heated debate, the Charter of the United Nations was finally completed and on June 26 it was signed by the representatives of fifty nations; later several other nations were admitted to membership. The Charter pledged the member nations to maintain international peace and security and to cooperate in establishing political, economic and social conditions favorable to the attainment of these objectives. Six major organs were created to accomplish the purposes of the United Nations: the General Assembly, the Security Council, the Economic and Social Council, the Trusteeship Council, the International Court of Justice, and the Secretariat.

The General Assembly, composed of delegates from all the member nations, considers any matter within the scope of the Charter except issues and disputes already on the agenda of the Security Council. The Security Council is composed of eleven members, of whom five— the United States, the United Kingdom, France, U.S.S.R., and China— are permanent and the other six elected; it is charged with the responsibility of maintaining peace and security, and to enforce its mandates it can call on the armed forces and for other assistance of member nations.

The Economic and Social Council established several agencies to carry on various aspects of its work. Among these, the United Nations Educational, Scientific, and Cultural Organization (UNESCO) is designed to promote international intellectual cooperation through the free exchange of information and ideas on education, art, and science. The Food and Agricultural Organization has the task of raising nutritional levels throughout the world. The International Labor Organization, formerly an agency of the League of Nations, attempts to improve working conditions in all countries. The function of the Provisional International Civil Aviation Organization is to unify international aviation procedures. The World Bank was placed under the jurisdiction of the Economic and Social Council. The World Health Organization coordinates the battle against disease and takes measures to raise the health standards of member nations, while the International Refugee Organization aids in relocating refugees and displaced persons.

EUROPEAN RECOVERY PLANS

The tremendous demand for American goods presented the need for a reduction in tariff rates, for without dollars secured from the sale of their products to the United States, foreign governments could not pay for their purchases in the United States except by borrowing dollars. An act of 1945 gave the President power to cut rates 50 per cent in addition to the 50 per cent authorized in the Reciprocal Trade Agreements Act of 1934. In 1947, the United States and twenty-two other nations, engaged in two-thirds of the world's commerce, agreed to cut tariff rates. The United States pledged itself to reduce duties on a large number of articles up to the 50 per cent permitted.

Later in 1947 another step was taken in lowering world trade barriers at a United Nations Conference on Trade and Unemployment held at Havana, Cuba. Representatives of sixty nations, engaged in 90 per cent of all international commerce, attended the conference. A charter was drawn up at the Havana meeting to create an International Trade Organization (ITO), which was to become an agency of the United Nations, responsible to the Economic and Social Council, after the charter was ratified by the member nations. The charter laid down a detailed code of rules to govern trade relationship, and the ITO was designed to promote world trade and to stimulate employment in order to raise living standards all over the world. In 1955, Congress gave the President power to reduce duties an additional 15 per cent.

Early in June, 1947, Secretary of State Marshall delivered an address at a Harvard Commencement in which he set forth the principles of American policy toward the postwar rehabilitation of Europe. He announced the intention of the United States to aid European nations in their recovery plans, and stated: "In considering the requirements for the rehabilitation of Europe, the physical loss of life, the visible destruction of cities, factories, mines, and railroads were correctly estimated, but it has become obvious during recent months that this visible destruction was probably less serious than the dislocation of

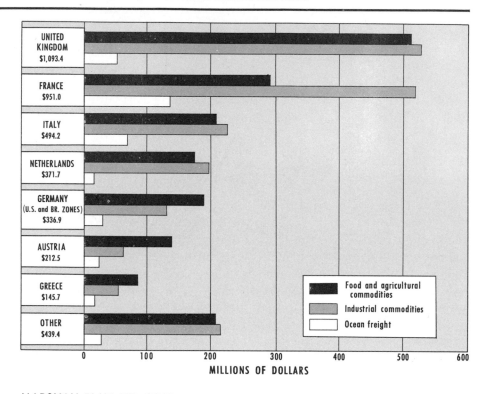

MARSHALL PLAN AID, 1948

European Recovery Program—American funds as allocated according to country and commodity group.

the entire fabric of European economy." By the summer of 1947, UNRRA had suspended operations in Europe, after having expended $3.5 billion, while during the two years after the war the United States had expended $10 billion in credits, grants, and loans for aid abroad. Yet economic recovery had made little headway.

Secretary of State Marshall suggested that European countries requiring American aid should cooperate in drawing up a program to present their needs. Britain and France quickly took up the suggestion which became known as the Marshall Plan. British Foreign Secretary Bevin and French Foreign Minister Bidault, after consulting Prime Minister Molotov of the Soviet Union, issued invitations on July 3, 1947, to all the European nations (except Spain) to participate in a conference at Paris for the purpose of discussing a unified reconstruction program.

On July 12, 1947, representatives of sixteen European nations met at Paris. By this time the Soviet Union had taken a hostile attitude toward the conference and, together with her eight satellites, declined the invitation. The Conference on European Economic Cooperation appointed a number of committees to study the needs of the various parts of Europe, including western Germany. At its final session in September, 1947, the conference adopted a report which called for a total of $21.78 billion in credits and loans from 1948 to the end of 1951. The report assumed that the International Bank for Reconstruction and Development and private investors would extend additional credits of a little more than $3.1 billion during the four-year period for the purchase of machinery and industrial equipment, thus reducing the necessary American aid to about $19 billion. The sixteen participating countries pledged themselves to internal financial and economic stabilization and to mutual aid among themselves. The program provided for achieving stabilized national currencies, lower trade barriers between the nations, common pools of power resources, and standardization on railroads. Production goals were set for agriculture, industry, and mining.

On receiving the report, President Truman summoned Congress and asked for more immediate aid to Britain, France, and Italy, and for $17 billion for the European Recovery Program (ERP), an amount to be expended by the summer of 1952, for the relief of European countries and for rebuilding European industries to make that continent self-supporting again. Such aid was in harmony with the United Nations Charter, and an economically strong Europe was essential to the prosperity of the United States. The young United Nations could not undertake such a program, and the United States therefore proposed to do so.

In accordance with the request of the President, Congress voted more than half a billion dollars for "stop-gap" aid to Britain, France, and Italy. In April, 1948, it passed the Foreign Assistance Act, which appropriated $5.3 billion for the first year of the European Recovery Program, and Congress took the attitude that additional appropriations would be made, beginning in 1949, on the basis of how well the plan worked. Most Americans believed that such European aid was necessary, though some objected, especially on the grounds that England and France, nationalizing many of their industries, were moving, together with other European countries, in the direction of establishing socialist states. Early in 1949, the Organization for European Economic Cooperation (OEEC) reported that much progress had been made among nineteen nations that had been aided by the economic recovery program and asked for several billions for the second year of operation. In April, President Truman signed a bill passed by Congress authorizing an expenditure of $5.430 billion to carry the European Recovery Program through June 30, 1950.

The threat of Russian aggression caused many nations to continue to keep large armies and navies. For the fiscal year from July 1, 1949, to June 30, 1950, the military budget of the United States reached $15 billion, an amount dictated largely by the necessity of keeping the nation strong against any military moves of Russia. The fear of Russian agression against the nations of western and northern Europe resulted in April, 1949, in the Atlantic Security Alliance, or North Atlantic Pact, which was sponsored by the United States. The North Atlantic Pact, ratified by the Senate in July, 1949, was the second multilateral defensive agreement signed by the United States at this time, the first being the Western Hemisphere Pact, made in September, 1947, at Rio de Janeiro; the terms of the two pacts were quite similar.

VALUE OF UNITED STATES FOREIGN AID, 1945 – 1959
(In billions of dollars)

		1945–1950	1951–1956	1957–1959
Net Nonmilitary Grants	Western Europe	10.9	5.4	0.6
	Asia, Africa, Near East	4.6	5.0	3.5
	Rest of World	1.6	0.6	0.7
	Total	17.1	11.0	4.8
Net Government Loans	Western Europe	8.1	0.2	−0.5
	Asia, Africa, Near East	0.7	0.8	0.6
	Rest of World	0.6	0.5	0.8
	Total	9.4	1.5	0.9
Net Military Grants	Western Europe	0.3	11.0	2.8
	Asia, Africa, Near East	1.4	5.1	4.1
	Rest of World	0.1	0.5	0.3
	Total	1.8	16.6	7.2
Grants and Loans: Net Total		28.3	29.2	12.9

Source: *Information Please Almanac, 1962*, p. 590.

The Department of State of the United States did everything possible to aid the consolidation of the European countries for the purpose of promoting confidence, peace, and future security. When the Marshall Plan ended in 1951, it was succeeded by the Mutual Security Agency (MSA), which emphasized the building of the defensive strength of the free nations. The work of the Mutual Security Program was later carried on by the Foreign Operations Administration (FOA). As a by-product of the Marshall Plan, some restrictions on trade between European countries were scaled down and a European Payments Union furthered trade between countries by providing commercial credits.

In 1950 Robert Schuman, a French statesman, proposed a merger of the iron, steel, and coal controls for western Europe, thus creating a market in a basic industry with 175,000,000 customers. France, Italy, West Germany, and the Benelux countries accepted the plan, but Britain refused to join until 1961. The European Coal-Steel Community was launched in 1952 when its Assembly met at Strasbourg, France. By pooling their coal, iron, and steel resources the six continental countries would be in a position to raise standards and also manufacture armaments for self-defense.

THE WESTERN HEMISPHERE

Undoubtedly the concern of the United States government over events in Europe and the Far East took attention from Latin America. While the Latin nations did not receive Marshall Plan aid, they were aided by loans from the United States government and the World Bank. In spite of the "good neighbor" policy, it continued to be popular in South and Central America to blame the United States for whatever was wrong, and in the United States there was a tendency to assume that these nations should support whatever policies were decided on in Washington. Prior to 1960 this smoldering or subsurface ill will appeared to have had little effect on United States-Latin-American trade and economic relations. Adjusted for changes in price and the size of the economies a rough generalization can be made that from 1947 to 1957 there was no significant change in the volume of either imports from, or exports to the Latin-American nations.

The most serious problems in the fifties came in Venezuela and Cuba. In Venezuela the problem was to preserve large United States oil and iron ore concessions. A strong radical movement continuously threatened nationalization of these resources. In 1959 Romulo Betancourt, a middle-of-the-road president, friendly to the United States, won a five-year term and managed to preserve the status quo. In Cuba the United States was less fortunate. Here the dictatorial and corrupt regime of Fulgencio Batista was overthrown early in 1959 by Fidel Castro. From the start Castro's ideas were too radical to suit the large United States property interests in Cuba, and the two governments became increasingly unfriendly. Within a year Castro had nationalized a large share of United States property and formed close ties with Russia; in retaliation President Eisenhower cut, and ultimately eliminated the Cuban sugar quota. These actions practically ended trade normally amounting to nearly a billion dollars a year, or over 10 per cent of the Latin-American total.

While politically the United States was worried by an enemy so close to its shores, and a number of citizens and corporations suffered large losses, two outlying parts of the United States and other Caribbean sugar countries gained. The revised sugar quotas gave increases to Hawaii and Puerto Rico and benefited other United States sugar growers. Puerto Rico also gained a large part of the valuable Cuban tourist trade.

In this same year of important hemispheric events Alaska and Hawaii became respectively the 49th and 50th states. Puerto Rico had been granted "commonwealth" status in 1950, which allowed autonomous internal government, but kept military and foreign affairs in the hands of the United States. Puerto Rico participated in agricultural benefits, and the United States gave the insular government the tariff duties collected on goods imported to it from foreign nations. Both independence and statehood parties existed, but Governor Muñoz Marin, the champion of the Commonwealth, continued to win over 60 per cent of the vote.

Meanwhile, Canada continually became closer to the United States. The northern defense of the continent was a joint undertaking; capital investors paid little attention to the international boundary; and total trade stood at about $7 billion a year by 1957.

FEDERAL FINANCES

In June of 1950 President Truman decided to prevent the conquest of South Korea by communist North Korea. With Russia absent, the Security Council of the United Nations agreed to support the United States action. Three years of fighting led to re-establishment of the prewar situation. The effect on United States defense expenditure, however, was of major importance and appeared to be permanent. The first year of the war Federal defense expenditures jumped $7 billion and in the next two years $25 billion more. This established a level of nearly $44 billion annually for defense. In succeeding years this amount was cut back a few billion dollars, but by 1960 military expenditures were again above $40 billion and headed upward.

The Korean War was financed on a pay-as-you-go basis. Sharp increases in excise, corporation, and personal income taxes were asked for by the President and made effective by Congress on October 1, 1950. A 30 per cent tax on excess profits above a 1946–1949 base went into effect and remained until January 1, 1954. There was sharp inflation in 1950, but it was caused by panicky buying rather than government spending.

People gradually became used to these high levels of taxation and defense spending, neither of which changed much during the next decade. In the thirties Federal taxes of all types paid by individuals had taken about 3 per cent of personal income. From 1951 on the figure ranged between 11½ and 12½ per cent. In 1954 an overhaul of Federal tax laws was completed. Removal of many inequities to business and individuals lowered revenue more than a billion dollars. The thousand-page bill, which President Eisenhower declared was the cornerstone of his legislative program, stressed encouragement to private enterprise. Business losses could be applied against the taxes of two previous years or carried forward over a seven-year period. Accelerated depreciation was allowed on new plants and equipment and double taxation of stock dividends was modified. For individuals, tax savings were provided on such items as estates, sick leave, dependents, and installment buying.

During the remainder of the Eisenhower administration and two years of the Kennedy administration there were only minor changes in tax policies. In each session of Congress tax cuts were demanded, and until 1963 the President resisted them in the cause of trying to balance the budget. There seemed to be no consistent tendency for the administration to use tax policy to counterbalance the swings of the business cycle. From 1946 to 1962 any counter-cyclical effects of Federal taxation appeared to be more from chance than from design. After carefully analyzing Federal fiscal policy E. Cary Brown concluded: "The generalization that all of us have made from time to time—that expansionary fiscal action will be taken promptly in a recession—and that, therefore, there is an inflationary bias in fiscal action is simply not borne out by the facts."[1] President Kennedy's proposal for tax reductions in 1963, however, gave new force to the earlier view.

[1] Ralph Freeman, ed., *Post War Economic Trends* (Harper & Brothers, 1960), p. 186.

In general the budget remained unbalanced. The net Federal debt declined slightly in four years of the Truman and two years of the Eisenhower administration, but rose over the period from $230 billion in 1946 to $286 billion in 1960. On a per capita basis, however, the debt generally declined from 1945 on, and in relation to gross national product it sank rapidly. Congress harassed the Treasury Department in its financing by placing limits on the size of the gross public debt, which had to be raised from time to time.

GOVERNMENT AIDS TO THE ECONOMY

One of the few marked changes in policy between the Truman and Eisenhower administrations involved hydroelectric power. President Eisenhower was opposed to federal construction of power dams if local government or private capital was available. Examples of the Eisenhower policy were the unsatisfactory effort to have a private company build a new dam in the Tennessee Valley, ultimately taken over by the city of Memphis, and three small private dams on the Snake River in place of one large federally-financed project. Pursuing this policy of decentralizing the development of resources, the President ordered the oil lands off the shores of Texas and California given to the respective states.

Construction of a deep water seaway through the upper St. Lawrence Valley to the Great Lakes urged by Canadian and middle-western interests for decades (p. 600) was finally approved by Congress in 1954. A St. Lawrence Seaway Development Co., financed by the United States and the St. Lawrence Seaway Authority of Canada, divided the work between them. Opened April 25, 1959, the Seaway ran 400 miles and cost half a billion dollars, the most extensive waterway project since the Panama Canal. Partly because of bad winters, the early economic effects of the Seaway were not as great as its opponents had feared or its backers had hoped.

The Reconstruction Finance Corporation that had loaned $49 billion to business without net loss during its twenty-one year life span was liquidated in 1954. The year before a Small Business Administration had been established to make limited loans and to provide advisory services to business. At the end of its first year of operation it had loaned or guaranteed loans for only $5,000,000; by 1959 the figure was still under half a billion. Thus, the government had largely withdrawn from competition with financial institutions in private lending, but was seeking to aid small enterprise that was not able to raise funds through commercial channels.

Queen Elizabeth II and President Eisenhower
at the opening of the St. Lawrence Seaway

Although Congress was under Republican control from 1947 to 1949 and 1953 to 1955, no important changes were made in the general policies affecting guarantee of homeowners' mortgages. Federal housing, however, was cut back to 45,000 units a year for the four years starting in 1955. In 1959, a Democratic Congress tried to force major extensions of the building program upon the President, but he vetoed two successive bills as "defective" and "inflationary," and Congress finally compromised on only 37,000 units a year for the next two years. The bill, however, increased mortgage guarantee funds by $8 billion, increased the amounts that homeowners could borrow, extended the time of repayment to 30 years, and increased funds for college housing and projects for the aged. In 1963, the Democrats passed a more liberal bill that authorized $4.9 billion in expenditures over a four-year period.

Federal aid to transcontinental railroads from 1862 to 1870, largely in the form of land, was paralleled after the Second World War by Federal grants for highway construction. Starting at about a quarter of a billion in 1946 the annual Federal subsidy had reached two billion in 1958. In that year Congress passed a bill sponsored by President

Eisenhower to spend an additional $25 billion during the next 12 years for a 41,000 mile interstate highway system. This would nearly equal the mileage of all railroad track built in the twelve years following the Civil War. For the highways covered by this bill the Federal government would put up 90 per cent of the cost. By 1960 it appeared that the program would cost nearly $40 billion instead of $25 billion. Thus the government in the interests of national defense and economic growth underwrote roads for trucks, buses, and countless other business and personal uses.

SOCIAL WELFARE

At the beginning of his first administration President Eisenhower created a new Department of Health, Education, and Welfare. Although divisions of opinion within Congress and between the President and Congress prevented important legislation for national health and limited aid to education to buildings, the department undoubtedly represented another milestone in the growth of the welfare state.

Social Security administration was placed in the new department. The amount and coverage of social security were increased by laws of 1954 and 1958. By the latter law almost all jobs were covered by either social security or special state or federal programs for their own workers. The medical profession and employees of certain non-profit organizations were the principal groups not covered by any compulsory government-administered program for old-age pensions. For social security, employers and employees were taxed equally on the latter's income up to $4,800 a year. The tax rates, starting at $2\frac{1}{2}$ per cent, were to advance in 1960, 1962, 1965, and 1969 until they reached $4\frac{1}{2}$ per cent each, or 9 per cent total. On this basis the system was expected to be self-sustaining. Maximum benefits for a husband and wife over 65 were $190.50 a month. Since taxpayers over 65 received double exemptions, this income would be tax free. A new law in 1961 made only minor changes in these provisions.

Thus, while socialism in the form of government ownership of the means of production had not advanced greatly since 1945, socialization of risk in the form of insurance, Federal subsidies, and aid to business was progressing steadily. By the standards of 1920, the United States of 1960 was an advanced social democracy.

CHAPTER 29

Money Markets, Banks, and Business Cycles

While economic development depends basically on resources, technology, entrepreneurship, and distribution of the resulting production, in a capitalist economy the mechanisms of the money market exert great influence. The supply of money, the ways of raising capital, and the means of financing demand all help to set the tempo of growth and select the avenues of development.

MONEY AND PRICES, 1914–1934

Money has a number of forms. As explained in Chapter 19, demand deposits in banks are potential money supply, and the rate at which checks are drawn and circulate is just as important as the circulation of currency or specie. Time or savings deposits can also be used as money, but since banks will not allow such deposits to be drawn against, frequently their rate of circulation as money is slow. By creating new deposits, bank loans or investments also add to the money supply. Thus the actual amount of currency and specie is important chiefly for its effect on limiting bank loans, investments, and deposits. The key elements are the amount of banking resources, the limits to credit expansion imposed by legal reserves, and the speed with which bank resources work as money.

631

CONSUMER PRICE INDEX, 1914 – 1934
(1947–1949 = 100)

Year	All Items	Year	All Items	Year	All Items
1914	42.9	1921	76.4	1928	73.3
1915	43.4	1922	71.6	1929	73.3
1916	46.6	1923	72.9	1930	71.4
1917	54.8	1924	73.1	1931	65.0
1918	64.3	1925	75.0	1932	58.4
1919	74.0	1926	75.6	1933	55.3
1920	85.7	1927	74.2	1934	57.2

Source: U.S. Bureau of the Census, *Historical Statistics of the United States*, *Colonial Times to 1957*, Washington, D.C., 1960, pp. 125–126.

From 1897 to 1914, in a period of general prosperity and increasing demand, both gold reserves and the use of bank deposits increased faster than the need for money in business transactions. This trend occurred in all the leading countries, and world prices rose year after year. From the beginning of the First World War inflation grew rapidly from the creation of government debt which was turned into demand deposits by having banks buy or lend on government bonds. In the United States bank deposits increased $11.2 billion between 1916 and 1919, and the consumer price index rose from 46.6 points to 74. As can be seen in the table above, after the sharp deflation of 1921 and 1922 the index remained fairly steady during the prosperous twenties.

This price stability was one of the misleading features of the boom in 1928 and 1929. In earlier American history prices had always risen from excessive demand during the peak of boom periods, but from 1926 to 1929 prices fell slightly. In retrospect, this demonstrated two factors: first, that the boom, in spite of its high levels of speculation, was not fully using the resources of the economy; and that in the absence of increased demand, the potential ability of the banking system to create more money did not raise prices.

THE PEAK OF SMALL UNIT BANKING

The desire of the businessmen and farmers of each local community to have their own bank had always run counter to the greater security, stability, and economy that would result from a few large banks with branches. Furthermore, the local people apparently resented Federal restrictions on the operation of their banks and therefore preferred state to national charters. In 1910 there were over 17,000 state-chartered banks or trust companies doing a commercial banking business, and only a little over 7,000 national banks. But the total assets of the national banks was $9.9 billion as against $9.4 billion for the others. In 1921 the increase in small state banks reached its maximum with nearly 23,000 out of a total of just over 31,000 commercial banks, and by this time their assets outstripped those of the national banks by nearly 50 per cent.

Since part of this spectacular rise in small banks came from wartime prosperity in agricultural areas, when farm incomes fell, there were too many banks for the amount of business. Also many banks in the poorer wheat areas like western Nebraska, the Dakotas, or Montana held mortgages that farmers could not meet. As a result, more banks failed every year during the generally prosperous twenties than had failed in any year since 1897. Most of the suspensions were among the state-chartered banks, but in the depressed areas there were national banks that found it impossible to keep going. In 1929 only 25,000 commercial banks were left, of which 7,500 were national.

The small decrease in national banks during the decade reflected mergers as well as suspensions. In states that allowed branch banking big banks such as Giannini's Bancitaly in California bought up smaller ones and merged them in more efficient chain operations. By 1929 nine states permitted branch-banking, but a majority of all branches of state banks were in California. Together with national banks, which could establish branches only in their home cities, the number of branch offices increased from 480 in 1920 to 3,350 in 1929. During the twenties the Chase Bank and the National City Bank of New York raced each other in attracting depositors, buying competitors, and opening branches to achieve and hold the title of the nation's largest bank.

The character of metropolitan banking business changed significantly between 1914 and 1929. Although banks from all over the country still kept deposits in the big banks of New York, in order to make payments there the Federal Reserve System eased the problem of transferring money, and made it less necessary for the "country" banks to draw on these New York funds to finance planting and harvesting, and easier for city banks to make payments to the West when they were needed. To this extent there was new stability in the banking system. But other new trends ran in the opposite direction.

In the prosperous years aggressive bank salesmen were winning new accounts for the big banks, but commercial loans were failing to keep pace with this growth in deposits. In earlier decades even big industrial companies had used bank loans to provide working capital, and in some cases renewable loans had financed expansion of the plant. In the twenties most of these companies were making high profits and able to finance expansion from earnings and security issues. As a result they paid off bank loans and, if they wanted additional money, found it better to raise it by selling stock that involved no fixed payments. One way for the banks to compensate for this lack of short-term loans was to buy securities; another way was to lend money on the basis of stocks or bonds. In a market that was presumed to be unusually stable, both of these expedients seemed a safe use of the depositors' money. On small loans this turned out to be the case, but unfortunately some of these loans were very large, such as $5,000,000 secured by the common stock of a single company. This amount of stock could not be sold in a rapidly falling market, so that when trouble came the loan was frozen. The banks also invested in mortgages on new urban properties which lacked the liquidity of small short-term loans. During the nine years 1921–1929, while the total of all other loans remained about stationary, members of the Federal Reserve System increased investments in securities by two-thirds, doubled loans on securities, and increased loans on urban real estate three and a half times.

Another trend that turned out to be dangerous had started before the war. Banks like the National City and the First National of New York that were active in investment banking set up security selling affiliates. In the twenties the other big banks followed their example. Theoretically there was no danger to depositors in having a bank engaged in marketing securities, but in practice the affiliate too often made a profit by selling securities of a somewhat speculative character to the bank. Here again, if the major security markets remained reasonably stable, any losses should have been moderate enough for the bank to absorb, but security markets did not maintain such stability. Thus, in spite of the Federal Reserve, the banking system during the twenties lost liquidity or the ability to convert assets into cash.

INVESTMENT BANKING

Billions of dollars in Liberty and Victory bonds in the hands of the investing public produced the easiest money market in history. Bondholders, convinced that business was prosperous and that stocks were likely to go up, were anxious to sell their governments and invest in common shares. In addition the top tenth of income receivers, who did practically all the investing in stocks, were receiving an increasing share of the national income. As a result the big investment banks that had controlled the security markets before the war lost power. In the easy market of the twenties new houses could handle issues of $100,-000,000. In addition the old "money trust" lacked the strong leadership supplied by Pierpont Morgan and his friends James Stillman of National City and George F. Baker of First National. The new generation of leaders in these banks seemed to be content to take a fair share of the business and to go with the general trends. As the easygoing atmosphere bred bad financial practices, the old houses were also involved.

Almost all these practices can be attributed, in part at least, to the ease with which securities could be sold. Foreign government bonds, for example, were popular because of their high yields, and investment houses literally urged weak governments to go further into debt so that a bond issue could be sold in the United States. A study of the history of bonds issued in the twenties shows that the later in the decade the issue appeared, the greater the likelihood of default in the thirties.

Since the public was anxious to invest in public utility stocks it was possible to set up "pyramided" holding companies. This device depended upon the fact that a company can be controlled absolutely by owning 51 per cent of its stock. By bringing the public in to own the other 49 per cent at each level in the pyramid of companies, it was

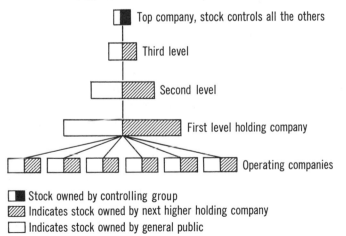

PYRAMIDED HOLDING COMPANY

possible for a million dollar investment in the top holding company to control operating companies at the bottom of the pyramid worth hundreds of millions.

The investment trust was a device to diversify the holdings of small investors. The latter bought shares in the trust. With the savings of the many small stockholders the managers of the trust could select a wide range of well-balanced investments. But they could also use the money to gain control of key companies and build personal power structures.

Basically the twenties was a great decade of innovation and improvement in finance. It was unfortunate that, without regulation, many of the new devices were misused. The pyramided holding company of two or three levels, for example, could be a useful device for efficient management, as well as for personal empire builders. Similarly, investment trusts demonstrated their usefulness to the small investor from 1935 on. The spectacular troubles with these novel mechanisms also obscure many other important developments. Consumer credit, for example, was used much more widely than ever before, and unsecured personal loans repayable in regular installments were pioneered by the Morris Plan. The elements missing in the twenties were a proper sense of trusteeship on the part of financial managers toward their depositors or stockholders and lack of necessary policing of financial transactions by the government.

THE NEW FEDERAL RESERVE SYSTEM

The early years of the Federal Reserve System were necessarily a period of experimentation. National banks (p. 424) had to become members, but the state banks and trust companies were not compelled to join, and with few exceptions remained on the outside. Therefore, the "system" only embraced about half of the banking resources and about a third of the banks. The First World War immediately presented the continuing problem that the Federal Reserve Board was never able to solve: the Treasury wanted low interest rates and easy money; preventing over-expansion of credit required higher rates and tight money. During the war the Board had to go along with the Treasury. After the war, during the highly inflationary boom the Board still refrained from tightening money while the Treasury was marketing Victory Bonds.

The founders of the system had thought that the principal control over business activity would be raising or lowering the rates that the Federal Reserve charged member banks for rediscount of eligible paper (p. 424). But this device could only be a direct control over commercial loans made against such paper, and as will be seen presently, not a very strong one. Furthermore, as member banks shifted more and more of their investment into securities and mortgages, control by the rediscount rate became weaker. A more forceful control, the one used for generations by the Bank of England, was the buying or selling of government bonds, known as open-market operations. The Federal Reserve first used this device as a control in the depression of 1922. By buying a large quantity of government bonds through a central committee the Reserve Banks put money in the hands of the previous holders, chiefly banks, which then presumably looked for new investments. Whether from this stimulation or not, the depression of 1922 was soon ended. This gave the Federal Reserve Board considerable confidence in open-market operations, but the problem of checking a runaway boom involved other factors.

The leading policy-maker in the system was Benjamin Strong, the governor of the Federal Reserve Bank of New York. While he was not a member of the central board in Washington, the board was inclined to take his advice. As the apparently baseless stock market boom mounted in 1927 and 1928, the national Federal Reserve Board wanted to raise discount rates and have the member banks sell bonds. But Strong reminded them of essentially the same type of problem the system had faced in the war: tight money could do harm as well as good. Business was only moderately prosperous, and there were two million unemployed. To make money tight might prevent businessmen from negotiating legitimate loans that would put men to work. Furthermore, a high rate would attract money from abroad and add to England's difficulty in maintaining a gold standard. Therefore, discount rates were kept low, and $435,000,000 worth of bonds were bought in open-market operations. In the midst of the dilemma, in 1928, Strong died. Late in that year the Board reversed its policy and recommended sharp increases in the discount rate. A high rate was put into effect in New York, but it was too weak a control to curb the strong spirit of speculation. Up to 1963 no one had devised a system for curbing speculation, and at the same time encouraging loans for normal business purposes.

THE BIG CRASH

Partly because the business cycle had been rather mild in its swings since 1897, and partly from faith that the old panics had come from money problems cured by the Federal Reserve, many people in the twenties were confident that the business cycle was under control. The break in prices in 1920 and the panic in March of 1921 were written off as inevitable results of the war. The Federal government had run at a deficit of $9 billion in 1919 and a surplus of nearly a billion in 1920, the drop in spending being equal to about a fifth of the national income. This government action alone might have been enough to cause a collapse. When the large government bond selling campaigns were over, the Federal Reserve System also sought to curb the boom. The Federal Reserve Bank of New York raised its discount rate from 4¾ per cent in 1919 to 7 per cent by June 1, 1920. These actions, plus a cessation of European buying now that the United States was no longer advancing large sums, were enough to explain the break. After reaching a peak in May, 1920, commodity prices declined and business began to slow down. Retail dealers, who had high-priced goods on their shelves, and manufacturers, who had costly raw materials on hand, were in a serious predicament. Banks contracted loans; railroad freight loadings and earnings declined; and factories closed down. By the spring of 1921 over four million persons were unemployed. Business failures numbering 6,450 in 1919 reached 22,400 in 1922. The average index number of wholesale prices of important commodities, using 100 for the 1913 level, reached 272 in May, 1920, and declined to 148 in June, 1921, remaining approximately at that level. The Federal Reserve System now came to the rescue, reducing discount rates and buying bonds. That this action coincided with a rapid recovery undoubtedly heightened public confidence that the economy could be controlled.

From 1923 to 1926 there was a period of increasing prosperity based on plant expansion, particularly in utilities, steel, and motors, and on urban building construction. Late in 1926 there was recession from this period of prosperity, featured by the spectacular collapse of a Florida real estate boom, but at the low point, toward the end of 1927, the dollar volume of business was only slightly below average. Again, businessmen felt confident that the situation was under control. In any explanation of the runaway stock market boom of 1928 and 1929, this element of over-confidence must be given great importance.

Millions of Americans had become familiar with the procedure of investment through their purchases of Liberty Loan bonds during the war, and the most venturesome had tried to emulate stock exchange traders as they bought "war babies" and other speculative stocks. In the period that followed, the public, spurred by visions of dazzling gains, became increasingly interested in the operations of the stock market. The trend of prices on the stock market had been upward since 1924. Recessions were not serious, and even those that occurred were taken by the speculating public as simply an idiosyncrasy of the market to be inevitably corrected within a short period of time. The easy money policy of the Federal Reserve System in 1927 to aid business and to help foreign nations in their relations with the United States encouraged increasing speculation. In spite of many unfavorable business trends, prices of stocks rose with alarming rapidity. Depression in several vital industries in addition to agriculture, technological unemployment, and the lag that was developing by 1928 in the building, steel, automobile, and oil industries were all danger signals to which political leaders and the public alike remained blind as they envisioned a future utopia of great material splendor.

From 1927 to 1929 prices on the stock exchange soared. Clerks, workingmen, and shopkeepers joined financiers and executives in buying securities that they felt sure could be sold at a profit. Professional men as well as widows and retired people staked the painful savings of years on stocks that seemed sure of doubling their money within a short time. Banks generally required that a "margin" of 25 per cent of the cost of the stock be paid in cash, but many brokers carried stocks for customers on much lower margins, the brokers, in turn, borrowing the necessary funds from the banks. As a result of public participation in the stock market, brokers' loans increased dizzily; the prices of stocks rose out of all relation to dividends; and financiers floated new securities to meet the demand. In 1929, corporations issued $8 billion in new securities, including $5 billion in common stock. Profits were attracted into the market, raising the price of existing securities instead of going into new productive investment; foreign investors aided the rise in the stock market while, at the same time, Americans sunk billions in foreign governmental and private securities. Favorable corporation reports and failure to recognize the growing stock market inflation gave the speculators a feeling of security. Bankers, manufacturers, and even economists interpreted the movement as the beginning of a new era to which the old ratios of earnings to capital values could not be applied. As we have seen, the Reserve Board tried to correct the situation by raising the discount rate, but speculation in stocks continued unabated. Direct pressure was brought to bear on member banks not to increase their loans to aid brokers. Loans were reduced but it did not break the speculative mania. It had become impossible to check the speculative fever.

Throughout the spring and summer of 1929 there were some market breaks, but in September many stocks were at all-time highs. The most severe crash did not come until October 29, 1929. On that day high-grade securities went tumbling down in the same manner as bogus mining stocks and more than 16,000,000 shares changed hands. Stock of the General Electric Company dropped forty-seven points; American Telephone and Telegraph Company, thirty-four points; and Westinghouse Electric and Manufacturing Company, thirty-five points. The stock exchanges of the country closed but were opened in a few days. Meantime, the bankers formed a pool to support the market. While temporarily successful to a certain degree, the bull market was ended, and the trend continued downward until prices reached an appalling low in 1932. But in 1929, United States Steel Corporation common stock, which had reached a high of $261.75, fell to $150; American Telephone and Telegraph Company stock fluctuated between $310.25 and $193.25, while Westinghouse Electric and Manufacturing Company stock ranged from $292.50 to $100.

The Panic of 1929 differed from earlier ones in that no money panic ensued. It was exclusively a stock market panic. The New York banks together with the Federal Reserve Bank met legitimate demands for credit. Liquidation was carried out in as orderly a manner as the terrible collapse in the prices of securities would permit. The catastrophe marked the end of an era in which many had lived in a fool's paradise. A new period followed during which painful adjustments had to be made.

REORGANIZING THE FINANCIAL SYSTEM

Since the stock market breaks in 1929 had been too rapid and severe for the banks to liquidate many of their large loans made against securities, they had to support an increasing burden of bad debts. Good bonds including those of the United States government sank in value, and some mortgages became temporarily worthless as the properties could not be sold. Bankers found themselves operating buildings and other businesses taken in foreclosure. National banks had to post reserves against loans in default. This was a drain on capital that even some of the biggest metropolitan banks could not stand. From 1930 through 1933 some 9,000 banks suspended payment, and the number of commercial banks fell to 14,000 of which about 5,500 were members of the Federal Reserve System.

The banking laws of the New Deal (pp. 570–573) guaranteed small deposits in banks meeting certain requirements, extended the powers of the national Federal Reserve Board to include control of margin rates on the stock exchanges, and control of rediscount and reserve rates in the various districts. But strong local opposition in Congress led by Senator Huey Long of Louisiana prevented the forcing of Federal Reserve membership on all banks. A majority of banks remained outside the system although they had only about a sixth of the commercial banking resources. Of 62 banks that failed in 1934, there were 53 without deposit insurance. In 1957 there were still 739 banks with over $10 billion in assets not covered by insurance. In all, the main core of banking had been greatly strengthened, and the percentage of annual failures reduced to a nearly negligible level, but a weak fringe of small-town banks still remained.

The divorce of investment from commercial banking, the Security Exchange Commission, and the Reconstruction Finance Corporation all reduced the influence of investment bankers. The big commercial banks liquidated their security affiliates. J. P. Morgan and Company elected to be a commercial bank and transferred its investment business to a new firm, Morgan, Stanley and Company.

The investment firms now lacked the resources of the big banks, and in addition, the SEC frequently compelled them to bid competitively for large security issues, a practice that Pierpont Morgan had virtually ended in the 1880's. The RFC, in a position to extend large loans that took the place of bond issues, was a more important source of capital than any investment house. The vast size of life insurance companies, and later on of pension funds, also led to much direct negotiation between companies needing money and these big investors. Metropolitan Life, for example, might easily take an entire bond issue for its own portfolio without recourse to investment bankers. The big companies still consulted the investment bankers, but their power to determine policy was largely gone. Furthermore, since no great upswing in private investment occurred, there was little new business for the investment houses.

UNSATISFACTORY RECOVERY

From 1933 to 1937 there was the longest sustained upswing in the history of the American business cycle. Industrial production, factory employment, and payrolls nearly doubled. In spite of this, private capital formation lagged, and nearly eight million workers were still unemployed. This led many to believe that the situation was chronic and that unemployment was an inevitable by-product of the machine age. Others, however, enthused by the rapid stride of recovery, felt that the problem would be largely, if not entirely, solved in time. But the decline that began in August, 1937, was more rapid than recovery had been. By the end of the year steel plants were operating only 25 per cent of their capacity. Capital goods industries as well as consumer goods industries were affected. The automobile, textile, and building trades, especially, were hard hit. Railroads were seriously affected and the number of railroad employees was reduced to a forty-year low of 913,000. Prices dropped, including agricultural prices. No serious panic ensued on the stock market or in business or finance. The stock market merely followed a general downward course to mid-1938.

Various reasons were given for the recession. Some people asserted that it was largely due to the curtailment of the pump-priming activities of the government; some, that it was the result of the failure of the government to balance the budget or to reduce the debt; some, that drastic taxation policies had been responsible; others blamed the excessive demands of labor which had been encouraged by the government. Government leaders put the blame on monopolistic practices of certain industrial and business enterprises. Undoubtedly the reduction of Federal funds for pump-priming contributed psychologically to the depression. These funds were cut from more than $3 billion annually in 1933–1936 to about $1 billion in 1937. But in reality, the increase in state and local expenditures more than compensated for the Federal reduction.

As a result of the recession, government spending and lending was renewed. The important New Deal agencies were again voted large sums. The WPA rolls were expanded; new plans of Federal and local public works were financed; and farmers received increased payments. The RFC advanced more loans to industrialists and businessmen. The Interstate Commerce Commission in March, 1938, permitted the railroads a 5 per cent increase in rates on farm and forest products and 10 per cent on most other commodities. Everything possible was done to combat the evils of the depression. In the summer of 1938 prices began to improve and within a year the trend in business activity and employment was definitely upward. But unemployment still stood at 9,500,000.

THE KEYNESIAN ANSWER

Clearly between 1929 and 1939 the laws of classic economic theory were not operating as they should. Money was plentiful, interest rates were the lowest on record, workers were looking for jobs, and still there was inadequate incentive to combine these factors into activities that would provide full employment. A British economist, John Maynard Keynes, put forth an explanation of the stagnation which became the most important twentieth-century change in economic theory and the basis for continued government economic action.

Keynes started by emphasizing the difference between the part of the national income spent for consumer goods, that is, for living purposes, and the portion spent for producer goods, that is, invested in further production. He contended that while expenditures for consumer goods depended on the size of the national income and its distribution between the rich and the poor, relations that changed but slowly, the amount spent on producer goods depended on business sentiment which was highly variable. Since national income could only increase in the long run from investment in producer goods, a fact that most businessmen and economists had always been willing to concede, such investment was too important a matter to be left to the vagaries of business sentiment. Looking at the situation in the thirties the Keynesian answer was that if businessmen were unwilling to invest sufficient amounts, the government should step in and apply stimulants by making key investments that would create demand for more producer goods.

There was another partially distinct line to the Keynesian reasoning: he asserted "that men are disposed, as a rule and on the average, to increase their consumption as their income increases, but not as much as the increase in their income." It followed from this that the more even the distribution of income, the greater the demand for consumer goods. Conversely, if the rich received more of the income, and estimates are that this had been happening in the twenties, demand would fall off. With stable or falling demand businessmen would find no profitable use for the savings of the rich.

This was close to the reasoning that had in fact guided some of the sponsors of the New Deal, but its appearance in a widely proclaimed book, published in New York in 1936, gave theoretical justification for the practical actions already taken. Keynes enjoyed the acceptance that comes to philosophers who justify what is being done, and little by little his ideas influenced almost all aspects of economic theory. He led economists to think in terms of national income and investment rather than money and price movements; he gave political leaders a basis for the new role of government in the welfare state. It was the experience of the results of high government spending and drastic income redistribution in the Second World War, however, that convinced Americans of the truth of the basic Keynesian propositions.

CONTROLLING THE NEW ORDER

The great problem of the thirties had been deflation—that of the forties and fifties was inflation. The change came with dramatic suddenness because of the Second World War. In 1940 the total assets of commercial banks stood at $68 billion, in 1945 the figure was $146 billion. The largest part of the increase, $58 billion, came from buying government bonds. Thus the money supply represented by bank deposits more than doubled during the war. In addition, the flight of gold to the United States, following the devaluation of the dollar in the mid-thirties, gave the Federal Reserve System greatly expanded backing for notes.

Price controls and rationing during the war kept these excess banking reserves and money supply from having their full effect on prices, although it should be noted that alongside the legal buying and selling that was shown in the price indexes, the black market had fantastically high, but unrecorded prices. The removal of controls, except for some local regulations on rent, in 1946 and 1947, together with excessive demand, allowed prices to register the change in the money supply. By 1948, the consumer price index was 72 per cent above 1940, and commodity prices had more than doubled. A mild recession in 1949 checked the upward movement, but panicky buying of commodities by consumers as well as producers during the early stages of the Korean War added some 10 per cent to the consumer price index. Continuing inflationary pressures, which will be discussed later, kept the trend generally upward to a point in 1960 which was 25 per cent higher than the peak in 1948.

The Federal government, meanwhile, was exercising controls to check the inflation. The Full Employment Act of 1946 (p. 618) had created a Committee of Economic Advisors to the President. This board had no power but might strongly influence executive action. Therefore, from 1946 on the mechanisms for economic control included the Treasury, the Federal Reserve Board, and the CEA. On the basis of the CEA recommendations and other information the President issued an annual Economic Report, and Congress, by setting up a Joint Committee on the Economic Report of the President, added a fourth government group interested in economic policy.

The multiplication of authorities with no head save the President probably illustrated a basic ambiguity in the role of government. It was trying to *control* the economy in the interests of *free* enterprise. Any real concentration of economic authority was politically unacceptable, and any controls that superseded the operations of the market, except in the case of agriculture, were regarded as contrary to American traditions. Thus the controls actually used were the same ones that the Federal Reserve had employed previously: (1) changes in the reserve requirements for banks; (2) changes in the rediscount rate; (3) open-market operations; (4) changes in margin requirements on the stock exchange; and (5) control of the conditions for granting installment credit. All operated through pressures on the money market, and if anyone were strong enough to resist these pressures, he could go his own way.

The CEA advised the President on the use of controls with the aims of lessening unemployment during recessions and curbing inflation during periods of prosperity. But the President was in no way compelled to follow the advice of the CEA. After some conflict with President Truman during his first administration the chairman of CEA, Edwin G. Nourse, resigned. Succeeding chairmen, Leon Keyserling during the Truman administration and Arthur F. Burns and Raymond J. Saulnier during the administrations of Eisenhower and

CONSUMER PRICE INDEX, 1935 – 1961
(1947–1949 = 100)

Year	All Items	Year	All Items	Year	All Items
1935	58.7	1944	75.2	1953	114.4
1936	59.3	1945	76.9	1954	114.8
1937	61.4	1946	83.4	1955	114.5
1938	60.3	1947	95.5	1956	116.2
1939	59.4	1948	102.8	1957	120.2
1940	59.9	1949	101.8	1958	123.5
1941	62.9	1950	102.8	1959	124.6
1942	69.7	1951	111.0	1960	126.5
1943	74.0	1952	113.5	1961	127.6

Sources: U.S. Bureau of the Census, *Historical Statistics of the United States, Colonial Times to 1957*, Washington, D.C., 1960, p. 125; and *The World Almanac, 1962*, p. 756.

Kennedy appear to have been in basic agreement with presidential aims, or vice versa. Even if the President and the CEA were agreed, they had no legal power over the Federal Reserve Board. To produce closer cooperation the Secretary of the Treasury, in 1958, started the practice of meeting with the chairman of the Federal Reserve Board, the chairman of CEA, and the President's assistant for economic affairs.

Regardless of the degree of cooperation there were several contradictory or uncontrollable forces influencing economic trends. The old contradiction between the Treasury's desire to sell bonds at high prices and low interest rates, and the Federal Reserve's desire to check inflation by tight money and high interest rates still occurred in the majority of the years after 1945, when the government ran a deficit. In 1946 and 1947, for example, the Federal Reserve could have checked inflation by selling government bonds, but in doing so they would have been competing directly with the Treasury. In the Eisenhower administration the Federal Reserve tightened money with the result that the government had to pay high interest rates on new bonds offered for sale.

A force strictly outside the control of government was increasing wage rates from labor-management negotiations. With most of the big "pace-setting" companies able to control the price of their products on the market it was easier to compromise with the demands of strong unions for higher wages than to resist. In fact, a few managements that did resist suffered severe losses to their competitors. Consequently, wages moved in only one direction—up.

Another uncontrollable element was purchasing by both consumer and businesses. There was no effective control over consumer decisions to purchase or not to purchase, or to go into debt. While the Federal Reserve had power to fix certain conditions for installment credit, the consumer was most likely to borrow without regard to terms during periods of inflation when the government would have him abstain. The table on p. 647 shows that rise of consumer indebtedness including home mortgages was a major inflationary force from 1946 on. Of a total of $736 billion indebtedness in 1957, all types of government owed $271 billion, corporations $244 billion, and individuals $221 billion. Business increases or decreases in inventory tended to accentuate cyclical swings. From 1949 to 1951, for example, when the government was trying to hold the line on the Korean War inflation, business inventory rose from $29 billion to $43 billion. As noted earlier, the sharp inflation in late 1950 appears to have been the result of stockpiling by both business and individual consumers.

Tightening the money supply was not only relatively ineffective in controlling the rise of individual indebtedness, but tight money also had bad effects on medium and small business. Big business could generally finance itself from retained earnings or security issues, whereas small business was dependent on the banks. Tight money, therefore, hurt small businesses in competition with big and added to the number of business failures. Viewed more basically, one cure for inflation was more goods, but tight money tended to curb production. During the generally inflationary fifties when the Federal Reserve was frequently tightening money, the amount spent, in real dollars, on new plant and equipment was on the average less than in the only moderately expanding twenties. In the fifties, it should be noted, more of the investment was in equipment and less in plant. This meant that depreciation would tend to be more rapid and continual replacement more necessary. But the figures indicate that inflation was more the result of consumer and government spending than of spending for producer goods.

Whether from better use of financial controls, the wiser buying of both businessmen and consumers, or the support given to the economy by military expenditures, pensions and unemployment insurance, or the combination of these and other forces, the business cycle was moderate in its swings. Peaks were reached in 1948, 1953, 1957, and 1959. Buoyed up by a long-term rising trend of activity, the recessions were mild. The increase or curtailment of manufacturers' inventories

VALUE OF INDIVIDUAL INDEBTEDNESS, 1946 – 1957

(In billions of dollars)

Year	Mortgage		Non-mortgage		Year	Mortgage		Non-mortgage	
	Farm	Non-farm	Farm	Non-farm		Farm	Non-farm	Farm	Non-farm
1946	4.9	32.5	2.7	20.5	1952	7.2	75.2	8.0	45.2
1947	5.1	38.7	3.5	23.5	1953	7.8	83.8	9.2	49.6
1948	5.3	45.1	5.5	27.3	1954	8.3	94.7	9.3	53.1
1949	5.6	50.6	6.4	31.2	1955	9.1	108.8	9.7	62.6
1950	6.1	59.4	6.2	37.2	1956	9.9	121.2	9.6	66.5
1951	6.6	67.4	7.0	38.8	1957	10.5	131.6	9.8	69.2

Source: U.S. Bureau of the Census, *Historical Statistics of the United States, Colonial Times to 1957*, Washington, D.C., 1960, p. 664.

and of housing activity rivalled business investment in initiating rises and falls. The stock market, continuously supported by the need of pension and insurance funds for investment, was not seriously involved in any of the swings. On occasion the market rose during downswings in business activity.

FOREIGN TRADE AND INVESTMENT

Foreign trade and private investment abroad from 1914 to 1957 involve a paradox: while the United States became the most important factor in world trade and finance, both foreign trade and private foreign investment became relatively less important in the economy of the United States; while the government of the United States became more internationally oriented, the economy of the nation became more self-sufficient. In 1913, the last normal trade year before the First World War, exports were equal to 6.2 per cent of the gross national product and imports to 4 per cent; from 1921 through 1929, exports averaged 5.1 and imports 4.2; for the eight years 1950 to 1957, exports averaged 4.2 and imports 3 per cent.

The same trends hold for foreign investment of private capital. In 1914 the United States private investment abroad, the only kind at that time, stood at nearly 10 per cent of gross national product. In the twenties the percentage rose, but generally declined from 1930 on, and stood at only 6.6 in 1950. High labor costs at home and relatively stable conditions abroad led to a return to somewhat higher levels of investment. In 1957, private capital invested abroad equalled 8.6 per cent of gross national product, but this was still below the level of 1914 and well below the level of the twenties. From the standpoint of annual flow of capital, more private funds came to the United States from 1950 to 1955 than were invested abroad by Americans. Up to 1957 in terms of real dollars only 1956 and 1957 surpassed the highest years of the twenties in volume of foreign investment. In these later years two-thirds of the money was spent for branch plant operations of United States firms. Clearly most Americans preferred to invest their money at home and leave foreign aid in the hands of the government. In view of the figures it scarcely needs to be added that in no year was private investment abroad comparable to the volume of Marshall Plan aid.

By 1957 so-called "direct" foreign investment, meaning investment in foreign plants or enterprises as distinct from buying the bonds of foreign governments, had a book value of only $25 billion, or about 5.2 per cent of the current gross national product. The 36 per

DISTRIBUTION OF UNITED STATES DIRECT
FOREIGN INVESTMENT, 1957

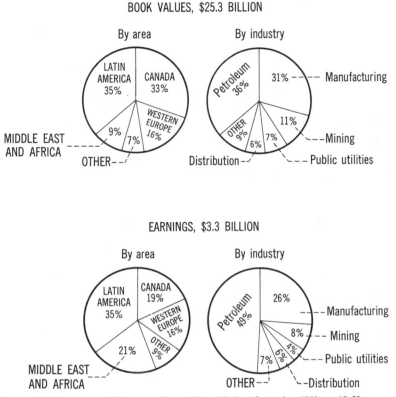

BOOK VALUES, $25.3 BILLION

By area   By industry

EARNINGS, $3.3 BILLION

By area   By industry

Source: U.S. Department of Commerce, *Survey of Current Business*, September, 1958, pp. 15–22.

cent of this total that was in oil properties, largely in Colombia, Venezuela, and the Middle East, earned nearly 50 per cent of the annual
return. North Africa was also regarded as promising oil territory. By
area, North and South America had absorbed more than two-thirds the
total direct investment, in most instances for the purpose of supplying
raw materials to the United States.

The lag in trade and foreign investment could no longer be laid
to the United States tariff. The Reciprocal Trade Agreements Act
(p. 505) and the subsequent Acts of 1945 and 1955 allowing the President to make additional reductions of 50 per cent and 15 per cent,
respectively, had opened the way for tariff cuts (p. 621). The General
Agreements on Tariff and Trade of 1947, 1952, and 1957 had lowered
the average of duties collected to 11 per cent, as compared with 52

per cent under the Hawley-Smoot Tariff of 1930–1933. Rather the change appeared to be the result of both Europe and the United States becoming more self-sufficient in the relative quantity of goods that had to be imported.

The character of both the United States and European imports had changed greatly since 1914. In that year hides, coffee, sugar, raw silk, and crude rubber were the chief imports to the United States. In 1957 the five leading imports were non-ferrous metals and ferroalloys, petroleum and its products, coffee, paper and pulp, and sugar. The rise of Canada as the principal nation trading with the United States had been a major factor in changing trade relations. Europe had provided the United States with nearly half its imports in 1914; by 1957 Latin America supplied a quarter of the total, a little more than Europe, and Canada almost as much. In exports the same regional shifts took place, but more gradually. In 1914, Europe had taken about half of the exports, and Canada and Latin America combined only about quarter. By 1957, Canada took a fifth of the exports, Latin America about a sixth, and Europe a little over a quarter. The rise of Canadian trade can also be seen as another indication of continental self-sufficiency.

The heavy surplus of exports in the twenties had represented a rapidly accumulating capital investment abroad. Unless more and more capital was exported each year, the time would come when the returns on previous investments would more than equal the new investment. But other items being equal, returns on investment would have to come from a surplus of imports. With the nearly prohibitive tariff rates of the decade it was hard to see how this adjustment could come about. The fifties did not present this potential problem. While export surpluses were proportionately larger than in the twenties, the difference did not represent an accumulating investment with foreign goods denied entry. In most years the surplus was about equalled by Marshall Plan aid and military expenditures abroad. In 1960 the United States was actually running a deficit in the international balance of payments, in spite of a large export surplus. If necessary, foreign aid could be adjusted to keep the balance in equilibrium.

BANKING IN THE NEW ORDER

While investment banking remained as an independent and profitable field of financial operation, the trend of history from 1940 on was against its ever regaining its earlier importance. Pension funds grew from $7 billion in assets in 1951 to $28 billion in 1960, and joined insurance companies as direct buyers of high-grade securities, without banking aid. The rich individual purchaser, a standby of the old investment houses for the sale of new stocks as late as the twenties, had practically disappeared. Of three and a half billion dollars in new common and preferred stock issued in 1960, individuals in the United States bought a negligible fraction, and pension funds took over half. Big companies continued to grow more self-sufficient in their financing and to need less new money in proportion to their total resources. In fact, new corporate securities for the seven years 1951 to 1957 had about the same real dollar value as in the years 1923 to 1929, which meant that in comparison with gross national product they were only about 40 per cent as large as in the earlier period.

Aside from direct purchasing of whole issues by big investors, security dealers faced a new type of competition in long-term bank and insurance company loans. In their reach for new business during the great depression, banks became willing to make "term" loans of five or ten years duration to companies with high credit ratings. Insurance companies might arrange to buy the loan from the bank at

ASSETS OF CORPORATE PENSION
FUNDS, 1951 - 1960

(In billions of dollars)

NET PURCHASES OF COMMON
AND PREFERRED STOCK, 1951 - 1960

(In billions of dollars)

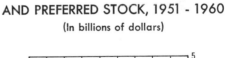
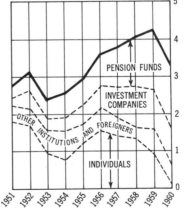

Chart includes all funds except those administered by the insurance companies, unions, and non-profit organizations.

Source: *The New York Times*, June 18, 1961, p. 10F.

Figures include buying for non-profit organizations, multi-employer plans, and also plans that are union-administered.

the end of five years and continue it for ten years more. Thus a loan could take the place of a bond issue. In 1955, one-third of all business loans by member banks of the Federal Reserve System were term loans.

Other important changes took place in bank investment port-folios. Throughout the century bank investments in securities had been gaining in relation to loans. We have noted how rapidly this change went on in the twenties. Government needs in the depression and the Second World War resulted in heavy investments in govern-ment securities. By 1945 bank holdings of United States government securities alone were worth between three and four times all loans. Now the business problem of the banks was to replace government securities by investments with higher yields. By 1953, loans rose above holdings of United States obligations for the first time, but the latter still comprised 76 per cent of all commercial bank investments in securities. Treasury bills of three months duration, first introduced in 1929, and Treasury certificates running nine to fourteen months, in-troduced during the Second World War, also made up about 90 per cent of the paper in the short-term money market. As a consequence bank earnings were greatly influenced by the interest rate on govern-ment obligations.

After the Second World War the packaged personal or consumer loan became an important part of bank investments. Until 1929, bank lending for consumer purposes had been to finance companies which assumed the burdens and risks. But again, to gain business in the depression, banks entered the field. While the overhead cost in paper work was high, interest returns ran 6 to 12 per cent, and defaults were few. By 1956, about 20 per cent of commercial bank loans took this form.

Real estate loans were the remaining important type of new busi-ness. The basic Act of 1863 had prohibited national banks from lend-ing on real estate. The Federal Reserve Act removed this restriction, and in the twenties banks made many real estate loans, particularly on large properties. But the small borrower still found it hard to meet the difference between the cost of construction of a new home and the amount the bank would lend. The Federal Housing Administration and later the Veterans Administration by guaranteeing mortgages running to 85 or 95 per cent of the value of the property, repayable in equal monthly installments, gave an enormous boost to real estate lending. During the postwar years this type of investment rose from a fifth to a quarter of all commercial bank loans.

The business structure of the banking system continued to develop in directions already clear in the twenties and thirties. By 1958 only 10 states completely prohibited branches, although 19 still confined them to one city or county. Meanwhile, Federal laws were modified to allow national banks under certain conditions the same freedom to create branches as the banks of the particular state enjoyed. Automation of bank accounting put an added premium on large-scale operation that was already favored by the cost of expert, specialized management. Although by forming syndicates small banks could handle sizable loans, the continuing prohibition against banks lending more than 10 per cent of the value of their capital to any one borrower favored the big banks. In fact, this provision had always tended to tie the banks of the nation to participation with the banks of the major metropolitan areas in the handling of big business loans.

In view of these pressures it is perhaps surprising that banks remained so numerous and competitive. In 1945 out of a total of 14,000 commercial banks, 1,000 had branches; in 1958, out of 13,600 banks, 1,900 had branches. In both years the average was about five offices for each bank with branches. Certain forces contrary to consolidation still sustained local banks. The people of the community generally preferred to do business with a locally-run office. The profits of many of the small banks were too low to tempt big business. Many of the same elements that allowed the local retail store to survive the competition of the chains sustained the local bank.

By 1960 this old and most continuously government-regulated business had made a tolerable adjustment to the new order. The average net profits of the four to five thousand national banks—the banks that had a majority of the banking resources—were as high from 1946 to 1957 as in any equally long period since 1869, when statistics began. The average net profit for the fifties was distinctly better than for the twenties. Most of the business, to be sure, was done by the big city banks and their branches. Many independent small town banks, however, kept going by the same policies they had historically pursued: low salaries, inadequate examination of risks, and reliance on community ties rather than salesmen to bring in business.

CHAPTER 30

The Big Change in Agriculture

Until 1870 agriculture had been the occupation of a majority of working Americans. As late as 1910 almost one-third of the labor force was in agriculture. Under these circumstances farming was not thought to be comparable to any other single occupation such as mining, transportation, or retail trade; rather it was the traditional way of life of the American people. The farmer was presumed to represent the American ideals of honesty, freedom, and independence in contrast to businessmen who were ethically and economically subservient to the market, or workers who could be dictated to by their employers. Politically agriculture was still far better represented than any other occupation.

From about 1940 to 1960 commercial agriculture changed rapidly into a business operation conducted by a small minority of the population with advanced technological equipment. The change came rapidly because of the demands of the Second World War and government programs; but basically it depended on the gradual development of gasoline powered machinery and the accumulation of scientific knowledge regarding seeds, soil, and nutrition. From 1910 to 1935 the increase in productivity per man-hour in agriculture was a moderate 25 per cent, in the next 25 years it rose over 100 per cent, and this figure greatly understates the increase on the most efficient farms. A

654

quarter of the farms turned out 85 per cent of the commercial product, and doubtless could have supplied the whole market if necessary. Thus while the agricultural labor force in 1960 was over 7.5 per cent of the total, it is quite probable that 3 per cent, working with an efficiency comparable to industry, could have met the demands for agricultural products.

MISUSED PROSPERITY

The history of United States farming from about 1900 on is one of failure to adjust either to changing scientific methods and technology or to the changing market, because habits of life and a traditional structure of ownership stood in the way. In the prosperity before the First World War demand was already shifting from grains toward citrus fruits, vegetables, and dairy products, but farmers, in spite of warnings from the Department of Agriculture, continued to expand their conventional cereal crops. With urban demand now growing faster than agricultural supply, all products were bringing better prices, and it was easy to be misled regarding long-run trends. During the first decade and a half of the twentieth century farm conditions became more prosperous and stable than they had been for nearly a century. When the war broke out in the summer of 1914, as international credits were disturbed, blockades established, German markets lost, and commerce upset, America's foreign markets for grains, cotton, and meats were seriously affected. Within a year, however, demands from the allied nations for farm products were threatening to outrun possible production. For six years there was pressure to grow more and more grain, perpetuating and accentuating the existing trend toward raising the wrong crops.

Prices rose rapidly at the beginning of the war, as the European demand for grain and other agricultural commodities began to increase. Wheat increased from ninety-seven cents a bushel in 1913 to a government-stabilized price of $2.20 after United States entry into the war and to $2.76 in 1919. Cotton, which occupied a precarious position in 1913, selling at eight cents a pound, rose to forty in 1919. Products such as wheat, cotton, tobacco, wool, hogs, and beans rose to prices before unknown. Some, including cattle, horses, hay, apples, and butter, made gains but did not soar. General levels, however, of all commodities were far higher than before the war.

The demand for American products spurred staple crop farmers to increased activities and to cultivating additional land. The government also aided the movement by loaning money at reduced rates of interest for the purpose of refunding old debts, and expanding production. In 1910 in the United States there was a farm mortgage indebtedness of $4.7 billion, a part of which was charged interest as high as 10 to 11 per cent. In 1916 Congress took steps to remedy this condition by the Federal Farm Loan Act which established twelve Federal land banks in as many districts under the general supervision of a seven-member board in Washington. It provided for Farm Loan Associations, organized among the farmers to guarantee the loans obtained from the banks, in which government and private funds were to be invested. The banks were authorized to make mortgage loans and to finance themselves by issuing tax-exempt bonds. Thus farmers in debt could borrow money at 5 or 6 per cent interest. Relieved of high rates of interest, many became too optimistic during the era of prosperity and went further into debt in order to expand. In 1921 farm mortgage indebtedness stood at $10.2 billion.

MALADJUSTMENT AND POLITICAL UNREST

The agricultural prosperity of the First World War ended in the depression of 1920–1921 when prices crashed. Wheat, which had sold at $2.76 a bushel in 1919, fell to $1.44 in December, 1920, and cotton dropped during the same period from forty cents a pound to fourteen cents. The serious decline of agricultural prices began in the summer of 1920. The blow struck the farmers in the fall of that year about the time that the grain crop was reaching the market. While industry generally recovered from the effects of the depression within a year or so, farm prices had fallen the most and recovered the least. The relative rigidity of the prices of manufactured goods and supplies that the farmer needed together with continuing high farm wages created a new and alarming disparity between farm income and costs.

The decline in agricultural prices was the result of large numbers of men from the disbanding armies in Europe going back to their farms to increase the world's supplies of grain. Americans had to compete more than ever before with such wheat-growing countries as Russia, Canada, Australia, and Argentina. The impoverishment of Europe and the resulting reduction of buying power was another factor that led to the rapid deflation of foreign trade, especially after the United States ended its policy of loans to foreign countries. Then, too, mechanization, including the use of tractors, trucks, automobiles, farm machinery, gas engines, and electric power, which had made rapid progress during the war, meant less demand for grain to feed work animals.

The distress of the staple crop farmers revitalized the National Grange and other agricultural organizations, while new ones sprang into being. The war had stimulated agricultural colleges and the Department of Agriculture to integrate their extension work to form local farm bureaus. In 1919 these clubs of farmers formed a national organization, the American Farm Bureau Federation. With the hard times of 1920, it set up an office in Washington, joining several farm organizations, represented at the capital, to form a strong pressure group. Pressure was brought to bear on lawmakers and administrators in the Federal and state governments to work in the interests of the farmers. As early as 1920 a new Farmer-Labor Party elected several members of Congress. The next year, members of Congress belonging to both major political parties organized a farm bloc under the leadership of Arthur Capper of Kansas, William S. Kenyon of Iowa, and the insurgent Robert M. La Follette of Wisconsin, to initiate and carry through legislation to benefit the farmers. In 1924, the plight of the farmers was largely responsible for a new Progressive Party (Conference for Progressive Political Action) under Senator Robert M. La Follette, which showed much strength in its 5,000,000 voters, especially in the twelve middle-western or far western states.

Widespread agricultural discontent together with able representation brought legislation aimed primarily at raising farm prices and granting farmers relief from the credit situation. The emergency tariff of 1921 and the Fordney-McCumber tariff of 1922 were designed to include protection to agricultural products such as wheat, corn, meat, wool, and sugar. But with a domestic surplus of staples the tariff wall had no effect on wheat, corn, or cotton prices, which continued their downward trend. Congress also enacted in 1921 the Futures Trading Act in an attempt to prevent the exchanges of the country from gambling on the nation's grain supply, while in 1922 and 1924 Cooperatives Acts were passed to exempt agricultural associations or cooperatives from prosecution under the antitrust laws. Another law, an Intermediate Credit Act (1923), established twelve credit banks in the Federal Land Bank cities for the purpose of advancing credit to farmers for periods from six months to three years—longer terms than usually made by commercial banks and shorter than the ordinary farm mortgage. They were empowered to rediscount commercial paper, the proceeds of which had been used for agricultural purposes, and they could also lend money directly to agricultural cooperative associations on notes secured by goods in storage or in transit. Such measures, however, were mere palliatives incapable of giving permanent relief.

Improved agricultural conditions in 1924 and 1925 were reflected in rising price levels, but the most persistent problem was that of surplus production. In an attempt to solve this problem, from 1924 to 1928, Congress considered legislation which received powerful and united support from the agricultural interests. In 1927, the McNary-Haugen bill was passed, but President Coolidge vetoed the measure. The next year it was passed again in modified form only to receive a second veto. The basic idea of the McNary-Haugen or equalization fee plan was to set aside that portion of an agricultural staple required to meet the domestic demand from the exportable surplus. The former was to be sold at a fixed domestic price—world price plus protective tariff duties. The surplus was to be bought by a government agency at the domestic price and sold in world markets for whatever it would bring. The difference between the higher domestic price and the world price obtained for the surplus was to be met by the farmers of each commodity in the form of a tax or equalization fee. Since an increase in surplus would mean a larger equalization fee, and thus a lower price to the producer, it was believed that overproduction would be automatically reduced.

President Coolidge vetoed both McNary-Haugen bills on the ground that price-fixing through the equalization fee would result in an "intolerable espionage" carried out by a "widespread bureaucracy," that it would encourage speculation, that it would favor only certain crops at the expense of others, and that dumping American surplus products on foreign countries would bring resentment and retaliation from them. Congress was unable to pass the measures over the President's veto. The administration supported a different plan, presented by Secretary of Agriculture Jardine, which encouraged and empowered cooperatives working through stabilization agencies to control production. Herbert Hoover endorsed the plan during the campaign of 1928.

A special session of Congress enacted the Agricultural Marketing Act in June, 1929, and the Federal Farm Board, backed by a revolving fund of $500,000,000, was created. The law aimed to provide agriculture with a mechanism for the orderly marketing of farm crops comparable to such mechanisms in other industries. To accomplish this, the board was authorized to encourage cooperatives and to establish stabilization corporations. By the end of 1929, the board became most concerned with the maintenance of prices. It created a Grain Stabilization Corporation and a Cotton Stabilization Corporation to purchase and hold wheat and cotton in an attempt to halt the downward trend of prices in these commodities. The world-wide depression hindered the government attempt to increase prices by withholding surpluses, and by the close of 1931, the attempt to stabilize the two great staples had failed. Of $377,737,000 spent in market purchases, one-half was lost through declining prices, while storage charges threatened to consume the remaining equities in the commodities. The attempts to raise prices of other products by buying surpluses and withholding them from market met with the same failure. By 1933, most of the $500,000,000 revolving fund had been spent or pledged, partly in a vain attempt to stabilize prices and partly in loans to cooperatives, chiefly to help them carry out holding operations. The attempts of the board to induce farmers to cut down production also failed. In 1932, with mounting surpluses and stagnant markets, Congress discussed production control and other plans which were incorporated later into New Deal legislation. Aid was granted to the farmers in 1932 when Congress amended the Federal Farm Loan Act of 1916, which among other things provided for a loan of $125,000,000 to the Land Banks. The Reconstruction Finance Corporation also advanced money to farmers to save their farms through the agency of regional agricultural cooperatives, but both the banks and the cooperatives set requirements for their loans that the really needy farmers could not meet.

THE NEW DEAL IN AGRICULTURE

None of the legislation prior to 1933 met the related problems of staple crop prices demoralized by large surpluses and mortgage payments that could not be met. By 1932 wholesale prices for nonagricultural products had fallen only 22 per cent below the 1929 level; those of farm products were 54 per cent lower. Farmers were using surplus corn for fuel in order to get rid of it. Wheat was bringing 49 cents a bushel, the lowest recorded price in the history of American farming.

The New Deal measures discussed on page 583 tried to meet the problem by: (1) limiting the production of staples through quotas voluntarily agreed to in return for parity payments; (2) interest-free crop loans that, in effect, turned surpluses over to the government; and (3) government guarantee of mortgages at rates that, with the new controls, farmers should be able to meet. The application of the program was aided by severe droughts in 1934 and 1936 and hampered by legal difficulties. The Agricultural Adjustment Act of 1938 (p. 584) however, stood the tests of judicial interpretation and made quotas, parity payments, and crop loans a continuing part of Federal agricultural policy.

The Agricultural Adjustment Act of 1938 included provisions de-

signed to broaden the market for farm products in the light of increasing competition with foreign countries and a consequent narrowing
of world markets. It was planned to do this through surplus diversion,
as for example, distributing commodities to distressed or stricken
areas and by finding new uses for agricultural products. To this end
the law authorized the establishment of four research laboratories
at Peoria, Illinois, in the New Orleans area, in the Philadelphia area,
and in the San Francisco area. The statute also set up the Federal Crop
Insurance Corporation, an agency of the Department of Agriculture.
With a capital stock of $100,000,000, it was empowered to write insur-
ance against losses from drought, flood, and insects for the wheat farmers of the country.

In order to carry out the broadened farm program, the Department
of Agriculture was reorganized in 1938. One of the principal changes
was the reorganization of the Bureau of Agricultural Economics as
a central agency to keep in touch with local, county, and state committees. It was charged with the duty of familiarizing itself with the
problems of all classes and interests in agriculture. It was expanded
to include trained personnel representing almost every major aspect
of modern agriculture. Among other changes in the Department was
the grouping of marketing activities and the appointment of a Director
of Marketing to coordinate that field. Another important change came
with the setting up of the Agricultural Program Board, composed of the
heads of action agencies, planning agencies, and several of the directors,
with the Land Use Co-ordinator as chairman. The duty of this Board
was to pass finally on all completed programs before they were put
into effect. One of the chief problems facing the Department of Agriculture was to coordinate its many and varied programs.

Between 1932 and 1937, farm income rose from $3.3 billion to
$7.2 billion. But by 1937, good weather had increased production and
the business recession had decreased consumption, defeating to a great
extent the attempts to develop a regulated program of restriction.
Despite reduced acreage of cotton, the crop in 1937 reached the unprecedented figure of 19,000,000 bales and the average price was but
eight cents a pound. The government took more than a fourth of it
as loan collateral and the 1938 crop was cut one-fifth. Record surpluses
of wheat resulted in 1937, and it was becoming more and more evident
that uncontrollable world conditions were complicating the American
program beyond solution. The world average price of wheat dropped
from ninety-six cents a bushel in 1937 to fifty cents a bushel in 1938,
compared to a parity price of $1.12. Large surpluses also appeared in

dairy products, fruits, and potatoes, although the picture was not so dark in connection with corn, livestock, and tobacco. Farm income for 1938 was about 18 per cent less than in 1937, in spite of an increase of Federal aid to agriculture. While the New Deal program had put a tax-supported floor under agricultural income, it had not met the basic problem of too many small farms. In fact, in so far as the government dealt with this problem, it favored an increase in subsistence farming for the unemployed.

The rapid rise of farm income from 1933 to 1937, however, led the more successful farmers to invest in new machinery and apply more scientific knowledge. This was reflected in a rise in the curve of productivity per man-hour that until 1960, at least, was to mount more rapidly than ever before. It took the Second World War with its demands for both farm products and manpower to begin to cut into the problem of uneconomically small farms and surplus agricultural labor. Between 1940 and 1946, four hundred thousand farms were merged in larger holdings, and employment on farms dropped 700,000. These were merely portents of the changes to come in the later forties, the fifties and the sixties, as agricultural workers found better jobs in industry.

UNITED STATES WHEAT SUPPLY AND DISTRIBUTION, 1952 – 1962

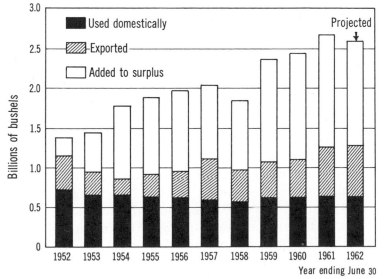

Source: U.S. Department of Agriculture.

Meanwhile, during the war years total farm acreage rose slightly and total farm product increased by more than 20 per cent.

CONTINUING PROBLEMS

Prosperity during the Second World War changed the situation of the farmer. His income rose rapidly in spite of government price controls, while his expenses increased only about two-thirds as fast. Farmlands and stock mounted in value. Farm mortgages were liquidated and farms operated by tenants fell from 2,400,000 in 1940 to 1,400,000 in 1950, reducing tenancy to 27 per cent of the total number of farms. Price controls over agricultural products were removed late in 1945 with the result that prices of farm products generally increased about 25 per cent. Yet even though the condition of the farmer had improved, industrial labor was better off than farm labor.

In the years from 1945 to 1960 the change in agriculture from a general American way of life to a specialized activity carried on with industrial machinery continued at a rapid rate. The number of farms which from 1910 to 1940 had remained fairly stable at about 6,500,000 now dropped to 3,700,000 by 1960, and average acreage per farm rose above 250. But in spite of a fall in the number of farm owners and workers, including family workers, to about 7,500,000, to a smaller number than those in manufacturing, trade, service, or government, large surpluses in production continued.

This rapid decline in the number of farms was stimulated by continuing opportunity for industrial jobs between 1945 and 1957. The latter permitted southern farmers, in particular, to end the leases of sharecroppers and use the land for raising cattle rather than cotton. Cotton production, now largely mechanized, moved to larger farms in the West. With continuing industrial opportunity the number of cultivators and workers would continue to fall.

Back of the sudden change in the relations of farm ownership and labor to farm product was the damming up of the forces for agricultural change prior to 1940 and their sudden release by the Second World War. New machines of many types attachable to all-purpose gasoline motors were now good investments for farmers. In 1940 only one farmer in four owned a tractor; by 1960 there were over a million more tractors than farms, and 35 per cent of the cultivators had two or more tractors. In the early thirties only one farm in ten had electricity, by 1960 nearly all farms were electrified. With electricity went radio, in favored areas television, and numerous labor-saving electrical appliances. Hybrid seeds that cost more than the regular varieties but

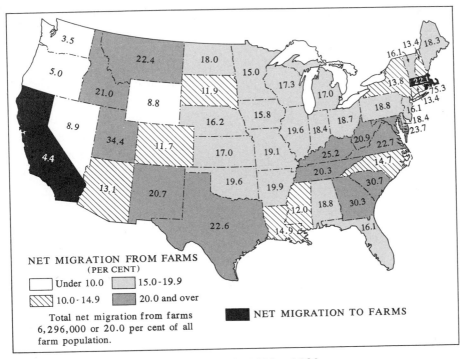

NET MIGRATION FROM FARMS
(PER CENT)

☐ Under 10.0	☐ 15.0-19.9
☒ 10.0-14.9	☐ 20.0 and over

Total net migration from farms
6,296,000 or 20.0 per cent of all
farm population.

■ NET MIGRATION TO FARMS

NET MIGRATION TO AND FROM FARMS, 1920 – 1930

could increase production by 20 per cent or more became the rule on successful farms. Farmers anxious to cash in on the war boom were willing to experiment with new fertilizers and methods that had developed from great advances in soil chemistry and biology since 1920. By selective breeding of poultry and live stock for meat, and by extra heavy feeding, it was possible to get more food and less waste from each animal. During the decade of the fifties man-hour productivity on farms increased an average of 6 per cent a year, a far higher rate than in industry.

All of these avenues to abundance, which removed any fear of long-run food shortage from the western world, were welcomed during the period of European reconstruction and the Korean War when farm income steadily mounted, but by 1953 American farmers were again facing declining income and mounting surpluses, and government was looked to for relief. The Eisenhower administration promised a "solid" agricultural plan that would include the principle of price supports and that would also build markets, safeguard farm income and protect consumers. The President stated that aside from the drought in some critical areas of the Great Plains states, agricultural problems stemmed from war-expanded production that exceeded market demand and reserve requirements.

The aim of the farm bill of 1954 was a system of more flexible price supports. From 1938 to 1942 the Secretary of Agriculture had been able to determine at his own discretion each year what percentage of "parity" should be regarded as a reasonable "floor" for each of the covered farm commodities. He was limited only by a minimum of 52 per cent and a maximum of 75 per cent. In selecting the support level he was guided chiefly by the supply situation in each particular commodity. During the Second World War in order to stimulate agricultural output the government passed emergency legislation which, among other things, set 90 per cent of parity as the fixed floor under basic agricultural commodities. In 1948 a conservative Congress gave the Secretary of Agriculture power after 1950 to lower support prices as production increased down to a minimum of 60 per cent of parity. If farmers failed to vote marketing quotas for any of the basic crops, support would drop to 50 per cent of parity. The law was slightly amended in 1949 to alter the means of computing parity, but the Korean War prevented the law from having much effect from 1950 to 1952 and supports remained at 90 per cent.

In the Republican farm bill of 1954 an administration anxious to move toward restoration of laissez faire was blocked by the powerful farm lobbies. When the bill finally passed, it made little alteration in the existing system. Wheat, corn, cotton, rice, and peanuts would get flexible props of from 82.5 per cent to 90 per cent of parity. While Secretary Benson lowered some supports, the change was too small to affect existing trends. Overproduction continued to make farm income decline.

In 1956 a new law for a "soil bank" allowed the Secretary to pay farmers for withdrawing acreage from production. This and other forces in 1957-1958 gave a temporary boost to farm income, but at the expense of the taxpayer. Farmers received payments for withdrawing acreage, some 38,000,000 acres, and then proceeded to grow more than ever before on the remaining land. As a result, agricultural benefit payments reached an all-time high of $6 billion, the government continued to store more and more surplus crops for which it had paid $8 billion, and income soon resumed its downward trend.

While government subsidies were keeping perhaps two million small farmers on their land, the most efficient proprietors, even in the staple crop areas, were finding it possible to make a profit from mass production at market prices and to make a fine addition to income from government subsidies. Other farmers in regions with favorable climate had long since abandoned the parity supported staples in favor of fruits, vegetables, dairy products, and other specialties. Some farmers were in fact tied into the business system in the same way as subcontractors in industry. They made annual contracts with big food processing companies to deliver products in certain quantities at set prices. The economic farm problem, therefore, was chiefly one of how to readjust the conditions of staple production to the market without either liquidating the uneconomic proprietors through the operation of supply and demand, or having the government exercise powers regarded as inconsistent with the free enterprise system.

CHAPTER 31

The Rise of Organized Labor

The history of labor from 1914 to 1960 has a sharp turning point in 1935. Up to that time organized labor in the United States was relatively weak and generally confined to the skilled crafts. Even at the peak reached in 1920 only 18.5 per cent of the nonagricultural workers were organized, and in normal years between 1910 and 1935 the percentage ran about 12. From 1935 on organized labor strongly aided by government undertook unionization of mass production industries and ultimately achieved a stable level with about one-third of the non-agricultural labor force organized.

POSTWAR BOOM

Organized labor emerged from the First World War more powerful than ever before and somewhat inclined toward radicalism. A total of about 5,000,000 union members in 1920, of whom 4,000,000 belonged to the American Federation of Labor bore witness to the effects of the war and the postwar boom. The dissatisfaction of labor as the rising cost of living forged ahead of the increases in wages had caused much unrest during the war, but serious trouble had been averted through the establishment and work of the National War Labor Board although many strikes occurred even in 1918. After the war, the discontent of labor, stimulated by the process of readjustment

666

to peacetime activities, together with the determination to restore real wage levels, if possible, resulted in a record number of strikes.

One of the most significant strikes after the war—one that illustrated the weakness of craft unionism in mass production—occurred in the steel industry.

For a generation attempts had been made to unionize that industry, but without success. Following the failure of a strike in 1909, the open shop generally prevailed in the industry. The First World War presented an opportunity to organize labor in the steel plants of the country. Led by the American Federation of Labor, twenty-four unions in 1918 established a Committee for Organizing the Steel Industry and a campaign was inaugurated. Attempts to negotiate with the steel companies failed. A strike to force recognition of the union, higher wages, and the eight-hour day began in September, 1919. About 400,000 men were involved altogether. The large number of such nationals as Yugoslavians, Czechoslovakians, Greeks, Italians, and Poles, as well as Welshmen, Englishmen, Irishmen, and Americans, working in the mills under such conditions as the twelve-hour day and seven-day week, the

DISTRIBUTION OF CHIEF OCCUPATIONS, 1900 – 1961
(In thousands)

Occupation	1900	1920	1940	1961
Professional, Technical	1,234	2,283	3,879	7,201
Managers, Proprietors	1,697	2,803	3,770	6,852
Clerical, Sales	2,184	5,443	8,432	14,539
Skilled Labor, Foremen	3,062	5,482	6,203	8,984
Operative	3,720	6,587	9,518	12,000
Laborers, except farm and mine	3,620	4,905	4,875	4,065
Private Household Workers	1,579	1,411	2,412	2,096
Other Service	1,047	1,901	3,657	6,603
Farmers, Farm Managers	5,763	6,442	5,362	2,800
Farm Laborers, Foremen	5,125	4,948	3,632	3,362

Sources: U.S. Bureau of the Census, *Historical Statistics of the United States, Colonial Times to 1957*, Washington, D.C., 1960, p. 74; and *The World Almanac, 1962*, p. 256.

extensive use by employers of black-listing, the employment of labor spies, and the control of the community life of the workers, both inspired and impeded the attempt at organization. Although all labor leaders agreed on the immediate aims of the strike, there was a division of opinion among them as to the ultimate plans of the labor movement. Disputes occurred over the merits of craft unionism over industrial unionism, skilled trade unionism over working class solidarity, and conservative unionism over revolutionary or radical unionism. The employers were not slow to take advantage of these divisions of opinion among the labor leaders, and they gave publicity to the differences.

An impartial commission of the Interchurch World Movement investigated conditions in the industry and reported that grievances of workers were real. The commission declared that it found an average work week of sixty-eight hours, the underpayment of unskilled labor, the military regimentation of workers, and the autocratic control of the industry by management. When the commission offered mediation, former judge Elbert H. Gary, chairman of the Board of Directors of the United States Steel Corporation, insisted that the result of a victory for unionism would be communism and a forcible division of property.

The strike was ill-timed and inadequately supported by the unwieldy number of craft unions involved. The cry of many workers, "In union there is strength," had little reality. Steel orders were on the decline, and the mills were successful in obtaining nonunion labor. The fears on the part of the public that sovietism was developing in the United States obscured the repudiation of collective bargaining by the employers. The strike collapsed and ended in January, 1920. Two years later, the United States Steel Corporation gave the workers the basic eight-hour day, and in the years that followed, steel workers received other concessions that they had demanded, although inflexible opposition to the unionization of the workers was maintained until 1937.

Among other strikes of the postwar period, the bituminous coal strike of 1919–1920 in the Indiana coal fields was serious. A federal commission adjusted the wage dispute, and the strike was temporarily ended. A threatened strike of anthracite miners in June, 1920, was averted by an agreement made between the employers and employees to submit differences to a commission for settlement. But in April, 1922, the miners of both bituminous and anthracite fields went on a strike which lasted five months, involving 500,000 union miners and 90,000 nonunion men. It was caused by the attempt of the mine owners to deflate war wages. Agreements were made whereby the workers

WORKERS INVOLVED IN STRIKES, 1927 – 1957

Year	Percentage of Employed Wage Earners Involved	Percentage of Annual Working Time Lost	Year	Percentage of Employed Wage Earners Involved	Percentage of Annual Working Time Lost	Year	Percentage of Employed Wage Earners Involved	Percentage of Annual Working Time Lost
1927	1.4	0.37	1938	2.8	0.15	1948	5.5	0.37
1928	1.3	0.17	1939	4.7	0.28	1949	9.0	0.59
1929	1.2	0.07	1940	2.3	0.10	1950	6.9	0.44
1930	0.8	0.05	1941	8.4	0.32	1951	5.5	0.23
1931	1.6	0.11	1942	2.8	0.05	1952	8.8	0.57
1932	1.8	0.23	1943	6.9	0.15	1953	5.6	0.26
1933	6.3	0.36	1944	7.0	0.09	1954	3.7	0.21
1934	7.2	0.38	1945	12.2	0.47	1955	6.2	0.26
1935	5.2	0.29	1946	14.5	1.43	1956	4.3	0.29
1936	3.1	0.21	1947	6.5	0.41	1957	3.1	0.14
1937	7.2	0.43						

Source: U.S. Bureau of the Census, *Historical Statistics of the United States, Colonial Times to 1957*, Washington, D.C., 1960, p. 99.

were to receive the old wages until March, 1923, and fact-finding commissions were provided for. A new strike threatened the anthracite industry in 1923 when the old contract expired. Then Congress took a hand. It authorized the Interstate Commerce Commission to control coal shipments in the emergency and to force down unjust prices. It provided for a coal director and created a coal commission to investigate. The commission recommended a law empowering the President to take over and operate the mines whenever operators and workers were deadlocked. At this point, President Harding appointed Governor Gifford Pinchot of Pennsylvania as mediator. He succeeded in effecting a settlement. In another strike lasting from September, 1925, to February, 1926, President Coolidge refused to interfere and the strikers lost.

In the summer of 1922, the railroad shopmen walked out because of a 12 per cent cut in wages, authorized by the Railroad Labor Board. The strike was an attack on the authority of the Board. Subpoenas issued to railroad managers and union heads were not obeyed. A White House conference produced no results, although an injunction of a Federal court, forbidding trespassing on railroad property, did. By September, an agreement was reached and the men returned to work. In 1926, the Railroad Labor Board was abolished, and railroad disputes were turned back to the interested parties for settlement. The law provided for adjustment through mediators and fact-finders without authority to enforce their decisions.

ANTIUNION PRESSURES

The dramatic decline of the American Federation of Labor from 4,000,000 members in 1920 to 2,900,000 in 1923 was accentuated by several factors besides severe unemployment in the depression of 1921 and 1922. The fear of radicalism that mounted to panicky heights among the upper classes made it easy for employer organizations to mobilize public opinion against unions. Newspaper advertisements warned against the closed shop; banks refused credit to firms dealing with union labor; employers' associations demanded the right to handle the labor relations of their members so that no contracts would be negotiated with unions; and spies, strike breakers, and company police were used more extensively than ever before. Antiunion sentiment affected the courts. Although the Clayton Act of 1914 had forbidden injunctions in labor disputes except where irreparable damage would be done to property, the courts used this loophole to justify scores of Federal injunctions. In 1928, the A. F. of L. published a list of 389 injunctions issued by Federal and state courts since 1919, and the list would doubtless have been much longer had methods less costly than appeal to the courts not been successful in many strikes.

Even in the prosperous years from 1923 to 1929 the A. F. of L. lost 100,000 more members. Dues were high, and as militancy declined, unions with substantial treasuries tended to fall under the control of officials interested mainly in money and power, or labor racketeers. The National Executive Council of the A. F. of L. still continued to resist association with the masses of unskilled labor. The A. F. of L. also failed to organize workers in the automobile industry and in the growing textile mills of the South, while at the same time it could not revitalize the Amalgamated Association of Iron, Steel, and Tin Workers. The death in 1924 of Samuel Gompers, whose leadership passed to the equally conservative but less able William Green, was another factor in the loss of power of the A. F. of L. Dissatisfaction, too, among the more radical elements caused difficulties which were to divide the organization in the next decade. But prosperity in most industries, industrial welfare programs, and profit-sharing plans, plus the fact that real wages were high, served to keep workers in a state of relative contentment. As labor organizations declined, the open shop triumphed, but not for long.

TECHNOLOGICAL UNEMPLOYMENT

Technological unemployment, the term used to denote unemployment which results from increasing mechanization, began to worry both intellectuals and labor leaders in the twenties. The problem was new only in its magnitude. The introduction of the blast furnace in the late Middle Ages, for example, interfered with the employment of those who had always crudely hammered out iron at Catalan forges. But it was in eighteenth-century England that serious antagonism to new inventions first developed. The power loom was assailed by those whose daily life and existence it directly affected and who could not see that ultimately it would create thousands of jobs for every one it destroyed. The results were machine-breaking riots, the persecution of inventors, and legal safeguards for old processes and various restrictions on new ones.

The changes in industry throughout the nineteenth and twentieth centuries showed a little more clearly the suffering brought to groups of workers because of their displacement by machines in various industries. In the United States, the linotype and cigar-molding machines were, at the time, outstanding examples. But it was in the decade or so following the First World War, as the machine came of age and as seeming prosperity fell on the country, that the serious effects of labor-saving machinery on those who were being displaced became more and more evident. Even in the most prosperous years of the "golden decade," more than 2,000,000 men were unemployed and many of these were out of work because of developments in production techniques. Skilled workers who were dislocated, especially the older men, found it difficult to adapt and adjust themselves to new positions and were forced to become laborers if they were fortunate enough to secure such jobs. This dislocation was obvious, for example, in the introduction of the hot-strip mill for the rolling of tin plate and sheet steel, which abolished more than 100,000 jobs in that industry. The same was true in many other industries as mechanization and scientific management produced more goods with fewer workers. In only a few cases at this time were any attempts made to retrain or transfer the employees to other positions. The influence of competitive practices and the power of labor organizations operate to prevent such planning.

While new processes have resulted in misery and suffering to large groups of workers, the long-time effects of the rapid mechanization of industry to the employment of workers is still a controversial issue. The electrical and automobile industries have opened up hundreds of thousands of new positions. Yet only sixty men were needed to do as much work in manufacturing in 1930 as 100 men had done in 1920. If new industries, such as the electrical and automobile trades, could be established periodically, there would be little question about the

UNEMPLOYMENT, 1926 – 1941

(In thousands of persons 14 years old and over)

Year	Unemployed	Year	Unemployed	Year	Unemployed
1926	880	1932	12,060	1937	7,700
1927	1,890	1933	12,830	1938	10,390
1928	2,080	1934	11,340	1939	9,480
1929	1,550	1935	10,610	1940	8,120
1930	4,340	1936	9,030	1941	5,560
1931	8,020				

Source: U.S. Bureau of the Census, *Historical Statistics of the United States, Colonial Times to 1957*, Washington, D.C., 1960, p. 73.

long-time gain to labor. It is, however, difficult to determine the full effects of changing technology on the general volume of employment and unemployment because such an analysis involves improvements in methods and management, changes in mechanical inventions, the varying prices of goods and services, problems regarding the migration of workers, and the effects of prosperity and depression upon industry.

LABOR IN THE DEPRESSION

The massive unemployment that started in 1930 was far more serious than any caused by technological displacement. Companies making capital goods such as machine tools or locomotives gradually dismissed most of their work force. Unskilled and part-time workers suffered severely, making unemployment higher among Negroes than whites. Many workers listed as employed were working short hours at reduced wages.

The Hoover administration did not deal directly with the labor problem, but the bipartisan National Industrial Recovery Act of 1933 (see p. 579) had provisions regarding wages, hours, and the right of collective bargaining. Section 7A of the law provided that all companies should enter into collective bargaining with their organized employees, but it did not clearly specify the conditions. The larger companies immediately started fulfilling the requirement by setting up company-sponsored unions and then bargaining with them. As a result, company union strength doubled from 1932 to 1935 and reached 2,500,000 in the latter year, as compared with 3,500,000 organized in national trade unions. Of companies with over 10,000 employees, 80 per cent had company unions.

The great opportunities for new organizing were in the mass-production industries that had resisted the craft system of the A. F. of L. General Johnson, the head of the National Recovery Administration, was not friendly to union labor and did little to enforce Section 7A for labor's benefit. After a short period his office was referred to by union leaders as the National Run Around. The group that controlled the Executive Council of the A. F. of L., mainly from the building trades, was opposed to industrial organization and failed to take advantage of the opportunities offered by the codes.

The Wagner Act in 1935 was explicit as to the right of a union representing a majority of the workers to bargain with the employer and placed restrictions on his interfering with union organizers. Furthermore, the National Labor Relations Board that administered the act was friendly to union contracts and higher wages. The door was now wide open to aggressive union activity.

Meanwhile, John L. Lewis of the United Mine Workers and some other A. F. of L. leaders, working in defiance of the views of President William Green and the Executive Council, had started drives for industrial organization. At the 1935 annual meeting of the A. F. of L. this group introduced a resolution for support of industrial unions in industries where a majority of the workers were under two or more union jurisdictions. In spite of the Biblical eloquence of Lewis, the resolution was defeated by the votes of 62 per cent of the delegates. Disregarding this defeat the leaders of eight unions set up a Committee for Industrial Organization and went to work. At the next annual meeting the A. F. of L. expelled these unions, and in 1937 the rebellious leaders plus men from other industries formed the Congress of Industrial Organizations.

Except for opening its membership to all crafts and levels of skill, the structure of the C. I. O. was much like that of the A. F. of L. It operated through state and local federations and was governed between annual meetings by an Executive Council and a president. Moreover, the A. F. of L., recognizing its defeat, started developing industrial unions. The real difference in the two organizations was in age and attitudes. The new movement appealed to younger, more radical leaders and organizers who for some years gave the C. I. O. higher morale and greater devotion to the cause of its members than could be expected from the entrenched rulers of the old unions.

Vigorous organizing campaigns were undertaken by the C. I. O. in steel, rubber, and motors. The sit-down strike, first used on a wide scale in Italy following the First World War and in France in 1936, was now tried in the United States by the United Automobile Workers and other industrial unions affiliated with the C. I. O. By the new technique strikers took possession of a plant, claiming that the sit-down strike was legal because it was "the most effective and least costly way" for workers to protect their rights. National attention was focussed on this type of strike when it was used in January, 1937, to force a complete suspension of work at the General Motors plant at Flint, Michigan. As sit-down strikes spread, law suits were instituted. In 1939, in the case of the National Labor Relations Board *vs.* Fansteel Metallurgical Corporation, the Supreme Court held that while workers had a right to strike, they had "no license to commit acts of violence or to seize their employer's plant" and that the sit-down strike was "illegal in its inception and prosecution." Following the decision this form of strike practically ceased in the United States, although "slow downs" took its place in many areas.

As a result of the 1937 organizing campaigns, the United States Steel Corporation, General Motors, and the Chrysler Corporation signed agreements. The independent steel companies held out for some time. The Republic Steel Company, Bethlehem Steel Corporation, Jones and Laughlin Steel Corporation, and others led by Tom Girdler of Republic and Eugene Grace of Bethlehem held out; but after strikes, violence, and hard-fought battles, they had to capitulate. The C. I. O. also established unions in other industries including the textile, electrical, radio, rubber, motor truck, and shoe industries as well as in sailors' and longshoremen's organizations. It attempted with less success to extend its unionism to agriculture through its organization of cannery, packing, and agricultural workers.

While the C. I. O. was developing, the expansion of union sentiment among the American working class aided the A. F. of L. Many employers, who had earlier refused to have anything to do with unions, fearing the militant C. I. O., now signed contracts with the A. F. of L. The two organizations fought each other in many parts of the country as they sought to unionize workers. President Roosevelt tried unsuccessfully to bring about a reunion of the two groups. By 1940, each organization claimed a membership of 4,000,000. Regardless of whether these figures were accurate or not, organized labor had made its greatest advances in history under the New Deal.

KEEPING PACE WITH INFLATION

After the outbreak of the war in Europe as prices and employment began to rise, strikes increased rapidly. In the first five months of 1941 strikes were five times greater than for the corresponding period of 1940. Some menaced the defense program and as a result the government temporarily took over three plants—those of the North American Aviation Company at Inglewood, California, the Federal Drydock and Shipbuilding Company at Kearny, New Jersey, and the Air Association Inc. at Bendix, New Jersey. A serious dispute occurred late in 1941 when John L. Lewis ordered a strike of 53,000 miners in the "captive" bituminous coal mines—those owned by and producing only for seven of the largest steel companies—which threatened to tie up the production of needed steel. The issue was finally settled by the acceptance of the closed shop by the companies involved. At the same time a nationwide strike was threatened by the railroad brotherhoods. It was averted by a government fact-finding agency, which granted a part of the demand for higher wages.

In return for their no-strike pledge during the war the C. I. O. and A. F. of L. were allowed maintenance of membership clauses in their contracts. As a result thousands of new workers recruited for defense purposes automatically joined unions, and subsequently union membership which had stood at 9,000,000 in 1940 rose to 15,000,000 by 1945. While there were no strikes officially called by the labor federations, there were wildcat work stoppages and threats of stoppage that exerted an upward pressure on wages. The War Labor Board granted the "Little Steel formula" of 15 per cent above January, 1941, and made numerous additional adjustments. While the official cost of living rose less than 25 per cent from 1941 to 1945, hourly rates in manufacturing advanced nearly 40 per cent, and in addition many workers steadily received overtime pay.

Large overtime pay was an obviously unstable element supporting the worker's standard of living, and its loss or the threat of its loss helped to bring on the labor crisis of 1946. With resumption of the right to strike the union leaders were bound to test the situation, and still harassed by price controls, management was bound to resist. During the year 1946, more than twice as many man-days of work, 116 million, were lost in strikes as in any other year in United States history.

The major strikes started late in 1945 when the United Auto Workers (C. I. O.) demanded a 30 per cent wage increase from General Motors. The strike continued for 113 days and ended only after a fact-finding board recommended to the President a general wage raise of 19.5 cents an hour, although an increase of 18.5 cents an hour was finally agreed upon. The strike cost $125,000,000 in wages and $600,-000,000 in lost production at a time when automobiles and trucks were scarce and in great demand.

Demands for large wage increases led to strikes in the electrical, telegraph, meat-packing, bituminous coal, and railroad industries. Settlements of these disputes were generally made on the basis of an increase to employees of 18.5 cents an hour. The bituminous coal strike was marked by the government seizure and operation of the mines from May, 1946, to June, 1947. In November, 1946, John L. Lewis refused to accept the plan worked out by Secretary of the Interior Julius A. Krug, and on the declaration by Lewis of "no contract, no work," 400,000 soft coal miners "stayed home." This led to a court injunction against Lewis and a trial for contempt of court when he failed to order the miners back to work. After seventeen days he called off the strike, but the government's injunction suit resulted in a fine in the United States District Court of $3,500,000 for the United Mine Workers and $10,000 for its president. Upon appeal, the Supreme Court ruled that both the union and its president were in civil and criminal contempt, but by a narrow decision (5–4), the nine justices held that the Norris-La Guardia Anti-Injunction Act of 1932 did not prevent the Federal government from using the injunction against labor unions under the circumstances. The Court confirmed the $10,000 fine against Lewis but reduced the union's fine to $700,000 if it would rescind its notice to the government of contract cancellation. This was done by Lewis on March 19, 1947.

The coal strike and the railroad strikes of 1946 resulted in a stiffening of the administration's attitude toward labor disputes. As the railroad strike began, President Truman told the nation that he would "have no alternative but to operate the trains by using every means within my power." The next day (May 25, 1946), as the President addressed a joint session of Congress on the dispute, a message was handed to him stating that the two brotherhoods which had held out against the President's compromise offer that included an increase of 18.5 cents an hour had signed the agreement and the strike was ended. In Congress, the Case Strike Control Bill, which had been considered for several months, was passed. The measure revived the weapons of court injunctions and suits against labor under the antitrust laws, prohibited by the Norris-La Guardia and Wagner labor acts. The new bill also provided for a Federal Mediation Board to intercede in labor disputes and for a sixty-day cooling-off period before a strike could begin. The President, however, feeling that the bill went too far, vetoed it, and the House sustained him. The President's request for a long-range congressional investigation into the causes of industrial disputes as a basis for permanent labor legislation was not considered.

With price controls ended, a pattern for a second round of wage increases in large industries was set peacefully in the spring of 1947 when the steel and auto workers' unions within the C. I. O. signed contracts with important companies for raises of about 15 cents an hour. The steel union made a two-year, no-strike contract and received a basic raise of 12.5 cents an hour plus another 2.5 cents for "fringe" items. While there were serious labor disputes, the number of strikes and the number of men involved by the latter part of 1947 had dropped considerably. In fact, to much of the public it seemed that big manufacturing companies, able to control prices in their markets, were too willing to avoid labor trouble by raising both wages and prices. It seemed that the emphasis of large-scale managerial enterprise on employee welfare presented a threat of continual inflation.

These fears, plus a Republican majority in the House of Representatives for the first time in fourteen years led to government action in 1947 to curb the power of organized labor. Congress passed the Labor-Management Relations (Taft-Hartley) Act over the veto of President Truman, and the legislatures of thirty states enacted measures limiting the privileges and regulating the activities of labor unions. The laws were fiercely fought by the American Federation of Labor, the Congress of Industrial Organizations, the Railroad Brotherhoods (though not directly affected by the Taft-Hartley law), and by many independent unions. Labor declared war on the legislators responsible for the laws, demanding their retirement and the repeal of the legislation.

The Taft-Hartley Act recognized the right of employees to organize and to bargain with management, but declared that the closed shop, making union membership a condition of employment, was illegal. The law set forth the conditions for collective bargaining and authorized the National Labor Relations Board, now increased from three to five members, to seek injunctions or restraining orders in cases of secondary boycotts, jurisdictional strikes, and the compulsory employment of additional help without specified duties. Unions were made liable for damages resulting from failure to live up to their contracts. Procedures were set up for delaying strikes that might create a national emergency. The books and records of unions were to be open to inspection, and union officials had to declare openly that they were not Communists, an issue that had become important especially in connection with several C. I. O. unions. Those who favored the new legislation insisted that it restored a fair balance between management and labor and eliminated abuses harmful to both and to the public. Labor leaders called it a "slave law," while President Truman condemned it as discriminatory against labor and predicted that it would promote friction, but he promised to administer the law fairly. In his campaign of 1948 the President pledged himself to do everything possible to secure its repeal.

Just after the Taft-Hartley bill became law, 400,000 soft coal miners began ten-day paid "vacations" which were legal under the agreement worked out between Secretary of the Interior Krug and John L. Lewis the previous year. The walkout again threatened to retard the steel and automobile industries and to tie up railroad transportation. After ten days Lewis signed a new wage agreement with the operators of the "captive" mines of the United States Steel Corporation, in spite of opposition from other operators, including those of the South, all of whom eventually signed the same contract. The new agreement raised the average miner's daily pay, reduced working hours from nine to eight, and provided benefits in vacation and welfare fund payments, as well as other concessions, including the right of the miners to work only when they were "able and willing." The contract showed that labor could win victories despite the Taft-Hartley law.

In 1947, Congress passed another measure, opposed by many labor organizations, particularly the C. I. O. It resulted from suits filed in 1946 and 1947 totaling more than $400 billion in claims for "portal-to-portal" pay, a term first used by the coal miners in maintaining that they should be paid for the time in which they traveled to and from the gate of a mine to the point where they actually worked. The claims of the various unions were based on a court interpretation of the Fair Labor Standards (Wage-Hour) Act. Congress took the view that the judicial interpretation was incorrect and that if applied it would bankrupt many industrial concerns. A measure which was finally adopted invalidated all "portal" claims not covered specifically by labor contracts and placed a two-year limit on future claims. President Truman signed the bill stating that he did not believe it undermined the basic wage-hour standard, as some critics of the bill claimed, but urged Congress to raise the legal minimum wages and to extend the wage-hour law to workers not covered by it.

UNION MEMBERSHIP IN THE UNITED STATES, 1915 – 1960
(In thousands)

Year	Union Membership	Year	Union Membership
1915	2,583	1940	8,717
1920	5,048	1945	14,322
1925	3,519	1950	14,300
1930	3,393	1955	16,802
1935	3,584	1960	17,049

Sources: U.S. Bureau of the Census, *Historical Statistics of the United States, Colonial Times to 1957*, Washington, D.C., 1960, p. 98; and *Statistical Abstract of the United States 1962*, Washington, D.C., 1962, p. 241.

Opposition to communism, aided by developments in the international situation, became an objective of many unions. At the 1947 Convention of the United Automobile Workers, Walter P. Reuther, the union's president, removed officials who were Communists and even those who had accepted Communist support. In 1950, eleven "Communist" unions were expelled from the C. I. O. Congress considered measures to outlaw the Communist party, but William Green, president of the A. F. of L., stated that he believed such a law would make martyrs of the Communists and suggested that foreign ideology be combatted by raising American living standards.

The cost of living reached a peak in 1948, and organized labor generally was able to secure a "third round" of wage increases, though not as large as the two that preceded it. Unimpeded by the Taft-Hartley law, a number of strikes occurred. The most significant was the spring coal strike, and once again John L. Lewis secured for the miners higher wages, an increase in the welfare fund, and the enforcement of the union's pension plan of $100 a month for every union miner sixty years of age or over with twenty-year service at the mines. A railroad strike was averted by a court injunction and intervention by the President, while maritime and longshoremen's strikes had serious results on both East and West coasts and on the Great Lakes. The General Motors Corporation averted a strike of its United Auto Workers union by granting an increase of wages which provided for tying wage rates to the cost of living as determined by the Bureau of Labor Statistics price index. As organized labor prepared for a "fourth round" of wage increases at the end of 1948 and beginning of 1949, unemployment increased somewhat, and it became obvious that supply had caught up with demand in a number of industries; the cost of living dropped slightly, but no sharp change in economic conditions was anticipated. The demands for increased wages became fewer, and many workers were satisfied with better social benefits. In the nation's basic industries, the rounds of pay increases had more than met the higher cost of living, but many "white collar workers" and others unaffiliated with unions received few pay raises and suffered as a result.

While the number of strikes totalled a few thousand each year, the most serious labor dispute of the fifties was the steel strike of 1952, carried on by the United Steel workers (C.I.O.). The strike had been postponed from time to time while the Wage Stabilization Board studied the case. The results, however, proved fruitless. A strike set for April 9 was called off when President Truman, instead of using the emergency powers of the Taft-Hartley law, seized and ran the steel industry, on the basis of emergency powers conferred during the Second

World War. Two months later the United States Supreme Court held the government seizure of the steel mills to be invalid. Then a strike occurred which was terminated by an agreement for wage increases, while the steel companies received permission to raise their basic steel ceiling by $5.20 a ton. The strike was the longest and costliest ever carried on in steel history. Production of about 17,000,000 tons of steel was delayed and the dispute cost the workers $350,000,000 in wages. Among other difficult labor disputes of the period were those carried on by the Commercial Telegraphers Union, the Railroad Brotherhoods, and the A. F. of L. International Council of Aluminum Workers.

While American unions had been successful in winning higher rates of pay, they had only in rare instances achieved guaranteed all-year-round income for their members, or the security of high severance pay. In 1952 the steel and auto unions of the C. I. O. made a "guaranteed annual wage" a major part of their demands. Employers were asked to put a percentage of wage payments into a guarantee fund which would be used to supplement government unemployment insurance. The chief automobile companies agreed to the plan in 1955, on the basis of supplementary payments for a 26-week period. While only a few other companies adopted the system, the campaign led management to plan still more carefully for uniform levels of production.

THE MERGER

By the mid-fifties neither the A. F. of L. or the C. I. O. were radical or crusading organizations. They no longer differed on the matter of industrial unionism. Both had industrial organizations and both had craft departments within their organizations to take care of certain skilled groups. Both had adopted Gomper's ideal of business unionism: using their resources for higher wages and shorter hours rather than for social or political reforms. Both had reached a fairly stable position in relation to the total labor force. From 1945 to 1960, union strength varied between 32 and 35 per cent of the nonagricultural labor force with no trend toward increase. Manufacturing labor was mainly organized, other types of labor were not, and as manufacturing employment was falling in relation to service activities, which were largely unorganized, the outlook for any rapid spread of unionism was not bright.

Not only did the leaders of the two big organizations become more alike in attitudes, but they also became more like the business executives with whom they dealt. The well-paid union leader was an organization man; he had accepted the capitalist system and found his place in it. Thus, while the union representatives might be tough and skillful bargainers, always trying to increase the issues subject to negotiation, they did not challenge ultimate managerial responsibility. They did not ask for representation on boards of directors or nationalization of industry.

With the death of the two elderly presidents, William Green of the A. F. of L. and Philip Murray of the C. I. O., it became possible to merge the organizations. George Meany, president of the A. F. of L., became the president of the combined body and Walter Reuther, head of the C. I. O., became the vice-president for industrial organization. This division of authority reflected the larger membership that the A. F. of L. brought to the union. The organizational structure of the two unions had been similar and the new A.F.L.-C.I.O. merely joined local groups together. But the new constitution gave the federation more power over the international unions than had existed before. The Executive Council, for example, adopted an Ethical Practices Code, and in 1957 expelled the Teamsters for violating it.

The new organization still faced many problems. Politically it was not strong enough to bring about quick repeal or substantial modification of the Taft-Hartley Act. In 1959, the Labor-Management Reporting and Disclosure Act, framed by Senator John F. Kennedy, gave the Federal government still greater power to protect the individual union member from corrupt or arbitrary use of power by either union or company officials. Union officials were to be elected by secret ballot. Unions had to render financial reports to the Secretary of Labor. The picketing of employers by rival unions was prohibited if the employer had already recognized a union. The jurisdiction of state labor boards was recognized for certain types of disputes. These and other provisions represented a mixture of liberal and conservative clauses resulting from congressional pressures, but the law went further in the Taft-Hartley direction of regulation of unions rather than restoring the union privileges and freedoms of the Wagner Act. Within the A.F.L.-C.I.O. the old rivalries between industrial and craft unions remained. Jurisdictional disputes between unions harassed the Executive Council and caused difficulties between Meany and Reuther. In addition, from 1958 to 1961 unemployment resulting from both the business cycle and technological change reduced the total membership from 15,000,-000 workers to 12,500,000.

LABOR IN THE WELFARE STATE

The real wages, security, and living conditions of labor improved so greatly between 1935 and 1960 that the effect was to create a new capital-labor relationship in United States society, and to hold out hope that higher levels of mass production would ultimately make such relations possible in many nations. From the beginning of the century on, advanced thinkers had talked of the necessity of high wages if mass production was to expand, but it took the Second World War to bring the lesson home to practical businessmen.

The only substantial gain in real wages between 1895 and 1935 had come when prices fell more rapidly than wage rates from 1920 to 1922. The gain was around 30 per cent. But from 1935 on average hourly earnings tended steadily upward, and in all but a few years of the period they kept ahead of price increases. By 1957, the average of real earnings for all occupations, including farm workers, was about 85 per cent above 1935, and real earnings in manufacturing were up nearly 100 per cent. Differences caused by geography and types of industry thwarted the efforts of unions to standardize wages. In 1958 weekly wages for production workers in manufacturing averaged over $100 in several Pacific coast cities and also in Michigan automotive centers, whereas they were around $55 in some cities in Maine, Massachusetts, and North Carolina.

Various types of "fringe benefits" asked for by unions from 1946 on, and generally granted by employers, together with Federal insurance totalled about one-fifth of all payrolls by 1957. A sample of 1,000 firms indicated that the legally required insurance payments were 4 per cent of payrolls; company or industry pensions or other benefit plans nearly 7 per cent; and paid holidays, vacations, sick leave, and rest periods over 9 per cent. During the sixties the government social security payments were scheduled to rise to nearly 5 per cent.

Hours of work declined slightly from 52 per week in 1914 to 48 in 1929. Then the effort to spread work during the depression reduced the average week to under 35 in 1934. The Fair Labor Standards Act of 1938 set the normal week at 40 hours, and except for much overtime during the Second World War, this remained the rule. Meanwhile, the labor of children under 15 or 16 had been restricted by all states as well as by the Federal government, and women's work was generally limited to eight hours a day.

But the increased buying power of the worker which enabled him to have an automobile, television set and other expensive machines, and the hours of work that gave him more time to enjoy them were only part of the big change. Mass-produced goods had become much more standardized, the cheaper automobiles looked and performed about as well as the most expensive ones, and the same type of change had taken place in other durable goods and in clothing. Prior to 1934 the average worker had no security beyond that provided by his own savings and public charity. In 1960, he had government unemployment insurance and old age benefits, and in many cases he belonged to private medical and pension plans. Before the great depression of the thirties only the thriftiest workers saved enough money to buy homes. From the Second World War on, houses with government guaranteed mortgages were available with little money down and low monthly payments on long-term mortgages. Furthermore, with an automobile the worker could live in the country, and a bus would take his children to an attractive consolidated school.

In the long view industrialism had been hard on the worker during the decades of rapid investment in basic production and transportation facilities. In the United States this stage was over by 1914, but the habits of thought which it inspired, such as the need for low rates of wages and higher rates of saving, lingered on. Only after the great depression and the Second World War was it evident that the growth of mass production depended primarily on increasing mass consumption. The new problem of the mid-twentieth century was adjustment to the need for more skilled and administrative employees and fewer manual workers. For those workers who lacked the ability to make this advance, there was the threat of early retirement or permanent unemployment.

This threat bore particularly heavily on Negro workers. During the First World War and from 1940 on, Negroes came in large numbers to the northern industrial cities. Most of these migrants came from localities that did not provide proper environment or enough education for Negroes to permit them to go on and acquire skills. The percentage of non-white males in the labor force, of which Negroes comprise over 90 per cent, fell over 10 per cent from 1920 to 1960, while the percentage of non-whites in the population as a whole rose about one per cent, standing at 11 per cent in 1960. Undoubtedly the waste of potential industrial manpower from improper education was extremely high among Negroes. These figures should not obscure great advances, however, in Negro status since 1940. By 1957, the number of skilled Negro workers had increased 181 per cent and the number in professional work 103 per cent, but it was still true in 1960 that no nation was educating the mass of its population adequately for the economic tasks to be performed.

CHAPTER 32

The Business Structure

The development of large-scale mass production with free enterprise as its ideal was a process of superimposing one business system upon another in which no earlier form of organization was wholly lost. In 1960 some textiles were still made in household workshops with family labor; some goods were still imported by small merchants with foreign agents; repairs on factory-made machines were still done by self-employed mechanics; retail trade was still predominantly a small shop family affair. On such holdovers from the business systems of early centuries were built the new institutions needed for mechanized transportation, nation-wide distribution, and mass production industry. The American business system, therefore, became increasingly complex and difficult to encompass by simple generalizations.

THE BUSINESS POPULATION

Before 1929 only those firms large enough and old enough to have ratings with Dun & Bradstreet can be counted. This group grew from 1,655,000 in 1914 to 2,213,000 in 1929. In the latter year the Office of Business Economics began a tabulation by industry of all firms having either one employee or an established place of business. The initial number was 3,029,000, or about a third larger than the Dun & Bradstreet list. Fluctuations in the annual count of firms indicate that both

685

depression and war were hard on small business, but that the number of firms increased rapidly in years of prosperity. At the bottom of the depression in 1933 there were only 2,782,000 enterprises left. The failures had been chiefly in manufacturing and construction. In whole-sale and retail trade, the loss in total firms was negligible. By 1936, the 1929 figure for total firms had been surpassed. The initial impact of the Second World War again reduced the business population by some 300,000 firms, but even by 1944 this number had been made up, and every year thereafter the business population increased until it reached 4,752,000 in 1962.

In both good years and bad, new enterprises were started in enor-mous numbers. Even in 1943, the most constricted year of the Second World War, there were 146,000 new firms, in 1950 about 350,000, and in 1957 over 400,000. At all periods most of the starts were in retail trade, but in the fifties there were about 60,000 new firms annually in

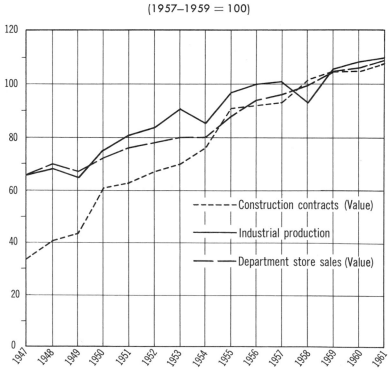

BUSINESS INDEX, 1947 – 1961

(1957–1959 = 100)

Construction contracts (Value)

Industrial production

Department store sales (Value)

Source: *The World Almanac, 1963*, New York, 1963, p.757.

manufacturing and slightly more in service enterprises. Three-quarters of all firms in the period after the Second World War were family enterprises with less than three employees. In 1951 less than one per cent of all firms, 36,800 to be exact, had one hundred or more employees, and the ratio of large firms to small was falling.

If, instead of counting firms, attention is focused on earnings the results are quite different. Earnings were only assembled for corporations, which numbered 20 to 25 per cent of all firms, and were chiefly the larger companies. In this top group the largest 5 per cent earned more than three-quarters of all corporate income.

During the fifty years before 1960 the statistical relations between large, medium, and small businesses remained remarkably stable. On the one hand the scale of operations needed to support national distributing organizations, advertising, and conveniently located plants or agencies increased, but as noted (p. 545), the economies of small-scale production also increased in many lines, and much service and trade still depended upon personal relations. The general trend over the whole period was toward mergers of firms in older industries with high fixed capital or heavy marketing costs, and the starting of many more firms in newborn types of manufacture, trade, and service. By far the greatest number of recorded mergers occurred in 1928 and 1929, with a record of 1,245 in the latter year. In fact, the late twenties was the period of maximum enthusiasm for merging companies. During the five years 1925 to 1929 there was an average of over 900 mergers a year, while from 1957 to 1961, in spite of favorable tax laws, less than 600 a year were recorded in a business population half again as big as in the late twenties.

Early in the century relationships developed that kept small enterprises alive and prosperous, at the expense of their owner-managers surrendering a part of their independence. Big companies had many allies attached to them by subcontracts, purchase of supplies, and joint participation in various types of venture. The Clayton Act forbade legal agreements tying suppliers to their major customers, but in fact, such relationships existed. If big company X regularly bought three-quarters of the product of company Y, the latter was not in a position to disregard the desires of X. In order to achieve some of the efficiency of large enterprise retailers entered into agreements with large wholesalers. Rexall drug stores, for example, were locally owned but centrally supplied.

Some market forces worked in favor of the thirty thousand-odd companies that could be called medium-sized businesses. These companies with from fifty to a couple of hundred employees could make products and give service that the large-scale operators could not afford to be bothered with. Medium-sized manufacturers could give special service, not matched by the big national producers, to retailers in the part of the country around the plant. Special sized boilers, castings, and other metal work, for example, was done in small foundries and shops with 50 or 100 employees. A "small" steel company with under 1,000 employees would take orders for small lots of special steel that big companies would not handle. The healthy continuance of intermediate-sized enterprise emphasized the essential inflexibility of mass production and of big companies.

Complicated statistical estimates of the degree of concentration of production in the hands of a few large companies in the major branches of manufacturing showed no general trend between 1947 and 1954. The writers of two scholarly studies of trends in monopoly during the first half of the century came to the conclusion that there had been no significant growth of monopoly since the government prosecutions of the Roosevelt and Taft administrations. Possibly such a trend might have developed after the Second World War as it had in the twenties, but a high wave of antitrust proceedings in the Truman and Eisenhower administrations—more than in the whole history of Federal law to that time—made companies cautious of the taint of monopoly.

Although monopoly may not have increased at all, and degree of concentration only moderately, the biggest United States companies became very large by world, or earlier domestic, standards. Bigness may be defined in so many ways that it is difficult to find any good basis for comparing companies in different types of business. Commercial banks, for example, have large assets, relatively few employees, and nothing quite comparable to gross sales. On the other hand, manufacturing companies, generally rated by amount of sales, have many employees and relatively low assets. Of the 500 leading industrial companies rated by sales, the smallest had sales in 1960 to $72,000,000. All but five of this group had over 1,000 employees and all but two over $20,000,000 in assets. There were probably somewhat fewer than five hundred banks, merchandizing firms, transportation companies, utilities, and insurance companies that could by varying measurements be rated as large as these industrial corporations.

The big business group could, therefore, be thought of very roughly as less than 1,000 firms, each of which had about a thousand employees or more, assets of over $20,000,000 sales or other annual

INCOME AND EMPLOYMENT IN MANUFACTURING AND TRADE, 1929 – 1957

Year	National Income Originating in:		Value Added by Manufacturing (In millions of dollars)	Employment (In thousands)		
	Wholesale Trade	Retail Trade and Automotive Services		Manufacturing	Wholesale Trade	Retail Trade and Automotive Services
	(In millions of dollars)					
1929	4,222	9,136	30,591	10,920	1,744	6,077
1933	1,781	3,704	14,008	9,149	1,393	5,038
1939	3,830	8,623	24,487	11,572	1,942	6,440
1947	11,651	25,690	74,290	14,323	2,635	8,376
1957	20,929	38,693	147,800	18,063	3,199	9,754

Sources: U.S. Bureau of the Census, *Historical Statistics of the United States, Colonial Times to 1957*, Washington, D.C., 1960, pp. 409, 518; and *Statistical Abstract of the United States*, 1962, p. 771.

returns of more than $50,000,000. This part of the business population, negligible in numbers, did a large part of American business. In the industrial field, where concentration was the highest, the top 500 accounted for 57 per cent of the industrial sales of 1960, 72 per cent of the profit, and employed about 13 per cent of the labor force. Adding those who worked for equally big nonindustrial concerns, perhaps one working American in five was employed by a big company.

DISTRIBUTING TO THE CONSUMER

Wholesale and retail trade have always made up the largest portion of the business population of proprietors and managers, but trade was behind agriculture and manufacturing in employment of labor up to the end of the Second World War and still one-third smaller than manufacturing in 1960. While the number of retail establishments declined in relation to all enterprises from 1929 to 1957, those in wholesale trade increased.

The general trends in the structure of wholesaling were a continuation of those noticeable in the late nineteenth century. As manufacturers grew larger and made their brands widely known through advertising, they had less need for energetic wholesalers. Retailers, needing the advertised product to satisfy customers, would order directly from a manufacturer's sales branch. Conversely, big retailers like chain stores could order in quantities that the manufacturer was willing to supply directly. Under these pressures wholesalers, jobbers, brokers, and factory agents became less important in many commodities. But other forces worked in an opposite direction. Where lines were highly varied, as in hardware, no ordinary retailer wanted to burden his shelves with complete stocks, and no producer wanted to set up the departments necessary to handle thousands of small orders. In other lines such as "high-styled" fabrics the wholesaler really organized the market, forecasting what would be wanted, financing its manufacture, and supplying the proper styles to retailers. Possibly by the 1960's a fairly stable balance had been reached, and the wholesaler would be able to hold the business that he still had.

All of the new developments in retail distribution that were to become popular in the twenties and thirties had their origins before the First World War. Chain stores and the cash and carry principle go back to the end of the nineteenth century—shopping centers to Kansas City in 1908 and self-service, at least, back to the Great Atlantic & Pacific Tea Company economy stores in 1913. A principle running through all of these developments was to get the customer to do some of the work of employees. Except for a limited use of vending machines there was no automation of the seller-consumer relation. Vending machines starting with gum and chocolate at the beginning of the century soon spread to cigarettes and after the Second World War to soft drinks. Progress was small in other lines, although many more items were sold through machines in Europe. The use of machines presented so many difficulties in packaging, preservation, pricing, and upkeep that in most lines they scarcely challenged self-service under the controlled conditions of a big market.

The major step toward elimination of sales employees came with the supermarket. Improving on the arrangements of the Piggly Wiggly self-service stores of the South, several Los Angeles merchants in the twenties arranged goods along aisles in large stores so that customers could help themselves and pay upon leaving. There was nothing strictly new in any single detail of the plan; the new element was the combination of large size, low prices, and nearly complete self-service. As the depression deepened in the early thirties vacant factories were converted into supermarkets, such as the Big Bear at Elizabeth, New Jersey, selling canned goods and other foods often bought at auction prices.

Over the next thirty years the supermarket came to be the major type of retail food store. They began to take on some of the features of the old-fashioned country general store, adding dry goods, liquors, and household and yard utensils. This growth was speeded up by the increasing use of the automobile for shopping, which allowed the customers of a big town or small city to reach a single supermarket.

In view of the obvious advantages of supermarkets, it is surprising that there were still so many small food stores in 1960. The number of all types of food stores had only declined a little over 20 per cent since 1929, and total employment had risen about 20 per cent. This meant, to be sure, that one-fifth fewer employees were taking care of nearly half again as many people, but compared with agriculture or industry the change was far from revolutionary.

Another gradual change in retailing from 1920 to 1960 was in the ownership and control of retail outlets. Corporate chains owning two or more stores increased during the twenties from 800 to 1,700, sold over a fifth of all merchandise, and seemed to be on their way to completely dominating the market. But in the thirties small retailers formed voluntary or cooperative chains with wholesalers, and checked the growth of corporate chains. Also a few states imposed special taxes on operations by out-of-state chains. The early supermarket ventures were independent, but by 1935 chains were moving into the field. In 1937, the A & P, for example, started opening supermarkets and in this way eventually cut their total number of stores by two-thirds. But in spite of opening supermarkets, chains in 1957 still did only about 20 per cent of all merchandising.

While food stores accounted for an increasing share of all chain store sales, rising from a third in 1929 to nearly half in 1960, chains were important in other fields of merchandising. Of these, department and variety stores, both old as chain organizations, did the most business. By the 1870's John Wanamaker had stores in both New York and Philadelphia, but the rapid growth came after 1900 when Woolworth spread its 5 and 10 cent variety stores all across the country and other competitors entered this market. In 1925 Sears, Roebuck Company, the old mail order house, started opening retail stores, and their rival, Montgomery Ward, followed suit in 1927. Essentially these outlets were department stores located in newer and cheaper parts of the cities, whereas the old department stores occupied high-priced locations in the center of town. To meet competition and to tap the rapidly growing metropolitan area markets, the downtown department stores began in the 1920's to establish suburban branches. Consequently, by 1960 most department stores were parts of either national or local chains.

In the years after the Second World War the growth of suburbs and the use of automobiles gave rise to a new organization of retail outlets—the shopping center. The center was also another example of the decentralization made possible by electricity and the automotive industries. Essentially, each center reproduced all the shopping and service facilities of a small town with its stores grouped around a parking area. The big, carefully-planned centers usually had one or more branches of well-known department stores in addition to food stores, specialty shops, and service facilities.

As noted earlier (p. 480), the greatest changes in advertising occurred between 1885 and 1910. By the 1930's all media except television, were well-explored, and all the basic types of appeal had been used. In fact, advertising expenditure reached a percentage of national income in 1910 and again in 1920 that was not equalled in any year up to 1960. During the prosperous twenties advertising increased in dollar value but, seen as a percentage of national income, it tended to fall slightly. Until the bottom of the depression in 1933 the decline in advertising expenditures was little greater than that of the national

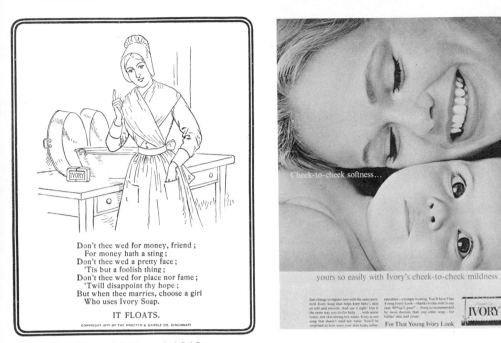

Advertising, 1899 and 1962

income, but when the latter rose again advertising lagged behind. Part of the lag was due to the fact that the national income or gross national product now included more government expenditure that involved negligible advertising, but even taking this into account, relative expenditure did not equal the 1920 peak.

Except for the rise of radio and television the use of media did not change greatly. As one would expect, radio and television cut into newspaper advertising. In 1936, a prosperous year, expenditures for newspaper space made up 44 per cent of the total and radio 6 per cent. By 1957, newspapers had fallen to 32 per cent, and radio and television had risen to 19 per cent.

In spite of much talk of the hidden persuaders of Madison Avenue, there was little change in the character of appeal. Already familiar with Freud, Adler, and Watson, who represented differing schools of new psychology, copy writers at the end of the First World War knew how to play upon fear, the desire for prestige, and other emotional factors. On the whole, governmental and industrial efforts at policing over the next forty years improved the honesty of advertising.

STABILIZING PRICES

Advertising was one device for maintaining a market based on the customer's confidence in a brand name rather than cheapness. All producers in highly capitalized mass production industries preferred to compete on the basis of qualities and particular characteristics rather than on price. From the nineteenth century on, industrialists sought to eliminate or control price competition through trade associations, pools, and trusts. The devices used after the First World War were only extensions and refinements of those used earlier.

Since the War Industries Board worked largely through trade associations in estimating possible supplies for the First World War, these organizations increased in number and strength. In the twenties many trade associations asked their members to state their prices in advance so that all could conform to an "open price policy." Insofar as members honestly adhered to the prices set by the leading producers, there would be uniform prices. The United States Supreme Court ruled in 1925 that as long as open prices were not used to raise prices or compel conformity the practice was not in restraint of trade.

In industries where a few producers dominated the market, the prices set by these leaders, usually much the same, would be followed by the lesser competitors. A leader such as United States Steel or General Motors would set its prices by a kind of cost-plus calculation, a level that would allow the smaller competitor a margin of profit under the "price umbrella." Prices set in this way were said to be "administered" rather than competitive.

The National Industrial Recovery Act of 1933 (p. 579), initially approved by both business associations and government, gave official approval to administered prices. Similarly the Agricultural Adjustment Administration gave farmers the benefit of calculated rather than competitive prices.

The nearly half of retail price that represented costs of distribution presented an irresistible temptation to profit from short-circuiting the usual process. Mail order houses had been an early step in this direction. In the twenties big city "discount houses" found they could make a profit selling at 15 to 20 per cent below the normal retail price. This cut was made possible by more direct avenues of purchase than were open to the neighborhood retailer and by dispensing with costly services such as credit, deliveries, turn-ins, repair, and salesmanship supplied by the small retailer. The discount house simply put goods on counters and let people take them for cash.

In the case of commodities that sold on the basis of brand names, small retailers pushed laws to compel the maintenance of uniform, advertised prices. In the thirties such goods made up only about 15 per cent of retail sales, but the movement was legally successful. Starting with California in 1931, forty-five states passed fair trade laws prohibiting more or less effectively the discounting of prices recommended by the producer. In 1937 Congress passed the Miller-Tydings Act which amended the Sherman Antitrust Law legalizing retail price fixing by the manufacturer on goods shipped in interstate commerce, providing the state involved had a fair trade law. The previous year, the Robinson-Patman Act, by prohibiting discrimination in price between large and small purchasers of goods to be shipped in interstate commerce, had tried to prevent supermarkets, discount houses, and chains from buying more cheaply than the small retailer.

In the sellers' market from 1942 to 1949 price maintenance was not important, but with the return of sharper competition and increased discounting the laws were successfully attacked in the courts. The judicial interpretation was that retailers were not bound by the law unless they had signed specific resale contracts. Since this was an unworkable procedure, the Miller-Tydings Act lost its force. The McGuire Act, passed by Congress in 1952, permitted manufacturers to put clauses obviating the necessity for signatures in resale contracts. The courts of seventeen states upheld the new law, but other state courts did not. In any case, price maintenance for many items, particularly durable goods, was almost impossible to enforce. Allowances for used articles turned in in trade, credit terms, and extras all made it difficult to say what price was really being paid. While stores in the United States still maintained the single price standard for inexpensive articles, the prices of expensive ones had become increasingly subject to bargaining. Economically this meant that fluctuations in price caused by shifts from buyers to sellers markets were borne by the middlemen and retailers more than by the producers.

Installment credit for practically all kinds of goods except food products, and for some services such as travel, introduced the rate of interest paid on the balance as an important element in price. By the fifties some department stores made a higher rate of profit from the interest on deferred payments than on the original mark-up of the goods. In 1929, at the end of the first great upswing in consumer credit, there was $3.2 billion in installment credit outstanding and $3.3 billion in loans and charge accounts. By 1957 the comparative figures were $34.2 billion and $11.1 billion. Even after adjustment for change in prices and population, this represented three to four times the real per capita consumer debt of 1929.

MANAGERIAL ENTERPRISE

By the mid-twentieth century the very large decentralized business corporation was an organization unique in the world's history. In 1960 the three largest industrial companies of the United States had over 200,000 employees each, and the largest, General Motors, had just under 600,000. Some perspective may be gained by noting that in time of peace the United States government never had 600,000 civilian employees before 1933, and that all the states combined never had 600,000 non-school employees before 1947. The biggest businesses, therefore, had bureaucracies that dwarfed in size all but the biggest governments. But there were other unique features of the big corporation besides its size. Most of the big industrial companies were business empires with dozens of plants making scores of diverse products; they were owned by thousands of stockholders who did not effectively participate in the control of their companies; and they were managed by professional executives with aims different from those of traditional businessmen.

While the particular characteristics of the widely-owned managerially-run company was most obvious in the biggest corporations, the general pattern fits several thousand smaller firms. The essential characteristics of managerial enterprise were domination of the board of directors by the officers of the company and selection of officers on the basis of executive ability rather than family connections or ownership of stock. A relatively small family-owned company, in which no important family stockholder wished to assume the burdens of management, might be run by professional executives. The family-dominated board could fire the executives, but if everything went smoothly the board would ratify the policies proposed by the outside professionals. Or stated more generally, the nonmanagement members of boards of directors were not usually well enough informed regarding company affairs to contradict executive policy. Thus, the directors who were supposed, as representatives of the owning stockholders, to control the company, came in practice to be an advisory committee for the management. In some large companies such as American Tobacco and Standard Oil of New Jersey, all members of the board of directors were officers of the company.

Banks or other organizations important to a particular company might be represented on its board and have considerable influence when decisions affecting such outside interests were made. After the changes of the New Deal period, the representatives of investment banking never wielded the arbitrary power that had earlier been enjoyed by the House of Morgan or other great banking interests. After 1920, the trend in the biggest companies was toward more and more managerial autonomy. Only when some powerful group of financiers bought control of the stock, as in the case of some of the railroads, or when management seemed unable to avoid receivership in bankruptcy, were executives likely to be overthrown by outside interests.

The professional manager was by training and interests a different type from the businessman who owned a small enterprise. While the professional might increasingly come from a lower-middle or working class family—about a quarter of the chief executives of 1952 had such origins as against a sixth 25 years earlier—he usually had attended college. Starting after graduation in a big company, he worked his way up through the ranks of lower and middle management. In many posts actual performance was hard to measure; cooperativeness, friendliness, and loyalty to the company were the things that his superiors could observe. "Getting along is the key to success," said the president of one of the biggest corporations.[1] In some positions a man's success could be checked by the accounting system, but he was also expected to produce a smooth running organization. Thus, the man who finally reached the top had been conditioned to think in terms of the welfare of the organization and its employees, and to derive his personal satisfaction from the approval of his fellow officers and the level of his salary as a mark of prestige within the organization.

In general, larger sales and higher profits were basic to the welfare of the company, so that business motives and language did not appear very different than in smaller enterprise. But there were many modifications that affected the conduct of business. The professional executive, who usually owned relatively little stock in the company, was more interested in the long-run welfare of the organization than in any immediate dividends. As Walter Gifford, president of American Telephone and Telegraph Company, said in 1926: "These men must take a long view ahead. They cannot decide questions merely on the basis of immediate advantage, because their company is going to be in business long after they are dead."[2] Aside from interest in the more

[1]Monroe J. Rathbone, "Standard Oil of New Jersey," quoted in *Time*, (January 27, 1961), LXXVII, p. 70.
[2]Thomas C. Cochran, *The American Business System* (Cambridge: Harvard University Press, 1957), p. 189.

remote future, an executive of forty who hoped to live on his company pension until he was ninety had a fifty-year interest in the welfare of the company.

In practical policy this long-run welfare view differed in several respects from the immediate profit view. An owner might decide to take all he could from an only moderately profitable enterprise and invest elsewhere, but management preferred large reserves to insure the welfare of the organization rather than large dividends. It was not uncommon for a big company to pay as little as one-third of net profits to the stockholders. Expenditures for research, consulting services, and new equipment were deductible from taxes and could strengthen the organization. Higher salaries and wages benefited management directly and built good morale. Justifiable as these expenses might be from an over-all economic or social view, professional management was accused by many stockholders of "conspicuous production" and of giving way too readily to union and employee pressures. In fact, the stockholder could suspect that since he had no direct relations with management and no operating function in the organization, he was likely to come out last in the division of earnings.

Only the very large companies with dominant positions in their markets fully illustrated these characteristics of managerial enterprise, but an increasing number of medium-sized companies were moving in the same direction. No exact statistical measures are possible, but some idea of the general increase in the size of companies, and hence the

PROFITS AND DIVIDENDS OF MANUFACTURING CORPORATIONS, 1947 – 1956
(In billions of dollars)

Year	Net Profits	Dividends	Year	Net Profits	Dividends
1947	9.7	4.2	1952	7.9	5.7
1948	10.6	4.6	1953	8.4	5.9
1949	8.8	4.9	1954	8.0	5.8
1950	12.2	6.1	1955	12.1	6.8
1951	9.8	5.7	1956	11.5	7.2

Source: *Economic Almanac, 1960*, p. 223.

probability of their demonstrating the characteristics of managerial enterprise, can be seen by comparing samples of 7,371 of the biggest companies taken as nearly as possible under identical conditions in 1928 and 1952. In the 1928 sample, 56 per cent of the firms had gross incomes of less than $5,000,000 a year. In the 1952 sample, only 17 per cent had incomes under $10,000,000. While prices had not quite doubled, the comparison shows the great growth in numbers of companies that were at least moderately big.

BUSINESS ADMINISTRATION

It was clear from an early date that the political science developed from government administration was not completely suited to business. Political science was basically concerned with power; business science assumed power at the top, and was concerned with the structure and procedures of administration. Before the First World War, when Frederick W. Taylor and his associates were approaching management from the angle of engineering efficiency, Harvard and the University of Pennsylvania initiated the systematic study of business administration. In the twenties most of the larger universities established schools of commerce or business. Increasingly the big companies became staffed by the graduates of these schools and advised by specialists in various aspects of administration.

Over the next thirty-odd years, the results could be seen in both the details of procedure and the over-all design of administration. In detail, administration became more specialized. There were more departments and more distinct divisions between staff specialists who advised and line officers who ran the processes. Expanding organizations were kept knit together by chief executive groups, officers conferences, company magazines (practically all big companies had such house organs by 1925), and employees and officers clubs. The latter allowed much discussion of policy over lunch and promoted a social life within the company. The increasing use of committees for policy-making after the twenties brought executives into closer contact with each other, educated the men on the way up, and gave a more democratic aura to decisions. There was also an effort, initiated in DuPont in 1919, to free top executives of routine responsibilities so that their whole time could be given to considerations of policy. This break between specific "know-how" and policy-making also meant that specialists in the latter could readily move from one type of industry to another. Organizations were constantly examining their procedures and calling in outside specialists to give objective appraisals.

In over-all design most big companies of 1920 were centralized organizations with single unified departments for special functions such as sales, production, maintenance, or engineering. Starting in the early twenties both DuPont and its close associate General Motors led the way in developing decentralized divisional structures. Semi-autonomous divisions suited the needs of companies that had used their earnings to buy firms making varied products. Producing refrigerators, for example, had little to do with automobiles, or high explosives with rayon. Divisions also suited an organization with many plants all over the country, but Alfred D. Chandler, the chief student of this development, contends that product diversification was a more important incentive than geographical spread.

There were varying degrees of decentralization, but ideally each unit was expected to operate as an independent company, relying on the parent firm for general policies, technical advice, and economies in buying and distribution. The success of each unit could be measured by elaborate accounting controls that when possible compared the results with those of nearly similar operations. The telephone company, of course, with thousands of nearly identical local exchanges, could use such controls with great precision, but General Motors was able to apply close comparison to its automobile divisions and make them keen competitors of each other. Such minute checking could be hard on the morale of local management, and by the fifties some big companies were simply having the results passed on to the executives involved and leaving improvement in operating efficiency initially up to them. Other stimulants designed to overcome the tendencies toward loss of initiative and too great valuation of security, present in all bureaucracies, were the new discoveries of research departments and other company specialists, bonuses for good performances and plans for stock purchases by management at favorable prices.

Coordination of these empires generally come through a holding company given over entirely to management, an officer-staffed board of directors with hard working committees, or a special council of top executives. The superiority of decentralization of operation and concentration of ultimate control by specialists in administration appeared to be demonstrated between 1935 and 1950 when this type of structure was adopted by most of the larger companies. In 1946, for example, Ford, hitherto the greatest monolithic company, avowedly copied the structure of General Motors.

EXTERNAL RELATIONS OF THE BIG COMPANY

Meanwhile, the external changes discussed in earlier chapters were making the problem of the position of the big company in society increasingly complex. State and Federal regulatory laws, higher taxes, new commissions, and in some cases, dependence on government contracts made the social and political influence of the company and its industry important. But knowledge of how to manipulate public opinion was also increasing. George Creel's Committee on Public Information in the First World War brought together specialists in publicity, advertising, and psychological theory. When the war was over some of these men such as Edward Bernays set up a new profession called public relations counselling. As the new counsellors gained clients the larger advertising agencies entered the field.

The aim of public relations, as distinct from advertising, was to create a favorable opinion of the industry and the company rather than to sell the product. Such tactics had been carried on by railroads and public utilities for decades, but systematic study of how to influence opinion carried on under a special name was new and in accord with the general trend toward increasing specialization in administration. The chief techniques of the twenties were: distribution of favorable news items to editors; preparation of magazine articles, often signed by company presidents, designed to interest the public in the achievements of business; educational moving pictures, occasionally shown in commercial theaters, but readily available to schools and associations; and an emphasis on "good will" advertising designed to sell ideas rather than products. During the twenties the news and educational material was taken by newspapers and magazines with only a little prodding from the agencies distributing it.

Even before the public relations advisers started emphasizing the importance of stockholders, A. T. & T., regulated in every state, had started an aggressive campaign to spread the holding of its stock. Using local employees as stock salesmen the telephone company increased its stockholders from about 100,000 in 1920 to over 200,000 in 1930, and to over 1,000,000 by 1950. This view of the value of the small stockholder as a political friend fitted well with recognition by 1920 that he lacked the power to influence management. In fact, the more stockholders the less likelihood of organizing them against executive policy. Consequently, companies split their stock to make shares easier to purchase in blocks of ten or twenty-five, and began writing public relations letters to the stockholder family. The earlier decree of the Federal

Communications Commission that companies with securities listed on public exchanges should issue reports was made into an asset. Reports were made attractive with color and illustrations, and generally included a description of the year's activities by the president or chairman of the board. Estimates of the number of individual stockholders in the United States in 1920 run well under 3,000,000, but by 1929 estimates placed them above 4,000,000. A much more accurate sampling by the New York Stock Exchange in 1955 placed the number of individual stockholders in nongovernment corporations at 8,280,000. While this figure meant that stockholding was widely spread among the top 10 per cent of receivers of income, it also meant that only 8 per cent of civilian adults owned stock. In other words, corporate stockholders were still a small minority.

The great depression taught public relations men the weaknesses of appeals to the public through newspapers and magazines. By the Second World War the accepted doctrine had become the "positive" approach. A company would be judged by what it did, not what it said. The public relations counsellor should see his job as a "two-way street" on which he persuaded the corporate executive to go the way the public desired, and the public to move in the direction favored by business. Several big corporations decentralized public relations and told local managers to take an active part in community affairs and to contribute the sums they deemed necessary to local welfare and civic movements.

The expenditure of company funds for civic, health, and educational purposes was also aided in the early fifties by court decisions holding that within reasonable limits such giving was in the interest of the stockholders and not a violation of the company charter. Big companies now began to set up scholarships, make grants to colleges and universities, and create nonprofit foundations. The latter were also useful as holding companies that could keep control of strategic blocks of company stock. As a result of these policies some of the dislike of absentee corporations that dominated the economic life of small cities died away, although businessmen and the public continued to prefer locally-owned enterprise.

After 1933, the need for dealing with more Federal regulatory boards and agencies, and from 1940 on the importance of defense contracts, led many companies and trade associations to seek to strengthen their influence in Washington. Lawyers who had previously been members of the regulatory boards and retired military men who had friends in the defense agencies made good Washington representatives. Such use of the talents of lawyers who had served in government had gone on since colonial days, but military influence hitherto had been relatively unimportant in time of peace.

BUSINESS AND THE ECONOMY

Granting that big companies, as we have defined them, were doing perhaps a quarter of the dollar volume of business and that their managers were the leaders of business opinion, what did this mean for economic welfare, stability, and growth? Had the nation in fact progressed in its business organization since the days of more active price competition by smaller firms?

Probably the basic answer in 1960 was that it was too soon to tell; that the new type of big business management was still too young and too experimental in policy to stand judgment. But certain effects seem clear. Big diversified corporations undoubtedly were more stable than the old small competitors. Careers with such companies offered a fairly high degree of security, as well as a great variety of occupations. But if a man were successful in his career, he was not likely to enjoy the feeling of security that comes from living for a long time in the same place; instead the company tended to become his community. Under pressure from labor unions and in recognition of the value of good morale, big companies paid high wages and salaries. Their higher administrators formed an elite based on both specialized knowledge and income.

Externally, the big company strove to gain a reputation for social responsibility and generally acted accordingly. There was much talk of higher business ethics, and in spite of some flagrant examples to the contrary, the role of the big business manager probably called for more reliability and honesty than that of the small competitor. The bureaucracy that inevitably accompanied bigness tended to diminish imaginative risk taking, but offsetting this was a rapidly increasing emphasis on research for new products and processes. Possibly the net result of the conflicting forces was a higher rate of innovation.

Whether managed in large units or small the factories of the United States and all other advanced industrial nations operated on the basis of increasing amounts of fixed capital per worker. From 1930 to 1960 the real value of capital in American manufacturing doubled, whereas the number of workers rose only 40 per cent. Furthermore, the equipment that represented the capital was proportionally more productive than in 1929. By 1957 the volume of output was $2\frac{1}{2}$ times that of the earlier year. The growing efficiency of industry and agriculture raised the income of the other sectors of the economy such as trade, service, and finance, and they, in turn, were operating on increasing amounts of capital per worker. The capital investment in manufacturing varied enormously by industry from $110,000 per worker in petroleum in 1956 to $3,600 in apparel and fabrics. The same type of variation appeared in nonmanufacturing activity, but there, comparisons are difficult. High capitalization obviously required big business units, while low investment per worker left the door open for small enterprise.

The period to 1960, at least, was one of capital scarcity. Rising consumer demand from wage increases, plus new technological developments in electronics, chemicals, and energy production required continuous large investment, tending in some years to outrun personal and institutional saving. This was a healthy condition from the standpoint of the business cycle and the general morale of a capitalist economy.

By 1961 average family income had risen above $7,000, and 30 per cent of families had $7,500 or more a year. These families lived in a more uniformly middle-class democracy than existed in earlier times. With factory wages higher than office clerical salaries, the social distinction between white and blue collar work had largely disappeared. Furthermore, most of the products that the average family bought had the same appearance and performance as more expensive models. Highly developed industrialism had largely standardized both production and consumption. With pensions and social security, and often many additional types of insurance, Americans could feel safer than the people of any previous generation from everything except nuclear war.

Bibliography

More than a list of suggested readings, but far from complete, this bibliography is designed to give the student a start on specialized reading. The monographs listed here, the bibliographical guides, and the indexes of the periodicals will, in turn, provide the more complete coverage needed for research.

Books in series are listed separately under appropriate headings, but the student of economic history should be aware of the publications of the National Bureau of Economic Research, The Twentieth Century Fund, The Brookings Institution, The National Industrial Conference Board, and the United States Bureau of the Census as the sources for most of the quantitative information that is available. Each student intending to specialize in either economic or general American history should have at hand *Historical Statistics of the United States: Colonial Times to 1957,* available from the United States Government Printing Office, Washington 25, D. C.

Many of the books listed here, and a considerable number of new titles each year, are available in paperback editions. To learn of these, consult R. R. Bowker Co., *Paperback Books in Print,* a quarterly publication.

BIBLIOGRAPHICAL GUIDES

Agricultural History, Yearly Bibliography (1954–   ); American Historical Association, *Index to the Writings on American History* (1956); American Historical Association, *Writings on American History* (1905–   ); Beers, H. P., *Bibliographies in American History: Guide to Materials for Research* (1942); Channing, Edward, Hart, A. B., and Turner, F. J., *Guide to the Study and Reading of American History* (1912); Daniells, L. M., comp., *Studies in Enterprise: A Selected Bibliography of American and Canadian Histories and Biographies of Businessmen* (1957); Edwards, E. E., *A Bibliography of the History of Agriculture in the United States,* United States Department of Agriculture, Miscellaneous Publications, No. 84 (1930); Edwards, E. E., *References on the Significance of the Frontier in American History* (1939); Handlin, Oscar, and others, comps., *Harvard Guide to American History* (1954); *Industrial Arts Index* (1913–   ); *Journal of Economic History,* bibliographies (1941–   ); Larson, Henrietta, *A Guide to Business History* (1948); Neufield, Maurice, *A Bibliography of American Labor Union History* (1958); Reynolds, L. G., and Killingsworth, C. C., *Trade Union Publications* (3 vols., 1945); Schleiffer, Hedwig, and Crandall, Ruth, *Index to Economic History: Essays in Festschriften, 1900–1950* (1953); Turner, F. J., and Merk, Frederick, *List of References on the History of the West* (1922).

PERIODICALS

Agricultural History (1927–   ); *American Economic Review* (1911–   ); *American Historical Review* (1895–   ); *Annals of the American Academy of Political and Social Science* (1890–   ); *Bankers' Magazine* (1847–   ); *Bulletin of the Business Historical Society* (1926–1954); *Business History Review* (1954–   ); *Commercial and Financial Chronicle* (1865–   ); *Debow's Review* (1847–1869); *Federal Reserve Bulletin* (1915–   ); *Hazard's United States Commercial and Statistical Register* (1840–1842); *Hunt's Merchants' Magazine and Commercial Review* (1839–1870); *Journal of Commerce* (1827–   ); *Journal of Economic and Business History* (1928–1932); *Journal of Economic History* (1941–   ); *Journal of Political Economy* (1892–   ); *Mississippi Valley Historical Review* (1914–   ); *Niles Weekly Register* (1811–1849); *Political Science Quarterly* (1886–   ).

ATLASES

Adams, J. T., ed., *Atlas of American History* (1943); *Harper's Atlas of American History* (1920); Lord, C. L., and E. H., *Historical Atlas of the United States* (1944); *Oxford Economic Atlas of the World* (2nd ed., 1959); Paullin, C. O., *Atlas of the Historical Geography of the United States* (1932); Shepherd, W. R., *Historical Atlas* (rev. ed., 1956).[1]

ENCYCLOPEDIAS AND DICTIONARIES

Adams, J. T., and Coleman, R. C., eds., *Dictionary of American History* (5 vols., 1940) and *Supplement* (1962); Johnson, Allen, and Malone, Dumas, eds., *Dictionary of American Biography* (20 vols., 1928–1936); Morris, Richard, ed., *Encyclopaedia of American History* (rev. ed., 1961); Seligman, E. R. A., *Encyclopedia of the Social Sciences* (15 vols., 1950-1935).

SOURCE COLLECTIONS

Bogard, E. L., and Thompson, C. M., *Readings in the Economic History of the United States* (1916); Bursk, E. C., Clark, D. T., and Hidy, R. W., eds., *The World of Business* (4 vols., 1962); Callender, G. S., *Selections from the Economic History of the United States, 1765–1860* (1909); Commager, H. S., *Documents of American History* (rev. ed., 1948); Commons, J. R., and Others, *Documentary History of American Industrial Society* (10 vols., 2nd ed., 1958); Flugel, Felix, and Faulkner, H. U., *Readings in the Social and Economic History of the United States* (1929); Hacker, L. M., *Major Documents in American Economic History* (2 vols., 1951); Hart, A. B., *American History Told by Contemporaries* (5 vols., 1897–1926); Manning, T. G., and Potter, D. M., *Government and the Economy: 1870 to the Present* (Published in separate paperback parts as *Select Problems in Historical Interpretation*) (1960); Schmidt, L. B., and Ross, E. D., *Readings in the Economic History of American Agriculture* (1925); Taylor, G. R., ed., *Problems in American Civilization: Readings Selected by the Department of American Studies, Amherst College.*

CHAPTER 1

EUROPEAN ORIGINS

Abbott, W. C., *Expansion of Europe* (2 vols., 1918); Barnes, H. E., *Economic History of the Western World* (1937); Cheyney, E. P., *The Dawn of a New Era, 1250–1453* (1936); Cheyney,

---

[1] In the case of texts that have come out in slightly revised editions, the general practice here will be to give the date of the original edition. If revisions or additions are of basic importance, the latest edition will be listed.

E. P., *European Background of American History* (1904); Clough, S. B., and Cole, C. W., *Economic History of Europe* (rev. ed., 1956); Heaton, Herbert, *Economic History of Europe* (rev. ed., 1948); Nef, J. U., *Industry and Government in France and England, 1540–1640* (1940); Newhall, R. A., *The Crusades* (1927); Newton, A. P., ed., *Travel and Travellers of the Middle Ages* (1926); Pirenne, Henri, *Economic and Social History of Medieval Europe* (1936); Setton, Kenneth, ed., *The Crusades* (2 vols., 1955, 1962); Thompson, J. W., *An Economic and Social History of the Middle Ages* (1928); Thompson, J. W., *An Economic and Social History of Europe in the Later Middle Ages* (1931).

THE COMMERCIAL REVOLUTION

Baker, J. N. L., *A History of Geographical Discovery* (1931); Brebner, J. B., *The Exploration of North America, 1492–1806* (1933); Day, Clive, *History of Commerce* (1936); De Roover, Raymond, *The Medici Bank* (1948); Gillespie, J. E., *A History of Geographical Discovery* (1933); Jacobs, Joseph, *Story of Geographical Discovery* (1904); Lane, F. C., *Andrea Barbarigo: Merchant of Venice, 1418–1449* (1944); Lane, F. C., *Venetian Ships and Shipbuilders of the Renaissance* (1934); Lybyer, A. H., "The Influence of the Ottoman Turks upon the Routes of Oriental Trade," American Historical Association, *Annual Report* (1914); Origo, Iris, *The Merchant of Prado* (1957); Packard, L. B., *The Commercial Revolution* (1927).

SPANISH EXPANSION

Bolton, H. E. and Marshall, T. M., *The Colonization of North America, 1492–1783* (1921); Chapman, C. E., *Colonial Hispanic America: A History* (1933); de Madariaga, Salvador, *The Rise of the Spanish American Empire* (1948); Fitzpatrick, F. A., *The Spanish Conquistadors* (1943); Hamilton, E. J., *American Treasure and the Price Revolution in Spain, 1501–1650* (1934); Haring, C. H., *Trade and Navigation Between Spain and the Indies in the Time of the Hapsburgs* (1918); Merriman, R. B., *The Rise of the Spanish Empire in the Old World and the New* (4 vols., 1918–1934); Morison, S. E., *Admiral of the Ocean Sea: A Life of Columbus* (1942); Moses, Bernard, *The Establishment of Spanish Rule in America* (1898); Prescott, W. H., *The Conquest of Mexico* (1843); Prescott, W. H., *The Conquest of Peru* (1847); Priestley, H. I., *The Coming of the White Man* (1929); Robertson, W. S., *History of the Latin-American Nations* (1922); Roscher, W. G. F., *The Spanish Colonial System* (1904); Shepherd, W. R., *Latin America* (1914); Simpson, L. B., *The Encomienda in New Spain* (1929); Wilgus, A. C., *The Development of Hispanic America* (1941).

PORTUGUESE EXPANSION

Beazley, C. R., *Prince Henry the Navigator* (1904); Jayne, G. K., *Vasco da Gama and His Successors* (1910); Martins, J. P. O., *The Golden Age of Prince Henry the Navigator* (Trans. by J. J. Abraham and W. E. Reynolds, 1914); Newton, A. P., *The Great Age of Discovery* (1932); Prestage, Edgar, *The Portuguese Pioneers* (1933); Stephens, H. M., *The Story of Portugal* (1903).

EARLY FRENCH COLONIZING EFFORTS

Biggar, H. P., *The Voyages of Jacques Cartier* (1924); Leacock, Stephen, *The Mariner of St. Malo* (1914); Munro, W. B., *Crusaders of New France* (1918); Packard, L. B., *The Age of Louis XIV* (1929); Parkman, Francis, *Pioneers of France in the New World* (1871); Windsor, Justin, *Cartier and Frontenac* (1894); Wrong, G. M., *The Rise and Fall of New France* (2 vols., 1928).

THE ENGLISH BACKGROUND

Ashley, William, *An Introduction to English Economic History and Theory* (2 vols., 1925); *Cambridge History of the British Empire,* I (1929); Cheyney, E. P., *A History of England from the Defeat of the Armada to the Death of Elizabeth* (2 vols., 1914, 1926); Gras, N. S. B., *An Introduction to Economic History* (1922); Lipson, Ephraim, *The Economic History of England* (3 vols., 1915–1931); Notestein, Wallace, *The English People on the Eve of Colonization, 1603–1630* (1954); Read, Conyers, *The Tudors* (1936); Salzman, L. F., *English Industries of the Middle Ages* (1923); Tawney, R. H., *The Agrarian Problem in the Sixteenth Century* (1912); Unwin, George, *Industrial Organization in the Sixteenth and Seventeenth Centuries* (1914); Usher, A. P., *An Introduction to the Industrial History of England* (1920).

CHAPTER 2

EARLY BRITISH EXPLORATIONS AND COLONIZING EFFORTS

Benson, E. F., *Sir Francis Drake* (1927); Brebner, J. H., *The Explorers of North America* (1933); Chatterton, E. K., *English Seamen and the Colonization of America* (1930); Chidsey, D. B., *Sir Humphrey Gilbert* (1932); Chidsey, D. B., *Sir Walter Raleigh* (1931); Connell-Smith, G., *Forerunners of Drake* (1954); Corbett, J. S., *Drake and the Tudor Navy* (2 vols., 1898); Cunningham, William, *Growth of English Industry and Commerce* (5th ed., 3 vols., 1910–1912); Gosling, W. G., *The Life of Sir Humphrey Gilbert* (1911); Hakluyt, Richard, *Principall Navigations, Voyages, Traffiques, and Discoveries of the English Nation* (16 vols., 1885–1890); Innes, A. P., *The Maritime and Colonial Expansion of England* (1931) Lingelbach, W. E., *The Merchant Adventurers of England* (1902); Parkes, G. B., *Richard Hakluyt and the English Voyages* (1928); Ramsay, G. D., *English Overseas Trade During the Centuries of Emergence* (1957); Scott, W. R., *Constitution and Finance of English, Scottish, and Irish Joint Stock Companies to 1720* (1912); Upcott, J. D., *Sir Francis Drake and the Beginnings of English Sea Power* (1927); Usher, A. P., *An Introduction to the Industrial History of England* (1920); Waldman, M., *Sir Walter Raleigh* (1928); Williamson, J. A., *Sir John Hawkins* (1927); Wood, W., *Elizabethan Sea-Dogs* (1918).

THE COLONIAL PERIOD

Adams, J. T., *Provincial America* (1927); Andrews, C. M., *The Colonial Period* (1912); Andrews, C. M., *The Colonial Period of American History* (4 vols., 1934–1938); Barck, Jr., O. T., and Lefler, H. T., *Colonial America* (1958); Becker, C. L., *Beginnings of the American People* (1915); Boorstin, Daniel, *The Americans: The Colonial Experience* (1958); Carman, H. J., *Social and Economic History of the United States* (2 vols., 1931, 1934); Chitwood, O. J., *A History of Colonial America* (1931); Dorfman, Joseph, *The Economic Mind in American Civilization, 1606–1865* (1946); Doyle, J. A., *English Colonies in America* (5 vols., 1882–1907); Gipson, L. H., *The British Empire Before the American Revolution* (9 vols., 1936–1956); Hall, M. G., *Edward Randolph and the American Colonies, 1676–1703* (1960); Holmes, V. B., *A History of the Americas* (1950); Jernegan, M. H., *The American Colonies, 1492–1750* (reissue, 1959); McDonald, W., ed., *Select Charters Illustrative of American History* (1904); Nettels, C. P., *The Roots of American Civilization* (1938); Osgood, H. L., *The American Colonies in the Seventeenth Century* (3 vols., 1904–1907); Osgood, H. L., *The American Colonies in the Eighteenth Century* (4 vols., 1924–1925); Pratt, J. W., *America's Colonial Experience* (1958); Saunders, J. B., *Early American History, 1492–1789* (1938); Smith, J. M., ed., *Seventeenth Century America* (1959); Tyler, L. G., *England in America, 1580–1652* (1904); Wertenbaker, T. J., *The First Americans, 1607–1690* (1927); Wright, L. D., *The Cultural Life of the American Colonies, 1607–1763* (1957).

THE NEW ENGLAND COLONIES

Adams, J. T., *The Founding of New England* (1921); Adams, J. T., *Revolutionary New England, 1691–1776* (1923); Bailyn, Bernard, *The New England Merchants in the Seventeenth Century* (1955); Banks, C. E., *The Planters of the Commonwealth* (1930); Baxter, J. P., *Sir Ferdinando Gorges and His Province of Maine* (3 vols., 1890); Brown, R. E., *Middle-Class Democracy and the Revolution in Massachusetts, 1691–1780* (1955); Burrage, H. S., *Beginnings of Colonial Maine* (1914); Calder, I. M., *The New Haven Colony* (1934); Clark, G. L., *A History of Connecticut* (1914); Dunn, Richard, *Puritans and Yankees: The Winthrop Dynasty of New England, 1630–1717* (1962); Fiske, John, *The Beginnings of New England* (1889); Fry, W. H., *New Hampshire as a Royal Province* (1908); Garvan, A. N. B. *Town Planning in Colonial Connecticut* (1951); Lord Arthur, *Plymouth and the Pilgrims* (1920); Morgan, Edmund, *The Puritan Dilemma: The Story of John Winthrop* (1948); Morison, S. E., *Builders of the Bay Colony* (1930); Richman, I. B., *Rhode Island: Its Making and Its Meaning* (2 vols., 1902); Rose-Troup, F. J., *The Massachusetts Bay Company and Its Predecessors* (1930); Weeden, W. B., *Economic and Social History of New England* (2 vols., 1891); Wertenbaker, T. J., *The Puritan Oligarchy* (1947); Willison, G. F.; *Saints and Strangers* (1945).

THE MIDDLE COLONIES

Brewster, William, *The Pennsylvania and New York Frontier: History from 1720 to the Close of the Revolution* (1954); Dunaway, W. A., *A History of Pennsylvania* (1935); Fisher, S. G., *The Quaker Colonies* (1919); Fiske, John, *Dutch and Quaker Colonies* (2 vols., 1899); Fletcher, S. W., *Pennsylvania Agriculture and Country Life, 1640–1850* (1950); Flick, A. C., ed., *History of the State of New York* (10 vols., 1933–1937); Goodwin, M. W., *Dutch and English on the Hudson* (1919); Hull, W. I., *William Penn and Dutch Quaker Migration* (1935); Innes, J. H., *New Amsterdam and Its People* (1902); Janvier, T. A., *The Dutch Founding of New York* (1903); Johnson, Amandus, *The Swedish Settlements on the Delaware, 1638–1664* (2 vols., 1911); Pomfret, J. E., *The Province of West New Jersey, 1607–1702* (1956); Sharpless, Isaac, *Two Centuries of Pennsylvania History* (1900); Tanner, E. P., *The Province of New Jersey, 1664–1738* (1908); Ward, C. L., *The Dutch and the Swedes on the Delaware, 1609–1664* (1930); Wertenbaker, T. J., *Founding of American Civilization: The Middle Colonies* (1938).

THE SOUTHERN COLONIES

Ashe, S. A., *History of North Carolina* (2 vols., 1908, 1925); Bridenbaugh, Carl, *Myths and Realities: Societies of the Old South* (1952); Brown, Alexander, *The First Republic of America* (1898); Bruce, P. A., *The Economic History of Virginia in the Seventeenth Century* (2 vols., 1895); Bruce, P. A., *The Virginia Plutarch* (2 vols., 1929); Crane, V. W., *The Southern Frontier, 1670–1732* (1928); Craven, W. F., *The Southern Colonies in the Seventeenth Century 1607–1689* (1949); Fiske, John, *Old Virginia and Her Neighbors* (2 vols., 1897); Holmes, Wendell, and Coulter, E. M., *History of the South* (1947); Jester, A. L., and Hiden, M. W., eds., *Adventurers of Purse and Person, Virginia, 1607–1625* (1956); Hall, C. C., *The Lords of Baltimore and the Maryland Palatinate* (1904); McCrady, Edward, *The History of South Carolina under the Proprietary Government, 1670–1719* (1897); Mereness, N. D., *Maryland as a Proprietary Province* (1901); Raper, C. L., *North Carolina, A Study in English Colonial Government* (1904); Stanard, M. N., *The Story of Virginia's First Century* (1928); Steiner, B. C., *Beginnings of Maryland, 1631–1639* (1903); Wertenbaker, T. J., *The Old South: The Founding of American Civilization* (1942); Wertenbaker, T. J., *The Planters of Colonial Virginia* (1922); Wertenbaker, T. J., *Virginia under the Stuarts, 1607–1688* (1914); Willison, G. F., *Behold Virginia: The Fifth Crown* (1951).

THE ETHNIC GROUPS

Adams, J. T., *Provincial Society* (1927); Aptheker, Herbert, *A Documentary History of the Negro People in the United States* (1951); Baird, C. W., *History of the Huguenot Emigration to America* (2 vols., 1885); Bernheim, G. D., *German Settlements in North and South Carolina* (1872); Bittinger, L. F., *The Germans in Colonial Times* (1901); Cunz, Dieter, *The Maryland Germans* (1948); Diffenderffer, F. R., *The German Immigration into Pennsylvania* (1900); Faust, A. B., *The German Element in the United States* (2 vols., 1909, 1927); Fenton, W. N., *American Indians and White Relations to 1830* (1957); Gladwin, H. S., *History of the Ancient Southwest* (1957); Glasgow, Maude, *The Scotch-Irish in Northern Ireland and in the American Colonies* (1936); Graham, I. C. C., *Colonists from Scotland: Emigration to North America, 1707–1738* (1956); Greene, E. B., and Harrington, V. D., *American Population Before the Federal Census of 1790* (1932); Green, L. J., *The Negro in Colonial New England, 1620–1776* (1942); Hanna, C. A., *The Scotch-Irish* (2 vols., 1902); Hansen, M. L., *The Atlantic Migration, 1607–1860* (1940); Hirsch, A. H., *The Huguenots of South Carolina* (1928); Huntington, Ellsworth, *The Red Man's Continent* (1919); Klees, Frederic, *The Pennsylvania Dutch* (1950); Knittle, W. A., *Early Eighteenth Century Palatine Emigration: A British Redemptioner Project to Manufacture Naval Stores* (1936); MacLean, J. P., *An Historical Account of the Setlements on the Scotch Highlanders in America* (1900); MacLeod, W. C., *The American Indian Frontier* (1928); O'Brien, M. J., *A Hidden Phase of the American Revolution* (1919); Peake, O. B., *History of the United States Indian Factory System, 1795–1822* (1954); Proper, E. E., *Colonial Immigration Laws* (1900); Radin, Paul, *The Story of the American Indian* (1934); Stafford, H. E., *Early Inhabitants of the Americas* (1949); Wissler, Clark, *The American Indian* (1922); Wissler, Clark, *Indians of the United States* (reissue, 1957); Wood, Ralph, ed., *The Pennsylvania Germans* (1942).

CHAPTER 3

GEOGRAPHIC ASPECTS

Atwood, W. W., *Physiographic Provinces of North America* (1940); Brigham, A. P., *Geographic Influences in American History* (1902); Brown, R. H., *Historical Geography of the United States* (1958); Deasy, G. F., *The World's Nations: An Economic and Regional Geography* (1958); Farrand, Livingston, *Basis of American History* (1904); Fenneman, N. M., *Physiography of Eastern United States* (1938); Hulbert, A. B., *Soil and Its Influence on the History of the United States* (1930); Jones, C. F., and Darkenwald, G. G., *Economic Geography* (rev. ed., 1954); Klimm, L. E., and Others, *Introductory Economic Geography* (3rd ed., 1956); McCarty, H. H., *The Geographic Basis of American Economic Life* (1940); Noyes, C. R., *Economic Man in Relation to his Natural Environment* (2 vols., 1948); Semple, E. C., and Jones, C. F., *American History and Its Geographic Conditions* (new ed., 1933); Smith, J. R., and Phillips, M. O., *North America* (1942); Whitbeck, R. H., and Thomas, O. J., *The Geographic Factor: Its Role in Life and Civilization* (1932).

THE ENGLISH ECONOMIC AND SOCIAL BACKGROUND

Ashley, W. J., *The Economic Organization of England* (1914); Cunningham, William, *The Growth of English Industry and Commerce* (5th ed., 3 vols., 1910–1912); Edwards, E. E., *American Agriculture: The First 300 Years* (1941); Gras, N. S. B., *An Introduction to Economic History* (1922); Gras, N. S. B., *A History of Agriculture* (1925); Lipson, Ephraim, *The Economic History of England* (3 vols., 1915–1931); Raleigh, S. L., and Onions, C. T., eds., *Shakespeare's England* (2 vols., 1917); Salzman, L. F., *England in Tudor Times; An Account of Its Social Life and Industries* (1926); Tawney, R. H., *The Agrarian Problem in the Six-*

teenth Century (1912); Trevelyan, G. M., *England Under Queen Anne* (3 vols., 1930–1934); Trevelyan, G. M., *England Under the Stuarts* (1904); Trotter, Eleanor, *Seventeenth Century Life in the Country Parish* (1919).

COLONIAL AGRICULTURE

Andrews, C. M., *Colonial Folkways* (1919); Bidwell, P. W., and Falconer, J. I., *History of Agriculture in the Northern United States, 1620–1860* (1925); Bruce, P. A., *Economic History of Virginia in the Seventeenth Century,* I (2 vols., 1895); Carrier, Lyman, *The Beginnings of Agriculture in America* (1923); Connor, L. G., *A Brief History of the Sheep Industry,* American Historical Association, *Annual Report* (1918); Craven, A. O., *Soil Exhaustion as a Factor in the Agricultural History of Virginia and Maryland, 1606–1860* (1926); Fletcher, Stevenson, *Pennsylvania Agriculture and Country Life, 1640–1840* (1950); Gray, L. C., *History of Agriculture in the Southern United States* (2 vols., 1933); Hawk, E. Q., *Economic History of the South* (1934); Jacobstein, Meyer, *The Tobacco Industry in the United States* (1907); Mark, Irving, *Agrarian Conflicts in Colonial New York, 1711–1775* (1940); Sanford, A. H., *The Story of Agriculture in the United States* (1916); Schafer, Joseph, *The Social History of American Agriculture* (1936); Schmidt, H. G., *Hunterdon: An Agricultural History* (1946); Taylor, C. C., *The Farmers' Movement, 1620–1840* (1950); Wertenbaker, T. J., *The Planters of Colonial Virginia* (1922); Woodward, C. R., *Ploughs and Politicks: Charles Reed of New Jersey and His Notes on Agriculture, 1715–1774* (1941).

LAND TENURE AND LAND SPECULATION

Akagi, R. H., *The Town Proprietors of the New England Colonies* (1924); Ballagh, J. C., "Introduction to Southern Economic History—the Land System," American Historical Association, *Annual Report* (1897); Barnes, V. F., "Land Tenure in English Colonial Charters in the Seventeenth Century," *Essays in Colonial History* (1931); Bond, B. W., Jr., *The Quit-Rent System in the American Colonies* (1919); Bruce, P. A., *Economic History of Virginia in the Seventeenth Century* (2 vols., 1895); Ford, A. C., *Colonial Predents of Our National Land System* (1910); Harris, Marshall, *Origin of the Land Tenure System in the United States* (1953); Havighurst, Walter, *Wilderness for Sale: The Story of the First Western Land Rush* (1956); Lewis, G. E., *The Indiana Company, 1763–1798: A Study in Eighteenth Century Frontier Land Speculation and Business Venture* (1941); Morris, R. B., *Studies in the History of American Law* (1930); Shepherd, W. R., *History of Proprietary Government in Pennsylvania* (1896); Weeden, W. B., *Economic and Social History of New England, 1620–1789* (2 vols., 1891).

COLONIAL LABOR

Ballagh, J. C., *Slavery in Virginia* (1902); Ballagh, J. C., *White Servitude in Virginia* (1895); Bassett, J. S., *Slavery and Servitude in the Colony of North Carolina* (1896); Brackett, J. R., *The Negro in Maryland* (1889); Commons, J. R., and Others, *History of Labour in the United States* (2 vols., 1918); Cooley, H. S., *A Study of Slavery in New Jersey* (1896); Donnan, Elizabeth, ed., *Documents Illustrative of the History of the Slave Trade to America* (3 vols., 1930–1932); Geiser, K. F., *Redemptioners and Indentured Servants in Pennsylvania* (1901); Greene, L. J., *The Negro in Colonial New England, 1620–1776* (1942); Herrick, C. A., *White Servitude in Pennsylvania* (1926); Jernegan, M. W., *Laboring and Dependent Classes in Colonial America, 1607–1783* (1931); McCormac, E. I., *White Servitude in Maryland* (1904); McCrady, Edward, "Slavery . . . South Carolina, 1670–1770," American Historical Association, *Annual Report* (1895); Morris, R. B., *Government and Labor in Early America* (1946); Phillips, U. B., *American Negro Slavery* (1921); Phillips, U. B., *Life and Labor in the Old*

South (1929); Smith, A. E., *Colonists in Bondage: White Servitude and Convict Labor in America, 1607–1776* (1947); Turner, E. R., *The Negro in Pennsylvania* (1911); Woodson, C. G., *The Negro in Our History* (1941).

CHAPTER 4

GENERAL WORKS ON COLONIAL INDUSTRIES

Bishop, J. L., *A History of American Manufactures from 1608–1860* (3 vols., 1866); Bolles, A. S., *Industrial History of the United States* (1887); Bridenbaugh, Carl, *The Colonial Craftsman* (1950); Clark, V. S., *History of Manufactures in the United States* (3 vols., 1929); Davis, J. S., *Essays in the Earlier History of American Corporations* (2 vols., 1917); Gipson, L. H., *The British Empire before the American Revolution*, II and III (1936); Keir, R. M., *Manufacturing* (1928); Moore, J. H. R., *Industrial History of the American People* (1913); Nettels, C. P., *The Roots of American Civilization* (1938); Tryon, R. M., *Household Manufactures in the United States, 1640–1860* (1917); Van Wagener, Jr., Jared, *The Golden Age of Homespun* (1953).

FOREST INDUSTRIES

Albion, R. G., *Forests and Sea Power* (1926); Coyne, F. E., *The Development of the Cooperage Industry in the United States, 1620–1940* (1940); Cross, A. L., *Eighteenth Century Documents Relating to the Royal Forests, the Sheriffs and Smuggling* (1928); Defebaugh, J. E., *History of the Lumber Industry of America* (2 vols., 1906–1907); Knittle, W. A., *Early Eighteenth Century Palatine Emigration: A British Redemptioner Project to Manufacture Naval Stores* (1936); Lord, E. L., *Industrial Experiments in the British Colonies of North America* (1898).

THE FISHERIES AND WHALING

Hawes, C. B., *Whaling* (1924); Hohman, E. P., *The American Whaleman* (1928); Innis, H. A., *The Cod Fisheries: The History of an International Economy* (1940, 1954); Jenkins, J. T., *A History of the Whale Fisheries* (1921); Judah, C. B., *The North American Fisheries and British Policy to 1713* (1933); Lounsbury, R. G., *The British Fishery at Newfoundland, 1634–1763* (1934); McFarland, R., *A History of the New England Fisheries* (1911); Middleton, A. P., *Tobacco Coast: A Maritime History of Chesapeake Bay in the Colonial Era* (1951); Morison, S. E., *Maritime History of Massachusetts, 1783–1860* (1921); Tower, W. S., *A History of American Whale Fishing* (1920).

MANUFACTURING, SHOP AND MILL INDUSTRIES

Allen, F. J., *The Shoe Industry* (1922); Bining, A. C., *Pennsylvania Iron Manufacture in the Eighteenth Century* (1938); Bruce, Kathleen, *Virginia Iron Manufacture in the Slave Era* (1931); Cole, A. H., *The American Wool Manufacture* (2 vols., 1926); Cole, A. H., and Williamson, H. F., *The American Carpet Manufacture: A History and an Analysis* (1941); Copeland, M. T., *The Cotton Manufacturing Industry of the United States* (1912); Hazard, B. E., *The Organization of the Boot and Shoe Industry in Massachusetts Before 1875* (1921); Kuhlmann, C. B., *The Development of the Flour-Milling Industry in the United States* (1929); Langdon, W. C., *Everyday Things in American Life, 1607–1776* (1937); Peterson, A. G., "Flour and Grist Milling in Virginia," *Virginia Magazine of History and Biography*, XLIII (April, 1935); Prime, A. C., *The Arts and Crafts in Philadelphia, Maryland, and South Carolina, 1721–1785* (1929); Rickard, T. A., *History of American Mining* (1932);

Storck, John and Teague, W. D., *Flour for Men's Bread: A History of Milling* (1952); Weeks, L. H., *A History of Paper Manufacturing in the United States, 1690–1916* (1916).

CHAPTER 5

COLONIAL MERCHANTS

Bailyn, Bernard, *The New England Merchants in the Seventeenth Century* (1955); Baxter, W. R., *The House of Hancock: Business in Boston, 1724–1775* (1945); Fairchild, Byron, *Mssr. William Pepperell* (1954); Gray, Edward, *William Gray of Salem* (1914); Hall, C. S., *Benjamin Tallmadge: Revolutionary Soldier and American Businessman* (1943); Harrington, V. D., *The New York Merchants on the Eve of the Revolution* (1935); Hedges, J. B., *The Browns of Providence Plantations* (1952); Hillyer, W. H., *James Talcott: Merchant and his Times* (1937); Morison, S. E., *Builders of the Bay Colony* (1920); Porter, K. W., *The Jacksons and the Lees: Two Generations of Massachusetts Merchants, 1765-1844* (2 vols., 1937); Schlesinger, A. M., *The Colonial Merchants and the American Revolution, 1763–1776* (1918); Sellers, Leila, *Charleston Business on the Eve of the Revolution* (1935); Tolles, F. B., *Meeting House and Counting House: The Quaker Merchants of Colonial Philadelphia, 1682–1768* (1948); Tooker, Elva, *Nathan Tooker: Philadelphia Merchant* (1955); White, P. L., *The Beekmans of New York in Politics and Commerce, 1647–1877* (1956).

THE FUR TRADE

Crane, V. W., *The Southern Frontier* (1929); Greenbie, Sydney, *Frontiers and the Fur Trade* (1929); Hanna, C. A., *The Wilderness Road* (1911); Innis, H. A., *The Fur Trade in Canada* (1930); Moloney, Francis X., *The Fur Trade in New England, 1620–1676* (1931); Phillips, P. C., *The Fur Trade* (2 vols., 1961); Vandiveer, C. A., *The Fur-Trade and Early Western Exploration* (1929); Volwiler, A. T., *George Croghan and the Westward Movement, 1741–1782* (1926); Wrong, G. M., *The Rise and Fall of New France* (2 vols., 1928).

COLONIAL COMMERCE

Andrews, C. M., *The Colonial Period* (1912); Bridenbaugh, Carl, *Cities in Revolt: Urban Life in America, 1743–1776* (1955); Bridenbaugh, Carl, *Cities in the Wilderness; The First Century of Urban Life in America, 1625–1742* (1938); Bassett, J. S., "The Relation Between the Virginia Planter and the London Merchant," American Historical Association, *Report,* I (1901); Day, Clive, *History of Commerce of the United States* (1925); Jernegan, M. W., *The American Colonies, 1492–1750* (1929); Johnson, E. R., Van Metre, T. W., Huebner, G. G., and Hanchett, D. S., *History of Domestic and Foreign Commerce of the United States* (2 vols., 1915); Keir, R. M., *The March of Commerce* (1927); Middleton, A. P., *Tobacco Coast: A Maritime History of the Chesapeake Bay in the Colonial Era* (1953); Morriss, M. S., *Colonial Trade of Maryland, 1689–1715* (1914); Schlesinger, A. M., *The Colonial Merchants and the American Revolution, 1763–1776* (1918).

WEST INDIAN COMMERCE

Andrews, C. M., *The Colonial Period of American History* (4 vols., 1934–1938); Harlow, V. T., *A History of Barbados* (1926); Newton, A. P., *The European Nations in the West Indies, 1739–1763* (1939); Pares, Richard, *War and Trade in the West Indies, 1700–1763* (1913); Parkes, Richard, *Yankees and Creoles: The Trades Between America and the West Indies before the American Revolution* (1956) Peabody, R. E., *Merchant Ventures of Old Salem:*

A History of the Commercial Voyages of a New England Family to the Indies and Elsewhere in the 18th Century (1912); Pitman, F. W., *The Development of the West Indies, 1700–1763* (1913); Thornton, A. P., *West India Policy under the Restoration* (1956); Williamson, J. A., *The Caribbean Islands under the Proprietary Patents* (1926).

COLONIAL FINANCE AND CURRENCY

Baxter, S. B., *The Development of the Treasury, 1660-1702* (1957); Behrens, K. L., *Paper Money in Maryland, 1727–1789* (1923); Bruce, P. A., *Economic History of Virginia in the Seventeenth Century* (2 vols., 1895); Bullock, C. J., *Essays on the Monetary History of the United States* (1900); Davis, A. M., *Colonial Currency Reprints* (4 vols., 1910–1911); Dewey, D. R., *Financial History of the United States* (rev. ed., 1956); Dorfman, Joseph, *The Economic Mind in America, 1606–1865* (1939); Gould, C. P., *Money and Transportation in Maryland, 1720–1765 (1915);* Hidy, Ralph, *The House of Baring in America: Trade, Finance, English Merchant Bankers at Work, 1763–1811* (1949); Nettels, C. P., *The Money Supply of the American Colonies before 1720* (1934); Phillips, Henry, Jr., *Historical Sketches of the Paper Money of the Colonies* (2 vols., 1865, 1866); Scott, Kenneth, *Counterfeiting in Colonial America* (1957); Shultz, W. J., and Caine, M. R., *Financial Development of the United States* (1937).

BRITISH POLICY AND COLONIAL LEGISLATION

Andrews, C. M., *The Colonial Background of the American Revolution* (1924); Ashley, W. J., *Surveys, Historic and Economic* (1900); Beer, G. L., *The Commercial Policy of England towards the American Colonies* (1893); Bining, A. C., *British Regulation of the Colonial Iron Industry* (1933); Giesecke, A. A., *American Commercial Legislation before 1789* (1910); Lord, E. L., *Industrial Experiments in the British Colonies of North America* (1898).

PIRACY, PRIVATEERING, AND SMUGGLING

Dow, G. F., and Edmonds, J. H., *The Pirates of the New England Coast, 1630–1730* (1923); Esquemeling, J., *The Buccaneers of America* (1931); Haring, C. H., *The Bucaneers in the West Indies* (1910); Hughson, S. C., *The Carolina Pirates and Colonial Commerce* (1894); Jameson, J. F., ed., *Privateering and Piracy in the Colonial Period* (1924); McClellan, W. S., *Smuggling in the American Colonies* (1912); Maclay, E. S., *History of American Privateers* (1924).

CHAPTER 6

MERCANTILISM AND BRITISH COLONIAL POLICY

Andrews, C. M., *The Colonial Background of the American Revolution* (1924); Bastable, C. F., *The Commerce of Nations* (1923); Beer, G. L., *British Colonial Policy, 1754–1765* (1907); Beer, G. L., *Commercial Policy of England Toward the American Colonies* (1893); Beer, G. L., *The Old Colonial System* (1913); Beer, G. L., *Origins of British Colonial Policy, 1578–1660* (1908); Dickerson, O. M., *The Navigation Acts and the American Revolution* (1951); Egerton, H. E., *A Short History of English Colonial Policy* (2nd ed., 1909); Giesecke, A. A., *American Commercial Legislation before 1789* (1910); Heckscher, E. F., *Mercantilism* (2 vols., 1935); Horrocks, J. W., *Short History of Mercantilism* (1925); Lord, E. L., *Industrial Experiments in the British Colonies of North America* (1898); Ritcheson, C. R., *British*

Politics and the American Revolution (1954); Schmoller, Gustav, *The Mercantile System and its Historical Significance* (1896).

BACKGROUND OF THE REVOLUTION

Adams, J. T., *Revolutionary New England, 1691–1776* (1923); Andrews, C. M., *The Colonial Background of the Revolution* (1924); Becker, C. L., *The Beginning of the American People* (1915); Becker, C. L., *The Eve of the Revolution* (1929); Belcher, Henry, *The First American Civil War, 1775–1778* (2 vols., 1911); Beloff, Max, ed., *The Debate on the American Revolution* (1950); *Cambridge History of the British Empire* (8 vols., 1929), I, *The Old Empire, from the Beginnings to 1783;* Clark, D. M., *British Opinion and the American Revolution* (1930); Dickerson, O. M., *The Navigation Acts and the American Revolution* (1951); Egerton, H. E., *Causes and Character of the American Revolution* (1923); Gipson, L. H., *The Coming of the Revolution, 1763–1775* (1954); Greene, E. B., *The Revolutionary Generation* (1943); Harper, Lawrence, *English Navigation Laws* (1939); Knollenberg, Bernhard, *Origin of the American Revolution, 1759–1776* (1960); McIlwaine, C. H., *The American Revolution* (1923); Miller, J. C., *Origins of the American Revolution* (rev. ed., 1959); Morgan, E. S., and Morgan, H. M., *The Stamp Act Crisis: Prologue to Revolution* (1953); Morgan, E. S., *The Birth of the Republic, 1763–1789* (1956); Morison, S. E., *The American Revolution, 1764–1788: Sources and Documents* (1923); Rossiter, Clinton, *Seedtime of the Republic* (1953); Schlesinger, A. M., *New Viewpoints in American History* (1922); Trevelyan, G. O., *The American Revolution* (4 vols., 1899–1907); Van Tyne, C. H., *The Causes of the War of Independence* (1922); Van Tyne, C. H., *The War for Independence* (1929); Wahlke, J. C., *Causes of the American Revolution* (1950).

ECONOMIC ASPECTS OF THE REVOLUTION

Bezanson, Anne, and Others, *Prices and Inflation during the American Revolution, 1770–1790* (1951); Cole, A. H., *Wholesale Commodity Prices in the United States 1700–1861* (1938); East, R. A., *Business Enterprise in the American Revolutionary Era* (1938); Jameson, J. F., *The American Revolution Considered as a Social Movement* (1926); Johnson, E. R., and Others, *History of Domestic and Foreign Commerce of the United States* (2 vols., 1915); Johnson, V. L., *The Administration of the American Commissariat during the Revolutionary War* (1941); Kraus, Michael, *Intercolonial Aspects of American Culture on the Eve of the Revolution with Special Reference to the Northern Towns* (1928); Mahan, A. T., *The Influence of Sea Power upon History, 1660–1783* (1917); Miller, J. C., *The Triumph of Freedom, 1775–1783* (1948); Nettels, C. P., *The Roots of American Civilization* (1938); Newcomer, L. N., *The Embattled Farmers: A Massachusetts Countryside in the American Revolution* (1953); Nevins, Allan, *The American States during and after the Revolution, 1775–1789* (1924); Russell, C. E., *Haym Solomon and the Revolution* (1930); Schlesinger, A. M., *The Colonial Merchants and the American Revolution* (1918); Van Doren, C. C., *Secret History of the American Revolution: History of Peace Negotiations* (1941); Weeden, W. B., *Economic and Social History of New England, 1620–1789* (2 vols., 1890).

FINANCING THE WAR

Bullock, C. J., *The Finances of the United States from 1775–1789* (1895); Dewey, D. R., *Financial History of the United States* (rev. ed., 1956); Ferguson, E. J., *The Power of the Purse: A History of American Public Finance, 1776–1790* (1961); Oberholtzer, E. P., *Life of Robert Morris* (1903); Sumner, W. G., *The Financier and Finances of the American Revolution* (2 vols., 1891); Ver Steeg, C. L., *Robert Morris: Revolutionary Financier* (1954).

ECONOMIC ASPECTS OF THE CONFEDERATION

Adams, H. B., *Maryland's Influence on Land Cessions to the United States* (1885); Adams, J. T., *New England in the Republic, 1776–1850* (1926); Bullock, C. J. *Finances of the United States, 1775–1789* (1895); Burnett, E. C., *The Continental Congress* (1941); Cochran, T. C., *New York and the Confederation* (1932); Dewey, D. R., *Financial History of the United States* (12th ed., 1936); East, R. A., *Business Enterprise in the American Revolutionary Era* (1938); Fiske, John, *The Critical Period of American History, 1783–1789* (1888); Jameson, J. F., *The American Revolution Considered as a Social Movement* (1926); Jensen, Merrill, *The Articles of Confederation* (1940); Jensen, Merrill, *The New Nation: A History of the United States during the Confederation, 1776–1790* (1961); Lightner, O. C., *The History of Business Depressions* (1922); McLaughlin, A. C., *Confederation and Constitution* (1905); McMaster, J. B., *A History of the People of the United States,* I (1883); Morison, S. E., *Maritime History of Massachusetts, 1783–1860* (1921); Nevins, Allan, *The American States during and after the Revolution, 1775–1789* (1924); Spaulding, E. W., *New York in the Critical Period* (1932); Wood, G. G., *Congressional Control of Foreign Relations during the American Revolution, 1774–1789* (1919).

MAKING THE CONSTITUTION

Brunhouse, R. L., *The Counter Revolution in Pennsylvania, 1776–1790* (1942); Crowl, Philip, *Maryland During and After the Revolution* (1943); Ferrand, Max, *Fathers of the Constitution* (1921); Farrand, Max, *Framing of the Constitution* (1913); Hockett, H. C., *The Constitutional History of the United States* (2 vols., 1939); McLaughlin, A. C., *The Confederation and the Constitution* (1905); McLaughlin, A. C., *A Constitutional History of the United States* (1935); Prescott, A. T., *Drafting the Federal Constitution,* (1941); Solberg, W. A., *The Constitutional Convention and Formation of the Union* (1958); Warren, Charles, *The Making of the Constitution* (1928).

ECONOMIC INTERPRETATION OF THE CONSTITUTION

Beard, C. A., *An Economic Interpretation of the Constitution of the United States* (1913); Beard, C. A., *The Economic Origins of the Jeffersonian Democracy* (1915); Bensen, Lee, *Turner and Beard: American Historical Writing Reconsidered* (1960); Brown, R. E., *Charles Beard and the Constitution* (1956); Ferguson, E. J., *The Power of the Purse: A History of American Public Finance, 1776–1790* (1961); Libby, O. G., *The Geographical Distribution of the Vote on the Federal Constitution* (1894); McDonald, Forrest, *We the People: The Economic Origins of the Constitution* (1958); Schlesinger, A. M., *New Viewpoints in American History* (1922).

CHAPTER 7

THE FRONTIER IN AMERICAN HISTORY

Alvord, C. W., *The Mississippi Valley in British Politics* (2 vols., 1917); Billington, R. A., and Hedges, J. B., *Westward Expansion: A History of the American Frontier* (rev. ed., 1960); Dodd, W. E., *Struggles for Democracy* (1937); Farrand, Livingston, *Basis of American History* (1904); Halsey, F. W., *The Old American Frontier* (2 vols., 1901); Holbrook, Stewart, *Yankee Exodus: An Account of Migration from New England, 1636–1850* (1950); Paxson, F. L. *History of the American Frontier, 1763–1893* (1924); Semple, E. C., and Jones, C. F., *American History and Its Geographic Condition* (rev. ed., 1933); Turner, F. J., *The Frontier in Amer-*

ican History (1920); Turner, F. J., *Rise of the New West* (1906); Turner, F. J., *Significance of Sections in American History* (1933); Turner, F. J., *The United States, 1830–1850* (1935).

DEVELOPING A NATIONAL LAND POLICY

Bond, B. W., Jr., ed., *The Papers of John Cleves Symmes* (1926); Carstensen, V. R., ed., *The Public Lands* (1963); Donaldson, Thomas, *The Public Domain* (1884); Harris, Marshall, *Origin of the Land Tenure System in the United States* (1953); Hibbard, B. H., *A History of the Public Land Policies* (1924); McKitrick, Reuben, *The Public Land System of Texas, 1823–1910* (1918); Robbins, R. M., *Our Landed Heritage: The Public Domain, 1776–1936* (1942); Sakolski, A. M., *The Great American Land Bubble* (1932); Sato, Shosuke, *History of the Land Question in the United States* (1886); Stephenson, G. M., *The Political History of Public Lands from 1840 to 1862; From Preemption to Homestead* (1917); Treat, P. J., *The National Land System, 1785–1820* (1910); Wellington, R. G., *The Political and Sectional Influence of the Public Lands, 1828–1842* (1914).

THE OLD NORTHWEST

Abernethy, T. P., *Western Lands and the American Revolution* (1937); Alden, C. H., *New Governments West of the Alleghenies Before 1780* (1897); Barrett, J. A., *Evolution of the Ordinance of 1787* (1891); Bond, B. W., Jr., *The Civilization of the Old Northwest* (1934); Buck, S. J., and Buck, E. H., *The Planting of Civilization in Western Pennsylvania* (1939); Buley, R. C., *The Old Northwest* (2 vols., 1950); Hinsdale, B. A., *The Old Northwest* (1899); Hubbart, H. C., *The Older Middle West, 1840–1880,* (1936); Hulbert, A. B., *Paths of Inland Commerce* (1920); Mathews, L. K., *Expansion of New England* (1909); Ogg, F. A., *The Old Northwest; A Chronicle of the Ohio Valley and Beyond* (1919); O'Mara, Walter, *The Savage Country* (1960); Roosevelt, Theodore, *Winning of the West* (4 vols., 1894–1896); Winsor, J., *The Westward Movement, 1763–1798* (1897).

THE OLD SOUTHWEST

Abernethy, T. P., *From Frontier to Plantation in Tennessee: A Study in Frontier Democracy* (1932); Ambler, C. H., *George Washington and the West* (1936); Henderson, Archibald, *The Conquest of the Old Southwest* (1920); Johnston, Mary, *Pioneers of the Old South* (1921); Roosevelt, Theodore, *Winning of the West* (4 vols., 1894–1896); Skinner, C. L., *Pioneers of the Old Southwest* (1919); Thwaites, R. G., *Daniel Boone* (1902); Whitaker, A. P., *The Mississippi Question, 1795–1803: A Study in Trade, Politics, and Diplomacy* (1934); Whitaker, A. P., *Spanish American Frontier, 1783–1795* (1927).

THE TRANS-MISSISSIPPI WEST

Arrington, L. J., *Great Basin Kingdom: An Economic History of the Latter-Day Saints* (1958); Barker, E. C., *The Life of Stephen F. Austin, the Founder of Texas, 1793–1836* (1925); Barker, E. C., *Mexico and Texas, 1821–1835* (1928); Bemis, S. F., *Diplomatic History of the United States* (1936); Callcott, W. H., *Santa Anna: The Story of an Enigma Who Once Was Mexico* (1936); Garber, P. N., *The Gadsden Treaty* (1923); Garrison, W. P., *Westward Extension* (1906); Gilbert, E. W., *Exploration of Western America, 1800–1850: An Historical Geography* (1933); Greer, L. H., *The Founding of an Empire* (1947); Greer, L. H., *Utah and the Nation* (1929); Goodwin, C. L., *The Trans-Mississippi West, 1803–1853* (1922); James, Marquis, *The Raven: A Biography of Sam Houston* (1929); Montgomery, R. C., *The White-Headed Eagle, John McLoughlin, Builder of an Empire* (1934); Paxson, F. L., *History of the American Frontier, 1763–1893* (1924); Riegel, R. E., *America Moves West* (rev.

ed., 1947); Rippy, J. F., *United States and Mexico* (1926); Schafer, Joseph, *The Social History of American Agriculture* (1936); Sears, L. M., *John Slidell* (1925); Sheridan, Richard, *Economic Development in South Central Kansas* (1956); Smith, H. N., *Virgin Land* (1950); Smith, Justin, *Annexation of Texas* (1911); Smith, Justin, *War With Mexico* (2 vols., 1919); Stephenson, N. W., *Texas and the Mexican War* (1921); Turner, F. J., *The Rise of the New West* (1906); Wade, R. C., *The Urban Frontier: The Rise of Western Cities, 1790–1830* (1959); Webb, W. P., *The Great Plains* (1931); Webb, W. P., *The Great Frontier* (1952).

PACIFIC COAST SETTLEMENTS

Billington, R. A., *The Far Western Frontier, 1830–1860* (1956); Chittenden, H. M., *The American Fur Trade of the Far West* (3 vols., rev. ed., 1935); Coman, Katherine, *Economic Beginnings of the Far West* (2 vols., 1912); Ghent, W. J., *The Early Far West, 1540–1850* (1931); Ghent, W. J., *The Road to Oregon* (1929); Laut, A. C., *Pioneers of the Pacific Coast* (1915); Porter, K. W., *John Jacob Astor* (1931); Skinner, C. L., *Adventurers of Oregon* (1920); Skinner, C. L., *Beaver, Kings, and Cabins* (1933); Winther, O. O., *The Great Northwest* (1947); Winther, O. O., *The Old Oregon Country: A History of Frontier Trade, Transportation, and Travel* (1950).

CHAPTER 8

DEVELOPMENT OF THE CORPORATION

Abbott, C. C., *The Rise of the Business Corporation* (1936); Blande, J. G., *Maryland Business Corporations, 1783–1852* (1934); Cadman, Jr., J. W., *The Corporation in New Jersey: Business and Politics, 1791–1875* (1949); Cochran, T. C., *Basic History of American Business* (1959); Davis, J. S., *Essays in the Earlier History of American Corporations* (2 vols., 1917); Dill, J. B., comp., *Corporation Act of New Jersey, with other General Acts Relating to Business Corporations* (1963); Dodd, E. M., *American Business Corporations until 1860, with Special Reference to Massachusetts* (1954); Evans, G. H., *Business Incorporations in the United States, 1800–1845* (1948); Handlin, Oscar, and Handlin, M. F., *Commonweath: A Study of the Role of Government in the American Economy, 1774–1861* (1947); Hartz, Louis, *Economic Thought and Democratic Thought: Pennsylvania, 1776–1860* (1948); Heath, M. S., *Constructive Liberalism: The Role of the State in the Economic Development of Georgia, 1776–1861* (1947); Hunt, B. C., *The Development of the Business Corporation in England, 1800–1867* (1936); Livermore, Shaw, *Early American Land Companies: Their Influence on Corporate Development* (1939); Primm, J. N., *Economic Policy in the Development of a Western State: Missouri, 1820–1860* (1954).

GENERAL WORKS ON TRANSPORTATION

Ambler, C. H., *A History of Transportation in the Ohio Valley* (1932); Bogart, E. L., *Internal Improvements and the State Debt in Ohio* (1924); Dunbar, Seymour, *History of Travel in America* (4 vols., 1915); Gebhard, W. F., *Transportation and Industrial Development in the Middle West* (1900); Goodrich, Carter, *Government Promotion of Canals and Railroads, 1800–1860* (1960); Hulbert, A. B., *Historic Highways of America* (16 vols., 1902–1905); MacGill, C. E., and Others, *History of Transportation in the United States Before 1860* (1917); Miller, J. A., *Fares Please; From Horse-Cars to Streamliners* (1941); Phillips, U. B., *History of Transportation in the Eastern Cotton Belt to 1860* (1908); Riegel, R. E., *America Moves West* (1930); Riegel, R. E., *Young America, 1830–1840* (1949); Taylor, G. E., *The Transportation Revolution, 1815–1861* (1961).

ROADS AND TURNPIKES

Duffus, R. L., *The Santa Fe Trail* (1930); Dunbar, Seymour, *History of Travel in America* (4 vols., 1915); Gard, Wayne, *The Chisholm Trail* (1954); Hulbert, A. B., *Historic Highways of America* (16 vols., 1902–1905); Hulbert, A. B., *The Old National Pike* (1901); Hulbert, A. B., *Paths of Inland Commerce* (1920); Jackson, W. T., *Wagon Roads West, 1846–1869* (1952); Seabright, T. B., *The Old Pike* (1894).

WATERWAYS

Baldwin, L. D., *The Keelboat Age on Western Waters* (1941); Dunaway, W. F., *History of the James River and Kanawha Company* (1922); Goodrich, Carter and Others, *Canals and American Economic Development* (1961); Harlow, A. F., *Old Towpaths, The Story of the American Canal Era* (1926); Jones, C. L., *Economic History of the Anthracite Tidewater Canal* (1908); Miller, Nathan, *The Enterprise of a Free People* (1962); Putnam, J. W., *The Illinois and Michigan Canal: A Study in Economic History* (1918); Sanderlin, W. S., *Great National Project: A History of the Chesapeake and Ohio Canal* (1948); Waggoner, M. S., *The Long Haul West: The Great Canal Era, 1817–1850* (1958); Ward, G. W., *The Early Development of the Chesapeake and Ohio Canal Project* (1889); Whitford, N. E., *History of the Canal System of the State of New York* (2 vols., 1906).

RISE OF THE STEAMBOAT

Ambler, C. H., *A History of Transportation in the Ohio Valley* (1932); Boyd, T. A., *Poor John Fitch: Inventor of the Steamboat* (1935); Dayton, F. E., *Steamboat Days* (1925); Dixon, F. H., *A Traffic History of the Mississippi River System* (1909); Dunbar, Seymour, *History of Travel in America* (4 vols., 1915); Flexner, James, *Steamboats Come True* (1944); Hulbert, A. B., *Paths of Inland Commerce* (1920); Hunter, L. C., *Steamboats on the Western Rivers: An Economic and Technological History* (1949); Lane, C. D., *American Paddle Steamboats* (1943); Petersen, W. J., *Steamboating on the Upper Mississippi: The Water Way to Iowa* (1937); Quick, Herbert, and Quick, E. C., *Mississippi Steamboating* (1926); Tyler, D. B., *The American Clyde: A History of Iron and Steel Shipbuilding on the Delaware from 1840 to World War I* (1958).

RAILROADS

Ackerman, W. K., *Early Illinois Railroads* (1884); Alexander, E. P., *Iron Horses: American Locomotives, 1829–1900* (1914); Bradlee, F. B. C., *The Boston and Maine Railroad* (1921); Brown, C. K., *A State Movement in Railroad Development* (1928); Carter, C. W., *When Railroads Were New* (1909); Cleveland, F. A., and Powell, F. W., *Railroad Promotion and Capitalization in the United States* (1909); Derrick, S. M., *Centennial History of South Carolina Railroad* (1930); Gates, P. W., *The Illinois Central Railroad and Its Colonization Work* (1934); Haney, H. L., *Congressional History of Railroads in the United States to 1850* (1908); Hungerford, Edward, *The Story of the Baltimore and Ohio Railroad, 1827–1927* (2 vols., 1928); Hunt, R. S., *Law and Locomotives* (1958); Johnson, E. R., *American Railway Transportation* (1903); Johnson, E. R., and Van Metre, T. W., *Principles of Railway Transportation* (1922); Kirkland, E. C., *Men, Cities, and Transportation: A Study in New England History, 1820–1900* (2 vols., 1948); Laut, A. C., *The Romance of the Rails* (1929); Miller, S. L., *Railway Transportation* (1924); Overton, R. C., *Burlington West: A Colonization History of the Burlington Railroad* (1941); Pierce, H. H., *Railroads of New York: A Study of Government Air, 1826–1875* (1953); Reizenstein, Milton, *Economic History of the Baltimore and Ohio Railroad* (1897); Riegel, R. E., *History of Western Railroads* (1926); Schotter, H. W.,

The Growth and Development of the Pennsylvania Railroad (1926); Stevens, F. W., *The Beginnings of the New York Central Railroad* (1926); Stover, J. F., *American Railroads* (1961); Thompson, Slason, *A Short History of American Railways* (1925).

COMMUNICATION

Hafen, L. R. H., *The Overland Mail, 1849–1860* (1926); Harlow, A. F., *Old Wires and New Waves: The History of the Telegraph, Telephone and Wireless* (1936); Hungerford, Edward, *Wells Fargo, Advancing the American Frontier* (1949); Mabee, Carleton, *The American Leonardo: A Life of Samuel B. Morse* (1943); Russel, R. R., *Improvement of Communication to the Pacific Coast as an Issue in American Politics, 1783–1864* (1948); Thompson, R. L., *Wiring a Continent: The History of the Telegraph Industry in the United States, 1832–1866* (1947); Wiltsee, E. A., *The Pioneer Miner and the Pack Mule Express* (1931); Wilson, Neil, *Treasure Express: Epic Days of the Wells Fargo* (1936); Winther, O. O., *Express and Stagecoach Days in California* (1936).

CHAPTER 9

BANKING AND CREDIT

Balinsky, Alexander, *Albert Gallatin: Fiscal Theories and Policies* (1958); Catterall, R. C. H., *The Second Bank of the United States* (1903); Dewey, D. R., *Financial History of the United States* (rev. ed., 1956); Dewey, D. R., *State Banking Before the Civil War* (1910); Conant. C. A., *History of Modern Banks of Issue* (rev. ed., 1915); Dunbar, C. F., *Chapters on the Theory and History of Banking* (1896); Ewing, F. B., *Forgotten Statesman: Albert Gallatin* (1959); Foulke, R. A., *The Sinews of American Commerce* (1941); Govan, T. P., *Nicholas Biddle* (1959); Gras, N. S. B., *The Massachusetts-First National Bank of Boston, 1784–1934* (1937); Hammond, Bray, *Banks and Politics in America from the Revolution to the Civil War* (1957); Holdsworth, J. T., and Dewey, D. R., *The First and Second Banks of the United States* (1910); Kinley, David, *The Independent Treasury of the United States and Its Relation to the Banks of the Country* (1910); Miller, H. E., *Banking Theories in the United States before 1860* (1927); Redlick, Fritz, *The Molding of American Banking: Men and Ideas* (2 vols., 1947, 1951); Schlesinger, Jr., A. M., *The Age of Jackson* (1945); Schultz, W. J., and Caine, M. R., *Financial Development of the United States* (1937); Smith, W. B., *Aspects of the Second Bank of the United States* (1953); Smith, W. B., *Economic Aspects of the Second Bank of the United States* (1953); Studenski, Paul, and Krooss, H. E., *Financial History of the United States* (1952); Summer, W. G., *History of Banking in the United States* (1896); Taylor, G. R., ed., *Jackson and Biddle* (1949); Warren, Charles, *Bankruptcy in the United States* (1935); Westerfield, R. B., *Money, Credit and Banking* (rev. ed., 1947).

DEPRESSION PERIODS

Barnett, Paul, *Business Cycle Theory in the United States, 1860–1900* (1941); Collman, C. A., *Our Mysterious Panics, 1830–1930; A Story of Events and the Men Involved* (1931); Lightner, O. C., *The History of Business Depressions* (1922); McGrane, R. C., *The Panic of 1837* (1924); Rothbard, M. N., *The Panic of 1819* (1962); Smith, W. B., and Cole, A. H., *Fluctuations in American Business, 1790–1860* (1935); Van Vleck, G. W., *The Panic of 1857* (1943); Wildman, M. S., *Money Inflation in the United States; A Study in Social Pathology* (1905).

CURRENCY AND FISCAL POLICY

Bolles, A. S., *The Financial History of the United States* (3 vols., 1884–1886); De Knight, W. F., *History of the Currency of the Country and of the Loans of the United States from the Earliest Period to June 30, 1900* (1900); Dewey, D. R., *Financial History of the United States* (rev. ed., 1956); Hepburn, A. B., *History of Coinage and Currency in the United States* rev. ed., 1915); Laughlin, J. L., *The History of Bimetallism in the United States* (rev. ed., 1897); Watson, D. K., *History of American Coinage* (1899); White, Horace, *Money and Banking Illustrated by American History* (rev. ed., 1914).

THE STOCK MARKET AND AMERICAN SECURITIES

Hedges, J. E., *Commercial Banking and the Stock Market before 1863* (1938); McGrane, R. C., *Foreign Bondholders and American State Debts* (1935); Medbery, J. K., *Men and Mysteries of Wall Street* (1870); Myers, M. G., *The New York Money Market: Origins and Development* (1931); Neil, H. B., *The Inside Story of the Stock Exchange* (1950); Warshow, R. I., *The Story of Wall Street* (1929).

CHAPTER 10

THE ENGLISH BACKGROUND

Ashton, T. S., *Iron and Steel in the Industrial Revolution* (1924); Botsford, J. B., *English Society in the Eighteenth Century* (1924); Daniels, G. W., *The Early English Cotton Industry* (1920); Fay, C. R., *Great Britain from Adam Smith to the Present Day* (1928); Hammond, J. L., and Hammond, B., *The Rise of Modern Industry* (1926); Mantoux, Paul, *The Industrial Revolution* (1928); Redford, A., *The Economic History of England, 1760–1860* (1931); Unwin, G., Hulme, A., and Taylor, G., *Samuel Oldknow and the Arkwrights* (1924); Usher, A. P., *An Introduction to the Industrial History of England* (1920).

INVENTIONS

Anderson, O. E., *Refrigeration in America: A History of New Technology and Its Impact* (1953); Burlingame, Roger, *Engines of Democracy* (1940); Burlingame, Roger, *March of Iron Men* (1938); Burlingame, Roger, *Machines that Built America* (1953); Bryn, E. W., *The Progress of Invention in the Nineteenth Century* (1900); Clark, V. S., *History of Manufactures in the United States* (3 vols., 1929); Cummings, R. O., *American Ice Harvest: A Historical Study in Technology, 1800–1918* (1949); Habakkuk, H. J., *American and British Technology in the Nineteenth Century: The Search for Labour-Saving Inventions* (1961); Kaempffert, Waldemar, ed., *A Popular History of American Inventions* (2 vols., 1924); Oliver, J. W., *History of American Technology* (1956); Roe, J. W., *English and American Tool Builders* (1926); Usher, A. P., *A History of Mechanical Inventions* (1954).

RISE OF THE AMERICAN FACTORY SYSTEM
AND INDUSTRIAL EXPANSION

Bishop, J. L., *History of American Manufactures from 1608–1860* (3 vols., 1866); Bolles, A. S., *Industrial History of the United States* (1878); Carman, H. J., *Social and Economic History of the United States* (2 vols., 1930–1934); Chamberlain, J. R., *The Enterprising Americans: A Business History of the United States* (1962); Clark, V. S., *History of Manufactures in the United States* (3 vols., 1929); Cochran, T. C., and Miller, William, *The Age of Enterprise: A Social History of Industrial America* (reissue, 1961); Cole, A. H., ed., *Industrial and Commercial Correspondence of Alexander Hamilton* (1928); Glover, J. G., and Cornell, W. B., eds., *The Development of American Industries: Their Economic Significance* (1941); Habakkuk, H. J., *American and British Technology in the Nineteenth Century: The Search for Labour-Saving Inventions* (1961); Hacker, L. M., *The Triumph of American Capitalism*

(1940); Hutcheson, Harold, *Tench Coxe: A Study in American Economic Development* (1938); Keir, R. M., *Manufacturing* (1928); Langdon, W. C., *Everyday Things in American Life, 1776–1876* (1928); Morris, R. B., ed., *The Basic Ideas of Alexander Hamilton* (1957); National Bureau of Economic Research, *Trends in the American Economy in the Nineteenth Century* (1960); North, D. C., *The Economic Growth of the United States, 1790–1860* (1961); Tryon, R. M., *Household Manufactures in the United States, 1640–1860* (1917); Wile, F. W., ed., *A Century of Industrial Progress* (1928).

SPECIAL INDUSTRIES

Armes, Ethel, *The Story of Coal and Iron in Alabama* (1910); Bruce, Kathleen, *Virginia Iron Manufacture in the Slave Era* (1931); Burgy, J. H., *The New England Cotton Textile Industry: A Study in Industrial Geography* (1932); Cameron, E. H., *Samuel Slater: Father of American Manufacturers* (1960); Cole, A. H., *The American Wool Manufacture* (2 vols., 1926); Cole, A. H., and Williamson, H. F., *The American Carpet Manufacture* (1941); Copeland, M. T., *The Cotton Manufacturing Industry in the United States* (1912); Coyne, F. B., *The Development of the Cooperage Industry in the United States, 1620–1940* (1940); Eavenson, H. N., *The Organization of the Boot and Shoe Industry in Massachusetts before 1875* (1921); Gibb, G. S., *Saco-Lowell Shops: Textile Machinery in New England, 1813–1949* (1950); Gibb, G. S., *The Whitesmiths of Taunton: A History of Reed and Barton, 1824–1943* (1943); Hammond, M. B., *The Cotton Industry* (1897); Knowlton, E. H., *Pepperell's Progress: History of a Cotton Textile Company* (1948); Kullmann, C. B., *Development of the Flour-Milling Industry in the United States* (1929); Layer, R. G., *Earnings of Cotton Mill Operatives, 1825–1914* (1955); Lomax, A. L., *Pioneer Woolen Mills in Oregon: History of Wool and Woolen Industry in Oregon, 1811–1875* (1941); Mitchell, Broadus, *The Rise of Cotton Mills in the South* (1921); Moore, C. W., *Timing a Century: History of the Waltham Watch Company* (1945); Navin, T. R., *The Whitin Machine Works since 1831: A Textile Machinery Company in an Industrial Village* (1950); North, D. C., *The Economic Growth of the United States, 1790–1860* (1961); Nystrom, P. H., *Textiles* (1916); Scherer, J. A. B., *Cotton as a World Power* (1916); Smith, T. R., *The Cotton Industry of Fall River, Mass.,* (1944); Swank, J. M., *History of the Manufacture of Iron in all Ages* (2nd ed., 1892); Ware, C. F., *The Early New England Cotton Manufacture* (1931); Weeks, L. H., *A History of Paper Manufacturing in the United States, 1690–1916* (1916); Williamson, H. F., *Winchester: The Gun that Won the West* (1952); Wolfbein, S. L., *The Decline of a Cotton City: The Story of New Bedford* (1944).

THE TARIFF

Ashley, P. W. L., *Modern Tariff History* (3rd ed., 1920); Macdonald, William, *Jacksonian Democracy* (1906); Rabbeno, U., *American Commercial Policy* (2nd ed., 1895); Stanwood, Edward, *American Tariff Controversies in the Nineteenth Century* (2 vols., 1903); Taussig, F. W., *The Tariff History of the United States* (8th ed., 1931); Taussig, F. W., *State Papers and Speeches on the Tariff* (1888); Wright, C. W., *Wool-Growing and the Tariff* (1910).

LABOR

Abbott, E., *Women in Industry* (1910); Beard, Mary, *A Short History of the American Labor Movement* (1920); Boone, Gladys, *The Women's Trade Union Leagues in Great Britain and the United States of America* (1942); Carlton, F. T., *History and Problems of Organized Labor* (rev. ed., 1920); Commons, J. R., and Others, *History of Labour in the United States* (4 vols., 1918–1935); Groat, G. G., *Organized Labor in America* (1916); Josephson, Hannah, *Golden Threads: New England's Mill Girls and Magnates* (1949); Sullivan, W. A., *Industrial*

Worker in Pennsylvania, 1800–1840 (1955); Ware, Norman, *The Industrial Worker, 1840–1860* (1924); Watkins, G. S., *An Introduction to the Study of the Labor Problem* (1922).

CHAPTER 11

FOREIGN COMMERCE AND THE AMERICAN MERCHANT MARINE

Abbot, W. J., *The Story of the Merchant Marine* (1919); Bates, W. W., *The American Marine* (1893); Bates, W. W., *American Navigation* (1902); Benns, F. L., *The American Struggle for the British West India Carrying Trade, 1815–1830* (1923); Buck, N. S., *The Development of the Organization of Anglo-American Trade, 1800–1850* (1925); Cartwright, C. E., *The Tale of our Merchant Marine* (1924); Clark, A. H., *The Clipper Ship Era, 1843–1869* (1910); Day, Clive, *History of Commerce of the United States* (1925); Dow, G. F., *Whale Ships and Whaling* (1925); Dulles, F. R., *The Old China Trade* (1930); Frederick, J. H., *The Development of American Commerce* (1932); Hutchins, John G. B., *The American Maritime Industries and Public Policy, 1789–1914; An Economic History* (1941); Johnson, E. R., Van Metre, T. W., Huebner, G. G., and Hanchett, D. S., *History of Domestic and Foreign Commerce of the United States* (2 vols. 1915); Keir, R. M., *The March of Commerce* (1927); McKee, M. M., *Ship Subsidy Question in United States Politics* (1922); Marvin, W. L., *The American Merchant Marine* (1902); Meeker, Royal, *History of Ship Subsidies* (1905); Morison, S. E., *Maritime History of Massachusetts, 1783–1860* (1921); North, D. C., *The Economic Growth of the United States, 1790–1860* (1961); Paine, R. D., *The Old Merchant Marine* (1919).

AMERICAN COMMERCE DURING THE EUROPEAN WARS, 1793–1815

Bemis, S. F., *Jay's Treaty: A Study in Commerce and Diplomacy* (1924); Galpin, W. F., *The Grain Supply of England During the Napoleonic Period* (1925); Heckscher, E. F., *The Continental System: An Economic Interpretation* (1922); Hyneman, C. S., *The First American Neutrality, 1792–1815* (1934); Jessup, P. C., *Neutrality, Its History, Economics, and Law* (4 vols., 1935–1936); Nussbaum, F. L., *Commercial Policy in the French Revolution* (1923); Sears, L. M., *Jefferson and the Embargo* (1927); Thomas, C. M., *American Neutrality in 1793* (1931).

THE WAR OF 1812

Babcock, K. C., *Rise of American Nationality, 1811–1819* (1906); Burt, A. L., *The United States, Great Britain, and British North America from the Revolution to the Establishment of Peace after the War of 1812* (1940); Coggeshall, George, *History of the American Privateers and Letters-of-Marque during Our War with England in the Years 1812, 1813, and 1814* (1856); Maclay, E. S., *A History of American Privateers* (1924); Mahan, A. T., *Sea Power in Its Relation to the War of 1812* (2 vols., 1905); Paine, R. D., *The Fight for a Free Sea* (1920); Pratt, J. W., *Expansionists of 1812* (1925); Roosevelt, Theodore, *Naval War of 1812* (1882); Updyke, F. A., *Diplomacy of the War of 1812* (1915); Zimmerman, J. F., *Impressment of American Seamen* (1925).

DOMESTIC COMMERCE AND INTERNAL TRADE

Albion, R. G., *The Rise of New York Port, 1815–1860* (1939); Atherton, L. E., *The Pioneer Merchant in America* (1939); Atherton, L. E., *The Southern Country Store* (1954); Carson,

Gerald, *The Old Country Store* (1954); Clark, T. D., *Pills, Petticoats and Plows: The Southern Country Store* (1946); Duffus, R. L., *The Santa Fe Trail* (1930); Gould, R. E., *Yankee Storekeeper* (1946); Huebner, G. G., and Hanchett, D. S., *History of Domestic and Foreign Commerce of the United States* (2 vols., 1915); Jennings, Sister Marietta, *A Pioneer Merchant of St. Louis, 1810–1820: The Business Career of Christian Welt* (1939); Johnson, E. R., and Others, *History of Domestic and Foreign Commerce of the United States* (2 vols., 1915); Johnson, L. A., *Over the Counter and On the Shelf: Country Storekeeping in America, 1620–1920* (1961); Jones, F. M., *Middlemen in the Domestic Trade of the United States, 1806–1860* (1937); Lippincott, Isaac, *Internal Trade of the United States, 1700–1860* (1916); Livingood, J. W., *The Philadelphia-Baltimore Trade Rivalry, 1780–1860* (1947); Martin, M. E., *Merchants and Trade of the Connecticut River Valley, 1750–1820* (1939); Mills, J. C., *Our Inland Seas, Their Shipping and Commerce for Three Centuries* (1910); Plumb, R. G., *History of the Navigation of the Great Lakes* (1911); Quaire, M. M., ed., *The Commerce of the Prairies* (reissue, 1926); Westerfield, R. B., *Early History of American Auctions* (1920); Wright, Richardson, Hawkers and Walkers in Early America (1927).

SHIPBUILDING AND SHIPS

Cutler, C. C., *Greyhounds of the Sea: The Story of the American Clipper Ship* (1930); Howe, O. T., and Matthews, F. C., *American Clipper Ships, 1833–1858* (1926, 1927); Kittredge, H. C., *Shipmasters of Cape Cod* (1935); Morison, S. E., *The Maritime History of Massachusetts, 1783–1860* (1921); Robinson, John, and Dow, G. F., *The Sailing Ships of New England* (1924).

CHAPTER 12

AGRICULTURE IN THE NORTH

Bailey, L. H., ed., *Cyclopedia of American Agriculture*, IV (1912); Bidwell, P. W., and Falconer, J. I., *History of Agriculture in the Northern United States, 1620–1860* (1925); Gates, Paul, *The Farmers' Age: Agriculture, 1815–1860* (1960); Hedrick, V. P., *A History of Agriculture in the State of New York* (1933); Hutchinson, W. T., *Cyrus Hall McCormick* (1936); Sanford, A. H., *The Story of Agriculture in the United States* (1916); Schafer, Joseph, *The Social History of American Agriculture* (1936); Wilson, H. F., *The Hill Country of Northern New England: Its Social and Economic History, 1790–1930* (1936); Woodward, C. R., *The Development of Agriculture in New Jersey, 1640–1880* (1927).

AGRICULTURE IN THE SOUTH

Craven, A. O., *Soil Exhaustion as a Factor in the Agricultural History of Virginia and Maryland, 1606–1860* (1926); Dickson, Harris, *The Story of King Cotton* (1937); Dodd, W. E., *The Cotton Kingdom* (1919); Eaton, Clement, *A History of the Old South* (1949); Gaines, F. P., *The Cotton Plantation: A Study in the Development and Accuracy of a Tradition* (1924); Gray, L. C., *History of Agriculture in the Southern United States* (2 vols., 1933); Hammond, M. P., *The Cotton Industry* (1897); Hawk, E. Q., *Economic History of the South* (1934); Jacobstein, Meyer, *The Tobacco Industry in the United States* (1907); Moore, J. H., *Agriculture in Ante-Bellum Mississippi* (1958); Phillips, U. B., *American Negro Slavery* (1918); Phillips, U. B., ed., *Plantation and Frontier, 1649–1863* (2 vols., 1910); Phillips, U. B., *Life and Labor in the Old South* (1929); Robert, J. C., *The Tobacco Kingdom: Plantation, Market, and Factory in Virginia and North Carolina, 1800–1860* (1938); Scherer, J. A. B., *Cotton As a World Power* (1916); Sitterson, J. C., *Sugar Country: The Cane Sugar Industry in the South, 1753–1950* (1953); Stephenson, W. H., *Basic History of the Old South* (1952); Turner, F. J., *The United States, 1830–1850* (1935); Weaver, Herbert, *Mississippi Farmer, 1850–1860* (1945).

IMPROVED AGRICULTURE

Allen, B. W., *Historical Background of the United States Department of Agriculture* (1940); Craven, A. O., *Edmund Ruffin: Southerner* (1932); Greathouse, C. H., *Historical Sketch of the United States Department of Agriculture* (1907); Hutchinson, W. T., *Cyrus Hall McCormick* (2 vols., 1930, 1935); Ivins, L. S., and Winship, A. E., *Fifty Famous Farmers* (1924); Johnson, T. C., *Scientific Interests in the Old South* (1936); McCormick, Cyrus, *The Century of the Reaper* (1931); McCormick, F. J., *The Development of Farm Machines* (1941); Rogin, Leo, *The Introduction of Farm Machinery in Its Relation to the Productivity of Labor in Agriculture of the United States* (1931); Thompson, Hallard, *The Age of Invention: A Chronicle of Mechanical Conquest* (1921); True, A. C., *A History of Agricultural Education in the United States, 1785–1925* (1929); Usher, A. P., *A History of Mechanical Inventions* (1954); Wik, R. M., *Steam Power on the American Farm* (1954).

AGRICULTURAL SOCIETIES AND THE AGRICULTURAL PRESS

Bardolph, Richard, *Agricultural Literature and the Early Illinois Farmer* (1948); Carmen, H. J., ed., *Jesse Buel: Agricultural Reformer* (1947); Carrier, Lyman, *Beginnings of Agriculture in America* (1923); Demaree, A. L., *The American Agricultural Press, 1819–1860* (1941); Kellar, H. A., ed., *Solon Robinson, A Pioneer and Agriculturist: Selected Writings* (1936); Neely, W. C., *The Agricultural Fair* (1935); Ogilvie, W. E., *Pioneer Agricultural Journalists* (1927); Wiest, Edward, *Agricultural Organization in the United States* (1923).

CHAPTER 13

BACKGROUND OF THE CIVIL WAR

Cole, A. C., *The Irrepressible Conflict* (1930); Cotterall, H. J., *Judicial Cases Concerning Slavery and the Negro* (1926); Craven, A. O., *The Coming of the Civil War* (2nd ed., 1957); Craven, A. O., *The Civil War in the Making, 1810–1860* (1959); DeBow, J. D. B., ed., *The Industrial Resources of the Southern and Western States* (3 vols., 1852–1853); Dumond, D. L., *The Secession Movement, 1860-1861* (1931); Foner, P. S., *Business and Slavery: The New York Merchants and the Irrepressible Conflict* (1941); Franklin, J. H., *The Militant South* (1956); Jenkins, W. S., *Pro-Slavery Thought in the Old South* (1935); Milton, G. F., *The Eve of Conflict: Stephen A. Douglas and the Needless War* (1934); Nichols, R. F., *Disruption of American Democracy* (1948); Nichols, R. F., *Stakes of Power, 1845–1877* (1961); Russel, R. R., *Economic Aspects of Southern Sectionalism, 1840–1861* (1924); Scherer, J. A. B., *Cotton as a World Power: A Study in the Economic Interpretation of History* (1916); Simms, H. H., *A Decade of Sectional Controversy, 1851–1861* (1942); Stampp, K. M., ed., *Causes of the Civil War* (1959); Syndor, C. C., *The Development of Southern Sectionalism, 1819–1848* (1948); Van Deusen, J. G., *Economic Basis of Disunion in South Carolina* (1928).

ECONOMIC CONDITIONS IN THE NORTH DURING THE WAR

Adams, E. D., *Great Britain and the American Civil War* (2 vols., 1925); Andreano, Ralph, ed., *The Economic Impact of the American Civil War* (1962); Barrett, D. C., *The Greenbacks and the Resumption of Specie Payments, 1862–1879* (1931); Bolles, A. S., *Financial History of the United States* (1886); Dewey, D. R., *Financial History of the United States* (rev. ed., 1956); Fite, E. D., *Social and Industrial Conditions in the North During the Civil War* (1910); Foner, P. S., *The New York Merchants and the Irrepressible Conflict* (1941); Larson, H. M., *Jay Cooke, Private Banker* (1936); Oberholtzer, E. P., *Jay Cooke* (2 vols., 1907); Pratt, E. A., *The Rise of Rail Power* (1916); Sumner, F. P., *The Baltimore and Ohio Railroad in the Civil War* (1939); Turner, G. E., *Victory Rode the Rails* (1953).

ECONOMIC CONDITIONS IN THE CONFEDERACY

Black, R. C., *The Railroads of the Confederacy* (1952); Bradlee, F. B. C., *Blockade Running during the Civil War and the Effect of Land and Water Transportation on the Confederacy,* Essex Institute *Collections,* LX (1925); Coulter, E. M., *The Confederate States of America, 1861–1865* (1950); Dewey, D. R., *Financial History of the United States,* (rev. ed., 1956); Eaton Clement, *A History of the Southern Confederacy* (1954); Lonn, Ella, *Salt as a Factor in the Confederacy* (1933); Moore, A. B., *Conscription and Conflict in the Confederacy* (1924); Owsley, F. W., *King Cotton Diplomacy* (1931); Robinson, W. M., Jr., *The Confederate Privateers* (1928); Schwab, J. C., *The Confederate States of America, 1861–1865: A Financial and Industrial History* (1901); Soley, J. R., *The Blockade and the Cruisers* (1890); Stephenson, N. W., *The Day of the Confederacy* (1919); Todd, R. C., *Confederate Finance* (1954); Wesley, C. H., *The Collapse of the Confederacy* (1922).

THE PLANTATION SYSTEM

Bassett, J. S., *The Southern Plantation Overseer as Revealed in His Letters* (1925); Cotterill, R. S., *The Old South* (1936); Dodd, W. E., *The Cotton Kingdom* (1919); Gaines, F. P., *The Southern Plantation, A Study in the Development and Accuracy of a Tradition* (1924); Gray, L. C., *History of Agriculture in the Southern United States to 1860* (2 vols., 1933); Hesseltine, W. B., *A History of the South, 1607–1936* (1937); House, A. V., ed., *Planter Management and Capitalism in Ante-Bellum Georgia: The Journal of Hugh Frazer Grant* (1954); Phillips, U. B., *Life and Labor in the Old South* (1929).

SLAVERY AND THE SLAVE TRADE

Bancroft, Frederic, *Slave-Trading in the Old South* (1931); Brawley, Benjamin, *A Short History of the American Negro* (1919); Brawley, Benjamin, *A Social History of the American Negro* (1921); Claridge, W. W., *History of the Gold Coast* (1915); Donnan, Elizabeth, ed., *Documents Illustrative of the History of the Slave Trade to America* (3 vols., 1930–1932); Dow, G. F., *Slave Ships and Slavery* (1927); DuBois, W. E. B., *The Suppression of the African Slave-Trade to the United States of America, 1638–1870* (1896); Elkins, S. N., *Slavery: A Problem in American Life* (1960); Flanders, R. B., *Plantation Slavery in Georgia* (1933); Franklin, J. H., *From Slavery to Freedom* (rev. ed., 1956); Gara, Larry, *The Liberty Line: The Legend of the Underground Railroad* (1961); McDougall, I. E., *Slavery in Kentucky, 1792–1865* (1918); Mooney, C. C., *Slavery in Tennessee* (1957); Phillips, U. B., *American Negro Slavery* (1918); Sellers, J. B., *Slavery in Alabama* (1950); Snydor, C. S., *Slavery in Mississippi* (1933); Stampp, K. M., *The Peculiar Institution* (1956); Stephenson, W. H., *Isaac Franklin, Slave Trader and Planter of the Old South* (1938); Taylor, O. W., *Negro Slavery in Alabama* (1958); Taylor, R. H., *Slave Holding in North Carolina: An Economic View* (1926); Trexler, H. A., *Slavery in Missouri, 1804–1865* (1914); Wesley, C. H., *Negro Labor in the United States, 1850–1925* (1927); Woodson, C. G., *Free Negro Heads of Families in the United States in 1830* (1925); Woodson, C. G., *The Negro in Our History* (1922).

ANTI-SLAVERY AND ABOLITION

Adams, A. D., *The Neglected Period of Anti-Slavery in America* (1909); Barnes, G. H., *Antislavery Impulse, 1830–1844* (1933); Barnes, G. H., and Dumond, D. L., *Letters of Theodore Dwight Weld, Angelina Grimke Weld, and Sarah Grimke, 1822–1844* (2 vols., 1934); Commager, H. S., *Theodore Parker, Yankee Crusader* (1936); Filler, Louis, *Crusade Against Slavery, 1830–1860* (1960); Fox, E. L., *The American Colonization Society, 1817–1840* (1919); Gara, Larry, *The Liberty Line: The Legend of the Underground Railroad* (1961); Garrison, W. P., and Garrison, F. H., *William Lloyd Garrison* (4 vols., 1885–1889); Hart, A. B., *Slavery and Abolition;* Macy, Jesse, *The Anti-Slavery Crusade* (1919); Siebert, W. H., *The Underground Railroad from Slavery to Freedom* (1898).

CHAPTER 14

HISTORY OF THE RAILROADS

Bogen, J. I., *The Anthracite Roads* (1927); Bradley, G. D., *The Story of the Santa Fe* (1920); Brownson, H. G., *History of the Illinois Central Railroad to 1870* (1915); Cleveland, F. A., and Powell, F. W., *Railroad Promotion and Capitalization in the United States* (1909); Daggett, Stuart, *Chapters on the History of the Southern Pacific* (1922); Daggett, Stuart, *Railroad Reorganization* (1908); Derrick, S. M., *Centennial History of South Carolina Railroad* (1930); Fish, C. R., *The Restoration of the Southern Railroads* (1919); Fogel, R. W., *The Union Pacific Railroad* (1960); Gates, P. W., *The Illinois Central and Its Colonization Work* (1934); Graebner, N. A., *Empire on the Pacific: A Study in Continental Expansion* (1955); Hedges, H. B., *Henry Villard and the Railways of the Northwest* (1930); Hilton, G. W., and Due, J. F., *Electric Interurban Railways in America* (1960); Hitt, R., Comp., *Street Cars and Interurbans of Yesteryear* (1960); Hungerford, Edward, *The Story of the Baltimore and Ohio Railroad, 1827–1927* (2 vols., 1928); Hungerford, Edward, *Men and Iron: The History of the New York Central* (1938); Kirkland, E. C., *Men, Cities, and Transportation: A Study in New England History, 1820–1900* (2 vols., 1948); Laut, A. C., *The Romance of the Rails* (2 vols., 1929); Locklin, D. P., *Economics of Transportation* (1938); Longstroth, C. S., *Railway Cooperation in the United States* (1899); Million, J. W., *State Aid to Railroads in Missouri* (1896); Mott, E. H., *Between the Ocean and the Lakes: A Story of the Erie* (1910); Overton, R. C., *Burlington West: A Colonization History of the Burlington Railroad* (1941); Overton, R. C., *Gulf to Rockies: The Heritage of the Fort Worth, and Denver-Colorado and Southern Railways, 1861–1898* (1953); Quiett, G. C., *They Built the West: An Epic of Rails and Cities* (1934); Reid, H., *The Virginia Railway* (1961); Riegel, R. E., *The Story of the Western Railroads* (1926); Ripley, W. Z., *Railroads: Finance and Organizations* (1915); Sanborn, J. B., *Congressional Grants of Land in Aid of Railways* (1899); Smalley, E. U., *The Northern Pacific Railway* (1883); Stover, J. F., *American Railroads* (1961); Stover, J. F., *The Railroads of the South, 1865–1900* (1955); Taylor, George, and Neu, Irene, *The American Railroad Network* (1956); Trottman, Nelson, *History of the Union Pacific* (1923).

EARLY RAILROAD PROBLEMS

Adams, C. F., *Railroads: Their Origin and Problems* (rev. ed., 1893); Adams, C. F., and Adams, Henry, *Chapters of Erie and Other Essays* (1886); Benson, Lee, *Merchants, Farmers, and Railroads: Railroad Regulation and New York Politics, 1850–1887* (1955); Campbell, E. G., *The Reorganization of the American Railroad System, 1893–1900* (1938); Cloud, D. C., *Monopolies and the People* (1873); Cochran, T. C., *Railroad Leaders, 1845–1890: The*

Business Mind in Action (1953); Daggett, Stuart, *Railroad Reorganization* (1908); Grodinsky, Julius, *The Iowa Pool: A Study in Railroad Competition* (1950); Hicks, F. C., ed., *High Finance in the Sixties* (1929); Hudson, J. F., *The Railways and the Republic* (1886); Jones, Eliot, *Principles of Railroad Transportation* (1924); Johnson, E. R., *American Railway Transportation* (1912); Johnson, E. R., and Van Metre, T. W., *Principles of Railways Transportation* (1922); Larrabee, W. F., *The Railroad Question* (1893); Pierce, Harry, *Railroads of New York: A Study in Government Aid* (1953); Ulmer, M. J., *Trends and Cycles in Capital Formation by United States Railroads, 1870–1950* (1954).

RAILROAD REGULATION

Benson, Lee, *Merchants, Farmers and Railroads: Railroad Regulation and New York Politics, 1850–1887* (1955); Buck, S. J., *The Agrarian Crusade* (1920); Buck, S. J., *The Granger Movement* (1913); Cunningham, W. J., *American Railroads: Government Control and Reconstruction* (1922); Dixon, F. H., *Railroads and Government: Their Relations in the United States, 1910–1921* (1922); Dixon, F. H., *State Railroad Control* (1896); Haines, H. S., *Problems in Railway Regulation* (1911); Haney, L. H., *A Congressional History of Railroads in the United States, 1850–1887* (1910); Meyer, B. H., *Railway Legislation in the United States* (1903); Sharfman, I. L., *The American Railroad Problem* (1921); Sharfman, I. L., *The Interstate Commerce Commission* (4 vols., 1931–1937).

BIOGRAPHIES OF RAILROAD LEADERS

Cochran, T. C., *Railroad Leaders, 1845–1890: The Business Mind in Action* (1953); Hedges, J. P., *Henry Villard and the Railways of the Northwest* (1930); Josephson, Matthew, *The Robber Barons* (1934); Keanan, George, *E. H. Harriman* (2 vols., 1922); Lane, W. J., *Commodore Vanderbilt: An Epic of the Steam Age* (1942); Lewis, Oscar, *The Big Four: The Story of Huntington, Stanford, Hopkins, and Crocker* (1938); Moody, John, *The Railroad Builders* (1919); Pearson, H. G., *An American Railroad Builder: John Murray Forbes* (1911); Pyle, J. G., *Life of James J. Hill* (2 vols., 1917); Schlegel, M. W., *Ruler of the Reading: The Life of Franklin B. Gowen, 1836–1889* (1947); Sullivan, O. M., *The Empire Builders* (1928).

INLAND WATERWAYS

Ambler, C. H., *History of Transportation in the Ohio Valley* (1931); Beasley, Norman, *Freighters of Fortune* (1930); Bennett, I. E., ed., *History of the Panama Canal: Its Construction and Builders* (1915); Bunau-Varilla, Philippe, *Panama: The Creation, Destruction and Resurrection* (1914); Dixon, F. H., *Traffic History of the Mississippi River System* (1909); Gjerset, Knut, *Norwegian Sailors on the Great Lakes* (1928); Goodrich, Carter, and Others, *Canals and American Economic Development* (1961); Harlow, A. F., *Old Towpaths* (1926); Hartsough, M. H., *From Canoe to Steel Barge on the Upper Mississippi* (1934); Ireland, Tom, *The Great Lakes—St. Lawrence Deep Waterways to the Sea* (1934); Johnson, E. R., *The Panama Canal and Commerce* (1916); Mills, J. C., *Our Inland Seas, Their Shipping and Commerce for Three Centuries* (1910); Plumb, R. G., *History of Navigation of the Great Lakes* (1910); Sanderlin, W. S., *Great National Project: A History of the Chesapeake and Ohio Canal* (1948); Waggoner, M. S., *The Long Haul West: The Great Canal Era 1817–1850* (1958); Whitford, N. E., *History of the Barge Canal of New York State* (1922).

COMMUNICATION

Casson, H. N., *History of the Telephone* (1910); Danielian, N. R., *A. T. & T.: The Story of Industrial Conquest* (1939); Harlow, A. F., *Old Wires and New Waves* (1936); Mackenzie,

Catherine, *Alexander Graham Bell* (1928); Page, A. W., *The Bell Telephone System* (1941); Stehman, J. W., *The Financial History of the American Telephone and Telegraph* (1925); Thompson, R. L., *Wiring a Continent* (1947).

CHAPTER 15

THE PASSING OF THE FRONTIER

Arrington, L. J., *Great Basin Kingdom: An Economic History of the Latter-Day Saints* (1958); Athearn, R. G., *William Tecumseh Sherman and the Settlement of the West* (1956); Babcock, K. C., *The Scandinavian Element in the United States* (1914); Billington, R. A., *Westward Expansion* (1949); Blegen, T. C., *Norwegian Migration in America* (1931); Boynton, P. H., *The Rediscovery of the Frontier* (1934); Branch, E. D., *Westward: The Romance of the American Frontier* (1930); Briggs, H. E., *Frontiers of the Northwest* (1940); Byrne, P. E., *Soldiers of the Plains* (1926); Clark, D. E., *The West in American History* (1937); Commons, J. R., *Races and Immigrants in America* (1907); Curti, Merle, and Others, *The Making of an American Community: A Case Study of Democracy in a Frontier County* (1959); Dick, Everett, *The Sod-House Frontier, 1854–1890* (1943); Fox, D. R., *Sources of Culture in the Middle West: Background vs., Frontier* (1934); Hough, Emerson, *The Passing of the Frontier,* (1918); Malin, J. C., *The Grasslands of North America: Prolegomena to Its History* (1947); Nelson, Lowry, *The Mormon Village: A Pattern of Technique of Land Settlement* (1952); Orth, S. P., *Our Foreigners* (1920); Paxson, F. L., *History of the American Frontier, 1763–1893* (1924); Paxson, F. L., *The Last American Frontier* (1910); Paxson, F. L., *When the West is Gone* (1930); Qualey, C. C., *Norwegian Settlement in the United States* (1938); Riegel, R. E., *America Moves West* (1930); Shannon, J. P., *Catholic Colonization on the Western Frontier* (1937); Sharp, P. F., *Whoop-Up Country: The Canadian-American West, 1865–1885* (1956); Turner, F. J., *The Frontier in American History* (1920); Turner, F. J., *The Early Writings of Frederick Jackson Turner* (1938); Van Avery, Dale, *Men of the Western Frontier* (1956); Webb, W. T., *The Great Plains* (1936); Winther, O. O., *The Great Northwest* (1947); Wittke, Carl, *We Who Built America* (1940); Wyman, W. D., and Droebert, C. B., *The Frontier in Perspective* (1957).

THE PUBLIC LAND SYSTEM

Calef, W. C., *Private Grazing and Public Lands: Studies in the Local Management of the Taylor Grazing Act* (1961); Donaldson, Thomas, *The Public Domain* (1884); Faulkner, H. U., *The Quest for Social Justice, 1898–1914* (1931); Foss, P. O., *Politics and Grass* (1960); Gates, P. W., *Fifty Million Acres: Conflicts over Kansas Land Policy, 1854–1890* (1954); Hibbard, B. H., *History of the Public Land Policies* (1924); Lokken, R. L., *Iowa Public Land Disposal* (1942); Nelson, Lowry, *The Morman Village: A Pattern of Technique of Land Settlement* (1952); McKitrick, Reuben, *The Public Land System of Texas, 1823–1910* (1918); Paxson, F. L., *When the West is Gone* (1930); Peffer, E. L., *The Closing of the Public Domain: Disposal and Reservation Policy, 1900–1950* (1951); Robbins, R. M., *Our Landed Heritage: The Public Domain, 1776–1936* (1942).

THE MINERAL KINGDOM

Bancroft, H. H., *History of Nevada, Colorado, and Wyoming, 1540–1888* (1890); Caughey, J. W., *The Gold Rush* (1948); Glasscock, C. B., *The Big Bonanza* (1931); Quiett, G. C., *Pay Dirt, a Panorama of American Gold Rushes* (1936); Quiett, G. C., *They Built the West* (1934); Rickard, T. A., *History of American Mining* (1932); Shinn, C. H., *The Story of the Mine*

(1901); Spence, C. C., *British Investments and the American Mining Frontier, 1860–1901* (1958); Trimble, W. J., *The Mining Advance into the Inland Kingdom* (University of Wisconsin *Bulletin* No. 638, 1914).

THE CATTLE AND SHEEP COUNTRY

Barnes, W. C., *The Story of the Range* (1926); Branch, E. D., *The Cowboy and His Interpreters* (1926); Branch, E. D., *Westward: The Romance of the American Frontier* (1930); Brown, Dee, *Trail Driving Days* (1952); Clemens, R. A., *The American Livestock and Meat Industry* (1923); Dale, E. E., *The Range Cattle Industry* (1930); Frantz, J. B., and Coate, Jr., Julian, *The American Cowboy: Myth and Reality* (1959); Gard, Wayne, *The Great Buffalo Hunt* (1959); Hough, Emerson, *The Story of the Cowboy* (2 vols., 1897); Nordyke, L., *Cattle Empire: The Fabulous Story of the 3,000,000 Acre XIT* (1949); Osgood, E. S., *The Day of the Cattleman* (1929); Peake, O. B., *The Colorado Cattle Industry* (1937); Pelzer, Louis, *The Cattleman's Frontier* (1936); Rollins, P. A., *The Cowboy* (1922); Streeter, F. B., *Prairie Trails and Cow-Towns* (1936); Thompson, J. W., *A History of Livestock Raising in the United States, 1607–1860* (1942); Wentworth, E. N., *America's Sheep Trails: History and Personalities* (1948); Wright, R. M., *Dodge City, The Cowboy Capital* (1913).

THE INDIANS

Byrne, P. E., *Soldiers of the Plains* (1926); Debo, Angie, *And Still the Waters Run* (1940); Fenton, W. N., *American Indian and White Relations to 1830* (1957); Fey, H. E., and McNickle, D'Arcy, *Indians and Other Americans* (1959); Foreman, Grant, *Indian Removal* (rev. ed., 1953); Harmon, G. D., *Sixty Years of Indian Affairs* (1941); Kinney, J. P., *A Continent Lost—A Civilization Won: Indian Land Tenure in America* (1937); Leupp, F. E., *The Indian and His Problem* (1910); Lindsay, Charles, *The Big Horn Basin* (1932); Meriam, Lewis, and Others, *The Problem of Indian Administration* (1928); Moorehead, W. K., *The American Indian in the United States* (1914); Priest, L. B., *Uncle Sam's Stepchildren: The Reformation of United States Indian Policy, 1865–1887* (1942); Reichard, G. A., *Dezba: Woman of the Desert* (1939); Schmeckebier, L. F., *The Office of Indian Affairs* (1927); Seymour, F. W., *The Story of the Red Man* (1929); Vestal, Stanley, *Sitting Bull* (1932); Wellman, P. I., *Death in the Desert, the Fifty Years' War for the Great Southwest* (1935).

CHAPTER 16

THE CONSERVATION MOVEMENT

GENERAL WORKS: Carter, J. F., *Remaking America* (1942); Chase, Stuart, *Rich Land, Poor Land; a Study of Waste in Natural Resources of America* (1936); Coyle, D. C., *Conservation An American Story of Conflict and Accomplishment* (1957); Douglas James, *Conservation of Natural Resources* (1909); Fanning, C. E., *Selected Articles on the Conservation of Natural Resources* (1913); Fletcher, H. F., *Ethics of Conservation* (1910); Freeman, O. W., *The Pacific Northwest, a Regional, Human, and Economic Survey of Resources and Development* (1942); Gregory, M. H., *Checking the Waste; a Study in Conservation* (1911); Gustafson, A. F., *Conservation in the United States* (1939); Hayes, S. P., *Conservation and the Gospel of Efficiency* (1961); Hynning, C. J., *State Conservation of Resources* (1939); Mitchell, L. S., *My Country 'Tis of Thee; The Use and Abuse of Natural Resources* (1940); Nourse, E. G., *America's Capacity to Produce* (1934); Parkins, A. E., and Whitaker, J. R., *Our Natural Resources and Their Conservation* (1936); Pinchot, Gifford, *The Fight for Conservation* (1910); Talbot, F. A., *Millions from Waste* (1920); Van Hise, C. R., *Conservation of Natural Resources in the United States* (1910); Van Hise, C. R., and Havemeyer, Loomis, *The Conservation of Our Natural Resources* (1930).

CONSERVATION AND RECLAMATION OF LAND

Bowie, A. J., *Practical Irrigation* (1908); Hibbard, A. H., *This Land of Ours* (1960); Jean, F. C., *Root Behavior and Crop Yield Under Irrigation* (1924); Kearney, T. H., and Shantz, H. S., *Water Economy of Dry Land Crops* (1912); Newell, F. H., *Irrigation in the United States* (1902); O'Donnell, I. D., *United States Reclamation Service* (1918); Sears, P. B., *Deserts on the March* (1935); Teale, R. P., *The Economics of Land Reclamation in the United States* (1927); United States Great Plains Committee, *The Future of the Great Plains* (1936); Yard, R. S., *Our Federal Lands: A Romance of American Development* (1928).

FORESTS AND FOREST POLICY

Cameron, Jenks, *The Development of Governmental Forest Control in the United States* (1928); Carhart, A. H., *National Forests* (1959); Dana, S. T., *Forest and Range Policy: Its Development in the United States* (1956); Fernow, B. E., ed., *Forest Influences* (1893); Fries, R. F., *Empire in Pine: The Story of Lumbering in Wisconsin, 1830–1900* (1951); Gates, P. W., *The Wisconsin Pine Lands of Cornell University* (1943); Holbrook, S. H., *Holy Old Mackinaw: A Natural History of the American Lumberjack* (1938); Ise, John, *The United States Forest Policy* (1920); Larson, Agnes, *White Pine Industry in Minnesota* (1949); Pinchot, Gifford, *The Fight for Conservation* (1910); Reynolds, A. R., *The Daniel Shaw Lumber Company: A Case Study of the Wisconsin Lumbering Frontier* (1957); United States Forest Service, *A National Plan for American Forestry* (2 vols., 1933).

CONSERVATION OF MINERAL LANDS

Gilbert, C. G., and Progue, J. E., *America's Power Resources; The Economic Significance of Coal, Oil and Water-Power* (1921); Ise, John, *Our Vanishing Oil Resources* (1929); Leith, C. K., *World Minerals and World Politics* (1931); Stahl, R. M., *The Ballinger-Pinchot Controversy* (1926); Van Hise, C. R., and Havemeyer, Loomis, *The Conservation of Our Natural Resources* (1930).

THE INLAND WATERWAYS MOVEMENT

Chisholm, G. G., *Inland Waterways* (1908); Department of Commerce, Bureau of Foreign and Domestic Commerce, *Inland Water Transportation in the United States*, Miscellaneous Series, No. 119 (1923); Dixon, F. H., *Traffic History of the Mississippi River System* (1909); Johnson, E. R., *Inland Waterways, Their Relation to Transportation* (1893); National Waterways Commission, *Final Report* (1912).

THE NATIONAL PARKS

American Scenic and Historic Preservation Society, *Scenic and Historic America* (1929); Gabrielson, I. V., *Wild Life Conservation* (1941); Good, A. H., *Park and Recreational Structures* (1938); Newhall, N. W., *Contribution to the Heritage of Every American* (1957); Playground and Recreation Association of America, *Park Recreation Areas in the United States* (1928); United States National Park Service, *Park Structures and Facilities* (1935).

CHAPTER 17

ECONOMIC PROBLEMS OF RECONSTRUCTION

Beale, H. K., *The Critical Year: A Study of Andrew Johnson and Reconstruction* (1930); Bowers, C. G., *The Tragic Era* (1929); Brooks, R. P., *Agrarian Revolution in Georgia, 1865–1912* (1914); Buck, P. H., *The Road to Reunion, 1865–1900* (1937); Caskey, W. M., *Secession and Restoration in Louisiana* (1938); Clayton, Powell, *Aftermath of the Civil War in Arkansas* (1915); Coulter, E. M., *Civil War and Readjustment in Kentucky* (1926); Davis, W. W., *The Civil War and Reconstruction in Florida* (1913); Dunning, W. A., *Reconstruction, Political and Economic* (1907); Fertig, J. W., *Secession and Reconstruction of Tennessee* (1898); Fleming, W. L., *Civil War and Reconstruction in Alabama* (1905); Fleming, W. L., *Documentary History of Reconstruction* (2 vols., 1906–1907); Fleming, W. L., *The Sequel of Appomattox* (1919); Flicken, J. R., *History of Reconstruction in Louisiana* (1910); Garner, J. W., *Reconstruction in Mississippi* (1901); Hamilton, J. G. de R., *Reconstruction in North Carolina* (1914); Hesseltine, W. B., *The South in American History* (2nd ed., 1960); Lonn, Ella, *Reconstruction in Louisiana After 1868* (1918); Nevins, Allan, *The Emergence of Modern America, 1865–1878* (1927); Patton, J. W., *Unionism and Reconstruction in Tennessee* (1934); Pike, James, *The Prostrate South; South Carolina under Negro Government* (new ed., 1935); Ramsdell, C. W., *Reconstruction in Texas* (1910); Randall, J. G., *The Civil War and Reconstruction* (1937); Simkins, F. B., *A History of the South* (1953); Simkins, F. B., and Woody, R. W., *South Carolina During Reconstruction* (1932); Staples, T. S., *Reconstruction in Arkansas* (1923); Thompson, C. M., *Reconstruction in Georgia, Economic, Social, and Political, 1866–1872* (1915); Thompson, Holland, *The New South; A Chronicle of Social and Industrial Evolution* (1919); Warmoth, H. C., *War Politics and Reconstruction* (1930); Woodward, C. V., *Reunion and Reaction: The Compromise of 1877 and The Era of Reconstruction* (1951).

AGRICULTURAL CHANGES

Bizzel, W. B., *Rural Texas* (1924); Brown, H. B., *Cotton: History, Species, Varieties, Morphology, Breeding, Culture, Disease, Marketing, and Uses* (1927); Bruce, P. A., *The Rise of the New South* (1905); Burkett, C. W., and Poe, C. H., *Cotton, Its Cultivation, Marketing, Manufacture, and the Problems of the Cotton World* (1906); Gee, W. P., and Corson, J. J., *Rural Depopulation in Certain Tidewater and Piedmont Areas of Virginia* (1929); Hawk, E. Q., *Economic History of the South* (1934); Jacobstein, Meyer, *The Tobacco Industry in the United States* (1907); Montgomery, R. H.: *The Cooperative Pattern in Cotton* (1929); Odum, H. W., *Southern Regions of the United States* (1936); Owsley, F. L., *Plain Folk of the Old South* (1949); Owsley, F. L., *King Cotton Diplomacy* (1931); Range, Willard, *A Century of Agriculture, 1850–1950* (1954); Scherer, J. A. R., *Cotton as a World Power* (1916); Tang, A. M., *Economic Development in the Southern Piedmont, 1860–1950: Its Impact on Agriculture* (1958); Tilley, N. M., *The Bright Tobacco Industry, 1860–1929* (1948); Vance, R. B., *Human Factors in Cotton Culture* (1929).

INDUSTRIAL CHANGES

Armes, Ethel, *The Story of Coal and Iron in Alabama* (1910); Boyd, W. K., *The Story of Durham* (1925); Brooks, R. P., *The Industrialization of the South* (1929); Bruce, P. A., *The Rise of the New South* (1905); Cappon, L. J., *Government and Private Industry in the Southern Confederacy*, Humanistic Studies in Honor of John Calvin Metcalf (1941); Copeland, M. T., *The Cotton Manufacturing Industry in the United States* (1923); Couch, W. I., *Culture in the South* (1934); Daniels, Jonathan, *A Southerner Discovers* the South (1938); Grady, H. W., *The New South* (1890); Hawk, E. Q., *Economic History of the South* (1934); Hesseltine, W. B., *A History of the South, 1607–1936* (1936); Jenkins, J. W., *James B. Duke* (1927); Kendrick, B. B., and Arnett, A. M., *The South Looks at Its Past* (1935); Lement, B. F., *The Cotton Textile Industry of the Southern Appalachian Piedmont* (1933); Mims, Edwin, *The Advancing South* (1926); Mitchell, Broadus, *The Rise of the Cotton Mills in the South* (1921); Mitchell, Broadus, and Mitchell, G. S., *The Industrial Revolution in the South* (1930); Odum, H. W., *Southern Regions of the United States* (1936); Potwin, M. A., *Cotton Mill People of the Piedmont* (1927); Ross, M. H., *Machine Age in the Hills* (1933); Spratt, J. S., *The Road to Spindletop: Economic Change in Texas, 1875–1901* (1955); Street, J. H., *The New Revolution in the Cotton Economy* (1957); Thompson, Holland, *The New South; A Chronicle of Social and Industrial Evolution* (1919); Vance, R. B., *Human Factors in Cotton Culture* (1929); Woodward, C. V., *Origins of the New South* (1951).

LABOR IN THE SOUTH

Banks, E. M., *Economics of Land Tenure in Georgia* (1905); Franklin, J. H., *From Slavery to Freedom* (rev. ed., 1956); Levinson, Paul, *Race, Class and Party* (1932); Potwin, M. A., *Cotton Mill People of the Piedmont* (1927); Sinclair, W. A., *The Aftermath of Slavery* (1905); Taylor, A. A., *The Negro in the Reconstruction of Virginia* (1926); Taylor, A. A., *The Negro in South Carolina During the Reconstruction* (1924); Vance, R. B., *Human Geography of the South; A Study in Regional Resources and Human Adequacy* (1932); Woodson, C. G., *The Negro in Our History* (1931).

CHAPTER 18

AGRARIAN UNREST AND THE GRANGER MOVEMENT

Atkeson, T. C., *Semi-Centennial History of the Patrons of Husbandry* (1916); Boyle, J. E., *Agricultural Economics* (1921); Buck, S. J., *The Agrarian Crusade* (1920); Buck, S. J., *The Granger Movement* (1913); Commons, J. R., and Others, eds., *A Documentary History of American Industrial Society* (1910); Dick, Everett, *The Sod House Frontier, 1854–1890* (1943); Doane, R. R., *The Measurement of American Wealth* (1933); Fine, Nathan, *Labor and Farmer Parties in the United States, 1828–1928* (1928); Haynes, F. E., *Third Party Movements Since the Civil War* (1916); Hedges, J. B., *Henry Villard and the Railways of the Northwest* (1930); Hibbard, B. H., *A History of Public Land Policies* (1924); Hicks, J. D., and Saloutos, Theodore, *Agricultural Discontent in the Middle West* (1951); Hunt, R. L., *A History of Farmer Movements in the Southwest, 1873–1925* (1935); Locklin, D. P., *Economics of Transportation* (1938); Merriam, C. R., *American Political Ideas, 1855–1917* (1920); Noblin, Stuart, *Leonidas La Fayette Polk: Agrarian Crusader* (1949); Paine, A. E., *The Granger Movement in Illinois* (1904); Rice, S. A., *Farmers and Workers in American Politics* (1924), Ross, E. D., *The Liberal Republican Movement* (1919); Saloutos, Theodore, *Farmers' Movements in the South, 1865–1933* (1960); Shannon, F. A., *America's Farmers' Movements* (1957); Taylor, C. C., *The Farmers' Movements, 1620–1920* (1953); Woodward, C. V., *Tom Watson, Agrarian Rebel* (1938).

AGRICULTURAL INVENTION AND ITS EFFECTS

Bailey, J. C., *Seeman A., Knapp: Schoolmaster of American Agriculture* (1945); Hutchinson, W. T., *Cyrus Hall McCormick* (2 vols., 1930, 1935); Kaempffert, Waldemar, ed., *A Popular History of American Invention*, 2 vols., 1924); Miller, M. F., *The Evolution of Reaping*

Machines (1902); Quaintance, H. W., *The Influence of Farm Machinery on Production and Labor* (1904); Rogin, Leo, *The Introduction of Farm Machinery in Its Relation to the Productivity of Labor in the Agriculture of the United States during the Nineteenth Century* (1931); Usher, A. P., *A History of Mechanical Invention* (1954); Wik, R. M., *Steam Power on the Farm* (1954).

THE GREENBACK MOVEMENT

Barnes, J. A., *John G. Carlisle, Financial Statesman* (1931); Barrett, D. C., *The Greenbacks and the Resumption of Specie Payments, 1862–1879* (1931); Dewey, D. R., *Financial History of the United States* (12th ed., 1936); McGrane, R. C., "Ohio and the Greenback Movement," *Mississippi Valley Historical Review*, XI (March, 1925); Mitchell, W. C., *Gold Prices and Wages Under the Greenback Standard* (1908); Mitchell, W. C., *History of the Greenbacks, 1862–1865* (reissue, 1960); Nevins, Allan, *Hamilton Fish: The Inner History of the Grant Administration* (1936); Noyes, A. D., *Forty Years of American Finance* (1909); Sharkey, R. R., *Money, Class, and Party* (1959); Shultz, W. J., and Caine, M. R., *Financial History of the United States* (1937).

FARMERS' ALLIANCES AND THE POPULIST MOVEMENT

Arnett, A. M., *The Populist Movement in Georgia* (1922); Clark, J. B., *Populism in Alabama* (1927); Fine, Nathan, *Labor and Farm Parties in the United States, 1828–1928* (1928); Fossum, P. R., *The Agrarian Movement in North Dakota* (1925); Haynes, F. E., *Third Party Movements since the Civil War* (1916); Hepburn, A. B., *History of Coinage and Currency in the United States* (1903); Hicks, J. D., *The Populist Revolt: A History of the Farmer's Alliance and the People's Party* (1931); Laughlin, J. L., *History of Bimetallism in the United States* (1897); McVey, F. L., *The Populist Movement* (1896); Martin, R. C., *The People's Party in Texas* (1933); Noyes, A. D., *Forty Years of American Finance* (1909); Paxson, F. L., *When the West Is Gone* (1930); Russell, H. B., *International Monetary Conferences in the United States* (1898); Saloutos, Theodore, *Farmers' Movements in the South* (1960); Shannon, F. A., *The Farmer's Last Frontier: Agriculture, 1860–1897* (1945); Sharp, J. A., *The Farmers' Alliance and the People's Party in Tennessee* (1938); Sheldon, W. D., *Populism in the Old Dominion: Virginia Farm Politics, 1885–1900* (1935); Simkins, F. B., *The Tillman Movement in South Carolina* (1926); Wiest, Edward, *Agricultural Organization in the United States* (1923).

GOVERNMENT AND AGRICULTURE

Benedict, M. R., *Farm Policies of the United States, 1790–1950* (1953); Cameron, Jenks, *The Bureau of Dairy Industry* (1929); Conover, Milton, *The Office of Experiment Stations* (1924); Davenport, Eugene, *The Relations Between the Federal Department of Agriculture and the Agricultural College and Experiment Stations* (1913); Halcrow, H. G., *Agricultural Policy of the United States* (1953); Higbee, E. C., *American Agriculture and Geography: Resources and Conservation* (1958); Powell, F. W., *The Bureau of Animal Husbandry* (1927); Ross, E. D., *Democracy's College: The Land-Grant Movement in the Formative Stage* (1942); Swann, H. T., *Two Blades of Grass: A History of Scientific Development in the United States Department of Agriculture* (1947); True, A. C., and Clark, V. A., *Agricultural Experiment Stations in the United States, 1607–1925* (1927); True, A. C., *A History of Agricultural Education in the United States, 1785–1925* (1929); True, A. C., *A History of Agricultural Experimentation and Research in the United States, 1607–1925* (1937); True, A. C., *A History of Agricultural Extension Work in the United States, 1785–1923* (1928); Wanlass, W. L., *The*

United States Department of Agriculture (1926); Weber, G. A., *The Bureau of Chemistry and Soils* (1928); Weber, G. A., *The Plant Quarantine and Control Administration* (1930).

AGRICULTURAL EXPANSION

Anderson, F. I., *The Farmer of Tomorrow* (1913); Clemen, A. R., *The American Livestock and Meat Industry* (1923); Dale, E. E., *Cow Country* (1942); Dyke, E. V., *Early Economic Conditions and the Development of Agriculture in Minnesota* (1915); Eckles, C. H., *Dairy Cattle and Milk Production* (5th ed. rev. by Ernest L. Anthony, 1950); Garland, Hamlin, *A Daughter of the Middle Border* (1921); Garland, Hamlin, *A Son of the Middle Border* (1922); Leschoier, D. D., *Harvest Labor Problems in the Wheat Belt* (1922), Malin, J. C., *Winter Wheat in the Golden Belt of Kansas* (1944); Pirtle, T. R., *History of the Dairy Industry* (1926); Prentice, E. P., *American Dairy Cattle: Their Past and Future* (1942); Schafer, Joseph, *Social History of American Agriculture* (1936); Shannon, F. A., *The Farmer's Last Frontier: Agriculture, 1860–1897* (1945); Sparks, E. S., *History and Theory of Agricultural Credit in the United States* (1932); Taylor, H. C., and Taylor, A. D., *The Story of Agricultural Economics in the United States, 1840–1932* (1952); Thompson, J. G., *The Rise and Decline of Wheat-Growing Industry in Wisconsin* (1909); Wright, Ivan, *Bank Credit and Agriculture* (1922); Wright, Ivan, *Farm Mortgage Financing* (1923).

CHAPTER 19

COMMERCIAL BANKING AND THE MONETARY SYSTEMS

Barnett, G. C., *State Banks and Trust Companies Since the Passage of the National Bank Act* (1911); Davis, A. M., *The Origin of the National Banking System* (1910); Dewey, D. R., *Financial History of the United States* (rev. ed., 1956); Gregory, T. E., *The Gold Standard and Its Future* (1932); Helderman, L. C., *National and State Banks, A Study of Their Origins* (1931); Hepburn, A. B., *History of Coinage and Currency in the United States* (rev. ed., 1915); Kinley, David, *The Independent Treasury System of the United States and Its Relations to the Banks of the Country* (1911); Noyes, A. D., *Forty Years of American Finance* (1909), Patterson, R. T., *Federal Debt Management Policies, 1865–1879* (1954); Shultz, W. J., and Caine, M. R., *Financial Development of the United States* (1937); Smith, J. G., *The Development of Trust Companies in the United States* (1927); Willis, H. P., and Edwards, G. R., *Banking and Business* (rev. ed., 1925); Winkler, J. K., *The First Billion; The Stillmans and the National City Bank* (1933).

DEPRESSION PERIODS

Corey, Lewis, *The House of Morgan* (1930); Collman, C. A., *Our Mysterious Panics, 1830–1930: A Story of Events and the Men Involved* (1931); Feder, L. H., *Unemployment Relief in Periods of Depression* (1936); Josephson, Matthew, *The Politicos, 1865–1896* (1938); Larson, H. M., *Jay Cooke, Private Banker* (1936); Lauck, W. J., *The Causes of the Panic of 1893* (1907); Lightner, O. C., *The History of Business Depressions* (1922); McCartney, E. R., *The Crisis of 1873* (1935); McMurry, D. L., *Coxey's Army* (1929); Noyes, A. D., *Forty Years of American Finance* (1909); Oberholtzer, E. P., *Jay Cooke, Financier of the Civil War* (2 vols., 1907); Philbrick, F. S., *The Mercantile Conditions of the Panic of 1893* (1902); Seligman, E. R., and Others, *The Currency Problem and the Present Financial Situation* (1908); Sprague, O. M. W., *History of Crises Under the National Banking System* (1910); Weberg, F. P., *The Background of the Panic of 1893* (1929); Wells, D. A., *Recent Economic Changes* (1889).

THE BUSINESS CYCLE

Adams, A. B., *Analyses of Business Cycles* (1936); Burns, A. F., and Mitchell, W. C., *Measuring Business Cycles* (1946); Douglas, P. H., *Controlling Depressions* (1935); Fels, Rendix, *American Business Cycles, 1865–1897* (1959); Hastings, H. B., *Costs and Profits: Their Relation to Business Cycles* (1923); Mitchell, W. C., *Business Cycles* (1913); Moore, H. L., *Generating Economic Cycles* (1923); Moore, H. L., *Economic Cycles: Their Law and Cause* (1914); Persons, W. M., *Forecasting Business Cycles* (1931); Pigou, A. C., *Industrial Fluctuations* (1927); Schluter, W. C., *Economic Cycles and Crises* (1933); Slichter, S. H., *Towards Stability: The Problem of Economic Balance* (1934); Wernette, J. P., *The Control of Business Cycles* (1940).
For other volumes, see Chapter 29.

MARKETING SECURITIES

Allen, F. L., *The Great Pierpont Morgan* (1949); Allen, F. L., *Lords of Creation* (1935); Brady, R. A., *Business as a System of Power* (1943); Brandeis, L. D., *Other People's Money* (1932); Burr, A. R., *The Portrait of a Banker: James Stillman* (1927); Clews, Henry, *Fifty Years in Wall Street* (1908); Corey, Lewis, *The House of Morgan* (1930); Edwards, G. W., *Evolution of Finance Capitalism* (1938); Garraty, J. A., *Right-Hand Man: George W. Perkins* (1960); Paine, A. B., *George Fisher, Banker* (1920); Pratt, S. S., *The Work of Wall Street* (3rd ed., 1921); Satterlee, H. L., *J. Pierpont Morgan: An Intimate Portrait* (1939); Wasson, R. B., *The Hall Carbine Affair* (1948); Willis, H. P., and Bogen, J. J., *Investment Banking* (1929).

THE FEDERAL RESERVE SYSTEM

Baker, R. S., *Woodrow Wilson, Life and Letters*, IV (1931); Burgess, W. R., *The Reserve Bank and the Money Market* (1927); Glass, Carter, *An Adventure in Constructive Finance* (1927); Hardy, C. O., *Credit Policies of the Federal Reserve System* (1932); Harris, S. E., *Twenty Years of the Federal Reserve Policy* (2 vols., 1933); Kemmerer, E. W., *The A B C of the Federal Reserve System* (1916); Laughlin, J. L., *The Federal Reserve Act, Its Origins and Problems* (1933); Spahr, W. E., *The Federal Reserve System and the Control of Credit* (1931); Warburg, P. M., *The Federal Reserve System: Its Origin and Growth* (2 vols., 1930); Weyforth, W. O., *The Federal Reserve Board* (1933); Willis, H. P., *The Federal Reserve System* (1923); Willis, H. P., and Steiner, W. H., *Federal Reserve Banking Practice* (1926).

CHAPTER 20

GROWTH OF INDUSTRY

Brady, R. A., *Business as a System of Power* (1943); Burns, A. F., *Production Trends in the United States Since 1870* (1934); Creamer, Daniel, *Capital and Output Trends in Manufacturing Industries, 1880–1948* (1954); Durand, E. D., *American Industry and Commerce* (1930); Fabricant, Solomon, *Output of Manufacturing Industries, 1899–1937* (1940); Glover, J. G., and Cornell, W. B., eds., *The Development of American Industries* (3rd ed., 1951); Gras, N. S. B., *Industrial Evolution* (1930); Hendrick, B. J., *The Age of Big Business* (1920); Industrial Commission, *Report of the Industrial Commission* (19 vols., 1902); Keir, R. M., *Manufacturing* (1928); Keith, C. K., *World Minerals and World Politics* (1931); Kuznets, Simon, Thomas, D. S., and Others, *Population Redistribution and Economic Growth, 1870–1950* (3 vols., 1957–1962); Mitchell, W. C., and King, W. I., *Income in the United States: Its Amount and Distribution, 1909–1919* (1921); National Industrial Conference Board, *A*

Graphic Analysis of the Census of Manufacturing, 1849–1919 (1923); Tarbell, I. M., *The Nationalizing of Business, 1878–1898* (1936); Thorp, W. K., *Business Annals* (1926); Walker, J. B., *The Epic of American Industry* (1949); Warshow, H. T., ed., *Representative Industries in the United States* (1928); Wile, F. W., ed., *A Century of Industrial Progress* (1928); Wright, C. D., *Industrial Evolution of the United States* (1897).

TECHNOLOGICAL CHANGE

Anderson, O. E., *Refrigeration in America: A History of a New Technology and Its Impact* (1953); Bryn, E. W., *The Progress of Invention in the Nineteenth Century* (1900); Dyer, F. L., and Martin, T. C., *Edison, His Life and Inventions* (2 vols., 1924); Habakkuk, H. F., *American and British Technology in the Nineteenth Century* (1962); Kaempffert, Waldemar, ed., *A Popular History of American Invention* (2 vols., 1924); MacLaurin, W. R., *Invention and Innovation in the Radio Industry* (1949); Oliver, J. W., *History of American Technology* (1956); Singer, Charles, and Others, *A History of Technology* (4 vols., 1954); Strassman, W. P., *Risk and Technological Innovation: American Manufacturing Methods During the Nineteenth Century* (1959); Usher, A. P., *A History of Mechanical Inventions* (1954); Woodworth, J. V., *American Tool Making and Interchangeable Manufacturing* (1905).

SPECIAL INDUSTRIES: AUTOMOBILES

Barber, H. L., *The Story of the Automobile* (1927); Denison, Melville, *The Power To Go* (1956); Greenleaf, William, *Monopoly on Wheels: Henry Ford and the Selden Patent* (1961); Kennedy, E. A., *The Automobile Industry* (1941); Nevins, Allan, and Hill, F. B., *Ford: The Times, The Man, The Company* (1954); Norwood, E. P., *Ford: Men and Methods* (1931); Pound, Arthur, *The Turning Wheel* (1934); Rae, J. B., *American Automobile Manufacturers: The First Forty Years* (1959); Seltzer, L. H., *A Financial History of the American Automobile Industry* (1928).

ELECTRICAL

Broderick, J. T., *Forty Years with General Electric* (1929); Federal Trade Commission, *The Electric Power Industry* (1929); Hardy, C. O., *Recent Growth of the Electric and Power Industry* (1929); Hammond, J. W., *Men and Volts: The Story of General Electric* (1941); Keating, P. W., *Lamps for a Bright America: A History of the Electric Lamp Industry* (1948); Lamme, B. G., *Benjamin Garver Lamme, Electrical Engineer: An Autobiography* (1926); MacLauren, Malcolm, *The Rise of the Electric Industry During the Nineteenth Century* (1943).

MINING

Barger, Harold, and Schurr, S. H., *The Mining Industry, 1899–1939* (1944); Gates, Jr., W. B., *Michigan Copper and Boston Dollars: An Economic History of the Michigan Copper Industry* (1951); Minnesota Historical Records Survey, *The Cuyuana Range: A History of the Minnesota Iron Mining District* (1940); Rickard, T. A., *A History of American Mining* (1932).

OIL

Beaton, Kendall, *Enterprise in Oil: A History of Shell in the United States* (1957); Clark, J. S., *The Oil Century: From the Drake Well to the Conservation Era* (1958); Gibb, G. S., and Knowlton, E. H., *The Resurgent Years: A History of Standard Oil Company (New Jersey), 1911–1927* (1956); Giddens, P. H., *The Birth of the Oil Industry* (1938); Giddens, P. H.,

Standard Oil Company (Indiana) (1955); Hidy, Ralph, and Hidy, M. E., *Pioneering in Big Business, 1882–1911* (1955); Johnson, A. M., *The Development of American Petroleum Pipelines: A Study in Private Enterprise and Public Policy, 1862–1906* (1956); Loos, J. L., *Oil on Stream: A History of Interstate Pipe Line Company, 1909–1959* (1959); Rister, C. C., *Oil: Titan of the Southwest* (1949); Montague, G. H., *The Rise and Progress of the Standard Oil Company* (1903); Sherman, R. B., *The Petroleum Industry: An Economic Survey* (1940); Stocking, G. W., *The Oil Industry and the Competitive System* (1929); Tarbell, I. M., *History of the Standard Oil Company* (2 vols., 1904); White, G. T., *Formative Years in the Far West: A History of Standard Oil Company of California and Predecessors Through 1919* (1962); Williamson, H. F., and Others, *The American Petroleum Industry: The Age of Illumination, 1859–1899* (1959).

STEEL

Daugherty, C. R., and Others, *Economics of the Iron and Steel Industry* (2 vols., 1937); Schroeder, G. G., *The Growth of the Major Steel Companies, 1900–1950* (1953); Smith, J. R., *Story of Iron and Steel* (1913); Swank, J. M., *History of the Manufacture of Iron in All Ages* (2nd ed., 1892); Wilgus, H. L., *A Study of the United States Steel Corporation in its Industrial and Legal Aspects* (1901).

OTHERS

Carosso, V. P., *The California Wine Industry* (1951); Clough, S. B., *A Century of American Life Insurance: A History of the Mutual Life Insurance Company of New York, 1843–1943* (1946); Cochran, T. C., *The Pabst Brewing Company* (1948); Davis, Pearce, *The Development of the American Glass Industry* (1949); E. I. du Pont de Nemours and Company, *The Autobiography of an American Enterprise* (1951); Dutton, W. S., *DuPont: 140 Years* (1951); James, Marquis, *The Metropolitan Life: A Study in Business Growth* (1947); James, Marquis, *Biography of a Business, 1792–1942: The Insurance Company of North America* (1942); Huck, Virginia, *Brand of the Tartan: The 3 M Story* (1955); Lief, Alfred, *It Floats: The Story of Proctor and Gamble* (1958); Miller, William, *The Book Industry* (1948); Scoville, W. C., *Revolution in Glass Making: Entrepreneurship in the American Industry, 1880–1920* (1948); Thornton, H. J., *The History of the Quaker Oats Company* (1933); Vatter, H. G., *Small Enterprise and Oligopoly: A Study of Butter, Flour, Automobile, and Glass Container Industries* (1955).

See also Chapters 10 and 25.

BIOGRAPHIES OF INDUSTRIAL AND BUSINESS LEADERS

Backer, P. W., *Charles Goodyear, Connecticut Yankee and Rubber Pioneer: A Biography* (1940); Carroll, J. C., *Armour and his Times* (1938); Carnegie, Andrew, *Autobiography of Andrew Carnegie* (1920); Chandler, A. D., *Henry Varnum Poor: Business Editor, Analyst, and Reformer* (1956); Firestone, H. S., *Men and Rubber* (1926); Flynn, J. T., *God's Gold: The Story of Rockefeller and his Times* (1932); Ford, Henry, *My Life and Work* (1922); Friess, C. M., *Joseph B. Eastman: Servant of the People* (1952); Grodinsky, Julius, *Jay Gould: His Business Career, 1867–1892* (1957); Harvey, George, *Henry Clay Frick: The Man* (1928); Hendrick, B. J., *The Life of Andrew Carnegie* (2 vols., 1932); James, Marquis, *Alfred I. du Pont: The Family Rebel* (1941); Jenkins, J. W., *James B. Duke: Master Builder* (1927); Josephson, Matthew, *The Robber Barons: The Great American Capitalists, 1861–1901* (1934); Leupp, F. E., *George Westinghouse: His Life and Achievements* (1923); Lief, Andrew, *Harvey Firestone: Free Man of Enterprise* (1931); Lowitt, Richard, *A Merchant Prince of the Nineteenth Century: William E. Dodge* (1954); Moody, John, *The Masters of Capital* (1919);

Myers, Gustavus, *History of the Great American Fortunes* (3 vols., 1910); Nevins, Allan, *Abram S. Hewitt: With Some Account of Peter Cooper* (1935); Nevins, Allan, *John D. Rockefeller* (2 vols., 1940); Nevins, Allan, *Study in Power: John D. Rockefeller, Industrialist and Philanthropist* (2 vols., 1953); Nevins, Allan, and Hill, F. B., *Ford: The Times, The Man, The Company* (2 vols., 1954–1956); O'Connor, Harvey, *Mellon's Millions* (1933); Prout, H. G., *A Life of George Westinghouse* (1921); Redlich, Fritz, *History of American Business Leaders* (1940); Rockefeller, J. D., *Random Reminiscences of Men and Events* (1933); Sloan, A. P., Jr., and Sparkes, Boyden, *Adventures of a White-Collar Man* (1941); Sward, Keith, *The Legend of Henry Ford* (1948); Tarbell, I. M., *The Life of Elbert H. Gary* (1925).

URBANIZATION

Allen, Hugh, *Rubber's Home Town: The Real-Life Story of Akron* (1949); Andrews, Wayne, *Battle for Chicago* (1946); Atherton, Lewis, *Main Street on the Middle Border* (1954); Belcher, W. W., *The Economic Rivalry Between St. Louis and Chicago, 1850–1880* (1947); Green, C. M., *American Cities in the Growth of the Nation* (1957); Green, C. M., *History of Naugatuck, Connecticut* (1949); Fargo, L. F., *Spokane Story* (1950); Hays, S. P., *Response to Industrialism, 1885–1914* (1959); McKelvey, Blake, *Rochester: The Flower City, 1885–1890* (1949); McKelvey, Blake, *Rochester: The Quest for Quality, 1890–1925* (1956); Parker, M. T., *Lowell: A Study in Industrial Development* (1940); Pierce, B. L., *A History of Chicago* (3 vols., 1937–1957); Schlesinger, A. M., *The Rise of the City, 1878–1898* (1933).

TARIFF

Ashley, P. W. L., *Modern Tariff History* (3rd ed., 1920); Stanwood, Edward, *American Tariff Controversies in the Nineteenth Century* (2 vols., 1903); Tarbell, I. M., *The Tariff in Our Times* (1911); Taussig, F. W., *Some Aspects of the Tariff Question* (1915); Taussig, F. W., *Tariff History of the United States* (8th ed., 1931); Wright, C. W., *Wool Growing and the Tariff; a Study in the Economic History of the United States* (1910).

CHAPTER 21

ORGANIZED LABOR

Beard, M. R., *A Short History of the American Labor Movement* (1920); Bimba, Anthony, *The History of the American Working Class* (1927); Boone, Gladys, *The Women's Trade Union Leagues in Great Britain and the United States of America* (1942); Brissenden, P. F., *The I.W.W., a Study of American Syndicalism* (1919); Carlton, F. T., *History and Problems of Organized Labor* (rev. ed., 1920); Carlton, F. T., *Organized Labor in American History* (1920); Catlin, W. B., *The Labor Problem in the United States and Great Britain* (1926); Commons, J. R., and Others, *History of Labour in the United States* (4 vols., 1918–1935); Commons, J. R., and Others, *Documentary History of American Industrial Society* (10 vols., 1910–1911); Douglas, P. H., Hitchcock, C. N., and Atkins, W. E., *The Worker in Modern Economic Society* (1923); Dulles, F. R., *Labor in America* (1960); Ely, R. T., *Labor Movement in America* (1905); Fine, Nathan, *Labor and Farmer Parties in the United States, 1828–1928* (1928); Foner, P. S., *History of the Labor Movement in the United States* (2 vols., 1948, 1955); Gambs, J. S., *The Decline of the I.W.W.* (1932); Groat, G. G., *Organized Labor in America* (1919); Harris, Herbert, *American Labor* (1939); Lauck, W. J., and Sydenstricker, E., *Conditions of Labor in American Industries* (1917); Lescohier, D. D., *The Labor Market* (1919); Levine, L., *The Women's Garment Workers* (1924); Lorwin, L. L., *The American Federation of Labor: History, Policies, and Prospects* (1933); Marot, Helen, *American Labor Union*

(1914); Mason, A. T., *Organized Labor and the Law* (1925); Mason, L. L., *The American Federation of Labor* (1959); Mitchell, John, *Organized Labor* (1903); Orth, S. P., *Armies of Labor* (1919); Perlman, Selig, *A History of Trade Unionism in the United States* (1922); Rayback, J. G., *History of American Labor* (1959); Reed, L. S., *The Labor Philosophy of Samuel Gompers* (1930); Saposs, D. J., *Left Wing Unionism* (1920); Spargo, John, *Syndicalism, Industrial Unionism and Socialism* (1913); Taft, Philip, *The A. F. of L. in the Time of Gompers* (1957); Ulman, Lloyd, *Rise of the National Trade Union* (1955); Ware, N. J., *The Labor Movement in the United States, 1860–1895* (1959); Wesley, C. H., *Negro Labor in the United States* (1927); Wolman, Leo, *Ebb and Flow in Trade Unionism* (1936); Wolman, Leo, *The Growth of American Trade Unions, 1880–1923* (1923).

LABOR DISPUTES

Adamic, Louis, *Dynamite: The Story of Class Violence in America* (1931); Adams, T. S., and Sumner, H. L., *Labor Problems* (1905); Coleman, J. W., *The Molly Maguire Riots* (1936); Commons, J. R., and Andrews, J. B., *Principles of Labor Legislation* (rev. ed., 1927); Cornell, R. J., *The Anthracite Coal Strike of 1902* (1957); David, Henry, *History of the Haymarket Affair* (1936); Dougherty, C. R., *Labor Problems in American Industry* (1933); Fitch, J. A., *The Causes of Industrial Unrest* (1924); Gambs, J. S., *The Decline of the I.W.W.* (1932); Ginger, Ray, *Altgeld's America* (1958); Griffin, J. I., *Strikes: A Study in Quantitative Economics* (1939); McMurray, D. L., *The Great Burlington Strike of 1888: A Case Study in Labor Relations* (1956); Peterson, Florence, *Strikes in the United States, 1880–1938* (1938); Watkins, G. S., *An Introduction to the Study of Labor Problems* (1922); Yellen, Samuel, *American Labor Struggles* (1936); Yoder, Dale, *Labor Problems and Labor Economics* (1933).

GOVERNMENT AND LABOR

Barnard, J. L., *Factory Legislation in Pennsylvania* (1907); Beckner, E. R., *A History of Labor Legislation in Illinois* (1929); Berman, Edward, *Labor and the Sherman Act* (1930); Berman, Edward, *Labor Disputes and the President of the United States* (1924); Carroll, M. R., *Labor and Politics: The Attitude of the American Federation of Labor toward Legislation and Politics* (1923); Edwards, A. M., *The Labor Legislation of Connecticut* (1907); Fairchild, F. R., *The Factory Legislation of the State of New York* (1905); Field, A. S., *The Child Labor Policy of New Jersey* (1909); Frankfurter, Felix, and Greene, Nathan, *The Labor Injunction* (1930); Gregory, C. O., *Labor and the Law* (1946); Groat, G. G., *Attitude of American Courts in Labor Cases* (1911); Gulick, C. A., Jr., *Labor Policy of the United States Steel Corporation* (1924); Mason, A. T., *Organized Labor and the Law* (1925); Persons, C. E., and Others, *Labor Laws and Their Enforcement with Special Reference to Massachusetts* (1911); Towles, J. K., *Factory Legislation of Rhode Island* (1908); United States Strike Commission, *Report on the Chicago Strike of June–July, 1894* (1895); Witte, E. E., *The Government in Labor Disputes* (1932).

IMMIGRATION

Abbott, Edith, *Historical Aspects of the Immigration Problem* (1926); Abbott, Edith, *Immigation: Select Documents and Case Records* (1924); Berthoff, R. T., *British Immigrants in Industrial America, 1790–1950* (1953); Commons, J. R., *Races and Immigrants in America* (1907); Davie, M. R., *World Immigration with Special Reference to the United States* (1936); Davis, J. D. *The Russian Immigrant* (1922); Davis, Philip, and Schwartz, Bertha, *Immigration and Americanization* (1920); Erickson, Charlotte, *American Industry and the European Immigrant, 1860–1885* (1950); Gamio, Manuel, *Mexican Immigration to the United States*

(1930); Gavit, J. P., *American by Choice* (1922); Handlin, Oscar, ed., *Immigration as a Factor in American History* (1959); Handlin, Oscar, *The Uprooted* (1951); Hanson, M. L., *The Immigrant in the American West* (1944); Hanson, M. L., *The Immigrant in American History* (1940); Higham, John, *Strangers in the Land, 1860–1925* (1955); Hoglund, A. W., *Finnish Immigration in America, 1880–1920* (1960); Hourwick, I. A., *Immigration and Labor* (1922); Jenks, J. W., and Lauck, W. J., *The Immigration Problem* (1917); Johnson, A. J., *The Battle Cry of Freedom: New England Immigrant Aid Company in the Kansas Crusade* (1954); National Industrial Conference Board, *Immigration Problems in the United States* (1923); Orth, S. P., *Our Foreigners* (1920); Schrier, Arnold, *Ireland and the American Emigration, 1850–1900* (1958); Wittke, Carl, *The Irish in America* (1956); Wittke, Carl, *We Who Built America* (1946).

WAGES AND WELFARE OF WORKERS

Brissenden, P. F., *Earnings of Factory Workers, 1899–1927* (1929); Bureau of Labor Statistics, Bulletin No. 499, *History of Wages in the United States from Colonial Times to 1928* (1929); Coombs, Whitney, *The Wages of Unskilled Labor in Manufacturing Industries in the United States, 1890–1924* (1926); Douglas, P. H., *Real Wages in the United States, 1890–1926* (1930); Douglas, P. H., *The Theory of Wages* (1934); Long, C. D., *Wages and Earnings in the United States, 1860–1890* (1960); Rees, Albert, *Real Wages in Manufacturing, 1890–1914* (1961).

BIOGRAPHIES OF LABOR LEADERS

Ginger, Ray, *Eugene V. Debs* (1949); Gompers, Samuel, *Seventy Years of Life and Labor* (reissue, 1957); Drinnon, Richard, *Rebel in Paradise: A Biography of Emma Goldman* (1961); Grossman, Jonathan, *William Sylvis: Pioneer of American Labor* (1945); Harvey, R. H., *Samuel Gompers: Champion of the Toiling Masses* (1935); Josephson, Matthew, *Sidney Hillman: Statesman of American Labor* (1952); Powderly, T. V., *The Path I Trod* (1940); Reed, L. S., *The Labor Philosophy of Samuel Gompers* (1950).

CHAPTER 22

GENERAL STUDIES OF BUSINESS ORGANIZATION

Clark, W. E., *The Trust Problem* (1917); Ely, R. T., *Monopolies and Trusts* (1900); Haney, L. H., *Business Organization and Combination* (rev. ed., 1913); Hendrick, B. J., *The Age of Big Business* (1920); Jenks, J. W., and Clark, W. E., *The Trust Problem* (rev. ed., 1929); Jones, Eliot, *The Trust Problem in the United States* (1921); Keezer, D. M., and May, Stacy, *The Public Control of Business* (1930); Moody, John, *The Truth About the Trusts* (1904); Nutter, G. W., *The Extent of Enterprise Monopoly in the U. S., 1899–1939* (1951); Ripley, W. Z., *Trusts, Pools, and Corporation* (rev. ed., 1916); Seager, H. R., and Gulick, C. A., *Trust and Corporation Problems* (1929); Snyder, Carl, *Capitalism the Creator: The Economic Foundations of Modern Industrial Society* (1940); Watkins, M. W., *Industrial Combination and Public Policy* (1927).

SPECIAL STUDIES OF LARGE COMBINATIONS

Anthracite Coal Strike Commission, *Report to the President on the Anthracite Coal Strike of May–October, 1902* (1903); Berglund, Abraham, *The United States Steel Corporation* (1907); Hidy, Ralph, and Hidy, M. E., *Pioneering in Big Business, 1882–1911* (1955); Jones, Eliot, *The Anthracite Coal Combination* (1914); Montague, G. H., *Rise and Progress of the*

Standard Oil Company (1903); Mussey, H. R., *Combination in the Mining Industry: A Study of Concentration in Lake Superior Ore Production* (1905); Nearing, Scott, *Anthracite: An Instance of National Resource Monopoly* (1915); Nevins, Allan, *Study in Power: John D. Rockefeller, Industrialist and Philanthropist* (2 vols., 1953); Federal Trade Commission, *Report of the Federal Trade Commission on the Petroleum Industry; Prices, Profits, and Competition* (1928); Tarbell, I. M., *History of the Standard Oil Company* (2 vols., 1904); Wilgus, H. L., *A Study of the United States Steel Corporation in its Industrial and Legal Aspects* (1901).

THE PROGRESSIVE ERA

Destler, C. McA., *American Radicalism, 1865–1901* (1946); Diamond, William, *Economic Thought of Woodrow Wilson* (1943); Dorfman, Joseph, *The Economic Mind in American Civilization, 1865–1918* (1949); Faulkner, H. U., *The Quest for Social Justice, 1898–1914* (1931); Fine, Nathan, *Labor and Farmer Parties in the United States, 1828–1929* (1928); Haynes, F. E., *Social Politics in the United States* (1924); Haynes, F. E., *Third Party Movements in the United States since the Civil War* (1916); Hays, Samuel, *The Response to Industrialism, 1885–1914* (1959); Hofstadter, Richard, *The Age of Reform* (1955); Link, A. S., *Woodrow Wilson and the Progressive Era, 1910–1917* (1954); Lloyd, Caro, *Life of Henry Demarest Lloyd* (2 vols., 1912); Lloyd, H. D., *Wealth Against Commonwealth* (reissue, 1936) (condensed version, 1963); Merriam, C. E., *American Political Ideas, 1865–1917* (1920); Mowry, G. E., *Theodore Roosevelt and the Progressive Movement* (1947); Rice, S. A., *Farmers and Workers in American Politics* (1924); Russell, C. E., *Bare Hands and Stone Walls* (1933); Steffens, Lincoln, *Autobiography of Lincoln Steffens* (2 vols., 1931); Wiebe, R. H., *Businessmen and Reform: A Study of the Progressive Movement* (1962); Wilson, Woodrow, *The New Freedom* (1913).

REGULATION OF BIG BUSINESS

Berman, Edward, *Labor and the Sherman Act* (1930); Clark, J. D., *The Federal Trust Policy* (1931); Hodges, E. P., *The Antitrust Act and the Supreme Court* (1941); Knauth, O. W., *The Policy of the United States Toward Industrial Monopoly* (1914); Taft, W. H., *The Antitrust Act and the Supreme Court* (1914); Thompson, M. R., *Trust Dissolution* (1919); Walker, A. H., *A History of the Sherman Law of the United States of America* (1910); Keezer, D. M., and May, Stacy, *Public Control of Business* (1931); Sharfman, I. L., *The Interstate Commerce Commission* (4 vols., 1931–1937); Thorelli, H. B., *Federal Antitrust Policy: Origination of an American Tradition* (1954).

MARKETING AND DISTRIBUTION

Appel, Joseph, *The Business Biography of John Wanamaker* (2 vols., 1930); Barger, Harold, *Distribution's Place in the American Economy Since 1869* (1955); Baxter, W. J., *Chain Store Distribution and Management* (1931); Emmet, Boris, and Jeuck, J. E., *Catalogues and Counters: A History of Sears, Roebuck and Company* (1950); Filene, E. A., *More Profits from Merchandizing* (1926); Gibbons, H. A., *John Wanamaker* (2 vols., 1926); Hower, R. M., *History of Macy's of New York, 1858–1919* (1943); Hower, R. M., *The History of an Advertising Agency: N. W. Ayer & Son at Work, 1869–1949* (rev. ed., 1949); Kirkland, E. C., *Industry Comes of Age* (1962); Mayfield, F. M., *The Department Store Story* (1949); Presbry, Frank, *History and Development of Advertising* (1929); Tebbel, J. W., *The Marshall Fields: A Study in Wealth* (1947); Twyman, R. W., *History of Marshall Field & Company, 1852–1906* (1954); Woolworth, F. W., and Company, *Fifty Years of Woolworth, 1879–1929* (1929).

See also Chapter 32.

CHAPTER 23

RISE OF THE UNITED STATES TO WORLD POWER

Beale, Howard, *Theodore Roosevelt and the Rise of America to World Power* (1952); Beard, C. A., *The Idea of National Interest* (1934); Bemis, S. F., *A Diplomatic History of the United States* (1936); Clark, Grover, *The Balance Sheets of Imperialism* (1936); Clark, Grover, *A Place in the Sun* (1936); Coolidge, A. C., *United States as a World Power* (1916); Culbertson, W. S., *International Economic Policies* (1925); Dulles, F. R., *America's Rise to World Power, 1898–1954* (1955); Dunn, R. W., *American Foreign Investments* (1926); Feis, Herbert, *Europe, the World's Banker, 1870–1914* (1930); Ferrell, R. H. S., *American Diplomacy: A History* (1959); Fish, C. R., *The Path of Empire* (1919); Halsey, F. M., *Investments in Latin America and the British West Indies* (1918); Jenks, L. H., *The Migration of British Capital to 1875* (1927); Johnson, E. R., Van Metre, T. W., Huebner, G. G., and Hanchett, D. S., *History of Domestic and Foreign Commerce of the United States* (2 vols., 1915); Lewis, Cleona, *America's State in International Investments* (1938); May, Ernest, *Imperial Democracy* (1961); Moon, P. T., *Imperialism and World Politics* (1927); Moore, J. B., *Four Phases of American Development, Federalism—Democracy—Imperialism—Expansion* (1912); Nearing, Scott, *The American Empire* (1921); Nearing, Scott, and Freeman, Joseph, *Dollar Diplomacy* (1925); Pettigrew, R. F., *The Course of Empire* (1920); Powers, H. H., *America Among the Nations* (1919); Viallate, Achille, *Economic Imperialism and International Relations During the Last Fifty Years* (1923); Williams, B. H., *Economic Foreign Policy of the United States* (1929); Williams, W. A., *The Tragedy of American Diplomacy* (1959); Willoughby, W. F., *Territories and Dependencies of the United States* (1905); Winkler, Max, *Foreign Bonds, An Autopsy* (1933).

THE WAR WITH SPAIN AND RELATIONS WITH CUBA

Beals, Carleton, *The Crime of Cuba* (1933); Benton, E. J., *International Law and Diplomacy of the Spanish-American War* (1908); Chadwick, F. E., *The Relations of the United States and Spain*, Vol. I, *Diplomacy* (1909); II and III, *The Spanish-American War* (1911); Chapman, C. E., *History of the Cuban Republic, a Study in Hispanic American Politics* (1927); Dennis, A. L. P., *Adventures in American Diplomacy, 1896–1906* (1928); Fairbanks, Frank, *The United States and Cuba* (1948); Ferrara, Orestes, *The Last Spanish War* (1937); Fitzgibbon, R. H., *Cuba and the United States, 1900–1935* (1935); Flack, H. E., *Spanish American Diplomatic Relations Preceding the War of 1898* (1906); Freidel, Frank, *The Splendid Little War* (1958); Jenks, L. H., *Our Cuban Colony* (1928); Millis, Walter, *The Martial Spirit: A Study of Our War with Spain* (1931); Olcott, C. S., *The Life of William McKinley* (2 vols., 1916); Pratt, J. W., *Expansionists of 1898* (1936); Rhodes, J. F., *The McKinley and Roosevelt Administrations, 1897–1909* (1922); Wilkerson, M. M., *Public Opinion and the Spanish American War* (1932); Wisan, J. E., *The Cuban Crisis as Reflected in the New York Press, 1895–1898* (1934).

PANAMA CANAL

Bennett, I. E., ed., *History of the Panama Canal, Its Construction and Builders* (1915); Bishop, J. B., *The Panama Gateway* (1913); Bishop, J. B., *Theodore Roosevelt and His Time* (1920); Bullard, Arthur, *Panama, the Canal, the Country and the People* (2d ed., 1914); Bunau-Varilla, Philippe, *From Panama to Verdun* (1940); Bunau-Varilla, Philippe, *Panama: The Creation, Destruction and Resurrection* (1914); Dennett, Tyler, *John Hay* (1933); Dennis, A. L. P., *Adventures in American Diplomacy, 1896–1906* (1928); DuVal, M. P., *Cadiz to Cathay* (1940); Hill, H. C., *Roosevelt and the Caribbean* (1927); Johnson, E. R., *The*

Panama Canal and Commerce (1916); McCain, W. D., *The United States and the Republic of Panama* (1937); Miner, D. C., *The Fight for the Panama Route: The Story of the Spooner Act and the Hay Herran Treaty* (1940); Parks, E. T., *Colombia and the United States, 1765–1934* (1935); Pringle, H. F., *Theodore Roosevelt* (1931); Perkins, Dexter, *The Monroe Doctrine, 1867–1907* (1937); Rippy, J. F., *The Capitalists and Colombia* (1931); Roosevelt, Theodore, *Theodore Roosevelt: An Autobiography* (1922); White, E. B., *American Opinion of France* (1927).

LATIN AMERICA AND THE CARIBBEAN AREA

Beals, Carleton, *Porfirio Diaz, Dictator of Mexico* (1932); Bemis, S. F., *The Latin American Policy of the United States* (1943); Buell, R. L., *American Occupation of Haiti* (1933); Callahan, J. M., *American Foreign Policy in Mexican Relations* (1932); Clark, J. R., *Memorandum on the Monroe Doctrine* (1930); Clark, V. S., and Others, *Porto Rico and Its Problems* (1930); Cochran, T. C., *The Puerto Rican Businessman* (1959); Dennis, A. L. P., *Adventures in American Diplomacy, 1896–1906* (1928); Dunn, F. S., *Diplomatic Protection of Americans in Mexico* (1933); Dunn, R. W., *American Foreign Investments* (1926); Gayer, A. D., Homan, P. T., and James, E. K., *The Sugar Economy of Porto Rico* (1938); Gruening, E. H., *Mexico and Its Heritage* (1928); Hackett, C. W., *The Mexican Revolution and the United States, 1910–1926* (1926); Haring, C. H., *South America Looks at the United States* (1938); Hill, H. C., *Roosevelt and the Caribbean* (1927); Jones, C. L., *Caribbean Backgrounds and Prospects* (1931); Howland, C. P., *Survey of American Foreign Relations* (1929); Inman, S. G., *Latin America, Its Place in World Life* (1937); Jones, C. L., *The Caribbean Since 1900* (1936); Kelsey, Carl, "The American Intervention in Haiti and the Dominican Republic," *Annals of the American Academy of Political and Social Sciences*, C (March, 1922); Kepner, C. D., and Soothill, J. H., *The Banana Empire; A Case Study of Economic Imperialism* (1935); Knight, M. M., *The Americans in Santo Domingo* (1928); Latane, J. H., *The United States and Latin America* (1920); McCain, W. D., *The United States and the Republic of Panama* (1937); Marsh, M. A., *The Bankers in Bolivia* (1928); Millspaugh, A. C., *Haiti under American Control, 1915–1930* (1931); Mixer, Knowlton, *Porto Rico* (1926); Munro, D. G., *The Five Republics of Central America* (1918); Munro, D. G., *United States and the Caribbean Area* (1934); Muzzey, D. S., *James G. Blaine* (1934); Perkins, Dexter, *The Monroe Doctrine, 1867–1907* (1937); Perkins, Dexter, *The United States and the Caribbean* (1947); Phelps, D. M., *Migration of Industry to South America* (1936); Pletcher, D. M., *Rails, Mining and Progress: Seven American Promoters in Mexico, 1867–1911* (1958); Pringle, H. F., *Theodore Roosevelt* (1931); Rhodes, J. F., *The McKinley and Roosevelt Administrations* (1922); Rippy, J. F., *The Capitalists and Colombia* (1931); Rippy, J. F., *Latin America and the Industrial Age* (1944); Rippy, J. F., *The United States and Mexico* (new ed., 1931); Robertson, W. S., *Hispanic-American Relations with the United States* (1923); Roosevelt, Theodore, *Theodore Roosevelt: An Autobiography* (1913); Rowe, L. S., *The United States and Porto Rico* (1904); Stimson, H. L., *American Policy in Nicaragua* (1927); Stuart, G. H., *Latin America and the United States* (3rd ed., 1938); Tansill, C. C., *The Purchase of the Danish West Indies* (1932); Tyler, A. F., *The Foreign Policy of James G. Blaine* (1927); Williams, M. W., *The People and Politics of Latin America* (new ed., 1938); Winkler, Max, *Investments of United States Capital in Latin America* (1929).

THE UNITED STATES AND THE PACIFIC

Aberlarde, P. E., *American Tariff Policy Towards the Philippines* (1947); Barrows, D. P., *History of the Philippines* (1924); Blount, J. H., *The American Occupation of the Philippines* (1912); Campbell, C. S., *Special Business Interests and the Open Door Policy* (1951); Clark, H. W., *History of Alaska* (1930); Callahan, J. M., *American Relations in the Pacific and Far*

East, 1784–1900 (1901); Coman, Katherine, *The History of Contract Labor in the Hawaiian Islands* (1903); Dennett, Tyler, *Americans in Eastern Asia* (1922); Dennett, Tyler, *John Hay* (1933); Dulles, F. R., *America in the Pacific* (1932); Elliott, C. B., *The Philippines* (2 vols., 1917); Field, F. V. (Ed.), *Economic Handbook of the Pacific Area* (1934); Forbes, W. C., *The Philippine Islands* (2 vols., 1928); Griswold, A. W., *The Far Eastern Policy of the United States* (1938); Grunder, G. A., and Livezey, W. E., *The Philippines and the United States* (1951); Harrington, Fred, *God, Mammon, and the Japanese, 1884–1905* (1944); Harrison, F. B., *The Cornerstone of Philippine Independence* (1922); Jenkins, Shirley, *American Economic Policy Toward the Philippines* (1954); LeRoy, J. A., *The Americans in the Philippines* (2 vols., 1914); Nichols, J. P., *Alaska . . . Under the Rule of the United States* (1924); Odate, Gyojer, *Japan's Financial Relations with the United States* (1922); Pratt, J. W., *Expansionists of 1898* (1936); Remer, C. F., *Foreign Investments in China* (1933); Reyes, J. S., *History of America's Economic Policy toward the Philippines* (1923); Roosevelt, Nicholas, *The Philippines: A Treasure and a Problem* (1926); Reyes, J. S., *Legislative History of America's Economic Policy toward the Philippines* (1923); Storey, Moorfield and Lichauco, M. P., *The Conquest of the Philippines by the United States, 1898–1925* (1926); Tansill, C. C., *The Foreign Policy of Thomas F. Bayard, 1885–1897* (1940); Treat, P. J., *Diplomatic Relations between the United States and Japan, 1895–1905* (2 vols., 1938); Willoughby, W. W., *Foreign Rights and Interests in China* (2 vols., 1927); Worcester, D. C., *The Philippines: Past and Present* (2 vols., 1914).

CHAPTER 24

THE UNITED STATES AND EUROPE

Ashley, P. W. L., *Modern Tariff History* (3rd ed., 1920); Denny, Ludwell, *America Conquers Britain* (1930); Feis, Herbert, *Europe the World's Banker, 1870–1914* (1930); Heindel, R. H., *The American Impact on Great Britain, 1898–1914* (1940); Hobson, C. K., *The Export of Capital* (1914); Jenks, L. H., *The Migration of British Capital to 1875* (1927); Shadwell, Arthur, *Industrial Efficiency: A Comparative Study of Industrial Life in England, Germany, and America* (1906); Southard, F. A., Jr., *American Industry in Europe* (1931); Stead, W. T., *The Americanization of the World* (1902); Taussig, F. W., *The Tariff History of the United States* (8th ed., 1931).

THE UNITED STATES IN THE WAR

GENERAL ACCOUNTS: Baker, R. S., *Woodrow Wilson: Life and Letters*, VII–VIII (1939); Bassett, J. S., *Our War with Germany* (1919); Clarkson, G. B., *Industrial America in the World War* (1923); Creel, George, *How We Advertised America* (1920); Crowell, Benedict, and Wilson, R. F., eds., *How America Went to War* (6 vols., 1921); Houston, D. F., *Eight Years with Wilson's Cabinet* (1926); Paxson, F. L., *American Democracy and the World War* (2 vols., 1936, 1939); Seymour, Charles, ed., *American Diplomacy During the World War* (1934); Seymour, Charles, *Woodrow Wilson and the World War* (1921); Slosson, P. W., *The Great Crusade and After: 1914–1928* (1930); Sullivan, Mark, *Our Times, V* (1933); Willoughby, W. F., *Government Organization in War Times and After* (1919); Wittke, Carl, *German-Americans and the World War* (1936).

WAR FINANCES AND WAR DEBTS

Bergman, Karl, *History of Reparations* (1927); Bogart, E. L., *Direct and Indirect Costs of the Great World War* (1919); Bogart, E. L., *War Costs and Financing* (1921); Clark, J. M., *The*

Costs of the World War to the American People (1931); Fleming, D. F., *The United States and World Organization, 1920–1923* (1938); Hardy, C. O., *Wartime Control of Prices* (1940); Hollander, J. H., *War Borrowing* (1919); Mock, J. R., and Larson, Cedric, *Words that Won the War: The Story of the Committee on Public Information, 1917–1919* (1939); Moulton, H. G., and Pavolsky, Leo, *War Debts and World Prosperity* (1932); Noyes, A. D., *The War Period of American Finance, 1908–1925* (1926); Williams, B. H., *Economic Foreign Policy of the United States* (1929); Winkler, Max, *Foreign Bonds: An Autopsy* (1933).

TRANSPORTATION 1917–1929

American Bureau of Shipping, *The American Merchant Marine* (1933); Culbertson, W. S., *Commercial Policy in War Time and After* (1919); Cunningham, W. J., *American Railroads: Government Control and Reconstruction Policies* (1929); Dixon, F. H., *The Railroads and Government: Their Relations in the United States, 1910–1921* (1922); Ellingwood, A. R., and Coombs, Whitney, *The Government and Railroad Transportation* (1930); Fraser, C. C., *The Story of Aircraft* (1939); Ford, L. C., and Ford, T. F., *The Foreign Trade of the United States* (1920); Frederick, J. H., *The Development of American Commerce* (1932); Hines, W. D., *War History of American Railroads* (1928); Hurley, E. N., *The Bridge to France* (1927); Leonard, N., *Railroad Consolidation under the Transportation Act of 1920* (1946); Kennedy, J. P., *An Economic Survey of the American Merchant Marine* (1937); Locklin, D. P., *Economics of Transportation* (1938); Locklin, D. P., *Railroad Regulation Since 1920* (1928); Magoun, F. A., and Hodgins, Eric, *A History of Aircraft* (1931); McAdoo, W. G., *Crowded Years* (1931); McCormick, V. C., *Report of the War Trade Board* (1920); McVeagh, Roger, *The Transportation Act, 1920: Its Sources, History and Text* (1923); Moulton, H. G., and Others, *The American Transportation Problem* (1933); National Industrial Conference Board, *The American Merchant Marine Problem* (1929); Savage, Carlton, *Policy of the United States Toward Maritime Commerce in the War* (1934); Sumner, P. J. H., *Aircraft: Progress and Development* (1935); Smith, D. H., and Betters, P. V., *The United States Shipping Board* (1931); Splawn, M. W., *Government Operations of Railroad* (1928); Zeis, P. M., *American Shipping Policy* (1938).

AGRICULTURE IN THE WAR

Dickson, M. R., *The Food Front in World War I* (1944); Hoover, Herbert, *American Epic*, Vol. 2, *United States Food Administration* (1960); Mullendore, W. C., *History of the United States Food Administration* (1941); Nourse, E. G., *American Agriculture and the European Market* (1924); Powell, E. A., *The Army Behind the Army* (1919); Surface, F. M., *American Pork Production in the World War* (1926); Surface, F. M., *The Stabilization of the Price of Wheat during the War* (1925); Surface, F. M., *The Grain Trade during the World War* (1928); Surface, F. M., and Bland, R. L., *American Food in the World War and Reconstruction Period* (1931); Van Hise, C. R., *Conservation and Regulation in the United States during the World War* (1917).

INDUSTRY AND LABOR

Berman, Edward, *Labor Disputes and the President of the United States* (1924); Clarkson, G. B., *Industrial America in the World War* (1923); Coombs, Whitney, *The Wages of Unskilled Labor in the Manufacturing Industries in the United States, 1890–1920* (1926); Crowell, Benedict, and Wilson, R. F., eds., *How America Went to War* (6 vols., 1921); Douglas, P. H., *Real Wages in the United States, 1890–1926* (1930); Friday, David, *Profits, Wages, and Prices* (1920); Gompers, Samuel, *American Labor and the War* (1919); Gompers, Samuel, *Seventy Years of Life and Labor* (2 vols., 1925); King, W. I., *The Wealth and Income of the*

People of the United States (1917); Lorwin, L. L., *The American Federation of Labor* (1933); Soule, George, *Prosperity Decade: From War to Depression, 1917–1929* (1947); Stephen, John, *Labor in Wartime* (1940); Watkins, G. S., *Labor Problems and Labor Administration in the United States During the World War* (1919); Willoughby, W. F., *Government Organization in War Time and After* (1919).

THE GOVERNMENT AND BUSINESS

Davenport, E., and Cooke, S. R., *The Oil Trusts and Anglo-American Relations* (1923); Denny, Ludwell, *We Fight for Oil* (1928); Henderson, G. C., *The Federal Trade Commission* (1924); Keezer, D. M., and May, Stacy, *Public Control of Business: A Study of Antitrust Law Enforcement, Public Interest Regulation, and Government Participation in Business* (1930); Mohr, Anton, *The Oil War* (1926); Watkins, M. W., *Industrial Combination and Public Policy* (1927); Williams, B. H., *The Economic Foreign Policy of the United States* (1929).

See also Chapter 32.

IMMIGRATION RESTRICTION

Clark, J. P., *Deportation of Aliens from the United States* (1931); Garis, R. L., *Immigration Restriction* (1928); Handlin, Oscar, *The Uprooted* (1951); Higham, John, *Strangers in the Land, 1860–1925* (1955); Howland, Charles, ed., *Survey of American Foreign Relations,* (1929); Stephenson, G. M., *History of American Immigration, 1850–1924* (1926); Wilcox, W. F., ed., *International Migrations: Interpretations* (1931).

THE POSTWAR PERIOD

GENERAL ACCOUNTS: Adams, J. T., *Our Business Civilization* (1929); Adams, S. H., *The Incredible Era* (1939); Allen, F. L., *Only Yesterday* (1931); Borsodi, Ralph, *This Ugly Civilization* (1929); Chase, Stuart, *Prosperity, Fact or Myth?* (1930); Dumond, D. L., *Roosevelt to Roosevelt: The United States in the Twentieth Century* (1937); Hacker, L. M., *American Problems of Today* (1938); Malin, J. C., *The United States After the World War* (1930); National Industrial Conference Board, *A Picture of World Economic Conditions at the Beginning of 1930* (4 vols., 1930); President's Research Committee on Social Trends, *Recent Social Trends* (2 vols., 1933); Schlesinger, Jr., A. M., *Crisis of the Old Order* (1957); Siegfried, André, *America Comes of Age* (1927); Slosson, P. W., *The Great Crusade and After, 1914–1928* (1930); Sullivan, Mark, *Our Times*, VI (1935).

CHAPTER 25

TRANSPORTATION

Barger, Harold, *The Transportation Industries, 1899–1946: A Study of Output, Employment, and Productivity* (1951); Cleveland, R. M. and Williamson, S. T., *The Road is Yours* (1951); Dearing, C. L., *American Highway Policy* (1941); Frederick, J. H., *Commercial Air Transportation* (1955); Hultgren, Thor, *American Transportation in Prosperity & Depression* (1948); Kennedy, E. A., *The Automobile Industry* (1941); Labatut, Jean, and Lane, W. J., eds., *Highways in Our National Life: A Symposium* (1950); Little, J. A., and Cunningham, H. M., *Historical Development of Transport Coordination and Integration in the United States* (1950); Nevins, Allan, and Hill, F. E., *Ford: Expansion and Challenge* (1957); Rae, J. B., *American Automobile Manufacturers* (1959); Smith, H. L., *Airways: The History of Commercial Aviation in the United States* (1942); Stover, J. M., *American Railroads* (1961).

OTHER INDUSTRIES

Archer, G. L., *History of the Radio to 1926* (1938); Banning, W. P., *Commercial Broadcasting Pioneer: The WEAF Experiment, 1922–1926* (1946); Codel, Martin, ed., *Radio and Its Future* (1930); Committee on Recent Economic Changes of the President's Conference on Unemployment, and a Special Staff of the National Bureau, *Recent Economic Changes* (2 vols., 1929); Daugherty, C. R., and Others, *The Economics of the Iron and Steel Industry* (2 vols., 1937); Fabricant, Solomon, *The Output of Manufacturing Industries, 1899–1937* (1940); Glover, J. G. and Cornell, W. B., *The Development of American Industries; Their Economic Significance* (3rd ed., 1951); Gould, J. M., *Output and Productivity in the Electric and Gas Utilities 1899–1942* (1946); Hall, C. R., *History of American Industrial Science* (1954); Harlow, W. A. F., *Old Wires and New Waves* (1936); Haynes, William, *The American Chemical Industry* (6 vols., 1945–1954); Jome, H. L., *Economics of the Radio Industry* (1925); Kenduck, J. W., *Productivity Trends in the United States* (1961); Levin, Maurice, and Others, *America's Capacity to Consume* (1934); Martin, T. C. and Coles, S. L., *The Story of Electricity* (2 vols., 1919-1922); Maclaurin, R. C., *Invention and Innovation in the Radio Industry* (1949); McDonald, Forrest, *Let There Be Light: The Electric Utility Industry in Wisconsin, 1881–1955* (1957); Nourse, E. G., and Others, *America's Capacity to Produce* (1934); Schubert, Paul, *The Electric World: The Rise of Radio* (1939); Siepman, Charles, *Radio, Television and Society* (1950).

RELOCATION OF PLANTS AND PEOPLE

Barber, Bernard, *Social Stratification* (1957); Behrans, C. F., *Commercial Bank Activities in Urban Mortgage Financing* (1952); Cohn, D. L., *Combustion on Wheels: An Informal History of the Automobile Age* (1944); Colean, M. L., *The Impact of Government on Real Estate Finance in the United States* (1950); Editors of *Fortune, The Exploding Metropolis* (1958); Goldstein, Sidney, *The Norristown Study* (1961); Goldstein, Sidney, *Patterns of Mobility 1919–1950* (1958); Goodrich, Carter, and Others, *Migration and Economic Opportunity* (1935); Greenhut, M. L., *Plant Location in Theory and Practice* (1956); Harriss, C. L., *History and Policies of the Home Owners' Loan Corporation* (1951); Hawley, Amos, *The Changing Shape of Metropolitan America: Decentralization Since 1920* (1956); Hobbs, A. H., *The Changing Shape of Metropolitan America, Differentials in Internal Migration* (1942); Isaccs, Julius, *Economics of Migration* (1947); Jaffe, A. J. and Stewart, C. D., *Manpower Resources and Utilization* (1951); Klaman, S. B., *The Postwar Residential Mortgage Market* (1961); Kuznets, Simon, Thomas, D. S., and Others, *Population Redistribution and Economic Growth, 1870–1950* (3 vols., 1957–1962); Landis, Paul, *Population Problems: A Cultural Interpretation* (2nd ed., 1954); Lynd, R. S. and H. M., *Middletown* (1929); Lynd, R. S. and H. M., *Middletown in Transition* (1937); Lively, E. E., and Taeuber, Conrad, *Rural Migration in the U.S.* (1939); National Industrial Conference Board, *Trends in Industrial Location* (1952); Rossi, Peter H., *Why Families Move: A Study in The Social Psychology of Urban Residential Mobility* (1955); Taylor, C. C., and Others, *Rural Life in the United States* (1949); Taeuber, Conrad, and Taeuber, I. B., *The Changing Population of the United States* (1948); Thompson, W. S., *Population Problems* (1942); Thornwaite, C. W., *Internal Migration in the U.S.* (1934); Wood, Robert C., *Suburbia: Its People and their Politics* (1959).

NEW TECHNOLOGY AND RESEARCH

Bureau of Labor Statistics, Dept. of Labor and Research and Development Board, Dept. of Defense *Industrial Research and Development: A Preliminary Report* (1953); Burr, Kendall, *Pioneering in Industrial Research: The Story of the General Electric Research Laboratory* (1957); Carter, C. F. and Williams, B. R., *Science in Industry* (1959); Dewhurst, F. W., and

Others, *America's Needs and Resources* (1955); Editors of *Fortune, The Mighty Force of Research* (1953); Editors of *Fortune, U.S.A.: The Permanent Revolution* (1951); Hall, C. R., *History of American Industrial Science* (1954); Howard, F. A., *Organizing for Technical Progress* (1957); Jerome, Harry, *Mechanization in Industry* (1934); Kouwenhoven, J. A., *Made in America* (1948); National Resources Planning Board, *Research: A National Resource* (1941); National Science Foundation, *Science and Engineering in American Industry: A Final Report on a 1953–1954 Survey* (1954); Perazich, George, and Field, P. M., *Industrial Research and Changing Technology* (1940); Silk, L. S., *Research Production* (1960).

ATOMIC ENERGY

Campbell, J. W., *The Atomic Story* (1947); Dahl, R. A., and Brown, R. S., *Domestic Control of Atomic Energy* (1951); Dean, Gordon, *Report on the Atom* (1953); Hewlett, R. G. and Anderson, O. E., Jr., *A History of the United States Atomic Energy Commission* (1962), I, *The New World, 1939–1946;* Hopkins, J. J., *World Wide Industrial Role of Nuclear Energy* (1956); Mullenbach, Philip, *Civilian Nuclear Power* (1963); Schurr, S. H., and Others, *Energy in the American Economy 1850–1975, Economic Study of its History and Prospects* (1961); Tybout, R. A., *Atomic Power and Energy Resource Planning* (1958); Warren, F. H., and Others, *Growth Survey of the Atomic Industry, 1958–1968* (1958).

SCIENTIFIC MANAGEMENT

Baritz, Loren, *The Servants of Power* (1960); Copley, F. B., *Frederick W. Taylor: Father of Scientific Management* (2 vols., 1923); Frankel, L. K., and Fleischer, Alexander, *The Human Factor in Industry* (1920); Gantt, H. L., *Organizing for Work* (1919); Gilbreth, F. B., *Motion Study* (1911); Gilbreth, F. B., *Fatigue Study* (1918); Gilbreth, F. B., *Primer of Scientific Management* (2nd ed., 1914); Hunt, E. E., ed., *Scientific Management Since Taylor* (1924); Mayo, Elton, *Human Problems of an Industrial Civilization* (1946); Myers, James, *Psychology and Industrial Efficiency* (1913); Nadworny, M. J., *Scientific Management and the Unions 1900–1932* (1955); Roethlisberger, F. J., *Management and Morale* (1941); Taylor, F. W., *Scientific Management* (1911); Taylor, F. W., *Shop Management* (1911); Thompson, C. B., *The Theory and Practice of Scientific Management* (1917).

AUTOMATION

Becker, E. R., and Murphy, E. F., *The Office in Transition* (1957); Bittel, L. R., and Others, *Practical Automation* (1957); Bright, J. R., *Automation and Management* (1958); Buckingham, W. S., *Automation: Its Impact on Business and People* (1961); Grabbe, E. M., ed., *Automation in Business and Industry* (1957); Jacobson, H. B., and Roucek, J. S., eds., *Automation and Society* (1959); Mann, F. C., and Hoffman, L. R., *Automation and the Worker* (1960); Walker, C. R., *Toward the Automatic Factory* (1957).

CHAPTER 26

DEPRESSION

Adams, A. B., *National Economic Security* (1936); Adams, A. B., *Our Economic Revolution* (1933); Adams, J. T., *Our Business Civilization* (1932); Allen, F. L., *Since Yesterday* (1940); Ayres, L. P., *The Economics of Recovery* (1933); Brookings Institution Study, *The United States in the Twentieth Century: The Recovery Problem in the United States* (1936); Clark,

J. M., *Strategic Factors in Business Cycles* (1934); Corye, Lewis, *The Crisis of the Middle Class* (1935); Corey, Lewis, *Decline of American Capitalism* (1934); Davis, Maxine, *The Lost Generation* (1936); Dumond, D. L., *Roosevelt to Roosevelt: The United States in the Twentieth Century* (1937); Firestone, J. M., *Federal Receipts and Expenditures during Business Cycles, 1879–1958* (1960); Galbraith, J. K., *The Great Crash* (1955); Hacker, L. M., *American Problems of Today* (1938); Hoover, Herbert, *Memoirs*, vol. 3 *The Great Depression, 1929–1941* (1952); Mills, F. C., *Economic Tendencies in the United States* (1932); Mitchell, Broadus, *Depression Decade: From New Era Through New Deal, 1929–1941* (1948); Moley, Raymond, *After Seven Years* (1939); Moulton, H. G., *The Formation of Capital* (1935); Moulton, H. G., *Income and Economic Progress* (1935); Patterson, E. M., *The World's Economic Dilemma* (1930); Robbins, L. C., *The Great Depression* (1931); Seldes, G. V., *The Years of the Locust: America, 1929–1932* (1933); Woofter, T. J., and Winston, E. E. B., *Seven Lean Years* (1939).

HOOVER POLICIES

Brandes, J., *Herbert Hoover and Economic Diplomacy* (1962); Ferrell, R. H., *American Diplomacy in the Great Depression* (1959); Hoover, Herbert, *Memoirs: The Great Depression, 1929–1941* (1952); Meyers, W. S., and Newton, W. H., *The Hoover Administration* (1936); Myers, W. S., *State Papers of Herbert Hoover* (1934); Tugwell, R. G., *Mr. Hoover's Economic Policy* (1932); Warrent, H. G., *Herbert Hoover and the Great Depression* (1959); Wilbur, R. L., and Hyde, M. A., *The Hoover Policies* (1937).

THE NEW DEAL

GENERAL ACCOUNTS: Beard, C. A., and Smith, G. H. E., *The Future Comes* (1934); Berle, A. A., and Others, *America's Recovery Program* (1934); Brogan, Denis, *The Era of Franklin D. Roosevelt* (1950); Brookings Institution, *The Recovery Program Problem in the United States* (1936); Burns, J. M., *Roosevelt: The Lion and the Fox* (1956); Conkin, P. K., *Tomorrow a New World* (1949); Dulles, E. L., *Depression and Reconstruction* (1936); Einaudi, Mario, *The Roosevelt Revolution* (1959); Ezekiel, M. J. B., *$2500 a Year: From Scarcity to Abundance* (1936); Fairchild, David, *The Economic Thought of Franklin D. Roosevelt* (1956); Friedel, Frank, *Franklin D. Roosevelt* (3 vols., 1952, 1954, 1956); Hacker, L. M., *A Short History of the New Deal* (1934); Hansen, A. H., *Full Recovery or Stagnation?* (1938); Hoover, Herbert, *The American Road, 1933–1938* (1938); Lindley, E. K., *Half Way with Roosevelt* (1936); Lippmann, Walter, *Interpretations, 1933–1935* (1935); Moulton, H. G., and Others, *The Recovery Problem in the United States* (1936); Perkins, Dexter, *The New Age of Franklin D. Roosevelt* (1950); President's Research Committee on Social Trends, *Social Trends in the United States* (2 vols., 1933); Rauch, Basil, *The History of the New Deal, 1933–1938* (1944); Robinson, E. E., *The Roosevelt Leadership, 1933–1945* (1955); Roosevelt, F. D., *The Public Papers and Addresses of Franklin D. Roosevelt* (Rosenman, S. J., ed., 13 vols., 1938–1950); Schlesinger, A. M., Jr., *Coming of the New Deal* (1957); Schlesinger, A. M., Jr., *The Politics of Upheaval* (1960); Tugwell, R. G., *The Industrial Discipline and the Governmental Arts* (1933); Tugwell, R. G., *The Battle for Democracy* (1934); Tugwell, R. G., *The Democratic Roosevelt* (1957); Wallace, H. A., *New Frontiers* (1934).

BANKING AND FINANCE

Allen, F. W., *The Lords of Creation* (1935); Blum, J. D., *From the Morgenthau Diaries: Years of Crisis, 1928–1938* (1959); Colt, C. C., and Keith, N. S., *28 Days: A History of the Banking Crisis* (1933); Eccles, Mariner, *Beckoning Frontiers* (1951); Editors of *The Economist* (London), *The New Deal: An Analysis and Appraisal* (1937); Everest, A. S., *Morgenthau:*

The New Deal and Silver (1950); Fisher, Irving, *The Stock Market Crash and After* (1930); Gayer, A. D., ed., *The Lessons of Monetary Experience* (1937); Hart, A. G., *Debts and Recovery, 1929–1937* (1938); Hirst, F. W., *Wall Street and Lombard Street* (1931); Johnson, G. G., *The Treasury and Monetary Policy, 1933–1938* (1939); Jones, J. H., and Angly, Edward, *Fifty Billion Dollars: My Thirteen Years with RFC, 1932–1951* (1945); Moulton, H. G., *Financial Organization and the Economic System* (1938); National Industrial Conference Board, *The New Monetary System of the United States* (1934); Paris, J. D., *Monetary Policies of the United States* (1932–1938); Pecora, Ferdinand, *Wall Street Under Oath* (1939); Ramsay, M. L., *Pyramids of Power: The Story of Roosevelt, Insull, and the Utility Wars* (1937); Reeve, J. E., *Monetary Reform Movements: A Survey of Recent Plans and Panaceas* (1943); Studenski, Paul, and Kroos, H. E., *Financial History of the United States* (1952); Sullivan, Lawrence, *Prelude to Panic, The Story of the Bank Holiday* (1936); Westerfield, R. B., *Our Silver Debacle* (1936); Young, J. P., *The United States Silver Policy, Foreign Policy Reports, XII, No. 8* (1936).

AGRICULTURE

Backman, Jules, *Government Price-Fixing* (1938); Blaisdell, D. C., *Government and Agriculture: The Growth of Federal Farm Aid* (1940); Conkin, P. K., *Tomorrow a New World: The New Deal Commodity Programs* (1960); Daniels, Jonathan, *A Southerner Discovers the South* (1938); Davis, J. S., *On Agricultural Policy, 1926–1938* (1939); Johnson, C. S., and Others, *The Collapse of Cotton Tenancy* (1935); Lively, C. E., and Taeuber, Conrad, *Rural Migration in the United States* (1939); Lord, Russell, *The Wallaces of Iowa* (1947); McWilliams, Carey, *Factories in the Field* (1939); McWilliams, Carey, *Ill Fares the Land* (1939); Nourse, E. G., and Others, *Three Years of the Agricultural Adjustment Administration* (1937); Richard, H. I., *Cotton and the A.A.A.* (1936); Wallace, Henry, *New Frontiers and Democracy Reborn* (1944); Wynne, Walter, Jr., *Five Years of Rural Relief* (1938); Zimmerman, C. C., and Whetten, N. L., *Rural Families on Relief* (1938).

INDUSTRY AND LABOR

Bernstein, Irving, *The New Deal and Collective Bargaining* (1950); Brooks, R. R., *Unions of Their Own Choosing* (1939); Daugherty, C. R., *Labor under the N.R.A.* (1934); Dearing, C. L., and Others, *The A.B.C. of the N.R.A.* (1934); Derber, Milton, and Young, Edwin, eds., *Labor and the New Deal* (1949); Harris, Herbert, *American Labor* (1939); Johnson, H. S., *The Blue Eagle from Egg to Earth* (1936); Levinson, Edward, *Labor on the March* (1938); Lorwin, L. L., and Wubnig, Arthur, *Labor Relations Boards; The Regulation of Collective Bargaining under the National Industrial Recovery Act* (1935); Lyon, L. S., and Others, *The National Recovery Administration: An Analysis and Appraisal* (1935); MacDonald, Lois, *Labor Problems and the American Scene* (1938); Moley, Raymond, *After Seven Years* (1939); Perkins, Frances, *The Roosevelt I Knew* (1946); Roos, C. R., *NRA Economic Planning* (1937); Stein, Emmanuel, and Others, *Labor and the New Deal* (1934); Stolberg, Benjamin, *The Story of the C.I.O.* (1938); Tead, Ordway, and Metcalf, H. C., *Labor Relations under the Recovery Act* (1933); Walsh, J. R., *The C.I.O.: Industrial Unionism in Action* (1937); Whitney, S. N., *Trade Associations and Industrial Control, A Critique of the N.R.A.* (1934).

RELIEF AGENCIES

Abbott, Grace, *From Relief to Social Security* (1941); Adams, Grace, *Workers on Relief* (1939); Anderson, Nels, *The Right to Work* (1938); Aronovici, Carol, *Housing the Masses* (1939); Brown, J. C., *Public Relief, 1929–1939* (1940); Douglas, P. H., *Social Security in the*

United States (1936); Ebenstein, William, *The Law of Public Housing* (1940); Galbraith, J. K., and Johnson, G. G., Jr., *Economic Effects of Public Works Expenditures, 1933–1938* (1940); Gayer, A. D., *Public Works in Prosperity and Depression* (1935); Harriss, C. L., *History and Policies of the Home Owners' Loan Corporation* (1951); Hopkins, H. L., *Spending to Save: The Complete Story of Relief* (1936); Howard, D. S., *The WPA and Federal Relief Policy* (1943); Ickles, H. L., *Back to Work: The Story of the P.W.A.* (1935); Isakoff, J. F., *The Public Works Administration* (1938); Lane, M. D., and Steegmuller, Francis, *America on Relief* (1938); Lutz, H. L., *Public Finance* (1936); Post, L. W., *The Challenge of Housing* (1938); Strauss, M. W., and Wegg, Talbot, *Housing Comes of Age* (1938); Whiting, T. E., and Woofter, T. J., Jr., *Summary of Relief and Federal Work Program Statistics, 1933–1940* (1941).

SOCIAL SECURITY

Asch, S. H., *Social Security and Related Welfare Programs* (3rd ed., 1959); Chamber of Commerce of the United States, *Social Security in the United States: Chamber Policies and Reports of Committees on Social Security* (1944); Cohen, W. J., ed., *War and Post-War Social Security* (1942); Douglas, P. H., *Social Security in the United States* (1939); Harris, S. E., *Economics of Social Security* (1946); International Labour Office, *Approaches to Social Security: An International Survey* (1942); Meriam, Lewis, *Relief and Social Security* (1946); National Planning Association: *Joint Standards on Social Security by Agriculture, Business, and Labor* (1944); Turnbull, J. G., and Others, *Economic and Social Security* (1957).

GOVERNMENT AIDS TO THE ECONOMY

Adams, Walter, and Gray, H. M., *Monopoly in America: The Government as a Promotor* (1955); Becker, J. M., *Shared Government in Employmnet Security* (1959); Copeland, M. A., *Trends in Government Finance* (1961); Fabricant, Solomon, *The Trend of Government Activity in the United States since 1900* (1952); Fainsod, Merle, and Gordon, Lincoln, *Government and the American Economy* (1948); Saulner, R. J., and Others, *Federal Lending and Loan Insurance* (1958); Steiner, G. A., *Government's Role in Economic Life* (1953).

CONSERVATION

Burns, Arthur, and Caine, W. E., *Electric Power and Government Control* (1948); Chase, Stuart, *Rich Land, Poor Land: A Study of Waste in Natural Resources of America* (1936); Dewhurst, J. F., and Others, *America's Needs and Resources* (1955); Galloway, G. F., *Planning for America* (1941); Gustafson, A. F., *Conservation in the United States* (1939); Harper, R. M., *Natural Resources of the Tennessee Valley Region in Alabama* (1942); Hubbard, P. J., *Origins of the TVA: The Muscle Shoals Controversy, 1920–1932* (1961); Hynning, C. J., *State Conservation of Resources* (1939); Kyle, H. E., *The Building of the TVA* (1958); Laidler, H. W., *Power Control* (1928); Lilienthal, D. E., *TVA* (1941); Martin, R. C., ed., *TVA: the First Twenty Years* (1956); Nixon, E. B., *Franklin D. Roosevelt and Conservation* (1957); Osborn, Fairfield, *Our Plundered Planet* (1948); Perloff, H. S., and Others, *Regions, Resources and Economic Growth* (1960); Selznick, Philip, *TVA and the Grass Roots* (1949); Voght, William, *Road to Survival* (1948).

FOREIGN TRADE AND TARIFF

Culbertson, W. J., *Reciprocity: A National Policy for Foreign Trade* (1937); Fetter, F. W., *The New Deal and Tariff Policy* (1933); Pearson, J. C., *The Reciprocal Trade Agreements Program: The Policy of the United States and Its Effectiveness* (1942); Tasca, H. J., *The*

Reciprocal Trade Policy of the United States (1938); Taylor, A. E., *The New Deal and Foreign Trade* (1935).

CHAPTER 27

BACKGROUND AND PREPARATIONS FOR WAR

Beard, C. A., *American Foreign Policy in the Making, 1932–1940* (1946); Beard, C. A., *A Foreign Policy for America* (1940); Cherne, L. M., *Your Business Goes to War* (1942); Department of State, *Peace and War: United States Foreign Policy, 1931–1941* (1942); De Servsky, A. P., *Victory Through Air Power* (1942); Drummond, D. F., *The Passing of American Neutrality, 1937–1941* (1955); Harris, S. E., *Economics of American Defense* (1942); Holmes, H. N., *Strategic Materials and National Strength* (1942); Kiplinger, W. M., *Washington Is Like That* (1942); Langer, W. L., and Gleason, S. E., *The World Crisis and American Foreign Policy* (2 vols., 1953); Lissitzin, O. J., *International Air Transport and National Policy* (1942); Porter, Catharine, *Crisis in the Philippines* (1942).

THE DEFENSE OF THE WESTERN HEMISPHERE
AND THE GOOD NEIGHBOR POLICY

Duggan, Laurence, *The Americas: The Search for Hemisphere Security* (1949); Guerrant, E. O., *Roosevelt's Good Neighbor Policy* (1950); Perkins, Dexter, *The United States and the Caribbean* (1947); Wells, Sumner, *Seven Decisions that Shaped History* (1951); Wood, Bryce, *The Making of the Good Neighbor Policy* (1961).

PRODUCTION DURING THE WAR AND AFTER

Armstrong, R. B., and Others, *Problems in Price Control: Changing Production Patterns* (1947); Baxter, J. P., *Scientists Against Time* (1946); Borth, Christy, *Masters of Mass Production* (1945); Bowden, Witt, *War and Postwar Wages: Prices and Hours, 1914–1923 and 1939–1944* (1946); Bureau of the Budget, *The United States at War* (1946); Campbell, R. F., *The History of Basic Metals Price Control in World War II* (1948); Cavers, D. R., *Problems in Price Control: Pricing Standards* (1948); Chandler, L. V., and Wallace, D. H., *Inflation in the United States, 1940–1948* (1951); Chandler, L. V., and Wallace, D. H., *Economic Mobilization and Stabilization: Selected Materials on the Economics of War and Defense* (1951); Civilian Production Administration, *Industrial Mobilization for War: History of the War Production Boards and Predecessor Agencies, 1940–1945, Vol. I; Program and Administration* (1947); Craf, J. R., *A Survey of the American Economy, 1940–1946* (1947); Gold, Bela, *Wartime Economic Planning in Agriculture* (1949); Harris, S. E., *Inflation and the American Economy* (1945); Janeway, Eliot, *The Struggle for Survival: A Chronicle of Economic Mobilization in World War II* (1951); Kuznets, Simon, *The National Product in Wartime* (1945); Lane, F. C., *Ships for Victory* (1944); Moulton, H. G., *Effects of Defense Program on Prices, Wages, and Profits* (1941); Murphy, H. C., *National Debt in War and Transition* (1950); Nelson, D. M., *Arsenal of Democracy: The Story of American Production* (1946); Novick, David, and Others, *Wartime Production Controls* (1949); Rose, J. R., *American Wartime Transportation* (1955); Stettinius, E. R., Jr., *Lend Lease: Weapon for Victory* (1944); Walton, Francis, *Miracle of World War II; How American Industry Made Victory Possible* (1956); Wilcox, W. W., *The Farmer in the Second World War* (1947); Woodbury, D. O., *Battlefronts of Industry: Westinghouse in World War II* (1948).

For further material on agriculture, see Chapter 30.

LABOR

Department of Labor, *Labor Year Book, Mobilizing Labor for Defense* (2 vols., 1951); De Schweinitz, Dorothea, *Labor and Management in a Common Enterprise* (1949); Dunlop, J. T., and Others, *The Wage Adjustment Board: Wartime Stabilization in the Building and Construction Industry* (1950); Peterson, Florence, *American Labor Unions: What They Are and How They Work* (1945); Riegelman, Carol, *Labour-Management Co-Operation in the United States; War Production: A Study of Methods and Procedures* (1948); Seidman, Joel, *American Labor from Defense to Reconversion* (1953); *Yearbook of American Labor, War Labor Policies* (1945).

CHAPTER 28

POSTWAR ECONOMY

Alderfer, E. B., and Michl, H. E., *Economics of American Industry* (1947); Anderson, B. M., *Economics and the Public Welfare* (1949); Berge, Wendell, *Economic Freedom for the West* (1946); Canterberry, E. R., *The President's Council of Economic Advisers* (1961); Clemence, R. V., and Lambie, J. R., *Economic Changes in America* (1954); *Economic Report of the President*—annually since 1946; Freeman, R. E., ed., *Postwar Economic Trends in the United States* (1960); Glover, J. G., and Cornell, W. B., *The Development of American Industries: Their Economic Significance* (1951); Hansen, A. H., *The American Economy* (1947); Hickman, B. G., *An Interpretation of Price Movements Since the End of World War II* (1958); Hickman, B. G., *Growth and Stability of the Postwar Economy* (1960); Leontief, W. W., *Studies in the Structure of the American Economy* (1953); Slichter, S. H., *The American Economy* (1948).

INTERNATIONAL AFFAIRS

Agar, Herbert, *The Price of Power: America Since 1945* (1957); Brogan, D. W., *America in the Modern World* (1960); Clark, J. M., *Guideposts in Time of Change* (1949); Cole, G. D. H., *World in Transition* (1949); Cortney, Philip, *The Economic Munich* (1949); Feis, Herbert, *The American Effort in China from Pearl Harbor to the Marshall Mission* (1953); Goldman, E. F., *The Crucial Decade and After: America, 1945–1960* (1962); Graebner, N. A., *The New Isolationism: A Study in Politics and Foreign Policy Since 1950* (1956); Goodrich, L. M., *Korea: A Study of United States Policy in the United Nations* (1956); Hansen, A. H., *America's Role in the World Economy* (1945); Harris, S. E., *Foreign Economic Policy of the United States* (1948); Hickman, B. G., *The Korean War and United States Economic Activity, 1950–1952* (1952); Ingram, Kenneth, *History of the Cold War* (1955); Marshall, G. C., *The Limits of Foreign Policy* (1954); Mikesell, R. F., *United States Economic Policy and International Relations* (1952); Mills, L. A., and Others, *The New World of Southeast Asia* (1949); Northrop, S. C., *European Union and United States Foreign Policy* (1954); Reischauer, E. O., *The United States and Japan* (1950); Reitzel, William, and Others, *United States Foreign Policy, 1945–1955* (1956); Romanus, C. F., and Sunderland, R., *Stillwell's Mission to China* (1953); Rostow, W. W., *The United States in the World Arena* (1960); Smith, R. A., *Philippine Freedom* (1958); Smith, R. F., *The United States and Cuba: Business and Diplomacy, 1917–1960* (1962); Speiser, E. A., *The United States and the Near East* (1947); Taft, R. A., *A Foreign Policy for Americans* (1951); Truman, H. S., *Memoirs* (2 vols., 1955); Westerfield, H. B., *Foreign Policy and Politics: Pearl Harbor to Korea* (1955); Williams, W. A., *American-Russian Relations, 1781–1947* (1952); Vinacke, H. M., *The United States and the Far East, 1945–1951* (1952).

FOREIGN AID

Bingham, J. B., *Shirt Sleeve Diplomacy: Point 4 in Action* (1954); Bowles, Chester, *American Politics in a Revolutionary World* (1956); Buchanan, N. S., and Lutz, F. A., *Rebuilding the World Economy* (1947); Enke, Stephen, and Salera, Virgil, *International Economics* (1951); Harris, S. E., *The European Recovery Program* (1954); Myrdal, Gunner, *An International Economy* (1956); Piquet, H. S., *Aid, Trade, and the Tariff* (1953); Price, H. B., *The Marshall Plan and its Meaning* (1955); Thorp, W. L., *Trade, Aid, or What?* (1954); Williams, J. H., *Money, Trade, and Economic Growth: In Honor of John Henry Williams* (1951).

UNITED NATIONS

Bloomfield, L. P., *The U.N. and United States Foreign Policy* (1960); Eichelberger, C. M., *U.N.: The First Fifteen Years* (1960); Finer, Herman, *The United Nations Economic and Social Council* (1946); Goodrich, L. M., and Hambro, E. J., *Charter of the United Nations: Commentary and Documents* (1946); Gross, E. A., *The United Nations: Structure for Peace* (1962); Rusdrill, R. B., *A History of the United Nations Charter: The Role of the United States 1940–1945* (1958); Wortley, B. A., ed., *UN: The First Ten Years* (1959).

CHAPTER 29

BANKING AND FINANCE

Behrens, C. F., *Commercial Bank Activities in Urban Mortgage Financing* (1952); Chandler, L. V., *Benjamin Strong: Central Banker* (1958); Clark, Evans, and Galloway, G. B., *The Internal Debts of the United States* (1933); Creamer, Daniel, and Others, *Capital in Manufacturing and Mining: Its Formation and Financing* (1960); Federal Reserve System, Board of Governors, *The Federal Reserve System: Its Purposes and Functions* (1947); Gesel, G. A., *Protecting Your Dollars: An Account of the work of the Securities and Exchange Commission* (1940); Goldsmith, R. W., *Financial Intermediaries in the American Economy Since 1900* (1958); Hickman, W. B., *The Volume of Corporate Bond Financing since 1900* (1953); Kemmerer, E. D., and Kemmerer, D. L., *ABC of the Federal Reserve System* (rev. ed., 1950); Klaman, S. B., *The Postwar Residential Mortgage Market* (1961); Koch, A. R., *The Financing of Large Corporations* (1943); Kuznets, Simon, *Capital in the American Economy: Its Formation and Financing* (1961); Macaulay, F. R., *Some Theoretical Problems Suggested by the Movements of Interest Rates, Bond Yields, and Stock Prices in the United States since 1856* (1938); Morton, J. E., *Urban Mortgage Lending: Comparative Markets and Experience* (1956); Robinson, R. I., *Postwar Market for State and Local Government Securities* (1960); Saulnier, R. J., and Jacoby, N. H., *Financing Equipment for Commercial and Industrial Enterprise* (1944); Ulmer, M. J., *Capital in Transportation: Communications and Public Utilities; Its Formation and Financing* (1960); Westerfield, R. W., *Money, Credit and Banking* (1947).

MONETARY POLICIES

Beyen, J. W., *Money in a Maelstrom* (1949); Brown, George, *The International Gold Standard Reinterpreted* (2 vols., 1940); Chandler, L. V., *Inflation in the United States 1940–1948* (1950); Chang, T. C., *Cyclical Movements in the Balance of Payments* (1951); Currie, Lauchlin, *The Supply and Control of Money in the United States* (1934); Fisher, Irving, *Stabilizing the*

Dollar (1934); Hart, A. G., *In Defense of the Dollar* (1953); Hart, A. G., *Defense without Inflation* (1951); MacDougall, Donald, *The World Dollar Problem* (1957); Nussbaum, Arthur, *A History of the Dollar* (1957); Paris, James D., *Monetary Policies of the United States 1932–1938* (1938); Studenski, Paul, and Krooss, H. E., *Financial History of the United States* (1952).

CONSUMER FINANCING

Bernstein, Blanche, *The Pattern of Consumer Instalment Debt, 1935–1936* (1940); Chapman, J. M., and Associates, *Commercial Banks and Consumer Credit* (1940); Coppock, J. D., *Government Agencies of Consumer Instalment Credit* (1940); Dauer, E. A., *Comparative Operating Experience of Consumer Instalment Financing Agencies and Commercial Banks, 1929–1941* (1944); Donaldson, E. E., *Personal Finance* (1948); Durand, David, *Risk Elements in Consumer Instalment Financing* (1941); Holthausen, D. McC., and Others, *The Volume of Consumer Instalment Credit, 1929–1938* (1941); Plummer, W. C., and Young, R. A., *Sales Finance Companies and Their Credit Practices* (1940); Phelps, C. W., *The Role of Sales Finance Companies in the American Economy* (1952); Saulnier, R. J., *Industrial Banking Companies and Their Credit Practices* (1940); Young, R. A., and Others, *Personal Finance Companies and Their Credit Practices* (1940).

THE BUSINESS CYCLE

Allen, F. L., *Lords of Creation* (1935); Burns, A. F., and Mitchell, W. C., *Measuring Business Cycles* (1946); Chase, Stuart, *Prosperity: Fact or Myth* (1929); Committee of the President's Conference on Unemployment, and a Special Staff of the National Bureau, *Business Cycles and Unemployment* (1923); Dobrovolsky, S. O., *Corporate Income Retention* (1951); Fisher, Irving, *The Stock Market Crash and After* (1930); Firestone, J. M., *Federal Receipts and Expenditures During Business Cycles* (1879–1958); Flynn, J. T., *Security Speculation* (1943); Galbraith, J. K., *The Great Crash* (1955); Hansen, A. H., *Full Recovery or Stagnation?* (1938); Hicks, John, *Rehearsal for Disaster: The Boom and Collapse of 1919–1920* (1961); Mitchell, W. C., *What Happens During Business Cycles: A Progress Report* (1951); Moore, G. H., *Business Cycle Indicators* (2 vols., 1961); National Industrial Conference Board, *Major Forces in World Business Depression* (1931); Ripley, W. Z., *Main Street and Wall Street* (1927); Robbins, L. G., *The Great Depression* (1933); Slichter, S. H., *Toward Stability: The Problem of Economic Balance* (1934); Wernette, J. P., *The Control of Business Cycles* (1940).

NATIONAL INCOME AND SAVING

Dillard, D. D., *The Economics of John Maynard Keynes* (1948); Goldsmith, R. G., *A Study of Savings in the United States* (2 vols., 1955); Keynes, J. M., *The General Theory of Employment, Interest and Money* (1936); Keynes, J. M., and Slichter, S. H., *The Means to Prosperity* (1933); Klein, L. R., *The Keynesian Revolution* (1947); Kuznets, Simon, *National Income: A Summary of Findings* (1940); Kuznets, Simon, *National Income and Its Composition 1919–1938* (1941); Kuznets, Simon, *Share of Upper Income Groups in Income and Savings* (1953); Lampman, R. J., *The Share of Top Wealth-Holders in National Wealth, 1922–1956* (1962); Leven, Maurice, *The Income Structure of the United States* (1938); Martin, R. F., *National Income in the United States, 1799–1938* (1939); Miller, H. P., *Income of the American People* (1955); Mitchell, W. C., and Others, *Income in the United States: Its Amount and Distribution* (2 vols., 1921, 1922).

TAXATION

Blough, Roy, *The Federal Taxing Process* (1952); Groves, H. M., *Postwar Taxation and Economic Progress* (1946); Paul, Randolph E., *Taxation in the United States* (1954); Ratner, Sidney, *American Taxation* (1942).

FOREIGN TRADE AND INVESTMENTS

American Management Association, *European Common Market* (1959); Bidwell, P. W., *What the Tariff Means to American Industries* (1956); Bloomfield, A. I., *Capital Imports and the American Balance of Payments, 1934–1949* (1950); Brown, W. A., *The United States and the Restoration of World Trade* (1950); Gardner, R. N., *Sterling-Dollar Diplomacy* (1956); Gordon, W. C., *International Trade: Goods, People, and Ideas* (1958); Horn, P. V., *International Trade* (rev. ed., 1945); Humphrey, D. D., *American Imports* (1955); Lewis, Cleona, *America's Stake in International Investments* (1938); Mintz, Ilse, *Deterioration of the Quality of Foreign Bonds in the United States, 1920–1930* (1951); Morgenstein, Oskar, *International Financial Transactions and Business Cycles* (1959); National Industrial Conference Board, *The International Financial Problem of the United States* (1929); National Industrial Conference Board, *Trends in the Foreign Trade of the United States* (1930); Vanek, Jaroslave, *The National Resource Content of United States Foreign Trade, 1870–1955* (1957); Whittlesey, C. R., *National Interests and International Cartels* (1946); Wilcox, Clair, *A Charter for World Trade* (1949); Williams, J. H., *Money, Trade, and Economic Growth* (1951).

CHAPTER 30

WORLD WAR I AND THE 1920's

Barger, Harold, and Lansberg, H. H., *American Agriculture, 1899–1939: A Study of Output, Employment, and Productivity* (1942); Benedict, M. R., *Farm Policies of the United States, 1790–1950* (1953); Black, J. D., *Agricultural Reform in the United States* (1929); Bogue, A. G., *Money at Interest: The Farm Mortgage in the Middle Border* (1955); Boyle, J. E., *Marketing Agricultural Products* (1925); Capper, Arthur, *The Agricultural Bloc* (1922); Davis, J. S., *The Farm Export Debenture Plan* (1929); Eliot, Clara, *The Farmer's Campaign for Credit* (1927); Engberg, R. C., *Industrial Prosperity and the Farmer* (1927); Gee, Wilson, *The Place of Agriculture in Our Life* (1930); Gee, Wilson, *The Social Economics of Agriculture* (1932); Grant, McDonnell, *Decline of Agrarian Democracy* (1953); Hacker, L. M., *The Farmer is Doomed* (1933); Hargreaves, M. W. M., *Dry Farming in the Northern Plains, 1900–1925* (1957); Huebner, G. G., *Agricultural Commerce* (2nd ed., 1924); Kile, O. M., *The Farm Bureau Through Three Decades* (1948); Kirkpatrick, E. L., *The Farmers Standard of Living* (1929); Lippincott, Isaac, *What the Farmer Needs* (1928); Morlan, Robert, *Political Prairie Fire: The Non-Partisan League, 1915–1922* (1955); National Industrial Conference Board, *The Agricultural Problem in the United States* (1926); Nourse, E. G., *American Agriculture and the European Markets* (1924); Ostrolenk, Bernard, *The Surplus Farmer* (1932); Seilgman, E. R. A., *The Economics of Farm Relief* (1929); Shidilier, J. H., *Farm Crisis, 1919–1923* (1957); Sparks, E. S., *History and Theory of Agricultural Credit in the United States* (1932); Taylor, H. C., and Taylor, A. D., *The Story of Agricultural Economics in the United States, 1840–1932* (1952); Tostlebe, A. S., *Capital and Agriculture: Its Formation and Financing since 1870* (1937); Wallace, H. C., *Our Debt and Duty to the Farmer* (1925); Warren, G. F., and Pearson, F. A., *The Agricultural Situation in the United States* (1924); Wiest, Edward, *Agricultural Organization in the United States* (1923).

AGRICULTURE AND THE NEW DEAL

Baker, O. E., and Others, *Agriculture in Modern Life* (1939); Barger, Harold, and Lansberg, H. H., *American Agriculture, 1890–1939: A Study of Output, Employment, and Productivity* (1942); Benedict, M. R., *Farm Policies of the United States, 1790–1950* (1953); Blaisdell, D. C., *Government and Agriculture: The Growth of Federal Farm Aid* (1940); Davis, J. S., *On Agricultural Policy, 1926–1938* (1939); Fite, Gilbert, *George Peek and the Fight for Parity* (1954); Gee, Wilson, *American Farm Policy* (1934); Halcrow, H. G., *Agricultural Policy of the United States* (1953); Jamieson, Stuart, *Labor Unionism in American Agriculture* (1946); Kile, O. M., *The Farm Bureau Through Three Decades* (1948); Lord, Russell, *The Wallaces of Iowa* (1947); McConnell, Grant, *The Decline of Agrarian Democracy* (1953); McWilliams, Carey, *Factories in the Fields* (1939); Norse, E. G., *Three Years of the Agricultural Adjustment Administration* (1937); Richards, H. I., *Cotton and the A.A.A.* (1936); Webb, J. N., and Brown, Malcolm, *Migrant Families* (1938).

THE CONTINUING AGRICULTURAL PROBLEM

Benedict, M. R., and Stine, O. C., *The Agricultural Commodity Programs: Two Decades of Experience* (1956); Benedict, M. R., *Can We Solve the Farm Problem: An Analysis of Federal Aid to Agriculture* (1955); Black, J. D., *The Rural Economy of New England: A Regional Study* (1950); Bogue, A. G., *Money at Interest: The Farm Mortgage in the Middle Border* (1955); Cochrane, W. W., *Farm Prices: Myth and Reality* (1958); Fulmer, J. L., *Agricultural Progress in the Cotton Belt since 1920* (1950); Gale, J. D., *Trade and Agriculture* (1950); Harding, T. S., *Two Blades of Grass: A History of Scientific Development in the United States Department of Agriculture* (1947); Haystead, Ladd, and Fite, G. C., *Agricultural Regions of the United States* (1955); Hicks, J. D., and Saloutos, Theodore, *Agricultural Discontent in the Middle West* (1951); Higbee, E. C., *American Agriculture: Geography, Resources, and Conservation* (1958); Horton, D. C., *Patterns of Farm Financial Structure: A Cross-Section View of Economic and Physical Determinants* (1957); Jesness, O. B., *Farm Price and Income Supports* (1950); Johnson, S. E., *Changes in American Farming* (1949); Jones, L. A., and Durand, David, *Mortgage Lending Experience in Agriculture* (1954); Nelson, Lowry, *American Farm Life* (1951); Schultz, Theodore, *Agriculture in an Unstable Economy* (1945); Soth, Lauren, *Farm Trouble in an Age of Plenty* (1957); Taylor, H. C., and Taylor, A. D., *The Story of Agricultural Economics in the United States, 1840–1932* (1932); Tostlebe, A. S., *Capital and Agriculture: Its Formation and Financing since 1870* (1937).

THE SOUTH

Aull, G. H., and Stepp, J. M., *The Postwar Outlook in an Agricultural-Industrial Area* (1945); Butler, C. P., and Crawford, D. E., *Farm Power Utilization and Costs on "Very Large" Farms in the South Carolina Piedmont* (1948); Butler, C. P., *Some Economic Effects of Cotton Acreage Diversions in the Piedmont Areas of Georgia and South Carolina* (1956); Chilton, S. J. P., *Rice Yields in Areas Improved by Application of Fertilizer* (1944); Clark, T. D., *The Emerging South* (1961); Daniels, Jonathan, *A Southerner Discovers the South* (1938); Efferson, J. N., *The Production and Marketing of Rice* (1955); Fulmer, J. L., *Agricultural Progress in the Cotton Belts Since 1920* (1950); Hoover, C. B., and Ratchford, B. U., *Economic Resources and Policies of the South* (1951); Johnson, C. S., and Others, *The Collapse of Cotton Tenancy* (1935); Logan, Rayford, and Others, *What the Negro Wants* (1944); Maclachland, J. M., and Floyd, Joseph, *This Changing South* (1951); Mims, Edwin, *The Advancing South: Stories of Progress and Reaction* (1927); Myrdal, Gunnar, *An American Dilemma: The Negro Problem and Modern Democracy* (2 vols., 1944); Odum, H. W., *Southern Regions of the United States* (1936); United States Presidents' Materials Policy Commission,

Resources for Freedom (5 vols., 1952); Woofter, J. T. J., Jr., *Landlord and Tenant on the Cotton Plantation* (1936).

CHAPTER 31

LABOR FORCE, EMPLOYMENT, AND MOBILITY

Anderson, H. D., and Davidson, P. E., *Occupational Trends in the United States* (1940); Bogue, D. J., *An Exploratory Study of Migration and Labor Mobility Using Social Security* (1950); Davidson, P. E., and Anderson, A. D., *Occupational Mobility in an American Community* (1937); Edwards, A. D., *Population in Relation to Resources and Employment Opportunities in South Carolina* (1945); Ducoff, L. J., and Hagood, M. J., *Labor Force Definition and Measurement* (1947); Durand, J. D., *The Labor Force in the United States, 1890–1960* (1948); Frazier, Franklin, *Black Bourgeosie* (1957); Frazier, Franklin, *The Negro Family* (1958); Gillen, P. B., *The Distribution of Occupations as a City Yardstick* (1951); Jaffe, A. J., and Carleton, R. O., *Occupational Mobility in the United States, 1930–1960* (1954); Lester, R. A., *Economics of Labor* (1941); Long, C. D., *The Labor Force Under Changing Income and Employment* (1958); McEntire, Davis, *The Labor Force in California: A Study of Characteristics and Trends in Labor, Force, Employment, and Occupations in California, 1900–1950* (1952); Mann, F. C., and Hoffman, L. R., *Automation and the Worker* (1960); Palmer, Gladys, *Labor Mobility in Six Cities* (1954); Parnes, H. S., *Research on Labor Mobility* (1954); Peterson, Florence, *Survey of Labor Economics* (1947); Reid, I. D., *The Negro Immigrant* (1939); Rogoff, Natalie, *Recent Trends in Occupational Mobility* (1953); Rose, A. M., *The Negro in Postwar America* (1950); Schwartz, Harry, *Seasonal Farm Labor in the United States* (1945); Scripps Foundation Studies in Population Distribution; Smyth, R. C., and Murphy, M. J., *Bargaining with Organization Labor* (1949); Stigler, G. J., *Trend of Employment in the Service Industries* (1956); Warner, W. L., and Abegglen, J. C., *Occupational Mobility in American Business and Industry, 1928–1952* (1955); Woytinsky, W. S., *The Labor Supply in the United States* (1938).

GOVERNMENT AND LABOR

Ashe, D. I., and Rifkin, G., *The Taft-Hartley Law* (1947); Bernheim, A. L., and Others, *Labor and Government* (1935); Bradley, P. D., ed., *Public Stakes in Union Power* (1960); Brinker, P. A., *The Taft-Hartley Act After Ten Years* (1958); Brown, E. C., *National Labor Policy* (1950); Calkins, Fay, *CIO and the Democratic Party* (1952); Daugherty, C. R., *Labor under the N.R.A.* (1934); Gaer, Joseph, *The First Round* (1944); Labor Relations Boards, *The Regulation of Collective Bargaining under the National Industrial Recovery Act* (1935); Leiter, R. D., *Labor Economics and Industrial Relations* (rev. ed., 1962); Lyon, L. S., and Others, *The National Recovery Administration, An Analysis and Appraisal* (1935); Metz, H. W., *Labor Policy of the Federal Government* (1947); Metz, H. W., and Jacobstein, Meyer, *A National Labor Policy* (1947); Millis, H. C., and Brown, E. C., *From the Wagner Act to Taft-Hartley* (1950); Seidman, Joel, *American Labor from Defense to Reconversion* (1953); Witte, E. E., *The Government in Labor Disputes* (1932); Wolf, H. D., *The Railroad Labor Board* (1927).

UNIONS AND BARGAINING

Bakke, E. W., *Mutual Survival: The Goal of Unions and Management* (1947); Bernstein, Irving, *The Lean Years: A History of the American Worker, 1920–1933* (1960); Chamberlain, N. W., *Collective Bargaining* (1951); Chamberlin, E. H., *An Economic Analysis of Labor*

Union Power (1948); Daugherty, C. R., and Parrish, J. B., *Labor Problems in American Society* (1952); Dulles, F. R., *Labor in America* (rev. ed., 1960); Foster, W. Z., *The Great Steel Strike and its Lessons* (1920); Goldberg, A. J., *AFL-CIO: Labor United* (1956); Interchurch World Movement, Commission of Inquiry, *Report of the Steel Strike of 1919* (1920); Larrowe, C. P., *Shape-Up and Hiring Hall* (1955); Leiserson, W. M., *American Trade Union Democracy* (1959); Lenz, Sidney, *Crisis of American Labor* (1959); Lumpkin, Katherine, ed., *Labor in Postwar America* (1949); Merritt, W. G., *Destination Unknown: Fifty Years of Labor Relations* (1951); Millis, H. A., *How Collective Bargaining Works* (1942); Mollenhoff, C. R., *Tentacles of Terror: The Teamsters Defy the Government* (1959); Morris, J. O., *Conflict Within the A.F. of L.* (1959); Perlman, Mark, *Labor Theories in America: Background and Development* (1958); Peterson, Florence, *American Labor Unions* (1952); Slichter, S. H., and Others, *The Impact of Collective Bargaining on Management* (1961); Slichter, S. H., *Union Policies and Industrial Management* (1941); Smyth, R. C., and Murphy, M. J., *Bargaining with Organized Labor* (1948); Taft, Philip, *The A.F. of L. from the Death of Gompers to the Merger* (1959); Taft, Philip, *Structure and Government of Trade Unions* (1954); Updegraff, C. M., ed., *Arbitration in Labor Disputes* (rev. ed., 1961).

LABOR LEADERS

Dayton, E. L., *Walter Reuther* (1958); Foster, W. Z., *From Bryan to Stalin* (1937); Ginzberg, Eli, and Carwell, Joseph, *The Labor Leader* (1948); Howe, Irving, and Widick, B. J., *The U.A.W. and Walter Reuther* (1949); Josephson, Matthew, *Sidney Hillman: Statesman of American Labor* (1952); Madison, C. A., *America's Labor Leaders* (1950); Mills, C. W., *The New Men of Power: American Labor Leaders* (1948); Raddock, M. C., *Portrait of an American: William L. Hutchison* (1955); Wechsler, J. A., *Labor Baron—A Portrait of John L. Lewis* (1944).

STANDARD OF LIVING

Balderston, C. C., *Profit Sharing for Wage Earners* (1937); Baker, Helen, *Employee Savings Programs: An Analysis of Recent Trends* (1937); Bendix, Rudolph, and Lipset,.S. M., *Class Status and Power* (1953); Cooke, M. L., and Murray, Philip, *Organized Labor and Production* (1946); McKelvey, J. T., *A.F.L. Attitudes Toward Production, 1900–1932* (1952); United States Department of Labor, *The Gift of Freedom: A Study of the Economic and Social Status of Wage Earners in the United States* (1949).

LABOR IN SPECIAL INDUSTRIES

Braun, Kurt, *Union-Management Co-operation: Experience in the Clothing Industry* (1947); Brazeal, B. R., *The Brotherhood of Sleeping Car Porters: Its Origin and Development* (1945); Carsel, Wilfred, *A History of the Ladies' Garment Workers' Union* (1940); Christies, R. A., *Empire in Wood: A History of the Carpenters' Union* (1956); Corey, Lewis, *Meat and Man: A Study of Monopoly, Unionism, and Food Policy* (1949); Dunn, R. R., *Labor and Automobiles* (1929); Fisher, Waldo, *Economic Consequences of the Seven-Hour Day and Wage Changes in the Bituminous Coal Industry* (1939); Hardy, Jack, *The Clothing Workers: A Study in the Conditions and Struggles in the Needle Trades* (1935); Hertel, D. W., *History of the Brotherhood of Way Employees* (1955); Hohman, E. P., *History of American Merchant Seamen* (1956); Howe, Irving, and Wedick, B. J., *The U.A.W. and Walter Reuther* (1949); Jensen, V. H., *Labor Relations in the Non-Ferrous Metal Industry up to 1930* (1950); Jensen, V. H., *Lumber and Labor* (1945); Lester, R. D., *The Musicians and Petrillo* (1953); Levine, Louis, *The Women's Garment Workers: A History of the International Ladies' Garment Workers' Union* (1924); Loft, Jacob, *The Printing Trades* (1944); McCaleb, W. F., *Brotherhood of Railway Trainmen* (1936); McDonald, D. J., and Lynch, E. A., *Coal and Unionism: A History of the American Coal Miners' Union* (1939); McGinley, J. J., *Labor Relations in the New York Rapid Transit Systems, 1904–1944* (1949); McPherson, W. H., *Labor Relations in the Automobile Industry* (1940); Nelson, James, *The Mine Workers' District 50: The Story of the Gas, Coke, and Chemical Unions of Massachusetts and their Growth into a National Union* (1955); Perlman, Mark, *The Machinist: A New Study in American Trade Unionism* (1961); Roberts, H. S., *Rubber Workers* (1944); Robinson, D. B., *Spotlight on a Union: The Story of the United Hatters* (1948); Schweppe, Emma, *The Firemen's and Patrolmen's Unions in the City of New York* (1948); Seidman, Joel, *The Needle Trades* (1942); Seybold, J. W., *The Philadelphia Printing Industry: A Case Study* (1949); Stolberg, Benjamin, *Tailor's Progress* (1944); Suffern, A. E., *The Coal Miners' Struggle for Industrial Status* (1926); Zaretz, C. E., *The Amalgamated Clothing Workers of America* (1934).

CHAPTER 32

MARKETING AND PUBLIC RELATIONS

Barger, Harold, *Distribution's Place in the American Economy since 1869* (1955); Bernays, E. L., *Public Relations* (1952); Boyd, H. W., Jr., and Others, *Contemporary American Marketing* (1957); Bridge, D. U., *Men and Methods of Newspaper Advertising* (1947); Brown, L. O., *Marketing and Distribution Research* (1955); Canfield, B. R., *Public Relations* (3rd ed., 1960); Creel, George, *How We Advertised America* (1920); Duddy, E. A., and Revzan, D. D., *Marketing* (1947); Dunlap, O. E., Jr., *The Radio in Advertising* (1931); Edwards, C. M., and Howard, W. H., *Retail Advertising Sales and Promotion* (1943); Emmet, Boris, and Jeuck, J. E., *Catalogs and Counters: A History of Sears, Roebuck and Company* (1950); Filene, E. A., *Next Steps Forward in Retailing* (1937); Finn, David, *Public Relations* (1960); Goldman, E. F., *Two-Way Street: The Emergence of the Public Relations Counsel* (1948); Heidingsfeld, M. S., and Blankenship, A. B., *Market and Marketing Analysis* (1947); Hepner, H. W., *Effective Advertising* (1949); Hettinger, H. S., *A Decade of Radio Advertising* (1933); Hower, Ralph, *The History of an Advertising Agency: N. W. Ayer & Son at Work, 1869–1949* (rev. ed., 1949); Kleppner, Otto, *Advertising Procedure* (1950); Luck, D. J., and Wales, H. G., *Marketing Research* (1952); Nielander, W. A., and Miller, R. W., *Public Relations* (1951); Pease, O. A., *The Responsibilities of American Advertising: Private Control and Public Influence, 1920–1940* (1958); Presbry, Frank, *The History and Development of Advertising* (1929); Stewart, P. W., and Dewhurst, J. F., *Does Distribution Cost Too Much?* (1939); Wingate, J. W., and Corbin, Arnold, *Changing Patterns in Retailing* (1956); Whyte, W. H., Jr., *Is Anybody Listening?* (1952).

See also Chapter 22.

BUSINESS STRUCTURE

Adams, Walter, and Gray, H. M., *Monopoly in America* (1955); Berle, A. A., Jr., *Power Without Property* (1959); Berle, A. A., Jr., and Means, G. C., *The Modern Corporation and Private Property* (1932); Bernheim, A. L., and Others, *Big Business: Its Growth and Place* (1937); Buchanan, N. S., *The Economics of Corporate Enterprise* (1940); Burns, A. R., *The Decline of Competition* (1936); Chudson, W. A., *A Pattern of Corporate Financial Structure: A Cross Sectional View of Manufacturing, Mining, Trade, and Construction, 1937* (1945); Cochran, T. C., *The American Business System* (1957); Dewhurst, F. W., and Others, *America's Needs and Resources* (1947); Drucker, P. F., *Concept of the Corporation* (1946); Hansen, Alvin, *The American Economy* (1957); Hansen, Alvin, *Economic Issues of the 1960's* (1960); Editors of *Fortune, U. S. A.: The Permanent Revolution* (1951); Jennings, W. W., *20 Giants of American Business* (1953); Kaplan, A. D. H., *Big Enterprise in a Competitive System* (1954); Laidler, H. W., *Concentration of Control in American Industry* (1931); Levin, H. J., ed., *Business Organization and Public Policy* (1958); Mayer, K. B., and Goldstein, Sidney, *The First Two Years: Problems of Small Firm Growth and Survival* (1961); Means, G. C., *The Corporate Revolution in America* (1962); Moulton, H. G., *Controlling Factors in*

Economic Growth (1949); Nelson, R. L., *Merger Movements in American Industry, 1895–1956* (1959); Nutter, G. W., *The Extent of Enterprise Monopoly in the United States, 1899–1939* (1951); Owens, R. N., *Business Organization and Combination* (1946); Ramsey, M. L., *Pyramids of Power* (1932); Rauschenbush, H. S., and Laidler, H. W., *The Power Control* (1928); Stocking, G. W., and Watkins, M. W., *Monopoly and Free Enterprise* (1951).

MANAGERIAL ENTERPRISE

Barnard, C. I., *The Functions of the Executive* (1938); Barnard, C. I., *Organization of Management* (1948); Blau, P. M., *Bureaucracy in Modern Society* (1956); Burnham, James, *The Managerial Revolution* (1941); Burnham, James, *Change and the Entrepreneur* (1949); Cochran, T. C., *The American Business System* (1957); Drucker, Peter, *The Practice of Management* (1954); Editors of *Fortune, U. S. A., The Permanent Revolution* (1951); Gordon, R. A., *Business Leadership in the Large Corporation* (1945); Knauth, O. W., *Managerial Enterprise* (1948); Supple, B. E., ed., *The Entrepreneur* (1958); Sutton, F. X., and Others, *The American Business Creed* (1956).

BUSINESS AND GOVERNMENT

Baldwin, W. L., *Antitrust and the Changing Corporation* (1951); Handler, Walter, *Antitrust in Perspective* (1957); Lyon, L. S., Watkins, M. W., and Abramson, Victor, *Government and Economic Life* (2 vols., 1939); Mund, V. A., *Government and Business* (1950); Rohlfing C. C., and Others, *Business and Government* (1953); Watkins, M. W., *Industrial Combination and Public Policy* (1927); Whitney, S. N., *Antitrust Policy: American Experience in Twenty Industries* (2 vols., 1955).

BUSINESS AND SOCIETY

Andrews, F. E., *Corporation Giving* (1952); Batchelor, Bronson, *The New Outlook in Business* (1940); Boulding, K. E., *The Organizational Revolution: A Study in Ethics of Economic Organizations* (1953); Bowen, H. R., *Social Responsibilities of the Businessman* (1953); Brandeis, L. D., *Business: A Profession* (1932); Business History Conference, Michigan State University, *America as a Business Civilization* (1962); Chase, Stuart, and Others, *Social Responsibility of Management* (1950); Clark, J. M., *Social Control of Business* (1926); Childs, Marquis, and Cater, Douglass, *Ethics in a Business Society* (1954); Clemens, E. W., *Economics and Public Utilities* (1950); Dennison, H. S., *Ethics and Modern Business* (1932); Dennison, H. S., and Galbraith, J. K., *Modern Corporation and Business Policy* (1958); Fine, Sidney, *Laissez-Faire and the General Welfare State* (1956); Flanders, R. E., *The Functions of Management in American Life* (1949); Hurff, G. B., *Social Aspects of Enterprise in the Large Corporation* (1950); Mason, E. S., ed., *Corporation in Modern Society* (1960); Merrill, H. F., ed., *Responsibilities of Business Leadership* (1948); Owens, R. M., *Business Management and Public Policy* (1958); Robinson, H. J., *Relativity in Business Morals* (1928); Ruml, Beardsley, and Geiger, Theodore, *Manual of Corporate Giving* (1952); Staley, Eugene, ed., *Creating an Industrial Society* (1952); Survey Research Center, University of Michigan, *Business From the Viewpoint of the Public* (1951).

MID-CENTURY CAPITALISM

Allen, F. L., *The Big Change* (1952); Barber, Bernard, *Social Stratification* (1957); Editors of *Fortune, U. S. A.: The Permanent Revolution* (1951); Galbraith, J. K., *American Capitalism: The Concept of Countervailing Power* (1952); Mills, C. W., *White Collar: American Middle Classes* (1951); Rostow, E. V., *Planning for Freedom* (1960); Warner, W. L., and Abegglen, J. C., *Occupational Mobility in American Business and Industry, 1928–1952* (1955).

Index

PICTURE SOURCES